Get the eBooks FREE!

(PDF, ePub, Kindle, and liveBook all included)

We believe that once you buy a book from us, you should be able to read it in any format we have available. To get electronic versions of this book at no additional cost to you, purchase and then register this book at the Manning website.

Go to https://www.manning.com/freebook and follow the instructions to complete your pBook registration.

That's it!
Thanks from Manning!

Xamarin in Action

CREATING NATIVE CROSS-PLATFORM MOBILE APPS

JIM BENNETT

MANNING
SHELTER ISLAND

For online information and ordering of this and other Manning books, please visit www.manning.com. The publisher offers discounts on this book when ordered in quantity. For more information, please contact

Special Sales Department
Manning Publications Co.
20 Baldwin Road
PO Box 761
Shelter Island, NY 11964
Email: orders@manning.com

Manning Publications Co.
20 Baldwin Road
PO Box 761
Shelter Island, NY 11964

Development editor: Elesha Hyde
Review editor: Aleksandar Dragosavljević
Technical development editor: Gary Park
Project editor: Kevin Sullivan
Copyeditor: Andy Carroll
Proofreader: Corbin Collins
Technical proofreader: Tomasz Cielecki
Typesetter: Dottie Marsico
Illustrator: April Milne
Cover designer: Marija Tudor

ISBN 9781617294389
Printed in the United States of America
1 2 3 4 5 6 7 8 9 10 – EBM – 23 22 21 20 19 18

To the amazing Nat and Evie,
for your unwavering love and support whilst I was glued to my laptop.

brief contents

contents

foreword

When Jim told me he was writing a book on Xamarin that was focusing on architecture, design, testing, and best practices, I could not have been more excited. I knew he was the perfect author for this style of book. The very first time I interacted with Jim, we were both creating C# bindings around Bluetooth beacon libraries for iOS and Android. I knew right away we would become great friends, and I'm glad he's joined Microsoft as one of our Developer Advocates to continue all of the great work he was doing in the community.

Xamarin in Action is a resource that I wish I'd had by my side when I was starting native cross-platform mobile development with Xamarin. This book walks you through the key fundamentals of what Xamarin is and how the technology works in Visual Studio, but it also guides you through best practices on building production-quality mobile applications. From design to architecture to deployment, by the end of this book you'll have a full grasp of mobile development with Xamarin and you'll surely have fallen in love with it just as much as I have.

When Jim asked me if I would write a foreword for his book, and I started to read the chapters, it brought me back to when I discovered Xamarin for the first time. This may be where you are right now, getting ready to start your mobile development career. I could think of no better way to introduce *Xamarin in Action* than by sharing my Xamarin journey with you.

I can vividly remember the moment that made me want to become a mobile developer, changing my life forever. It was the fall of 2010, and I was attending my first developer conference, the Professional Developers Conference in Redmond, Washington, at Microsoft headquarters. While there, I was introduced to Azure, the future of cloud computing, and was handed my first smartphone. This tiny supercomputer not only fit into my pocket, but also enabled me to craft full-blown applications in C# from Visual Studio that I could ship to people around the globe. It blew my mind. In that instant, I knew I was done writing printer software and needed to move to Seattle to be closer to the action.

Before I knew it, I'd accepted a job at a small startup, moved my life across the country, and started my role as the sole mobile developer. On my first day, I was tasked with creating native iOS, Android, and Windows applications in only two months. I remember immediately freezing up, as I tried to figure out what I'd gotten myself into, and how I was going to accomplish this as a C# developer who didn't know Objective-C or Java. I knew I would have to find a cross-platform framework if I was going to be successful, and that it would need to integrate into my existing development workflow and tools and, of course, be powered by C#. This was when I discovered the Xamarin platform. I didn't waste any time in downloading the tools and started crafting my first native iOS and Android apps in C# and Visual Studio!

From my very first File > New experience, I was in love with Xamarin. It gave me everything I could ask for in a platform, including native performance, access to every single native API in C#, and a full native user interface that I could craft right from Visual Studio. Xamarin truly made building cross-platform native apps fast, easy, and fun, and I never looked back. After successfully shipping those initial apps in just a few months (and several more over the next few years), I was so in love with Xamarin that I accepted a job with the company as a developer advocate, so I could focus all my energy on helping developers around the world transform their careers with the power of Xamarin.

It's not hyperbole when I say that I absolutely love this technology and know that it can transform your business to be more productive and agile when crafting mobile applications. It even has the power to change your entire career. I'm living proof.

JAMES MONTEMAGNO
Principal Program Manager,
Mobile Developer Tools, Microsoft

preface

I've been involved in technology most of my life, and every year is more exciting for a technologist than the last. Innovations keep coming faster and faster, making it sometimes hard (and always expensive) to keep up. One of the most exciting innovations of the last decade has been the rise of the smartphone. The technology world changed the day Steve Jobs announced the iPhone, and it has been going from strength to strength ever since. I've been an avid iPhone user from the start, and I even wrote a couple of apps using Objective-C during the iPhone's early years. The biggest thing I learned from that experience was that writing mobile apps is cool, but using Objective-C is painful.

Fast-forward a few years, and I was a bored C# developer. I'd been building trading systems for years, desktop apps designed to help other people make a lot of money with unexciting technology, and I needed a change. At the start of my career I was passionate about coding, writing code in my spare time and devouring books and training courses. After a number of years in finance, that passion was dying. I looked around for something to fire it back up, and I found the answer—Xamarin.

I'd spent years learning C#, and with Xamarin I could use those skills to build mobile apps for both iOS and Android. No longer would I have to write Objective-C code for iOS and Java code for Android. The world of mobile development had been opened up to developers like me using C#, a language I not only was very comfortable with, but also actively enjoyed using. I decided that Xamarin was the technology for me, bought myself a license, signed up for Xamarin University, quit my job, and spent four months in a co-working space learning Xamarin. I was hooked, and since then I haven't looked back. I've been so passionate about the technology that I wanted to tell the world how easy it is to build cross-platform mobile apps.

One question that kept coming up in the community was, "How do I build a production-quality app?" There are many great guides on how to use the iOS and Android SDKs, but no end-to-end documentation on how to go from an idea to a working, tested, shipped app—documentation that takes advantage of design patterns like MVVM not only to build testable code, but also to take advantage of Xamarin's most powerful capability: the ability to share large portions of your code between platforms. That was the inspiration for this book. Xamarin is a better way to write, test, monitor, and deploy mobile apps, and this book aims to show you how.

acknowledgments

This book has involved a huge amount of work over the past year and a bit. But in spite of the countless hours I put in, it would never have happened without a lot of hard work from some amazing people. This book isn't the creation of a great writer; instead, it's the result of an enthusiastic developer standing on the shoulders of giants, and it is these giants to whom I owe a huge amount of thanks.

First, I'd like to thank the team at Xamarin for creating a product that has excited me beyond any technology that I've worked with before—especially Miguel de Icaza, Nat Friedman, and Joseph Hill for founding such an awesome company to create an awesome product; James Montemagno for kick-starting my involvement with the Xamarin community by inspiring me to write and speak; Jayme Singleton for her great work building the Xamarin community and supporting all its members; and Mikayla Hutchinson for always being happy to help no matter what dumb questions I ask her.

On the community side, I'd like to thank the Xamarin MVP community, past and present, for welcoming me to the fold, being on hand to answer questions, and supporting my writing, with special thanks to Dave Evans for giving me my first chance to speak at a meetup—a defining moment in my community involvement. Part of what has made this book so easy to write is the amazing framework that is MvvmCross, so I'd like to also thank the MvvmCross team for their hard work and support, especially Martijn van Dijk.

This book wouldn't have been one-tenth as good as it is without the constant support, feedback, and teaching of my development editor at Manning Publications, Elesha Hyde. The techniques you've taught me have made me a better communicator, writer, and mentor, and I've been incredibly appreciative of your guidance every time there was a bump in the road. I hope I've done you proud.

I'd also like to thank the reviewers who took time to read the manuscript at various stages in its development: Andreas Berggren, Davide Fiorentino lo Regio, Dennis Sellinger, Eric Sweigart, Gareth van der Berg, Jason Smith, Jesse Liberty, Karthikeyarajan Rajendran, Krishna Chaitanya Anipindi, Lokeshwar Reddy Vangala, Mario Solomou, Michael Lund, Narasimha Baliga, Patrick Regan, Philip Taffet, Prabhuti Prakash, Riccardo Moschetti, Richard Lebel, Stefan Hellweger, Steve Atchue, Thomas Overby Hansen, and Zorodzayi Mukuya. This book is much better because of your feedback. I'd especially like to thank Gary Park and Tomasz Cielecki (another member of the great MvvmCross team) for their thorough technical review and their constant feedback.

Part of this book was written while fueled up on coffee and pancakes, so I'd like to thank Sarah and the team at Soulshine in Browns Bay, New Zealand, for fueling my writing every Saturday morning. The majority of this book was written while working for a small but incredible company in New Zealand called EROAD, and I would love to thank them for supporting my efforts, especially Jared Langguth for giving me a chance to write Xamarin apps all day, every day, and Sam Williams for continuously showing me the world of development from a different perspective.

Finally, there's no way this book could have happened without the love and support of my family. My parents first got me into programming at an early age (even helping copy out ZX Spectrum source code listings from books and magazines), and they've always inspired me to do my best at everything I do and to always do what I love. Thank you both for being there for me my entire life. My biggest thanks have to go to my wife, Nat, and my daughter, Evie. Nat—thank you for being by my side as I followed my passions wherever in the world they took us, and for supporting such a huge personal project. Evie—thank you for being excited that Daddy was teaching people to write apps for iPads. I hope one day you find something that excites and drives you the way Xamarin mobile development has me. I love you both.

All the good parts of this book are thanks to these amazing people. All the mistakes are mine and mine alone.

about this book

Xamarin in Action has been written to help you build production-quality mobile apps—five-star apps that are well architected, well tested, and deployed to the store with analytics and crash monitoring. This book covers the journey from idea to delivery, ensuring that you build your apps the right way. It doesn't try to replicate information that's easily available online in API docs; instead, it focuses on the concepts of a well-built cross-platform Xamarin app, bringing together all the information you need without bogging you down.

Who should read this book

Xamarin in Action is for developers who want to build cross-platform mobile apps using C#, either because it's a language they know, or because they want to take advantage of the cross-platform capabilities of Xamarin. This book assumes a small amount of C# knowledge, but all C# developers from beginner to advanced will be able to use it to learn how to build mobile apps. Even if you're an experienced native iOS or Android app developer using Objective-C or Java, this book will help you easily transition to building Xamarin apps. The underlying architecture of a Xamarin app is very different from a native app, and so are the technologies and tools available. This book will help teach you how to build apps using a cross-platform architecture and the tooling inside Visual Studio.

How this book is organized

This book is split into three parts covering 16 chapters. Part 1 covers the architectural concepts behind a well-written cross-platform Xamarin app, with a Hello World example app to get you started:

- Chapter 1 discusses Xamarin and the benefits of building Xamarin mobile apps. It also looks at the development lifecycle, covering all the steps in building production-quality mobile apps.
- Chapter 2 starts by looking at MVVM (model-view–view model), the design pattern for building good-quality, testable, cross-platform apps, and then looks at the structure of a Xamarin app. It then covers creating a basic Hello World cross-platform mobile app.
- Chapter 3 dives into MVVM in more detail, looking at the different layers from model, through view model, to view. It then covers the application layer and navigation patterns.
- Chapter 4 revisits the example Hello World app from chapter 2, diving deeper into how the MVVM design pattern was used to build the app. It then looks at expanding the app using cross-platform Xamarin plugins.
- Chapter 5 is all about multithreading, covering the threading considerations involved when building mobile apps and introducing async and await, a feature of C# that makes it easy to build clean and easy-to-read multithreaded code.

Part 2 builds on this architecture and shows you how to build cross-platform apps starting with the cross-platform code and moving on to platform-specific UI code. You'll take a couple of examples from the design stage through to fully working iOS and Android apps:

- Chapter 6 introduces the two example apps that will be built throughout the rest of part 2. It looks at how to design an app, considering what code goes in what layer in the MVVM design pattern. Finally, it covers creating solutions for the example apps and looks at the project and application properties for a Xamarin mobile app.
- Chapter 7 focuses on the model layer, including building simple models, building more complex model layers with services and repositories, and accessing SQLite databases and web services. It also introduces unit testing, showing how easy it is to unit-test well-structured code.
- Chapter 8 moves up a layer and covers view models. It considers how state and behavior are represented, covering properties, commands, and value conversion. It also shows how to test UI logic using unit testing.
- Chapter 9 covers the view and application layers and starts the process of building the Android version of one of the example apps. It covers Android resource files, layouts, UI controls, and activities.
- Chapter 10 focuses on the second of the example Android apps, covering recycler views for showing lists of data and multiscreen navigation. It then shows how to add polish to an app by creating app icons and splash screens.
- Chapter 11 moves from Android to iOS, working on the application and view layers of the first example app, covering view controllers, UI controls, storyboards, and auto layout and constraints.

- Chapter 12 covers how to build the second example iOS app, looking at table views and multiscreen navigation. It then covers app icons and launch screens.

Part 3 covers making a working app production-ready and shipping it to users:

- Chapter 13 looks at how to run apps on real devices, including setting up Android devices for developers, configuring iOS devices, and generating iOS provisioning profiles.
- Chapter 14 covers UI testing, the ability to write and run automated tests that interact with your app the way a real person would.
- Chapter 15 introduces Visual Studio App Center, showing how it can be used to build your apps, run UI tests against devices in the cloud, and set up your apps to track usage information and crashes.
- Chapter 16 covers the final stage in an app's journey: delivery to users. It looks at using App Center to provide beta test builds to selected users and then shows how to finally publish apps to the Google Play store and Apple App Store.

This book is sequential, with later chapters building on concepts explained in the previous chapters. It takes you on a journey from idea, through architectural concepts, to building up each layer, and finally to testing and publishing your app. You'll find it easier to read the first two parts from start to finish, rather than dipping in and out of different chapters. Part 3 can be read out of order, depending on your needs.

About the code

This book contains many examples of source code, both in numbered listings and inline with normal text. In both cases, source code is formatted in a `fixed-width font like this` to separate it from ordinary text. In some cases, the original source code has been reformatted; I've added line breaks and reworked indentation to accommodate the available page space in the book. In rare cases, even this wasn't enough, and listings include line-continuation markers ➥. Additionally, comments in the source code have often been removed from the listings when the code is described in the text. Code annotations accompany many of the listings, highlighting important concepts.

Source code is available for all chapters in this book, with the exception of chapters 1 and 3. Each chapter has one or more solutions, showing the example app or apps discussed in that chapter, with all the source for the chapter fully implemented and working. For example, chapter 7 has two apps with model layers that can be tested using unit tests, but not a runnable app. By chapter 9, the first example app will run and be fully working on Android.

All the source code has been tested using Visual Studio 2017 both on Windows (with the Xamarin workload installed) and Mac based on the 15.4 release published in October 2017. You'll need to ensure that you have the Android SDK v7.1 or later installed. (The latest one is installed by default, but if you installed a long time ago, you may need to update your SDK.) You'll also need Xcode 9 or later installed on your Mac for iOS builds.

The source code for this book is available for download from the publisher's website at https://www.manning.com/books/xamarin-in-action.

Software and hardware requirements

The most basic requirement for building Xamarin apps is a computer running Visual Studio. Windows users will need Visual Studio 2017 with the Xamarin workload installed. When you install VS2017 with the Xamarin workload, everything you need should be installed for you, although it's always worth ensuring you have updated to the latest version of Visual Studio and updated your Android SDK to the latest stable version.

Mac users will need the latest version of Visual Studio for Mac installed. The installer should install and configure everything you need, with one exception—Xcode. You'll need to install Xcode from the Mac App Store. It's also worth ensuring everything is up to date, with the latest stable versions of VS for Mac, the Android SDK, and Xcode installed.

If you want to build iOS apps from a PC, you'll need access to a Mac with Visual Studio for Mac installed, either on your network or via a cloud service such as MacinCloud.

To publish to the stores, you'll need developer accounts with both Google Play and Apple. These aren't free. Currently, the Google Play developer account is a one-time fee of $25, and the Apple developer program is $99 per year. You'll be able to run your code on Android emulators and iOS simulators as you develop, but it's always worth having real hardware to test on, especially when you prepare to release to the stores.

Online resources

If you need additional help:

- The forums at https://forums.xamarin.com are a great place to ask questions.
- There is a vibrant Xamarin community Slack team that you can join at https://xamarinchat.herokuapp.com/, full of Xamarin developers and support engineers.
- As always, Stack Overflow (https://stackoverflow.com/) has the answers to most things you'll want to know, and lots of top-notch Xamarin developers are on hand to answer any additional questions you may have.

Book forum

Purchase of *Xamarin in Action* includes free access to a private web forum run by Manning Publications where you can make comments about the book, ask technical questions, and receive help from the author and from other users. To access the forum, go to https://forums.manning.com/forums/xamarin-in-action. You can also learn more about Manning's forums and the rules of conduct at https://forums.manning.com/forums/about.

Manning's commitment to our readers is to provide a venue where a meaningful dialogue between individual readers and between readers and the author can take place. It is not a commitment to any specific amount of participation on the part of the author, whose contribution to the forum remains voluntary (and unpaid). We suggest you try asking the author some challenging questions lest his interest stray! The forum and the archives of previous discussions will be accessible from the publisher's website as long as the book is in print.

About the author

JIM BENNETT is a Senior Cloud Developer Advocate at Microsoft, specializing in cloud-connected Xamarin apps. He has decades of experience building desktop and mobile apps, mainly using C# and other Microsoft technologies. For the past four years, he has been heavily involved in developing cross-platform mobile apps using Xamarin, both at work and as personal projects. He's a regular speaker on mobile development at meetups and conferences, contributes to open source, and blogs about and evangelizes Xamarin whenever he can. He's a former Xamarin and Microsoft MVP, he's passionate about sharing knowledge and helping others to learn, and when he's not playing with his young daughter, he's happy to spend hours discussing mobile development over Thai food and good beer or whisky.

about the cover illustration

The illustration on the cover of *Xamarin in Action* bears the caption "Bostandji bachi." The literal translation is "chief gardener," but the Bostandjis of the Turkish sultan had powers and responsibilities ranging far beyond the sultan's gardens to his palaces and supervising the police of the capital. The illustration is taken from a collection of costumes of the Ottoman Empire published on January 1, 1802, by William Miller of Old Bond Street, London. The title page is missing from the collection, and we've so far been unable to track it down. The book's table of contents identifies the figures in both English and French, and each illustration also bears the names of two artists who worked on it, both of whom would no doubt be surprised to find their art gracing the front cover of a computer programming book 200 years later.

The collection was purchased by a Manning editor at an antiquarian flea market in the "Garage" on West 26th Street in Manhattan. The seller was an American based in Ankara, Turkey, and the transaction took place just as he was packing up his stand for the day. The Manning editor didn't have on his person the substantial amount of cash that was required for the purchase, and a credit card and check were both politely turned down. With the seller flying back to Ankara that evening, the situation seemed hopeless. What was the solution? It turned out to be nothing more than an old-fashioned verbal agreement sealed with a handshake. The seller proposed that the money be transferred to him by wire, and the editor walked out with the bank information on a piece of paper and the portfolio of images under his arm. Needless to say, we transferred the funds the next day, and we remain grateful and impressed by this unknown person's trust in one of us. It recalls something that might have happened a long time ago.

The pictures from the Ottoman collection, like the other illustrations that appear on Manning's covers, bring to life the richness and variety of dress customs of two centuries ago. They recall the sense of isolation and distance of that period—and of every other historic period except our own hyperkinetic present. Dress codes have changed since then certainly, and the diversity by region, so rich at the time, has faded away. It's now often hard to tell the inhabitant of one continent from that of another. Perhaps, viewed optimistically, we've traded a cultural and visual diversity for a more varied personal life. Or a more varied and interesting intellectual and technical life.

We at Manning celebrate the inventiveness, the initiative, and, yes, the *fun* of the computer business with book covers based on the rich diversity of regional life as it was two centuries ago, brought back to life by the pictures from this collection.

Part 1

Getting started with Xamarin

The traditional way to build a mobile app is to write it twice: once in Objective-C or Swift for iOS, and then again in Java for Android. This is a huge waste of time, duplicating code across two languages. Luckily some of the most innovative engineers in the world (according to *Time* magazine) have a solution—Xamarin.

Xamarin is a platform from Microsoft that allows you to build and ship iOS and Android apps using .NET. It's also part of a thriving mobile ecosystem containing everything from mobile-specific cloud resources from Microsoft, DevOps tools, and a huge community of open source software. At its most basic, it's a way to use the same language and technology across iOS and Android, allowing you to reuse large amounts of code and third-party libraries across two very different mobile platforms. The best practices around Xamarin are focused on keeping this amount of code-sharing as large as possible.

This first part of the book covers the architectural concepts behind a well-written cross-platform Xamarin app, focusing on the incredibly popular MVVM design pattern. A good architecture will help you reuse the most code possible, so it's worth investing the time to learn these concepts, avoiding wasting time writing swathes of code twice. Patterns such as MVVM allow you to test your code faster and easier using unit tests, catching bugs earlier in the development cycle and reducing the time manually testing (and bug fixing) further down the development cycle. These are the foundations you'll need to build production-quality mobile apps.

Chapter 1 starts by discussing Xamarin and the benefits of building Xamarin mobile apps. It also looks at the development lifecycle, covering all the steps in building production-quality mobile apps.

Chapter 2 looks at the MVVM design pattern as a way to increase your code reuse, and to build a well-architected, testable app. Then it covers the creation of a Hello World app that uses a popular MVVM framework.

Chapter 3 dives into MVVM in more detail, looking at the different layers from model, through view model, to view. It then covers the application layer and navigation patterns.

Chapter 4 revisits the example Hello World app from chapter 2, diving deeper into how the MVVM design pattern was used to build the app. It then looks at expanding the app, using cross-platform Xamarin plugins.

Chapter 5 is all about multithreading, covering the threading considerations involved in building mobile apps. It also introduces async and await, a feature of C# that makes it very easy to build clean and easy-to-read multithreaded code.

1 Introducing native cross-platform applications with Xamarin

This chapter covers

- What a Xamarin app is
- The mobile-optimized development lifecycle
- Building production-ready cross-platform apps

Back in 2000 Microsoft announced a new software framework called .NET, along with a new programming language called C#. Not long after this, a company called Ximian (founded by Miguel de Icaza and Nat Friedman) started working on Mono, a free implementation of the .NET framework and the C# compiler that could run on Linux.

Fast forward 16 years, and Nat Friedman is standing on stage at the Xamarin Evolve conference giving the keynote talk—physically in front of sixteen hundred mobile developers and virtually in front of tens of thousands more. He's speaking about how Xamarin enables a mobile-optimized development lifecycle. Xamarin (the company that grew out of the ashes of Ximian and that provides tools and technology to build cross-platform mobile apps) had just been bought by Microsoft for a rumored half a billion U.S. dollars, and had become a key part of Microsoft's "mobile first, cloud first" strategy.

Xamarin is now a well-known term among the mobile developer community, and it's starting to be well known in other Microsoft-based developer circles. But what do we mean when we talk about Xamarin mobile apps, and what does Xamarin give us above and beyond other tools?

1.1 Introducing Xamarin mobile apps

To really see the benefits of Xamarin mobile apps, we first need to look at how apps are built using vendor-provided development environments, or other cross-platform tools like Cordova, and compare them to what Xamarin offers. We can do this by looking at two main types of developers—an indie developer working on an app in their spare time, and a corporate development team building an app for their customers. We'll start by considering what their differing needs are in terms of platform support, and then we'll compare the possible options.

Our example indie developer has come up with the idea of the millennium for a killer app, FlappyFoo, that they want to sell to consumers on an app store. Our example large corporation, FooCorp, wants to build a DailyFoo app to help their customers.

Figure 1.1 outlines the four different mobile development platforms you could choose from:

- Vendor-specific apps using the development environments from Apple and Google
- Cordova
- Xamarin native using Xamarin.iOS and Xamarin.Android
- Xamarin.Forms

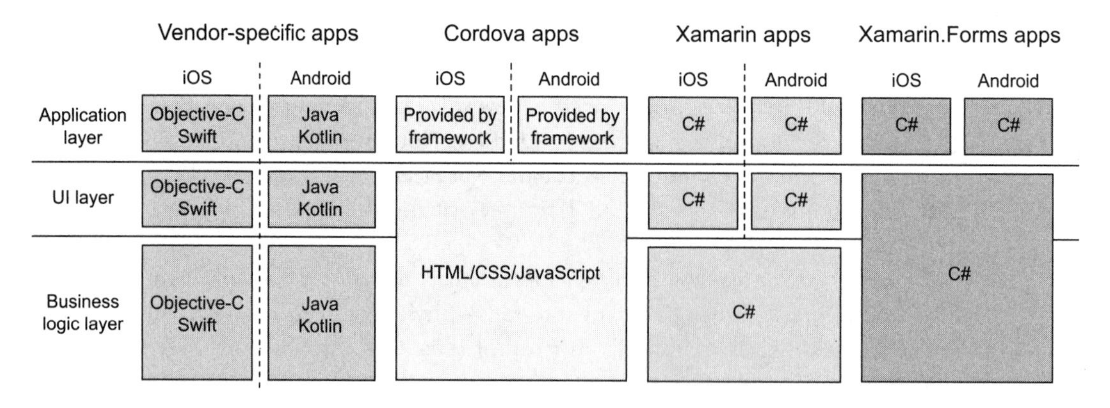

Figure 1.1 A comparison of the different mobile-development platforms

This diagram shows the programming languages used and where code can be shared for each layer of the app—from the application layer (the thin wrapper around the rest of the app that makes it into something that can be run on each platform), down through the UI layer to the business logic layer. The boxes are not to scale—they're just a representation of the layers. Your app could be heavy on UI but light on logic, so the UI layer would be bigger, or vice versa. Let's look at each of these in more detail.

1.1.1 Vendor-specific native apps

Each OS comes with a different set of APIs, a different paradigm for building the user interface, a different way of handling user interactions, and, most frustratingly, a different programming language (or choice of languages) for you to use. If you want to build an app for Apple's iOS-based devices such as iPhones and iPads, you need to program in either Objective-C or Swift. For Android phones and tablets, you need to program in Java (with Kotlin support coming soon).

For each platform you'll end up building the entire app from the user interface layer right down to any in-app business logic all in the vendor's preferred language, as shown in figure 1.2.

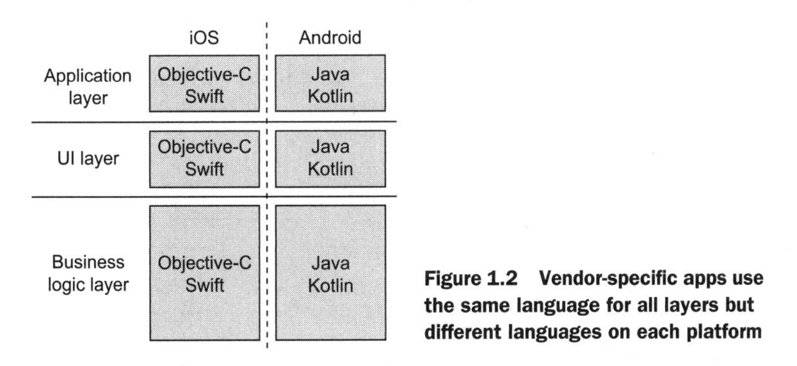

Figure 1.2 Vendor-specific apps use the same language for all layers but different languages on each platform

For our indie developer, this is a big problem. For FlappyFoo to be a success, it will need maximum reach, and this means both iOS and Android versions. To achieve this, the indie developer will have to learn two programming languages, and there's more to learn than just the language syntax—they'll have to learn different tools, different ways of getting access to third-party code, the different words developers use to express each concept, and the different design patterns that make up standard apps. This is a big task.

Even if the indie developer is a polyglot and is happy in multiple environments, there's still the issue of time. They'll have to code the same app twice, implementing the same logic in different languages. Time to market is key, and if the developer hits only one platform to start with, there's nothing to stop copycats from flooding the other platform quickly. FlappyFoo may dominate the iOS app store but could lose serious revenue to FlappyBar from another developer on Android.

For our corporate team, the biggest issue is cost. To reach multiple platforms usually means one team per platform with the associated developer and organizational costs. This can be especially problematic if you consider the difficulties in finding, hiring, and retaining good developers. Ideally you want to be able to release simultaneously on all platforms, and to replicate each new feature to both platforms and release them simultaneously. This is hard if you've managed to employ five Android developers but only two iOS developers (a common scenario as it's much easier to find Java developers in the corporate environment to help with Android versions than it is to find Objective-C or Swift developers).

Thinking of the corporation's customers who use DailyFoo every day to track their Foo, the last thing we want is for them to change platform, find out that the new platform's version is missing a killer feature from DailyFoo, and jump ship to MyBar from BarCorp.

It's not all bad, though. The one thing you can always be sure of when writing an app using the vendor-provided tools is that you're always building a truly native application that will be as high performance as possible and that supports everything the OS and devices have to offer. Whenever an OS update is released, the tooling is always updated to match, giving you access to all the newest features that your users will want to have. This is an important consideration, as app users are fickle. They'll quickly drop an app for a competitor if it's not up to scratch, it's slow, clunky, or just not well integrated into their device.

1.1.2 Cordova

As already mentioned, using multiple languages and development tools is a headache. One popular way around this is using Cordova. This is a set of tools that allows you to create web applications using HTML, JavaScript, and CSS to build a mobile website, which is then wrapped in an app and packaged up for each platform, as shown in figure 1.3.

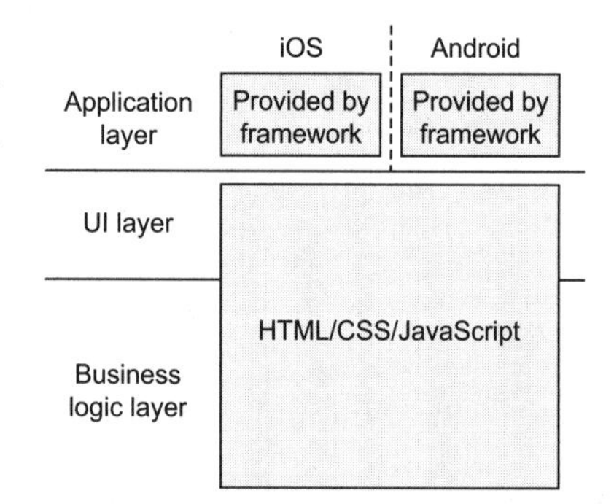

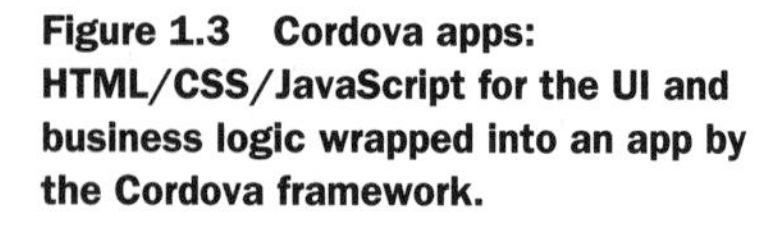
Figure 1.3 Cordova apps: HTML/CSS/JavaScript for the UI and business logic wrapped into an app by the Cordova framework.

This has the big upside of a common language and development environment—one toolset for the indie developer to learn, or one team in a corporate environment. The downsides, though, can seriously outweigh this upside. First, you aren't creating a native app—you're creating a web app. This means that the widgets you see in the user interface are HTML widgets styled to look like native components. This might fool your users now, but if an OS update changes the style, your apps won't keep up without a rebuild and will look out of date. Second, the OS and device-specific features that are available to the native developer won't be available to a Cordova developer.

The tooling does its best to provide some lowest-common-denominator plugins to allow hardware and OS access, but these are written with the aim of being cross-platform, so they only support the features common to both platforms. They're also later to market. If the vendor releases a new feature you want to take advantage of, you'll have to wait for the Cordova plugin to be created to support it, and this may never happen.

Thinking of our indie developer, if they use Cordova to build FlappyFoo, it could easily run slowly, especially on older devices. This can lead to a swath of one-star reviews, a lack of sales, and the developer going hungry. Cordova apps also run in a browser, so they're limited by the speed and feature set of that browser—newer versions of the OS might have a fully featured, fast browser but older versions might be lacking. This can lead to different capabilities or different levels of performance on the same device but with different OS versions—something that's very hard to test on the hugely fragmented ecosystem of Android.

For our corporate development team building DailyFoo, an app that's slow or that looks out of date once an OS update comes out can create a negative image of the FooCorp brand. If the MyBar app from the rival BarCorp supports 3D touch on iOS, and DailyFoo doesn't due to a lack of support from Cordova plugins, our fickle customers might easily be tempted to switch.

1.1.3 Xamarin native apps

In my mind, Xamarin is the clear winner because it combines the best of both the previous methods. Fundamentally, Xamarin provides a set of .NET wrappers around the native OS APIs based on Mono—the cross-platform implementation of .NET that grew out of Ximian. This provides a .NET framework for Android and iOS, with libraries and a C# compiler for each platform. It means you can write apps in C# that target each mobile platform natively, and because you're using a single programming language, you can easily abstract out all your business logic (anything that doesn't interact with the device directly) into a set of libraries that can be shared between platforms. You can even abstract out a lot of the UI logic by using design patterns like MVVM (model-view–view model, which you'll learn about in more detail in chapter 2). Figure 1.13 shows the code split and sharing between each layer.

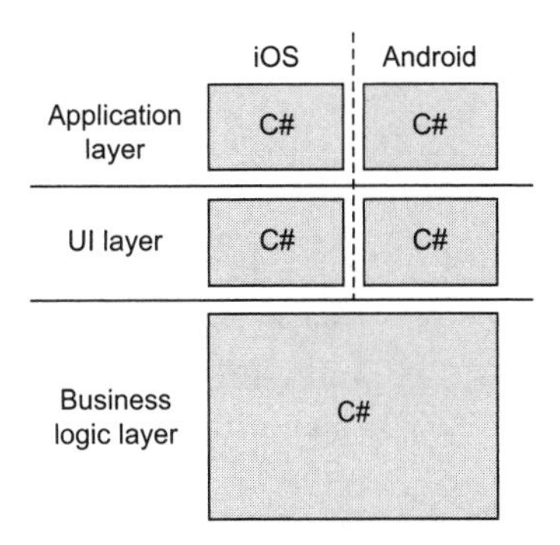

Figure 1.4 Xamarin apps are written in C#, so you can share common business logic and also have platform-specific UIs.

Let's take a closer look at those last points, as this is important and is the key reason in my mind for using Xamarin:

- Xamarin provides wrappers around *native* APIs.
- Xamarin provides a *compiler* for each platform to produce native code.

This is key. The native APIs are wrapped in C# code so you can call them from your C# code. You write your apps using the same idioms and classes as pure native code, but using C#. On iOS you have a `UIViewController` class for each screen, but this is a C# class, not the Objective-C one from the iOS SDK that you code against. On Android, each screen is derived from a class called `Activity`, but it's a C# class that wraps the Java `Activity` class from the Android SDK.

The code you write is compiled code as well—this isn't sitting inside some emulator on the device; it's compiled to native code that interacts with the same libraries as an app written in the vendor's language of choice and compiled with their tools. This means your app is truly native. It uses native widgets on the UI, has access to every device and OS feature the native API has access to, and is as fast as a native app.

XAMARIN APPS == NATIVE APPS This is the killer feature of Xamarin apps. They're written in C# and they have access to all the features of that language, to a large part of the .NET framework that desktop developers are used to, and to a whole host of third-party code. But the end result is native code—the same as that created in Objective-C or Swift on iOS, or Java on Android.

On iOS the C# compiler takes your code and produces a native iOS binary using an Ahead-Of-Time (AOT) compiler (figure 1.5).

On Android it creates IL code (the same as for C# apps running on Windows), which is compiled at runtime using just-in-time (JIT) compilation (figure 1.6). This is provided by a Mono runtime that's built into your app and installed with it (but don't worry, you only get the bits of the Mono runtime you need, thanks to a very good linker). Xamarin also has an AOT compiler for Android, but at the time of writing, it's still very much experimental.

WHAT ABOUT OTHER LANGUAGES? You can also write your apps using F# if you prefer a more functional style of programming. F# is fully supported for iOS and Android apps. If VB.NET is your thing, you can build .NET Standard class libraries using it and call these from your iOS and Android apps built using C# or F#. Those options are outside the scope of this book, though—here we'll just focus on C#.

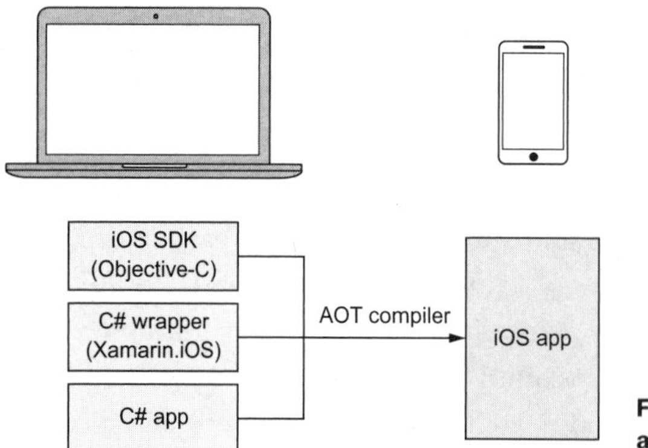

Figure 1.5 Xamarin.iOS uses an ahead-of-time compiler.

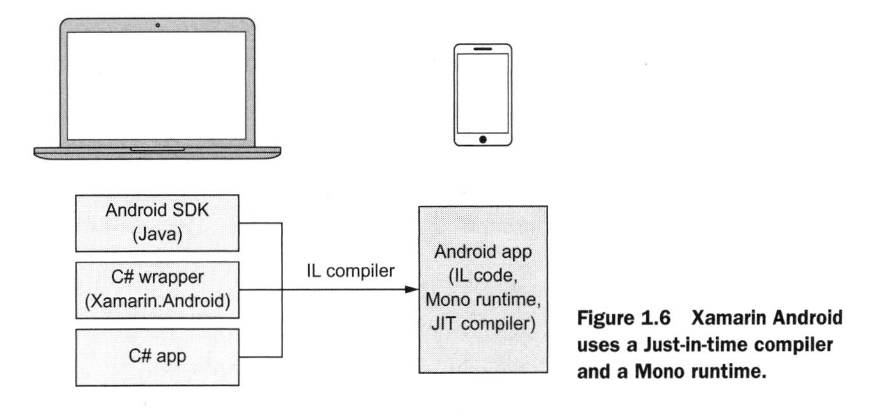

Figure 1.6 Xamarin Android uses a Just-in-time compiler and a Mono runtime.

Because the language of choice is C#, the code libraries written to share code between iOS and Android can also be shared with a UWP (Universal Windows Platform) app, so you can easily target Windows 10 devices from desktops to tablets to phones to the XBox One if you so desire.

For our indie developer, this is good news. They only have one language to learn, and they only have to write the bulk of their app once, and then write the device-specific layer once per platform they want to support. This gives a faster time to market, which is vital for consumer apps. It also means the core logic code is tested the same way on all platforms, bugs are fixed once, and improvements and new features are created with fewer changes.

For our corporate development team, this is also a good thing as it means fewer developers and less cost. Ideally there would be some developers who specialize in the platform-specific idioms of each supported OS who can work on the UI or device-specific logic, but the core of the development team can build the business logic once in a single language. It's also easier to build the development teams because C# developers are easy to find—much easier than Objective-C developers. The advantages for the indie developer also apply here—less code to test and faster to market with bug fixes and new features.

This is not a total utopia. Xamarin developers still have to write the UI layer and anything that interacts with the device using platform-specific C# code and they still need to understand the idioms of each platform, but they only have one language to support. One syntax, one toolset, one way of using third-party code.

It's easy to look at this and think of it as a partial failure—something that misses the mark by not being totally cross-platform—but that's really one of its strengths. By having C# platform-specific APIs, you get the best of what the device has to offer. You aren't limited to a common subset; instead you can write each platform's app in a way that makes the most of the features of those devices. It also means you have access to everything—when iOS adds a new feature, Xamarin wraps its API and it's available to you pretty much the same day. Your apps can be targeted to each platform, so they look and feel like a pure, native app and take advantage of the unique features that make Android and iOS so different, but behind the scenes you're sharing around 75% of your code base. Table 1.1 shows some examples of this code sharing.

Table 1.1 The amount of code in two popular apps reused between iOS and Android

	iCircuit (http://icircuitapp.com)	TouchDraw (http://elevenworks.com/home)
iOS	70%	61%
Android	86%	72%

There's one downside to using Xamarin for your mobile apps—you're dependent on them wrapping the SDKs and ensuring that the compilers work on all required platforms. There's an overhead to wrapping the SDKs, and although Xamarin has got very, very good at it, there can still be a gap between an API being made available from Apple and Google and Xamarin having it wrapped. This is usually not an issue, as both Apple and Google release beta versions early enough for Xamarin to have time to deal with any quirks.

The only thing that has been a problem is when the underlying compiler requirements change. This happened recently with Apple Watch apps: originally they were compiled native code, but for watchOS 2 the Apple compiler changed to output bytecode instead of native code. It took a long time for Mono to catch up and be able to compile working watchOS 2 apps. This is the biggest risk with Xamarin—that Apple or Google could completely change how they build apps, and by the time Xamarin catches up, your app could have been late to market with a cool new feature or device support.

Now that Xamarin is owned by Microsoft, I can see this being less of an issue as they'll have more resources to throw against such a problem.

1.1.4 *Xamarin.Forms*

Xamarin also offers a more cross-platform solution called Xamarin.Forms that attempts to bring code reuse up to 95–98% by abstracting out the UI and device-specific code layers. Unlike Cordova apps that use HTML, Xamarin.Forms apps are still native apps. It uses an abstraction that sits on top of the iOS and Android platforms and provides a lowest common denominator experience, providing features that are common to both platforms. By doing this, you can get up to 98% code reuse. This is shown in figure 1.7.

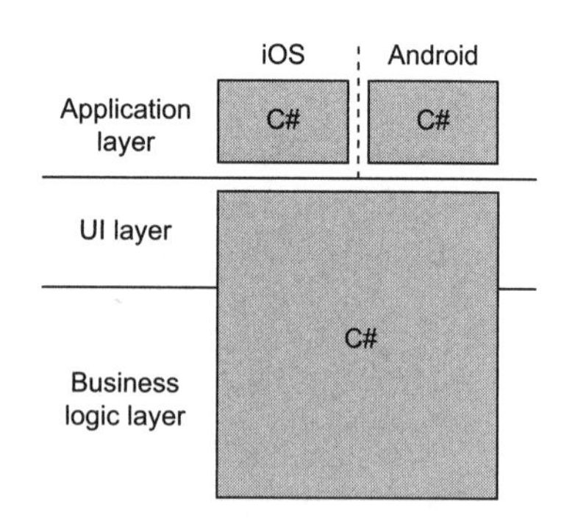

Figure 1.7 Xamarin.Forms apps have a cross-platform UI to share even more code.

This abstraction is done using a set of UI classes that represent features common to both, and when the app is run, these are translated to the native equivalents behind the scenes. For example, each screen you see is a `Page`, and this is rendered on iOS using a `UIViewController` and on Android using an `Activity`. If you add a `Button` to this page, it's a `UIButton` on iOS and a `Button` widget on Android. Unlike Cordova, which uses HTML to provide the cross-platform capability, Xamarin.Forms uses the actual, native controls, so you get a true native experience. If the OS updates the look of the buttons, your Forms apps will look like the new version. This abstraction is exposed not only as a set of C# classes you can use from your C# code, but you can also define your UI using XAML—a variant of XML originally defined by Microsoft for building UIs.

XAML allows you to define your UI using a more declarative syntax, similar in nature to HTML, and it's very familiar to developers from a Windows desktop background who are used to building apps with WPF. If you've built WPF or Windows 10 apps, you'll probably have come across XAML before. Xamarin.Forms uses a slightly different variant of XAML than WPF/Windows 10, but most of the concepts are the same. This similarity will increase over time because Microsoft is in the process of defining XAML Standard, a single XAML syntax that will be used across all the Microsoft XAML tooling.

The downside is that you're building one app for all platforms. Although it tries to be as native as possible by using native controls, you can't easily get around platform-specific idioms. For example, if you have an app that has two screens to work on, you'd navigate on Android using a drawer exposed by a hamburger menu, whereas on iOS you'd use tabs. This difference isn't easy to implement in Forms without a lot of custom logic and custom UIs. If you want to go further than the lowest common denominator (for example, adding platform-specific behavior to one control on one platform) then you'd need to write a custom renderer for it—code that maps from the Forms controls to the underlying control.

Forms does try to abstract away device-specific features like maps or the camera using plugins, but again it's a lowest common denominator model. The camera plugin won't give you live photos on iOS, and the maps plugin doesn't give you the same amount of control as Google Maps on Android.

For our indie developer, Forms might not be the best choice—the amount of work it would take to make an app look and feel like a true native experience might outweigh the time savings by maximizing code reuse.

For corporate developers, it might be a better option. Certainly for in-house apps, where you don't always need a killer native experience, it's a great tool, but for consumer apps it might not provide all the features needed. I'm sure over time it will carry on getting better and better—it's under heavy development at the moment—but it's not quite there yet for a great consumer app.

This book focuses on native Xamarin mobile apps, but the principles of MVVM that we'll cover also apply to Xamarin.Forms apps.

1.1.5 Xamarin developer tools

As I've shown, Xamarin is far and away the best choice for mobile development—it gives you the power and performance of a native app, providing access to everything in the SDKs and on the devices, and it uses C# as a common language on all platforms so you can share the majority of your code base. So how do you go about building a Xamarin app?

For pure native apps, tooling is provided by the vendors: iOS apps are built using Xcode on the Mac, and Android apps are built using Android Studio on Mac/Windows/Linux.

For Xamarin apps, the best IDE around is Microsoft's 20-year-old Visual Studio. It comes with a ridiculous number of features and tools, and it has a huge range of extensions to provide all manner of new features. It's available as a community edition for indie developers and small teams for free, and it tiers up from there depending on how big your team is, what your support needs are, and whether you want enterprise features like profilers or embedding assemblies (you can compare the different tiers at www.visualstudio.com/vs/compare/). Xamarin is fully built into Visual Studio, providing a totally native experience where you can create a new app that targets iOS or Android just as easily as you can create a desktop WPF app or a class library. You can easily reference other projects, add in NuGet packages, and do everything with these project types that you can do with any native Windows project. From there you can build your Xamarin Android app and run it on an emulator (Visual Studio provides a number of built-in Android emulators) or on a real device. You can also build and run a Xamarin iOS app, albeit with some Apple-related restrictions.

Apple's licensing rules for its SDK, compiler, and build tools require that you build on a Mac. Seeing as our Xamarin apps wrap the SDKs and compile down to native code using the Apple toolchain, you have to have a Mac. Luckily Xamarin iOS on Windows takes away the pain of this and provides support inside Visual Studio on Windows for building and debugging iOS apps using a remote Mac—all you need is a Mac with Xamarin installed that you can connect to, and the magic just happens. Visual Studio connects to the Mac to compile your code. The iOS SDK on the Mac includes an iPhone/iPad simulator, which you can use to test your app, and a debugger that allows you to debug apps running on a device connected via USB to your Mac, so initially you still had to test your apps either by running the simulator on the Mac or using a device plugged into it. But Xamarin now has that covered as well—at least for simulators. It can share the screen from the simulator to your Windows box so you can debug on a simulator as if it were all available on Windows. This means the Mac you need for building need not be next to you, or even on the same network. There are cloud services that can rent you time on Macs, such as Mac In Cloud (www.macincloud.com). You can use these for building your apps, and you can test these apps by debugging through Visual Studio on a simulator that's screen-shared back to your Windows box. Figure 1.8 shows an overview of this process. You only need access to a physical Mac if you want to test on a real device.

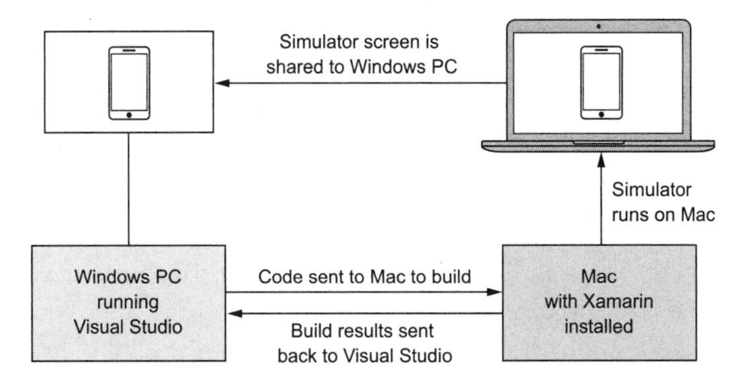

Figure 1.8 Visual Studio can connect to a Mac locally or in the cloud to build and debug iOS apps in a simulator.

So far, so cool. We're building cross-platform mobile apps on Windows. But one of the founding principles of the Mono project that inspired the Xamarin we know and love is being able to run on different platforms, and Xamarin has you covered there. Visual Studio is now available on the Mac, albeit in a cut-down version compared to Visual Studio on Windows. Xamarin used to have an IDE called Xamarin Studio, and this became the basis of Visual Studio for Mac. Visual Studio for Mac supports building iOS and Android apps, as well as macOS apps, tvOS apps, and ASP.NET Core websites. It has Azure integration allowing you to build both the mobile and web components of your app ecosystem, and even to debug both mobile and web components inside the same debugging session. Visual Studio on the Mac has the same licensing as for Windows, so it's free for indie developers and small teams, with paid plans available for larger teams.

Which tool you use really depends on personal preference and the platforms you want to support. In this book we'll be covering Visual Studio on both Windows and Mac.

> **CROSS-PLATFORM ALL THE THINGS!** One other awesome thing to note is that Microsoft has changed recently from a closed company that was Windows only to one that supports open source and multiple platforms. They've even open sourced parts of the .NET framework and the compiler and have made it cross-platform. This means that bits of Mono are slowly being replaced with the Microsoft implementations from their .NET framework. It also means that the compiler in Visual Studio is the same on Windows as on Mac, with both using the open source Roslyn compiler. When you compile on the Mac, it's the same compiler as on Windows.

1.1.6 Mobile-optimized development lifecycle

So far we've covered Xamarin apps, and, to a lot of people, this is what Xamarin is—a .NET framework and compiler for iOS and Android based on Mono. But as well as providing the tools to build cross-platform apps, Xamarin also provides the tooling you need to do a lot more than just write the code.

One of the biggest concepts in the development world in recent years is DevOps—the cultural shift to a model where development and operations are combined. Some of the aims of DevOps include enabling individuals to be involved in all parts of the development and release cycle, automating as much as possible, and moving to a continuous delivery model where code can be checked in, built, and tested automatically and shipped to production with minimal human input. DevOps is a massive topic, well outside the scope of this book, but there are a number of tools, either provided by Xamarin or well integrated with other Xamarin tools, that can be used to help implement a good DevOps strategy.

During the Xamarin Evolve conference in April 2016, one of the main themes of the keynote was the mobile-optimized development lifecycle (as illustrated in figure 1.9). During this keynote, a number of tools, both from Xamarin and their new parent company Microsoft, were discussed. It was pretty clear that this was a key focus for Xamarin as a company, and it's only been growing with the introduction of Visual Studio App Center and the greater push towards DevOps. This is important as we consider how to build production-quality mobile apps.

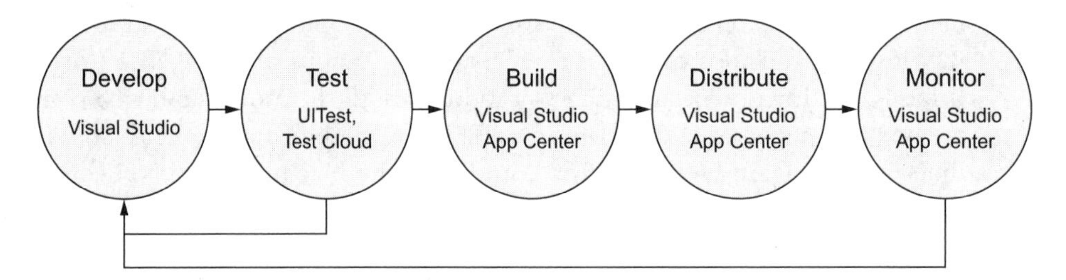

Figure 1.9 The mobile-optimized development lifecycle is a continuously iterating cycle of develop, test, build, distribute, and monitor.

1.2 Creating production-quality mobile apps

It's a long journey from a back-of-the-napkin idea to a fully working, deployed app of sufficient quality to be usable and not get bad reviews. It's easy for developers to jump straight into coding, as this is the part we love, but if you want to build an app that's successful, you have to consider the whole software-development lifecycle. There's no point in diving into the code and building something that doesn't look good or work well because you haven't considered the design of your finished app. During coding, you have to keep testing and monitoring in mind so that you code in a way that supports them. For anything more than a prototype, you have to think about the whole lifecycle before you write a single line of code. This lifecycle is very similar to the mobile-optimized development lifecycle talked about at Xamarin Evolve, but it adds a few more steps.

In this book we'll be building a production-quality app, so let's look at the stages a mobile app will need to go through on this journey. We'll see what Xamarin can (or can't) help with.

Starting with an MVP

> *If you are not embarrassed by the first version of your product, you've released too late.*
>
> —Reid Hoffman

It's good practice when building a mobile app to start with an MVP—a minimum viable product. This is the smallest, simplest, fastest-to-market version you can deliver. Once this is in consumers' hands, you can monitor how it's used and deliver features based on what real people want. A lot of people think an app must be full-featured, based on their idea of what a full feature set is, to be successful, but your users might know better. It's better to get an app out quickly and iterate based on real-world feedback, because it's very easy to be wrong about what an app should have.

For example, Flickr started out as an online role-playing game with a photo-sharing tool, and only the photo-sharing part now survives. Be prepared to pivot!

1.2.1 Design

Designing an app is hard, especially for developers with no formal design training. We've all seen some pretty shocking UIs, mainly for in-house apps where developers have thrown all the content and controls onto the screen and left it at that. In the consumer mobile world, this is no longer an option. Users can jump ship to another app that does the same things as yours in the time it takes to download a few megabytes of data from an app store. They have no loyalty to your app, and a bad app can remove loyalty to your business.

For example, if you're a bank and people use your app to interact with their accounts every day and the experience is bad, they'd rather change their bank than keep using your bad app. You can get away with it in a corporate environment where your users are in-house and have to use whatever you put in front of them, but be prepared for complaints that may not be good for your career progression—especially if the CEO is one of the users.

There are several things to consider when designing an app:

- *Consistency*—Does your app look and work like other apps on the same platform, especially the ones provided by the OS vendor.

  For example, Android apps should follow the activity stack with the Back button doing what you'd expect. iOS apps should use tabs to switch between popular actions.

- *User experience*—Is your app easy to use and intuitive? A user should be able to just pick it up and know how to use it without any training. Being consistent with other apps can help with this.

  For example, avoid custom icons for buttons or menu items. Instead, use ones that are industry standard or just use text. No one cares that you think having your own custom icons will help promote your brand and make an app look like it's yours. Instead, they'll dump it if they can't understand how to use it.
- *Flow*—Does your app flow well? Is there an easy flow for a user to use the app? When one action naturally leads to another, the journey between the actions should be short and concise.

  For example, if your app is for taking photos, the options for editing or sharing a photo should be on the same screen where you view the photo you've taken, not buried in a menu that involves multiple steps to navigate.
- *Good looks*—Does your app look good, are any images well drawn and appropriate for the device size, is all text clear and readable, and are the colors consistent and appropriate?

  For example, an app could be run on a small phone, large phone, "phablet," small tablet, or large tablet. Any text on the screen must be readable in all formats, images must be sized to look good on all device sizes, and on-screen items should be spaced so that it's clear what the user is looking at without UI elements blending into each other due to lack of space.
- *Accessibility*—Is your app accessible to users with differing abilities?

  For example, if a user increases the default font size, is the app still usable? Are any audio alerts also available as visual alerts? Some of this is dependent on your target audience (for example, there is not much you can do to make a music player accessible to a deaf person), but a well-designed app will consider all possible users.

It might seem odd to introduce design now, at the start of the book, but it's an important thing to think about when you build your app. Although Xamarin provides you with the tools you need to write cross-platform apps sharing your core code, you still have to build the platform-specific layer, which includes different UI code for iOS and Android. As part of this UI layer, you need to consider what makes each platform different, and design each UI accordingly. For your app to be a success, it needs to be intuitive and look good on each platform, and part of this is consistency with what users of each platform are used to. I can't overemphasize the word *consistency* enough—your app shouldn't only be consistent with the platform but with itself. Any difference will cause user confusion, leading to a bad experience.

Ideally you either need skill as a designer, or access to someone with that skill. This can be easy in a corporate environment, but maybe not so easy for an indie developer doing everything on their own. The good news, though, is that the different OS vendors have you covered. They've all published a set of guidelines on how to build apps that not only look and work well, but are also consistent with other apps on that platform. Google has Material Design, Apple has its Human Interface Guidelines. We'll come back to these later in this book when we look at building UIs.

USABILITY

One of the key things about design is how usable your app is. An app that looks slick but is impossible to use is probably worse than an app that is bad to look at but works well. When you are designing your app the relevant platform guidelines can help ensure some consistency with other apps, but you are still responsible for ensuring a great user experience. While you are thinking of design also try out your user experience virtually—either with online tools (of which there are plenty) or simple tools like paper prototypes. With these you can mock up the UI and how it works and actually try it out—have people use the virtual or paper version as if it was a real app and see if it is natural to them. If they see the first screen of your app and have no idea what to do then you could lose a customer. Sometimes you only have seconds to draw a user in before they decide your app is no good and delete it, so it's vital to make those first user interactions simple and obvious. One very popular book on user experience design sums up the most important principle in its title: *'Don't make me think!'*.

1.2.2 Develop

This is the fun part—the bit we as developers love the most. Despite it being the best bit, it can also be less fun if we don't have good tools to help. A good developer can code in a raw text editor, but it's painful when you're used to a full-featured IDE. Luckily, as Xamarin developers, we're spoiled. On Windows there is Visual Studio, which is in my mind the best IDE around, especially when coupled with extensions like ReSharper from JetBrains. On Mac there's Visual Studio for Mac, which uses the same compiler platform as Visual Studio on Windows. These IDEs give you code completion, easy-to-use refactorings, and in-editor indications of suspect or erroneous code. They also provide full debugging support for Xamarin apps running either in an emulator/simulator or on an actual device.

Seeing as all Xamarin apps are .NET apps using a platform-specific .NET framework, you have access to a whole host of libraries built by third-party developers that are also built on the .NET framework. Despite the differences between .NET on Windows, iOS, and Android, there's a core subset that's common to all platforms, so any libraries that target this subset can be used in all your apps, and any libraries that target a particular platform can be used against that platform. This gives you access to a wealth of code that does all manner of things, from connecting to databases, handling JSON, and constructing unit tests to providing frameworks for application development. Access to these is provided by a packaging tool called NuGet (pronounced New-Get)—these libraries are packaged into a zip file with multiple libraries separated by whichever platform they target. At the time of writing, there are almost 57,000 unique packages available on NuGet.org, and the tools to use these packages are built into Visual Studio. You simply right-click, select Manage NuGet Packages, and from there install whatever you need. We'll look at these a bit more later because they'll be used in the apps built throughout this book.

Testing is an important part of coding—all good coders will write unit tests as they code, if not before. Luckily Visual Studio on Windows and Mac helps in this endeavor, providing a way to run or debug tests. With live unit testing in Visual Studio on Windows, or extensions like ReSharper with dotCover or NCrunch, you can even see in the editor which lines of code are covered by tests, color-coded to indicate which tests pass and which fail, and with the tests continuously running so it moves from red to green as you write code. You can also get IDE extensions to use things like behavior-driven design (BDD), which allows you to write your tests in natural language.

When you code your app, you need to think about testing all the time, to the point of choosing design patterns that help keep your code separated enough that it can be tested easily and thoroughly. When we look at how to actually build an app later in this book, we'll be using MVVM, a design pattern that enables this, and we'll think about testing at every step.

All these tools make coding a lot of fun and reduce the drudge work by making it easy to automate writing boilerplate code and easy to refactor, so you're never fighting with your code to improve it.

1.2.3 Test

Testing really goes hand in hand with coding. It's something that should be continuous, and ideally automated. Testing every feature of your app takes a long time, and sometimes it's very difficult to test every scenario, including the edge cases. If you can automate this, not only does it save time but it means you can fully test your app at every stage of development. That way you can catch bugs as soon as they appear, so you know what changes introduced them and you can fix them while these changes are fresh in your mind. If you don't know about them till the end of development, it's a lot harder to determine what caused the bug and find a fix.

The ability to run unit tests inside your IDE is a good thing because you have to think about how to test your code as you write. There are three types of testing to think about: unit testing, UI testing, and manual testing.

UNIT TESTING

Unit testing is testing units of code, with a unit being the smallest possible isolatable piece of code. These are black-box tests against the contract of a class, designed to test that class in isolation. If that class has dependencies on other classes, those dependencies should be mocked out and given predefined behavior to ensure you're just testing the one class in isolation.

For example, say you have a `Counter` class that has a `Count` property and an `IncrementCount` method. The behavior of the class is that when you call `IncrementCount`, the `Count` value goes up by 1. Here you can write a test that creates the class, calls `IncrementCount`, and verifies that the `Count` has gone up by 1 and only 1. If it doesn't go up, the test fails; if it goes up by anything other than 1, the test fails. You don't care about the implementation of the class—how it increments is of no interest, as this could change at any time. You just care about the contract—that `IncrementCount` increments the `Count` by 1. Once this test is written, you can be sure this method works, and if a bug appears in your app that looks like the `Count` is incremented by 2, you can easily see that if the unit test passes, the error is elsewhere in your app.

Another example would be a `SaveCount` method on your `Counter` class that saves the count to a web server by making a REST call passing some JSON. If your class is well written, it shouldn't talk to the web server directly but abstract that out to another class (we'll call it `WebService`) that actually makes the call. Your class just needs to construct the JSON and tell the other class which REST endpoint to use, passing it the JSON. In this case when you construct your `Counter` class instance, you have to pass it the `WebService` instance so it has something to call. As is, this isn't well separated into a unit for testing, but we can change that.

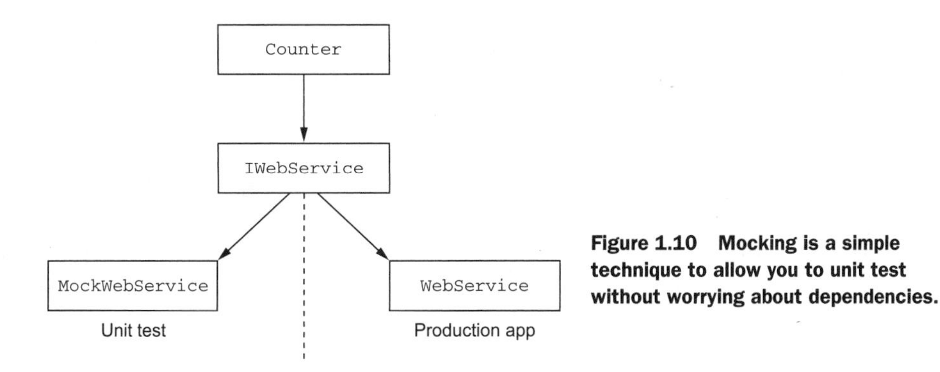

Figure 1.10 Mocking is a simple technique to allow you to unit test without worrying about dependencies.

If the `WebService` class implements an interface, `IWebService`, that defines the method to make the server call, you can instead pass the interface in when you construct your `Counter`. By doing this, you can mock the interface in your unit test—that is, have inside the test another object that implements the interface that you have control of. This way, you can call the `SaveCount` method and then inspect the call that was made to your interface and verify that the correct endpoint was called with the correct JSON.

UI TESTING

UI testing is the complete opposite of unit testing. Here you're considering your app as a whole and testing it as if you were a real user interacting with the app. Xamarin provides a tool called UITest to enable this. It's a library that allows you to write tests that look like unit tests and that are run using NUnit (a popular unit-testing tool), but these tests will launch your app on an emulator/simulator or physical device and perform interactions like tapping or swiping and allow you to query the UI to verify that everything works as expected.

For example, in an app that has a count shown in a label and a button that you tap to increment the count, you could write a UI test that launches the app, reads the value of the count label, taps the button, then re-reads the label, ensuring that the value has increased. Xamarin UITest does this by finding items inside the visual tree (the representation of the UI on screen) based on their name, ID, or contents. Once it finds these, you can read data or perform actions like tap, so a test could find the count label based on it having an ID of `Count` defined inside the Android layout or iOS storyboard, and it could read the text property from there. UI tests can also call backdoors—these are special methods embedded in your app to allow you make your tests more easily. You can use these to do things like prepopulate data to avoid performing lots of repetitive steps in the UI, or to emulate situations that are hard to do through a UI test, like switching off WiFi on Android to test connectivity issues.

Once you have UI tests that run and pass on an emulator or your physical device, it would be nice to run them on more devices. One of the downsides to mobile development is the large number of possible devices and OS versions. On iOS this isn't such an issue because most people keep their OS up to date, and there's only a small range of devices. On Android it's a massive problem as there are thousands of possible devices, and OS updates aren't available to all due to manufacturer and carrier-provided tweaks. If Google updates Android, the device manufacturer needs to take that update and apply it to their version of Android and give it to the carrier, who then needs to apply it to their version before it's available to be installed on the device. In a lot of cases, the manufacturer or carrier won't do this, especially for older devices, meaning there's massive fragmentation of OS versions on Android. At the time of writing, 85% of iOS devices are on the latest version of iOS. On Android, only 7.5% are on the latest, with 20% one version behind, 16% two versions behind, 33% three versions behind, and the remainder on even earlier versions.

What Xamarin provides to get around this is a service called Test Cloud. This is thousands of physical devices from different manufacturers with different OS versions set up in a data center, and you can rent time on these devices to run your UI tests. This way you can cover a wide range of device sizes and OS versions, and when you review the results you see not only which tests pass or fail, but you can get screenshots of every step, so you can see how the UI looks. This can be invaluable when you have a bug that only manifests itself on one OS or one screen size and you don't have an emulator or physical device available that replicates it. This is integrated into Visual Studio—one click to deploy your test and run it in the cloud.

MANUAL TESTING

Yup, you're on your own with this one. Manual testing means you have to interact with your app to try everything out. Ideally, if you've implemented good unit and UI tests, you've verified that your app works correctly. Manual testing should then be a quick sanity check to ensure any edge cases that can't be tested using automation (such as launching external apps) are working. You should also manually test as you go along, to verify the usability of the app, verifying the user experience. Automated tests can verify whether something works correctly, but you still need to interact with the app yourself to see if things work intuitively. After implementing each feature in the app, you should try it out to make sure it follows your app's design (as well as the design guidelines for each app), and to ensure it's easy to use and gives good feedback.

For usability testing you should also consider hallway testing—going up to people and getting them to try the app out and see what feedback they give. When you do this, you should try to mimic the real-world experience as much as possible. Just give them the app and leave them to it with no help, much like an end user who has just downloaded it from the app store. If they can't work out how to use your app, you may need to reconsider the user experience.

1.2.4 Build

Continuous integration (CI) is the process whereby you continuously integrate your code changes into the core codebase and test it each time. In its simplest form, it's having something that detects when code is changed inside your source code repository (such as on GitHub or BitBucket), builds your app, and runs your tests so you can see straightaway if you've broken the build or introduced a bug. This is a huge topic so I won't cover it in much detail here, but I'll touch on some areas that are relevant to Xamarin developers. There are a number of different CI tools around, and they all have some degree of support for Xamarin apps (even the most basic ones support Xamarin, because the tooling works from the command line).

There are hundreds of possibilities for the kinds of builds you could set up from a CI system. For example, you could have a check-in build that monitors your source code repo, and every time new code is checked in, it builds it and runs all your unit tests. You could then have another build that runs at the same time every night, getting the latest code, building it, running the unit tests, and then running all of the UI tests locally. Finally, you could have a release build that's triggered manually, which gets the code, builds it, runs the unit tests, runs the UI tests, and (if all passes) packages the build up and deploys it to the app store.

The main thing you want with these builds is the continuous feedback loop—every check-in should be verified to see that it builds and the tests pass; if there are any errors, the person checking in the code should be notified so they can fix the error directly. Some CI systems can even take this further and provide precommit builds—the code you want to commit is built and tests are run, and only if everything passes is the code committed. If the build or tests fail, the commit is rolled back.

When choosing a CI system, you need to consider how good their support is for Xamarin apps and how much time you want to spend configuring them. Jenkins, for example, is a free tool and is fantastic for Java apps, but its Xamarin support is nonexistent at the time of writing, so setting up builds is a lot of work. Other tools have Xamarin support out of the box, so it's easy to set up. The main one for Xamarin apps is Visual Studio App Center.

App Center (https://appcenter.ms) is described as "Mission Control for your apps." You can connect to it using a GitHub or Microsoft account, point it to a Git repository in GitHub, VSTS, or BitBucket, and then it's trivial to set up builds. You choose which type of app to build (iOS or Android), choose a branch to build from, point it at your solution or project file, choose the build configuration, and away it goes. You can also add signing certificates to allow your builds to run on real devices, and even launch your app on a device once it's built as a sanity check to ensure that it works.

1.2.5 Distribute

You've designed your app, coded it up, tested it, and built it. Now you need to get it into the hands of your users. You could submit it to the relevant app store, but first it's good to put it in the hands of beta testers.

App Center allows you to set up alpha and beta users and distribute your app directly to them. Once they have your app, you can push out updated builds as you fix bugs or make tweaks, and when they relaunch the app your users will be prompted to install these updates. This is direct to the users you want to do the testing, it's not an open marketplace. Your users will only be able to download your app if they're registered against it, so you have complete control of the distribution.

1.2.6 Monitor

Once your app is released and being used, you should monitor it. If your users are experiencing crashes, you can expect a slew of one-star reviews that will drive potential new users away. Your app will have bugs in it (that's a fact of software development), but if you can monitor for these and fix the issues as soon as possible, you can minimize the impact. If you know that crashes have happened, you can do something about it immediately, and that will help with your app downloads. Remember, your customers won't file bug reports and eagerly await a fix. They'll just download another app that does the same thing as yours.

For the Xamarin developer, it's easy to monitor for crashes using App Center. You can integrate the App Center SDK into your app as easily as installing a NuGet package and adding one line of code. This will track all crashes and upload stack traces to the App Center site so you can quickly see the line of code where it happened, get it fixed, and get a new version deployed. This is an invaluable tool—the quicker you can fix a crash, the less chance you have of losing users.

In addition, App Center allows you to do user and event tracking so you can see not only the demographics of your audience but also how they're using your app. Again, this can be important in making your app as good as possible. If a particular feature of your app is being used regularly, then it's something to work on and improve. If a feature is never used, then either it's not wanted by your users or not obvious, so you can strip it out or make it easier to discover. If your app is popular in a particular country, you can add native language support for that country if it's not there already. You can also track the path a user takes through your app, and if popular features are hidden behind a lot of interactions, you can change the user experience to surface those features more quickly.

All this is easy to add to your Xamarin app—just one line of code per user action to track what they're doing. Demographic data comes as soon as you enable the SDK. If you capture the right data and use it correctly, you'll have a powerful tool to help shape your app.

1.3 Rinse and repeat...

Monitoring is the final step in the mobile-optimized development lifecycle, a cycle that repeats with every iteration of your app. It's no good resting on your laurels after a release; it's time to fix bugs and add new features. Figure 1.11 sums up the steps.

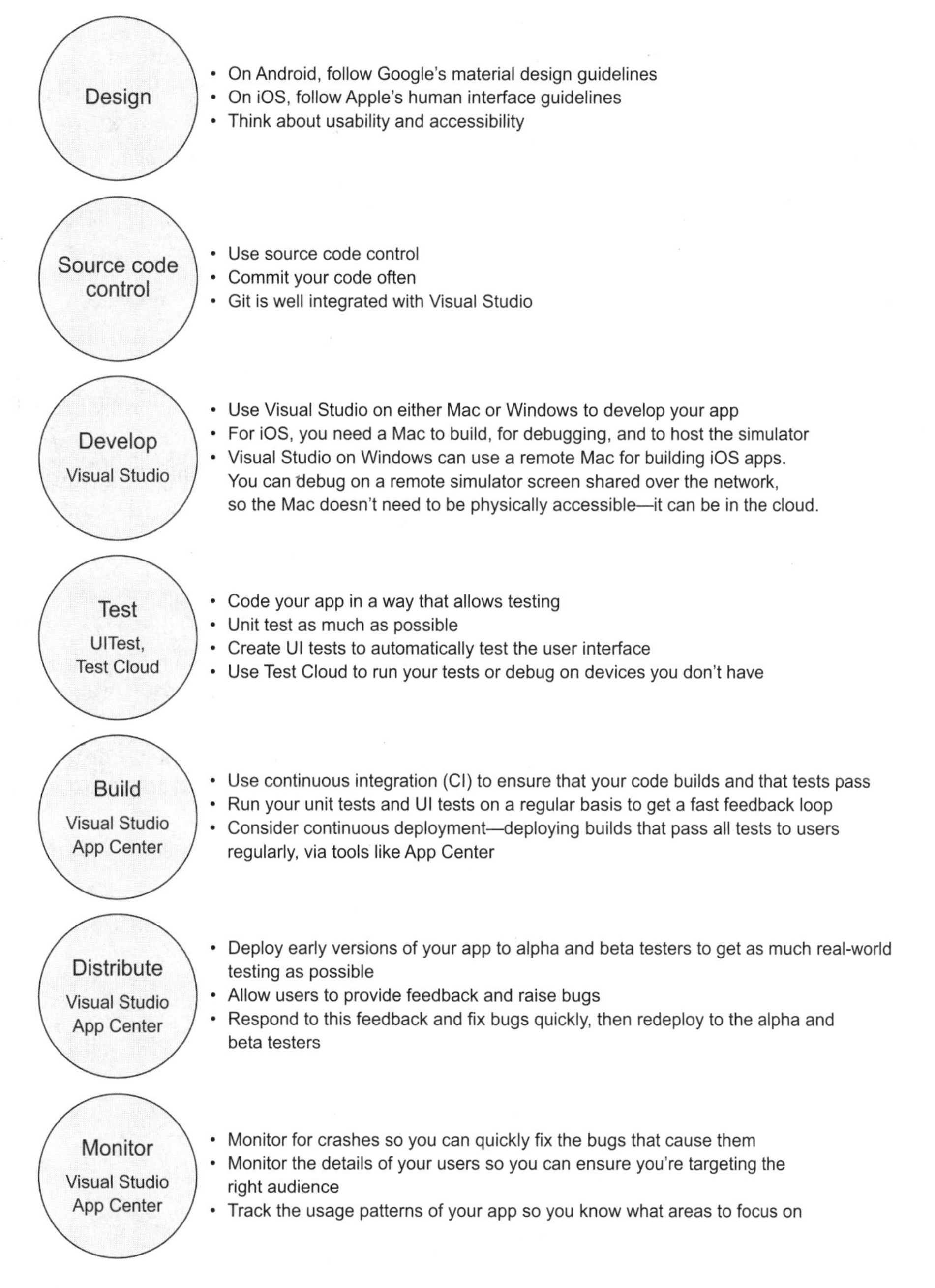

Design
• On Android, follow Google's material design guidelines
• On iOS, follow Apple's human interface guidelines
• Think about usability and accessibility
Source code control
• Use source code control
• Commit your code often
• Git is well integrated with Visual Studio
Develop
Visual Studio
• Use Visual Studio on either Mac or Windows to develop your app
• For iOS, you need a Mac to build, for debugging, and to host the simulator
• Visual Studio on Windows can use a remote Mac for building iOS apps. You can debug on a remote simulator screen shared over the network, so the Mac doesn't need to be physically accessible—it can be in the cloud.
Test
UITest, Test Cloud
• Code your app in a way that allows testing
• Unit test as much as possible
• Create UI tests to automatically test the user interface
• Use Test Cloud to run your tests or debug on devices you don't have
Build
Visual Studio
App Center
• Use continuous integration (CI) to ensure that your code builds and that tests pass
• Run your unit tests and UI tests on a regular basis to get a fast feedback loop
• Consider continuous deployment—deploying builds that pass all tests to users regularly, via tools like App Center
Distribute
Visual Studio
App Center
• Deploy early versions of your app to alpha and beta testers to get as much real-world testing as possible
• Allow users to provide feedback and raise bugs
• Respond to this feedback and fix bugs quickly, then redeploy to the alpha and beta testers
Monitor
Visual Studio
App Center
• Monitor for crashes so you can quickly fix the bugs that cause them
• Monitor the details of your users so you can ensure you're targeting the right audience
• Track the usage patterns of your app so you know what areas to focus on

Figure 1.11 A summary of all the steps for each cycle of a production app

Keep your cycles small so it's easy to change direction based on feedback from your monitoring or your users. But don't make them so small that your users are updating their apps too often (next-day release is important for fixing bugs, but keep features updates at least a week apart). Regular updates are important because they make your users feel like your app is here to stay, and they're good for promoting your app, as the stores highlight recently updated apps.

Now that you've seen this lifecycle in detail, it's time to put some of this into practice and write some code that demonstrates the power of Xamarin apps. In the next chapter we'll look at a design pattern that can help you build cross-platform Xamarin apps by increasing the amount of cross-platform code that can be shared across iOS and Android apps. Then we'll follow tradition and build a cross-platform Hello World application.

Summary

In this chapter you learned

- Xamarin native apps are apps built in C# using a version of the .NET framework based on Mono that's been customized to run on iOS and Android and using libraries that wrap the native device SDKs.
- Xamarin apps are better than native apps written using the vendor tools because you get all the power of a native app with all the features of the device and OS, but they're written in a common language, allowing you to share common logic and code between apps on different platforms.
- Xamarin has tools for the mobile-optimized development lifecycle, covering developing, testing, building, distributing, and monitoring.
- There's more to a production-quality mobile app than just coding. You first need to consider the design of your app to ensure that it's suitable for the platform you're targeting. You also need to code it well, ensure it's fully tested, build it in a reproducible way, deploy it, and monitor it for issues once it's in the wild.

2 *Hello MVVM—creating a simple cross-platform app using MVVM*

This chapter covers

- What MVVM is and why it's the best choice for cross-platform Xamarin apps
- What the MVVM design pattern is all about, and why you'd want to use it to maximize your cross-platform code
- Getting set up with Xamarin and the MvvmCross extension
- Creating HelloCrossPlatformWorld, your first Xamarin mobile app
- Running your app on iOS and Android

Typically at this point in a book, it's traditional to build a Hello World app to show off the technology in question. For this book, though, I'm going to go slightly against tradition and start by discussing the MVVM (model-view–view model) design pattern. Then we'll get our hands dirty with some code toward the end of this chapter.

WE'RE DISCUSSING MVVM FOR CROSS-PLATFORM XAMARIN APPS The principles discussed in this chapter are for using MVVM with Xamarin apps. Although these follow the principles for MVVM on other platforms, such as desktop Windows apps or the web, there's a lot more to it for Xamarin apps. If you've done MVVM before (maybe with WPF) it's still worth reading this chapter as there are some important differences.

2.1 What are UI design patterns?

Over time, developers have come across and solved the same problems again and again. Out of this has come a set of abstract solutions that can be applied when building your code. These are known as *design patterns*—repeatable solutions to common problems that occur when designing and building software.

Building apps that interact with the user through a user interface (UI) is no different. There are standard problems that developers want to solve, and a number of patterns have come about as solutions to these problems.

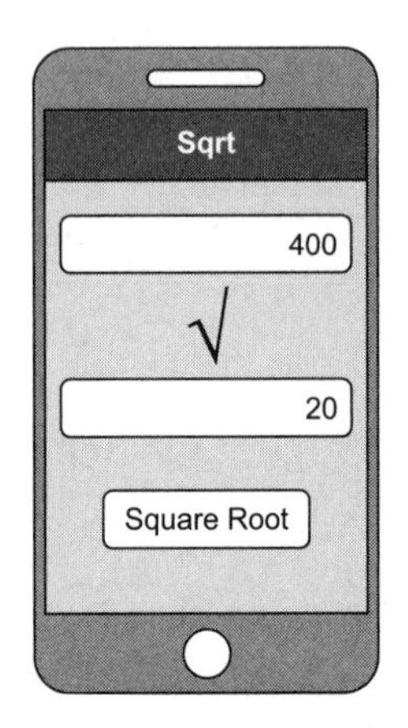

Figure 2.1 A simple square-root calculator app that calculates the square root of a given number

Let's consider a simple square-root calculator app called Sqrt that has a text box you can put a number in, and a button. When you tap the button, it calculates the square root of the number in the text box and shows the answer on a label. An example of this app is shown in figure 2.1.

The simplest way to write this app is to wire up the button to an event that takes the value directly from the text box, calculates the square root, and writes the value to a label. All this can be done in the code-behind file for the UI. Simple, and all in one class. The following listing has some pseudocode for the kind of thing you might write.

Listing 2.1 Pseudocode for adding numbers by wiring to the UI directly

```
MyAddButton.Click += (s, e) =>
{
   var number = double.Parse(NumberTextBox.Text);
   var sqrt = Math.Sqrt(number);
   MyResultLabel.Text = sqrt.ToString();
}
```

- Listens for the Click event of the button
- The number comes from reading the value from the Text property of the text box.
- Once the square root is calculated, the Text property of the label is set directly.

Although this seems simple, it has a number of flaws.

First, this isn't easily testable. You can only test this app by updating the value in the text box and tapping the button. It would be better if you could write unit tests so you could programmatically test the code, covering multiple cases including edge cases, such as missing inputs or large or negative numbers. This way you could run a set of automated tests quickly and repeatably every time you change your code.

Second, this isn't cross-platform. One of the reasons for building apps using Xamarin is so that parts of your app can be written in shared code that works on both iOS and Android. If your calculation is wired directly to the view, you can't do this. Think back to the layers introduced in chapter 1, shown in figure 2.2.

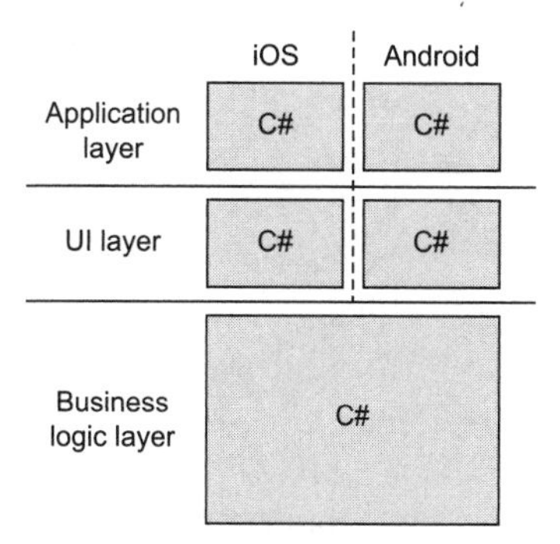

Figure 2.2 Xamarin apps are written in C# so you can share any common business logic while having a platform-specific UI.

In a Xamarin app we have three layers:

- *Application layer*—This is a small part of the code that makes your app runnable on each platform and has different platform-specific implementations for iOS and Android.
- *UI layer*—The UI layer also has separate platform-specific implementations for iOS and Android.
- *Business logic layer*—The business logic layer is shared between the two platforms.

To fit the calculator code into this structure, you'd need to have your calculation code in the cross-platform business logic layer, and the button, text box, label, and all the wiring in the UI layer. This is the kind of problem all UI developers come across on a daily basis, and, as you'd expect, there's a design pattern to help with this—MVVM.

2.2 MVVM—the design pattern for Xamarin apps

MVVM (model-view–view model) is the most popular design pattern for cross-platform apps built using Xamarin, and it has a history of being a very successful design pattern for building Windows desktop apps using WPF, Silverlight apps, and now Windows 10 UWP apps. It has even made its way onto the web with frameworks like knockout.js using it. When Xamarin designed Xamarin.Forms, whose goal was to have as much code sharing as possible, the principles of MVVM were baked into the underlying framework right off the bat.

Think back to the three layers in the Xamarin app. These three layers enable a reasonable amount of code sharing, but we can do better. In the UI layer there are really two layers—the actual UI widgets, and some logic around these widgets. For example, we could put some logic around the answer label to make it only visible once the square root has been calculated. This expands our three layers to four.

Figure 2.3 shows the how the layers would look if we could move this UI logic into shared code. If we did this, the label in our example would be in the UI layer, and the logic that decides whether it should be visible or hidden would be in the cross-platform UI logic layer. This is a great way to do things—we're maximizing code reuse by abstracting the UI logic into cross-platform code.

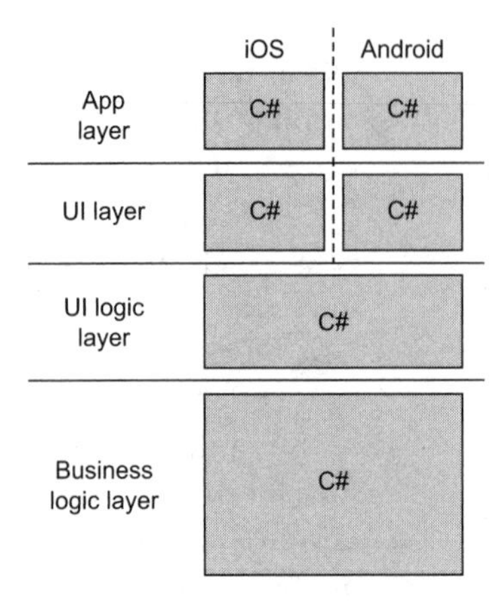

Figure 2.3 To maximize code reuse, it would be good to have UI logic in shared code.

MVVM helps with this splitting-out of the UI and its logic. This pattern is named based on the three layers that you use in your app, as shown in figure 2.4. Let's look at these layers in the context of our calculator example:

- *Model*—Your data and business logic.

  The model is the data, business logic, and access to any external resources (such as web services or databases) defined in terms of the domain, and this maps to the business logic layer in our Xamarin app. In our example, the model contains the number, the logic to calculate the square root, and the result.
- *View*—The actual UI, buttons, text controls, and all other widgets.

  The view is the UI with all its widgets and layouts, and this maps to part of the UI layer and holds the UI widgets (the text box, button, and label). This is a passive view, so it doesn't have any code to get or set the values or to handle events, such as the button click.
- *View model*—The UI data and logic.

  For our calculator app, this has properties that represent the numbers on the model—the input value and the result. It also has a command property that wraps the square root calculation logic on the model into an object (more on commands in the next chapter). The view model knows about the model but has no knowledge of the view.

In addition to these three layers, it has a *binder*, a binding layer that you can think of as glue that connects the view model to the view. This removes the need to write boilerplate code to synchronize the UI—the binder can watch for changes in the view model and update the view to match, or update the view model to match changes made by the user in the UI. This binder is loosely coupled rather than tightly coupled, and the connection is often made based on wiring up properties in the view and view model based on their names (so in the case of a binding between a property called `Text` and a property called `Name`, at runtime the binder will use reflection to map these string values to the underlying properties).

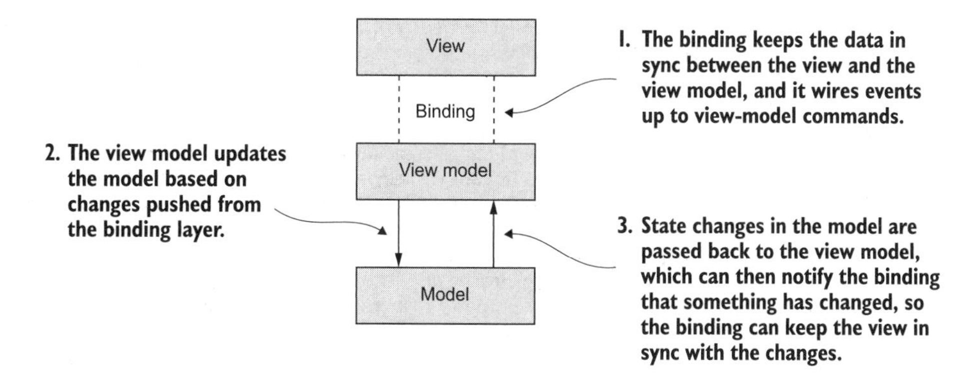

Figure 2.4 MVVM has a model, a view model, a view, and a binding layer that keeps the view and view model in sync and connects events on the view to the view model.

> **Reflecting on reflection**
>
> If you've never heard of reflection before, it's a part of the C# API that allows you to query details about a class—you can discover properties, fields, methods, or events. Once you've found out the details, you can also execute code. For example, you can find a property based on its name and then get the value of that property from a particular instance of that class. Reflection is also common in other languages such as Java—C# reflection is basically the same as Java reflection.
>
> This is great for binding—if you bind a property called `Name`, the binding code can use reflection to find a property on your view-model class with that same name, and then it can get the value on your view-model instance.

For our calculator app, the binding would wire up the text box, button, and label on the UI to the equivalent properties and a command on the view model.

There's a bit of magic involved in making this binder work, and this is usually implemented in an MVVM framework—a third-party library that gives you a set of base classes providing the implementation of this pattern. I cover how this works later in this chapter.

> **MVVM FRAMEWORKS** There are multiple MVVM frameworks that work with Xamarin native apps, such as MvvmCross, MVVM Light, and Caliburn.Micro. Although each one has differences, they all follow the same basic principles and do roughly the same things. Later in this book we'll be using MvvmCross, but everything in this book is applicable to most frameworks.

For example, as shown in figure 2.5, we could have a text box on our calculator app UI that's *bound* to a `Number` property. This means that at runtime it will try to find a public property called `Number` on the view model that it's bound to using reflection,

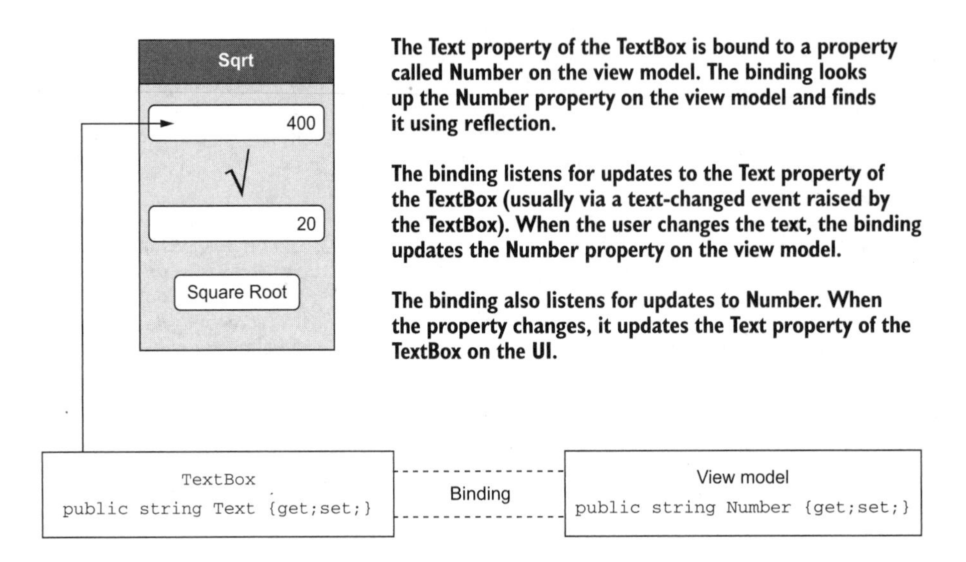

Sqrt
400
√
20
Square Root
The Text property of the TextBox is bound to a property called Number on the view model. The binding looks up the Number property on the view model and finds it using reflection.
The binding listens for updates to the Text property of the TextBox (usually via a text-changed event raised by the TextBox). When the user changes the text, the binding updates the Number property on the view model.
The binding also listens for updates to Number. When the property changes, it updates the Text property of the TextBox on the UI.
TextBox
public string Text {get;set;}
Binding
View model
public string Number {get;set;}

Figure 2.5 Binding keeps the value on the view in sync with the value in the view model.

and it will show the string contained in that property in the text box. If the user changes the value inside the text box, it will update the value of the `Number` property to match what the user has typed in. Conversely, if the value of the `Number` property on the view model changes, the binding will update the text box to match.

The binder doesn't care what the underlying class type is of the view model you're using, just that it has a public property called `Number` that it can extract the value from. In some of the MVVM frameworks, it doesn't even care if the property is there or not. If it can't find the property, it just treats it as an empty value. This loose coupling is what makes MVVM especially powerful—it allows view models to be completely agnostic to the view, so you can write unit tests against the view model that simulate the UI without worrying about UI code getting in the way. It also supports code reuse, so a view could be glued to any view model that has properties with the names it's expecting.

Figure 2.6 expands on the previous figures by showing how these layers map to the three layers of MVVM:

- *App layer*—The app layer is one that doesn't really come under the pure MVVM design pattern, but the different MVVM frameworks do provide some application-layer features. This allows us to have some cross-platform code in our app layer that can control app logic, such as which view is shown first and how the different classes in the app are wired together, such as defining which view model is used for each view.
- *UI layer*—The UI layer is our view layer, and this is platform-specific code.
- *Binding*—The binding between the UI layer and the UI logic layer is the binder—the glue that connects the UI layer to its logic layer. This is usually a

mix of cross-platform and platform-specific code provided by a third-party framework.

- *UI logic layer*—The UI logic layer is our view-model layer. It provides logic for the UI and other device interactions in a cross-platform way. Part of this logic is value conversion—converting from data in your domain objects to data on the UI. For example, you could model a user in your domain with a first name and last name but on the UI want to show the full name. The view model will provide this value conversion by concatenating the names and giving one string value that will be shown by the UI.

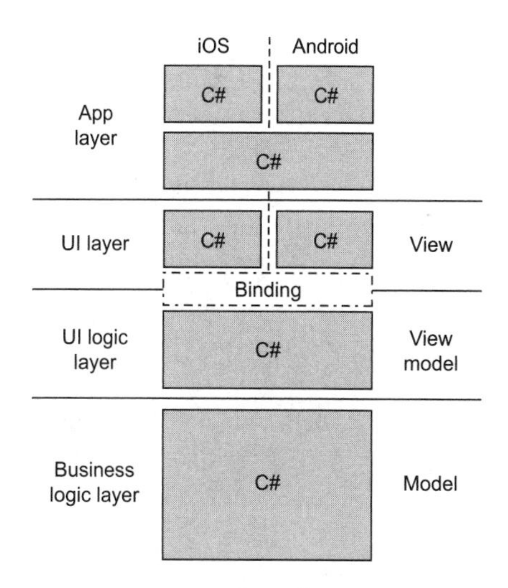

Figure 2.6 The different layers of MVVM fit with the different layers of a Xamarin app.

- *Business logic layer*—The business logic layer is the model layer. This contains data, domain objects, logic, and connectivity to external resources such as databases or web services. Again, this is cross-platform.

A QUICK HISTORY LESSON MVVM has been around since 2005 and was developed by two architects from Microsoft, Ken Cooper and Ted Peters. It was primarily created for use with the new UI technology stack coming out of Microsoft called WPF, and it leverages the data binding that was a key feature of WPF. In WPF you write your UI using XAML, a UI-based markup language, and in this XAML you can bind the properties of a UI widget to properties defined in the data context of the view—essentially the view model. This allowed UI/UX experts to design the UI using more designer-based tools, and to simply wire the widgets, based on their names, to code written independently by developers.

2.3 What is cross-platform code?

Some of the layers in our MVVM-based app use cross-platform code—specifically, part of the app layer, the UI logic (view-model) layer, and the business logic (model) layer. The reason for this is simple—we're building an app for both iOS and Android, so the app will need to work the same way on both platforms, use the same type of data, and have roughly the same UI logic. It makes a lot of sense to build this once and use the same code on both apps—code that we write once and can run on iOS and Android. The term *cross-platform code* has come up a lot already in this book, and it will continue to be a theme throughout. But what exactly do we mean when we talk about cross-platform code in C#?

Cross-platform native apps are not truly cross-platform

In the Xamarin world we talk of cross-platform native apps, but these are not true cross-platform apps where exactly the same app will run on all platforms. Neither is it cross-platform in that all the code runs on all platforms (with a hidden app layer).

What I mean here is that we have two apps, one that runs on iOS and one that runs on Android, both developed using the same language and sharing a large portion of the code. They're cross-platform in that the business logic (and ideally the UI logic) is truly cross-platform, and the smallest possible device-specific UI and feature layer is built to be platform-specific.

The MVVM design pattern is very well suited to helping you get as much code-sharing as possible.

2.3.1 .NET Standard class libraries

When Microsoft released the .NET Framework, they provided a set of APIs that work on Windows, and with each version of the framework they added more APIs that developers can use. Over time, support for more platforms was added, such as Microsoft's Silverlight (apps running in a browser) or the Windows Store (apps running in a sandbox and distributed via a Microsoft app store). These different platforms didn't provide the same capabilities, so code written against the core .NET Framework might not work on Silverlight if it required APIs that Silverlight didn't (or couldn't) implement. The initial solution to this was portable class libraries (PCLs)—libraries that targeted a common subset of the .NET APIs that would run on all platforms. Xamarin took advantage of this, using the same model to allow you to write portable class libraries that targeted the subset of the .NET Framework that runs on iOS or Android.

This worked after a fashion, but it caused a lot of confusion. PCLs come in *profiles*—a profile being a defined subset that will work on a particular combination of platforms. One profile would work on iOS, Android, and Windows under .NET 4.5, whereas another would also run on iOS and Android but require .NET 4.6. This meant that not only would you need to choose the right profile for the platforms you were targeting, but you'd also need any third-party libraries to also target a compatible profile. If your profile included .NET 4.5 on Windows, you couldn't use a library that used a profile that needed .NET 4.6, for example.

Things are now a lot better, thanks to a new initiative from Microsoft called .NET Standard. This is an attempt to standardize the different .NET platforms into a versioned set of APIs. Each platform, such as Xamarin iOS, Xamarin Android, or the .NET Framework on Windows implements a particular version of the standard, as well as all previous versions. This is an inclusive standard, so if a platform supports .NET Standard 1.6, it also includes 1.5, 1.4, and so on, all the way back to 1.0. The idea behind this is simple—each version has more APIs available than the previous version, and your code can use libraries that target the same or an earlier version of the standard. For example, if your code targets .NET Standard 1.6, you can use a library that targets 1.4. You can think of the .NET Framework on Windows as the most complete set of APIs, and each .NET Standard version as a more complete implementation of the full .NET Framework.

You can read more on .NET Standard libraries, and see what version of the standard is implement by which version of each platform on Microsoft Docs at http://mng.bz/sB0y. At the time of writing, Xamarin iOS and Android supports version 2.0, so you can use code that targets 2.0 or earlier from your Xamarin apps. Be aware, though, that targeting higher versions may limit the platforms you support. At the time of writing, UWP only supports 1.4, so if you decide to add a UWP project to your Xamarin apps to support Windows 10, you'll need to ensure the core projects used by your app target 1.4 or lower.

These .NET Standard libraries are perfect for the cross-platform layer in your Xamarin apps. The set of APIs that .NET Standard libraries implement includes all the bits that would work on all platforms—collections, Tasks, simple I/O, and networking. What isn't included is anything that's specific to a platform, such as UI code. This is left up to platform-specific code to implement. .NET Standard is just an API specification, it's not the actual implementation. Under the hood, the code that makes up the subset of the .NET APIs isn't the same on all platforms, each platform implements their features using the native API that the platform provides. But the interface to it—the classes and namespaces—are the same.

When you write your cross-platform app, you want as much code as possible inside .NET Standard libraries, as this is the code that's shared. Thinking again about the layers in our app, you can easily see which layers would live in a .NET Standard library, as shown in figure 2.7.

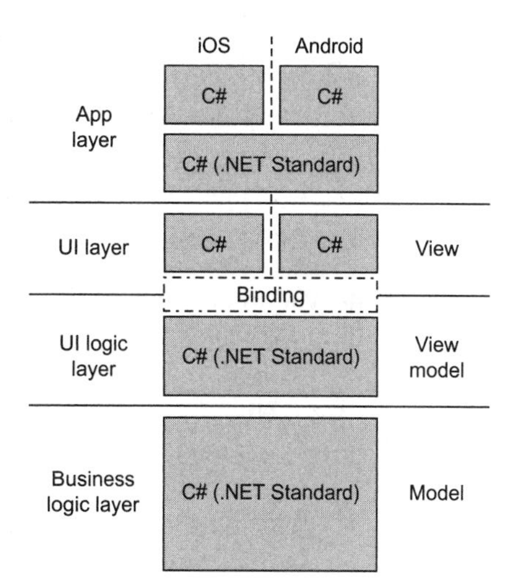

Figure 2.7 The cross-platform layers in a mobile app are implemented in .NET Standard libraries.

To map this to the project structure you're probably used to in a C# solution, you'd have (at least) three projects. One (or more) would be a .NET Standard project containing all your cross-platform UI and business logic code. Another would be an iOS app project that contains the iOS application code and the iOS UI code. And the last would be an Android app that contains the Android-specific UI and application code. This is illustrated in figure 2.8.

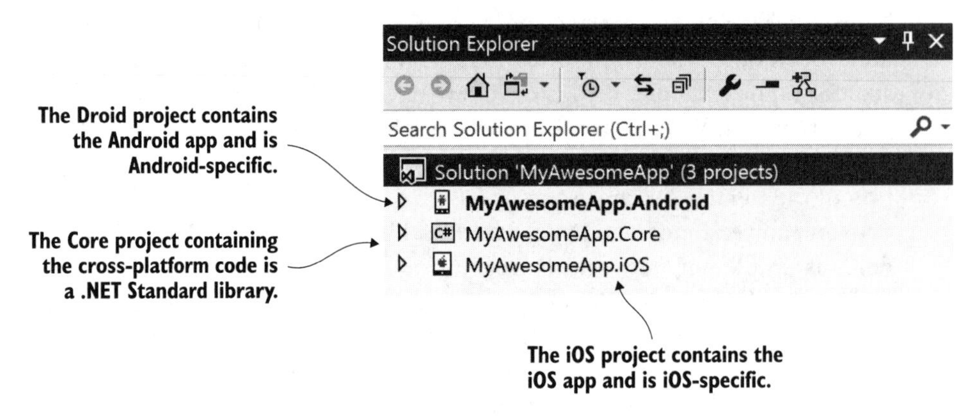
The Droid project contains the Android app and is Android-specific.
The Core project containing the cross-platform code is a .NET Standard library.
The iOS project contains the iOS app and is iOS-specific.
Solution Explorer
Search Solution Explorer (Ctrl+;)
Solution 'MyAwesomeApp' (3 projects)
MyAwesomeApp.Android
MyAwesomeApp.Core
MyAwesomeApp.iOS

Figure 2.8 A typical cross-platform app would contain a .NET Standard library with the core code, an Android app with Android-specific code, and an iOS app with iOS-specific code

Now that you've seen some of the basics, let's build a simple example app using the MvvmCross MVVM framework.

2.4 Getting started—creating your first solution

As promised, you're now going to create a Hello World app—a simple app that doesn't do very much but allows you to be sure your development environment is working correctly, and to see how simple it is to create a working app. Because the big strength of Xamarin is to allow you to create cross-platform apps with a large amount of code sharing, you're going to create two apps: one for iOS and one for Android. They will share a common core library with all the business logic—inasmuch as you can have business logic in a Hello World app. You'll also leverage what you've learned in this chapter and build it using MVVM. The MvvmCross framework you'll be using here will save you writing a lot of boilerplate code. This framework is hugely popular with developers building cross-platform Xamarin apps, and it's very actively maintained and enhanced.

> **MVVMCROSS** We'll be covering what you need to know about MvvmCross to build your example apps in this book. If you want to read more about it (or contribute to the framework—it's fully open source and welcomes contributions) then head to https://mvvmcross.com.

We'll be following these steps to achieve this:

- *Creating and running a new cross-platform app*—We'll be creating a cross-platform MvvmCross app using a Visual Studio extension that we'll be installing. Once this solution has been created, we'll fire it up on iOS and Android as a sanity check.
- *Proving the code is cross-platform*—Just to prove we have a cross-platform app with shared code, we'll be tweaking the code in one place and seeing the effect it has on both apps.

Despite using MvvmCross here and in the apps we'll build in later chapters, the aim is not to lock you into this framework. We'll only be using some small parts of it, and the principles behind those parts are pretty standard for the MVVM pattern. These principles are easy to apply when using other frameworks, such as MVVM Light.

2.4.1 Requirements—what hardware or software do you need for each mobile platform?

In chapter 1 we discussed Xamarin's platform support and the tooling you can use. Here's a quick refresher:

- If you have a Windows PC, you need to install Visual Studio 2017 and ensure the "Xamarin" workload is ticked in the installer.
- If you have a Mac, you need to install Visual Studio for Mac, which includes Visual Studio as well as the iOS and Android Xamarin components, the Android SDK, and Google's Android emulator. You also need to install Xcode from the Mac App Store for iOS development.
- If you want to develop iOS apps using Visual Studio on Windows, you need to have access to a Mac with Xamarin and Xcode installed.
- Always install or upgrade to the latest stable versions of all components, such as the latest version of VS 2017, the latest VS for Mac, the latest Xcode, and the latest Android SDK and tools. To install the latest Android SDK and tools, you'll need to use the Android SDK manager, available from Visual Studio by going to Tools > Android > Android SDK Manager on Windows or Tools > SDK Manager on the Mac.

This book doesn't cover installation

The Visual Studio installers change pretty often, so it's hard to keep up with them in print. Although this book does outline what's needed, it doesn't cover installation and configuration in detail.

At the time of writing, the Visual Studio for Mac installer gives you everything you need on Mac, including Android SDKs and emulators. The only extra thing you need to install is Xcode from the Mac App Store to build iOS apps.

On Windows, the Visual Studio 2017 installer installs everything, as long as you tick the right options for cross-platform development, Android SDKs, and emulators, which change a bit with each update. If you're using a Windows virtual machine on your Mac to run Visual Studio, you'll need to enable your virtual machine to host a nested virtual machine if you want to run the Android emulators—check the VM documentation for how to do this. If you use a PC, you'll need an Intel CPU with virtualization enabled (most modern CPUs have this). The system requirements for running the emulators are listed at the Android Studio site (http://mng.bz/hkXV).

> ***(continued)***
> If you get stuck, Xamarin has great documentation on its website (https://aka.ms/XamDocs) covering everything you need for installation and setup. The site also has helpful forums with a great community of users, and Xamarin's own engineers if you get a particularly strange problem. And obviously, there's always Stack Overflow.

At this point I'm going to assume you already have everything you need installed. If not, now would be a good time to do it.

For this little test app, we're only going to test on the Android emulator and iOS simulator, so don't worry if you don't have a physical device to use. If you do have a physical device, then put it to one side for now and just use the emulator/simulator as there's a bit of device setup you need to do to run and debug apps on real devices. On Android this is simple, but on iOS it's a bit more complicated. We'll be discussing this in chapter 13.

As previously mentioned, we'll be using the MvvmCross framework, and luckily for us there's an extension available for Visual Studio that allows us to create a new cross-platform solution. This solution contains a core library and platform-specific apps for all supported platforms (so on Visual Studio for Mac you get an iOS app and an Android app; on Windows it's iOS, Android, WPF, and UWP). Seeing as we'll be installing an extension, and the projects we create will need NuGet packages, you'll need internet access. This may sound obvious, but if you're in a coffee shop, now would be a good time to grab their WiFi password.

2.4.2 Creating the solution

Let's look at how to install the extension and create our first solution.

CREATING THE SOLUTION USING VISUAL STUDIO FOR MAC

From Visual Studio, select Visual Studio > Extensions. This will bring up a dialog box to allow you to add or remove extensions. From here, select the Gallery tab, ensure the repository is set to Visual Studio Extension Repository, and look for MvvmCross Template Pack under IDE Extensions, or by using the search (see figure 2.9). Select this and click Install. Then click Install on the dialog box that pops up.

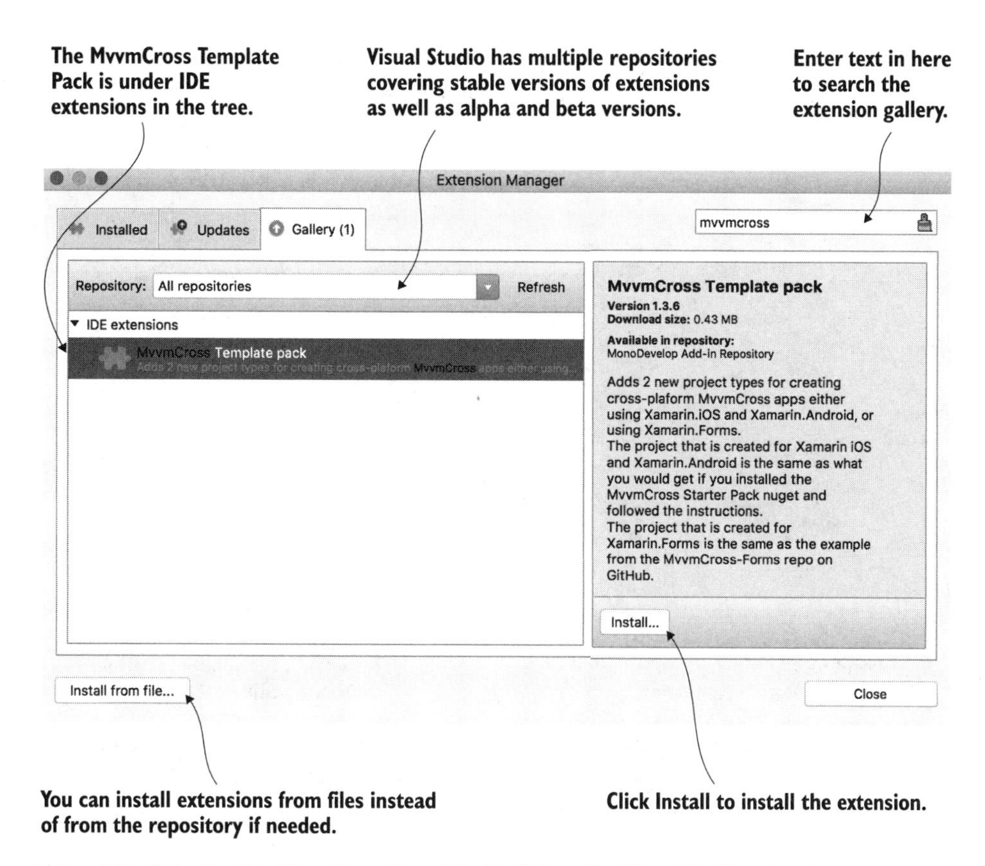

Figure 2.9 Selecting the MvvmCross Template Pack from the Visual Studio extension manager

Once this is installed, it's a good idea to restart Visual Studio, as the new solution type won't appear in the right place until you do.

Once Visual Studio is restarted, you can start creating a new solution. You can access the New Solution dialog box in three ways.

- From the menu by going to File > New > Solution
- Using the keyboard shortcut Shift-Command-N (⇧+⌘+N)
- By clicking the New Project button at the bottom of the Get Started page shown when you open Visual Studio for the first time. Whichever way you choose, you'll then be presented with the New Solution dialog box (figure 2.10).

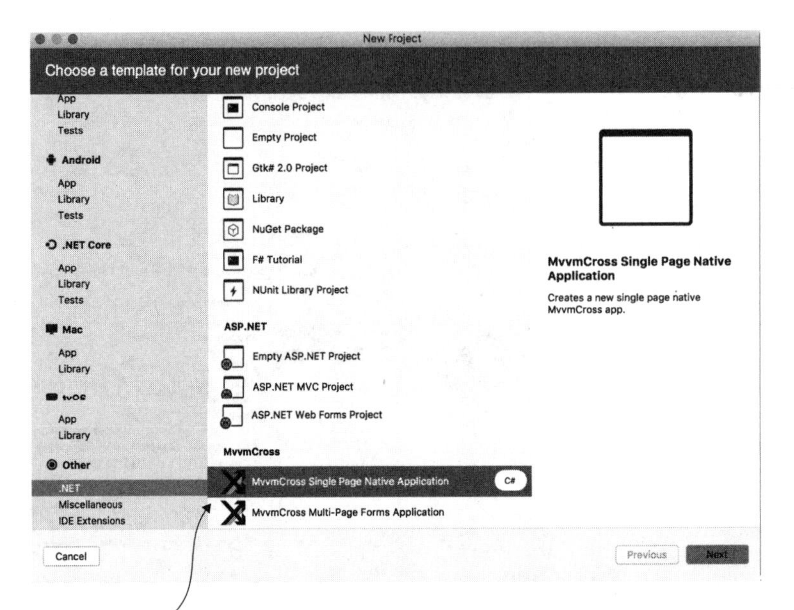

Select Other >.Net, then select MvvmCross Single Page Native Application from the MvvmCross section.

Enter the project name here. By default, the solution is given the same name as the project.

Visual Studio will, by default, create all the files needed to push this to a Git repository, even creating an appropriate .gitignore file for you.

You can change the folder the project is created in here.

Figure 2.10 The New Solution dialog boxes showing the MvvmCross cross-platform app solution template, and setting the project name

From this dialog box select Other > .NET from the left-side list, and then select MvvmCross Single Page Native Application from the list in the middle. Click Next. On the next screen enter `HelloCrossPlatformWorld` as the project name and click Create.

This will create a new solution for you containing three projects: a .NET Standard core project (HelloCrossPlatformWorld.Core), an iOS app (HelloCrossPlatformWorld.iOS), and an Android app (HelloCrossPlatformWorld.Droid), as shown in figure 2.11. Once the solution has been created, it will try to download all the NuGet packages it needs—you'll see the status bar at the top showing Adding Packages. This may take a while, depending on the speed of your internet connection, and you may be asked to agree to some license agreements as they download. You'll need to let them fully download before building the apps.

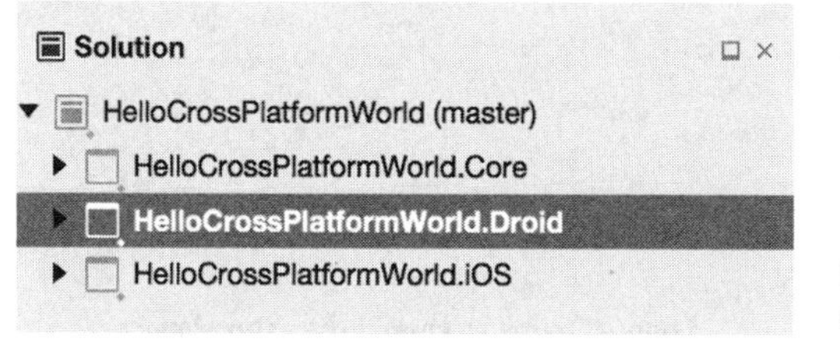

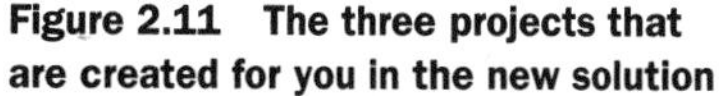

Figure 2.11 The three projects that are created for you in the new solution

WHY NOT HELLOCROSSPLATFORMWORLD.ANDROID The convention for Android apps is to use "Droid" in their names instead of Android. This is because the project name becomes the default namespace, and if you have "<something>.Android" in your namespace, you can get a clash with the global "Android" namespace. You end up littering your code with global::Android.<whatever> in using directives or types, making it harder to read. Stick to .Droid, it's easier!

CREATING THE SOLUTION USING VISUAL STUDIO FOR WINDOWS

From Visual Studio select Tools > Extensions and Updates. Select the Online section on the left, and use the search box to search for MvvmCross for Visual Studio (figure 2.12). There are multiple extensions with the same and similar names, so ensure the one you install is named "MvvmCross for Visual Studio" and is at least version 2.0. Select it and click the Download button, and click Install in the dialog box that pops up.

Once this is downloaded, you'll be prompted to restart Visual Studio to install the extension, so close Visual Studio and wait for the extension installer to finish. After this has finished, restart Visual Studio, and you can create the new solution in two ways:

- From the File menu by selecting File > New > Project
- By clicking the New Project option from the Start section of the Start Page that's shown whenever you open Visual Studio

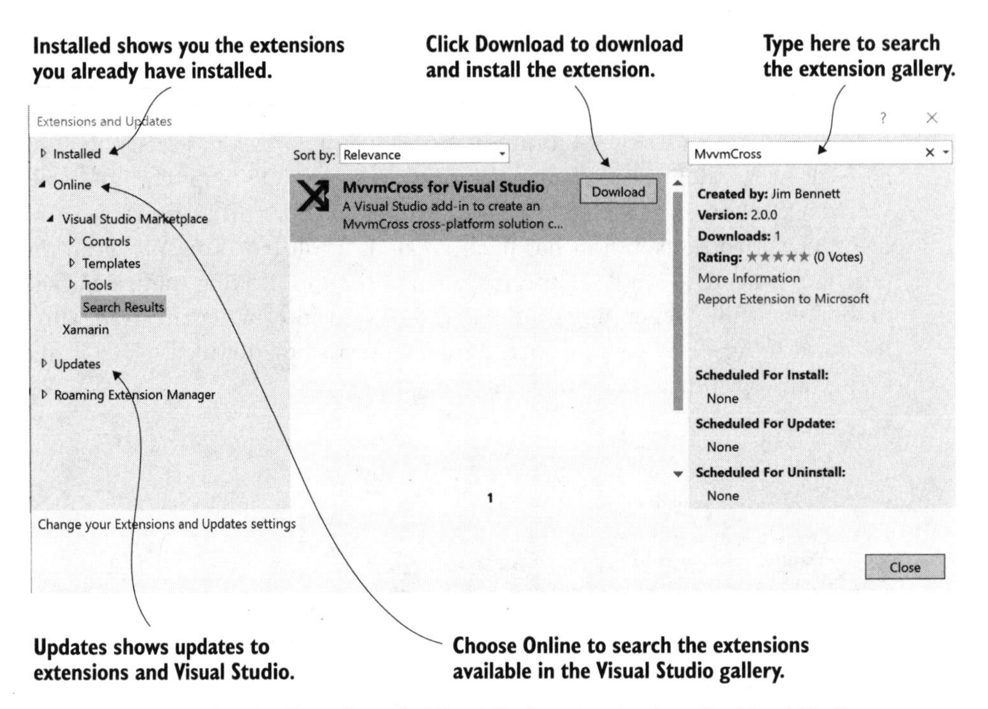

Figure 2.12 Selecting the MvvmCross for Visual Studio extension from the Visual Studio Extension manager

From the New Project dialog box (shown in figure 2.13), select the MvvmCross section under Visual C# on the left, choose MvvmCross Single Page Native Application from the list in the middle, enter HelloCrossPlatformWorld as the project name, and click OK. Windows has problems with paths longer than 256 characters, and some of the directories that will be created when your app is built have long names, so you may want to ensure your solution is created in a folder close to the root of a drive. If you do it in C:\Users\<username>\Documents\visual studio 2017\Projects, your path may be too long.

This will create five projects for you: a .NET Standard core project, an iOS app, an Android app, and a couple of Windows apps covering WPF and UWP. We're only interested in supporting iOS and Android here, so you can delete the Universal Windows and WPF projects by selecting them and pressing Delete or using Remove from the right-click context menu. This will leave you with the same three projects as on Visual Studio for Mac: the core project, the iOS app, and the Android app, as shown in figure 2.14.

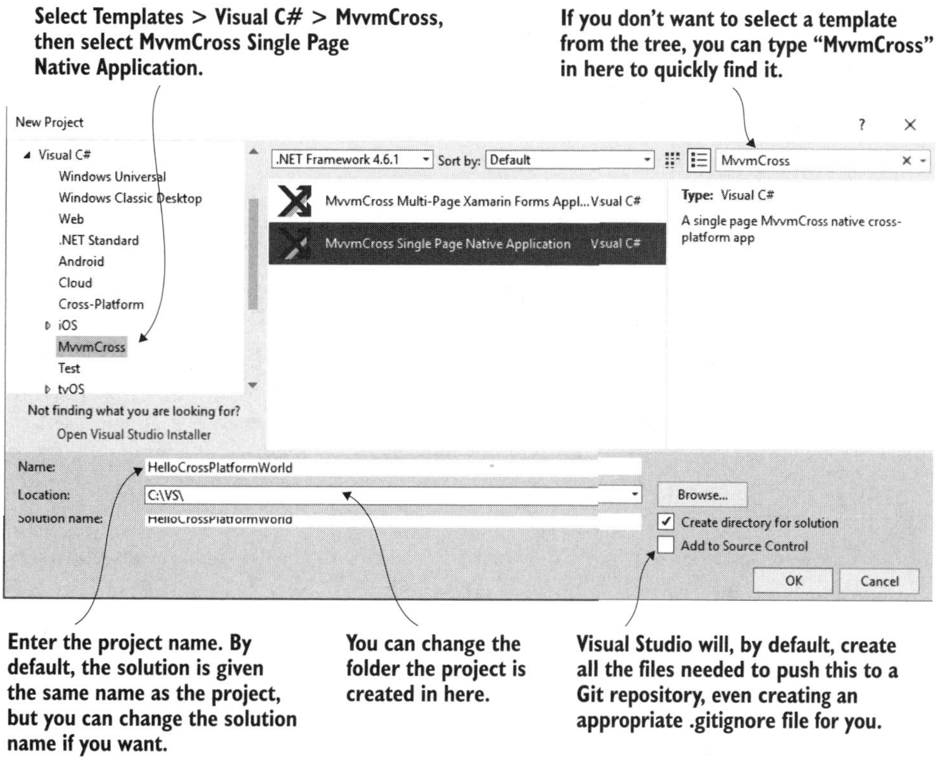

Select Templates > Visual C# > MvvmCross, then select MvvmCross Single Page Native Application.

If you don't want to select a template from the tree, you can type "MvvmCross" in here to quickly find it.

Enter the project name. By default, the solution is given the same name as the project, but you can change the solution name if you want.

You can change the folder the project is created in here.

Visual Studio will, by default, create all the files needed to push this to a Git repository, even creating an appropriate .gitignore file for you.

Figure 2.13 The New Project dialog box, where you can create your new solution

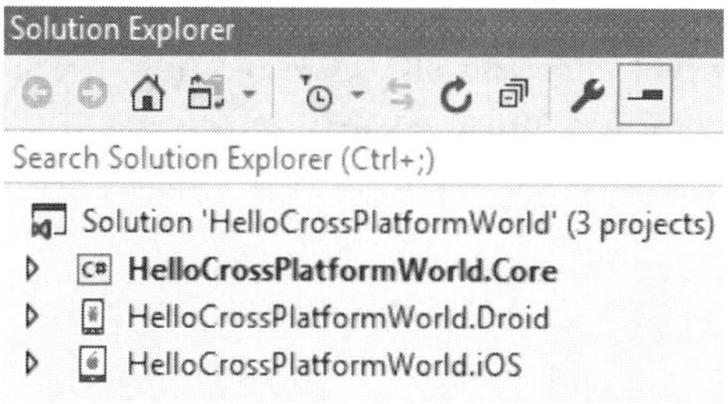

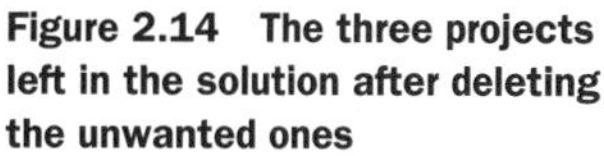

Figure 2.14 The three projects left in the solution after deleting the unwanted ones

> ### Connecting Visual Studio to a Mac for iOS development
> I won't be covering this in detail here, as this is well documented in Xamarin's "Getting Started" guide, on the developer site at http://mng.bz/KbiM, and it could potentially change between the time of writing and when you are reading this.
>
> Essentially, though, you need to allow remote login on a Mac that already has Xamarin and Xcode installed. Visual Studio then connects to this Mac to build your iOS app. The process is pretty simple, and if you use a Mac hosted in the cloud, your provider should be able to provide instructions about how to set it up.

2.4.3 *What have we just created?*

The MvvmCross extension has given us three projects that we care about. We have a cross-platform core project and two app projects. These projects reference MvvmCross NuGet packages providing the MvvmCross MVVM framework.

> **When you create this project, the NuGet packages may not be the latest**
>
> NuGet packages are versioned. You can install version 1.0 of a package from the public NuGet server, and later the author could update it to version 1.1. You can then easily update the NuGet package from inside Visual Studio.
>
> Be wary though. Sometimes packages may not be backwards compatible. The Mvvm-Cross extension may not always install the latest versions of the MvvmCross NuGet packages, and if you update them, the code created by the extension will probably still work, but there are no guarantees.

The core project is a combination of two of our layers—the cross-platform business logic layer and the cross-platform UI logic layer. These layers don't need to exist in separate projects—they're just conceptual layers. The core contains a view model for the app plus some cross-platform application logic (we'll discuss the application layer in the next chapter). Figure 2.15 shows the structure of this project in the solution pad.

You'll notice here that we don't have any models. In this simple example, the model is just a `string` that's wrapped up inside the view model (and we'll play with this string a bit later). This isn't normal—in a real-world case, the view model would need something in the model layer so that it could represent the model layer's state and behavior. For now though, as this is a trivial Hello World, there's no model layer.

The platform-specific app and view layers, as well as the binding, live inside the two app projects—one for iOS and one for Android—as the code for these apps is

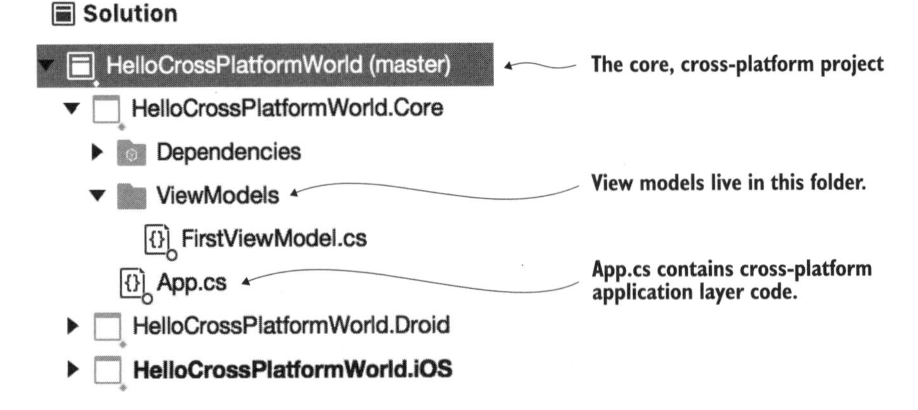

Figure 2.15 The structure of the cross-platform core project

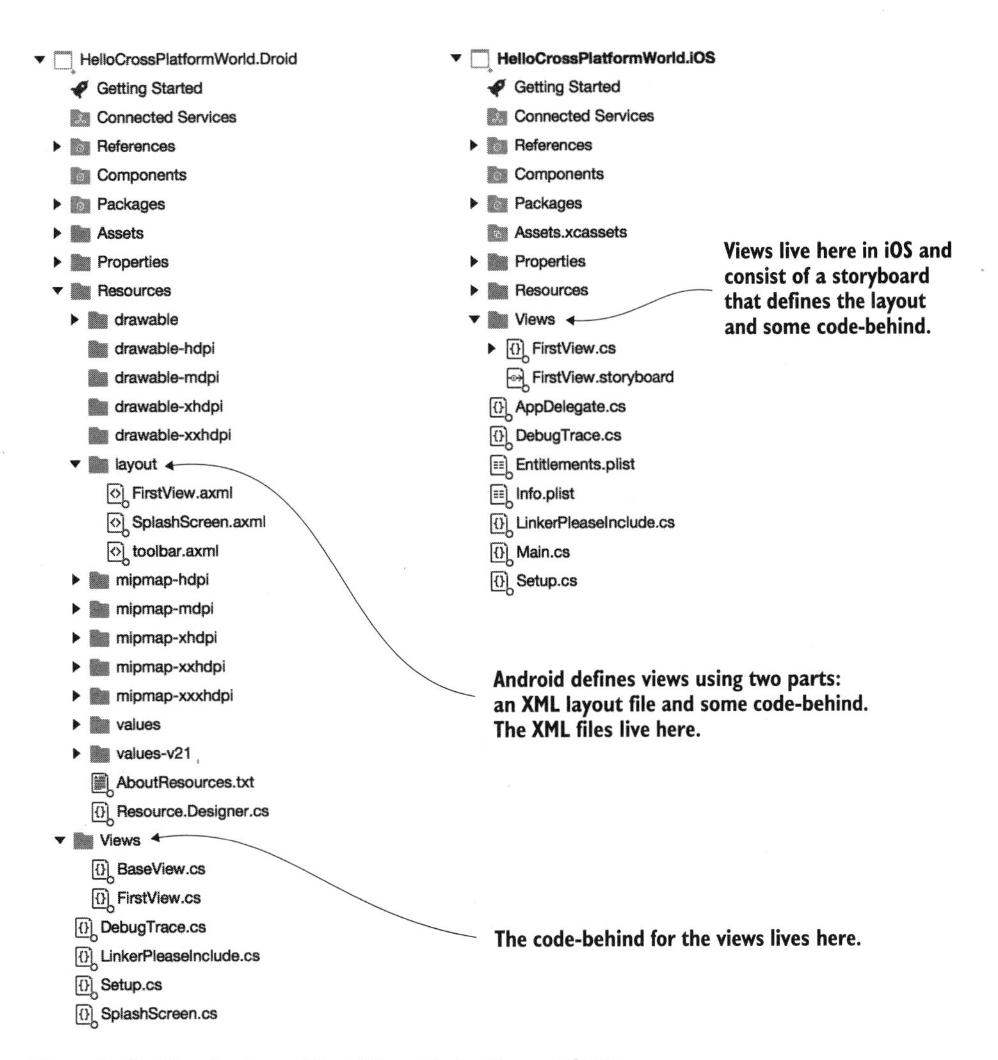

Figure 2.16 The structure of the iOS and Android app projects

platform-specific. The structure is shown in figure 2.16. In the upcoming chapters we'll go into more detail about how Android and iOS define their application layers and their views.

2.4.4 Building and running the apps

We have two apps now, so let's run them and see what happens. Figure 2.17 shows what you'll see when they're running. In both cases we have an app that has an editable text box and a label. If you change the text in the text box, the label will be updated instantly.

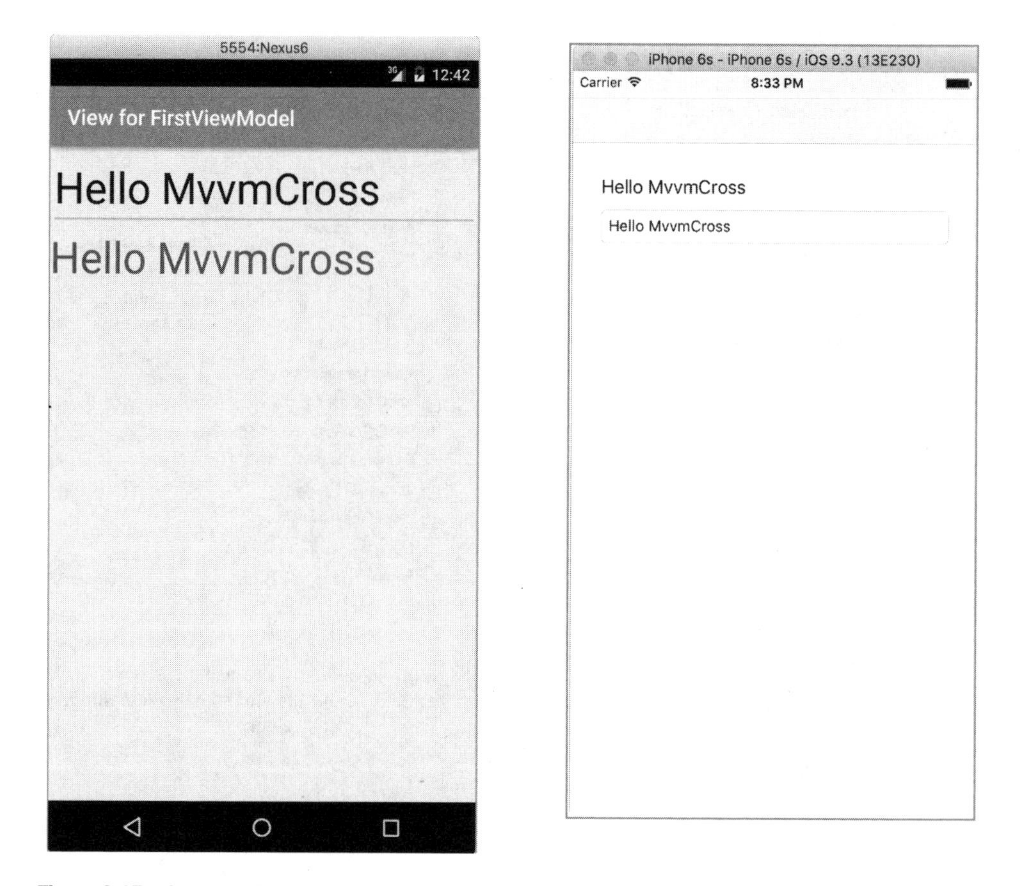

Figure 2.17 Our Hello Cross-Platform World apps running on both Android and iOS

When you used the MvvmCross extension to create the solution, it created these two apps for you, both using some shared common code.

ANDROID

Let's start by taking the Android app for a spin.

> **SWITCHING FROM MAC TO WINDOWS** The project and solution files created by Visual Studio for Mac are fully compatible with Visual Studio on Windows, and vice versa. This means if you use one tool and want to change to the other, you can. It also means you can load anyone else's solution, regardless of what tools were used to create it.

The first thing to do is to ensure the Android app is the startup project, so right-click it and select Set as Startup Project. Once this is selected, you'll see options for choosing the device to run it on in the menu.

On Visual Studio for Mac (on the left in figure 2.18), you'll see two drop-down menus in the top left, and from the second one you can choose the device to run on—

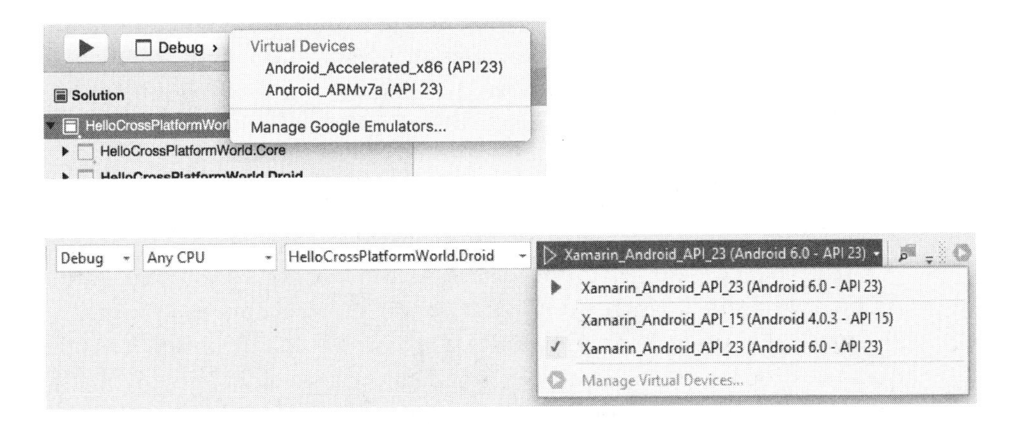

Figure 2.18 The Android device selection menus

an emulator or a physical device (if you have one plugged in). Visual Studio uses the emulators from Google and installs and configures two of these by default. You should select the Accelerated x86 emulator, as this will be faster on a Mac; ARM-based emulators run about 10 times slower than the x86 version.

Visual Studio for Windows installs the Visual Studio Emulator for Android as part of its installer (assuming the option was ticked when you ran the installer), and it will configure a few of these inside Visual Studio for you to use.

These emulators come in different hardware types and different Android OS versions. You'll need to use an x86-based emulator (it's much faster than the ARM version), and all the x86 emulators are basically the same in terms of hardware, just using a different version of the Android OS. For now, just choose the latest OS version, and run the app either by clicking the Run button on the toolbar, or by choosing Run > Start Debugging on Visual Studio for Mac or Debug > Start Debugging on Windows. Sit back and relax as your app is built and the emulator is launched.

Be aware that the first time your app builds, it will take a very long time—there are a number of SDK files that Xamarin needs to download in order to build an Android app, and it downloads these the first time your app is built with no feedback in the output except that it's building. Don't kill the build—if you do, you may have to manually clean up half-downloaded zip files. If you do get errors about corrupt zip files, you can find information on how to fix them in Xamarin's Android Troubleshooting guide at http://mng.bz/MKSQ.

DON'T RUN MORE THAN ONE ANDROID EMULATOR Android emulators can be a bit fussy sometimes, as they run inside virtual machines. If you try to run more than one, they can freeze up and not start. If you ever get this happening—the emulator screen stays black and nothing happens—quit it and close all other emulators you have running, and try again.

This app doesn't do much. It just shows off the very basic features of MvvmCross. If you change the text in the text box, the label below will update to reflect this. We'll dive into what's happening a bit more later, but for now you're over the first hurdle—you have an app that runs. Let's crack on with iOS.

iOS

Building and running the iOS app is very similar to Android. First, ensure the iOS app is the startup project, just as you did for the Android app.

Next you need to select the device to run on. This is slightly different from Android. Android always builds the same code for emulators and physical devices, so all you need to do is choose the device. On Visual Studio for Mac, this is the same—from the drop-down menu choose a simulator or a physical device if one is available (on the left in figure 2.19). From here, select the iPhone simulator of your choice, though a recent one is always good.

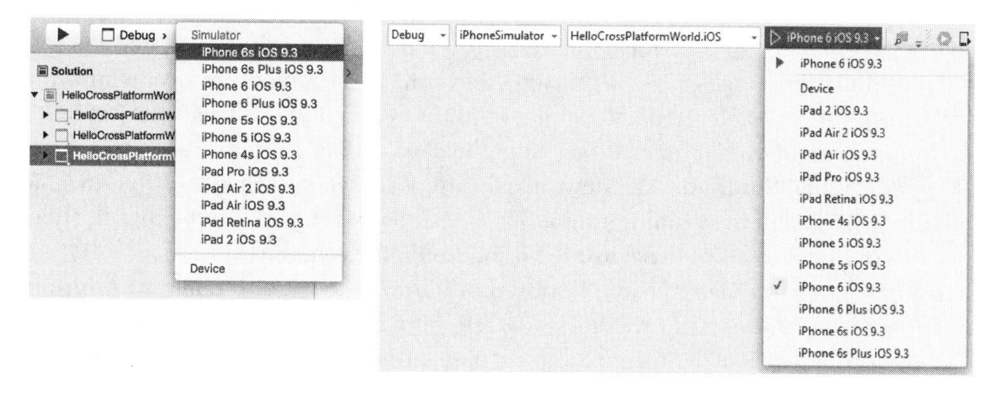

Figure 2.19 The iOS device selection menus

Visual Studio for Windows is similar, though it breaks this out into two drop-down menus—one to choose either a physical device or a simulator, and another that shows the available devices or simulators (on the right in figure 2.19). In this case, choose iPhoneSimulator from the first menu, and select the simulator of your choice from the second.

Once the appropriate simulator is selected, run the app. If you're using Visual Studio for Mac, the simulator will run on your Mac. If you're using Windows, the simulator will either launch on your Mac, or on your Windows PC if you have the iOS simulator for Windows installed.

Once the simulator fires up, you'll see the basic MvvmCross sample app. This is identical to the Android app—edit the text and the label updates to match. Awesome—your Xamarin app is running on iOS without any extra work.

2.5 Is this really a cross-platform app?

One of the big upsides of Xamarin is being able to write cross-platform apps—separate apps for each platform with shared core code. The question on your lips now is probably "is this what we're seeing here?" The answer is yes! The iOS and Android projects have part of the application layer (the code to actually run an application), and the view layer (the UI is defined in platform-specific code), but the core of everything is in a shared core project. This is pretty simple to prove, so let's make a simple code change to demonstrate it.

In the apps you've run on Android and iOS, you have a text box with "Hello MvvmCross" in it, and a label that matches this text, updating whenever the text changes. Let's now change the initial value of this text.

In the Core project there's a ViewModels folder (figure 2.20), and inside this is a view-model class called `FirstViewModel` (in the FirstViewModel.cs file). Look at the `hello` field, and you'll see it's initialized to `Hello MvvmCross`. Update this to be `Hello Xamarin in Action` as follows.

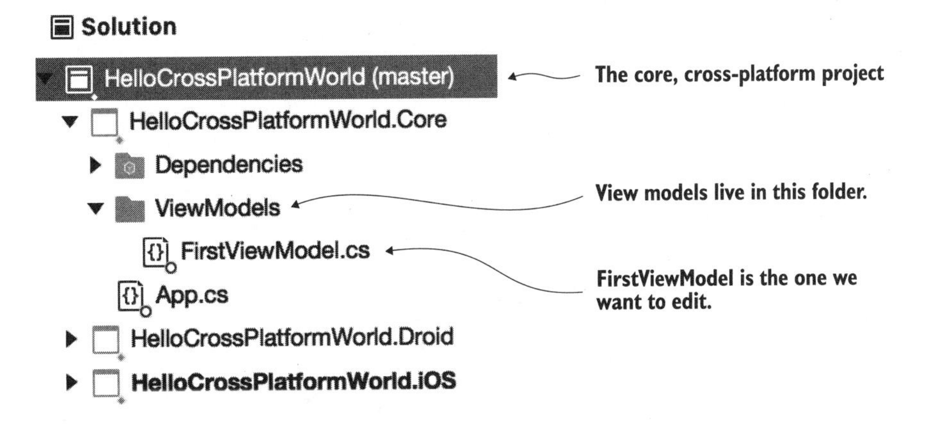

Figure 2.20 The structure of the core project showing the location of the `FirstViewModel` class

Listing 2.2 Updated `hello` field in `FirstViewModel`

```
string hello = "Hello Xamarin in Action";
```

This is a one-line code change in one file in shared code. If you build and run the Android and iOS apps now, you'll see that both have the new text showing in the text box and label, as in figure 2.21.

The apps look the same and work the same. The only difference is the original string value that's shown on startup.

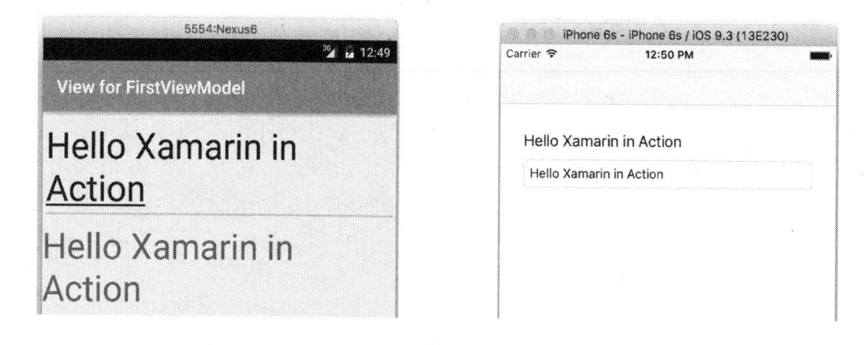

Figure 2.21 Both sample apps showing the new text, changed by changing only one line of code

So how does this all work? Let's look at this solution to see how it fits into our layers. This app has two views, one on iOS and one on Android, a view model in shared cross-platform code, and a `string` that acts as a model (figure 2.22).

Before we can go into much more detail about what's happening here, there's a lot more about MVVM we need to discuss. In the next chapter we'll take that deeper dive into MVVM, and once you've seen in more depth how MVVM works we'll look in more detail at the code we've just built.

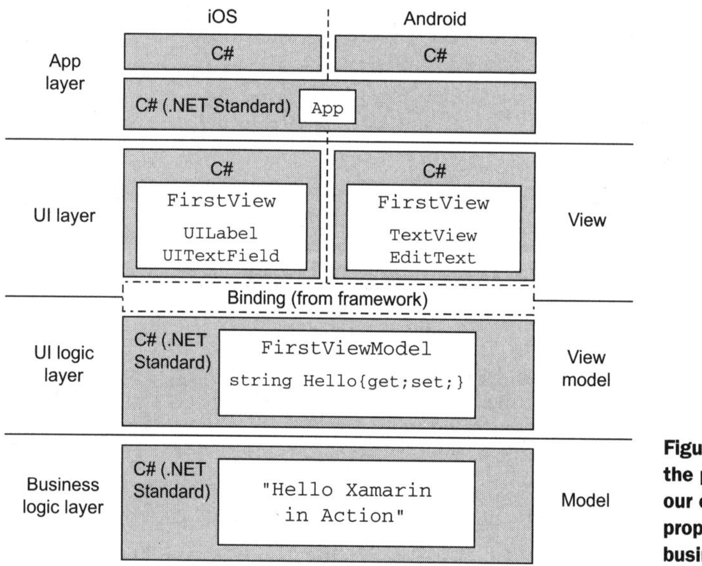

Figure 2.22 Our UI code is in the platform-specific UI layer; our core class with its string property is in the cross-platform business logic layer.

Summary

In this chapter you learned that

- A number of design patterns have evolved over time to help in making better UI applications. The latest incarnation of these, MVVM, is very well suited to building Xamarin apps, as it maximizes the amount of cross-platform code in our apps.
- A cross-platform Xamarin app is not totally cross-platform. Instead it's an app where all platforms are written in the same language (C#) so that you can share a large portion of your code.
- Cross-platform code is written in .NET Standard libraries that provide access to a subset of .NET that works on all platforms.
- The MVVM pattern consists of three layers. You can write two of these layers, the model and the view model, once inside a .NET Standard library and share the code between your iOS and Android apps.

You also learned how to

- Use an extension in Visual Studio to create a cross-platform Xamarin app, with projects for iOS and Android, and a .NET Standard library core project for shared code.
- Run these apps inside the iOS simulator and Android emulator.

3 MVVM—the model-view–view model design pattern

This chapter covers

- A more detailed look at what's in the model, view model, view, and binding layers
- How a view model provides cross-platform UI logic by modeling state and behavior
- Using property-changed notifications
- Using commands
- How the binding layer glues the view and view-model layers together
- Value conversion in the view model and value converters
- What happens in the application layer
- Navigation patterns for MVVM apps

In the previous chapter we looked at the MVVM UI design pattern, before creating our first cross-platform example app. We're going to examine that example app in a lot more detail, but first we need to look at the layers in an MVVM app in more depth. To do this we'll take an example calculator app (figure 3.1) and look at how we'd write this using MVVM.

To understand how to build this app we need to look at how the user will interact with the UI, and see how those interactions move up and down through the layers of MVVM. Figure 3.2 shows a high-level overview.

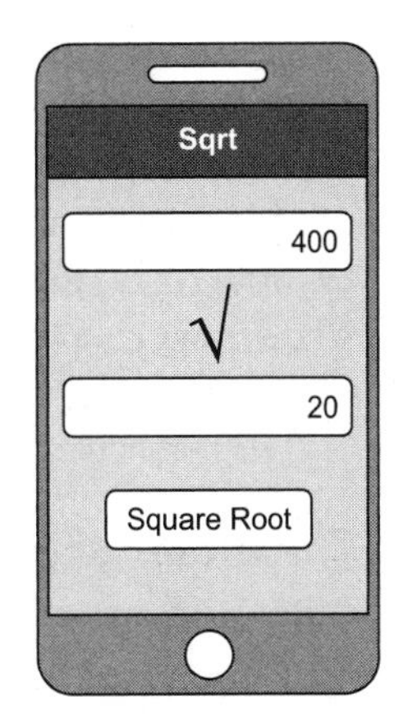
Sqrt
400
√
20
Square Root

Figure 3.1 A simple square-root calculator app that calculates the square root of a given number

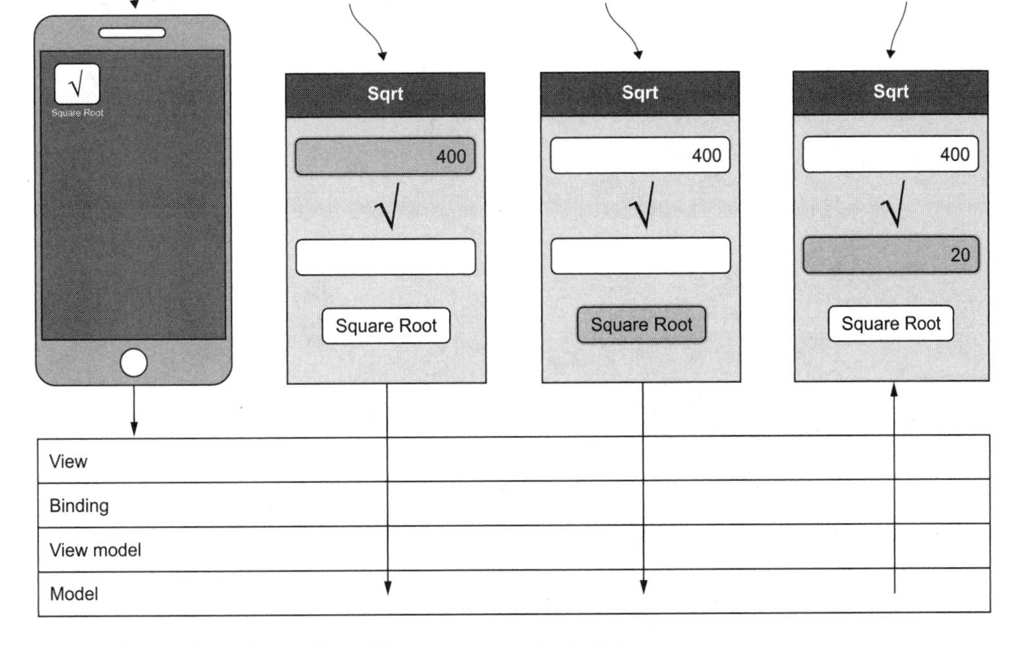
1. The app launches, creating the model, view, view model, and binding.
2. The user enters the number 400 into a text box, and this value is propagated down through the layers until it ends up as a number on the model.
3. The user taps the Square Root button, and this action is propagated down through the layers to the model, where the square root is calculated.
4. The result of 20 is calculated in the model, and the value propagates back up through the layers until it's shown on the UI as text on a label.
Square Root
Sqrt
400
√
Square Root
20
View
Binding
View model
Model

Figure 3.2 A typical user interaction with our square-root calculator

At the end of this chapter, we'll revisit this app diagram, breaking each layer apart and seeing all the interactions that take place between each layer. This chapter is theory rather than practice, but it's important in understanding how to structure your app to get the most out of the cross-platform capabilities that Xamarin offers. The code examples here are simple examples and pseudocode, not parts of a fully working app. In the next chapter we'll be taking what you learn here and using it to understand and build on the example app you built in the previous chapter.

Let's start by looking at how this app could be split between the different layers.

3.1 The model layer

The model layer is a cross-platform layer that represents your data, your business logic, and your access to external resources such as databases or web services. The simple calculator app doesn't need to access any external resources, but if you did need to persist data to a database or interact with web services, you'd do this in the model layer.

In our calculator example, the model layer would contain a square-root calculator class that takes a number, calculates the square root, and makes the result available, similar to the structure shown in figure 3.3.

The following listing shows a possible implementation. The class has a number property, `Number`, a `Sqrt` method that calculates the square root of the number, and a read-only `Result` property that stores the result.

Listing 3.1 A possible implementation of `SquareRootCalculator`

```
public class SquareRootCalculator
{
   public double Number {get; set;}
   public double Result {get; private set;}

   public void Sqrt()
   {
      Result = Math.Sqrt(Number);
   }
}
```

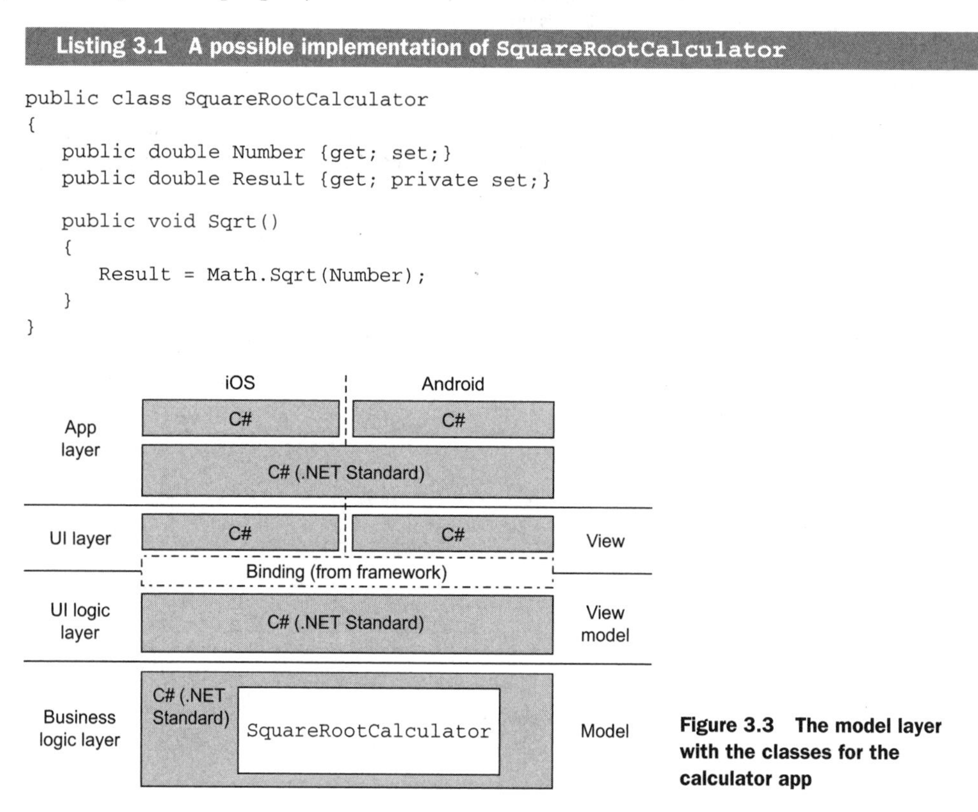

Figure 3.3 The model layer with the classes for the calculator app

The model layer is a layer—it contains one or more classes working together. As you'll see later in this chapter, you'll usually have one view whose name is suffixed with `View` for a screen (for example, `SquareRootView`), and one view model for that view with a name suffixed with `ViewModel` (such as `SquareRootViewModel`). It's normal to assume that there should be a corresponding `Model` class providing the data and business logic for that view model, but this doesn't have to be the case. If you want to write your code that way, go ahead, but don't feel you have to.

There are many ways to build the model layer following many different patterns and practices (such as domain-oriented or data-centric approaches). How you build this layer is up to you, but there are a few main principles you should stick to to make this layer the first *M* of MVVM:

- *The code should be cross-platform*—One of the reasons for using this pattern is that it allows you to reuse as much code as possible.
- *The code should be testable*—Another key reason for using MVVM is testability—the segregation of the UI from its logic means you can unit-test that logic, and this same principle should apply here. Your model layer should be testable using unit tests—your classes should be well written with single responsibilities so tests can be clearly defined.

  Again, thinking of our calculator app, the `SquareRootCalculator` class is very easy to unit-test. You could write tests that set different values for `Number`, call `Sqrt`, and verify the `Result` property. This is a trivial example, but even in a more complicated app you'll need to ensure that it's testable. This way you can ensure your model works without having to always build and run your app.
- *The model should represent data and business logic at the domain level, not the UI level*—This is an important principle of the model layer—it should represent your data and logic at a level that makes sense to your domain. Any value conversion of the data in business terms to UI terms shouldn't be performed at this layer.

  Thinking again about our calculator app, the UI controls for entering values and showing them usually deal with `string` values. Strings are no good here as you need to calculate using numbers, so the model should always think in terms of numbers. The other layers can deal with strings and conversions.

UNIT TESTING Unit testing is a massive topic, worthy of a book in its own right, so I won't be going into much detail about it here. All I will be covering is how to approach writing your app using MVVM to help with writing your unit tests. If you want to read more on this topic, I recommend *The Art of Unit Testing*, Second Edition, by Roy Osherove (Manning, 2013).

3.2 The view-model layer

The view-model layer (the VM at the end of MVVM) is the UI logic layer. This layer is responsible for two things:

- *Value conversion*—From data in the model layer represented in a way that makes sense to your domain to the way data is represented in the UI
- *UI logic*—Such as logic that determines when to show data and when and how to navigate between different views

There are a few basic principles behind a good view model:

- Just like the model layer, it should be cross-platform.
- Again, like the model layer, it should be easily testable using unit tests. You want to have as high-quality an app as possible, so being able to test the UI logic quickly and thoroughly using unit tests will help you achieve this goal.
- It must be bindable. Binding is the glue that connects the view model to the view, and the view model will need to implement features such as property-changed notifications that allow the binding layer to be aware of changes so that it can keep the UI and view model in sync.
- It should be stateless. The view model is a value conversion and logic layer. It's not a data store, so its state should always come from the model layer. When the UI changes the state (such as when a text box is updated) the binding tells the view model that something has changed and that the view model is responsible for updating the state in the model.

The view model is the meat of the MVVM pattern, and it will usually map one-to-one against the different screens or to different sections of each view. In our calculator app, we want a view model that wraps the model, called `SquareRootViewModel` (figure 3.4). If we had an app with multiple screens, maybe one for square roots and one for cube roots, we'd also have two view models, `SquareRootViewModel` and `CubeRootViewModel`, each accessing the model layer. Because our model layer is a layer and doesn't map one-to-one with view models, we could have both square root and cube root in the same model class, and that one model would be used by both view models.

3.2.1 State and behavior

When considering a UI, there are really two things to think about—state and behavior.

- *State* is the information you see on the screen, be it actual data, like text and numbers, or a representation of the app's state, such as buttons being disabled or validation errors being shown around text boxes. State is a representation of the data in the model in a way that maps to the UI, using *properties*, just like the properties you'd put on a class.
- *Behavior* is the actions that happen when a user interacts with the UI. The view model is the implementation of this. Behavior is represented using *commands*, objects that encapsulate some kind of logic, which is fired by interacting with the UI in a way that executes the command.

Think of driving a car. You're driving at a certain speed, as indicated by the speedometer. By pressing the accelerator you go faster; by pressing the brake you go slower.

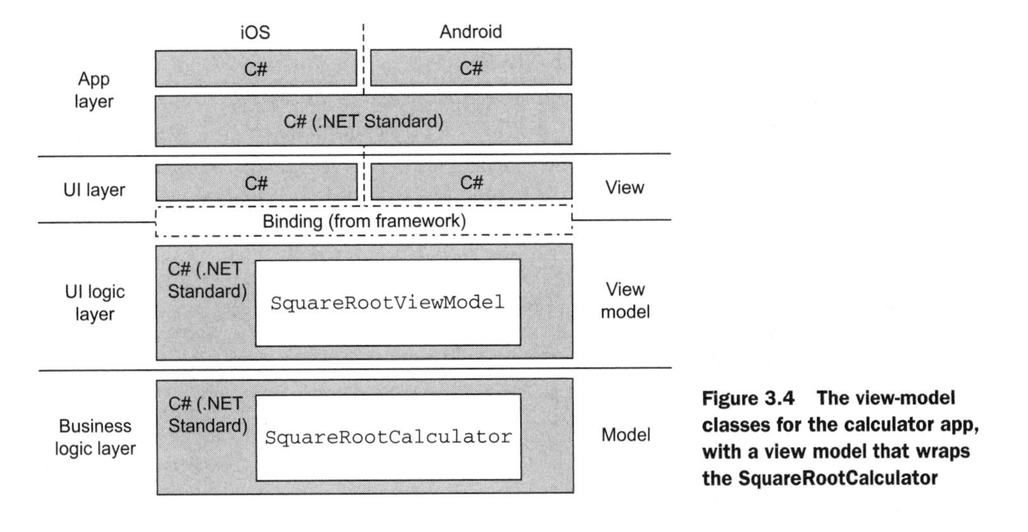

Figure 3.4 The view-model classes for the calculator app, with a view model that wraps the SquareRootCalculator

The *state* is the speed—represented in miles or kilometers per hour. The car determines its speed by measuring the speed of rotation of the driveshaft and converting this value into a vehicle speed. In this case, the driveshaft speed measurement is exposed to the speedometer as a representation of the driveshaft speed but it's converted mathematically to the vehicle speed.

The *behavior* is the ability to change speed by pressing the accelerator or brake. When you press the accelerator, the engine allows more fuel/air in, making the engine go faster. When you press the brake, the wheels are slowed down using friction. The representation of how to increase speed is pressing on the accelerator pedal. The representation of how to decrease speed is pressing on the brake pedal.

The speedometer represents the engine speed, and the pedals represent the behavior of changing speed, all in a driver-friendly way. This is analogous to our MVVM layers. The model is the mechanicals of the car, and the view is the speedometer and pedals. The view model represents the vehicle speed and speed-change behavior to the speedometer and pedals in a way that's consistent with the view.

If we consider our square-root app, we have one number and the ability to tap a button to calculate the square root and see the result. The *state* here is the number we want to calculate the square root of, as well as the result. The *behavior* is a command that encapsulates the logic to calculate the square root. By tapping the button, you *command* the view model to do something that does this calculation.

It probably sounds a bit contradictory to say that the view model represents state and behavior after saying that one of the basic principles is that it should be stateless. Let's examine what's meant by both things.

The view model represents the state of the UI in that all the values and logic that define the data shown in the UI come from the state of the view model as exposed to the view layer. The values in text box and label come from properties on the view model. The setting that defines whether a control is visible or hidden comes from the properties of the view model. In this sense, the view model provides a representation of the state of the model layer to the UI.

As a class, though, the view model should be stateless, in that it gets its state from the model layer and shouldn't hold on to this state itself. The values in the text box and label are read from the view model, but the original source is the model layer (figure 3.5). At any time you should be able to recreate the view model from the data in the model layer, because it will not store any state itself.

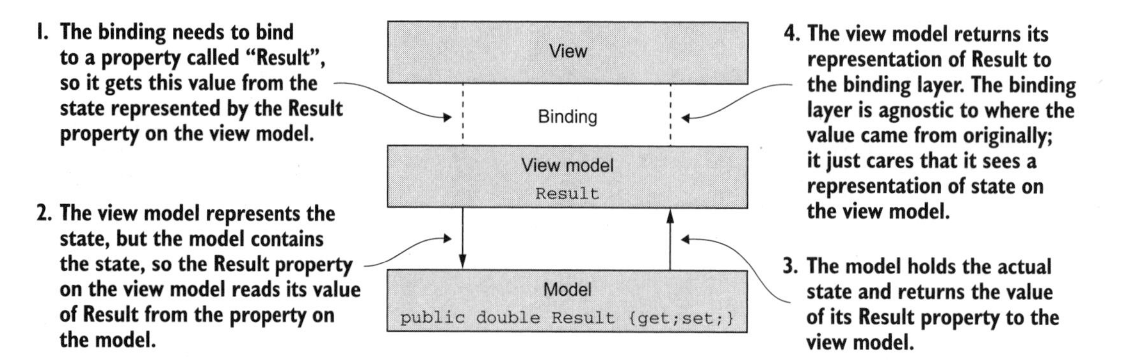

1. The binding needs to bind to a property called "Result", so it gets this value from the state represented by the Result property on the view model.
2. The view model represents the state, but the model contains the state, so the Result property on the view model reads its value of Result from the property on the model.
View
Binding
View model
Result
Model
public double Result {get;set;}
4. The view model returns its representation of Result to the binding layer. The binding layer is agnostic to where the value came from originally; it just cares that it sees a representation of state on the view model.
3. The model holds the actual state and returns the value of its Result property to the view model.

Figure 3.5 The view model is a representation of the state shown in the model.

The real state is in the model layer, and the view model converts that state into state that's appropriate for the view layer. The view model *represents* the state, but the model *contains* the state. By having the view model as a representation, you can return the state directly or perform value conversions on the state before returning it to the binding layer.

PROPERTIES AND CHANGED NOTIFICATIONS

In its simplest form, a property of a view model is the same as any other property you may have used in C# code. It has a getter and a setter—methods that return some data or set the data. Internally in these methods, it could just return or update values, or it could have some logic. In its simplest form, a property can get and set a value on the model, as shown here.

Listing 3.2 Pass-through property that gets and sets first number value on the model

```
public class SquareRootViewModel
{
   SquareRootCalculator sqrtCalc;

   public double Number
   {
      get { return sqrtCalc.Number; }
```

- The SquareRootViewModel view model class. The convention is to name view models with the suffix "ViewModel".
- The view model has an instance of the model stored as a private field.
- The view model exposes the number to be used in the calculation through the Number property.
- The getter for the Number property is a simple pass-through—it just returns the value of the property on the underlying model.

```
        set { sqrtCalc.Number = value; }
    }

    public double Result
    {
        get { return sqrtCalc.Result; }
    }
}
```

The setter is also a simple pass-through, setting the value on the underlying model.

The Result is also a pass-through, but it's read-only on the model so it's only a getter, not a setter.

So far, so simple. In fact, you're probably wondering why we bother with a view model at all if it just calls straight in to the model. The reason for using a view model is because view models support property-changed notifications—the raising of an event to tell anyone who's interested that a property has changed. Remember the binding layer? This keeps the UI in sync with the underlying data, and part of keeping this in sync is being aware of when things change. Figure 3.6 is a recap of binding, highlighting this.

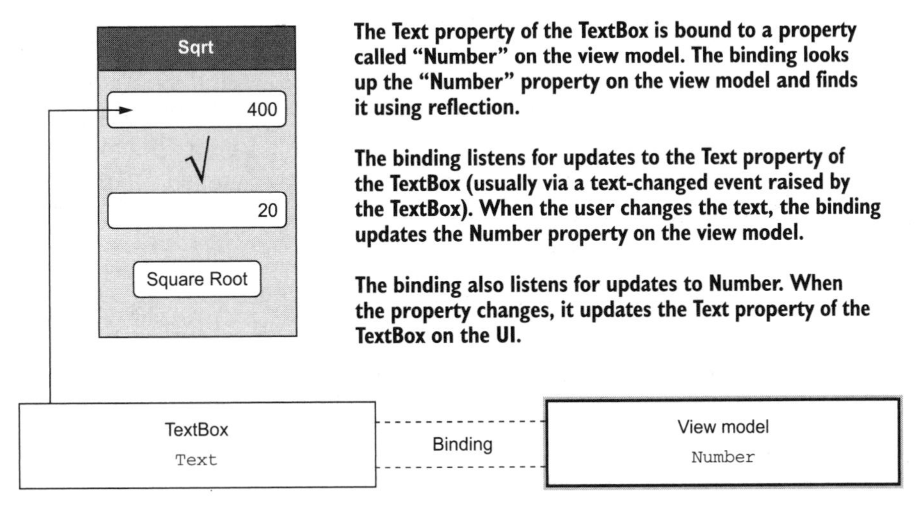

Sqrt
400
√
20
Square Root
The Text property of the TextBox is bound to a property called "Number" on the view model. The binding looks up the "Number" property on the view model and finds it using reflection.
The binding listens for updates to the Text property of the TextBox (usually via a text-changed event raised by the TextBox). When the user changes the text, the binding updates the Number property on the view model.
The binding also listens for updates to Number. When the property changes, it updates the Text property of the TextBox on the UI.
TextBox
Text
Binding
View model
Number

Figure 3.6 The binding listens to changes in the view model and updates the view accordingly.

The way the binding layer does this is through property-changed notifications. These are events raised by the view model telling anyone who's interested that a property has changed. In our case, the binding layer is interested, so it listens to these notifications. When it gets one, it will read the new value of the property and update the UI to match.

The standard way of implementing property-changed notifications in C# is though an interface called `INotifyPropertyChanged`. This interface has been around since .NET 2.0 (over a decade ago), and has only one member, an event called `PropertyChanged`, which uses the standard event-handler delegate, passing an object that defines the sender and some event arguments. These arguments are of type `PropertyChangedEventArgs`, and this type only has one member of note—`PropertyName`, the name of the property that has changed as a `string`. The following listing shows this interface.

Listing 3.3 The `INotifyPropertyChanged` interface

```
public interface INotifyPropertyChanged
{
   event PropertyChangedEventHandler PropertyChanged;
}
```

This event doesn't include the value that's changed, just the name. The binding layer will subscribe to this event, and when it's raised it will get the name of the property from the event args, find the UI control (or controls) that's bound to a property of that name, read the new value from the view model, and update the UI.

> **NOTIFYING THAT ALL PROPERTIES HAVE CHANGED** By convention, if you use an empty string or null as the property name in the event args when raising this event, it tells the binding layer that everything has changed, so it should reread all values and update the UI. Be warned, though; not every MVVM framework will obey this convention.

We can update the view model example to implement this. When the number changes, or the result of the square root changes, we need to notify the binding of this change via a property-changed notification. One thing to note here is that your view model should only notify if something has actually changed—if the value hasn't changed, the event shouldn't be raised.

Let's add a `Sqrt` method for our view to illustrate this.

Listing 3.4 Adding property-changed notifications to our view model

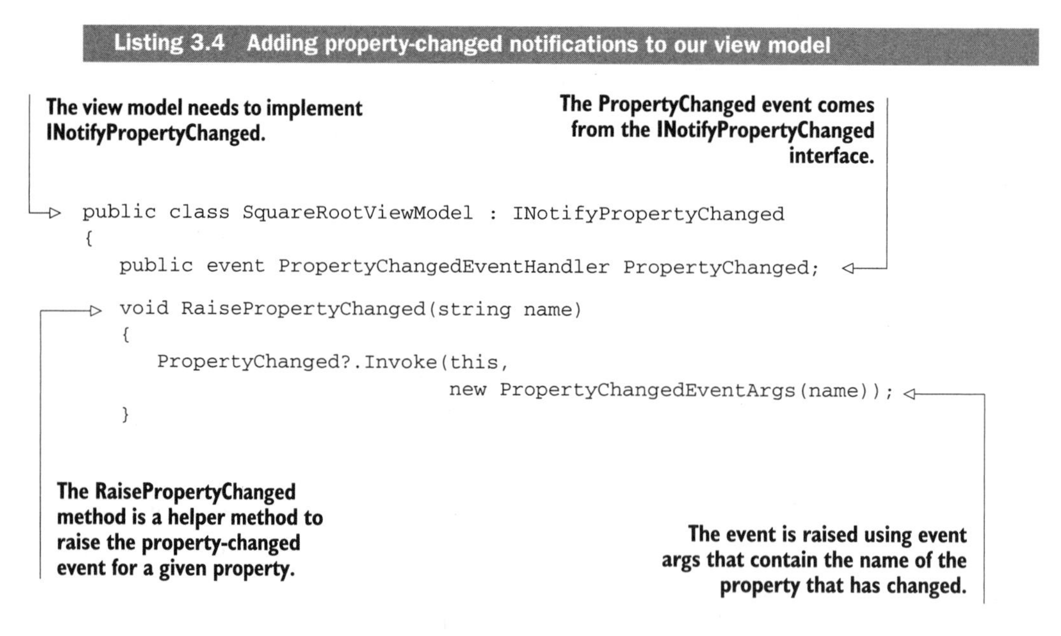

The view model needs to implement INotifyPropertyChanged.
The PropertyChanged event comes from the INotifyPropertyChanged interface.
The RaisePropertyChanged method is a helper method to raise the property-changed event for a given property.
The event is raised using event args that contain the name of the property that has changed.


```
public class SquareRootViewModel : INotifyPropertyChanged
{
   public event PropertyChangedEventHandler PropertyChanged;

   void RaisePropertyChanged(string name)
   {
      PropertyChanged?.Invoke(this,
                              new PropertyChangedEventArgs(name));
   }
```

```
    public double Number
    {
       get { return sqrtCalc.Number; }
       set
       {
          if (sqrtCalc.Number == value) return;
          sqrtCalc.Number = value;
          RaisePropertyChanged("Number");
       }
    }

    public void Sqrt()
    {
       sqrtCalc.Sqrt();
       RaisePropertyChanged("Result");
    }
    ...
}
```

After the Number property changes, a property-changed event is raised.

After the Sqrt method on the model is called, the Result property is updated so the event is raised.

When the Number property is set, the new value is compared to the old one, and if the value hasn't actually changed, nothing happens: no update and no property-changed notification.

Simplifying `RaisePropertyChanged` using an attribute

C# defines an attribute called `CallerMemberName` that you can set on a string parameter of a method, and it tells the compiler to use the name of the calling method or property as the value for this parameter. This means you can define your property-changed method as follows:

```
void RaisePropertyChanged([CallerMemberName]string name = null)
```

Then you can call it using `RaisePropertyChanged()` from inside your property setter, without passing any explicit value for `name` to the method. The name of the property this is called from will be automatically set as the `name` parameter. For example, if you call this from inside the setter of the `Number` property, the value of the `name` parameter will be "Number". A number of MVVM frameworks, including MvvmCross, use this for their raise-property-changed methods.

Property-changed notifications are the way to tell the binding layer that something has changed. You can notify about any property at any time—you don't have to notify about the property being changed. For example, if your view model had two properties for a person's first and last names, and a property that reflected their whole name as a concatenation of the first and last names, you'd want any changes to either the first or last name to raise a property-changed notification for the whole name, as shown in the following listing.

Listing 3.5 Property-changed notifications can be raised for any property at any time

```
public string Name
{
   get { return FirstName + " " + LastName; }
}

public string FirstName
{
   get { return model.FirstName; }
   set
   {
      if (model.FirstName == value) return;
      model.FirstName = value;
      RaisePropertyChanged("FirstName");
      RaisePropertyChanged("Name");
   }
}
```

The Name property is dependent on the values of FirstName and LastName.

Because of this dependency, when FirstName changes, it raises a property-changed notification for itself and for the Name property.

COLLECTIONS AND COLLECTION-CHANGED NOTIFICATIONS

In addition to using individual properties, there's a standard way in C# of notifying the binding layer that the items in a collection have changed: using a similar interface called `INotifyCollectionChanged`. This is generally used with list controls—UI widgets that show a list or table of data. Just like with `INotifyPropertyChanged`, the binding layer subscribes to an event, and when it receives this event, it will tell the list control to reload the changes.

Unlike `INotifyPropertyChanged`, this isn't an interface that the view model defines; instead, this is at the property level. The view model will expose a property of a type that implements `INotifyCollectionChanged`, and when the binding layer binds this property to a corresponding property on the list control, it will also subscribe to the event on that property.

An example of this, with an app that shows a list of names, is shown in figure 3.7. This interface just contains one member, an event called `CollectionChanged`. This uses the standard event-handler delegate with event args of type `NotifyCollectionChangedEventArgs`. The following listing shows this interface.

Listing 3.6 The `INotifyCollectionChanged` interface

```
public interface INotifyCollectionChanged
{
   event NotifyCollectionChangedEventHandler CollectionChanged;
}
```

These event args contain a number of properties allowing you to describe the changes that have been made to the collection. This, in turn, allows the bound list control to respond appropriately if possible.

For most use cases, though, you don't need to worry too much about this because there's a nice helpful collection that's already part of the .NET Framework that handles all of this for you—`ObservableCollection<T>`. The collection is derived from the

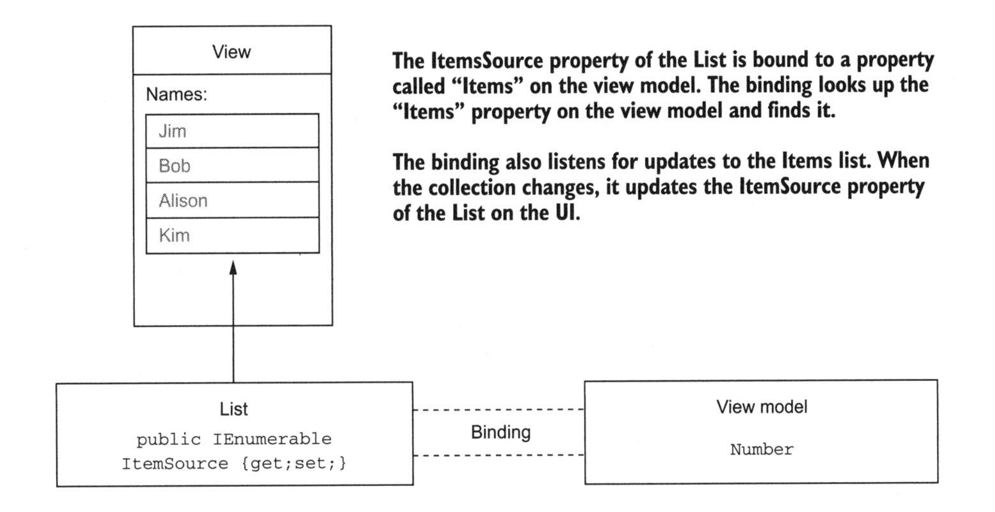

Figure 3.7 Collections can be bound to list controls, and when the collection changes, the list control on the UI is updated.

generic `List<T>` and implements `INotifyCollectionChanged`. When you perform any action that changes the list, it will raise the event with the correct arguments.

When the underlying `ObservableCollection` changes (such as when an item is added to it), the event is raised, and the binding detects this and tells the list control to update and show the changes. This is shown in figure 3.8.

Be aware, though, that `ObservableCollection` will raise the `CollectionChanged` event for all changes, so if you're adding thousands of items, the UI will update thousands of times, which can slow or even lock up your UI. It's probably better in this case to create a new collection, add all the values to it, and then set your property to this

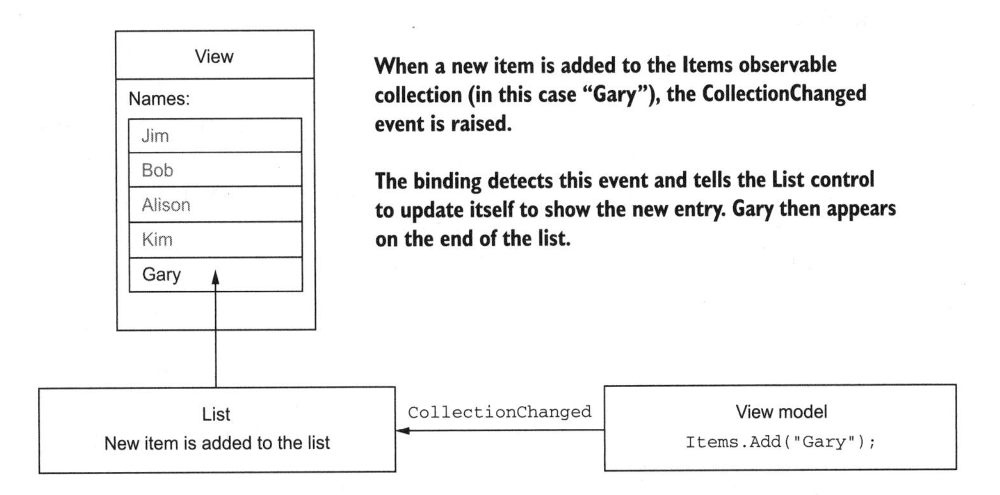

Figure 3.8 When an observable collection is updated, an event is raised and the binding detects this and tells the UI to update.

new collection—leading to only one UI update. The following listing shows an example of this.

Listing 3.7 Creating a new collection and updating the property

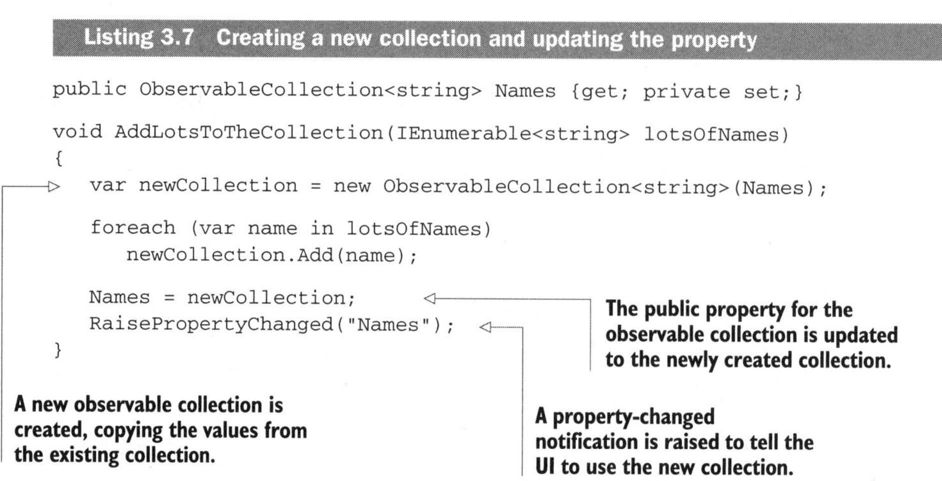

```
public ObservableCollection<string> Names {get; private set;}

void AddLotsToTheCollection(IEnumerable<string> lotsOfNames)
{
    var newCollection = new ObservableCollection<string>(Names);

    foreach (var name in lotsOfNames)
        newCollection.Add(name);

    Names = newCollection;
    RaisePropertyChanged("Names");
}
```

The public property for the observable collection is updated to the newly created collection.
A new observable collection is created, copying the values from the existing collection.
A property-changed notification is raised to tell the UI to use the new collection.

OTHER IMPLEMENTATIONS OF `ObservableCollection` CAN MAKE THIS EVEN EASIER
There are a number of implementations of `ObservableCollection` available in various open source projects that provide better support for bulk operations by blocking the collection-changed event until all operations are complete. One such implementation from MvvmCross is `MvxObservableCollection`, which has an `AddRange` method that suppresses the collection-changed event, adds all the items passed to the method, and then raises the collection-changed event. This collection also provides methods for bulk deletes and replacements and for suppressing the collection-changed event while you perform custom operations.

COMMANDS

The properties of the view model define its state, so the next thing to look at is how behavior is defined. The standard way to define behavior in MVVM is using the *command pattern*. In this pattern, everything needed to perform an action is encapsulated in an object, and you tell this object that you want it to perform its action at a certain time, giving it any extra information it needs about the particular time it's run.

Think of a genie—your wish is its command. You tell the genie that you want a coffee, and it obeys your command using its magic, and poof, a coffee appears, as shown in figure 3.9.

You can think of the command pattern the same way. The command is an object that encapsulates the ability to perform an action, such as a genie who encapsulates the ability to grant your wish. You execute the command with an optional parameter, commanding the genie to bring you coffee. The command then performs the action—the genie brings you coffee.

In the C# world, `ICommand` is the interface for an object that implements this command pattern. It has a method you can invoke to execute the command with a parameter, a method you can call to see if you can execute the command with a parameter,

Figure 3.9 Commanding a genie to bring you coffee. It would have been eternal wealth, but coffee was easier to draw.

and an event that gets raised when your ability to execute the command changes as shown in the following listing.

Listing 3.8 The `ICommand` interface

```
public interface ICommand
{
   void Execute(object parameter);
   bool CanExecute(object parameter);
   event EventHandler CanExecuteChanged;
}
```

As shown in figure 3.10, you can think of `Execute` as a method that commands the genie to grant your wish, and the `parameter` as the thing you wish for. Traditionally, a genie will only grant three wishes, so figure 3.11 shows that `CanExecute` will return `true` while you have wishes remaining, but after your third wish will return `false`. The `CanExecuteChanged` event is like the genie telling you after your third wish that you've run out of wishes (and disappearing in a puff of smoke back into the lamp).

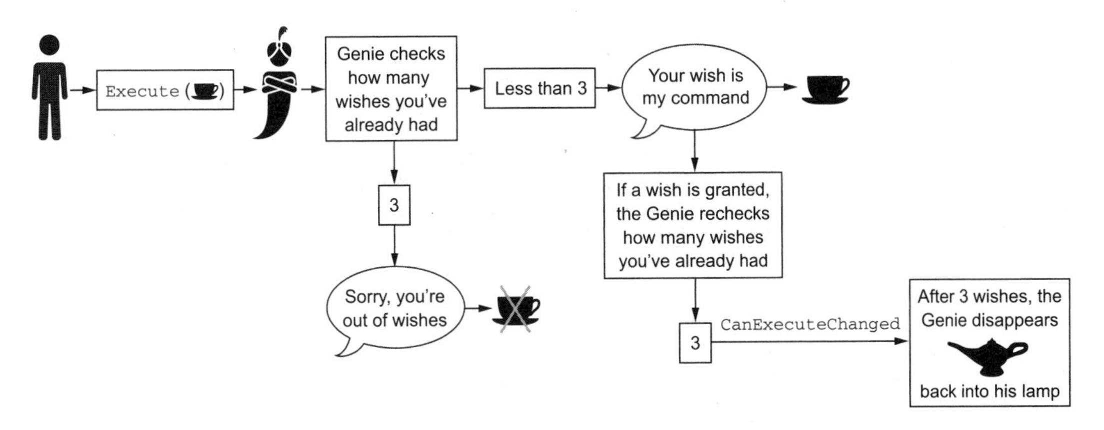

Figure 3.10 Our genie is like the `ICommand` interface—we can make a wish (`Execute`) and see when we've run out of wishes (`CanExecuteChanged`).

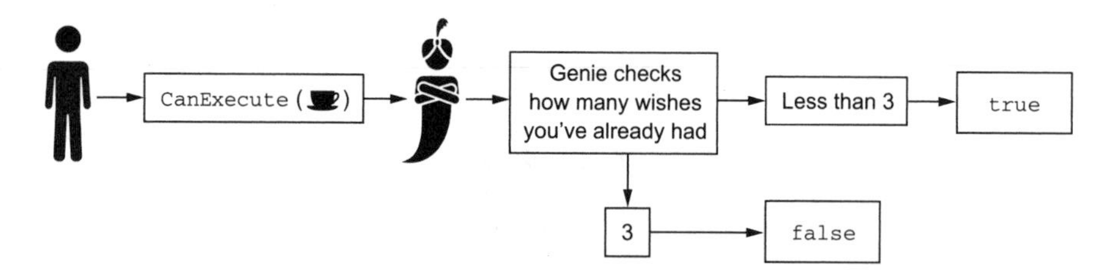

Figure 3.11 We can also ask the genie if we can have any more wishes (`CanExecute`).

The command is exposed as a property on the view model, and the binding layer will have a way to wire up the command to a widget on the UI.

The classic use case is with a button. Buttons usually have a click event, or a similar event that's run when the button is tapped. When a button is bound to a command, the click event will `Execute` the command. The enabled state of the button would also be bound to the `CanExecute` method, so if `CanExecute` returns `true`, the button is enabled, and if it returns `false`, the button is disabled. This would be evaluated when the button is first bound and every time the command raises the `CanExecuteChanged` event. This is shown in figure 3.12.

In our calculator app, the Square Root button would be bound to a command that, when executed, calls the `Sqrt` method on the model. If you haven't entered a number into the text box, you can't calculate a square root, so in this case the `CanExecute` will return `false` and the button will be disabled. Once you enter text, the `CanExecuteChanged` will be raised to tell the binding to re-evaluate `CanExecute` and enable the button.

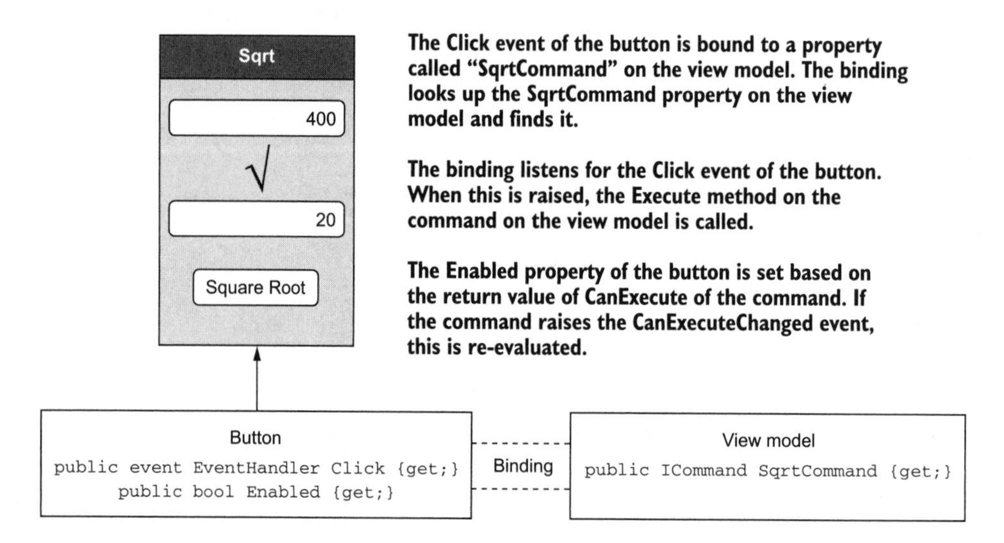

Figure 3.12 Events such as button clicks can be bound to commands, and these commands are executed when the event is raised.

Commands don't return a result, they just run and return once they've finished. The way to return a result, if one is required, is by making changes to the state of the view model and raising a property-changed event. Some commands don't need to update a state because they don't do anything that requires feedback on the current UI. Commands that do need to update, such as saving data and indicating that the data has been saved, will do it by updating a property that causes the UI to change.

Usually you don't need much fancy logic with a command—just create a command object and give it a method to run when it's executed. Unfortunately (and somewhat surprisingly) there isn't a default `ICommand` implementation built into the .NET Framework that does this. Luckily there are plenty of example implementations around the internet and others are built into the various MVVM frameworks. These commands usually take in an `Action` that provides the method to run on execution, and optionally a `Predicate` (a method that returns a Boolean) to use for the implementation of `CanExecute`. They also provide a method you can call to raise the `CanExecuteChanged` event.

In our calculator view model, we can change the `Sqrt` method shown in listing 3.4 to a command, as follows.

Listing 3.9 Adding a command to the view model

```
public class SquareRootViewModel : INotifyPropertyChanged
{
   ...
   public ICommand SqrtCommand {get; private set;}
   public SquareRootViewModel()
   {
      SqrtCommand = new MvxCommand(o =>
         {
            sqrtCalc.Sqrt();
            RaisePropertyChanged("Result");
         });
   }
}
```

The Sqrt method has been removed, and a new property of type ICommand has been added, called SqrtCommand.

Creates a new instance of the command

In the constructor for the view model, the `SqrtCommand` is set to a new instance of `MvxCommand`, the command class from MvvmCross that takes an `Action<object>` to execute (`Execute` takes an `object` as its parameter, so the action needs to have an `object` parameter). The action is invoked when the command is executed, and in this example the action calls `Sqrt` on the model and raises a property change to indicate the `Result` has changed.

3.2.2 Value conversion

The model contains data in a way that's relevant to the domain or business logic; the UI handles data in a format that can work with the widgets on screen. Some of the time these formats will be the same, but other times they won't match.

When they don't match, the view model will need to convert the state of the model to a state that the UI can use. The view model will represent the state of the model using the converted values. Similarly, if the UI is updated, this needs to be reflected by updating the state represented by the view model. This means setting a value using data in the format relevant to the UI, and then converting it to the format used by the model. It's the view model that's responsible for this value conversion.

As you've probably noticed in our square-root calculator, the model deals with numbers as doubles. This is the business layer, so doubles are fine. UIs, on the other hand, don't normally deal in doubles. Text boxes like the one used for entering the number usually deal in strings, and so do labels like the one we're using to show the result.

This is where the view model comes in—part of its job is value conversion from the model layer to the UI layer. In this case it should be responsible for converting from strings in the UI to numbers in the model and vice versa.

Let's look at how the view-model class code should work.

Listing 3.10 Handling value conversion from the model (doubles) to UI (strings)

```
public class SquareRootViewModel
{
   ...
   public string Number
   {
      get { return sqrtCalc.Number.ToString(); }
      set
      {
         if (value == Number) return;
         sqrtCalc.Number = double.Parse(value);
         RaisePropertyChanged("Number");
      }
   }

   public string Result
   {
      get { return sqrtCalc.Result.ToString(); }
   }
}
```

The Number property on the view model is a string.

To return a string, the getter calls ToString() on the double value from the model.

Compares the value to the existing value using the property on the view model instead of the property on the model. The value is a string, so you need to compare it with a string instead of the double on the model.

To set a double on the model, the setter parses the string into a double. This could fail, so in the real world you'd need to ensure the string value is always a valid number— most UI text boxes can limit which characters the user can enter to numbers and decimal points.

Again, to return a string the view model calls ToString() on the value from the model.

VIEW MODELS ARE RESPONSIBLE FOR VALUE CONVERSION The layers above the view model think in terms of the UI, and the layers below think in terms of the business logic and domain. The view model is responsible for converting from one to the other as data passes through this layer.

The model layer has data as doubles. The view-model layer converts these values to strings, and represents the state of the model layer through string properties. This state is in the right format for the UI layer, so the binding layer can set the text on the UI controls to these string values. Once a string value on the UI is updated, the binding layer updates the string representation of the number on the view model, which converts the value to a double and updates the data on the model.

There are times where you might want platform-specific value conversion rather than cross-platform conversion in a view model, and you can do this using a value converter. We'll look at these later in the chapter.

3.2.3 Testability

Like the model layer, the view-model layer should be built with testability in mind. View models not only provide cross-platform logic, but when they're well built you can write unit tests to verify that their logic is correct: one code base for this logic, one set of tests, one place to find and fix bugs. This is one of the major reasons behind the original invention of MVVM—you can write unit tests against your UI logic. It's very easy to do thanks to the way view models encapsulate state and behavior. You can test user interactions with the UI by writing test code that replicates the way the binding would update the view model.

For example, to test a user typing into a text box, you don't actually need a text box. Instead you can write code that acts like the binding layer and sets the value of the property on the view model that would be bound to the text box. To test updates coming to the UI from the view model, you just need to listen for property-changed or collection-changed events, and when these happen verify that the property or collection has the correct value. To test a user clicking a button, you just need to execute the command and verify what happens.

When building your view models, you should always think about unit testing. Your view models should be well decoupled and use techniques like interface over implementation, the same as for models. It's also worth seeing what your MVVM framework offers to help you with this. For example, some frameworks provide a messenger to allow your view models to communicate indirectly with other view models (or other classes in your app) without having to be aware of each other.

To improve the testability of the `SquareRootCalculator` view model, we should decouple it from the model by exposing an interface on the model and passing an instance of that interface when the view model is constructed inside our app. From a unit test, we can create a mock model that implements this interface, and then use this when we construct the view model. This way we have complete control over what the model will do in the test.

As mentioned earlier, unit testing is a huge topic, and mocking is an important part of it. It's outside the scope of this book, but if you always build your model and view-model layer code to prefer interface to implementation, you'll be well set up for unit testing.

3.3 The view layer

Put simply, the view layer is the UI. Everything that has to be platform-specific because it deals with UI widgets is in the view layer. This layer should be as thin as possible and just contain code to define which widgets are needed on screen and the values of any of their properties that won't change based on logic inside the view model. When you're building your view, if you find yourself adding any logic, move it to the view model.

Thinking back to our calculator example, we'd need to create two views called `SquareRootView`, one in the iOS app and one in the Android. This naming is in keeping with the convention of the view and view model having the same name with a different suffix, as shown in figure 3.13.

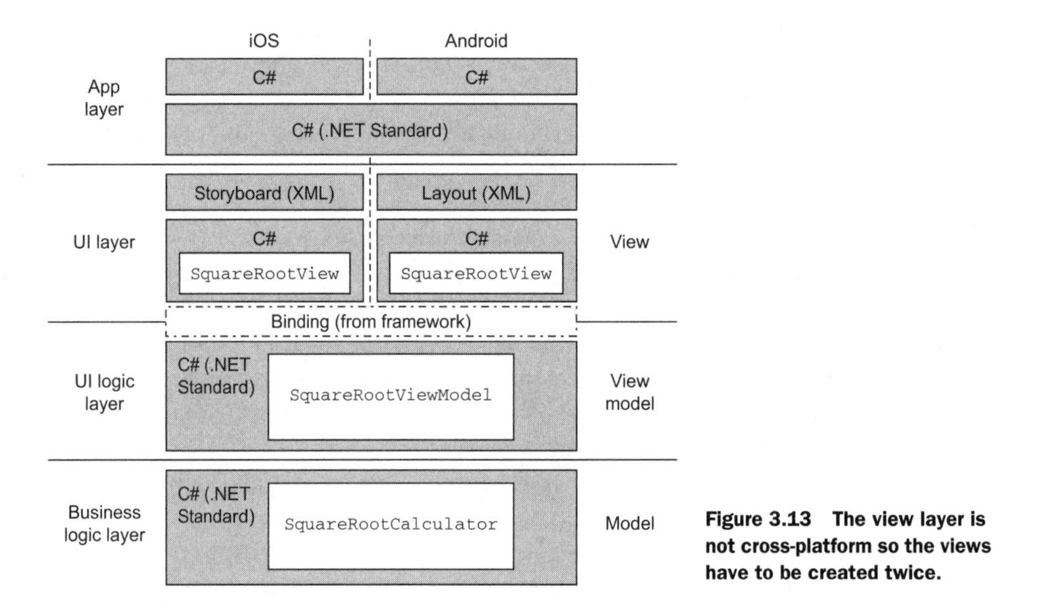

Figure 3.13 The view layer is not cross-platform so the views have to be created twice.

As this layer isn't cross-platform, you can add all the fancy UI goodness you want in this layer—nice looking widgets, animations, effects, and anything else you want that's specific to the platform to make your UI look amazing. Just remember that because this layer isn't cross-platform, everything has to be written twice, once for iOS and once for Android, so everything that can be shared (such as logic) should be shared in the view-model layer.

On both iOS and Android, there are two parts to any UI:

- *A layout file*—Contains details of the widgets defined in XML and can be used with a visual designer. Android calls these layout resources; iOS has two types of these, storyboards and XIB files.
- *A code-behind file*—Provides any logic needed by the UI and defines its lifecycle (such as when the view is shown and when it's hidden). On Android this is called an *activity*; on iOS this is a *view controller*.

We'll look at these layout and code-behind files in more detail in chapters 9 through 12 when we look at building UIs for iOS and Android.

There's not much more to add about the view layer in terms of MVVM. Most of the magic of MVVM is in the view-model layer, so the only thing to consider here is what you can put in the view-model layer and what has to be in the view layer. As a good rule of thumb, you want to do as much as possible in the layout file, and as little as possible in the code-behind. If you're adding code that can't be in the layout file for whatever reason, you should consider whether it's generic logic that should be in the view model (and therefore shared between platforms) or if it's platform-specific and must be in the view layer. For example, if you're showing or hiding a label based on the value of a property in the view model, the logic for this should also be in the view model. If, on the other hand, you're choosing which of a set of platform-specific animations you'll use based on a property in the view model, this logic would go in the view layer—albeit ideally in a separate, self-contained class that could be unit-tested.

3.4 Binding

Binding is the magic that links together the view and the view model in a loosely coupled way. It's responsible for connecting properties on the view to properties on the view model and keeping them in sync, and for connecting events on the view to commands on the view model so that these commands are run when the user interacts with the UI. When binding, you link up a named property on the view to a named property on the view model, and behind the scenes the binding framework will find the actual properties with the given names and wire them up—setting the view to match the value in the view model, and monitoring for changes so it can keep these values in sync.

There's nothing in the .NET Framework to help bind everything together. Instead, you have to either write the logic yourself or use a framework such as MvvmCross, MVVM Light, or Caliburn.Micro to do it.

There are a couple of binding concepts to be aware of—what the source and target are, and what the binding mode is. You also need to be aware that binding isn't really cross-platform, so it can help if you need to bind to properties whose types aren't supported in your cross-platform code.

3.4.1 Source and target

When you bind a view to a view model, you connect a target to a source:

- The *source* is the original source of data (the view model).
- The *target* is the original target of the data (the view).

It's easy to see how these definitions can be confusing—for a text-entry box on a new-user screen, the "source" of the data could be considered what the user enters, but from a binding perspective the source is always the view model and the target is always the view.

You will often hear the term *binding source* mentioned, and this refers to the view model. The binding source is also sometimes referred to as the *binding context* (Xamarin.Forms uses this name) or *data context* (if you've done WPF before, you'll recognize this).

3.4.2 Binding mode

There are four possible modes for binding:

- *One time*—The binding happens once when the view is bound. The value in the view is set from the property in the view model once, and all changes are ignored. This is useful for static text or images that can't change.
- *One way*—The binding goes from source to target only. Every time the view model changes, the view is updated. This makes sense for static controls such as labels where the value in the view can never be user-updated, but the view model may update due to changes from the model layer (such as getting a new value from a web service).
- *One way to source*—The binding goes from target to source only. Every time the value on the view changes, the view model is updated. This isn't used very often.
- *Two way*—The binding goes from source to target and target to source. Every time the property on the view model changes, the value on the view is updated, and every time the value on the view changes, the property on the view model is updated. For controls like text boxes, tick boxes, or radio buttons, this is usually the default binding mode.

3.4.3 Binding is not cross-platform

Binding is platform-specific, and it's always set in the view layer. It needs to be, as it needs to understand the UI widgets to be able to set the data on them and listen for updates.

In our square-root calculator, we need to bind the text box that the user uses to enter the number to the `Number` property on the view model, bind the button to the `SqrtCommand` property, and then bind the result label to the `Result` property.

The binding has to be platform-specific to understand the UI widgets well enough to monitor for view-layer value changes. In figure 3.14 the binding needs to know how to detect changes to the text in the text box (for example, by handling a text-changed event), and how to detect a tap on the button (by handling a click event). On the view-model side, the binding will listen for property-changed notifications from the `INotifyPropertyChanged` interface to know when the view model has been updated. Once it gets this notification, it needs to know how to instruct the UI to update, such as knowing how to tell the label to show the result.

❶ The Text property of the TextBox is bound to a property called "Number" on the view model. The binding finds Number and sets the Text property to be that value.

The binding knows about text boxes, so it listens to the TextChanged event. When this is raised, it will read the value in Text and set the Number property on the view model to that value.

The binding listens to the PropertyChanged event on the view model. When this is raised for the Number property, it reads the value and sets it on the Text property of the text box.

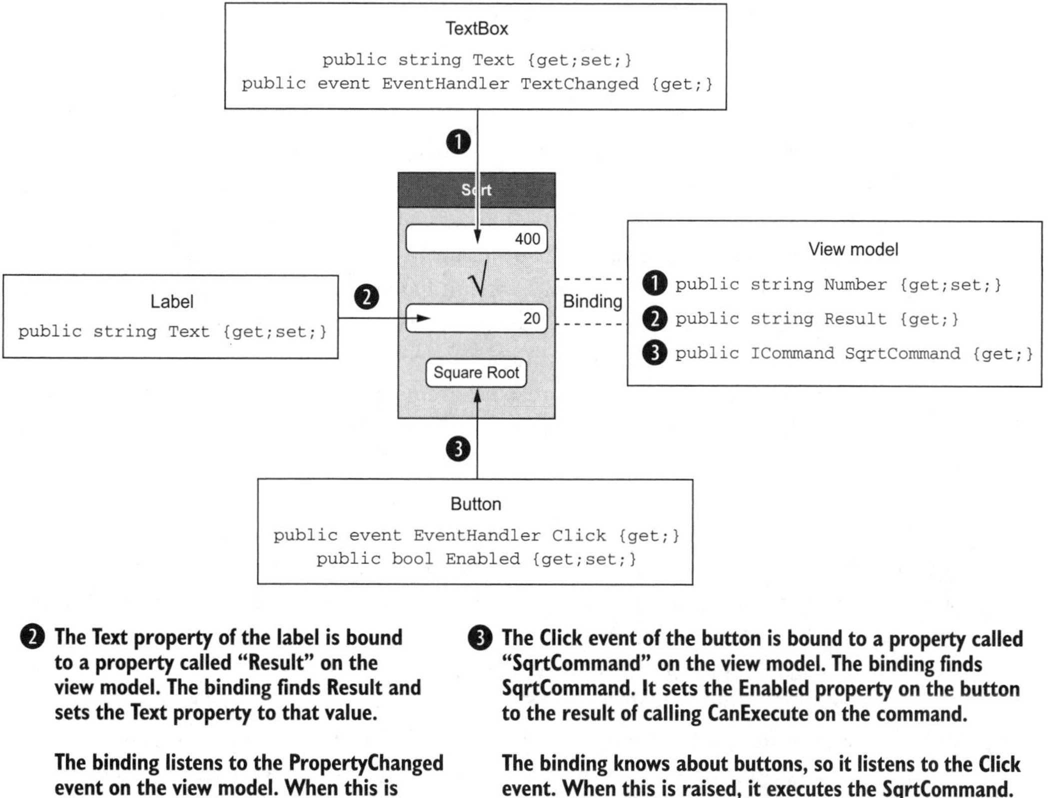

❷ The Text property of the label is bound to a property called "Result" on the view model. The binding finds Result and sets the Text property to that value.

The binding listens to the PropertyChanged event on the view model. When this is raised for the Result property, it reads the value and sets it on the Text property of the label.

❸ The Click event of the button is bound to a property called "SqrtCommand" on the view model. The binding finds SqrtCommand. It sets the Enabled property on the button to the result of calling CanExecute on the command.

The binding knows about buttons, so it listens to the Click event. When this is raised, it executes the SqrtCommand.

The binding listens to the CanExecuteChanged event on the command. When this is raised, it re-evaluates CanExecute and sets the Enabled property on the button accordingly.

Figure 3.14 Binding connects the view and view model together in a loosely coupled way, but it needs to be platform-specific to know which properties and events in the view layer to use.

BINDING USES REFLECTION, SO MAKE SURE YOUR PROPERTIES ARE VISIBLE Binding needs to be able to find the properties on the source and target (view model and widget). How good the binding framework is at finding these depends on the framework, but it's a good general practice to make your properties public and to verify how the framework works.

3.4.4 Value converters

Binding your cross-platform view model to your platform-specific code is great, but what about the times when types and even values are different between platforms? For example, with text boxes on both iOS and Android, you can bind the text to a string property in your view model—this works on both platforms. The problem comes if you want to show or hide the text box. On Android, visibility is controlled by an enum called `ViewStates`; on iOS it's a Boolean called `Hidden`. Normally on your view model, you want a readable property such as `ShowLabel` that returns `true` for the widget being visible and `false` for it being hidden. This doesn't map to the Android enum or the iOS `Hidden` property (it's the inverse, because on iOS `true` means the widget is *hidden*, so not visible).

The way around this is through value converters. As you might recall, the view model is a value-conversion layer (as well as a UI logic layer) so it can do some things, but because it's cross-platform it can't convert values to platform-specific ones. This means we must have a small part of our value conversion in platform-specific code, using *value converters*. These are classes with the singular purpose of converting from view-model types to view types, and converting back from view types to view-model types. Although we want to keep as much UI logic in cross-platform code as we can, platform-specific value converters are sometimes necessary, as they have to know about the platform-specific implementations, and they can be encapsulated in a way that makes them unit-testable.

When binding, you can tell the binding framework to use a particular value converter. When a property on the view model is updated, the binding framework reads the new value from the view model, converts the value using the value converter, and sets the converted value on the view. Conversely, when the view updates, the binding framework will read the value from the view, convert it back using the value converter, and set the value on the view model. This is shown in figure 3.15.

In contrast to property-changed notifications, there isn't a standard interface for value converters available everywhere. Microsoft defined one called `IValueConverter` for use in WPF applications, but this isn't available in .NET Standard libraries, iOS, or Android apps. Instead, a number of MVVM frameworks provide their own versions, which are identical.

In MvvmCross there's `IMvxValueConverter`. This interface is identical to `IValue-Converter` and has two methods—`Convert` to go from source to target (converting the view-model value to one the widget is expecting), and `ConvertBack` to go from target to source (converting from the widget value to one the view model is expecting). This interface is shown in the following listing. To create a value converter, you can implement this interface in your class and pass your class to the binding layer.

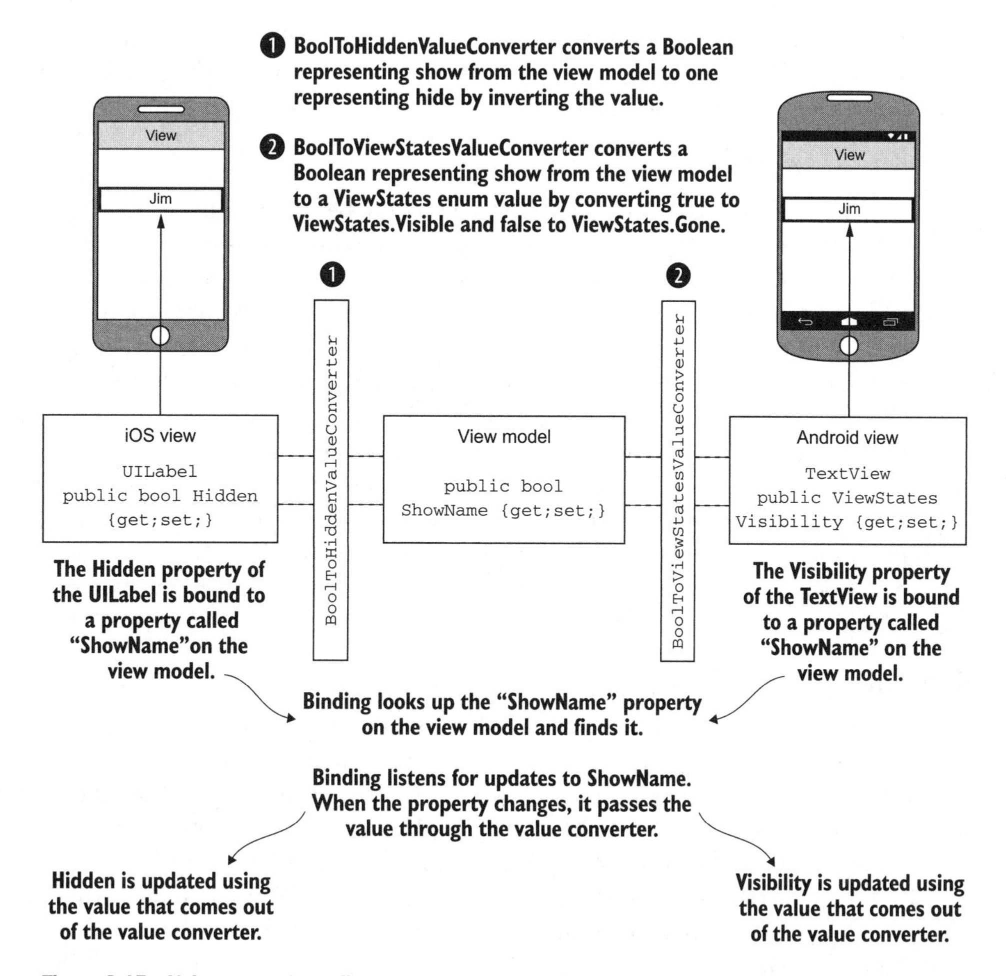

Figure 3.15 Value converters allow you to convert a value from the view model to a type that the view is expecting.

Listing 3.11 The `IMvxValueConverter` interface

```
public interface IMvxValueConverter
{
   object Convert(object value, Type targetType,
                  object parameter, CultureInfo culture);

   object ConvertBack(object value, Type targetType,
                      object parameter, CultureInfo culture);
}
```

Converts changes from the source (view-model) value to the target (view) value

Converts changes from the target (view) value to the source (view-model) value

The first parameter in both these methods (`value`) is the value you want to convert. These methods then return the converted value. The `targetType` parameter tells you what type the method should convert to, though this is normally ignored as value converters are usually pretty specific.

The `parameter` parameter can be useful if you want to have the value converter support a few different conversions and tweak the behavior when it's called. For example, you could have a value converter that converts numbers that represent amounts of money to strings in particular currencies, and use `parameter` to specify what currency to use (such as £ or $). The `culture` parameter is useful if you're supporting multiple languages, because it allows you to change your output based on the current localization settings. For example, if you're converting a number to a string, you can change the decimal symbol to either a period or a comma based on the user's country by passing the culture info to the `ToString` method on the number.

As with commands, no value converters are provided out of the box with the .NET Framework, but most MVVM libraries provide a few standard ones, such as converting Booleans to visibility flags. For example, MvvmCross provides `MvxVisibilityValueConverter` to map `true` values to visible and `false` values to invisible, and `MvxInvertedVisibilityValueConverter` to do the opposite.

3.5 The application layer

Most of the application layer is provided for you by the platform-specific code that's built into the Xamarin iOS and Android SDKs. When you create your app projects, a few files will be autogenerated for you, containing some application configuration. Any modifications to this will generally be platform-specific changes, such as handling notifications on iOS or wiring up background services on Android.

There are some small things that can be configured in cross-platform code, but this depends very much on your MVVM framework. The main thing you can control here is the startup process.

Normally, the main Android activity or iOS view controller that's loaded on application startup is defined at the application level, but a good MVVM framework will allow you to define this in cross-platform code. This is usually done by specifying the first view model to use. This allows you to put logic in the application layer that can be shared across both platforms and be unit tested.

A good example of a situation in which you might do this is an app that requires a user login. When the app is first loaded, your shared application code can see if there's already a valid user account from some shared user-management code. If there is a valid account, it can load the main screen of your app from its view model, and if not, it can load the login screen view model. If this logic is in cross-platform code, you'll only have to write this once, not once per platform.

In addition, the application layer can define how the different classes in your app are connected. For example, it can ensure that the `SquareRootViewModel` is constructed automatically using an implementation of `SquareRootCalculator` as the `ISquareRootCalculator` constructor parameter.

3.6 Navigation

The view-model layer provides as much UI logic as possible, and part of this UI logic is related to navigation—the act of moving from one screen to another in the app.

Imagine a company directory app that has two screens: one with a list of employees, and one that shows the details about an employee. The app provides navigation from the list to a single employee—when you tap on a person's name in the list on the first screen, a new screen shows the details about that person, as shown in figure 3.16.

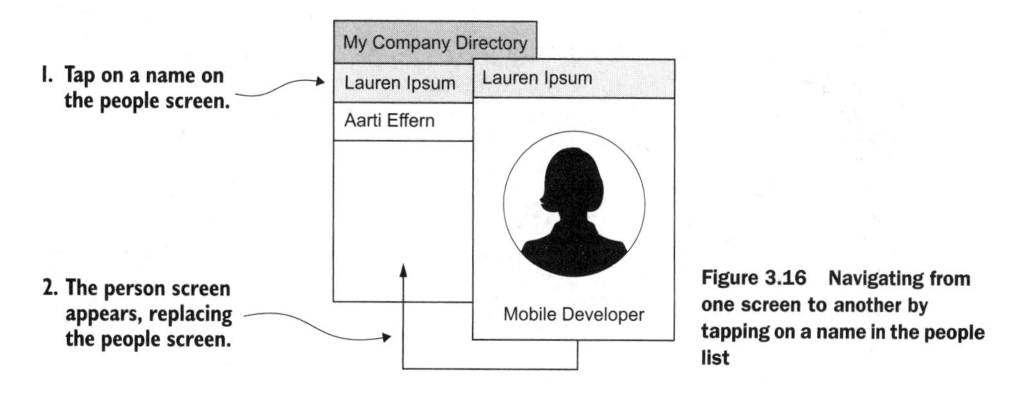
1. Tap on a name on the people screen.
2. The person screen appears, replacing the people screen.
My Company Directory
Lauren Ipsum
Aarti Effern
Lauren Ipsum
Mobile Developer

Figure 3.16 Navigating from one screen to another by tapping on a name in the people list

This kind of navigation is cross-platform in that regardless of how the UI is updated, we want to provide this navigation on both platforms. Both platforms will show the new screen and pass it data about which person was selected. The implementation on each platform is very different.

- *Android* conceptualizes each screen as a separate activity that the user is undertaking, and the user has to express an intent to change their activity.
- *iOS* thinks about each screen as a view on a part of the app, and the user segues from one view to another.

Both implementations mean the same thing from the user's perspective—you see a different screen—but the terms used and the underlying classes and method calls are very different.

What is a "screen"?

Many different terms are used to define what we see on an app. At any one time, your app will fill the screen of the device and display some UI widgets showing state or providing behavior. At various times in your app, usually when you tap something, the whole screen is replaced with another full screen of widgets.

In this book I'll use the term *screen* to refer to each distinct full screen UI, so in our calculator app there's just one screen showing the square-root calculator. In the company directory app, there would be two screens—the first one showing the list of people, and the second showing the details of a specific person.

To see how we can solve this problem in a cross-platform way using MVVM, we first must consider what we really mean when we think of the screens in an app from an MVVM perspective. When we see a screen in our app, what we're really seeing is a view and a view model—the view provides the UI widgets, and the view model provides the state and behavior. When we change screens, we're changing both the view and view model that are shown. So what controls this changing of screens? Which layer handles the navigation?

You can have multiple views and view models in a screen

In our simple examples, there's one view and one view model per screen, but nothing stops you from having more. You could have a screen made up of multiple parts, and each part would be its own view and view model.

For example, with the company directory app on a tablet in landscape orientation, there would be enough space to have the list of people on the left side and the details about the person on the right. That's one parent view showing two views and view models. In portrait orientation, the app would show one view and view model for the list, and tapping on a person would replace that view with the person view and view model.

Something has to ensure that the right view model is bound to the right view, so there needs to be a link between the view and the view model. There are two ways of doing this: view-first and view-model–first. Both of these approaches rely on there being something, usually in the app layer, that defines these links.

3.6.1 View-first

View-first means the view is the driver behind the navigation (figure 3.17). At app startup, the app layer will load a view, and when the view is loaded, something (maybe some code in the app layer, or even in the view itself) will create the corresponding view model and bind it up. When you navigate to another screen, the view is responsible for this. It will know which view it needs to navigate to and will show that view, which in turn causes its view model to be created and bound up.

3.6.2 View-model–first

View-model–first means the view model is the driver behind the navigation (figure 3.18). The app layer will load a view model at app startup, and this loading of the view model will cause the view to be created, bound to the view model, and shown. When you navigate to another screen, the view model is responsible for this. It will know which view model to navigate to and will interact with something (usually provided by the MVVM framework you're using) to create the new view model and its associated view.

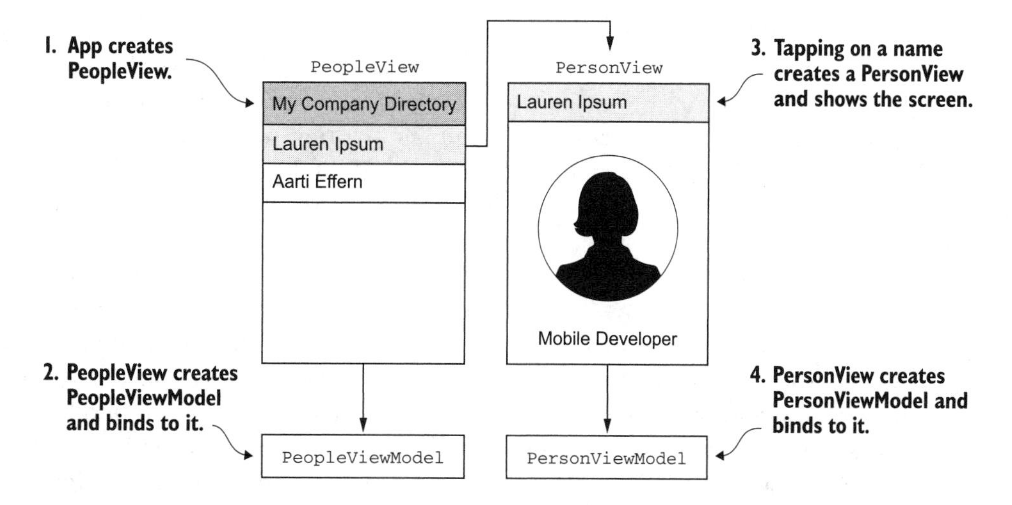

Figure 3.17 View-first navigation—the view drives the creation of view models and navigates to other views.

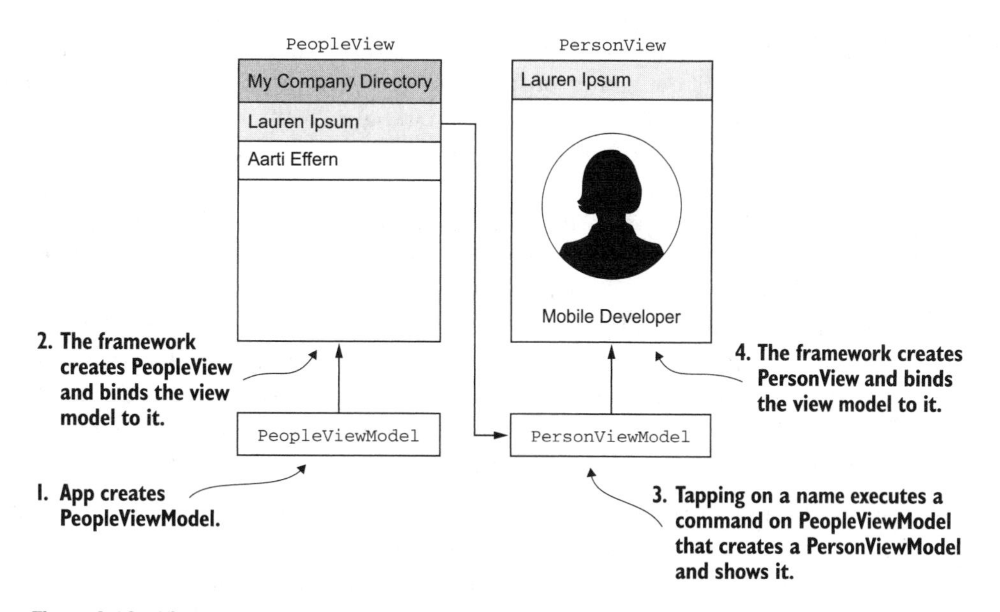

Figure 3.18 View-model–first navigation—the view model drives the creation of views using the MVVM framework and navigates to other view models.

3.6.3 Which one to use?

The most popular approach by far is view-model–first. If you have the logic to load views in the view layer, you have more platform-specific code, and this platform-specific code is hard to test except manually. Writing unit tests against UI code is harder than writing them against non-UI code. If the logic is in the view model, you have more logic in your cross-platform layer, so there's less code to write and more code that you can unit-test.

Most MVVM frameworks provide a navigation service of some description—a service that allows you to navigate to different views or view models. This service is always exposed via an interface that you can use from your view models (and mock out for testing) and it allows you to navigate in a way that's not tightly coupled to a view class. In some frameworks, this is done by navigating to a view model, and in others it's by navigating using a key (such as a unique string value) that has been linked to a view and view model. MvvmCross navigates via view model, and it's this navigation we'll be using in this book.

3.7 Revisiting the square-root calculator app

You've seen the square-root calculator app broken down layer by layer, so let's take a moment to step back and view the bigger picture, using a bigger picture. At the start of the chapter I presented a figure that showed user interactions with the app. We're now in a position to expand on this figure, filling in all the different interactions between the different layers. This is shown in figure 3.19.

Take a moment to study this diagram and follow the flow through the app. It shows a lot of what we've talked about already.

The app starts up and launches a view and view model, ideally using view-model–first navigation. As these are created, the binding wires up the state and behavior on the view model to the UI—the properties are bound to a text box and a label, and the command is bound to a button. As the user enters text, the view model is updated via the binding, which in turn pushes the value to the model. Clicking the button executes a command that calculates the square root and raises a property-changed notification. This property change is detected by the binding, which updates the UI.

This flow seems simple, but it encompasses the bulk of MVVM:

- The model is a separate layer that has business logic and uses properties of types that make sense in the business domain.
- The view model wraps the model layer and exposes state and behavior to the layers above, converting the state from business types to UI types.
- The binding sits above the view model and "glues" it to the view.
- The view exposes the state and behavior via widgets on the screen that the user can understand and interact with.

We have a model layer that's distinct, cross-platform, unit-testable, easier to maintain, and easier to evolve. We also have a view-model layer that's distinct, cross-platform,

❶ The app starts and the view and view model are created.

❷ The binding layer looks up the properties on the view and view model. It adds event handlers for the text, changing in the number text box and the click of the Add button. It also adds an event handler for the property-changed event on the view model. Finally, it sets the values on the view based on the values in the view model.

❸ Number gets/sets Number on the model, converting from a double on the model to a string on the view model. Result gets Result from the model, converting it to a string. The SqrtCommand wraps a call to Sqrt on the model.

❹ The user types “400” into the text box.

❺ The binding detects the text box’s text-changed event, reads the value inside the text box, and passes it to the property on the view model.

❼ The user taps the Square Root button.

❽ The binding detects the button-tap event and executes the SqrtCommand on the view model.

❿ The view model raises a property-changed event with the property name Result. The binding detects the event and reads the property.

⓬ The binding reads the value of Result and sets it on the result text box.

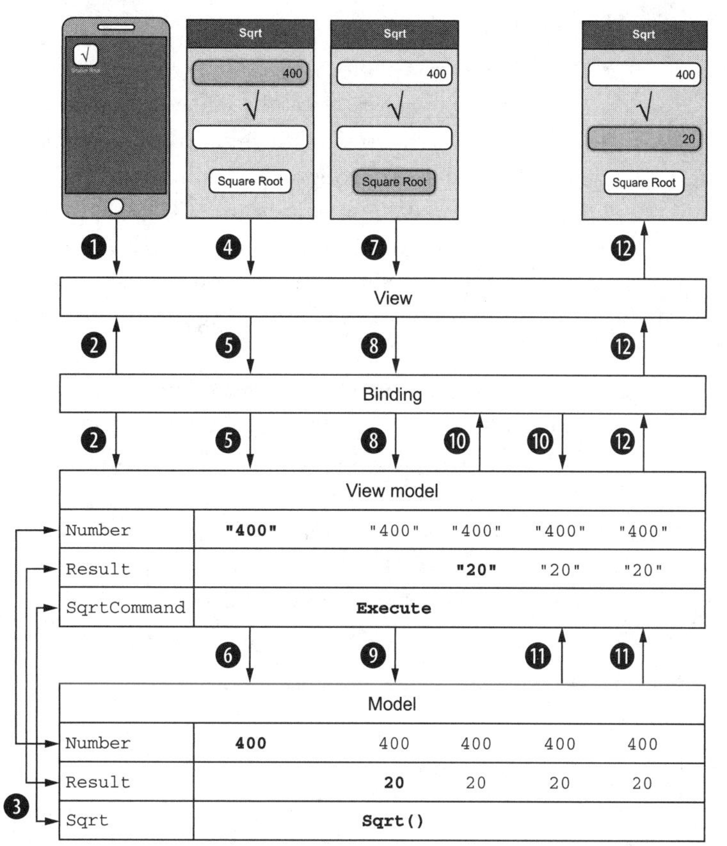

❻ The view model converts the string value of “400” to a double value of 400 and passes it through to the Number property on the model.

❾ The SqrtCommand on the view model wraps the Sqrt method on the model. When the command is executed, the Sqrt method is called and the Result is set to 20.

⓫ The view model reads the double value of Result and converts it to a string.

Figure 3.19 The complete square-root calculator, showing the interactions between all the layers of MVVM

unit-testable, easier to maintain, and easier to evolve. We have a binding layer and a thin UI layer that's platform-specific.

Now you're armed with more knowledge about MVVM. In the next chapter we'll take a look back at the Hello World example from chapter 2 and see what's happening in the code. We'll also extend the app using a cross-platform Xamarin plugin to make it say "Hello" to you.

Summary

In this chapter you learned that

- Models are cross-platform and unit-testable, and they represent data at the business-logic or domain level, not at the UI level.
- View models are cross-platform and unit-testable, and they represent state and behavior through properties and commands. View models act as a conversion layer between data or actions at the UI level and data or methods in the model.
- The platform-specific view layer and the cross-platform view model communicate though a binder, a loosely coupled layer that's usually provided by a framework that keeps the view (binding target) and view model (binding source) in sync.
- To navigate between different screens in your app you can use view-first navigation to have the view manage the navigation, or view-model–first navigation to have the view model manage it. View-model–first is preferable, as you can unit-test this navigation.
- The .NET Framework has some interfaces and classes that help to implement your app using MVVM, but to fully implement the pattern you can use a third-party framework such as MvvmCross, MVVM Light, or Caliburn.Micro.

4 Hello again, MVVM—understanding and enhancing our simple MVVM app

This chapter covers

- A detailed look into the code of the Hello Cross-Platform World app from chapter 2
- MvvmCross classes that provide a base implementation of a view model, a command, and some cross-platform app logic
- How to use MvvmCross to bind iOS and Android views to the view model
- Using Xamarin plugins to add cross-platform wrappers around platform-specific functionality
- Using inversion of control to loosely couple your code for unit testing
- Creating and binding a command
- Adding code to the view model to make your app speak to you

4.1 A deeper dive into our Hello Cross-Platform World app

Now that we've covered MVVM in detail, it's a good opportunity to review the Hello Cross-Platform World app you built in chapter 2 to see what the code does, and how it fits into the layers for a Xamarin app. You built the app using the MvvmCross extension, which created a simple Hello World app in which editing the value in a text box updated a label to match. It was a cross-platform app, and we proved this by changing a string in the core project and seeing that both apps were updated.

Let's start working through the model layers from the bottom up.

4.1.1 The model

Starting from the bottom up, let's think about the model. This is a simple app with a single string value, so there really isn't a model layer as such. You can think of the `hello` string field as the model.

There's not much else to look at here, so let's jump to the more important view-model layer.

4.1.2 The view model

In the HelloCrossPlatformWorld.Core project, you have a view model called `FirstViewModel` (figure 4.1). This view model "wraps" the model (the `hello` string) and exposes its value through its state—by exposing a property called `Hello`.

The first thing you may notice about this view model is that it has a base class—`MvxViewModel`. This class is provided by MvvmCross (all MvvmCross classes start with `Mvx` and interfaces start with `IMvx`), and it gives you a basic implementation of a view model. The main thing that it provides is property-changed notifications—it implements `INotifyPropertyChanged` and has some methods to raise the `PropertyChanged` event.

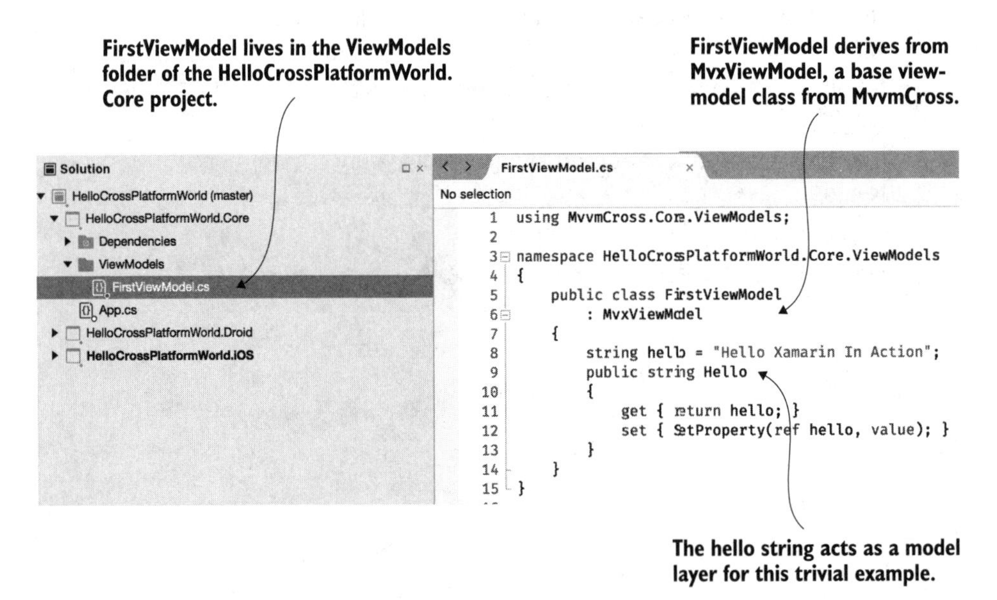

Figure 4.1 The structure of the core project showing the location of the `FirstViewModel` class

If you look at the `Hello` property, you may also notice something interesting in the set method.

Listing 4.1 Setting a value and raising a property-changed event

```
public string Hello
{
   get { return hello; }
   set { SetProperty(ref hello, value); }
}
```

Normally in a view model, you'd check whether the field was different from the value, and if so you'd set the field and raise the `PropertyChanged` event. Here, though, we're calling a method, `SetProperty`. This comes as part of `MvxViewModel` and wraps the usual set logic—it will check the value and only update the property and raise the property-changed event if it's different. You also may notice that the string is passed by `ref`. This means that a reference to the actual string field is passed instead of a copy, so that inside the `SetProperty` method you can update the value of the field. It doesn't provide any extra magic, it's just there to save on typing—three lines of code become one.

This method will also return a Boolean value—`true` means the value changed and was updated; `false` means it wasn't updated. This is helpful if you need to perform other actions if the value changed, such as raising property-changed notifications for other properties that use this value.

4.1.3 The application layer

Before we look at the view, it's worth taking a brief tour of the application layer. Mvvm-Cross provides some code in the application layer: some is platform-specific in the two app projects, and some is cross-platform in the core project. At the moment, all we really care about is the cross-platform part. This is in a class called `App` inside App.cs, as shown in figure 4.2.

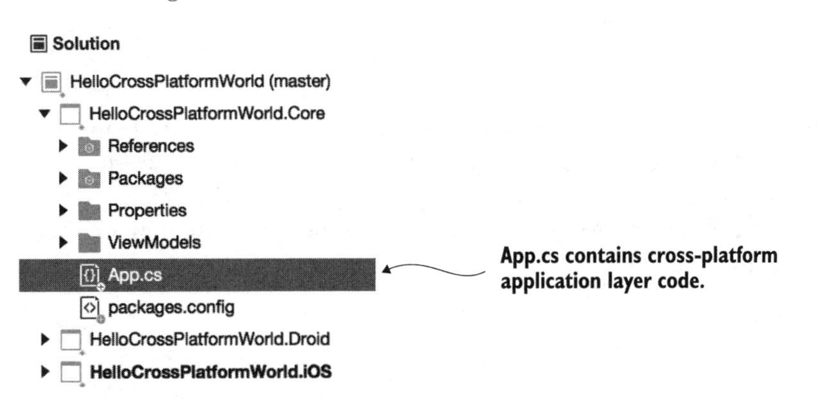

Figure 4.2 The cross-platform application layer code lives in App.cs in the core project.

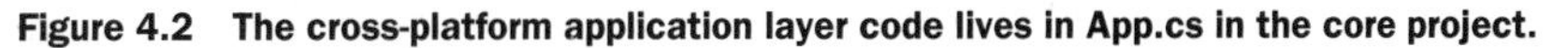

The `App` class is derived from `MvxApplication`, an MvvmCross base application class. This implements just one method—`Initialize`. The line in here that's of interest to us is the following.

Listing 4.2 Registering the view model shown on app start

```
RegisterNavigationServiceAppStart<ViewModels.FirstViewModel>();
```

This `RegisterNavigationServiceAppStart` call tells the MvvmCross application code that when the app starts up, the first thing to show is the `FirstViewModel`. If you remember back to MVVM navigation in the last chapter, you'll see that this is view-model–first navigation—the view model is registered as the app starts, so it's the first thing shown on launch. To show this view model, MvvmCross will look for the corresponding view and show that.

You need to tell MvvmCross which view is the right view for each view model. Luckily, though, you don't need to explicitly tell it; you can do it by the name. By convention, the view and view model have the same names except for the suffix, and MvvmCross uses this to determine which view to show for each view model. There are other ways to tell it if you don't want to follow this convention, but for now we'll stick to the naming convention. The view model here is called `FirstViewModel`, so to show it MvvmCross will look for a view called `FirstView`.

Once the view is loaded, a new instance of the view-model class is created, and this is set as the binding source of the view.

4.1.4 The view

Our view layer is split across the two app projects, so let's look at them one by one, starting with Android.

THE ANDROID VIEW

In the Android project, the Android view is defined as an `Activity`, which uses a layout file to define the UI. (`Activity` is the Android code-behind class for a full-screen window; we'll look at these in more detail in chapter 9.)

The view activity lives inside a folder called Views, and it's called `FirstView` (figure 4.3). Each `Activity` can build its UI in code, but more normally it loads the UI from a layout resource—an XML file that defines the widgets and layout containers (special widgets that don't have any visible components but are used to lay out other widgets, such as to arrange one below another in a vertical stack). The `FirstView` activity contains nothing of interest to us here. The interesting bit is inside FirstView.axml—the layout resource that it loads.

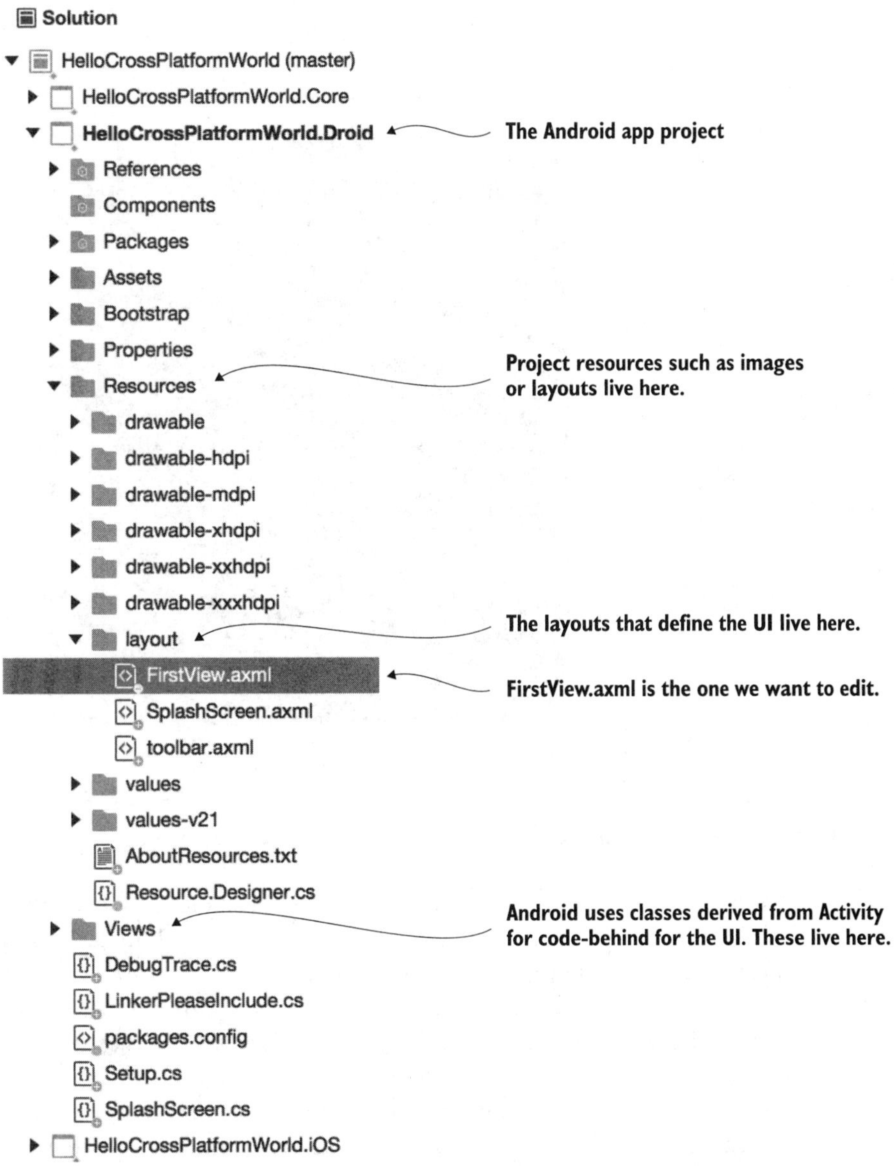

Solution
- HelloCrossPlatformWorld (master)
  - HelloCrossPlatformWorld.Core
  - **HelloCrossPlatformWorld.Droid** ← The Android app project
    - References
    - Components
    - Packages
    - Assets
    - Bootstrap
    - Properties
    - Resources ← Project resources such as images or layouts live here.
      - drawable
      - drawable-hdpi
      - drawable-mdpi
      - drawable-xhdpi
      - drawable-xxhdpi
      - drawable-xxxhdpi
      - layout ← The layouts that define the UI live here.
        - FirstView.axml ← FirstView.axml is the one we want to edit.
        - SplashScreen.axml
        - toolbar.axml
      - values
      - values-v21
      - AboutResources.txt
      - Resource.Designer.cs
    - Views ← Android uses classes derived from Activity for code-behind for the UI. These live here.
    - DebugTrace.cs
    - LinkerPleaseInclude.cs
    - packages.config
    - Setup.cs
    - SplashScreen.cs
  - HelloCrossPlatformWorld.iOS

Figure 4.3 The structure of the Android app project showing the location of the FirstView.axml layout file

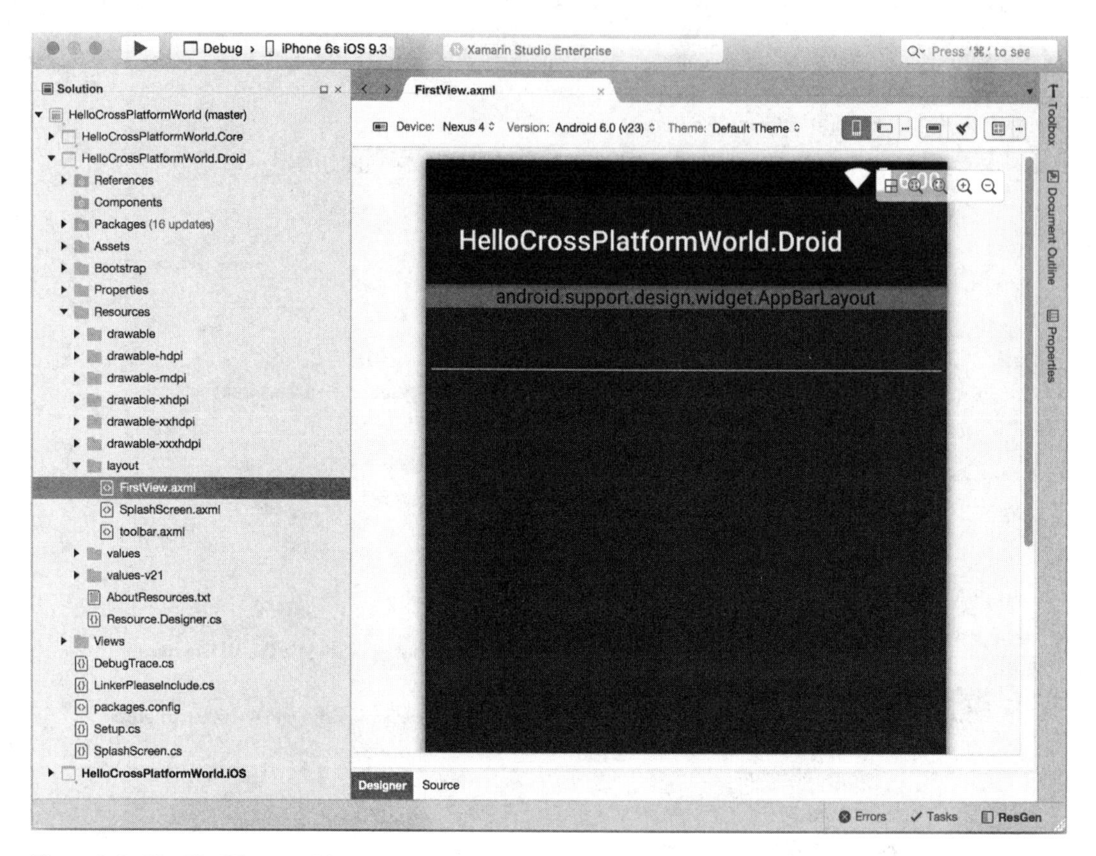

Figure 4.4 The FirstView.axml in the designer view

In the Android project is a folder called Resources that holds any resource files the app needs, such as images, strings, and layout files. You can find the layouts in the layout folder. If you look in there, you'll see the layout for our first view—FirstView.axml. If you open this layout resource, you'll get a tabbed view with one tab for a designer (figure 4.4) and one for the raw source (figure 4.5). It's the source view we're interested in.

In this Source tab, you'll see a number of nodes in the XML that each represent a visual element. Some are layouts, which are elements that hold other elements and lay them out a certain way, and some are widgets. We'll go into these in more detail in chapter 9. For now, these are the basics of the items in this layout:

- `RelativeLayout`—A layout element that allows you to position its children relative to the container or to each other. For example, you could put something at the top of the container, or put something below a particular element.
- `FrameLayout`—A layout that contains either a single item or items that are laid out one on top of the other (on the Z axis, so coming "out" of the screen).
- `LinearLayout`—A layout that stacks items either horizontally or vertically.

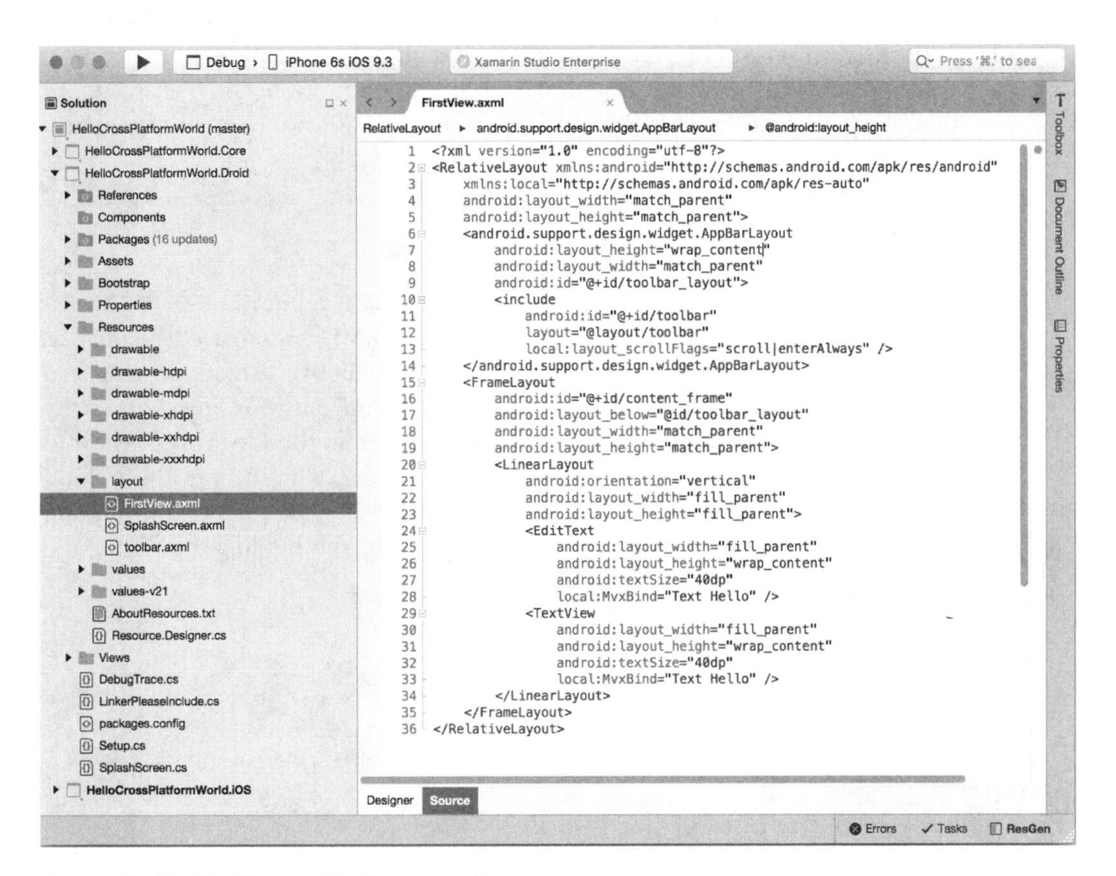

Figure 4.5 The FirstView.axml in the source view

- `EditText`—A text-entry control.
- `TextView`—A static-text control.

The two nodes we're interested in, `EditText` and `TextView`, are shown in the following listing.

Listing 4.3 Binding widgets in the layout resource to the view model

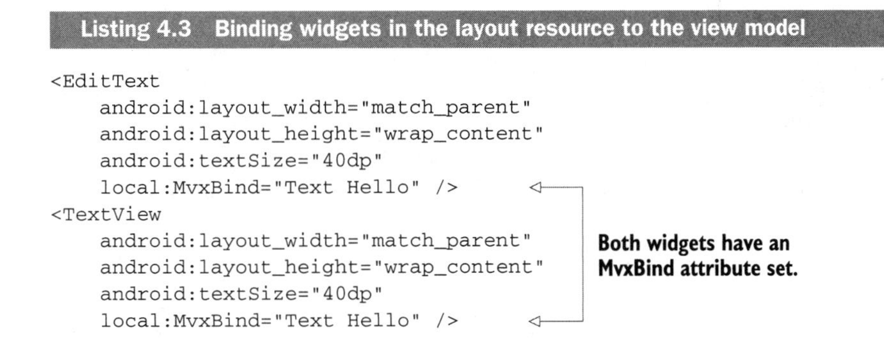

```
<EditText
    android:layout_width="match_parent"
    android:layout_height="wrap_content"
    android:textSize="40dp"
    local:MvxBind="Text Hello" />
<TextView
    android:layout_width="match_parent"
    android:layout_height="wrap_content"
    android:textSize="40dp"
    local:MvxBind="Text Hello" />
```

Both widgets have an MvxBind attribute set.

The `EditText` is an editable text box—a text-entry control. `TextView` is static text—a label. In the XML for these controls, you'll see a number of attributes set that are in the `android` namespace. These are standard control properties such as their sizing. In addition, both of these controls have an interesting attribute in the `local` namespace.

Listing 4.4 MvvmCross uses an attribute to specify binding in Android layout files

```
local:MvxBind="Text Hello"
```

As you might expect from the attribute name, `MvxBind` is an attribute from Mvvm-Cross that does binding. It comes from the `local` XML namespace (defined as `xmlns:local="http://schemas.android.com/apk/res-auto"`), which is a special namespace used to refer to all the resources that come from your app—either the code you've written, or code from external libraries, such as the MvvmCross Android NuGet packages. By setting these `MvxBind` attributes, you're telling MvvmCross to bind the `Text` property on both controls to a property called `Hello` on the binding source—an instance of `FirstViewModel`. Figure 4.6 shows this binding.

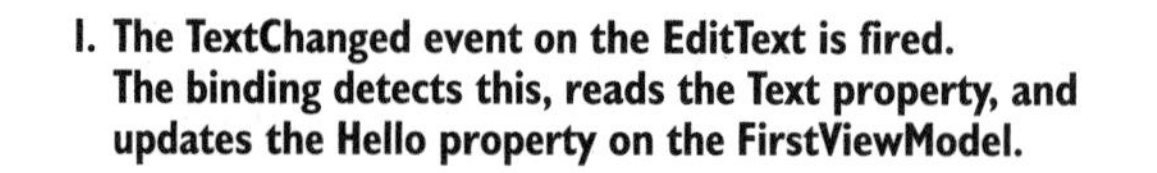

1. The TextChanged event on the EditText is fired.
The binding detects this, reads the Text property, and
updates the Hello property on the FirstViewModel.

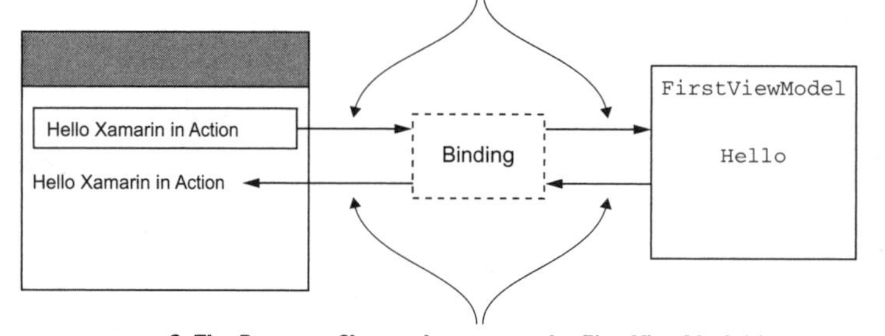

Figure 4.6 Binding detects the event on the view and updates the view model, and it detects events on the view model and updates the view.

THE IOS VIEW

Like Android, iOS has two files for a view: a designer file that defines the UI widgets and layout, and a view controller file that provides the code-behind (we'll look at these in more detail in chapter 11). These live in the Views folder in the Hello-CrossPlatformWorld.iOS project (figure 4.7).

Unlike in Android, the layout files (in this case, FirstView.storyboard) in iOS are not very human-readable and are not meant to be edited in source. Instead, you should use the designer to edit them. This means that you can't add your binding

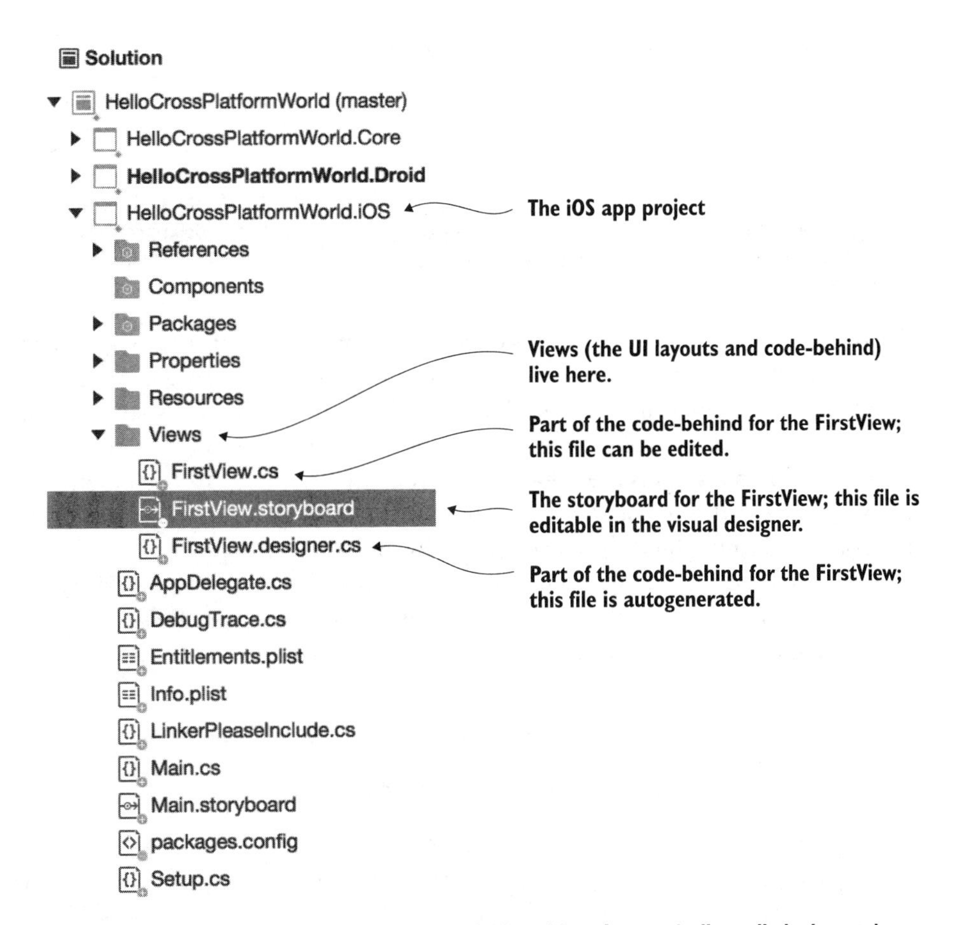

Figure 4.7 The views in iOS live in the Views folder with a view controller called `FirstView` and a storyboard called FirstView.storyboard.

using attributes the way you did in Android. Instead you can add the binding in the code-behind—in the `FirstView` view controller, located in FirstView.cs.

Let's now look at the important parts of this code.

Listing 4.5 On iOS, binding is done in the view controller

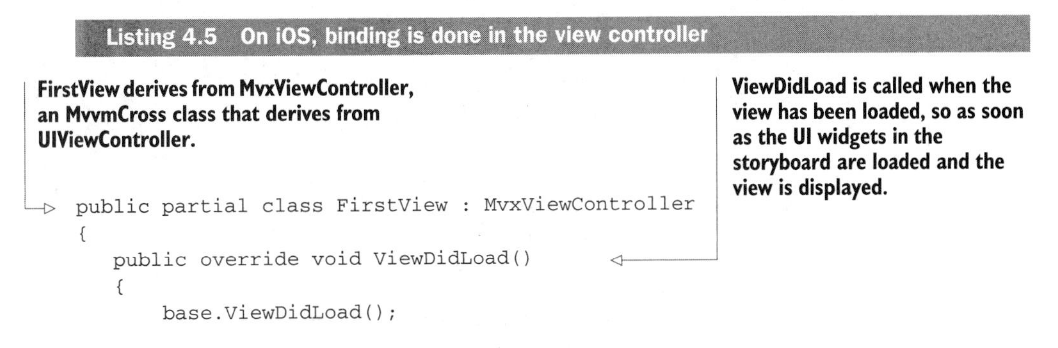

FirstView derives from MvxViewController, an MvvmCross class that derives from UIViewController.
ViewDidLoad is called when the view has been loaded, so as soon as the UI widgets in the storyboard are loaded and the view is displayed.

```
public partial class FirstView : MvxViewController
{
   public override void ViewDidLoad()
   {
       base.ViewDidLoad();
```

```
        var set = this.CreateBindingSet<FirstView, FirstViewModel>();
        set.Bind(Label).To(vm => vm.Hello);
        set.Bind(TextField).To(vm => vm.Hello);
        set.Apply();
    }
}
```

A binding set is a group of bindings for a view and view model.

The Label is bound to the Hello property on the view model.

The TextField is also bound to the Hello property on the view model.

Once the binding set is created, it can be applied to set the initial values and start listening for changes.

This code shows the `FirstView` class derived from `MvxViewController`—a MvvmCross view controller class that in turn derives from the base iOS `UIViewController`. View controllers are responsible for the lifecycle of the view—when it's shown, when it's hidden, and various states in between. In this case, we're hooking into when the view is loaded (and all widgets are created) by overriding the `ViewDidLoad` method. Once the view is loaded, the code creates a binding set—a collection of bindings between the controls and the binding source (the view model).

If you double-click to open FirstView.storyboard, it will open in a designer. In this you'll see a single view with two controls: a label and a text box. If you click on each, you'll see that they both have names, as shown in figure 4.8.

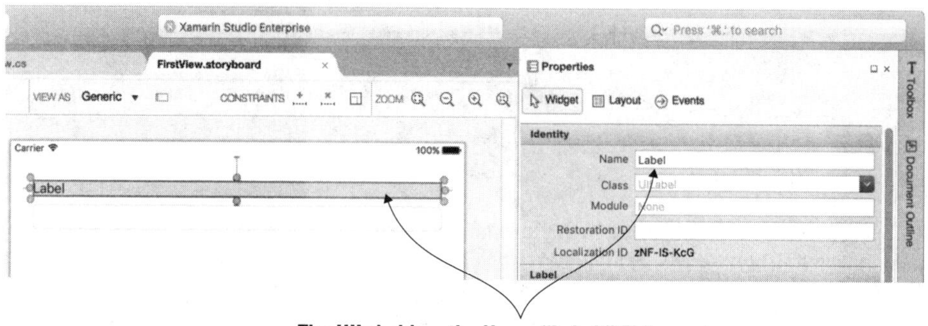

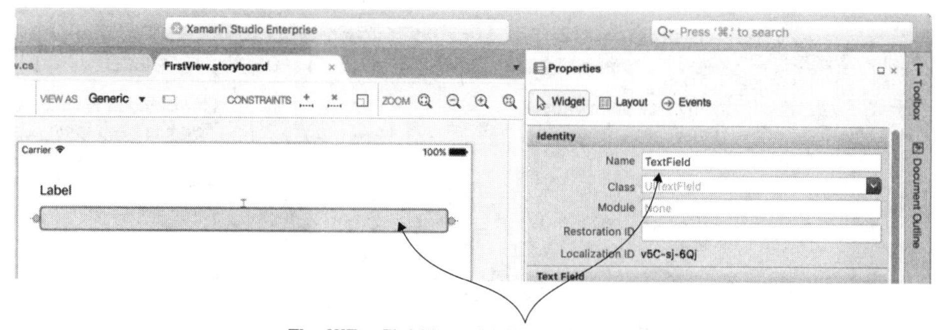

Figure 4.8 The iOS storyboard has two controls: one called `Label` and one called `TextField`.

You may have noticed that as well as FirstView.cs and FirstView.storyboard, there's also a file called FirstView.designer.cs. This is autogenerated every time you change the storyboard, and it contains mappings from items on the storyboard to properties of the `FirstView` class. If you open it, you'll see the two properties shown in the following listing.

Listing 4.6 UI widgets named on storyboards are defined as properties

```
[Outlet]
[GeneratedCode("iOS Designer", "1.0")]
UIKit.UILabel Label { get; set; }

[Outlet]
[GeneratedCode("iOS Designer", "1.0")]
UIKit.UITextField TextField { get; set; }
```

These properties represent the label and text box on the storyboard. The attributes on them tell the tooling that these properties are autogenerated from the storyboard designer (so there's no point in touching this code because your changes will be lost the next time the storyboard changes) and that it's an `Outlet`—the iOS term for a property that represents something on a storyboard. These two properties are of type `UILabel`, which is the iOS class for a static text label, and `UITextField`, which is the iOS text entry box.

FirstView.designer.cs contains a class called `FirstView`, just like the FirstView.cs file, but both class declarations are marked as `partial`. If you haven't come across this before, it's a way of saying that multiple files have pieces of the same class, and that the compiler should stick it all together in one class when it compiles. It's great for code like this—we can write one file and have another that's autogenerated based on a UI designer, and both files come together to define the class.

Looking back to the binding code, we'll bind these two properties to properties on the view model inside FirstView.cs, as follows.

Listing 4.7 Binding iOS widgets to the view model

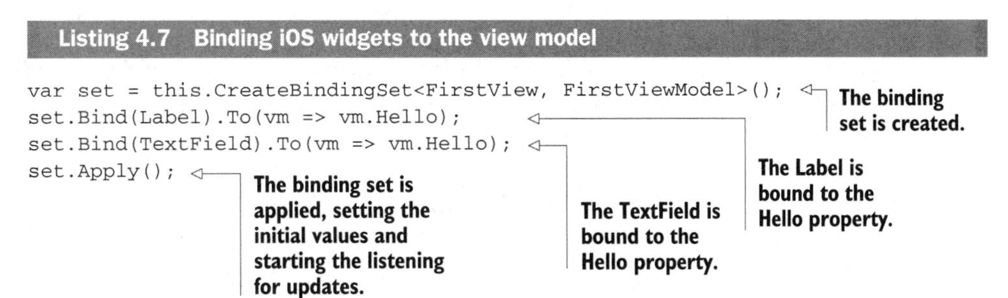

This code starts by creating a binding set, of type `MvxFluentBindingDescriptionSet`—another MvvmCross class. This binding set is typed based on the view and the view model, and once created it can be used to bind controls to properties on the view model.

When you bind to UI widgets, there's usually only one property or event you're interested in. Labels show static text, so the majority of the time you're only interested in binding this text. The same goes with text boxes—usually you're only interested in binding to the text. With buttons you normally only want to bind to the click event. Because of this, MvvmCross has some shortcuts, allowing you to bind to a widget without specifying the property you're interested in, and it will automatically pick the most appropriate one.

That is what you're seeing here. Unlike in the Android example, these bindings aren't to a particular property on the label and text field. Instead they're bound directly to the widgets, and they automagically pick the right property to bind to. In the Android example, this is less easy because the binding was expressed as an attribute in the XML file, but because we're forced to create the binding in code on iOS, we can take advantage of this.

Also unlike Android, the definition of the property on the view model (`.To(vm ? vm.Hello)`) doesn't appear to be to a string representation of the property. Instead, it's some kind of lambda function that points to the property. There isn't any real magic here—it uses this expression to get the name of the property to bind to from code. You can still set a string value of `"Hello"` instead if you wish, but by doing it this way you get IntelliSense code completion to help choose the right property and compiler checking if you update a property's name and forget to change it here. (If you use the built-in refactorings to rename the property, it also gets updated here automatically.)

Once this binding set is created, you `Apply` it to bind the initial values and listen for updates. Apart from the different syntax, this works the same way as on Android—events on the UI controls cause the view model to be updated, and property-changed events from the view model cause the view to be updated.

> **THIS SYNTAX CAN ALSO BE USED IN ANDROID** You can bind Android in code in exactly the same way as iOS if you want to. The attributes in the layout XML are just another way to do it.

Now that you've seen MVVM in action with a real-world example, and you understand what's happening in the app, let's expand on our example by adding some more features, providing you with some hands-on exposure to more bits of MVVM.

4.2 Expanding on our Hello World app

In the tradition of typical first apps, we're going to change our Hello World app to ask for the user's name and then say hello to them. Seeing as this is a mobile app and we have access to a lot more than a boring old console, we won't be displaying some text to say hello—we can make the app say hello by using the iOS and Android text-to-speech engines.

These are the steps we're going to take:

- Add a cross-platform plugin from Xamarin to help connect to the text-to-speech engines on each platform.
- Add a button to the UI.
- Add code in our cross-platform layer that's wired up to the button to run the text-to-speech engine.

4.2.1 Using .NET Standard plugins to access device-specific code

As you've already seen, we want as much code as possible in the shared layers. The problem occurs when we want to do something that's device-specific, such as getting our app to speak using a text-to-speech engine. The concept is very generic—we want to call a speak method and have it read the words over the device's audio output. The implementation, however, isn't generic. Android has an API for text to speech, and so does iOS, but the APIs are not at all the same. What we need is a way to call a generic speak method, and have the implementation worry about the platform-specific implementations.

Luckily for us there is such a thing that uses a pattern called *bait and switch*. What we can do is create three libraries, each targeting a different thing—one .NET Standard, one Android-specific, and one iOS-specific. These libraries will have the same assembly names, namespaces, and classes in each. The only difference is the implementation. The .NET Standard implementation will do nothing, the iOS one will implement the functionality using iOS APIs, and the Android one will implement it using Android APIs. To use these libraries, we reference the .NET Standard version from the .NET Standard project, the iOS version from the iOS project, and the Android version from the Android project.

At compile time, the .NET Standard core project is built against the .NET Standard implementation of the library, the iOS app against the iOS implementation, and the Android app against the Android implementation. Each library contains the same namespaces and classes, just different implementations. Runtime is where the magic happens. The compiler sees that the assemblies have the same names, and in the output directory the one referenced by the app "wins." So when you're compiling the iOS app, the final output directory will contain the version of the assembly that was referenced by the iOS app itself—the iOS library with the iOS implementation. For Android it's the same. Remember, these libraries have the same assembly names, so only one can be in the output directory. When the app is run and a call is made to the library, it can only be resolved to the platform-specific one, as that's the only version available. This means both the app code and the core project will call the platform-specific version.

Figure 4.9 shows this in action in our text-to-speech example. Calls to `Speak` are compiled against the assembly that's referenced, and at runtime the actual call is made to the version that's referenced by the app project.

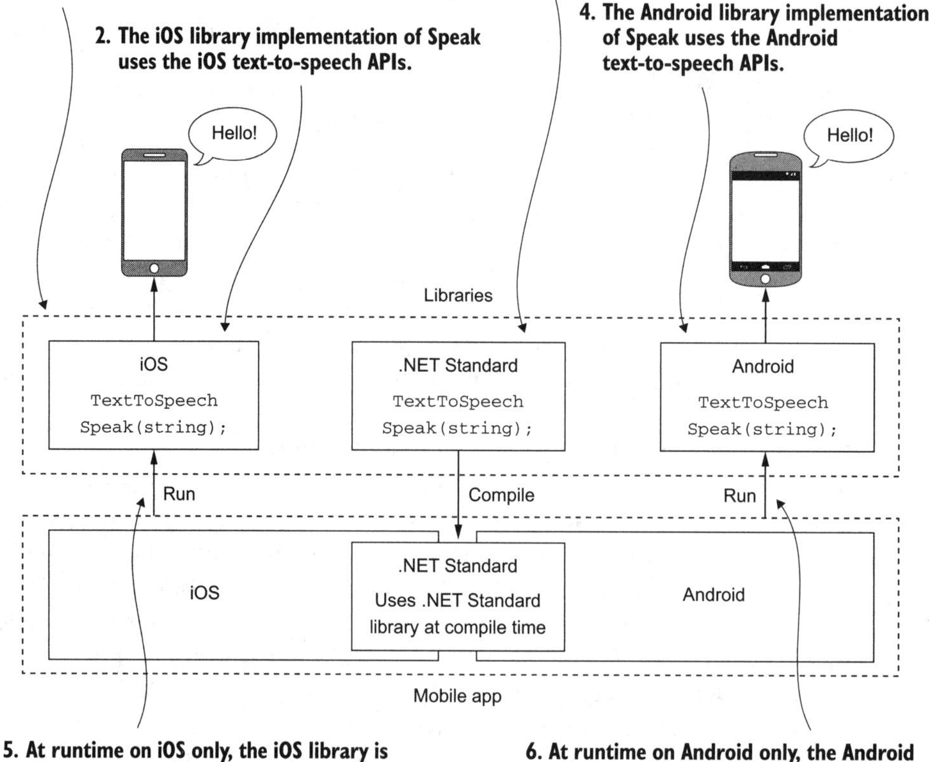

Figure 4.9 Using bait and switch with a text-to-speech plugin to compile against a .NET Standard version and then use the platform-specific code at runtime

This is a popular pattern used by a number of cross-platform NuGet packages. Xamarin itself provides a number of plugins—NuGet packages that provide access to device-specific functionality using the same bait and switch pattern. The text-to-speech example is taken from one of Xamarin's plugins, and they have other plugins to access other device services, such as the camera. The limitation with these is they have to represent the lowest common denominator so that the functionality works on all platforms—there's no point in adding camera functionality for live photos, for example, because this is only available on iOS and wouldn't work on Android.

4.2.2 *Installing the Xamarin text-to-speech plugin*

Installing this plugin is really easy—you do it using the NuGet package manager.

On Visual Studio for Windows, right-click the solution in the Solution Explorer and select Manage NuGet Packages for Solution. This will open the NuGet package manager in the workspace (figure 4.10). Select Browse, and in the search box enter *TextToSpeech*. In the list of packages that appears, select the one labeled "Xam.Plugins.TextToSpeech". The current version at the time of writing is 3.0.1, so select this version from the package settings on the right (later versions may work, but to ensure the following code works, use version 3.0.1). Select all the projects in the projects list and click the Install button on the right side. This will install the NuGet package into all three projects—the core project, the iOS app, and the Android app.

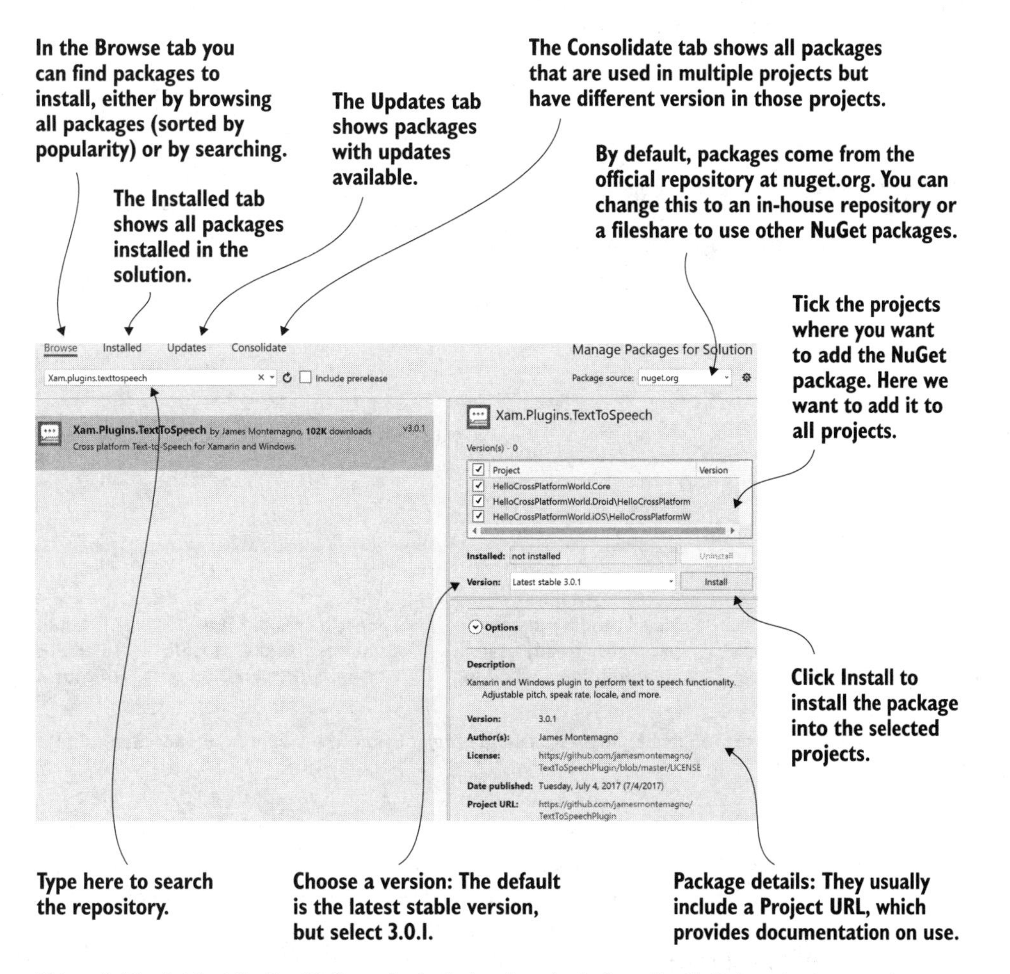
In the Browse tab you can find packages to install, either by browsing all packages (sorted by popularity) or by searching.
The Installed tab shows all packages installed in the solution.
The Updates tab shows packages with updates available.
The Consolidate tab shows all packages that are used in multiple projects but have different version in those projects.
By default, packages come from the official repository at nuget.org. You can change this to an in-house repository or a fileshare to use other NuGet packages.
Tick the projects where you want to add the NuGet package. Here we want to add it to all projects.
Click Install to install the package into the selected projects.
Type here to search the repository.
Choose a version: The default is the latest stable version, but select 3.0.1.
Package details: They usually include a Project URL, which provides documentation on use.
Browse
Installed
Updates
Consolidate
Manage Packages for Solution
Xam.plugins.texttospeech
Include prerelease
Package source: nuget.org
Xam.Plugins.TextToSpeech by James Montemagno, 102K downloads
v3.0.1
Cross platform Text-to-Speech for Xamarin and Windows.
Xam.Plugins.TextToSpeech
Version(s) - 0
Project
Version
HelloCrossPlatformWorld.Core
HelloCrossPlatformWorld.Droid\HelloCrossPlatform
HelloCrossPlatformWorld.iOS\HelloCrossPlatformW
Installed: not installed
Uninstall
Version: Latest stable 3.0.1
Install
Options
Description
Xamarin and Windows plugin to perform text to speech functionality. Adjustable pitch, speak rate, locale, and more.
Version: 3.0.1
Author(s): James Montemagno
License: https://github.com/jamesmontemagno/TextToSpeechPlugin/blob/master/LICENSE
Date published: Tuesday, July 4, 2017 (7/4/2017)
Project URL: https://github.com/jamesmontemagno/TextToSpeechPlugin

Figure 4.10 Adding the TextToSpeech plugin to all projects from the NuGet package manager

For Visual Studio for Mac, the process is similar but a bit longer—you have to add the NuGet package to each project separately. Right-click on the core project and select Add > Add NuGet packages. From the dialog box that pops up (shown in figure 4.11), search for "TextToSpeech", check the box next to Text to Speech Plugin for Xamarin and Windows, select version 3.0.1 from the drop-down menu on the bottom right, and click Add Package. Repeat this process for the iOS and Android projects. Luckily the NuGet package manager shows any packages already in use at the top, so after adding it to one project, it will appear at the top of the list for the other projects.

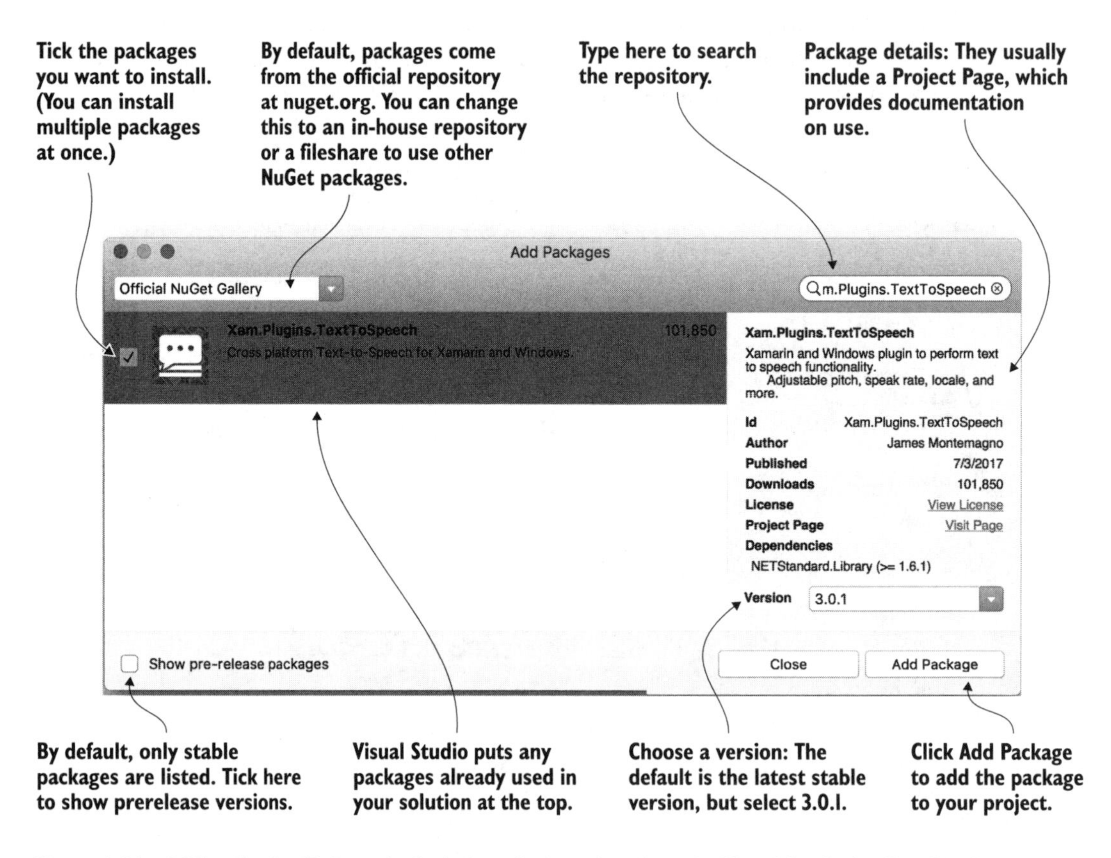
Tick the packages you want to install. (You can install multiple packages at once.)
By default, packages come from the official repository at nuget.org. You can change this to an in-house repository or a fileshare to use other NuGet packages.
Type here to search the repository.
Package details: They usually include a Project Page, which provides documentation on use.
Add Packages
Official NuGet Gallery
m.Plugins.TextToSpeech
Xam.Plugins.TextToSpeech
Cross platform Text-to-Speech for Xamarin and Windows.
101,850
Xam.Plugins.TextToSpeech
Xamarin and Windows plugin to perform text to speech functionality.
Adjustable pitch, speak rate, locale, and more.
Id Xam.Plugins.TextToSpeech
Author James Montemagno
Published 7/3/2017
Downloads 101,850
License View License
Project Page Visit Page
Dependencies
NETStandard.Library (>= 1.6.1)
Version 3.0.1
Show pre-release packages
Close
Add Package
By default, only stable packages are listed. Tick here to show prerelease versions.
Visual Studio puts any packages already used in your solution at the top.
Choose a version: The default is the latest stable version, but select 3.0.1.
Click Add Package to add the package to your project.

Figure 4.11 Adding the TextToSpeech plugin to a single project from the Visual Studio for Mac Add Packages dialog box

THERE'S AN EXTENSION TO HELP There's an extension for Visual Studio for Mac called NuGet Package Manager Extensions that provides solution-level package management. This extension allows you to install or update packages for multiple projects at the same time.

4.2.3 *Adding the cross-platform code*

To add the code to speak the hello message, make the code changes shown in the following listing to the `FirstViewModel` class in FirstViewModel.cs in the HelloCrossPlatformWorld.Core project. This is the same place you updated the hello message in chapter 2. This listing shows the complete class, not just the changes.

Listing 4.8 Updated `FirstViewModel` with code for speaking

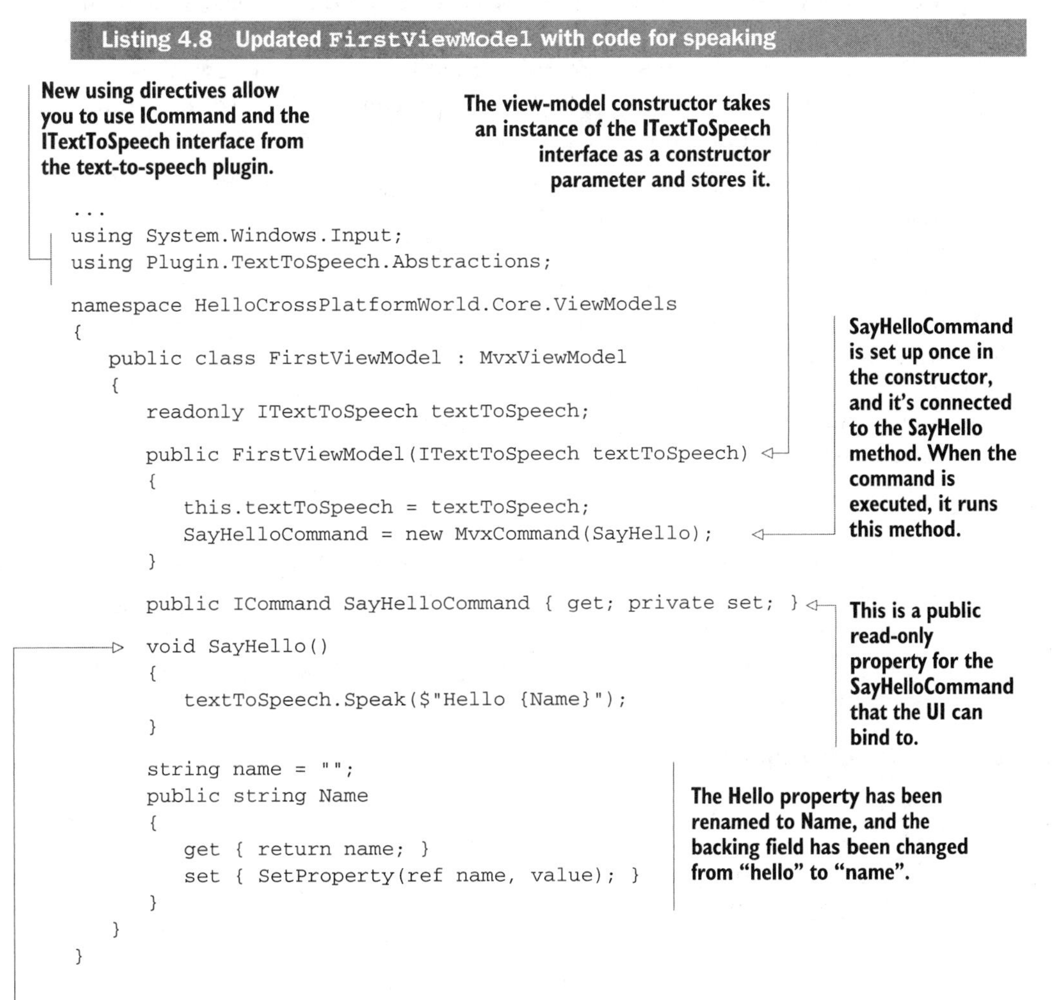

```
...
using System.Windows.Input;
using Plugin.TextToSpeech.Abstractions;

namespace HelloCrossPlatformWorld.Core.ViewModels
{
   public class FirstViewModel : MvxViewModel
   {
      readonly ITextToSpeech textToSpeech;

      public FirstViewModel(ITextToSpeech textToSpeech)
      {
         this.textToSpeech = textToSpeech;
         SayHelloCommand = new MvxCommand(SayHello);
      }

      public ICommand SayHelloCommand { get; private set; }

      void SayHello()
      {
         textToSpeech.Speak($"Hello {Name}");
      }

      string name = "";
      public string Name
      {
         get { return name; }
         set { SetProperty(ref name, value); }
      }
   }
}
```

New using directives allow you to use ICommand and the ITextToSpeech interface from the text-to-speech plugin.
The view-model constructor takes an instance of the ITextToSpeech interface as a constructor parameter and stores it.
SayHelloCommand is set up once in the constructor, and it's connected to the SayHello method. When the command is executed, it runs this method.
This is a public read-only property for the SayHelloCommand that the UI can bind to.
The Hello property has been renamed to Name, and the backing field has been changed from "hello" to "name".
The SayHello method makes a call to the text-to-speech interface that was passed to the constructor to speak the hello message.

These are the changes to the view model:

- A constructor parameter has been added to take and store an instance of the `ITextToSpeech` interface.
- The existing `Hello` property and its backing field have been renamed so you can use them to store the user's name.

- A new method has been added, `SayHello`. This method makes a call to the `Speak` method on the .NET Standard text-to-speech library (remember that at runtime it will use the platform-specific implementation) using a string built up from the `Name`. This method call will make your app say "Hello [Name]" out loud, using the text-to-speech engine on the device.
- A new read-only property called `SayHelloCommand` has been added. In the constructor, this command is created as an `MvxCommand`, a class that implements `ICommand` and comes from MvvmCross. This command class takes an `Action` as a constructor parameter, and when the command is executed, the `Action` is invoked. In this case the `Action` is a call to the `SayHello` method.

One of the most useful and interesting changes is the addition of a constructor parameter that takes an instance of `ITextToSpeech`. Passing in an interface is a great way of making your code better. First, you're segregated from the implementation of the text-to-speech platform. If you wanted to use a different implementation, you could, as long as it implemented the same interface. Second, and most importantly, you can unit-test this. Remember, testing is one of the key benefits of using a pattern like MVVM, and having the view model interact with the `ITextToSpeech` interface rather than a concrete implementation allows you to use a mock implementation in your unit tests, which can validate that the correct calls are made. Without this, you can't unit-test, you can only manually test that the right thing was called by listening for the spoken text.

The obvious question now is how you pass this implementation into the constructor in your app. You've changed the constructor, but where do you change the call to the constructor to add the new parameter? The answer is that you don't, at least not directly. Instead you use a little bit of magic called *inversion of control* that can create your view model for you and pass the right thing to the constructor.

4.2.4 Inversion of control

Think about making coffee at home. You need coffee, hot water, milk, sugar, and some form of machinery. You're in control of the coffee-making process—you know which cupboard you keep your coffee in, where in the fridge the milk lives, and how to operate your coffee-making technique of choice (grinder, French press, espresso maker, or whatever). You're in control, but that means you have to know everything (figure 4.12).

Now imagine you've decided it's too much like hard work, so instead you pop out to the local coffee shop to get your morning cup of wake-up juice. Suddenly you don't have to worry about beans, milk, kettles, French presses, or other coffee paraphernalia. Instead you just ask for coffee and receive a hot cup of a tasty caffeinated beverage. You're no longer in control—you've given this control up to the barista (figure 4.13). In return for this lack of control, you now have an easy way to get coffee. You've inverted that control from you to elsewhere—they could change beans or change their coffee machine and you wouldn't know or care. As long as you get your coffee, you're happy.

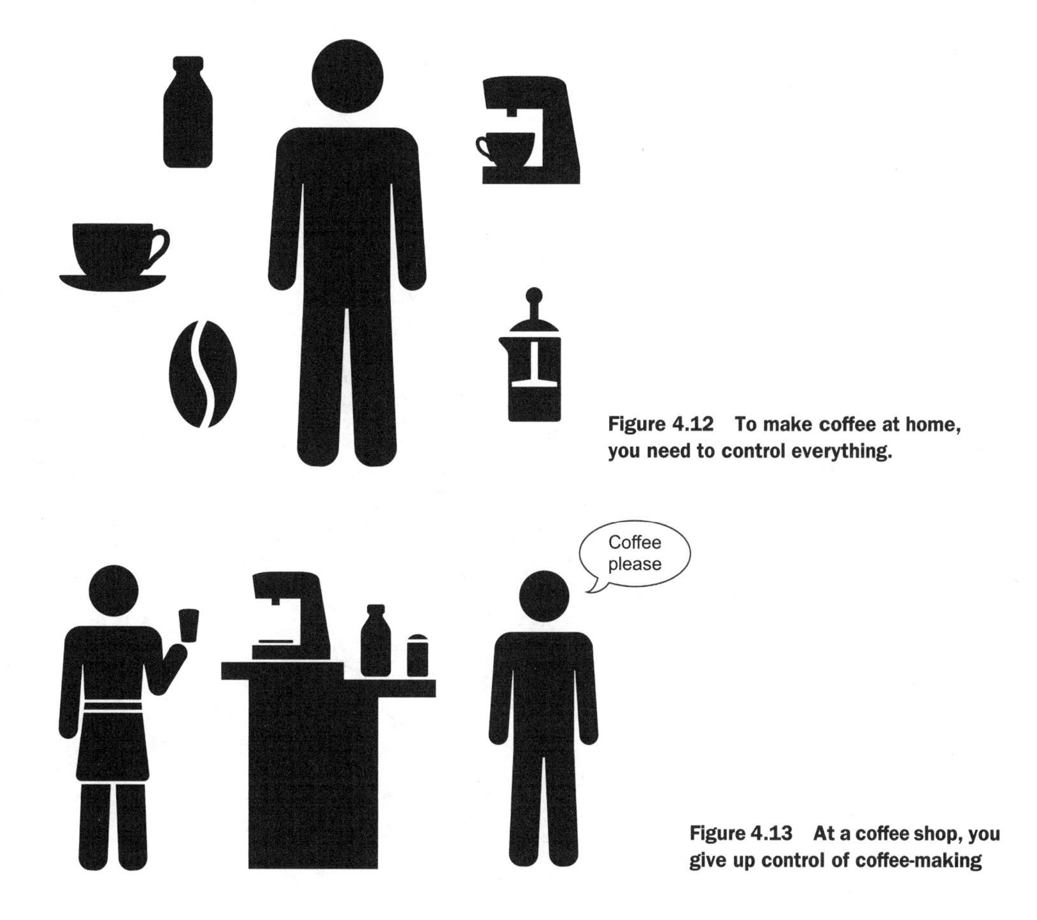

Figure 4.12 To make coffee at home, you need to control everything.

Figure 4.13 At a coffee shop, you give up control of coffee-making

In code, we can do the same thing, as shown in the following listing. Imagine a theoretical class that makes coffee at home, and a person class that uses it.

Listing 4.9 A class that makes coffee

```
public class MakeCoffeeAtHome        <-- The coffee-making class
{
   public Coffee MakeCoffee()
   {
   }
}
                                     A class that represents a
                                     person who desperately needs
public class Person              <-- coffee (such as the author)
{
   public void WakeUp()
   {
      var coffeeMaker = new MakeCoffeeAtHome();   <-- When the WakeUp method is
      Drink(coffeeMaker.MakeCoffee());                called, the Person constructs an
   }                                                  instance of MakeCoffeeAtHome
                                                      and uses it to make coffee
```

```
    public void Drink(Coffee coffee)
    {
    }
}
```

In this listing there's a class called `MakeCoffeeAtHome` that makes coffee, and a class called `Person` that constructs the coffee maker and calls it to get coffee. This code is very tightly coupled—the `Person` class is in complete control of the coffee-making. The downside is that `Person` is in complete control, which means that if anything changes, we'll have to change the `Person` class. For example, another developer might add a constructor to the `MakeCoffeeAtHome` class so that it takes a logger to track the amount of coffee being drunk—if that happened, this code would break. Similarly, if we wanted to change to buying coffee from the local coffee shop instead of making it ourselves, we'd need to rewrite our `Person` class. Another consequence of the code being tightly coupled is that we can't unit-test the `Person` class in isolation; we can only test it with the `MakeCoffeeAtHome` class.

It would be better if we could invert the control and make it the responsibility of something else to construct the coffee maker and pass it to the `Person`. This is shown in the following listing.

Listing 4.10 Changing `Person` to take a coffee maker as a constructor argument

```
public class Person
{
    MakeCoffeeAtHome coffeeMaker;
    public Person(MakeCoffeeAtHome coffeeMaker)
    {
        coffeeMaker = coffeeMaker;
    }

    public void WakeUp()
    {
        Drink(coffeeMaker.MakeCoffee());
    }
}
```

The coffee maker is no longer constructed by the Person. Instead it's passed in to the constructor.

The coffee maker passed to the constructor is used to make coffee.

This is a bit better—we've given up control of constructing the `MakeCoffeeAtHome` class, so that if the class needs to change its constructor, the `Person` class doesn't break. Let's take this one step further in the next listing and use an interface, so that `Person` becomes easier to unit-test.

Listing 4.11 Passing an interface to the `Person` constructor argument

```
public Interface IMakeCoffee
{
    Coffee MakeCoffee();
}
```

An interface used to define something that can make coffee

```
public class MakeCoffeeAtHome : IMakeCoffee
{
   public Coffee MakeCoffee()
   {
   }
}

public class Person
{
   IMakeCoffee coffeeMaker;
   public Person(IMakeCoffee coffeeMaker)
   {
      coffeeMaker = coffeeMaker;
   }
}
```

The MakeCoffeeAtHome class implements this interface.

The Person class no longer cares about the actual type of the coffee maker. It just needs something that implements the IMakeCoffee to be passed in to the constructor, and it can use this to make coffee.

This is better—we have an `IMakeCoffee` interface that's passed to the `Person` class. We can now unit-test the `Person` class in isolation by mocking the interface. We can also now change from making coffee at home to buying it from a coffee shop without changing the `Person` class; we just need a different implementation of the `IMakeCoffee` interface, as in the following listing.

Listing 4.12 A different implementation of the `IMakeCoffee` interface

```
public class CoffeeShop : IMakeCoffee
{
   public Coffee MakeCoffee()
   {
   }
}
```

CoffeeShop also implements the IMakeCoffee interface, so Person could be constructed using this, and when it makes coffee, the coffee shop would be making it.

So far so good. We've inverted control of the coffee maker to somewhere else, and this is one of the key parts of the *inversion of control* (IoC) design pattern—giving up control of how your code is wired together. The question now is where has this control gone to? Passing `IMakeCoffee` in as a constructor parameter is all well and good, but what is going to do this? Where in the code do we call this constructor?

What we need is a magic box. Something we can ask to give us a `Person` and have it create the `Person` automagically. All it would need to know is which coffee maker to use. We could tell it once to use a `CoffeeShop` when an instance of `IMakeCoffee` is needed, and then whenever we ask for a `Person`, we'd get one created using `CoffeeShop` as the constructor parameter. The `Person` doesn't care what's used to construct it, only that it's constructed with something that implements `IMakeCoffee`. Once we've told the magic box to use a `CoffeeShop`, we can stop thinking about how to construct the `Person` and just have one created for us.

The good news is that we can use an inversion of control container to do this hard work for us. This is a container class that you can think of as the magic box. You tell it what types you have (this is referred to as *registering* types), and when you ask for an instance of a type, it will look at the constructor of that type, create anything it needs, and pass them in when constructing the type you wanted. Essentially, it injects the dependency at construction time, so this concept is referred to as *dependency injection*—using a tool such as an IoC container to push dependencies into a class either by using constructor parameters (constructor injection) or by setting properties after construction. Figure 4.14 shows this.

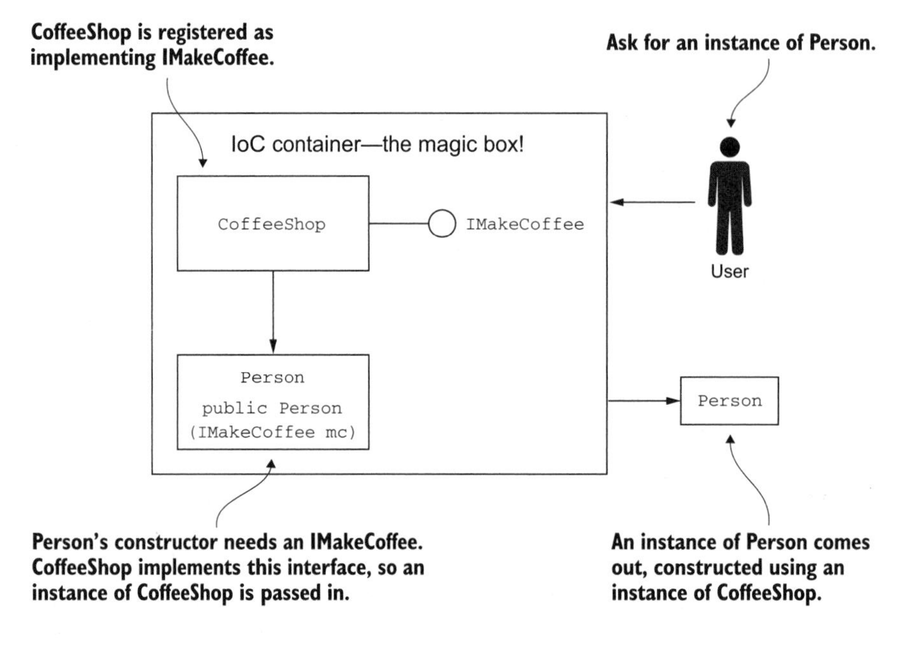
CoffeeShop is registered as implementing IMakeCoffee.
Ask for an instance of Person.
IoC container—the magic box!
CoffeeShop
IMakeCoffee
User
Person
public Person
(IMakeCoffee mc)
Person
Person's constructor needs an IMakeCoffee. CoffeeShop implements this interface, so an instance of CoffeeShop is passed in.
An instance of Person comes out, constructed using an instance of CoffeeShop.

Figure 4.14 The magic box that is an IoC container—you tell it what types you have, and when you ask for an instance of a type, any dependencies are resolved and then injected into the constructor of the type you've requested.

Let's think about this in terms of our Hello World app. If you compile the code with the changes we made to the `FirstViewModel`, you'll notice that it compiles with no problems. We've added a new constructor parameter but this doesn't break the code.

This is because MvvmCross uses an IoC container for everything it does. You never explicitly create a view or a view model yourself; instead, you rely on the built-in MvvmCross IoC container to do it for you. The built-in MvvmCross startup code will find all your view models and register them inside the IoC container, so you don't have to do anything with them. Remember the App.cs file with its call to `RegisterNavigationServiceAppStart<ViewModels.FirstViewModel>()`? This tells the MvvmCross framework that when the app starts up it needs to do the following:

1. Create this view model by requesting it from the container.
2. Create the corresponding view by finding a class with the same name as the view model (but with a `View` suffix).
3. Set the view model on the view to be the view model from the container.
4. Show the view.

MvvmCross.Platform.Exceptions.MvxIoCResolveException has been thrown

Failed to resolve parameter for parameter textToSpeech of type ITextToSpeech when creating HelloCrossPlatformWorld.Core.ViewModels.FirstViewModel

Show Details

Figure 4.15 The exception thrown when MvvmCross can't resolve a type from its IoC container

Our code compiles fine, but will it run? Nope. If you try it, the app will throw an `MvxIoCResolveException`, as shown in figure 4.15.

The `MvxIoCResolveException` type tells us that the MvvmCross framework was unable to resolve a type from the IoC container. The exception message tells us that the exception occurred when constructing the `FirstViewModel` class as it couldn't find an implementation of `ITextToSpeech` in the container to use as the constructor parameter. These exception messages are pretty easy to debug—they clearly state which parameter type is missing and which class was being constructed when it failed to find the type.

This is easy enough to fix—we need to register an instance of this interface with the IoC container before the view model is created. The text-to-speech plugin has a static class `CrossTextToSpeech` with a `Current` property that returns an implementation of the `ITextToSpeech` interface. We can register this in the container so that every time this interface is requested, this static instance is returned.

The place to do this is inside the cross-platform application class, which lives in the root folder of the HelloCrossPlatform.Core project in a class called `App` inside a file called App.cs. This `App` class derives from `MvxApplication`, an MvvmCross base application class that handles cross-platform application setup. The following listing shows the code change you need to make to the `App` class, so go ahead and update your code.

Listing 4.13 Adding registration of the text-to-speech plugin to the App class

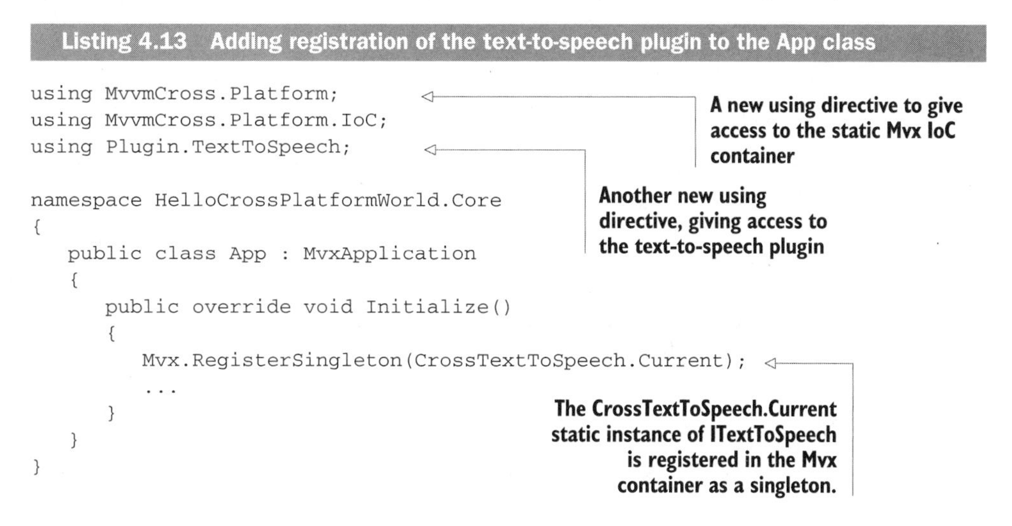

```
using MvvmCross.Platform;
using MvvmCross.Platform.IoC;
using Plugin.TextToSpeech;

namespace HelloCrossPlatformWorld.Core
{
   public class App : MvxApplication
   {
      public override void Initialize()
      {
         Mvx.RegisterSingleton(CrossTextToSpeech.Current);
         ...
      }
   }
}
```

A new using directive to give access to the static Mvx IoC container
Another new using directive, giving access to the text-to-speech plugin
The CrossTextToSpeech.Current static instance of ITextToSpeech is registered in the Mvx container as a singleton.

This change calls `RegisterSingleton` on the `Mvx` container, passing the static instance of the `ITextToSpeech` interface. `RegisterSingleton` tells the container that we only ever want one instance of this interface—every time it's requested, it will always return the same instance. Every time our view model is created, we get a new view model, but the same instance of the text-to-speech plugin gets passed to the constructor.

Now when our app starts up and the `FirstViewModel` is created, the container will find the `ITextToSpeech` instance and pass it into the constructor. We've inverted control of how our view model interacts with the text-to-speech plugin by taking it away from the view model and putting it inside our framework.

FINDING OUT HOW TO USE A PLUGIN OR NUGET PACKAGE When you're using a NuGet package for the first time, the hardest thing can be finding out how it works and how to use it. Most good NuGet packages are documented either on their own website or via a ReadMe inside the GitHub repo for the source. There's usually a link to this documentation shown in the NuGet package manager. For the text-to-speech plugin, the docs are on GitHub at https://github.com/jamesmontemagno/TextToSpeechPlugin.

This is a very powerful pattern. MvvmCross registers any view model derived from `MvxViewModel` as part of its default startup, and we registered the `ITextToSpeech` interface in the container manually. As a result, any time the view model is needed, it's created with the right constructor parameter. By registering everything we need via an interface inside an IoC container, we end up with loosely coupled code. This isn't just limited to view models—ideally this should be used in your model layer as well. This allows you to easily write unit tests against any class you want, mocking all the interfaces as you need them.

IoC all the things!

One other awesome thing to be aware of is that you don't have to register inside your core project—you can just as easily register inside your platform-specific code. This way you can provide access to platform-specific code via an interface.

A popular example of this would be a dialog service—something you can call to show a message popup to the user. You could define an interface for this inside your core project and create two platform-specific implementations, one in iOS and one in Android. Each implementation would use the relevant platform-specific code to show a message popup.

Once you have the core interface and two platform-specific implementations, you can register them inside the platform-specific part of the application layer. In addition to the cross-platform `MvxApplication` class, MvvmCross also has some platform-specific setup code derived from `MvxAndroidSetup` on Android and `MvxIosSetup` on iOS. You can find these inside the two Setup.cs files, one in the root of the Android app, the other in the root of the iOS app, and in there you can register classes in the `Mvx` container. At runtime your core project references the interface, and this is resolved to the platform-specific version.

Now that our core code is set up, let's add a button to the UI, connect that to our command, and make the app really say, "Hello!"

4.2.5 Wiring up the Android UI

There are two steps in wiring up the Android UI—first, add a button to the UI, and then wire it up to match the changes we've made. We'll start with the UI.

Start by opening up the FirstView.axml resource from the layout resource folder (figure 4.16). To wire up the new changes, you need to change the binding in the `EditText` and `TextView` to use the renamed `Name` property, and add a button to speak "Hello." The following listing shows the changes to the two elements inside `LinearLayout` and the new element you need for the button.

```
▼ layout
    FirstView.axml
    SplashScreen.axml
    toolbar.axml
```

Figure 4.16 The structure of the layout folder inside the resources folder of the Android app project, showing the location of the FirstView.axml layout file

Listing 4.14 The changes inside `LinearLayout` from line 20 onwards

```
<LinearLayout
   android:orientation="vertical"
   android:layout_width="match_parent"
   android:layout_height="match_parent">
   <EditText
      android:layout_width="match_parent"
      android:layout_height="wrap_content"
      android:textSize="40dp"
      local:MvxBind="Text Name" />
   <TextView
      android:layout_width="match_parent"
      android:layout_height="wrap_content"
      android:textSize="40dp"
      local:MvxBind="Text Name" />
   <Button
      android:layout_width="match_parent"
      android:layout_height="wrap_content"
      android:textSize="40dp"
      android:text="Say Hello"
      local:MvxBind="Click SayHelloCommand"/>
</LinearLayout>
```

- The binding for the EditText is changed to the new Name property.
- The binding for the TextView is changed to the new Name property.
- This button is new and is bound to the new SayHelloCommand that you just added to your view model.

Changing from `Hello` to `Name` updates the binding to look for a property on the view model called `Name` instead of one called `Hello`. This matches the name change we've just made.

The button binds something called `Click` to something called `SayHelloCommand`. MvvmCross is smart enough to know that `Click` is an event, so it expects this to be bound to an `ICommand`. At runtime when the button is tapped, the `Click` event is fired and `Execute` is called on the command.

THERE'S A DESIGNER YOU CAN USE IF YOU DON'T LIKE XML The designer tab is just that—a visual designer for laying out your UI. You can use it to add the button: just drag it on from the toolbar, and you should be able to position it in the `LinearLayout` below the other controls. You can then set the `text` and `textSize` in the Properties window and only dive into the XML to add the `MvxBind` attribute.

If you build and run this (but don't build all as you'll get a compiler error for the iOS project that we'll fix later), you'll see the new UI with the new button (shown in figure 4.17). Enter your name, tap the Say Hello button, and assuming you have the volume turned up, you'll hear the app saying hello to you! Exciting stuff, getting an app to talk using shared code (unless you're in a crowded coffee shop and everyone is now staring at you). To prove it's shared, lets get iOS talking to us as well.

Figure 4.17 The new Android app with its Say Hello button

4.2.6 *Wiring up the iOS UI*

Setting up the Android UI is pretty easy—just add another node to the XML. I'd love to be able to say iOS was just as easy, but that would be a lie. iOS is a downright pain when it comes to the UI. It used to be easy when there were only one or two screen resolutions, but now that there are multiple iPhone and iPad screen sizes, it's hard.

When there was only one screen size, everything was based on a concept called *frames*—you'd set the exact pixel location and size of every control (essentially defining where the frame of the control would be). The first retina iPhones were also easy—you used the same "pixels," and the OS just doubled everything. Now that there are a few more resolutions and screen sizes, everything uses something called *autolayout*, where you specify a set of rules called *constraints* for each control, and the layout is calculated based on these rules and the size of the screen.

For example, you could set a constraint saying "make my button use half the screen width and be fixed to the left side halfway up." On every screen size, the button would be in the same place relative to the screen—on the left side halfway up, regardless of the height of the screen. This does make for nice layouts, but setting these rules can be painful. I'll cover this in more detail in chapter 11, so for now just follow these "simple" instructions to get a new button on the screen.

Open the FirstView.storyboard file from the iOS project's Views folder (figure 4.18). We'll talk about storyboards in more detail in chapter 11, but for now think of it as a visual designer for your view. This will show the view as a large white box displaying the text entry control and label.

Figure 4.18 The structure of the Views folder in the iOS app project, showing the location of the FirstView storyboard

When the designer opens up, go to the toolbox. On Visual Studio for Mac, this should appear as a tabbed pad on the right side. If it's not there, you can open it using View > Pads > Toolbox. On Visual Studio for Windows, it should be docked on the left. If it's not there, you can show it using View > Toolbox.

Type *button* into the search bar on the toolbox, and drag a button to below the text entry control, as in figure 4.19.

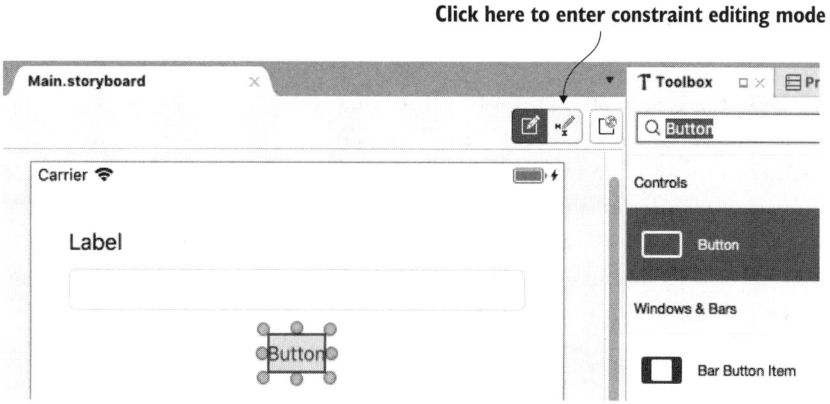

Click here to enter constraint editing mode

Figure 4.19 Dragging a button to the storyboard

Once the button is there, click the Constraint editing mode button to enter a mode where you can set the constraints. This will change the highlighting so you have a set of I-bar handles around the button instead of the circle handles.This is shown in figure 4.20.

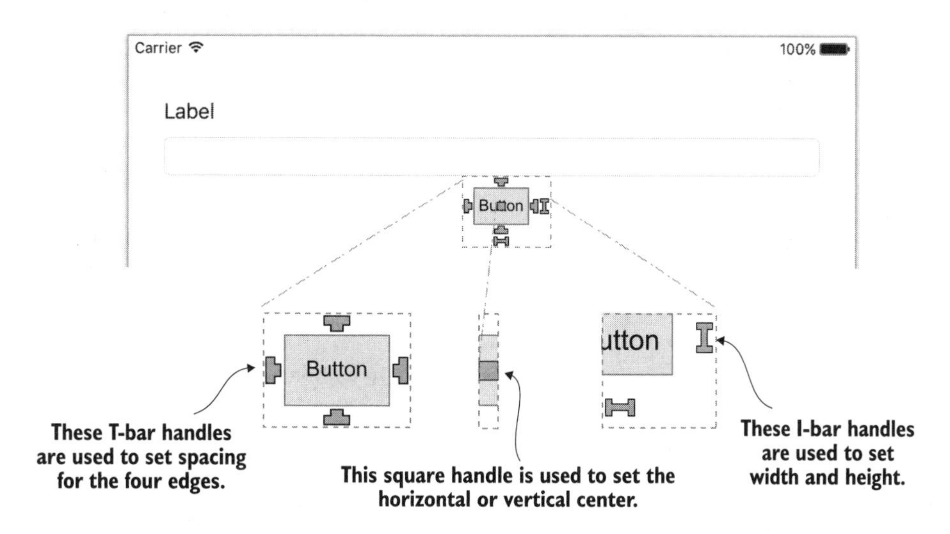

Figure 4.20 The constraint handles for constraining the size, distance to other controls, and center alignment

Once these handles are visible, you can drag them to create the constraints. As you drag them, you'll see various widgets in the view either light up or be highlighted with dashed lines. These are guides that show what you can constrain the properties of the button to. Essentially, these constraints allow you to fix the position of the button, its size, or its center point relative to other widgets, or relative to the screen. The highlights on screen show you what you can set that particular constraint to.

To get your button looking nice and sitting below the text field for all screen sizes, you'll have to constrain three things—the top of the button, its width, and its horizontal center:

1. Drag the top T-bar handle (the one that looks like a very short T on the top in the middle) over the text entry box. The top, middle, and bottom of the text entry box and label will turn to dashed green lines, with the one that the mouse is over highlighted in blue. Drop the T-bar on the bottommost dashed line of the text entry box. This sets a top constraint of a certain distance from the bottom of the text entry box. Don't worry about the value of this distance for now.
2. Drag the bottommost I-bar handle (the one that looks like an I on its side or a squashed H, not the one that looks like an upside-down T) onto the text entry box above. When you do this, the screen will turn blue and the other controls will be green. When you drag it over the text entry box, that will turn blue and the rest of the screen will be green—this is the time to release the mouse button or trackpad. This sets a width constraint to match the width of the text entry box.
3. Drag the square handle in the middle of the button to the middle of the screen width-ways, just below the button. The screen will change so the outline of the other controls are dashed green lines, with two other dashed green lines down the horizontal middle and across the vertical middle of the view. Drop it on the green line down the horizontal middle. This will constrain the middle of the button to the middle of the screen.

Figure 4.21 shows these steps.

When you're done, the button will have an orange highlight to it, as shown in figure 4.22. This is the designer's way of telling you the button will be in a different place at runtime. You can fix this by telling the designer to position the control based on the constraints. To do this, exit constraint editing mode by clicking the Frame Editing Mode button (the first button in the constraints section), then update the frames using the Update Constraints From Frames button (the last button in the constraints section). The button you've added should resize to be the same width as the text entry box, sitting slightly below it.

The constraints themselves will be shown in the Layout tab of the Properties pad, which can be shown in Visual Studio for Mac using View > Pads > Properties if it's not already displayed on the right side. On Windows it's in the Properties window, which should be docked on the right side, but if not you can display it using View > Properties Window. These tabs show the layout rules applied. The top spacing to the text

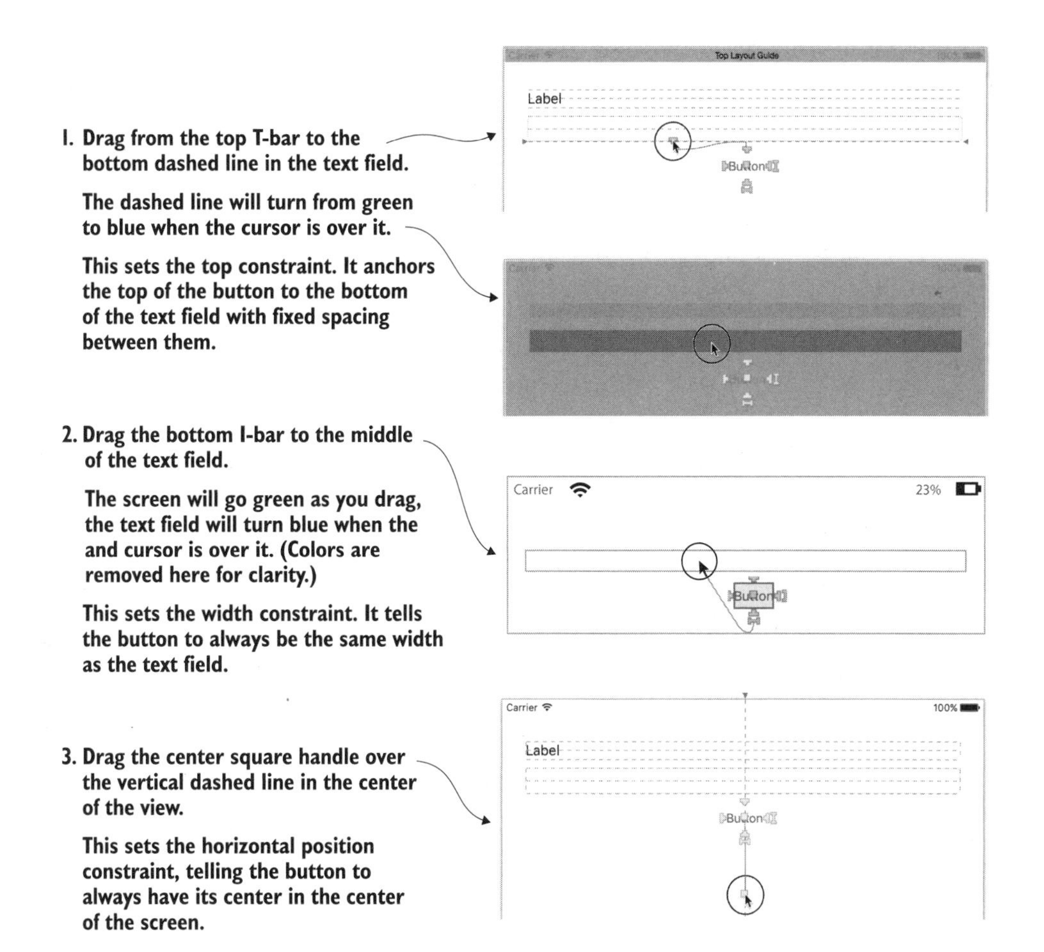

1. Drag from the top T-bar to the bottom dashed line in the text field.
The dashed line will turn from green to blue when the cursor is over it.
This sets the top constraint. It anchors the top of the button to the bottom of the text field with fixed spacing between them.
2. Drag the bottom I-bar to the middle of the text field.
The screen will go green as you drag, the text field will turn blue when the and cursor is over it. (Colors are removed here for clarity.)
This sets the width constraint. It tells the button to always be the same width as the text field.
3. Drag the center square handle over the vertical dashed line in the center of the view.
This sets the horizontal position constraint, telling the button to always have its center in the center of the screen.
Top Layout Guide
Label
Carrier
23%
Carrier
100%
Label

Figure 4.21 The three steps to set up the constraints—set the top constraint, the width constraint, and the horizontal center constraint.

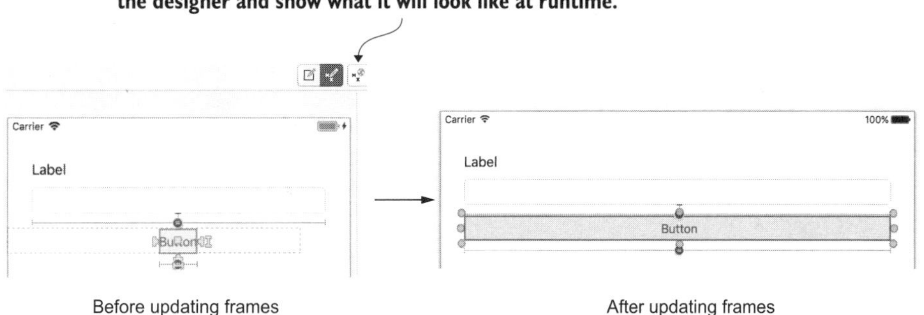

Figure 4.22 Lay out the constraints and click the Update Frames to Match Constraints button to see what the view will look like at runtime.

field is set to a constant value, the width of the button is set to the width of the text field, and the horizontal center of the button is set to the center of the superview—that's the view that contains it (in this case, the whole screen).

If you followed the previous instructions, you should have constraints like those shown in figure 4.23. The value in the Top Space To constraint may be different from the `14` shown in the figure because this value depends on where you dropped the button, but the rest should be the same. If yours doesn't match, the easiest fix is to delete the button and try again.

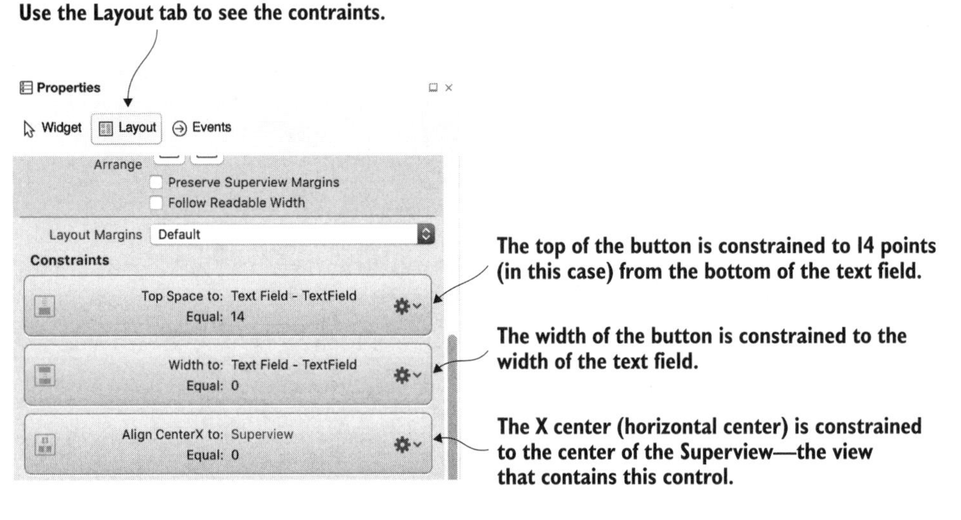

Figure 4.23 The constraints showing in the Properties pad

Once the layout is defined, you can set the text and the name of the button in the Widget tab of the Properties pad. Set the `Name` property in the Identify section to "SayHelloButton" and the `Title` property in the Button section to "Say Hello". Setting the title updates what's shown in the button; setting the name will create a property in the code-behind for that button. You can see these values set in figure 4.24.

Let's now bind this new button in the view to the command on the `FirstViewModel` in our core project. If you open FirstView.cs and look in the `ViewDidLoad` method, you'll see the code that binds the original `Hello` property to UI widgets. Make the changes in the following listing to bind the existing controls to the new `Name` property, and to wire up the button to the `SayHelloCommand`.

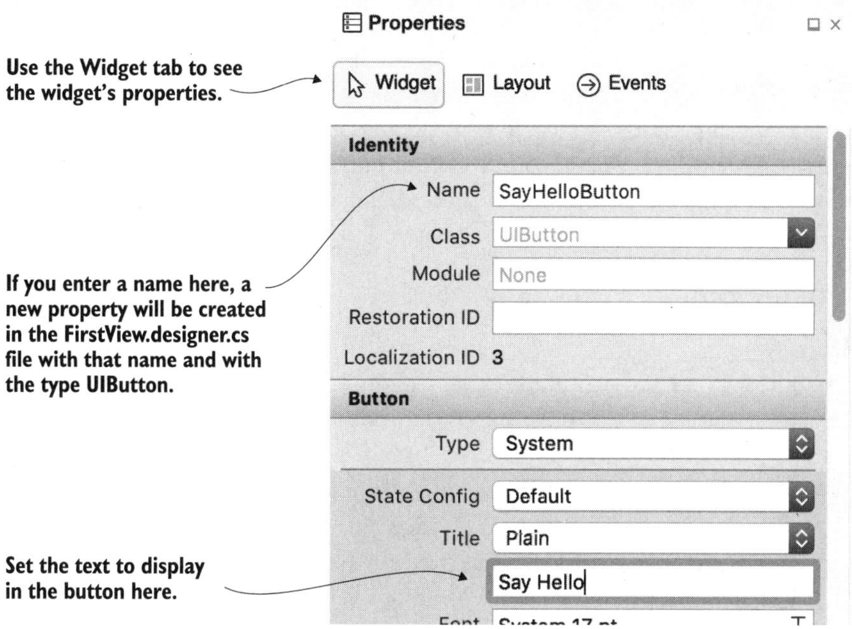

Use the Widget tab to see the widget's properties.

If you enter a name here, a new property will be created in the FirstView.designer.cs file with that name and with the type UIButton.

Set the text to display in the button here.

Figure 4.24 Setting the widget properties for the button

Listing 4.15 Updated `ViewDidLoad` method, binding the new properties and button

```
public override void ViewDidLoad()
{
   base.ViewDidLoad();

   var set = this.CreateBindingSet<FirstView, FirstViewModel>();
   set.Bind(Label).To(vm => vm.Name);
   set.Bind(TextField).To(vm => vm.Name);
   set.Bind(SayHelloButton).To(vm => vm.SayHelloCommand);
   set.Apply();
}
```

The Label is bound to your new Name property.

The TextField is bound to your new Name property.

The new UIButton named SayHelloButton is bound to your new SayHelloCommand.

As with the `UITextField` and `UILabel`, MvvmCross has some smarts around `UIButton`—the underlying type of a button on iOS. The standard event you'll wire up to on a `UIButton` is `TouchUpInside`, so by default this event is bound to the command. You can override this if you want, by explicitly specifying it, but in this case you want the default, so you don't need to give an event name.

And that's it—there's no logic as such because everything is in the core project. There's just new UI bits and some binding. If you run this now, enter your name, and tap the Say Hello button, you'll hear your app say hello to you!

One thing to notice with the text-to-speech is that when you make the call to speak, it returns immediately and the UI isn't locked up while the app is talking. You can test this out by editing the text while the app is talking. Unfortunately, this isn't always the case—it's very easy to call a method in your command that takes a long time to run (such as hitting a web service), and if you aren't careful, your UI will be unresponsive during this call. Even worse, your app could be terminated by the OS if it's unresponsive for too long. I'll discuss this in more detail and look at how you can handle multiple threads in your apps in the next chapter.

Summary

In this chapter you learned that

- MvvmCross apps are built using the different layers of MVVM, and MvvmCross has code for each layer, such as the base view-model and command types, binding, and support for view-model–first navigation.
- Plugins can provide extra device-specific functionality to your apps that's accessible from your cross-platform code.
- Inversion of control is a great pattern that allows you to define loose coupling between classes, making it easier to change them without breaking existing code, and making the classes easier to unit test.
- Having a mobile app talk to you with only a few lines of cross-platform code is really cool!

You also learned how to

- Find and add plugins easily using the NuGet package manager.
- Add new controls to an Android UI by making simple changes to an XML file (although you can use the designer).
- Add new controls on iOS and position them using constraints through the designer, giving a really nice UI layout at the cost of complexity.
- Easily wire up controls to your view model using binding, allowing the same code to be called from UI widgets on both iOS and Android.

5 What are we (a)waiting for? An introduction to multithreading for Xamarin apps

This chapter covers

- What is a thread, and what is multithreading?
- What the UI thread is, and why it's special
- Using tasks to run code on background threads
- Using `async` and `await` to make your code cleaner

When building apps, you always want to give your users the best experience possible. The world of mobile apps is highly competitive, with app users willing to drop your app for a competitor if you offer them a bad experience. There are many ways to provide this bad experience, but one of the worst is having an app with a slow, lagging UI, or one that locks up and becomes unresponsive. Fortunately, fixing apps that lag or lock up is relatively easy, and in this chapter we'll look at ways to do this.

This chapter takes a dive into multithreaded code for mobile apps, covering the UI thread, `Task`, and `async`/`await`. If you're an experienced C# UI developer (maybe from years of building desktop WPF apps), you've used tasks before, and if all your code uses `async` and `await`, you can feel free to skip this chapter. If your experience of multithreaded code is not UI-based, or not in C#, then read on! There are some quirks to be aware of when writing UIs that use multiple threads, and there are some awesome tools in the C# toolbox that can help.

5.1 Why do we need multithreaded code?

Think about an email app (something you probably use on a regular basis). This app shows your current emails, and as you're using it, it will go off to your email provider and download any new emails. All this happens seamlessly—the UI of the app is responsive at all times, allowing you to read and delete messages at the same time as the app is fetching or sending new emails.

This is a nice app experience, and something most app users take for granted. Apps will download data without interrupting what you're doing as a user, maybe giving some feedback to show you that it's doing something in the background, or showing some dummy data while the app starts up. Figure 5.1 shows some examples of this.

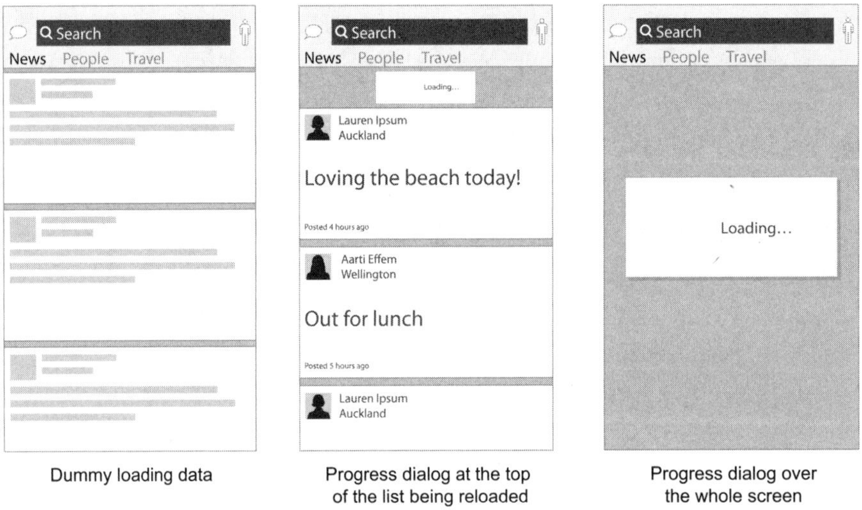

Dummy loading data

Progress dialog at the top of the list being reloaded

Progress dialog over the whole screen

Figure 5.1 Apps performing operations in the background, such as loading data, usually have some kind of indicator showing that something's happening.

USERS CAN NOTICE ANYTHING LONGER THAN ABOUT 100–200 MS Studies have been done into what users perceive as a noticeable lag, and they've found that anything over around 100–200 ms is noticeable as a brief delay. Microsoft now recommends that anything taking longer than 200 ms be done in the background, and they've followed this philosophy in the .NET framework, making anything longer than that async. Google and Apple recommend anything longer than 100 ms be run in the background. You can read more on this in

Jakob Nielsen's "Response Times: The 3 Important Limits" article on the Nielsen Norman Group website: www.nngroup.com/articles/response-times-3-important-limits/.

You may have also seen apps that don't provide such a nice experience and lock up the UI for a short while. If they lock it up for too long, you may have killed the app yourself, or in the case of Android seen a nice dialog that offers to kill it on your behalf. This is something that we, as app developers, want to avoid.

The basic principle is simple—keep the screen and widgets working while you're loading data in the background. But what does this mean? What is "the background," and how can we as app developers load data in this way?

Let's start by taking a quick look at the problem before we look at the solution. For the purposes of illustration, we'll look at our Hello Cross-Platform World app from chapter 4. In this app we bound a command in the view model to a button, to say hello to the user. But let's pretend that before the app can say hello to the user, it needs to make a call to a web service to do something.

Making a call to a web service from a mobile app can be slow, especially over a poor cellular connection (remember, millions of smartphone users are based in the developing world, where network speeds are much slower than the 4G that some countries have). We'll change our code to call a method that does nothing for a few seconds, to simulate this long call to a web service.

Make the following change in `FirstViewModel`, inside the FirstViewModel.cs file in the HelloCrossPlatformWorld.Core project.

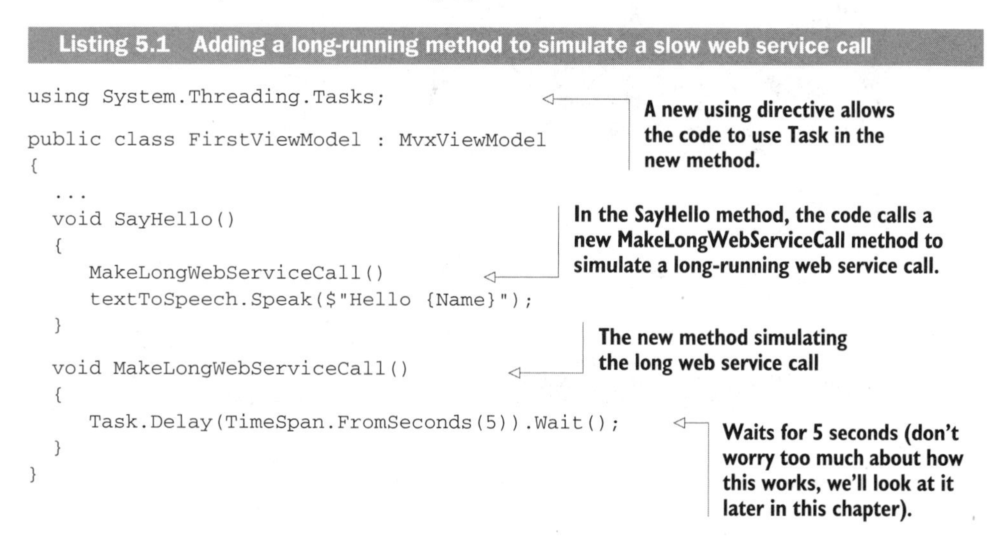

Listing 5.1 Adding a long-running method to simulate a slow web service call

```
using System.Threading.Tasks;

public class FirstViewModel : MvxViewModel
{
   ...
   void SayHello()
   {
      MakeLongWebServiceCall()
      textToSpeech.Speak($"Hello {Name}");
   }

   void MakeLongWebServiceCall()
   {
      Task.Delay(TimeSpan.FromSeconds(5)).Wait();
   }
}
```

A new using directive allows the code to use Task in the new method.
In the SayHello method, the code calls a new MakeLongWebServiceCall method to simulate a long-running web service call.
The new method simulating the long web service call
Waits for 5 seconds (don't worry too much about how this works, we'll look at it later in this chapter).

Make this change and run the app (either on iOS or Android). If you tap the Say Hello button, you'll see the whole app lock up for five seconds before it says hello to you. If you type in the text box, nothing will happen for those five seconds; the text will only appear after the five seconds are up. If this was an email client, and it locked up for that much time while downloading an email, it would be a very bad experience. If that happened while a user was trying to delete the current email, and nothing happened when they tapped the Delete button, they might tap it again, and again, and again. Once the app became responsive again, these multiple taps might turn into multiple deletes, deleting too many emails. Not a good experience.

Let's take this a bit further and imagine that our app needed to make many calls to this web service, taking even longer. Change the timeout to 60 seconds using the code in the following listing and run this on Android (not iOS this time).

Listing 5.2 Increasing the timeout to 60 seconds

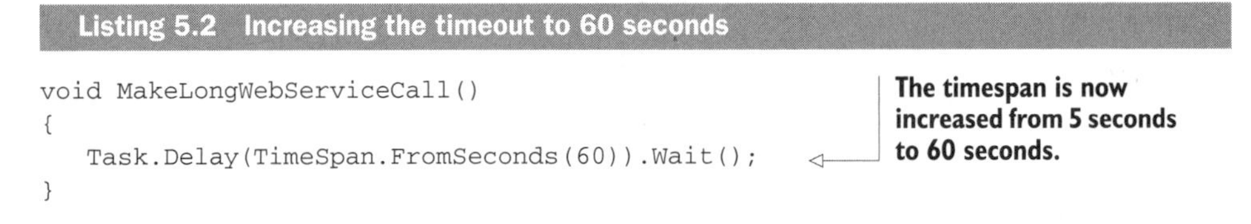

```
void MakeLongWebServiceCall()
{
   Task.Delay(TimeSpan.FromSeconds(60)).Wait();
}
```

The timespan is now increased from 5 seconds to 60 seconds.

Not only will your app be unresponsive for a really long time, but the OS will step in and tell the user that the app isn't responding, asking them if they want to wait or close the app (figure 5.2).

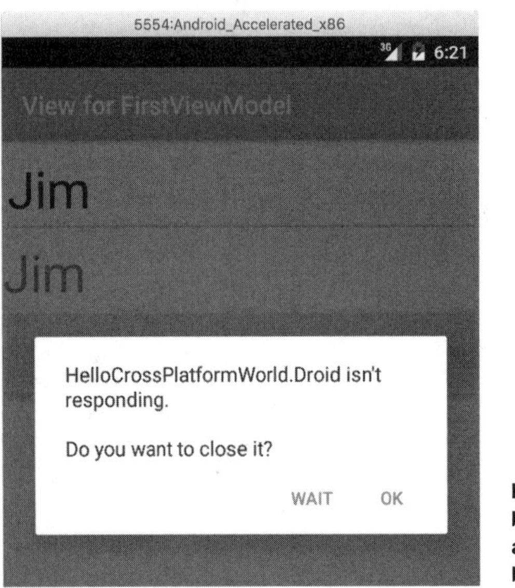

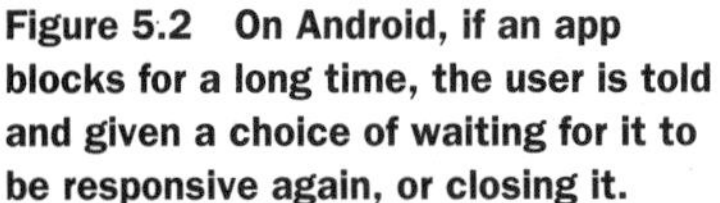

Figure 5.2 On Android, if an app blocks for a long time, the user is told and given a choice of waiting for it to be responsive again, or closing it.

Most users will tap OK at this point to close the app. If this happens too often, few users will come back to your app. Instead they'll download and use a competitor's app. Only Android gives this option—on iOS the app just locks up.

In the email app example, emails are downloaded in the background while the app is still usable. Ideally we'd want to do the same thing in our app—our long-running web service call should happen in the background so that the app remains responsive.

But what do we mean when we say we want things happening *in the background*? How can we use this "background" to run code? The answer lies in the world of threads and multithreaded code.

5.2 What are threads?

As regular app users, we've all seen things happening in the background—tweets downloading while we're reading other tweets, and emails appearing while we're writing new emails. You've probably heard of threads and multithreaded code, but what do these terms mean? Before we look into how we can get our apps to remain responsive while making long web service calls, let's look at what a thread actually is.

5.2.1 Buying coffee

Imagine you head out to buy coffee for your team at work, and you go to a really slow, inefficient coffee shop that only has one person working in it. You queue up, and when it's your turn you give your order to the barista, one coffee at a time. You order one coffee, the barista makes it, you order the next, the barista makes it, you order the next, and so on, and so on. Once you have your coffees you pay for them. You end up standing there for a long time getting bored, and either you finally get your coffees or you leave. Either way you're not happy because you were gone from the office for such a long time (and maybe even less happy because you got bored waiting and didn't end up with any coffee in return for your efforts). It's not just you—the people behind you in the queue might also get bored and leave before they've even ordered (figure 5.3).

Figure 5.3 When you're waiting for a large coffee order in a badly run coffee shop, you might just give up before you get your coffee.

Let's look at a timeline of how this might happen, as shown in figure 5.4. As you can see, there's a lot of waiting around for each coffee to be made before you can finally pay and take your coffees. You order, wait, order, wait, order, wait…

How could the coffee shop improve? The first thing they could do would be to take your order up front, then make your coffees, and then call you once they're done. You place your order, leave your name, and have time to yourself to read the news or surf

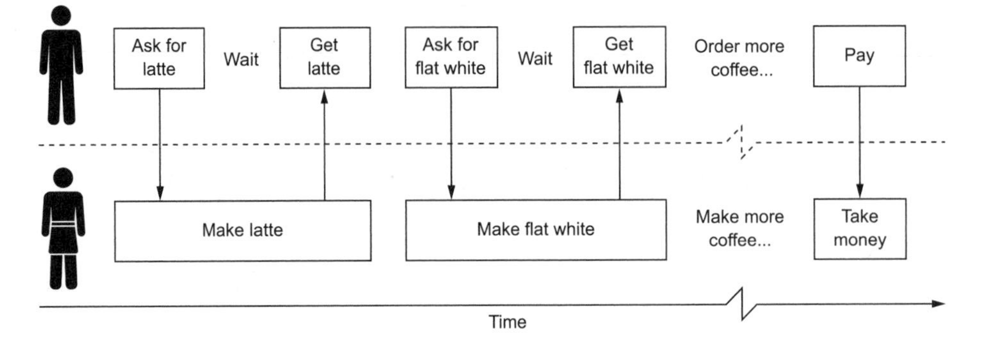

Figure 5.4 Ordering one coffee at a time and having it made, then ordering another takes a long time.

the internet. Then, when your coffees are ready, the barista would call out your name and you'd pick up your coffees. Figure 5.5 shows the timeline of this approach.

This is slightly better—it still takes the same amount of time to get your coffees, but at least you're not as bored as before, and you're less likely to give up and leave before you get your coffee. This is no better for the rest of the queue, though. Those poor, thirsty people will have to wait just as long for a tasty caffeinated beverage.

What else could the coffee shop do? How about adding more people? If they employed another barista, the coffee could be made a bit quicker. One barista could take the order, and the other could make the coffee. Figure 5.6 shows the timeline for this better scenario.

This doesn't make it better for us, but makes it a bit better for the other customers—they can now order while our coffee is being made, and they can also go off and do other things while they wait. It's better because customers aren't waiting in line bored for so long, but it still takes the same amount of time to make everyone's coffee.

Let's have one more go at making it better by adding additional baristas, as shown in figure 5.7. This is even better—not only can all the customers place their orders and then do whatever they like, instead of standing in a queue, but multiple coffees can be made at the same time, meaning each customer gets their coffee quicker.

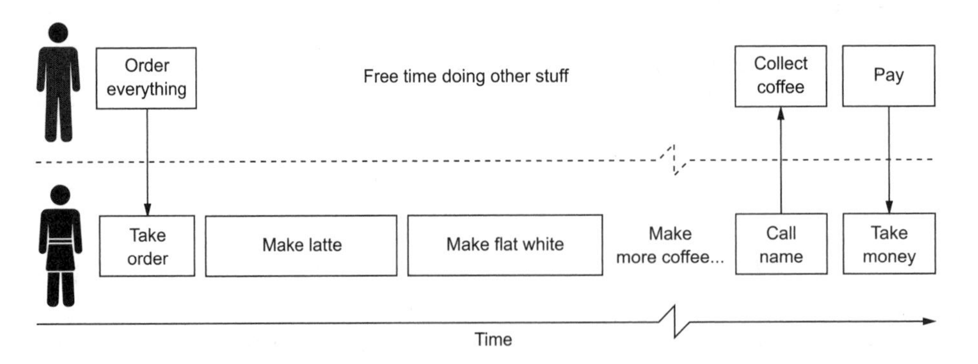

Figure 5.5 If you can place your coffee order up front, you're free to do other stuff while it's being made.

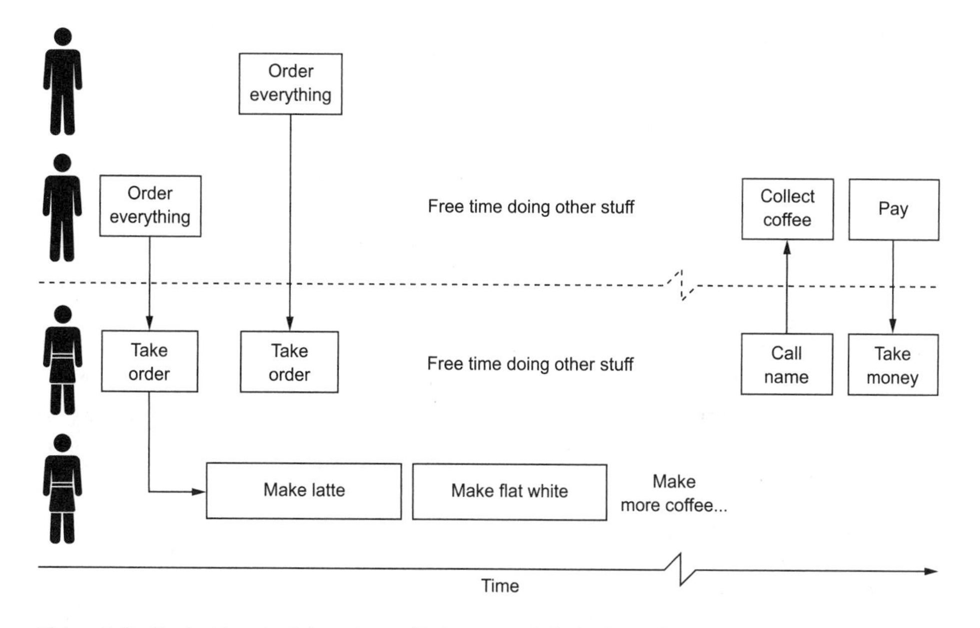

Figure 5.6 Having two baristas means that one can take orders while the other makes coffee.

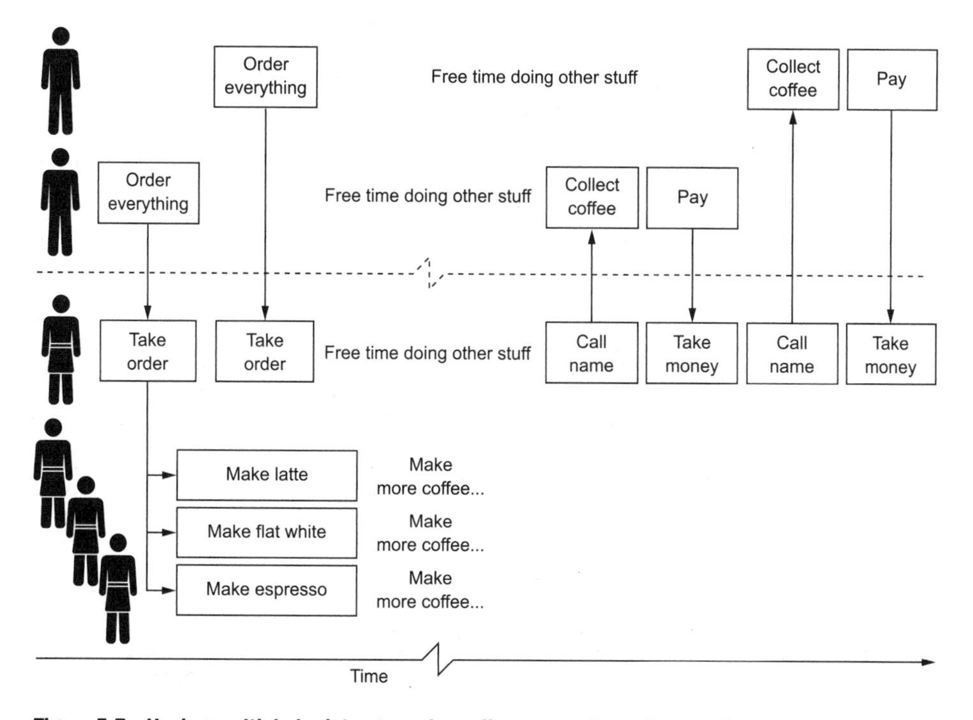

Figure 5.7 Having multiple baristas to make coffee means the orders can be made more quickly.

This is a great model for a coffee shop—and coincidentally a great model for software as well.

5.2.2 So what is a thread?

You can think of the staff members in the coffee shop as different threads—each one is working on a separate thing at the same time. They have a series of tasks to do, and they do them in order (a thread, like a barista, can only do one thing at a time). When they have nothing to do, they just stand there doing nothing, waiting for something else to do.

In computing terms, a thread is a thread of execution—a way for an app to split the code it's executing into one or more simultaneously running tasks. When an app runs, it runs using at least one but usually more threads. Every application, be it a mobile app, desktop app, console app, or website, runs in at least one thread. Just as a coffee shop with no staff wouldn't be able to make any coffee, there's no way for your code to run without a thread.

An email app will have one thread for the user interface, which will run the UI code allowing the user to interact with a list of emails, tap one to read it, write a reply, or perform other tasks the user wants to do, as shown in figure 5.8. It will also have one or more background threads for talking to the email provider—downloading emails or sending ones you've just written. These background threads will only interrupt the thread that runs the UI when they need to, such as when a new email has

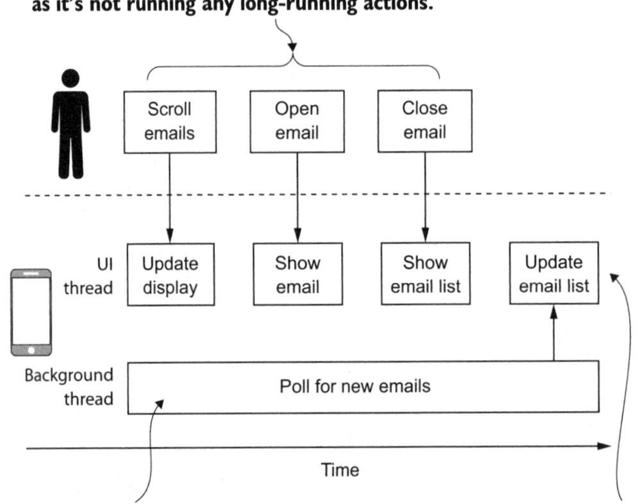

Figure 5.8 In an email app there will be a UI thread that keeps the UI responsive and a background thread to download emails.

been downloaded and the list of emails needs to be updated. Think of an email app as the server in our coffee shop example, but serving up emails instead of coffee. The baristas are running around in the background fetching emails instead of drinks, sending them, doing whatever tasks are needed, and only interrupting the server when they need to (such as letting the server know when an email has been downloaded, instead of when a coffee is ready).

This division of work into multiple threads isn't something that happens automatically. You need to explicitly tell your app to use multiple threads, in the same way that a coffee shop has to employ multiple baristas to make coffee. *Multithreaded* is the term that describes code that uses multiple threads to handle its workload. Our ideal coffee shop is multithreaded—it has multiple baristas (threads) creating coffee at the same time (executing code at the same time).

Multiple threads don't always mean multiple things are happening at once

If you have two threads executing code, this code may or may not be running at the same time.

Your mobile device probably has a multicore processor, which means it has a chip that you can think of as being more than one chip glued together. It can have two bits of code running at the same time by having multiple cores running different code—one core runs one thread and one runs the other.

In addition, though, it can run multiple threads on the same processor by giving one thread a bit of processing time, and then pausing it and giving the other thread some processor time. It's smart, so if one thread has to wait on something, like reading from the network, it can use that waiting time to run the other thread.

If you're feeling geeky and want to learn more, Google "preemptive multitasking".

5.2.3 A quick roundup

Let's take a quick moment to review all this, as it's important stuff:

- All code runs in a thread, and a thread runs code in sequence.
- An app can have multiple threads, each running different code at the same time.

This sounds simple, but the devil's in the details. Threading is actually a massive topic (with scary terms like *mutexes*, *semaphores*, and *critical sections*), worthy of a book in its own right. Luckily for us C# programmers, we don't need to worry too much about these details. But there are a few basic concepts you'll need to know about, and a few language constructs to learn about that encapsulate all the hard stuff, allowing us developers to get on and write code.

What you really need to know about are the two different types of threads (UI and background threads), tasks, and `async`/`await`. Let's start with the two types of threads.

5.3 UI thread and background threads

In our coffee shop, we have two different types of employees—a server who interacts with the customer, and baristas who take instructions from the server and make coffee. In our email app example there are two types of threads—one that runs the user interface (UI), and one or more that perform operations in the background, such as fetching emails. All mobile apps are the same as the email app, having these two types of threads. These thread types, like the two types of coffee shop employees, are actually very distinct and have very different characteristics.

5.3.1 The UI thread

The UI thread is something you hear a lot about when you're building applications with a user interface. It's the main thread inside your app (you'll often hear the UI thread referred to as the *main thread*)—the server at the counter who takes your coffee order. When buying coffee, you only interact with one person who takes your order and calls you when your coffee is ready, and it's the same with the UI thread. When your user interacts with the user interface of your app, they're interacting with the UI thread. If that one server is busy doing something else, you can't interact with them to order coffee until they're free. The same goes for the UI thread—if it's busy, you can't do anything else on that thread until it's free.

The UI thread has a simple but important job—running the user interface. It's responsible for everything the UI does. If you type a letter into a text box, the UI thread detects the keypress, runs the code to draw the new character on the screen, and raises the text-changed event. If you update a control, the UI thread is responsible for updating the screen, including calculating how controls should be laid out and what should be shown. The UI thread runs animations, transitions between views, and shows popups. Every interaction with the user via the screen and every change to the screen is handled by this one thread.

You never need to create the UI thread—it's created for you by the OS when your app starts up, and it stays around till your app is closed.

A barista can only do one thing at a time. If a coffee shop has a single barista who makes one coffee at a time, the customer has to wait for each coffee to be made. In the same way, a thread can only do one thing at a time. It runs its tasks sequentially, so the thread can't do the next task until the previous task is complete, even if one task takes a long time (figure 5.9).

The UI thread works using a queue of messages that it processes in order, and these messages can come from the OS or from your code. When you touch a control or type text, the OS detects this, creates a message, and sends it to the UI thread. The UI thread then handles the message when it's finished with the previous messages in its queue.

This is easy enough to demonstrate—launch the modified Hello Cross-Platform World app that you changed earlier in this chapter, enter some text, tap the Say Hello button, and enter more text while the app isn't responding. Try this on iOS, or if you

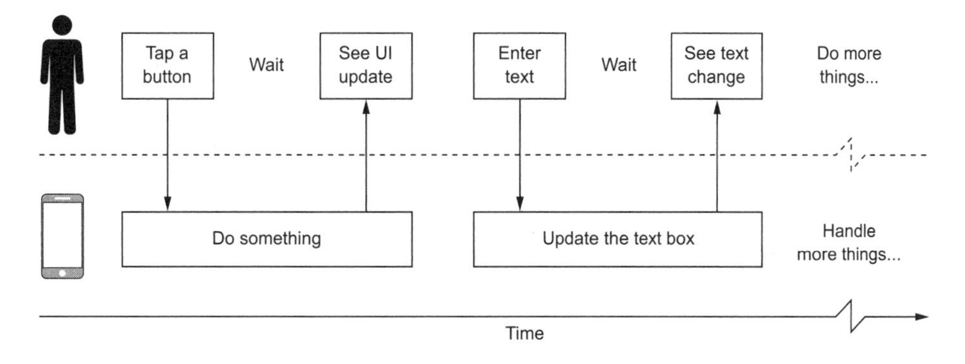

Figure 5.9 The UI thread handles input from the user sequentially, so it has to finish handling one input before it can handle another.

prefer to do it on Android reduce the wait time from 60 seconds down to about 20 seconds to avoid the OS warning message. You'll see the UI lock up for the wait time, and as you type, nothing will appear on screen. When the wait has finished, you'll suddenly see everything you've typed appear in the text box.

When you tap on the button, a message is raised by the operating system, which is then handled by the UI thread, raising the click event (figure 5.10). This event was bound to a command defined using an `Action`, which means the `Action` is also run on the UI thread. Our action paused for a few seconds, meaning the UI thread was also paused for a few seconds. For those few seconds, the UI was totally unresponsive because it was busy in the pause. It can only do one thing at a time, so if it's busy waiting, it can't respond to the messages from the OS in response to user input. Every-

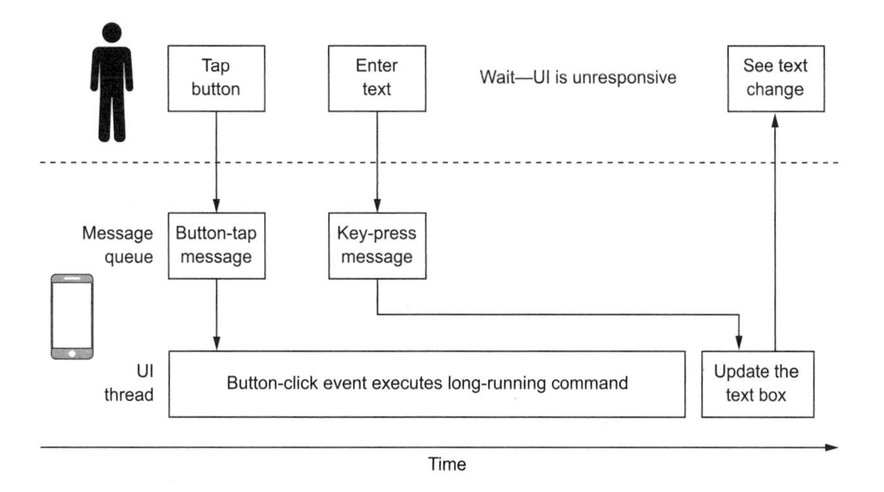

Figure 5.10 The UI thread handles messages from the OS resulting from user interactions, and if it takes too long to handle a message, the UI appears unresponsive.

thing to do with the UI has to wait. Once the time is up and the command finishes, the UI can then carry on processing the next message in its queue.

> **IF A BUTTON DOESN'T WORK, USERS WILL TAP IT TILL IT DOES** If an app freezes, users are likely to hammer the buttons or keyboard repeatedly until the app responds, leading to your app handling all these events when the UI thread is freed up. This could lead to app behavior that the user doesn't expect—if they tap a Delete button in an email client and the app doesn't respond, they could tap it a few more times and end up deleting more emails than they expected.

The UI thread lives as long as your app does, and your app only lives as long as the UI thread. If an exception is thrown inside the UI thread and it's not handled, the thread is terminated and your app dies. For example, in an email app, if a connection to the server can't be established and an exception is thrown on the UI thread and not handled properly, the app would die. Obviously this isn't a good thing. It leads to one simple rule—don't allow uncaught exceptions on the UI thread.

In the previous chapters, we looked at the layers of MVVM, and the UI fits very much into the view layer. Threads, however, don't fit into these nice simple layers—they can span all layers. You can run code in the UI thread that starts in the view (such as in a button click), then runs code in the view-model layer (such as the command that handles the click), which then makes a call into the model layer. The code in each layer will run in the UI thread. If this code is fast (less than 100–200 ms), this isn't a problem, but ideally anything slower shouldn't be in the UI thread, but should instead be run in a background thread to remove any obvious lag or lock-up in the UI.

5.3.2 Background threads

The UI thread is the single thread that runs the user interface. Background threads, on the other hand, are threads that perform tasks in the background, such as downloading emails. These are our baristas—they're given something to do by the server, and they go off and do it, only interrupting the server when they need do, such as after the coffees are made. In the same way, you can fire off background threads from your UI, and these go off and do their thing, only interrupting the UI thread if they need to, such as when an email is downloaded and the UI needs to update to show this.

Unlike the UI thread, background threads can be created, run code, and die without killing the app. If a background thread is locked up doing something, the app remains responsive. If it takes multiple minutes to download your email, nothing locks up in your app (and no nasty messages are displayed on Android asking the user if they want to close the app).

Also unlike the UI thread, you have to explicitly create background threads in your code. Luckily for us as C# developers, this isn't as hard as you might think, and once again it follows the model of our coffee shop.

5.4 Using tasks to run code in the background

So far we've established that you ask the server for coffee, and then the baristas make it. Let's dig a bit deeper into this.

You order a number of coffees, and the server takes the order and writes each item down on a ticket. These tickets are passed over to the baristas who actually handle them, usually by pinning them to a board. Each ticket represents a task for the baristas to do—for example, make coffee, make tea, or warm up a muffin. The baristas handle these tasks one by one, and once they're finished they put the item on the counter so the server can see that the order is progressing and then call you once everything is done. The server creates tasks; the baristas handle these tasks and let the server know when they're done.

This model works for one barista, two baristas, three, four ... as many as you have space for (figure 5.11). Baristas themselves could also create tasks for other people, such as the person who washes the dishes—shouting through to them to ask for more cups when they get low. The barista carries on making coffee while the dishwasher is preparing the clean cups, so no one is waiting. Baristas could even give tasks to the server, such as asking them to check an order, interrupting the server's ability to interact with customers while they complete the task given to them.

You can also think of an email app as something that would create tickets internally to track work to be done. For example, once the app loads it will create a ticket to download a list of new emails that will be handled by something. Once this list is downloaded, it can create tickets to download the full contents of each new email.

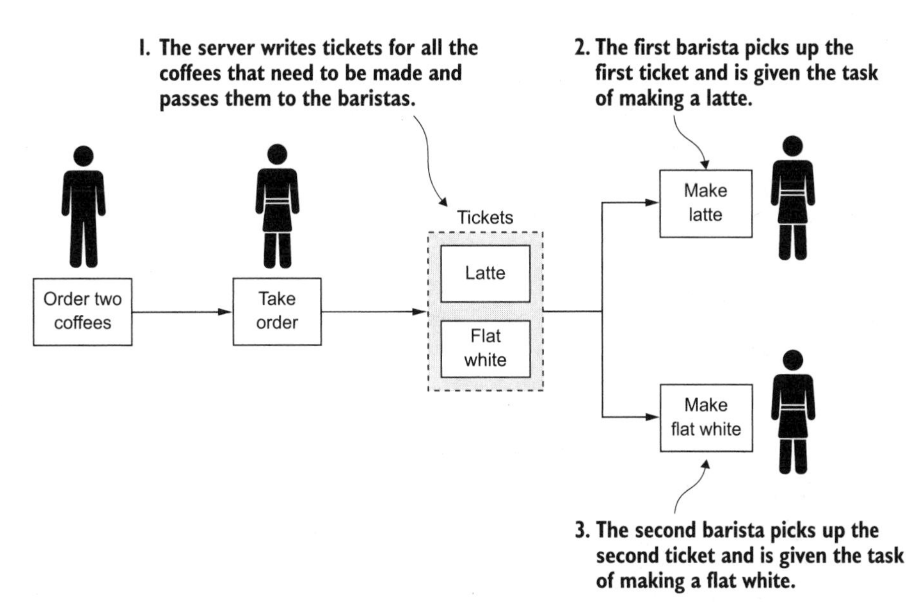

Figure 5.11 When you order coffee from the server, they give the baristas different tasks to do, such as making a latte or a flat white.

In C# you can create "tickets" and pin them to the .NET equivalent of the pin board so that something can pick them up and run them. These tickets are called *tasks*, and they're handed out by a task scheduler to be run on either a background thread or the UI thread.

5.4.1 Task and Task<T>

In our coffee shop there are tasks that get assigned to baristas or dishwashers or the server. In the .NET framework there are also tasks, represented by a class called `Task` (which lives in the `System.Threading.Tasks` namespace). This class is similar to a command in that it wraps an action that can be run. Unlike a command, these actions can only be run once, and they're not triggered by a user action but by a task scheduler that triggers the action on an appropriate thread. There's also `Task<T>`, which wraps a func that returns an instance of `T`. This is used if you need to get a return value from your task, such as a list of emails downloaded from an email server.

When a server creates a ticket for a cup of coffee, the next available barista will pick up this ticket and make the coffee (this is like a `Task<T>` with a return value of a cup of coffee). The scheduling of coffee making is handled by the board that the tickets are pinned to—baristas grab the next available ticket and start making the coffee. If each coffee takes the same amount of time to make, the baristas will end up taking tickets in turns, but if one coffee takes longer than another, one barista might end up taking two or three tickets in a row before the other barista is finished making the slower coffee and is available to pick up a ticket.

In this example, the pin board is a task scheduler. Tasks are created against a particular task scheduler, and this scheduler runs them on the relevant thread. By default, tasks use a scheduler that runs the tasks on a background thread (we'll look at another task scheduler later in this chapter). The default task scheduler has a pool of background threads and uses the next available one to run the next task—just as the next available barista picks up the next coffee ticket. This abstracts away a lot of complications, including creating and managing threads. You don't have to do anything yourself—the task scheduler does it all for you.

You can create a `Task` by just newing up an instance and passing it an `Action` to run as the constructor parameter. For `Task<T>`, you pass it a `Func<T>`. Once it's created, you can call `Start()` to run it. `Task` even has a static factory method, `Run`, that takes an `Action` or `Func<T>` as a parameter, creates the `Task` or `Task<T>`, and runs it automatically. By default, these new tasks will all run in a background thread because they use the default task scheduler (figure 5.12).

Earlier in this chapter we tweaked the Hello Cross-Platform World app to wait for a short while before speaking, to simulate a long-running web service call. This locked up the UI, so let's change the code to use a `Task` to run the long call in the background. Make the code changes shown in the following listing, and run the app.

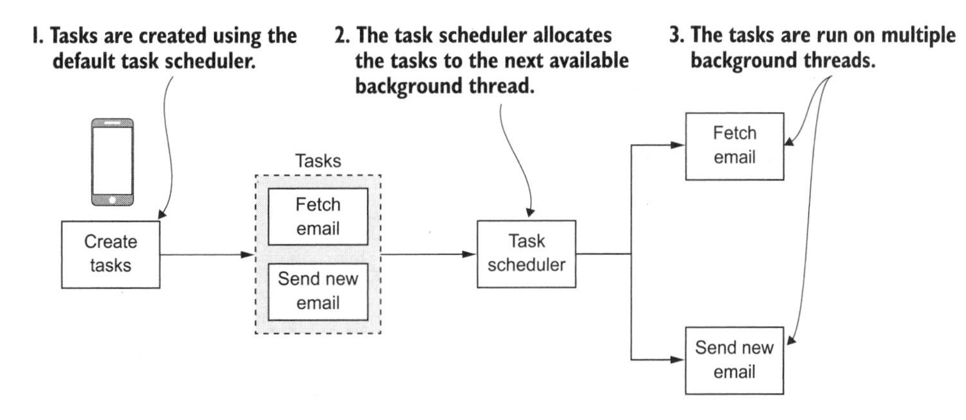
1. Tasks are created using the default task scheduler.
2. The task scheduler allocates the tasks to the next available background thread.
3. The tasks are run on multiple background threads.
Create tasks
Tasks
Fetch email
Send new email
Task scheduler
Fetch email
Send new email

Figure 5.12 The task scheduler takes tasks and runs them on the appropriate thread.

Listing 5.3 Keeping the UI responsive by using a task

```
void SayHello()
{
   var task = new Task(() => MakeLongWebServiceCall());
   task.Start();

   textToSpeech.Speak($"Hello {Name}");
}
```

The existing call to MakeLongWebServiceCall is converted to an Action and is passed to the constructor of the Task.

The task is started.

If you tap the Say Hello button now, you'll see that the app remains responsive during the wait. You'll also hear the app say hello to you straight away.

In this code you're creating a `Task` that will use the default task scheduler so it'll run on a background thread, and you're passing it an `Action` to run. The call to `Start` will tell the task scheduler to start running this task in the background. This call returns immediately—it doesn't wait for the `Task` to complete. The construction of the `Task` happens on the UI thread (remember, the command that calls `SayHello` is called from a button tap, which is handled on the UI thread), but the execution happens in the background, which is why the rest of the method runs straightaway (figure 5.13). We can simplify the code by using the static `Task.Run` method, which wraps the construction and starts it in one call, as shown in the following listing.

Listing 5.4 Creating a new task and running it, instead of using the `Start` method

```
void SayHello()
{
   Task.Run(() => MakeLongWebServiceCall());
   textToSpeech.Speak($"Hello {Name}");
}
```

Task.Run is the same as creating a task and calling Start.

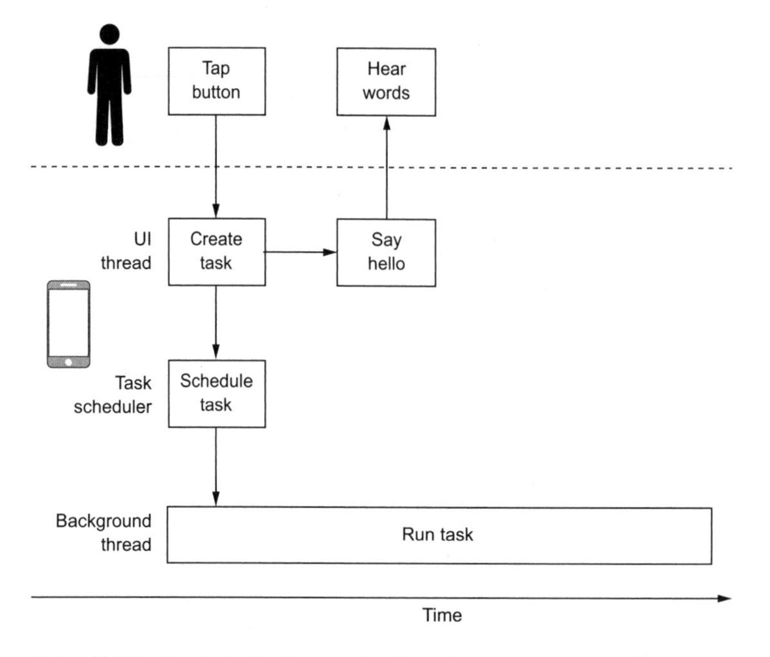

Figure 5.13 Running a task executes its code on a background thread.

This is a nice pattern, but what if we wanted the app to say hello after the long method has finished? For example, in an email app we'd want code that would go off to the email provider and download emails, and once they're downloaded it would tell the user, in true Tom Hanks/Meg Ryan style, that they've got mail. If the message came before the emails were downloaded, you'd have an unhappy app user.

Again, as C# developers we can do this easily, using task continuations.

5.4.2 Chaining tasks

Suppose one of our baristas needs both clean cups and more coffee beans, with the cups being more urgent—they have only two cups, but enough beans for five more cups of coffee. They could ask a dishwasher to get them both, one after the other—get some clean cups then get some more beans. The task to fetch more cups comes first, and once it's complete the dishwasher can collect more beans (figure 5.14).

In an email app we'd want to do something similar—first the app would log in, then it would download a list of all the new emails, and then it would start downloading the content of the new emails. All these tasks have to happen in order (after all, the app can't download the content of the emails before it knows which new emails to get content for) and they must happen in the background so that the UI remains responsive.

We can do this with our tasks in code: create a task to run some code, and tell it that once it's complete, another task should be run to execute other code. This is thanks to a method on `Task`—`ContinueWith`. This method takes an `Action<Task>` as

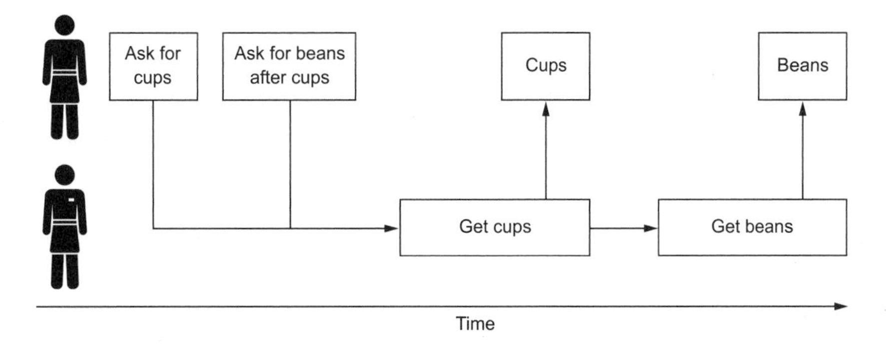

Figure 5.14 Tasks can be chained, such as asking a dishwasher to bring more cups and then fetch more coffee beans.

its parameter and returns a new `Task` to run that action. This new `Task` starts as soon as the original `Task` is complete, and the original `Task` is passed to the action as its parameter. If the original task was a `Task<T>`, the `ContinueWith` would take an `Action<Task<T>>` as its parameter. In this action, you can add the code you want to run after the task is complete. This is often referred to as *task continuation*.

We can use this in our example app to say hello to the user after the long-running method has completed. The following listing shows the code for this, so make this change and run the app.

Listing 5.5 After a task has completed, it can start running another task

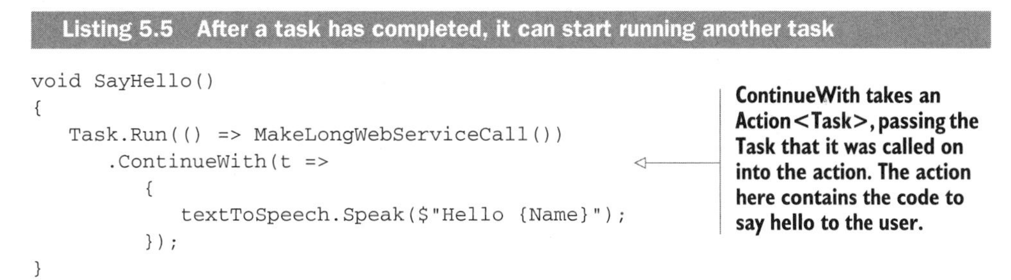

```
void SayHello()
{
   Task.Run(() => MakeLongWebServiceCall())
       .ContinueWith(t =>
          {
             textToSpeech.Speak($"Hello {Name}");
          });
}
```

ContinueWith takes an Action<Task>, passing the Task that it was called on into the action. The action here contains the code to say hello to the user.

As expected, the app will say hello to the user after a delay (feel free to adjust the delay in `MakeLongWebServiceCall` to something like 5 seconds to speed up your waiting time). During this delay, the app will remain responsive because everything is happening on a background thread, thanks to the default task scheduler.

Like `Task<T>`, `ContinueWith` can also create a task with a return value, so it can return `Task<T>` instead of just `Task`. To do this, instead of passing in an `Action<Task>` or `Action<Task<T>>`, you can pass in a `Func<Task, T>` or `Func<Task<T>, TResult>`. These continuations, just like tasks, can have a return value, but they run in the background.

How do we get the return value from a task if it's not like a method that returns a value? We can get it from the task's `Result`.

5.5 Task results

In our coffee shop, some tasks have a result that comes back to the creator of the task, and some don't. If a barista is tasked with making coffee, the result is a cup of coffee passed back to the server. If a dishwasher is tasked with cleaning up the floor, there's no result to pass back.

Tasks in C# are the same, and you can set the type of result by using a type argument. `Task` has no result and is like the dishwasher mopping the floor. `Task<T>` has a result of type `T` and is like the barista making coffee. This `Result` is only available once the task is finished—you can't get a cup of coffee before the barista has made it.

An email app could create a task to download a list of all the new emails that need to be downloaded. This list could be returned in the result of the task, and it would be iterated through in other tasks to download the contents of each email.

There are three ways to get the result of a task: keep polling to see if it has finished, force the task to wait, or use a continuation.

5.5.1 Polling to see if the task has finished

You can periodically poll the `Task<T>`, checking the `IsCompleted` property, and if it's `true`, the task has finished and you can get the `Result` (figure 5.15).

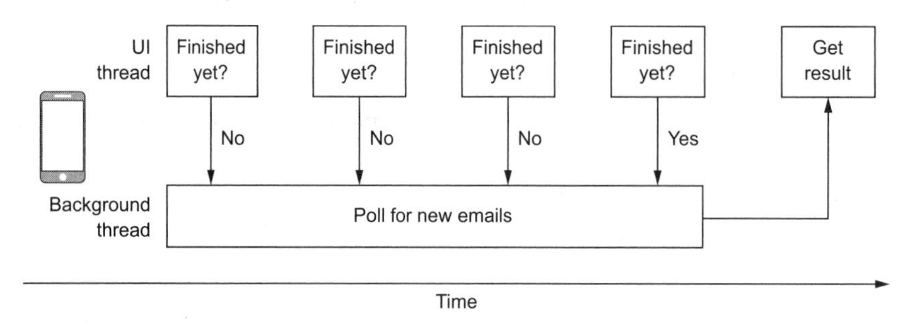

Figure 5.15 Tasks can be continuously polled to see if they've finished.

This isn't always ideal as you need to run code to do the polling. This technique isn't often used.

5.5.2 Waiting on the task

`Task` has a method called `Wait` that blocks until the task is finished, and you can call this to force your code to wait until the task has finished, as shown in figure 5.16. This often isn't ideal as it defeats the purpose of running tasks by using blocking code, but sometimes it's useful. It's something that must be avoided on the UI thread, of course, or you'll end up with an unresponsive app.

A good example of using this approach would be when preloading data, such as an email. An email app could quickly load the sender and subject details of all new emails and then kick off a task to load the contents of each email. If the email is downloaded

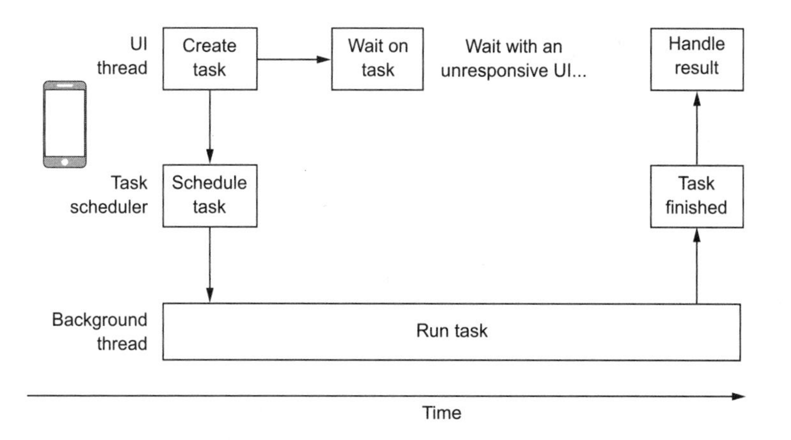

Figure 5.16 Waiting on a task blocks until the task has finished

before the user taps on it to view the contents, the app can just show the contents. If the email hasn't fully downloaded, the app could show a progress dialog while calling `Wait` on a background thread (so the UI remains responsive). Once the email is fully downloaded, the `Wait` call will return and the app can show the email's contents.

> **YOU'VE SEEN WAIT BEFORE** `Wait` might sound familiar because we've used it before. In the `MakeLongWebServiceCall` method in the examples we've been working through, there was a call that was waited—`Task.Delay(TimeSpan.FromSeconds(5)).Wait();`.
>
> `Task.Delay` is a factory method that creates and returns a new `Task` that does nothing but wait for a period of time (in the first version of this method, this was 5 seconds). The call to `Wait` blocks until this new task is finished, so until the 5 second delay is up.
>
> `Task.Delay` can be useful if you want something to run after a fixed period of time, such as polling for new emails every minute.

5.5.3 *Getting the result from a continuation*

The best way to get the result is by using a continuation—if you're interested in the `Result` of a `Task<T>`, it's usually because you want to do something with the result as soon as the original task has completed (figure 5.17).

When you use `ContinueWith`, the continuation task isn't started until the previous task has finished, and the `Action<Task<T>>` that you pass in is called using the now-finished task as its parameter. At this point, you can access the `Result`.

In our hypothetical email app we could use this for the user login—once the task that logs the user in to their email provider finishes, it will often return some kind of authorization token that can be passed to a continuation to be used to load emails for that user.

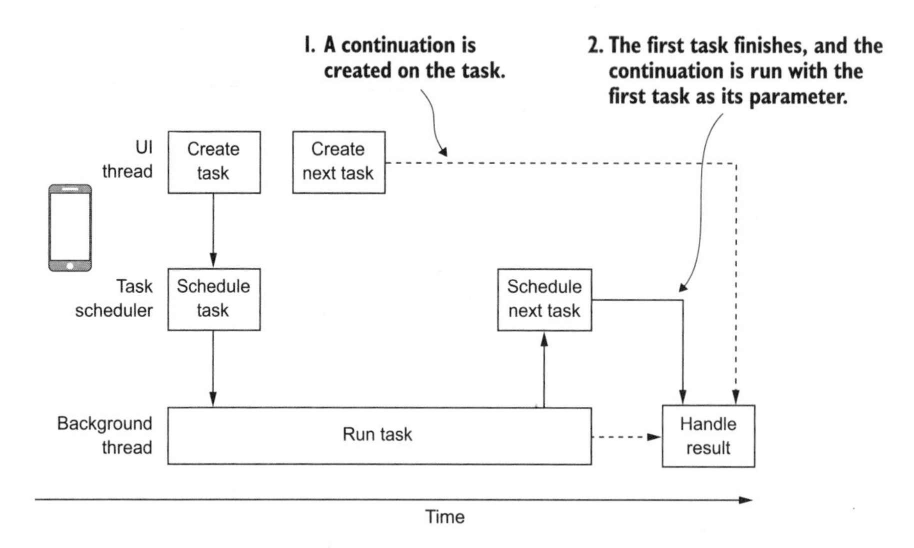

Figure 5.17 Continuations are a good way to handle the result of a task because they run after the task is complete and have access to the result of the original task.

5.5.4 Task exceptions

When a barista makes coffee, we naturally think of the happy path—they're tasked with making our coffee, and we get it once it's made. There's also the sad path—the coffee machine is broken, there are no more beans, or the barista has had enough and quits on the spot. These sad paths lead to the result of no coffee and an apology from the server.

The same could happen in our email app—it could go off to the email provider to get email, but if the device has no connection, the result wouldn't be a list of new emails; instead it would be a loss-of-connection message.

These sad paths are exceptions. We try to run a task, make coffee, or download email, and something goes wrong so our task isn't completed as expected. We don't have a result, and we have a reason for the failure. The same happens with C# tasks—if they don't succeed due to an exception, we don't have a result. Instead we have a *failed* task—also referred to as a *faulted* task.

When a task completes due to an exception, the `IsCompleted` property is set to `true`, and so is the `IsFaulted` property. In addition, the `Exception` property is set to an `AggregateException`, wrapping the exception thrown inside the task. If you don't do anything with this exception, it will be rethrown on the finalizer thread (a thread used by the garbage collector), causing your app to terminate. There are a couple of things you can do to stop this from happening:

- Call the `Wait` method on the task, and this method call will rethrow the exception so you can handle it appropriately.

- Access the `Exception` property—even if you do nothing with it, just reading the value will stop the exception from being rethrown on the finalizer thread.

The right thing to do is to catch these exceptions and handle them gracefully, but problems arise if you use a continuation. How can you tell the continuation that something has failed? You could catch the exception and report the failure via the `Result`, using a value that has an explicit meaning of failure, but this isn't always the best or easiest way.

Instead, the better way is not to catch the exception at all. A task is complete once the code is finished, either because the code has all run successfully, or because there was an unhandled exception. Either way, `IsCompleted` will be `true` because the code has completed. In the case of an exception, however, the `Result` will be the default value for the type (for example, `null` for classes, `0` for numbers), the `IsFaulted` property will be set to `true`, and the `Exception` property will be set to an `AggregateException` that wraps the exception that was thrown. If the code finished without an exception, `IsFaulted` will be `false` and the `Exception` property will be `null`. We can use these values in our continuation to see how the task ended and act accordingly. The following listing shows some pseudocode for this.

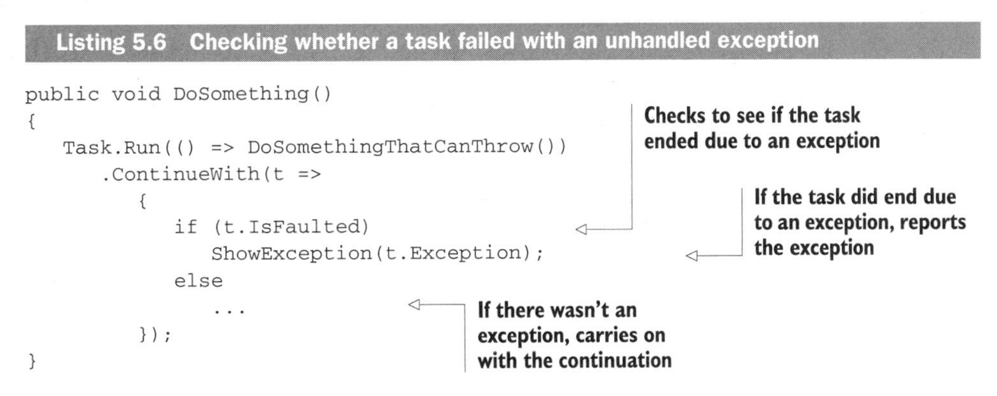

Listing 5.6 Checking whether a task failed with an unhandled exception

```
public void DoSomething()
{
   Task.Run(() => DoSomethingThatCanThrow())
      .ContinueWith(t =>
         {
            if (t.IsFaulted)
               ShowException(t.Exception);
            else
               ...
         });
}
```

Checks to see if the task ended due to an exception
If the task did end due to an exception, reports the exception
If there wasn't an exception, carries on with the continuation

Your code should always check to see if the task faulted, and if it did, you should always access the `Exception` property at least once. If you do this, you can ensure that the exception isn't rethrown when the task is finalized, killing your app.

5.6 Updating the UI

In our coffee shop, the server is the single point of interaction. The customer gives their order to the server, the server gets the baristas to make the coffee, and the server calls the customer once the coffee is ready and hands it over (figure 5.18). This is good from a customer perspective—they can go off and do whatever they want, and once their coffees are ready, one person calls them and they collect their coffees. If every time a barista finished making a single coffee they called the customer, a customer who ordered multiple coffees would be going back and forth between reading the news and collecting coffee.

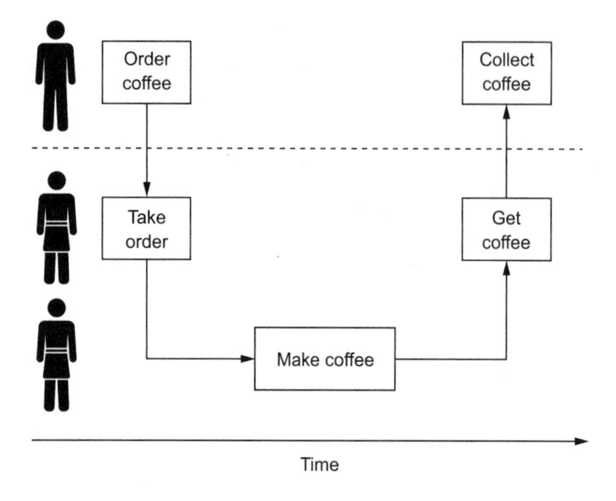
Order
coffee
Collect
coffee
Take
order
Get
coffee
Make coffee
Time

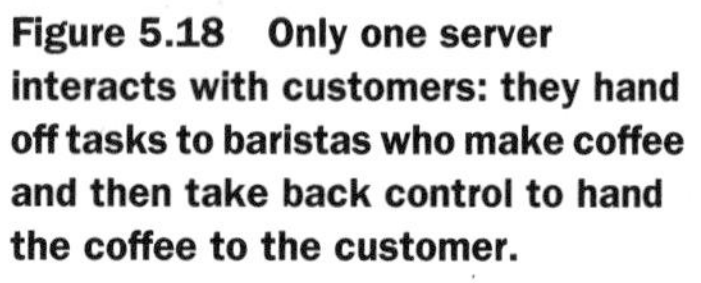

Figure 5.18 Only one server interacts with customers: they hand off tasks to baristas who make coffee and then take back control to hand the coffee to the customer.

In our coffee shop, the server is the one point of contact with the customer. The same is true of the UI—only the UI thread can update the UI. It's the only thread that can update controls, change layouts, or load new screens. This is enforced; if you try to update the UI from a background thread using a task, you'll get an exception. For example, if a task is run to download all new emails in an email app, the app's UI will need to be updated once the task is done to show these new emails. The code to update the UI will need to be on the UI thread—if it's inside the download task, and therefore running on a background thread, it will crash the UI.

Let's see this in action. We'll jump up a layer from the view model to the view and knock up a simple code example to show this by updating the iOS UI from a task. Revert all the changes you've made to `FirstViewModel` in this chapter, and then in `FirstView` (inside FirstView.cs in the Views folder of the HelloCrossPlatform-World.iOS project) make the change shown in the following listing.

Listing 5.7 Updating the UI from a background thread will give an exception

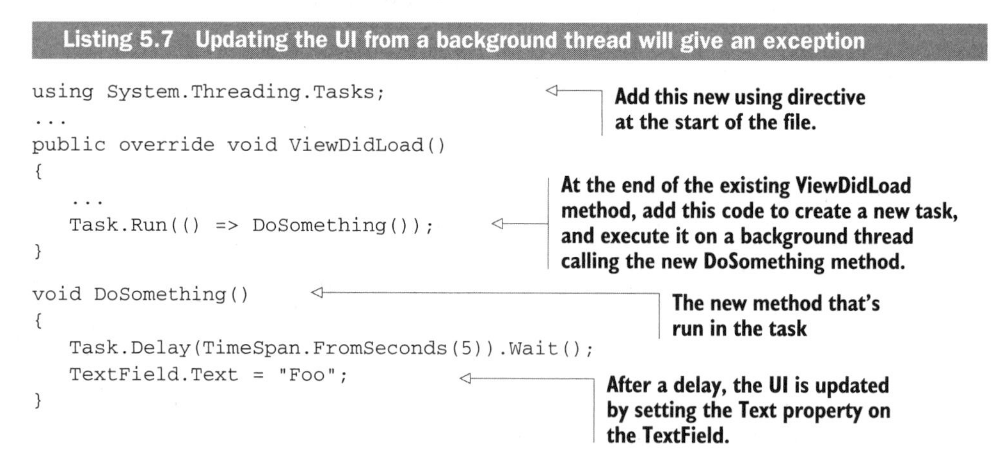

```
using System.Threading.Tasks;
...
public override void ViewDidLoad()
{
   ...
   Task.Run(() => DoSomething());
}

void DoSomething()
{
   Task.Delay(TimeSpan.FromSeconds(5)).Wait();
   TextField.Text = "Foo";
}
```

Add this new using directive at the start of the file.
At the end of the existing ViewDidLoad method, add this code to create a new task, and execute it on a background thread calling the new DoSomething method.
The new method that's run in the task
After a delay, the UI is updated by setting the Text property on the TextField.

This code looks like it does something in the background and then updates the UI to show "Foo". But if you run the iOS app, it won't do quite what you might expect.

If you are using Xcode 8 with the iOS 10 SDK, you'll get a nice exception, shown in figure 5.19.

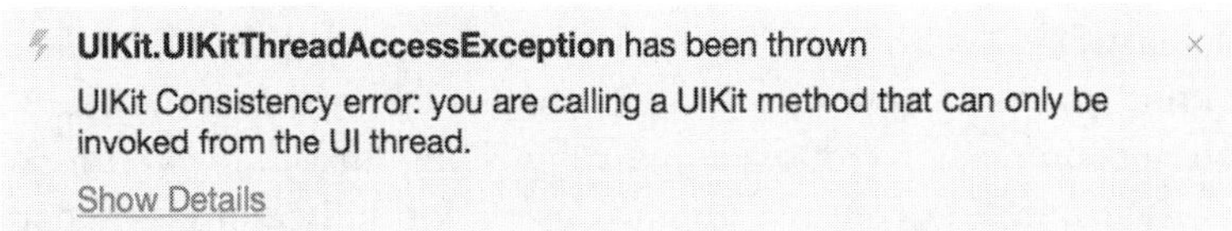

UIKit.UIKitThreadAccessException has been thrown
UIKit Consistency error: you are calling a UIKit method that can only be invoked from the UI thread.
Show Details

Figure 5.19 Updating the iOS UI from a background thread gives a thread-access exception.

This exception tells us that we're on the wrong thread. We're calling a `UIKit` method that can only be invoked from the UI thread (`UIKit` is the name Apple gives to the classes that it uses for UIs).

If you are using Xcode 9, then, instead of an exception, nothing will happen. Xcode 9 has moved the checks from exceptions in code to a Main Thread Checker, which is both a standalone app as well as a tool integrated into the Xcode debugger. At the time of writing, this tool hasn't been integrated into the Xamarin debugger. The upside of this change is that your app won't crash if a UI control is updated off the UI thread. The downside is that UI updates might be missed.

How can we update the UI from code running on a background thread?

5.6.1 *The UI task scheduler*

In our coffee shop we have two types of people who can do work. We have a server who deals with customer interaction, and baristas and dishwashers who work behind the scenes to make coffee, make tea, or wash cups. These two groups are very distinct and have very specific roles and limitations. You only have one server as a single point of contact for the customer, but the behind the scenes staff can scale based on demand—you'd need more baristas during the morning coffee rush than at the end of the day.

You can think of threads in a similar way. When a thread is created, it lives inside a *synchronization context*. A synchronization context is a group of one or more threads that share the same characteristics, so if some code can run on one thread inside that context, it can run on any thread. This is just like our coffee shop staff—all baristas have the same characteristics and can make coffee, but only the server can interact with the customer. When the task scheduler executes a task, it does so using a particular synchronization context, just as tasks in our coffee shop are given to specific people. Baristas pick up tasks to make coffee, dishwashers pick up tasks to get more cups, and the server picks up tasks to give the finished coffee to the customers.

By default, a task will be scheduled by the default task scheduler, which will use threads from the *default synchronization context* (also referred to as the *thread pool synchronization context*), which means it runs the tasks using one of the many pooled background threads available. These background threads are created for you by the task scheduler, so there's nothing you need to do in your code to use them. These threads share the same characteristics—they all run in the background, and they're all stopped when the UI thread stops. This is the default type of thread used when you create a task using `Task.Run` or you construct a new instance of `Task` or `Task<T>`.

There's another synchronization context that's of interest to us—the UI thread synchronization context. This context contains only one thread, the UI thread. Unlike the default synchronization context, which is used by the default task scheduler, the UI thread synchronization context isn't easily available from a static property. Instead we have to use a static method on the `TaskScheduler` class, `FromCurrentSynchronizationContext()`. This will always return the synchronization context for the current thread that it's called on. If you call this from a task running in the background, you'll get back the default scheduler, but if you call it from the UI thread, you'll get back a task scheduler that you can use to run your tasks on the UI thread (figure 5.20).

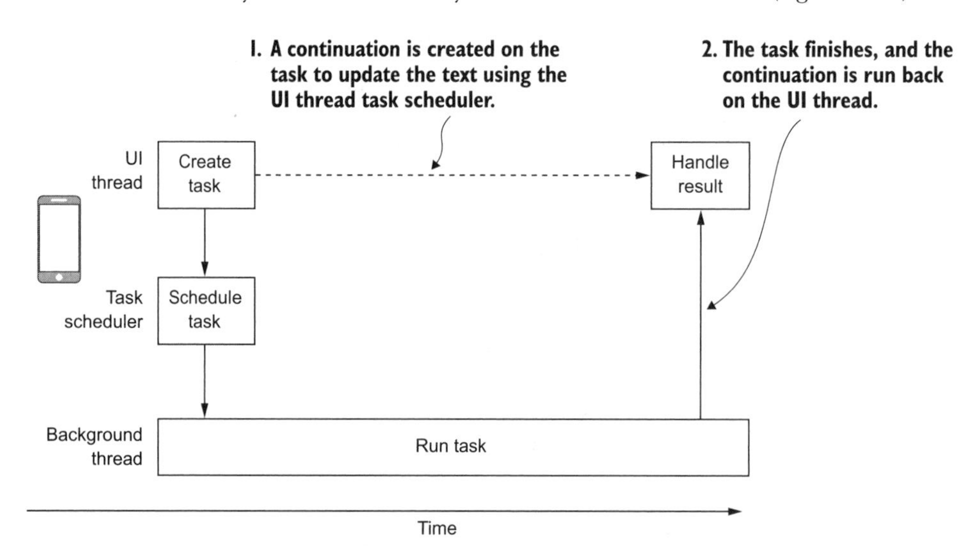

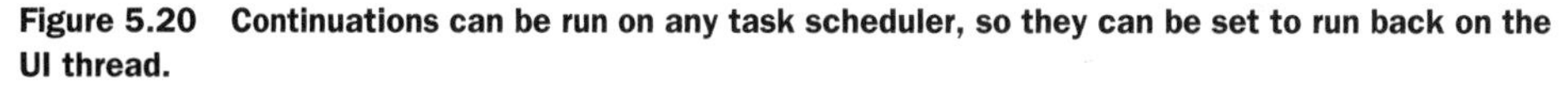

Figure 5.20 Continuations can be run on any task scheduler, so they can be set to run back on the UI thread.

This task scheduler will put your code onto the message queue that the UI thread processes. Your code will sit in this queue behind any other messages that the UI thread is already processing, such as UI events. Once the messages in front have been processed (if any), your code will be run.

MARSHALING YOUR CODE ONTO THE UI THREAD You'll often hear the term *marshaling* when talking about multithreaded code. Marshaling essentially means running code on a different thread—so, for example, when you run a task using the UI task scheduler, you're marshaling your code onto the UI thread.

The usual pattern here is to create a task on the UI thread that does some work in the background, and use a task continuation to execute some more code back on the UI thread by telling the continuation which task scheduler to use. The following listing shows how to do this.

Listing 5.8 Using the UI task scheduler allows the UI to be updated from a task

```
public override void ViewDidLoad()
{
   ...
   var scheduler =
      TaskScheduler.FromCurrentSynchronizationContext();
   Task.Run(() => DoSomethingLong())
      .ContinueWith(t => TextField.Text = "Foo", scheduler);
}

void DoSomethingLong()
{
   Task.Delay(TimeSpan.FromSeconds(5)).Wait();
}
```

When calling ContinueWith, you can pass in a task scheduler that you can use to run the task.

The UI update has been removed from the DoSomething method as it's now in the continuation.

If you make this change, build, and run this, once again everything will work. Let's break this down into steps:

1. The UI thread requests the task scheduler for the current synchronization context, which will be the task scheduler for the UI thread.
2. The UI thread creates and runs a task.
3. The UI thread sets up a task continuation, giving it an action to run and passing in the UI thread task scheduler. `FromCurrentSynchronizationContext` is evaluated before the task is set up, so it would be called on the UI thread and the resulting value would be passed to the call to `ContinueWith`, which sets up the continuation.
4. The default task scheduler runs the first action on a background thread.
5. When this action is complete, the UI task scheduler runs the continuation action.

5.6.2 Using the power of MVVM

If you have a view model with a command that's bound to a UI control, such as a button, when the user clicks the button, the code inside the command is run on the UI thread. By using continuations that use the UI task scheduler, you can write code inside your command that executes on a background thread and then comes back to the calling thread to perform any actions that will cause the UI to be updated. Depending on the MVVM framework you're using, though, you may not need to worry too much about marshaling your code back onto the UI thread.

One way that you can cause the UI to update is by property-changed notifications—you bind a UI control to a property on the view model, update the property, raise a property-changed notification, and the UI will update. This UI update has to be done on the UI thread.

Luckily, all the good MVVM frameworks take care of this. In the binding layer, the property-changed event is detected, the value to set is read, and the binding layer will run the UI update on the UI thread, regardless of what thread is used to raise the property-changed notification (figure 5.21). You can see this by changing your code to update the property on the view model instead of updating the UI directly. If you do this from a background thread, you can see the UI update with no exception being thrown. The following listing shows this change.

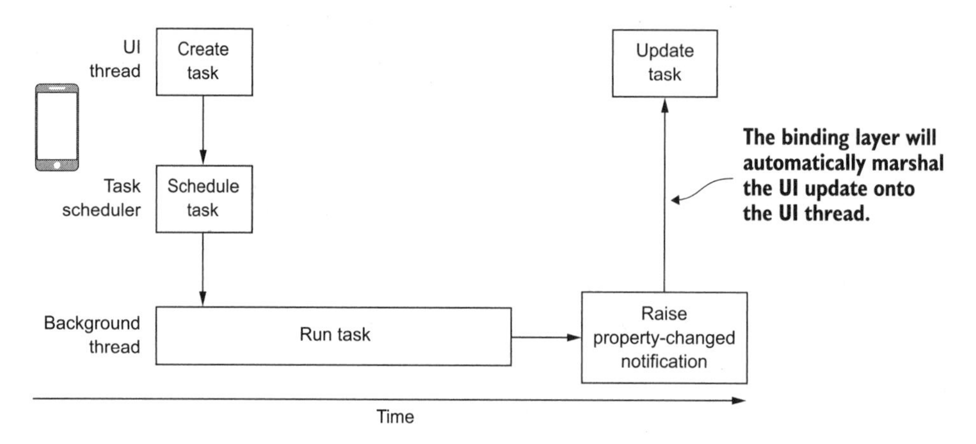

Figure 5.21 When a property-changed event is detected, the binding layer will marshal the call to update the UI onto the UI thread automatically.

Listing 5.9 Binding automatically marshals property changes into the UI thread

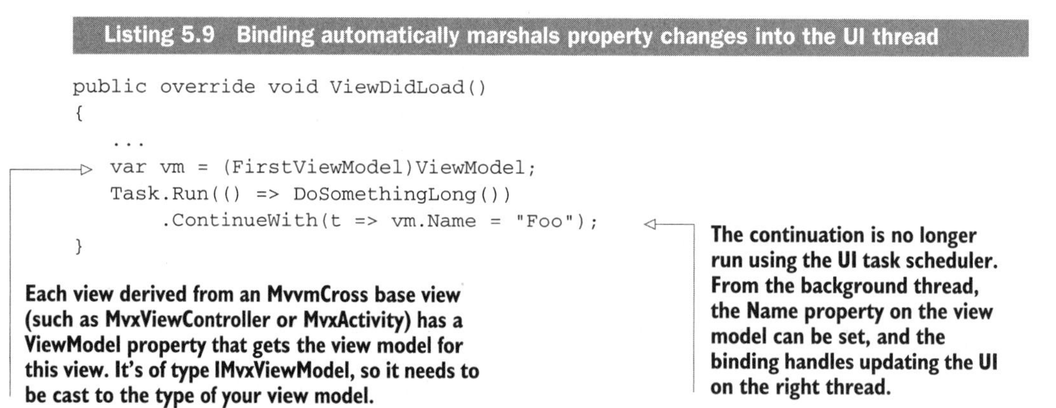

```
public override void ViewDidLoad()
{
    ...
    var vm = (FirstViewModel)ViewModel;
    Task.Run(() => DoSomethingLong())
        .ContinueWith(t => vm.Name = "Foo");
}
```

Each view derived from an MvvmCross base view (such as MvxViewController or MvxActivity) has a ViewModel property that gets the view model for this view. It's of type IMvxViewModel, so it needs to be cast to the type of your view model.
The continuation is no longer run using the UI task scheduler. From the background thread, the Name property on the view model can be set, and the binding handles updating the UI on the right thread.

If you make this change and run the app, you'll see the UI update. This is one of the powers of a good framework like MvvmCross—abstracting away the hard stuff, leaving you to focus on what your code should do instead of the complexities of how it should be done.

AVOID THE CAST TO FIRSTVIEWMODEL BY USING GENERICS The MvvmCross base views are also available in a generic form that takes a type argument for the view-model type. If you use these, the `ViewModel` property will be of the correct type and you won't need the cast to `FirstViewModel`. To see this in action, change the base type of the iOS view to `MvxViewController<FirstViewModel>`. You can then change the continuation to be `ContinueWith(t => ViewModel.Name = "Foo");`.

It's pretty clear that tasks are really rather useful. They allow you to package up some code and fire it off to be run on another thread. Then you can create another task to be run back on the calling thread once the first one completes. This is quite a popular pattern with UI apps—run code *x* in the background, and then run code *y* back on the UI thread. It's not perfect, and the way you handle return values and exceptions either by waiting on the task to complete or using a continuation can be downright clunky.

The good news for us C# developers is that, as a part of C# 5, Microsoft has added cool new features to make this a whole lot easier—`async` and `await`.

5.7 Async and await

In C# 5.0 two new keywords were added, `async` and `await`. These don't do anything in terms of code; instead, they're compiler hints, telling the compiler to handle code marked with these keywords differently. *Async* is short for *asynchronous*—code that can run multiple things at the same time. You'll often hear of multithreaded code referred to as *asynchronous code*.

5.7.1 The async and await keywords

The aim of the `async` and `await` keywords is to enable you to take the pattern of "run code *x* in the background then run code *y* back on the current synchronization context" and simplify it. You mark a method as `async`, and when you call other `async` methods from this method, you mark the calls to run them with `await`. The `await` tells the compiler that somewhere in the method that you're calling, some work will be done on a background thread using a task, and to hold off running the rest of the calling method until the awaited method has finished what it's doing. In the meantime, the current thread can process other code, and once the awaited method completes, the rest of the calling method finishes.

AWAIT DOESN'T CREATE A BACKGROUND THREAD FOR YOU There's a common misconception around `async` and `await` that they will actually run your code in the background. This isn't the case. Before we start digging into this in more detail, it's important to be aware of this.

Let's start with a simple code example in the view layer inside our iOS app. We'll make the app wait and then update the UI. Start by changing the `FirstView` class, in FirstView.cs in the HelloCrossPlatformWorld.iOS project, by reverting the previous changes made in this chapter and making the change shown in the following listing.

Listing 5.10 Running tasks in background doesn't affect when rest of code runs

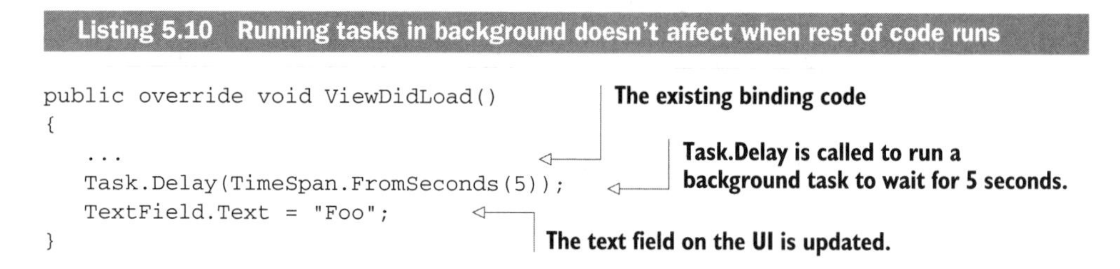

```
public override void ViewDidLoad()
{
   ...
   Task.Delay(TimeSpan.FromSeconds(5));
   TextField.Text = "Foo";
}
```


Read through the flow of this method. The OS calls a number of lifecycle methods when screens are displayed—methods that are called when a screen appears, disappears, or goes to other states. One of these lifecycle methods on iOS is `ViewDidLoad`, which is called by the OS as soon as the view has fully loaded and is shown on screen. This call runs on the UI thread as you've already seen, and it sets up the bindings in the existing code that we haven't changed, starts a task that waits for 5 seconds in the background, and then updates the UI (figure 5.22). If you run this code, you'd see what you expect—the UI shows "Foo" in the text field straightaway because the wait happens in a task—off on another thread.

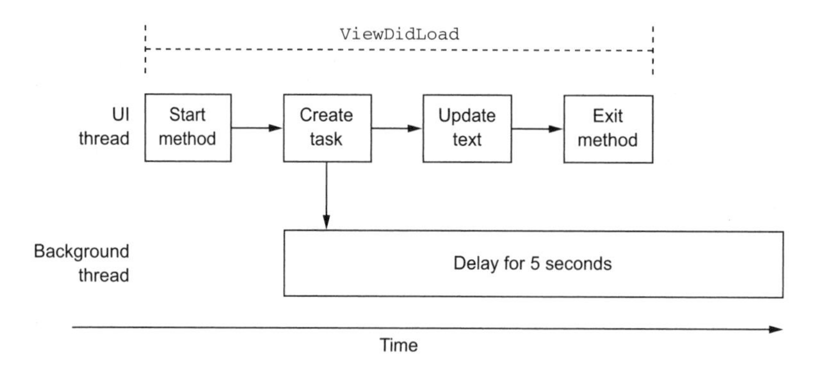

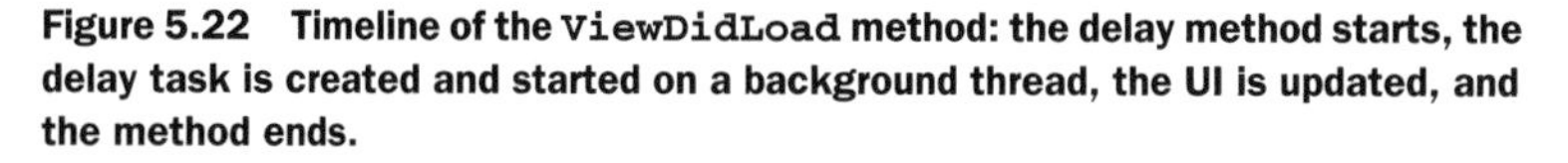

Figure 5.22 Timeline of the `ViewDidLoad` method: the delay method starts, the delay task is created and started on a background thread, the UI is updated, and the method ends.

It would be better if the UI were updated after the 5-second wait, but without the UI locking up for those 5 seconds. Let's make a couple of small changes to this method to achieve this in the following listing.

Listing 5.11 Adding `async` and `await` to our method

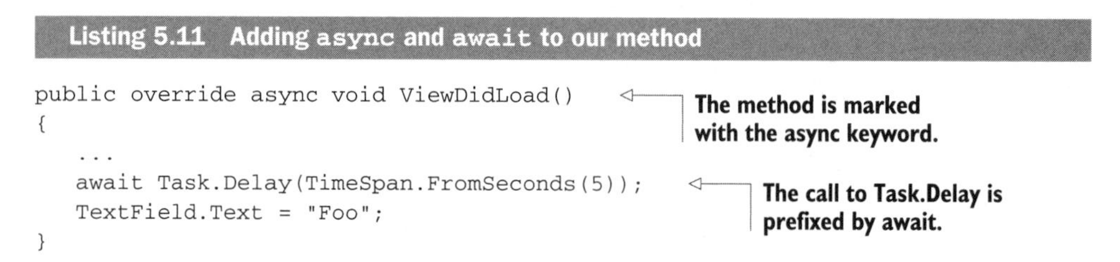

```
public override async void ViewDidLoad()
{
   ...
   await Task.Delay(TimeSpan.FromSeconds(5));
   TextField.Text = "Foo";
}
```

Make these code changes and run the code again. The app will start up, wait 5 seconds, and then update the text field. During the 5 seconds before the text field is updated, try to interact with the app to see if the app is responsive. You'll notice that it is. Unlike calling `Wait` on your task, which blocks the thread for the 5 seconds, this doesn't block. The call to `ViewDidLoad` by the OS returns as soon as the call to `Delay` is made, and the rest of the method call is called back on the original (UI) thread later (figure 5.23).

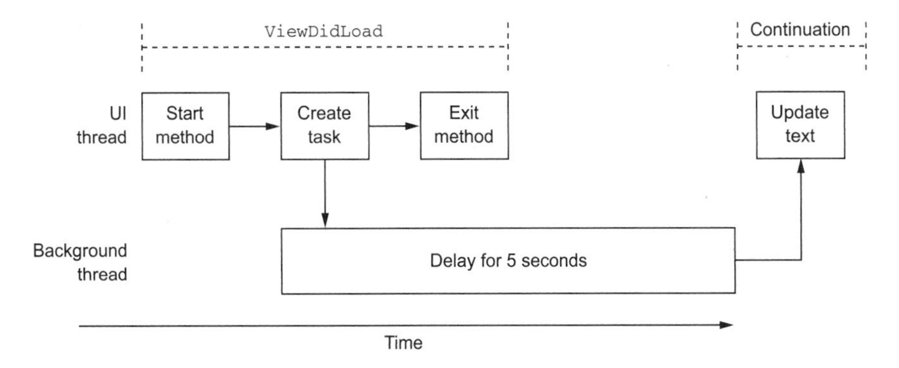

Figure 5.23 If you `await` the delay task, the `ViewDidLoad` method finishes as soon as the `await` is called, with the remainder of the method being called in a continuation back on the original thread.

The basic principle here is you can mark a method as `async` to tell the compiler that you're planning on using `await` in your method. Then you call `await` on a task (either one you create or one that's returned by a method) and the compiler, behind the scenes, will take the rest of the code in the method and put it in a continuation using the original synchronization context as the thread to run the continuation on.

> **AFTER AWAIT, THE CODE WILL RUN ON THE SAME SYNCHRONIZATION CONTEXT** The code before and after an `await` will run on the same synchronization context, but not necessarily the same thread. The UI synchronization context has a single thread, so if you await a method from the UI thread, the code that comes after it will run on the UI thread; if you await from a background thread, the code after the `await` may run on a different background thread.

You can think of the behavior of the code in listing 5.11 as analogous to the code in the following listing.

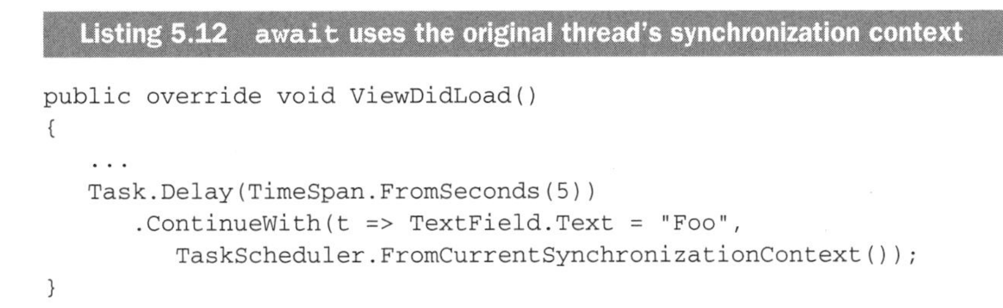

Listing 5.12 `await` uses the original thread's synchronization context

```
public override void ViewDidLoad()
{
   ...
   Task.Delay(TimeSpan.FromSeconds(5))
      .ContinueWith(t => TextField.Text = "Foo",
         TaskScheduler.FromCurrentSynchronizationContext());
}
```

What's the big upside to async and await? First, it makes your code much easier to read. Imagine if instead of having one call to ContinueWith you had five. That would be harder to read than just using await. Second, and probably most importantly, you can use return values and exceptions as if there were no continuations involved.

Thinking again of our email app example, when the user launches the app, it needs to call a web service to authenticate the user and then get back an authentication token. Once authenticated, it needs to call another web service, passing the authentication token, to download a list of new emails, and then it needs to download the full contents of each new email, again passing the authentication token. At each stage it will want to update the UI: once you're logged in it would show the emails, when it has downloaded the list of new emails it will display a summary, and as each email is fully downloaded the UI will be updated to show the details of each email. If at any time these actions were to fail with an exception (such as if there was no network connectivity, a common occurrence with mobile apps), the code would need to stop downloading emails and handle the exception, maybe by showing a message to the user. The following listing contains some pseudocode for this, using continuations.

Listing 5.13 Pseudocode for downloading emails and updating the UI

```
public void HandleLogInAndDownloadEmails()
{
   string token = null;
   Task.Run(() => LogIn())                    // Starts a task to log in
      .ContinueWith(t1 =>                     // Creates a continuation back on the UI thread
      {
         if (t1.IsFaulted)                    // If the original task threw an exception, shows it
            ShowException(t1.Exception);
         else
         {
            UpdateUIAfterLogIn();             // If the original task didn't throw an exception, updates the UI
            Task.Run(() => DownloadEmailList(token))   // Starts a continuation for downloading the emails, and so on, and so on
               .ContinueWith(t2 =>
               {
                  if (t2.IsFaulted)
                     ShowException(t2.Exception);
                  else
                  {
                     UpdateUIWithNewEmails();
                     foreach (var email in t2.Result)
                     {
                        Task.Run(() => DownloadEmail(token, email))
                           .ContinueWith(t3 =>
                           {
                              if (t3.IsFaulted)
                                 ShowException(t3.Exception);
                              else
                                 UpdateUIWithDownloadedEmails();
                           }, TaskScheduler.FromCurrentSynchronizationContext());
                     }
                  }
```

```
            }, TaskScheduler.FromCurrentSynchronizationContext());
        }
    }, TaskScheduler.FromCurrentSynchronizationContext());
}
```

This is very complicated code, partly because we're switching threads so often and partly because we need to keep querying the `Task` passed into the continuation for any exceptions and for the return value.

Not only can `async` and `await` remove the need for continuations, but they also help with return values and exceptions. As you already know, you can call `await` on a `Task`, but what's powerful about `await` is that it can return the result of a `Task<T>`. If you `await` a `Task`, there's no return value, so the `await` doesn't return anything, but if you `await` a `Task<T>`, the return value of the call is an instance of `T`, the one returned by the task. If your task throws an exception, it's normally swallowed up and only made available through the `Exception` property on the `Task` passed to the continuation. But if you use `async` and `await`, the `Exception` gets thrown as if you weren't in a task.

Let's rewrite listing 5.13 to do this, as follows.

Listing 5.14 Using `async` and `await` to clean up our code

```
public async Task HandleLogInAndDownloadEmails()
{
    try
    {
        var token = await Task.Run(() => LogIn());
        UpdateUIAfterLogIn();
        var emails = await Task.Run(() => DownloadEmailList(token));
        UpdateUIWithNewEmails();
        foreach (var email in emails)
        {
            await Task.Run(() => DownloadEmail(token, email));
            UpdateUIWithDownloadedEmails();
        }
    }
    catch (Exception ex)
    {
        ShowException(ex);
    }
}
```

- The method now returns Task and is decorated with the async keyword.
- The token is returned from the task thanks to the await call.
- The UI can be updated because we're back on the calling thread (the UI thread) after awaiting the task. We can continue this pattern for the rest of the method.
- The whole method can be wrapped in a try/catch because await takes care of throwing any exceptions.

The code in the preceding listing does the same as the code in listing 5.13, but it's cleaner and easier to read. It also seems to have a return type of `Task`, but it doesn't seem to return anything. Let's look at why this is by looking at how we write `async` methods.

5.7.2 Writing your own async methods

In the listings we've just looked at, the methods were marked with the `async` keyword, which tells the compiler that the method will contain calls to `await` tasks. If you don't have this keyword in your method, you can't `await`. You can try this quickly by removing the `async` keyword from the `ViewDidLoad` method you changed earlier. Take it out and your app won't compile.

MARKING METHODS AS ASYNC

You can't just mark any method as `async`—you can only use it on methods that have a return type of `void`, `Task`, or `Task<T>`, and you can't use it on methods without parameters or ref parameters. The `async` keyword isn't part of the method signature, so you can't use it in interfaces, but you can add it when you're overriding methods—you've seen this already when you added it to the override of `ViewDidLoad` in the iOS app. When you have an `async` method, the usual intent is for the caller to `await` it, and for this to happen the method must have a return type of `Task` or `Task<T>`—remember, you can only call await on a task, so if your method is a void method, there's nothing to await on.

When you mark the method as `async`, you don't actually return an instance of `Task` or `Task<T>`; you just return nothing or an instance of `T`, and the compiler does the rest for you, wrapping everything in a task so that the method can be awaited. You saw this in listing 5.14—the `HandleLogInAndDownloadEmails` method was marked as returning a `Task` but it didn't have an explicit return value.

You can mark a method that returns `void` as `async`, but this method can't be awaited as there's no task to await. This isn't normally an issue because there's no return value to worry about, but be aware that if you call an `async void` method, it may not complete before the rest of your code runs because some parts of it will run in the background. Ideally, you should never mark a `void` method as `async` unless you have no other choice, such as with event handlers or overriding existing methods.

If you override a `void` method and make the override `async`, you need to be aware that all the code won't be finished before the method returns. For example, overriding a method like `ViewDidLoad` on the iOS view controller and making it `async` will mean that the method will return once the first background task starts running. If you had some code in it to set up the UI, such as creating bindings, and if this code comes after the awaited task, it won't be run until the task completes. This could mean that your user will be using an app with a incomplete UI until the background task completes. It's good practice to only await methods after all your UI setup is complete, or to show some form of progress to the user so they're aware something is happening and that they need to wait.

Let's take our last example and in the following listing write some async methods to make the code cleaner.

Listing 5.15 Using `async` to make your code cleaner

```
async Task<string> LogIn() {}

async Task<IEnumerable<Email>> DownloadEmailList(string token){}

async Task DownloadEmail(string token, string email){}
```

The methods to load data are marked as async.

```
public async Task HandleLogInAndDownloadEmails()
{
   try
   {
      var token = await LogIn();          <-- There are no more calls to Task.Run.
      UpdateUIAfterLogIn();
      var emails = await DownloadEmailList(token);
      UpdateUIWithNewEmails();
      foreach (var email in emails)
      {
         await DownloadEmail(token, email);
         UpdateUIWithDownloadedEmails();
      }
   }
   catch (Exception ex)
   {
      ShowException(ex);
   }
}
```

In this listing, the code is a lot cleaner, and it's now the responsibility of the methods that are called to create the tasks that run in the background.

Remember, just using `async` and `await` won't create the tasks for you—you're still responsible for this, either directly by creating the task or indirectly by awaiting on another method that creates a task. For example, in the case of hitting a web service, there's a NuGet package available from Microsoft called `HttpClient` that will do this for you—it has some `async` methods that you can await that will create the task and run the web call in the background, so all you need to do in your code is mark your methods as `async` and `await` all the calls. This is one of the downsides of `async` and `await`, you have to mark everything as `async` and return tasks. If your web service call is buried ten calls down the call stack, all ten calls must be awaited and must return tasks.

> **WHAT ABOUT ACTION AND FUNC?** Just like methods, lambdas can be marked as `async`, and can `await` tasks. This means you can create `async` actions and funcs using the same keywords, using syntax like `var myAction = new Action(async () => await MyMethod());` or `var myFunc = new Func<int>(async () => await MyIntMethod());`.

RETURNING TASKS INSTEAD OF USING ASYNC AND AWAIT

Async methods have a return type of `Task` or `Task<T>`, but you never actually return the task yourself. Instead, you await other methods that return tasks and return the relevant type, and the compiler weaves its magic over your code to manage all the `await` statements and actually return a task at the end of the method that can be awaited by the calling code.

If you only have one call in your method that you await, and it's the last (or only) thing your method does, then instead of marking your method as async and awaiting the call, you can simply return the task. See the following two listings.

Listing 5.16 Using an async method when you could return a Task

```
public async Task MakeCoffee()
{
   await myCoffeeService.MakeCoffee();
}
```

In this code, the MakeCoffee method is async, but all it does is await a call to myCoffeeService.MakeCoffee(). To write less code, you can drop the async modifier and just return the result of the call instead of awaiting it.

Listing 5.17 Returning a Task instead of awaiting it

```
public Task MakeCoffee()
{
   return myCoffeeService.MakeCoffee();
}
```

This code is functionally identical, and in fact is marginally faster. Using await means the compiler has to generate code to track the threads in use and ensure that the code after the await happens on the correct thread. And it has to do this for all async methods in the current call stack. If you just return the task, this extra code is not needed. It's good practice to always return a task if your async method only awaits the last method call.

CONFIGUREAWAIT

When you await a call to an async method, you're telling the compiler that you want to ensure that all code after the await runs on the same synchronization context as the code before the await. The compiler creates code to capture the current synchronization context, calls a method that's awaited, and then runs the rest of the current method using the original synchronization context. There's a small compiler overhead to this—capturing the synchronization context and switching back to it.

There are times, though, when you don't care what thread the remainder of the code in your current method runs on. For example, you might have a method that awaits a database call, then does some CPU-intensive processing on the data, returning results to a calling method that updates the UI. The processing can be done on any thread—it's only the update to the UI that needs to happen on the UI thread. The following listing shows some pseudocode that illustrates this.

Listing 5.18 Performing a long calculation on the UI thread

```
public async Task CalcAndUpdate()
{
   var result = await Calc();          <-- From the UI thread, await a call to Calc
```

```
    myLabel.Text = result;
}

public async Task Calc()
{
    var data = await LoadData();
    return PerformLongCalculation(data);
}
```

Back on the UI thread, update a label

From the UI thread, await a call to LoadData

Back on the UI thread, perform a calculation

In this code, the call to the `LoadData` method will load data on a background thread, and then `Calc` will switch back to the current synchronization context (the UI thread) to run the calculation. We don't care which thread the `PerformLongCalculation` call actually runs on, just that the label update happens on the UI thread. What we can do is make a call to a method to tell the compiler that we don't want to switch synchronization contexts after the `await`, and the rest of the `Calc` method can run on whatever thread `LoadData` used to run. We can do this using the `ConfigureAwait` method on `Task`.

Listing 5.19 Using `ConfigureAwait` to avoid switching contexts

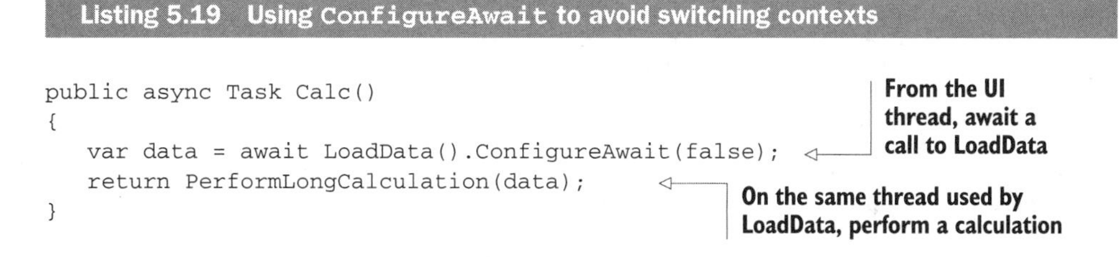
From the UI thread, await a call to LoadData
On the same thread used by LoadData, perform a calculation

```
public async Task Calc()
{
    var data = await LoadData().ConfigureAwait(false);
    return PerformLongCalculation(data);
}
```

By calling `ConfigureAwait(false)`, we're telling the compiler to remain on the same thread used by the call we're awaiting, but just for the remainder of the current method, until another `await`. When we return to `CalcAndUpdate`, the code will switch back to the calling synchronization context. Passing `true` to `ConfigureAwait` tells the compiler that you do want to switch back to the original synchronization context—which is the same as not calling it.

By identifying any awaited methods in code that will never need to interact with the UI thread and marking them with `ConfigureAwait`, you can make a small performance improvement. Not only does this save CPU time by avoiding storing the original synchronization context and reverting back to it later, but if your code constantly switches back to the UI thread to do simple work that could be run on a background thread, it can slow down your UI. It's generally a good idea to mark all calls you await with `ConfigureAwait` in any classes that don't interact with the UI, such as classes in your model layer.

5.7.3 Async commands

We've looked at building short, concise `async` methods that will `await` on other `async` methods, which in turn will `await` on calls to something like `HttpClient`, which will create tasks to hit a web service on a background thread. This is a nice pattern, but how do we call our new `async` method in the first place? As you've already seen, we can override a void method on our view, mark that as `async`, and `await` our new method there. We could also wire up an event to a login button, mark the event handler as `async` (remember, event handlers are always void methods), and await our method. Neither of these is really MVVM, so instead we could jump down into the view-model layer and call the method inside a command that we can bind to our view, either on a button-click or other event, such as a screen loading. Because our method is `async`, we need a new type of command—an async command.

As you've seen already, the commands in the view model start on the UI thread, so to run code in the background you need to create tasks. Luckily for us, all the good MVVM frameworks have asynchronous implementations of `ICommand` that we can use. In the case of MvvmCross, there's `MvxAsyncCommand`. Unlike `MvxCommand`, which takes an `Action` as its parameter, `MvxAsyncCommand` takes a `Func<Task>`—a call that returns as a task that can be awaited.

Let's see this in action. First, revert all the changes you've made to `FirstView` in the iOS app in this chapter, and make the changes shown in the following listing to `FirstViewModel`.

Listing 5.20 Creating an async command

```
public FirstViewModel(ITextToSpeech textToSpeech)
{
   this.textToSpeech = textToSpeech;
   SayHelloCommand = new MvxAsyncCommand(() => SayHello());
}

async Task SayHello()
{
   await Task.Delay(TimeSpan.FromSeconds(5));
   textToSpeech.Speak($"Hello {Name}");
}
```

The command you're creating is now an MvxAsyncCommand, and it takes a Func<Task>. You can pass it a method that returns a Task.

The SayHello method is marked as async and returns a Task. Remember, you don't explicitly return an instance of Task—the compiler handles it for you.

Calling await on Task.Delay will await the 5-second call.

After the 5-second delay, the call to say hello is made.

If you run this and tap the button, you'll get the 5-second delay before hearing the app say hello, and at all times the app remains responsive. The method run by the command is an `async` method that awaits the call to `Task.Delay`, which in turn delays for 5 seconds on a background thread before running the code to say hello back on the UI thread.

5.8 Make your app feel responsive

As you've seen so far, it's relatively easy to make your app responsive by executing long-running tasks on a background thread. Unfortunately, this isn't enough to make your app a five-star experience. Not only do you need to do things in the background, but you also need to show visible feedback to the user that something is happening, so they know that they need to wait.

There are a few popular ways to show feedback: using some form of spinner control in line with your UI while allowing user interactions to continue, using progress dialogs that cover the screen and block activity until the progress is complete, or showing dummy loading data, as in figure 5.24. An email app might use all of these methods to show progress in different ways at different times. When the app starts up, it will need to authenticate the user, so it might show dummy data while this is happening. Then once you're logged in, it could show your email list with a spinner at the top to show that it's loading more emails. Finally, if you tap a new email that hasn't been fully downloaded, it might show a progress dialog, showing that you're blocked from reading the email until it has fully downloaded.

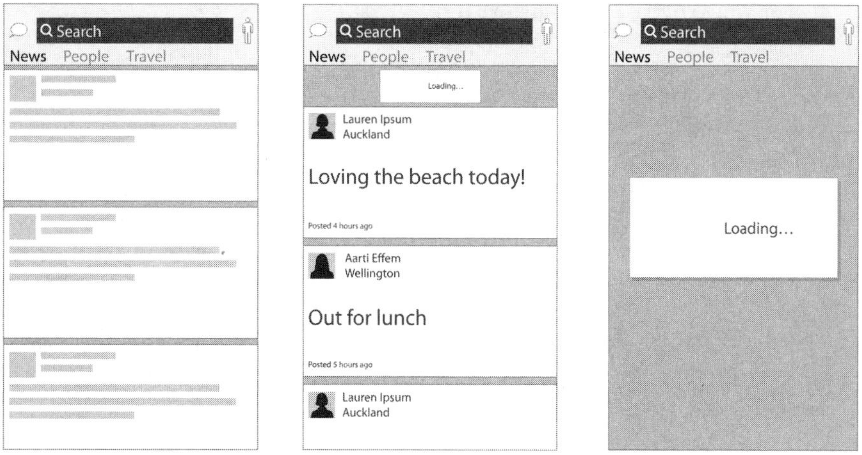

Dummy loading data

Progress dialog at the top of the list being reloaded

Progress dialog over the whole screen

Figure 5.24 If your app looks like it's doing something during a long operation, the user will be happier than if your app looks unresponsive.

How you display progress to the user is very much dependent on your app. On Android there's a `ProgressDialog` class that creates a dialog that sits in the middle of the screen, very much like the third example in figure 5.24. On iOS you have to hand-roll this or use a third-party component, but it has a simple property you can set to show a spinner in the status bar. Creating pull-to-refresh lists is easy on both platforms—it's built into the various list controls or included in easily accessible helpers. Creating dummy loading data is something you'll need to write yourself, as it would be specific to your app.

You should always think about how to give feedback to your user when doing work in the background. If your app appears to be doing nothing when it's loading, you probably need to add some user feedback. Ideally you should write this code in a platform-specific class and expose the ability to show and hide progress indicators via an interface that you make available to your view models via IoC, like the `ITextToSpeech` interface in chapter 4. This way your commands can use it to show feedback, just like in the following pseudocode.

Listing 5.21 Showing feedback to the user during a long-running command

```
public class MyViewModel : MvxViewModel
{
   IProgressService progressService;

   public MyViewModel(IProgressService progressService)
   {
      this.progressService = progressService;
      DoSomethingLongCommand = new MvxAsyncCommand(() => DoSomethingLong);
   }

   public ICommand DoSomethingLongCommand {get; private set;}

   async Task DoSomethingLong()
   {
      progressService.ShowProgressFeedback();
      try
      {
         ...
      }
      finally
      {
          progressService.HideProgressFeedback();
      }
   }
}
```

An instance of IProgressService is passed in through constructor injection and stored in a field. This interface has platform-specific implementations to show some form of progress feedback to the user, and to hide that feedback once the long-running action is complete.

Before a long-running action starts, the progress feedback is shown to the user.

After the long-running action is complete, the progress feedback is hidden. This is done in a finally block so that if the command throws an exception, the feedback is still hidden.

5.9 It's time to start building things

Over the last few chapters, we've gone through MVVM looking at the cross-platform model and view model, the binding and the view. We've looked at property-changed notifications and commands and seen how to run code in multiple threads. These are important principles that make up the foundations of building high-quality cross-platform mobile apps.

Now you're ready to start building apps for real. In the next part of this book we'll start looking at building an app from the ground up, starting with designing the app, the UI, the user flows through the app, and the structure of the code.

Summary

In this chapter you learned

- When building apps, you need to keep the UI responsive or users will stop using your apps. To do this, you can use tasks to write asynchronous code that runs in background threads instead of on the main UI thread.
- The UI thread is where everything on the UI happens. Exceptions on this thread can kill your app, and updating the UI from another thread will throw exceptions.
- C# has some awesome features that make it easy to write clean code that runs in the background.
- As well as keeping your UI responsive, you need to show feedback to the user that something is happening.

You also learned how to

- Run code in a background thread using a `Task`.
- Use continuations to run multiple tasks, including marshaling tasks back onto the UI thread.
- Handle exceptions thrown inside tasks using continuations.
- Use `async` and `await` to make your code more readable.

Part 2

Building apps

Now that you're familiar with the MVVM design pattern and how it can be used to build testable, reusable code, this part of the book expands on that knowledge. It shows how you can build cross-platform apps on iOS and Android, starting with the cross-platform code and moving on to platform-specific UI code, taking a couple of example apps from design through to fully working apps. This part moves up, layer by layer, though MVVM, before diving into the Android and iOS UIs.

Chapter 6 introduces two example apps that will be built throughout the rest of this part. It looks at how to design an app, focusing on what code goes in what layer in the MVVM design pattern. Finally, it covers creating the solutions for the example apps and looks at the project and application properties for a Xamarin mobile app.

Chapter 7 focuses on the model layer. You'll see how to build simple models and more complex model layers with services and repositories, and you'll learn how to access SQLite databases and web services. It also introduces unit testing, showing how easy it is to unit-test well-structured code.

Chapter 8 moves up a layer and covers view models. It considers how state and behavior are represented, covering properties, commands, and value conversion. It also shows how to test UI logic using unit testing.

Chapters 9 and 10 cover the view and application layers on Android, recycler views for showing lists of data, and multiscreen navigation. It then shows how to add polish to an app by creating app icons and splash screens.

Chapters 11 and 12 focus on iOS, working on the application and view layers of the first example app, covering view controllers, UI controls, storyboards, and auto layout and constraints, table views, and multiscreen navigation. It then covers app icons and launch screens.

After you've finished these chapters, you'll have working iOS and Android apps that will be made production-ready in the third part of this book.

6 Designing MVVM cross-platform apps

This chapter covers

- Preparing for building cross-platform apps by considering the differences between iOS and Android
- Designing the flows a user will take in an app, including which layer and which thread to use
- Creating the solution for an app
- Configuring the properties for your app, including SDK versions and linker settings

In the first part of this book we looked at the foundations of an MVVM-based cross-platform mobile app. We looked at what the different layers in MVVM are all about and how to structure your code inside them. We also looked at how threads work in mobile apps and how you can keep your apps responsive when performing long-running actions. Now it's time to think about how you can start building a cross-platform mobile app.

As developers, we're often tempted to start a new app by firing up our IDE and clicking File > New Project. But a little planning goes a long way, so before we start creating any code, let's first think about what we're building and then think about how to build it. Then we can create a new solution and look at how it differs from the kinds of solutions most C# developers are used to.

Throughout this part of the book we'll be looking at two app examples—one very simple and one slightly more complex—and I'll use these apps to introduce the ideas and concepts you'll need to know to build production-quality cross-platform apps using Xamarin and MVVM. In this chapter we'll talk about designing these apps: you'll see how to create the solutions for them, and I'll explain these solutions in detail. The next few chapters will explain how you can build up your Xamarin apps layer by layer, from the model, to the view model, to the view, looking at our two example apps and at other features you can add to your apps in each layer.

6.1 Introduction to designing a cross-platform app

The Facebook app is popular on iOS and Android, catering to millions of users worldwide. On both platforms it offers the same functionality, but the way it offers its features is different on each platform. Figure 6.1 shows what these apps look like at the time of writing.

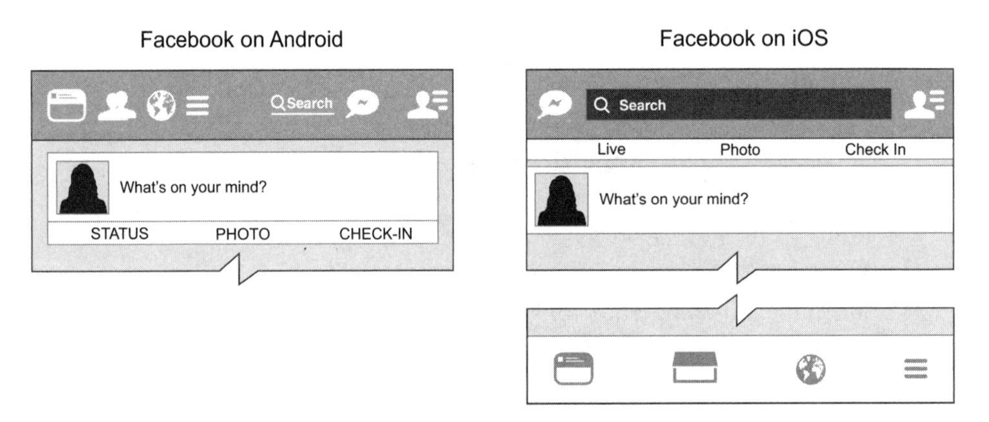

Figure 6.1 Apps like Facebook look and work differently on iOS and Android.

On Android, all the buttons are on the top of the screen. This is because Android has its three navigation buttons at the bottom of the device, either as physical or software buttons. If an app has buttons just above these navigation buttons, it's too easy to accidentally tap a navigation button when you meant to tap an app button, so Android apps don't have buttons on the bottom as a good design practice.

iOS, on the other hand, doesn't have easy-to-tap buttons at the bottom—it has a hardware home button, allowing the iOS Facebook app to have some of its buttons on the bottom. These buttons are used to select different views: your news feed, marketplace, notifications, and settings. They're tab buttons, each one representing a new tab in a tab control. (Tab controls consist of a number of pages indicated by tab buttons in a bar, and tapping a tab button shows the page represented by that tab, similar to the tabs on folders in a filing cabinet.)

On Android, swiping from right to left or left to right changes tabs; swiping on iOS won't change tabs, but swiping in the Facebook app will slide the screen out to show the Messenger screen (making it look like the Messenger screen is below the main screen—following the iOS human interface guidelines on depth). This is a simple but important difference—Android has tabs at the top with swiping to change tabs, whereas iOS has tabs at the bottom without swiping.

These differences may seem small, but they're important. They involve navigation paradigms that are common to each platform, making the apps consistent with other apps on their own platforms, whether they're apps that come with the OS or from third parties. This means a new user can start using an app and already have an idea how to navigate it.

With Xamarin you can build an app for multiple platforms in one Visual Studio solution with lots of shared code, but you have to be careful with your UIs. You shouldn't always build identical apps on both platforms; instead, tailor the user interface and user experience on each platform. You'll want to maximize code reuse, but not necessarily reuse the same UIs.

Luckily, some of this complexity is abstracted away from you—if you create tabs in your apps using out-of-the-box tab controls, you'll get the appropriate behavior, as shown in figure 6.2. The problems come when you need something that doesn't come from an out-of-the-box control.

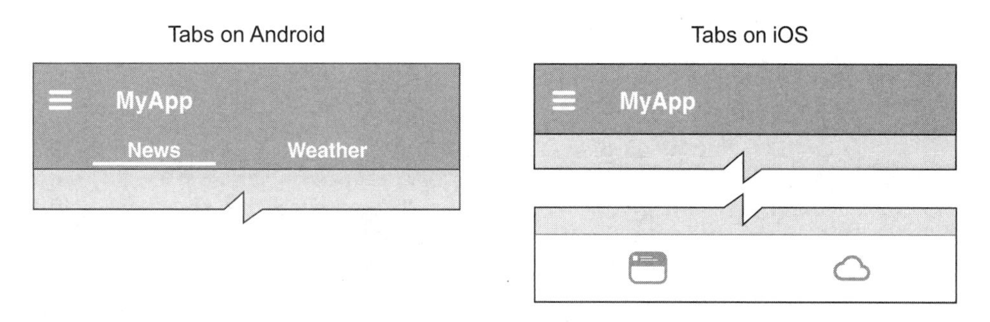

Figure 6.2 Using out-of-the-box controls ensures your app will have a consistent look and feel with the rest of the OS.

Google has released a Gmail app for both Android and iOS (figure 6.3). On iOS, to write a new email you tap a button on the top toolbar. This is pretty standard for iOS apps, using the top toolbar for action buttons. On Android it does something different—instead of having a button on the top toolbar, it has a floating action button (FAB). This is a round button near the bottom right of the screen (a little bit up from the bottom to avoid the risk of accidentally tapping a navigation button), and it uses a

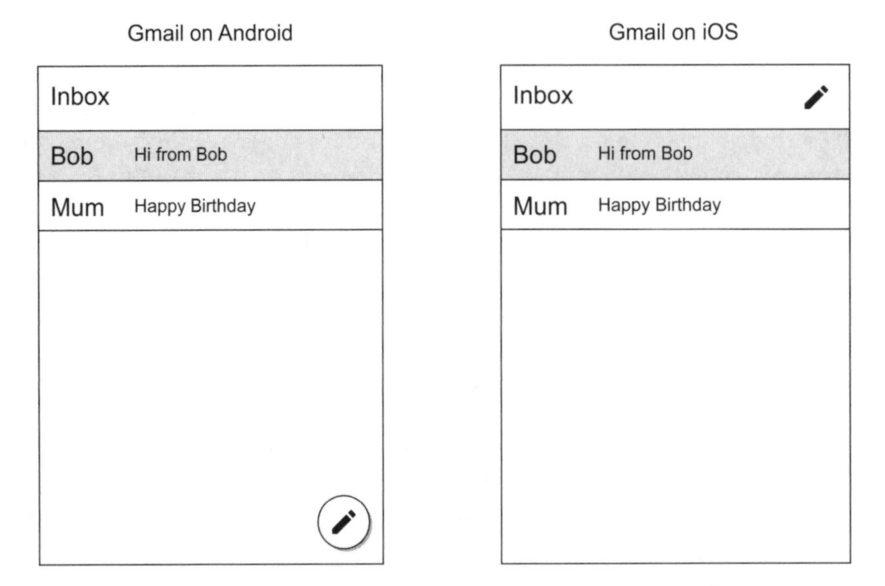

Figure 6.3 Android and iOS have different paradigms for the most popular action a user might do—iOS uses toolbar buttons, whereas Android favors the floating action button.

shadow effect (referred to as *elevation* in Android-speak) so it looks like it's floating above the page. This is a standard Android UI paradigm—a lot of Android apps use a FAB for the most common action on a particular screen.

Mobile apps are constantly changing

At the time of writing, Gmail uses the iOS toolbar button and Android FAB. This may change in future releases because Google is really trying to push its own design standard. It's worth getting a few apps on different platforms and looking at their differences to get an understanding of how apps can provide the same functionality in different ways.

Android has also released a bottom-navigation component, to provide iOS-like tabs at the bottom. This is pretty recent, but it may mean that Android apps will start to support bottom navigation.

These differences aren't provided for free by out-of-the-box controls. Instead, they're different controls added in different ways. On iOS the developers had to explicitly add a toolbar button, and on Android they had to add the FAB.

As developers of cross-platform apps, we have to keep these differences in mind. It's easy as a consumer to use one platform and get used to the way it works, but to be a successful cross-platform developer, you'll need to get used to both platforms so you can always think of your UIs in terms of each platform.

With this in mind, let's now start to think about the design for a couple of apps. One will be a single-screen square root calculator. The other will be a multiscreen counter app (an app that you can use to count different things, like how many cups of coffee you've had). We'll take both these apps through from design, to looking at the code structure, to creating a new solution and structuring the code.

6.2 Designing the UI and user flows

For the rest of this and the upcoming chapters, we're going to focus our attention on a couple of app examples. One is a simple square root calculator (like the example from chapter 2), which we'll call SquareRt, in keeping with the current trend for naming things by taking normal words and losing vowels. The other will be a counter app supporting multiple counters, and we'll call this one Countr. Let's look at these in turn and consider the design of their UIs and user flows. Later you'll see how this maps to the architecture of each app.

When I refer to the *UI*, I'm referring to the user interface presented to the user. By *user flows*, I'm referring to the user's experience—the actions the user can take to flow through the app, the interactions they have with the UI, and the results of these interactions on screen.

6.2.1 SquareRt—a simple app for calculating square roots

The aim of this app is to let the user enter a number and then to calculate its square root. It's a fairly simple task, so we don't need a complex UI. This is also the kind of app that could be the same on both iOS and Android.

Apple requires high-quality apps

This is a simple app example for illustration, and not something that you should ever build and try to submit to the app stores. Google has a fairly lax attitude toward the quality of apps that can be submitted, whereas Apple is fairly draconian (although both are strict about offensive material or copyright violations). If your app doesn't do anything of value (such as just calculating a square root), it's very likely to be rejected from the app store. According to Apple's App Store guidelines, there are "lots of serious developers who don't want their quality apps to be surrounded by amateur hour."

You can read Apple's "App Store Review Guidelines" at http://mng.bz/525T. The Google guidelines are at http://mng.bz/KQbE.

Before we can start cutting code, we need to think about what to build. Thinking about the UI is a good way to divide up the code. We're using MVVM after all, so we need to consider the model layer, the views, and their corresponding view models. Once we know what UI we need, we can start to define our views, and then the view models.

A good way to define the UI is to think about the user flows—what actions the user will want to take, and what the results of these actions will be. Once you have these actions, you can start to map them to the UI and define what your UI should look like. Let's draw a simple flowchart of the only user flow through the SquareRt app, shown in figure 6.4.

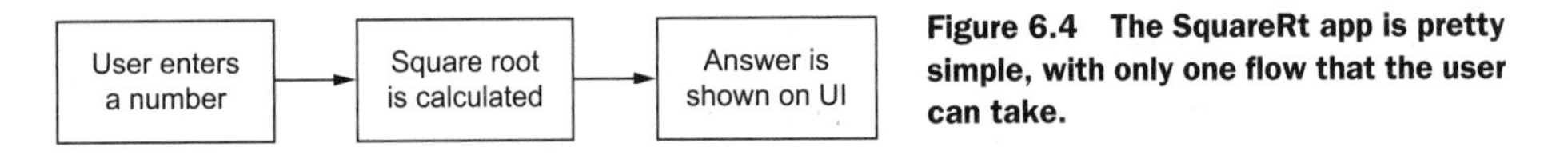

Figure 6.4 The SquareRt app is pretty simple, with only one flow that the user can take.

This flow is very simple—the user can only use this app for one thing. They need a way to enter a number, something in the app needs to calculate the square root, and then the square root is presented to the user. The UI for this is relatively easy to imagine—you need a way to enter the number, a way to kick off the calculation, and a way to show the results. Figure 6.5 shows some options.

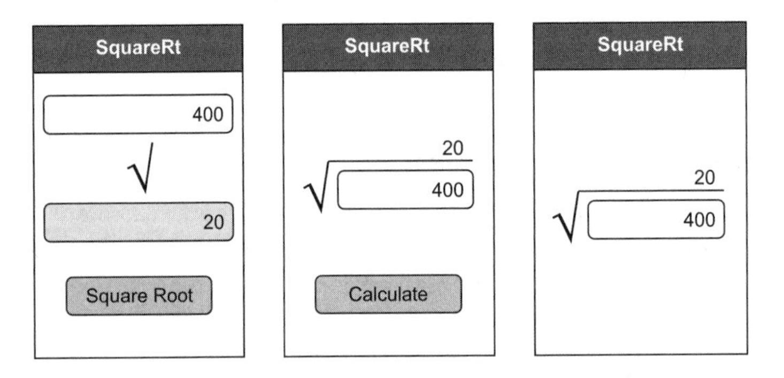

Figure 6.5 Some possible UIs for SquareRt, a simple square root calculation app

The first two UIs in figure 6.5 have a text box where the user can enter the number, and a button that kicks off the calculation. The third removes the button—from a user perspective, if they're entering a number, they obviously want to see the square root, so the app could calculate it automatically every time the value in the text box changes. This is a good option to consider—the less the user has to do, the better the experience.

We're going to use the third UI in this book (figure 6.6), but it's a good exercise to think about the other UIs, or to consider other designs of your own, as we delve deeper into designing this app.

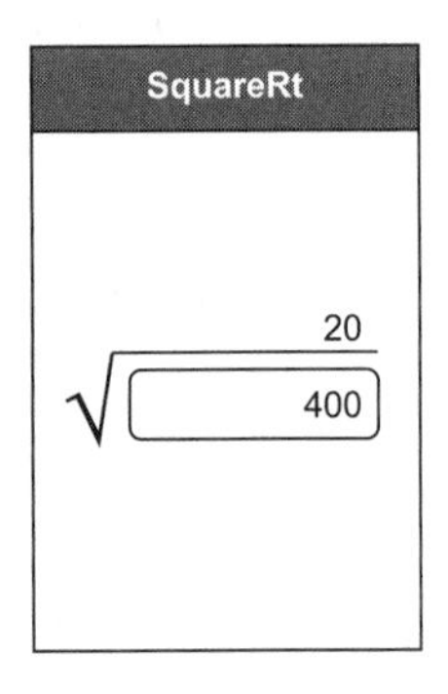

Figure 6.6 Our final UI for the SquareRt app

6.2.2 Countr—an app for counting multiple things

The SquareRt app is a very simple example, but most apps are a lot more complicated. Our second example is an app called Countr that allows the user to define multiple counters, and to increment them whenever they want, such as to track the number of cups of coffee they've had, or the number of times they've been out for a run. This app will need to show multiple counters, will need the ability to add or delete a counter, and will need a simple way to increment each counter. Figure 6.7 shows these user flows.

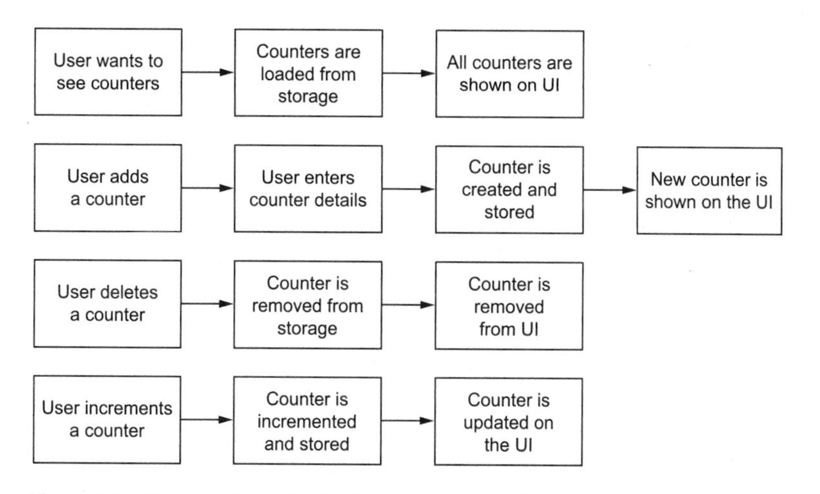

Figure 6.7 The user flows for the Countr app—showing, adding, deleting, and incrementing counters

Showing lists is a very popular thing to do in mobile apps. Think about the apps you use most often—probably most of them deal with lists or grids of data. Email apps show a list of emails, Facebook shows a list of posts, Twitter shows a list of tweets, messaging apps like WhatsApp show lists of messages. In all these apps you have a scrollable list of data. You read what's on the page and then "push" the items up by swiping up on the screen to see what's below. This is a popular paradigm, so we'll use it for our Countr app, with the main part of the UI showing a list of counters.

As you've already seen, Gmail on iOS and Android have different ways for the user to create a new email—a toolbar button on iOS and a FAB on Android. We'll follow this convention in our app with the iOS version having a toolbar button to add a new counter, and the Android version having a FAB to do the same thing.

Often apps with lists use swiping to delete—email apps allow you to swipe an email to the left to display a Delete button below the email, which you can tap to delete. This paradigm would be good for deleting counters.

Another thing you see with lists is buttons against each item, allowing you to perform some action, such as retweeting a tweet in the Twitter app or liking a post in

Facebook. Again, this is a popular paradigm, so we'll use this in our Countr app to increment a counter.

Unlike with our simple SquareRt app, the Countr app will have different UIs on iOS and Android, at least when it comes to adding counters. This is something you always have to keep in mind—Xamarin allows you to build cross-platform apps, but you should always build the UIs in a way that's right for each platform. Cross-platform core, and a platform-specific UI. Don't be tempted to build one UI for both platforms—if it goes against the standard UI of one platform, it will only confuse users.

Figure 6.8 shows the different UIs we can use for this app on both iOS and Android.

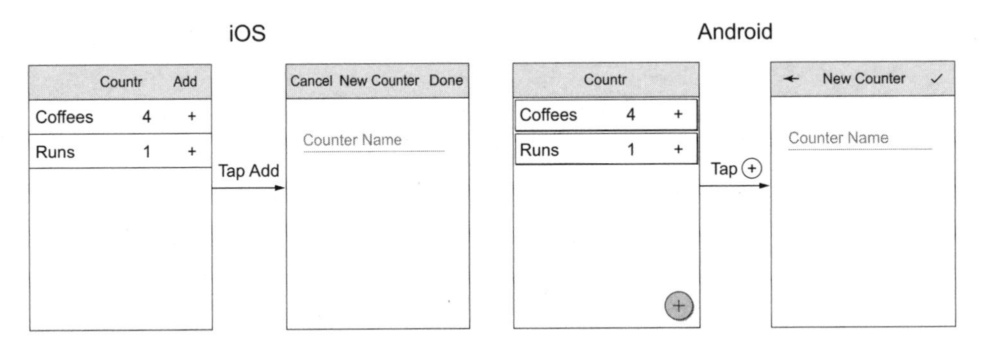

Figure 6.8 iOS and Android UIs for the Countr app with different UI conventions on each platform, such as an Add button in the toolbar on iOS, but a FAB on Android

6.2.3 Defining user flows and UIs

We've just looked at the user flows for our two example apps. But the hard part can be defining these flows, so how do you go about doing it? I like to use these steps:

1. Start by thinking about the high-level actions that the user will want to use your app for, such as counting something.
2. From these high-level actions, think about how they can get the app in a state where they can perform these actions, such as adding a counter so that they can count something, and showing all the counters to see what they can count.
3. Think about the ancillary tasks they might want to perform around this state, such as deleting a counter.
4. Think about the steps the user takes to perform each task or action, such as viewing counters, and the end results, such as seeing the counters.
5. Think about the general tasks your app needs to do in order to go from the starting point to the end result, such as loading counters from some kind of storage.

By following these steps, you should be able to build some simple flowcharts for your app, like the ones you've seen already. The flowchart should start with the high-level action the user's trying to achieve, starting from the place in your app where the user will likely be when they kick off these actions. Then it should go through one or more steps to achieve this action, either user-based steps (something the user has to do) or system steps (something the app does). Finally, it ends with a result that may or may not involve the user.

Figure 6.9 shows a simple example. The user wants to see counters, and the end result is that the counters are shown. The step required to get there is to load counters from storage.

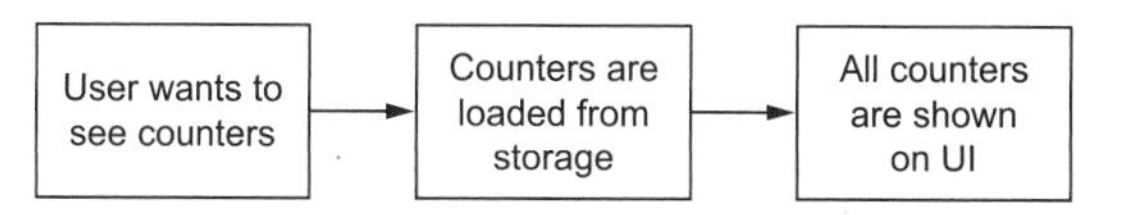

Figure 6.9 The steps for showing counters—the user wants to see them, the app loads them, the app displays them to the user.

Once you have these flows, it's easy to start mapping them to a UI. Your UI needs to provide a way to kick off each flow and provide the result. In this example, the UI needs a way to kick off loading the counters from some kind of storage when it's opened and then showing all the counters. This means you need a UI with a control that can show a collection of data, and the normal way to do this is using a vertically scrolling list control. When you're thinking about how to represent tasks and results on your app's UI, take a look at how other apps do it—sometimes there are standard ways, like lists, that you can use to make your app easy to use. After all, if you're using a popular UI paradigm, your users will probably already be used to it, so they'll be comfortable in your app.

The Countr example demonstrates that you can create cross-platform apps that have the same user flows, but with different UIs. I can't stress enough how important it is to always consider the differences between the UI paradigms on iOS and Android. Using Xamarin, you can build cross-platform apps, but that doesn't mean your apps have to be exactly the same on both platforms. It's worth spending time getting to know how each platform works so that when you design your apps, you can keep these differences in mind—even if the difference is as simple as using a FAB on Android and a toolbar button on iOS.

There are many opinions about how to build a mobile app with a good user experience—the topic is worthy of a book in its own right (such as *Usability Matters* by Matt Lacey, Manning, May 2018), but as a simple starting point I recommend looking at your app the way we've looked at our two examples. Start by considering the user flows—think about the interactions your user will have with your app. Then think about how you can map those interactions to the UI in a way that makes sense on each platform. It's also good to think about how the user can achieve each flow in as few steps as possible, in a way that makes sense on each platform.

We've now designed the user flows and sketched out the UIs, so let's look at converting these into an architecture that follows the MVVM design pattern.

6.3 Architecting the app

Now that we've worked out what the UI should be, it's time to start thinking about the architecture. As you've seen in the preceding chapters, there are three layers and two thread types to think of. You have to consider what goes in the model layer, what goes in the view-model layer, and what goes in the view layer. And for the code in the model and view-model layers, you need to consider what code needs to run on the UI thread and what can run in the background.

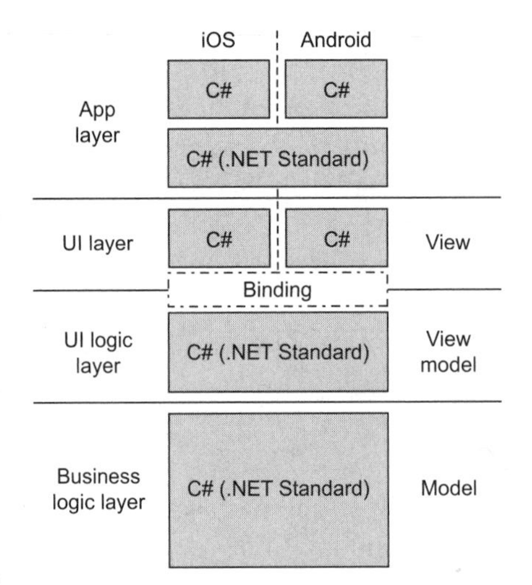

Figure 6.10 MVVM has three layers, with the view layer being platform-specific and the view-model and model layers being cross-platform.

6.3.1 Which layer?

As you start thinking about the structure of your code, you need to consider which layers the different parts of the code go in. Think back to the layer diagrams from previous chapters, as shown in figure 6.10. Remember that the code responsible for UI interactions encompasses the view layer, the view-model layer, and the binding—the view is the platform-specific UI widgets, and the view model is the cross-platform UI logic bound to the view.

SquareRt

For SquareRT, we want as much code as possible in the model and view-model layers. This is cross-platform code that's shared between the Android and iOS apps, and we only want to write it once and reuse it on both platforms.

Let's see how the SquareRt app code can be divided up between layers. We can take the user flow we've defined and map it across the layers. This is shown in figure 6.11.

What we see from this exercise is that we need one view with a control that a user can enter text into and one control to show the result. We also need a corresponding view model that can bind to those controls, and a model layer that can do the calculation. This very quickly leads to three classes that are the main structure of our app, as shown in figure 6.12.

Countr

Let's repeat the same exercise with our Countr app, mapping the flows we've already defined into our three MVVM layers. This is shown in figures 6.13 and 6.14.

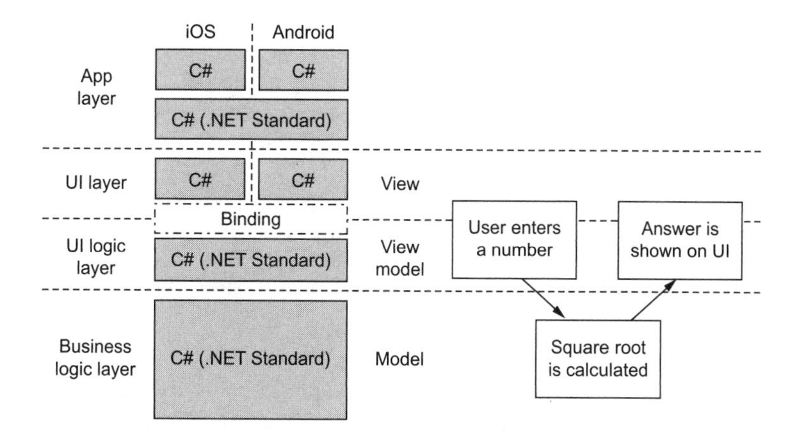

Figure 6.11 User flows can map to the MVVM layers, with user interactions spanning the view and view-model layers.

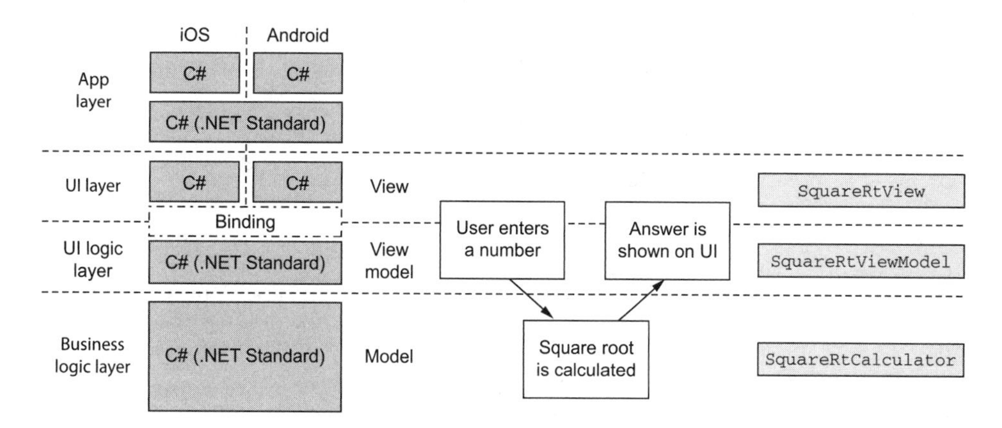

Figure 6.12 Once you've mapped user flows to the MVVM layers, you can map classes to these as well.

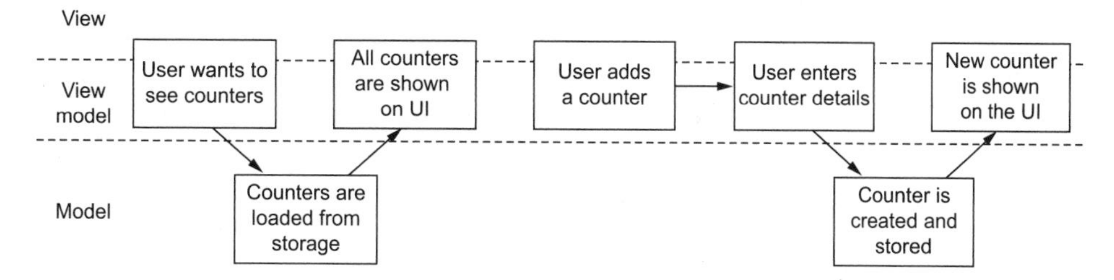

Figure 6.13 Mapping showing and adding counters to the view, view-model, and model layers

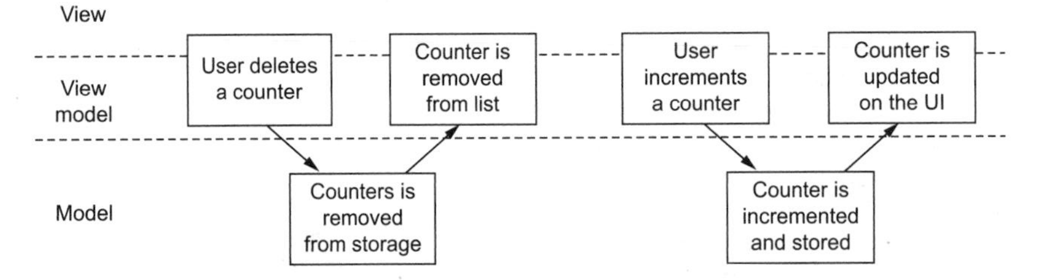

Figure 6.14 Mapping incrementing and deleting counters to the view, view-model, and model layers

Again, just like with SquareRt, you can see a pattern of classes in these layers. We need to display a list of counters that can be manipulated (such as adding and deleting them), so we need a view and view model for the UI, as well as some kind of service class in the model layer that stores and retrieves the counters from some kind of storage. We also need something in the UI to add a new counter and enter its details, so we need a view and view model for this new counter. This gives us the classes shown in figure 6.15.

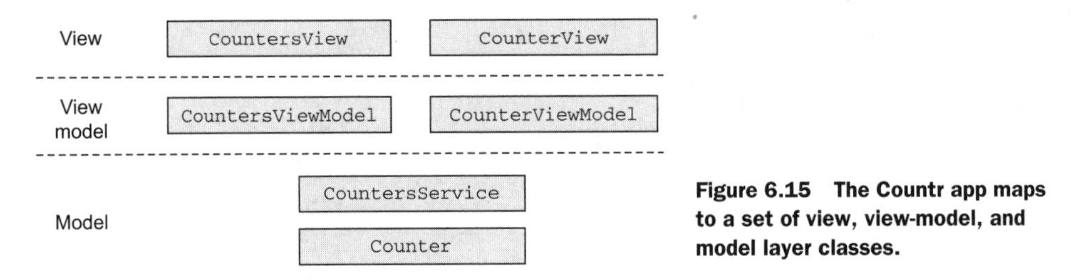

Figure 6.15 The Countr app maps to a set of view, view-model, and model layer classes.

DIVIDING APPS INTO LAYERS

Once you've worked out your user flows, it should be obvious which parts of the flow involve the UI and which parts don't. Any direct interaction with the user needs some kind of UI, and anything else doesn't. This means it's relatively simple to map user flows to the MVVM layers. Anything that involves the UI lives in the view and view-model layers (the UI in the view layer, and the state and behavior in view models), and the core business logic lives in the model layer. Your flow could switch between layers as many times as necessary—user does *x*, app does *y* in the background, it asks the user to confirm on the UI thread, does *z* in the background, and then shows the user a result.

The process of adding a counter needs something in the UI layer that the user can interact with to start the add flow, such as an Add button in the view and a command to handle it in a view model. Next, the user needs to give the counter a name, so there needs to be some kind of UI, such as a new screen with a text box where the user can enter the name, and a corresponding view model to get this name. Then the app needs to create the counter and store it somewhere, and this is handled in the model layer. Finally, the user needs to see the new counter in the list, so the UI for showing the list of counters needs to be updated, which means an update in a list of counters stored in a view model, which is reflected in a view.

6.3.2 *Which thread?*

We've divided our example apps up into layers to match the MVVM design pattern, so the next thing to do is think about multithreading. As you saw in the previous chapter, it's important that our app remains responsive, so we should start thinking now about what thread our code runs on.

There's a very simple rule to follow here—if the UI lags or is unresponsive for more than about 200 ms, the user will notice a perceptible lag. More than this and it feels like the app has locked up, and it can take only a few seconds before a user is fed up waiting and kills your app. You should always run any action that could take more than about 100 ms on a background thread.

Of course, this isn't always easy to judge, especially when you're in the process of developing your app. Most developers have high-powered versions of the latest and greatest devices, but most users don't. What takes 50 ms on your top-of-the-range iPhone 7 might take 500 ms on an old iPhone 4s. Making a web call might be almost instantaneous when calling a development web service running on your development machine and accessing it over WiFi, but it might take multiple seconds in the real world using 3G.

Here are some good basic guidelines:

1. Always test on a poor device—you can pick up older devices for not very much money, either through clearance sales or secondhand from sites like eBay or Craigslist. It's worth having a device with the lowest specs you want to support for testing.
2. Always assume anything involving the network will run slowly, so always make network calls on a background thread.
3. When storing anything locally, or retrieving anything from a database such as SQLite (a popular mobile database that comes as part of iOS and Android) or from a file, always do this in the background.
4. If you're not sure, do it in the background.

A good way to work out which code needs to run on the UI thread or a background thread is to take each task and ask yourself a few questions: does it involve the UI, does it need external resources, is it slow? Figure 6.16 shows a flowchart for this.

If you map your user flows by following this flowchart, you should be able to easily work out in which thread your code should be run.

ANDROID HAS A TOOL THAT CAN HELP CHECK YOUR CODE Android has a strict mode that you can enable to get feedback on your code, to see if it's running in the correct thread. You can use this to get feedback about whether an action is taking too long on the UI thread. There are more details on `StrictMode` in the Android developer's reference: http://mng.bz/nDI5.

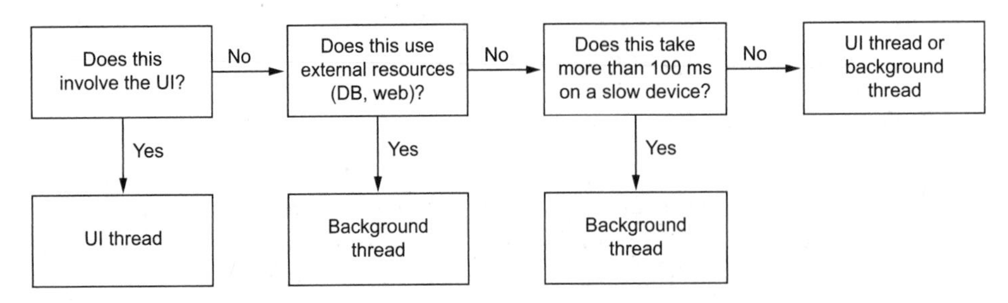

Figure 6.16 If your code involves the UI, it needs to run on the UI thread, but if it uses external resources or is slow, it should run on a background thread.

When using third-party code, such as NuGet packages or Xamarin components, it's always good to check whether the code has any async methods. For example, if you use `HttpClient` from the `System.Net.Http` namespace in the .NET Framework, you'll see it has methods like `GetAsync`, which returns a `Task<HttpResponseMessage>`. Whenever an async method is exposed, you can usually be sure that internally it will create a `Task` to run long-running actions on a background thread. You can await this from the UI thread, and your app should remain responsive because the `HttpClient` handles the threading for you. Obviously, there are no guarantees, so it's good to check the behavior first.

Let's now think about the threading requirements of our example apps. We'll take each user flow and consider what needs to happen to achieve it. From there, we can work out if each part of the flow needs to run on a background thread.

SQUARERT

The user flow for the SquareRt app has three parts—two that involve the UI (getting the initial number and showing the result), and one that involves a calculation. Although this is a relatively complex calculation, it's pretty quick—it will run in fractions of a millisecond, so we don't have to think about background threads at all. Everything can run on the UI thread (figure 6.17).

COUNTR

Unlike SquareRt, Countr does a bit more than just a single calculation. It includes a simple calculation—incrementing a counter, which could be run on the UI thread

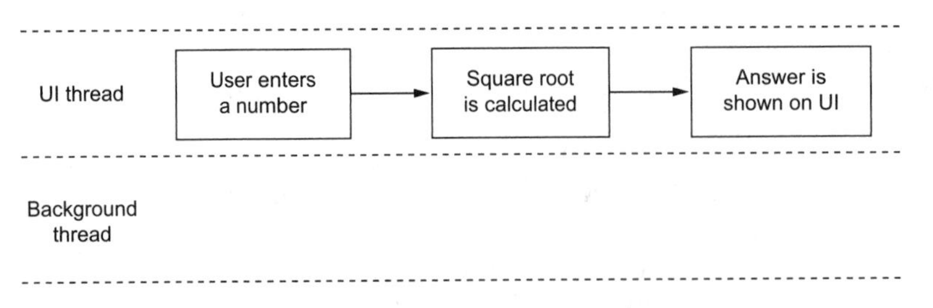

Figure 6.17 The SquareRt app doesn't do anything that needs to run in a background thread.

without any issues—but "storage" is the key word in these user flows when thinking about threading. We haven't discussed the storage of data yet (we'll look at storage in the next chapter), but any kind of storage involves making a call to something potentially slow. If you write to a SQLite database, or a file, or a web service, it's good practice to do it in a background thread to shield your UI from anything that might make it unresponsive.

FILESYSTEM ACCESS CAN BE SLOW It's often assumed that saving files by writing to flash memory in a mobile app is fast, because the hardware involved is pretty quick. Although this is generally true, the flash memory has a filesystem on top of it that may not be the best at handling concurrency. If it's busy performing a large file operation, such as saving a downloaded update, your fast disk access might wait a short time before running, making the save take longer than expected.

In the user flows, you can do anything that involves the UI on the UI thread, and anything that involves storage on a background thread. Even though the calculation to increment a counter is fast, we still need to think about doing it on a background thread because the result of the calculation will need to be stored. Figure 6.18 shows how the incrementing of a counter would be handled across the UI thread and a background thread.

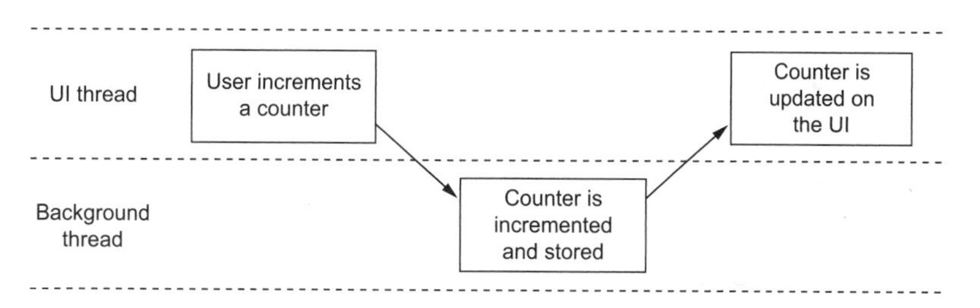

Figure 6.18 The Countr app needs to access storage, so it's better to do this on a background thread before coming back to the UI thread to display the results.

6.3.3 *Mapping code to layers and threads*

We've looked at how to map user flows onto MVVM layers and threads, and this is a good exercise to go through as you start out building cross-platform mobile apps. Figure 6.19 shows a layout you can use to help map your user flows and code. Print out or photocopy a few copies, or grab the SVG version from this book's Git repository to use with your favorite drawing tool if you'd like to save paper.

You should start by thinking about the distinct actions your user would want to perform with your app, as we've discussed. Then break them apart into separate steps—what would a user do step by step, and what would the app do step by step. Draw these flows on the diagram, thinking about which layer each should go into—UI interactions go on the view layer with the corresponding view model, and steps the app takes

View	UI thread	
View Model	UI thread	
	Background thread	
Model	UI thread	
	Background thread	

Figure 6.19 To help work out which layer or thread to use, try mapping your user flows on this diagram.

internally go in the model layer. As you put things into the view-model and model layers, think about the threading—should they be on the UI thread or a background thread? Steps that need external resources or that are slow always go on a background thread.

Have a go at mapping our two example apps using this diagram and the flows defined earlier (check appendix A to see how I did it). Then think about your own app ideas and try mapping those. If you've used MVVM before and built UI-based apps, you might find that you already think about these layers and threads automatically, so you don't need to use this diagram. But if this is all new to you, it's a good reference point.

Now that we've thought about how to put the code in the correct layers and threads, we're ready to create our solutions. It's time to fire up Visual Studio on your platform of choice and get ready to code!

6.4 Creating the solutions

Once you've created a rough app architecture based on the sort of classes you want, what layer those classes represent, and what thread your code should run on, it's time to fire up your IDE and create the actual solutions. In the rest of this chapter, we're going to create solutions much like we built the Hello Cross-Platform World example in earlier chapters. Then we'll look at at some new concepts that are important in mobile app development—app property files, SDK versions, and linking.

Everything in the remainder of this chapter is relevant to both SquareRt and Countr, and over the next few chapters we'll start writing the code to turn the new solutions into fully working apps. We'll just be creating the solution for SquareRt here, but everything we'll discuss is relevant to both apps, so repeat the process for Countr when you're done with SquareRt.

The first thing to do is to create a new solution. We'll be using the same Visual Studio extension we used in chapter 2 and creating the same project type. Name your project SquareRt (or come up with your own name, of course). In Visual Studio for Mac, create an MvvmCross Single Page Native Application from the Other > .NET section. On Windows, choose MvvmCross Single Page Native Application under Visual C# > MvvmCross, and delete the Universal Windows and WPF projects.

Now that you have your solution, let's take a look at some of the ways that the projects in this solution will differ from what you've seen before in C# projects, such as desktop or ASP.NET web applications. Mobile apps are different from other C# applications—they run on devices with limited hardware and with an OS that changes dramatically every year. This means your apps need to be very aware of the OS version and what APIs are available, as well as be as small as possible. They also expose a whole raft of properties to the OS and app stores via a file in the app package that provides information about your app. Let's start by looking at how these app properties are set.

6.5 Application properties

When you build and ship your mobile app, you have to bundle some information inside your app. This is used by both the relevant app store and the OS to get information about your app, such as its name, icon, supported OS version, and app version number. Both iOS and Android ship an XML file containing this information.

We'll look at a number of these properties here, but not the app icon. Mobile apps have to run on devices of all shapes and sizes, so there are some complications when it comes to images, and we'll look at these for Android in chapter 9 and iOS in chapter 11.

6.5.1 Android manifest

The AndroidManifest.xml file in the Properties folder of the solution is shipped with your app package and provides information about your app to the Google Play Store and the Android OS. This includes which SDK version you're targeting (more on this later in the chapter), what permissions your app needs, the app's name, its version, ID, and icon. In a native Java Android application built using Android Studio from Google, the manifest will also contain information about the classes that make up your app.

Luckily, as Xamarin developers, we don't need to worry about explicitly adding this information to the manifest XML file. Instead we mark the relevant classes with attributes, and these get added automatically to the copy of the manifest file that's packaged inside the compiled application at build time. Again, this will be covered in chapter 9, but you may have seen this already in the `FirstView` activity in the FirstView.cs file in the Views folder of the Android app—this class was marked with an `Activity` attribute (`[Activity(Label = "…")]`), indicating that at build time it should be added to the manifest as an activity with a particular label.

Although this is an XML file, there's really no need to manually edit the XML. Visual Studio comes with an editor for this: you can access it in Visual Studio for Mac from the Project Options dialog or by double-clicking the AndroidManifest.xml file in the Properties folder (figure 6.20); on Windows you can access it from the project Properties tab (right-click the app and select Properties). If you open it by double-clicking the file in the Solution Pad in Visual Studio for Mac, it opens in a tab with two subtabs—one to edit the file using the same editor as the Project Options dialog, and the other showing the raw XML (figure 6.20). In Visual Studio, double-clicking the file in the Solution Explorer opens a tab with just the raw XML.

There are several items of interest to us now:

- Application name
- Package name
- Version number
- Version name
- Required permissions

The AndroidManifest.xml file lives in the Properties folder.

Figure 6.20 The Android Manifest file in the Solution Pad and in the editor

APPLICATION NAME

The application name is the name of your application both in the Google Play Store and on your device. You'll notice in figure 6.20 that this is set to `@string/Application-Name`, which is a resource reference. You'll see these a lot in Android apps—rather than hard-code a value, you reference a resource. These resources are in the Resources folder, which contains a subfolder called values containing an XML file, string.xml. If you open this file, you'll see the following.

Listing 6.1 strings.xml contains strings that can be used anywhere in your app

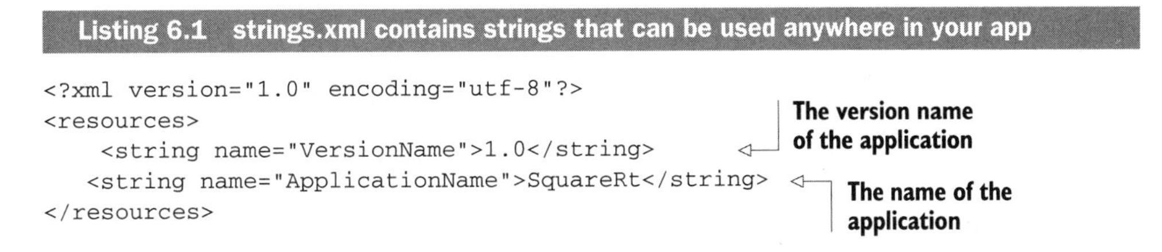

```
<?xml version="1.0" encoding="utf-8"?>
<resources>
    <string name="VersionName">1.0</string>
   <string name="ApplicationName">SquareRt</string>
</resources>
```


If you want to rename the app, you can edit the value of `ApplicationName` in this XML file, and the app will automatically be renamed next time you compile.

We'll cover these more in chapter 9, but the main reason for using resource files for storing values is so that you can localize your app easily. In this example we only have one strings.xml file, but you can have multiple resources based on the locale of the app's user—one file for U.S. English users, one for Chinese users, one for French users, and so on. By containing all your strings in one file, it's easy to get your app translated—there's only one XML file to translate. Localization is outside the scope of this book, but you can find more information in Android's "Localizing with Resources" API guide: http://mng.bz/fb7Y.

PACKAGE NAME

The package name is the unique name for your application package, and it's used to identify your app on the Google Play Store. When you want to push app updates to the store, this package name identifies which app is being updated. The normal form for this name is to use your company or personal domain name reversed, suffixed with an identifier for your app. For example, if I were creating this app for publication, I'd have a package name of `io.jimbobbennett.squarert`. Once your app has been published to the store, you can't change this value, or the Play store will think you're publishing a different app.

Unlike the application name, there's no need to define this in the strings.xml file because this will never change to match a locale. Once this name is set and your app is published, you can't change it, so be sure to set it correctly before publishing.

VERSION NUMBER

This is the version number of your package (also referred to in the XML as the version code). This number is used by the Google Play Store and the device to track upgrades—if the package on the store has a higher version number than the one on the device, the app can be upgraded. You can only push to the store an updated package with a higher version number than the one already in the store—it doesn't have to be 1 higher, you can increment it by however much you want, it just needs to be higher.

There's a limit on this number—it's a large limit (2,100,000,000 to be exact), but it can easily be reached if you use automated build tools that increment this number or set it to values based on the current time or source code revision number. Once it's reached, you can no longer upgrade your app, so be careful with large numbers.

VERSION NAME

This is your internal version name for your app, and it's a string that can be set in the manifest or in the string.xml resource file, as shown earlier in listing 6.1. Most developers use a multipart version so that they can internally track releases. You can set this to whatever is relevant to you.

REQUIRED PERMISSIONS

When you're building mobile apps, you can closely integrate your app with the features of the device as well as with other apps that come built into the OS, such as a camera, contacts, and calendars. Obviously, there are privacy concerns with this—you wouldn't want a malicious app accessing your private details and uploading them to a server somewhere, so both Android and iOS require your app to request permissions from the user before you can do certain things. Android has a changing permission model—on older OS versions, you'd specify the permissions you needed in the application manifest, and at install time the user would be prompted to give your app these permissions (and, at update time, if your app needed new permissions, the user would be asked to confirm them before updating). In newer versions of the Android OS, you can also ask for some permissions at runtime, explicitly popping up a dialog asking the user's consent before doing something.

The required permissions section allows you to request permissions up front by ticking the boxes against the permissions that your app requires. These permissions are shown to the user at install time, and the user has to agree to them before your app can be installed. It's always good to request as few permissions as you need, or users might refuse to install your app. Certainly any permissions that don't appear relevant will cause a user to pause before installing. For example, our SquareRt app doesn't need permissions to access the user's contacts or photos, and seeing a request for these permissions would definitely make a user refuse to install the app!

6.5.2 iOS info.plist

Like Android, iOS also has a properties file that ships with the app package, called info.plist (*plist* is short for *property list*). The info.plist file can be edited using a built-in editor by double-clicking the file (figure 6.21), or on Visual Studio on Windows from the iOS App project Properties tab.

The info.plist file in the iOS app contains the application settings that the OS needs to know about, such as the name, icons, supported orientations (portrait or landscape). This is an XML file that you can modify directly if you're so inclined, but Visual Studio has an editor that makes it easy to manipulate. The editor has three tabs: Application, which allows you to change the main application settings; Advanced, which configures things like the document types your app supports for extensions or URL types so your app can handle being launched for links; and Source, which is a key/value type editor for editing raw values without having to interact with the XML. The XML syntax isn't simple—you have to define nodes based on types, so you need to know what type to use for what value. This editor is a great help, and even the Source tab makes it easy for you by using the right types automatically.

Unlike Android, permissions aren't requested here. Instead, some permissions are granted by default (such as internet access) and others are requested at runtime.

These are the fields we care about:

- Application name
- Bundle identifier
- Version
- Build
- Devices
- Device orientations

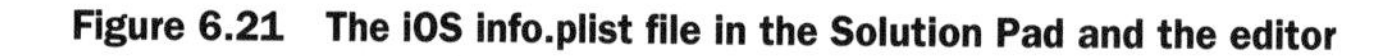

The info.plist file lives in the root of the iOS app.

Figure 6.21 The iOS info.plist file in the Solution Pad and the editor

APPLICATION NAME

As the name suggests, this is the application name that will be shown in the app store, and by default it's used as the name on the iOS SpringBoard. Unlike Android, you can't reference a string resource for this; it has to be set in the info.plist file on the Application tab. You can, however, localize it. See the "iOS Localization" Xamarin documentation for more information: http://mng.bz/6B91.

On the iOS SpringBoard, your app really doesn't have much space to display a name, and if the name is too long, it'll be truncated and end with ellipses. You can usually get 12 characters or so, but your app name might be longer.

Luckily the display name shown for your app on the SpringBoard can be different from the one shown on the store, so you can shorten it to fit. To change this, flip to the Source tab and you'll see a couple of values—Bundle Display Name and Bundle Name. Bundle Name is the name of your app on the app store, and Bundle Display Name is the name on the SpringBoard. You could set your bundle name to "SquareRt Square Root Calculator", and set the display name to "SquareRt". Be aware, though, that if you update the Application Name on the Application tab, both of these values will be updated to match.

Bundle identifier

The bundle identifier is a unique identifier for your app, and it's essentially the same as the Android package name—even down to the convention of using a reversed domain name suffixed with the app name. Once it's set on the app store, the bundle identifier can't be changed, and ideally you won't want to ever change it. Your app is signed with a certificate and a private key based on this bundle identifier, so if you change the identifier, the signing profiles won't work and will need to be re-created. We'll walk through doing this in chapter 13, but be warned, it's not a nice process!

Version

Version is a string representation of a three-part version number (usually something like major.minor.revision, such as 1.0.4) and it must be incremented each time you update the app on the store. This is the public version number that's shown on the store.

Build

Confusingly, iOS has a second one-, two-, or three-part version number that's used to define the build number. This is an internal build number, so it's not shown in iTunes, but it is used to determine if the app has been updated—just like the version code on Android. For example, if you're working on a release you want to publicly call 2.5.3, you'd submit an app with the version set to 2.5.3 and the build set to anything you like, such as 1. If this version gets rejected by Apple, you'd fix the issue and then upload a build with the same version (2.5.3) but a different build (such as 2) so that the public version stays the same but iTunes will know that you've submitted a new version.

Although this build number can consist of up to three parts, it's usually simpler to use a single build number and increment it with every build.

Devices

This field allows you to chose the type of device you want to target—iPhone, iPad, or both. This means that you can target a particular platform—for example, if you're building an app that only makes sense on a larger device, you can limit it just to iPad.

Device orientations

All mobile devices can be easily rotated, and a good app should work well in all orientations or it should be locked to one orientation (something you see a lot in games—they only work in landscape). By ticking the different boxes, you can choose which orientations to support.

6.6 SDK versions

Every year at Apple's WWDC (Worldwide Developers Conference) the senior VPs at Apple unveil the new and awesome features of the next version of iOS—the operating system for iPhones, iPads, and iPod Touches. The iPhone has been around for ten years and has seen eleven different versions of the OS in that time, going from a game-changing phone to a pocket supercomputer. The same is true for Android—fourteen versions of the OS in eight years. Currently the operating systems have a major update at least every year (more often for minor updates), and each update brings a whole range of new APIs that you can use and deprecates older ones. Each OS release comes with a newer version of the SDK providing these APIs, so new OS releases are often referred to as new SDKs. This is different from the previous OS models that C# developers would be used to—new Windows versions come out every few years, and updates to the .NET Framework are also few and far between (although this is a model that's changing, with Windows 10 having regular updates).

As a developer, you want to use the latest features where possible, but you still want to support older devices potentially running older OS versions. Supporting older OS versions is less of a concern on iOS, where within weeks of a new OS being released, the majority of users update, but it's a big concern on Android. When Google released Android, it was open source, so device manufacturers added their own features to the OS before passing it to the carriers who also sometimes added their own features. This means that when Google releases a new version of Android, or even a security patch, not every device can install the update straightaway. Instead they have to wait for the manufacturer to update their version, and possibly for the carrier to issue an update as well. For new devices this does happen, but for older devices that are no longer made, the updates may never be available. This results in the Android ecosystem being particularly fragmented.

iOS 10 was released in September 2016, and by November it was on 79% of devices (figure 6.22), iOS 9 was on 17%, and the remaining 4% were on older OS versions (data from Mixpanel, https://mixpanel.com/trends/). This means most app developers can target the most recent two versions (iOS 9 and 10 at the time of writing), and not worry about their app working on earlier versions.

On the other side of the mobile fence, the picture is not so rosy—Android Nougat has been out for the same length of time but is on less than 1% of devices (figure 6.23), with the majority being on Marshmallow, Lollipop, and even 19% of users on KitKat. Not only are users on older versions, but most of these users won't be able to upgrade—for example, I have a two-year-old tablet purchased from a major retailer in

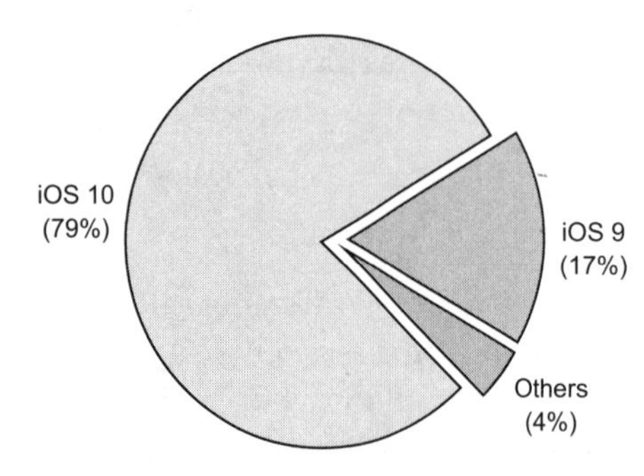

Figure 6.22 iOS users upgrade often, with 79% of users being on the latest iOS version two months after launch.

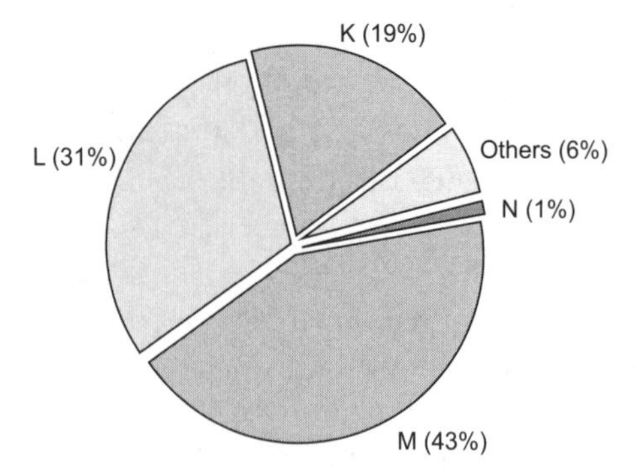

Figure 6.23 Android users don't (or can't) upgrade as often as iOS users, with 1% being on the latest Android version two months after launch.

the UK that's running Android Lollipop and will never be updated. This means that, as cross-platform mobile developers, we need to support a lot more versions of Android than we do of iOS.

6.6.1 Android SDK versions and the SDK manager

When you install Xamarin, it will also install the Android SDK for you. These are the libraries and tools used by Xamarin to compile Android apps, and they're the same tools that the native development IDE (Android Studio) uses.

You can see what's installed by going to Tools > SDK Manager from Visual Studio for Mac, or going to Tools > Android > Android SDK Manager from Visual Studio in Windows. This will load the Android SDK Manager, showing what versions of the Android tools and SDKs are installed, as well as the images for creating Android emulators. From here you can download new SDKs, download new emulator images, and update the versions of the build tools.

One of the downsides of Xamarin development is that there are a lot of moving pieces, some controlled by Xamarin, and others not (such as the Android SDKs). This means it's easy to get weird errors just by using combinations of the different tools that don't quite work together. As a general rule, I find it better to keep the SDK up to date with the latest stable version.

Android SDKs are referred to in three different ways—by version number, by API level (which can cover multiple version numbers), or by alphabetical confectionary-based nickname (with some names covering multiple API levels). This is as confusing as it sounds, and developers will mix and match their terminology. Google only supports (as in, provides security patches for) KitKat and above, and at the time of writing the latest version generally available is Nougat (with Oreo being rolled out to a limited set of Google devices). Table 6.1 shows how the names match up to API levels and to versions for the most recent versions.

Table 6.1 The different Android code names, API levels, and versions for the most recent and popular versions

Name	API level	Version
Jelly Bean	16–18	4.1–4.3.1
KitKat	19	4.4–4.4.4
Lollipop	21–22	5.0–5.1.1
Marshmallow	23	6.0–6.0.1
Nougat	24–25	7.0–7.1.1
Oreo	26	8.0

IMPROVEMENTS WITH APPCOMPAT AND GOOGLE PLAY SERVICES It's not all bad in the Android world. Google is working to back-port new features to older Android versions using a thing called AppCompat (providing libraries for using newer features on old OS versions) and by moving out a lot of the core APIs into a set of Google services called Google Play Services. This means you can still access newer features on older devices. This will be covered more in chapter 9.

SETTING THE ANDROID SDK VERSION FOR THE APP

As already mentioned, the APIs available to Android developers change over time. Nothing is ever deleted; instead, out-of-date APIs are marked as obsolete and new APIs are added. For example, Android has a text-to-speech class, `TextToSpeech` (http://mng.bz/T5u2). This has a method on it called `Speak` with two overrides. One override was added in API 21, and the other was deprecated as of API 21. Not only was it deprecated, but it also no longer works on devices running Lollipop (API 21) or above.

When you build a Xamarin Android app, you can choose three different Android SDK versions—the one to build against, the minimum your app should support, and the target version that your app is intended to run against:

- The minimum API is used at install time—the Google Play store won't let users install an app that has the minimum set to a version higher than the device is using.
- The build version is the SDK that's used when compiling, so you can only use APIs that are available in that version.
- The target version is used at runtime to ensure that everything works smoothly.

With the `TextToSpeech` API, if you wanted to use it in an app that supports KitKat and above, you'd need to set your minimum version to API 19, and then compile against a later version. This way your app will run on any device with KitKat and above, but you'd be able to call both APIs. Xamarin only binds the libraries from API 15 and above—you can target older versions if you want, and your app should run, but the compiler won't check that APIs that don't exist on those versions aren't called.

Obviously there's a problem here—there are two different overrides of a method: one that only runs on APIs 19 and 20, and one that only runs on APIs 21 and above. What can you do? First, when a method is deprecated, it's marked with the C# `Obsolete` attribute, so if you're compiling against a later SDK, you'll get a compiler warning if you call this method. This can really help you see what's no longer available, and this is a good reason to have warnings set to errors on your release builds! Second, you can query the SDK version at runtime and call different code depending on which OS version you're running against. The following listing shows an example of this.

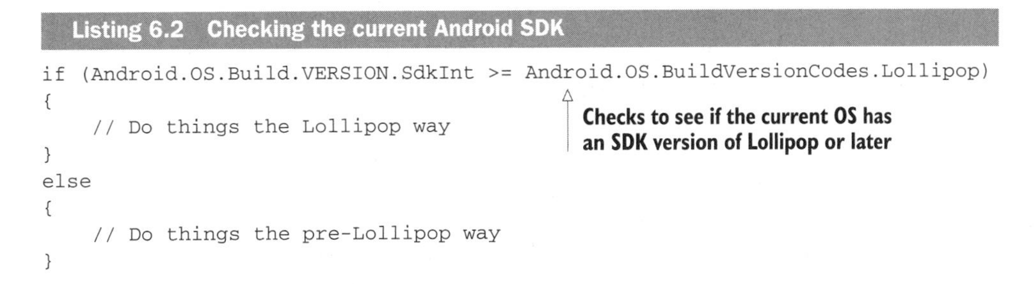

Listing 6.2 Checking the current Android SDK

```
if (Android.OS.Build.VERSION.SdkInt >= Android.OS.BuildVersionCodes.Lollipop)
{
    // Do things the Lollipop way
}
else
{
    // Do things the pre-Lollipop way
}
```

Checks to see if the current OS has an SDK version of Lollipop or later

A check is made against the current OS build, and if it's Lollipop or later, one code branch is run. If not, another is run. In the Lollipop and higher branch, the new `Speak` method is called; in the branch for versions prior to Lollipop, the old override can be called (and wrapped in an appropriate `#pragma` directive to suppress the warning).

> **Warnings should be errors in release builds**
>
> Warnings are the compiler's way of suggesting something might be wrong, such as a field being declared but not used, a variable being compared to itself in an `if` statement, or a deprecated API being used.
>
> To keep your code clean, it's advisable to set all warnings as errors for your release builds so that you can't compile an app for release without fixing all warnings. You can set this by ticking Treat Warnings as Errors in the Compile tab of the project Properties tab (project Options dialog for Visual Studio for Mac) for release builds. For debug builds, this doesn't matter so much, because it's easy to get warnings during development that you'll clean up once your code is ready.
>
> If you get a warning that you want to ignore instead of having it as an error (such as calling an obsolete API inside an SDK version check), you can wrap the offending line of code in a directive to tell the compiler to ignore it:
>
> ```
> #pragma warning disable
> // call obsolete code here
> #pragma warning restore
> ```
>
> Tells the compiler to ignore all warnings from here onwards (`#pragma warning disable`)
>
> Tells the compiler to stop ignoring warnings from here onwards (`#pragma warning restore`)
>
> You can read more about this in Microsoft's C# Guide, at http://mng.bz/8f0K.

Let's look at this example in the context of the three different versions:

- *Target framework*—This is the version of the Android SDK you're compiling against. You can only use APIs that are available in this version. If you use an API that wasn't introduced until a later version, your app won't compile. Normally this is set to Use Latest Installed Platform, which means that it will compile against the latest version that's installed from the Android SDK manager.

- *Minimum Android version*—This is the lowest Android version that your app will support. Your app won't be available to devices with a lower version, so those users won't be able to install it from the Google Play store. This doesn't mean that there are any compiler checks to ensure it will work—you can have your target as a later version and call APIs that aren't available in the minimum version. In this case your app will crash, so you need to make sure that if you call any newer APIs, you use runtime SDK checks, like the one shown in listing 6.2.
- *Target Android version*—This is the version of the SDK that you've tested your application against. This tells the Android OS not to enable any compatibility behaviors to help your app work. This is outside the scope of this book, and it's easiest to leave this as Automatic, to use the same version as the target framework.

SETTING THE SDK VERSIONS USING VISUAL STUDIO FOR MAC

The target framework is a compiler setting, so this is set in the project options. You can access this by double-clicking on your project in the Solution Pad (SquareRt .Droid or Countr.Droid for this chapter's examples), or by right-clicking the project, selecting Options, and then selecting the General tab from the Build section (figure 6.24).

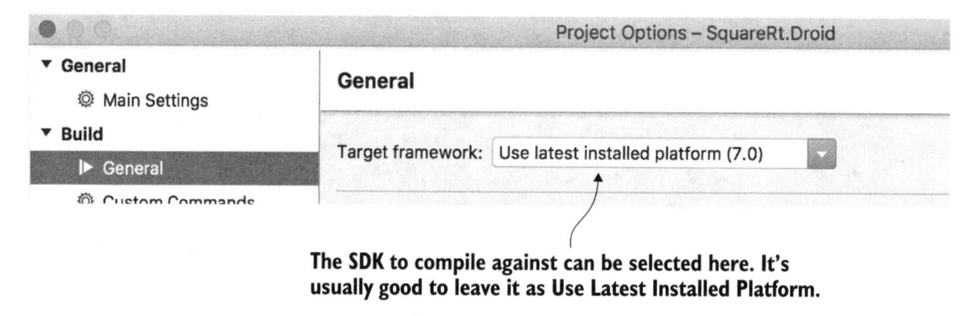

Figure 6.24 The SDK to compile against can be chosen from the Project Options.

The minimum Android version and target SDK version aren't used at compile time. Instead, they're checked at install time and runtime, which means they need to be set in the Android manifest file (figure 6.25).

The two settings we care about in this file are the Minimum Android Version and Target Android Version. The minimum should be set to the lowest version you want to support. Unless there's a particular API your app needs to use, I recommend setting this to KitKat to target the most devices. This is the default setting for new Xamarin Android apps. The target should be left as Automatic to use the latest installed platform.

SETTING THE SDK VERSIONS USING VISUAL STUDIO FOR WINDOWS

Unlike Visual Studio for Mac, Windows Visual Studio doesn't have an explicit editor for the AndroidManifest.xml file. Instead you can set the SDK versions from the project

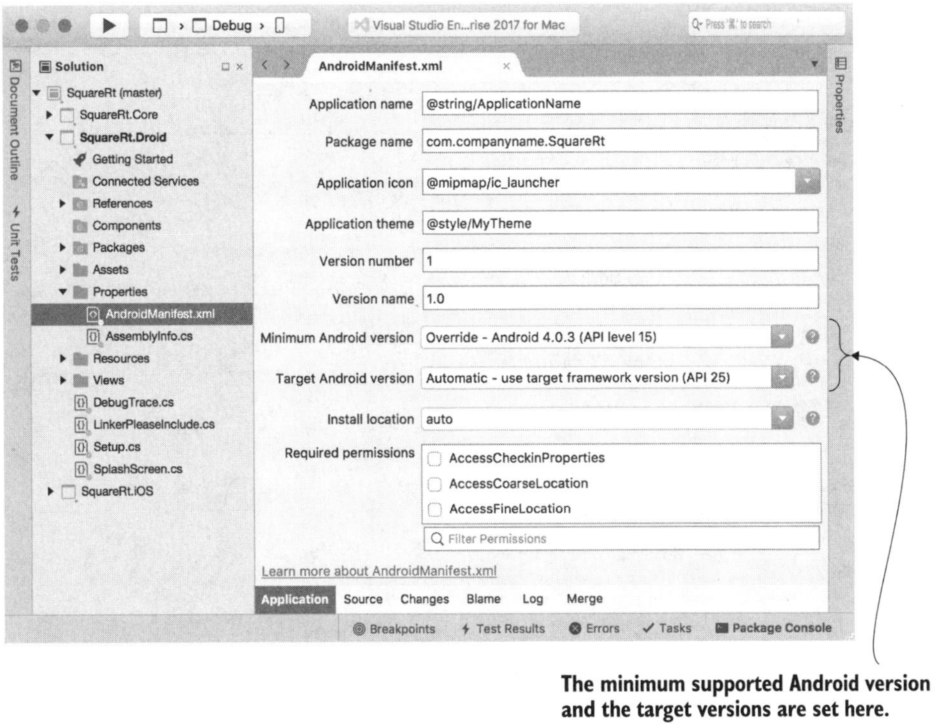

The minimum supported Android version and the target versions are set here.

Figure 6.25 The Android manifest editor

Properties tab (figure 6.26). Open these by right-clicking the project in the Solution Explorer (SquareRt.Droid or Countr.Droid in this chapter) and selecting Properties, or by selecting the project and pressing Alt-Enter. From the properties, select the Application tab to configure the Target Framework to compile against, and select the Android Manifest tab to configure the minimum and target SDK versions.

RUNNING AGAINST A PARTICULAR SDK VERSION

When Xamarin is installed, it will install the Android SDK for you. In the process, it will install some system images for different Android devices and create emulators for them using a version of the SDK that may not be the latest. The installed version may vary over time, so it's always worth installing the latest available stable SDK (at the time of writing this is 26—Oreo). Each year Google will roll out a new version starting with a beta version of the SDK, so unless you need to test against this beta, you should avoid installing and using it.

At the time of writing, Xamarin creates emulators running Marshmallow (API 23). This means that when you run your Android app, you can run it on an emulator targeting Marshmallow (figure 6.27)—you already did this back in chapter 2 when testing out the Hello Cross-Platform World app.

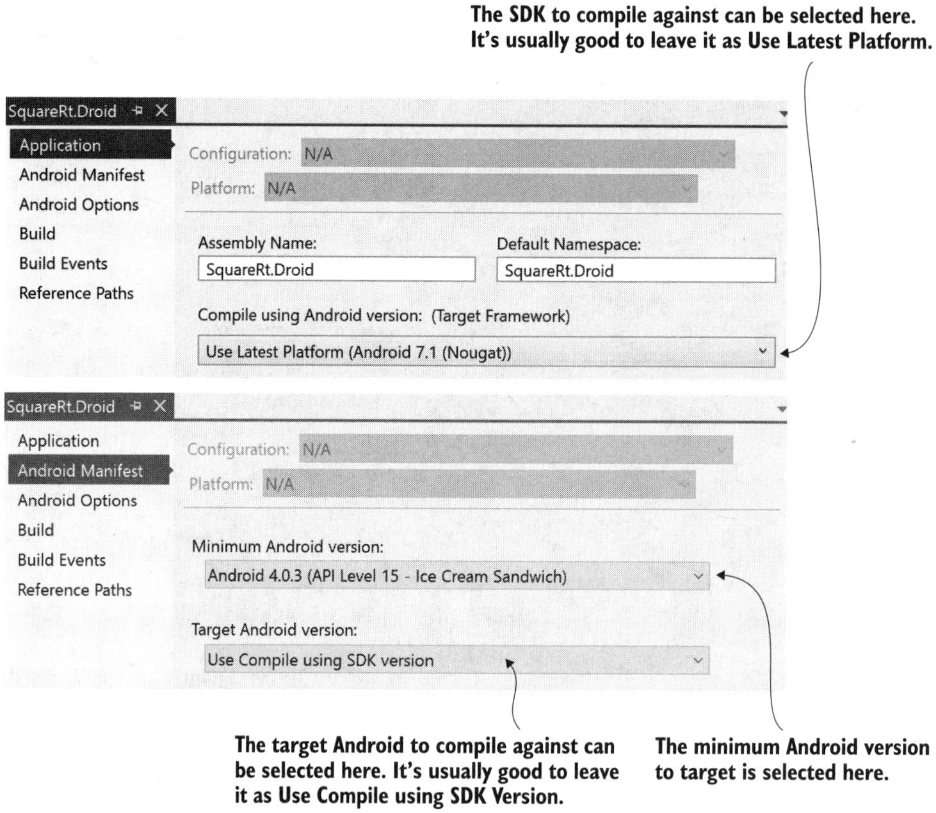

Figure 6.26 The Visual Studio Android properties

You can find more information on configuring emulators in the "Android SDK Emulator" section of the Xamarin documentation, including how to create emulators using different versions of the SDK (http://mng.bz/4CZX).

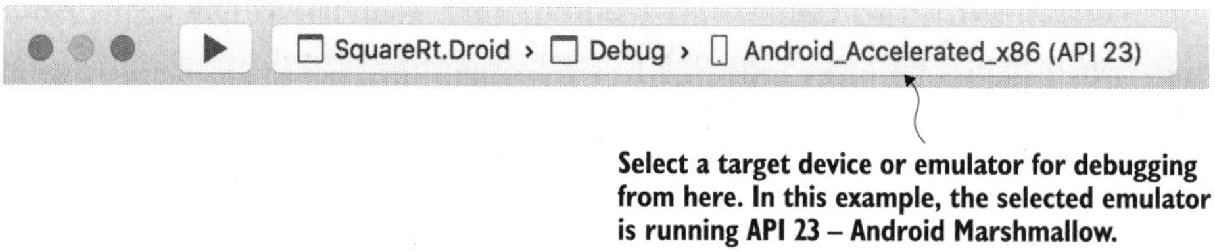

Select a target device or emulator for debugging from here. In this example, the selected emulator is running API 23 – Android Marshmallow.

Figure 6.27 Setting the target Android device

6.6.2 iOS SDK versions

Setting iOS SDK versions is much, much simpler than Android. For starters, the OS names match the SDK versions, and there's only one version number, not a version number, API level, and highly sugary codename. When you build iOS apps, you always build against the latest SDK; the only option you have is to choose the minimum version that your app will support. On iOS you only need to support two versions—the latest and the previous. This will cover a large proportion of the iOS user base. This is helped by the fact that Apple supplies the latest SDK version and will only accept submissions of apps to the store using a recent version of the SDK.

Where Android has an SDK manager to allow you to install multiple versions of the Android SDK, iOS has a much simpler model. Apple always wants you to use the latest SDK version, and that's pretty much all you can install. Every time you update Xcode (Apple's development environment that contains the tools Xamarin needs to build iOS apps) you always get the latest SDK to compile against, and the macOS App Store will always try to keep you on the latest version of Xcode. The way to compile against older versions of the SDK is to install older versions of Xcode, something that Apple doesn't support.

That's compiling taken care of—you always compile against the latest version of the SDK. As with Android, though, your apps can run on older versions of the SDK. You can control the minimum version that's supported, and you can check at runtime what OS your app is running on and call the relevant APIs.

SETTING THE MINIMUM SUPPORTED SDK

To control the minimum supported version, you can set the Deployment Target in your iOS app's info.plist file. This file lives in the root of the iOS app, and if you double-click it, it will open in a property editor. You can edit the raw XML if you want, but it's a complicated schema, so it's easier to use the property editor.

The field of interest here is the Deployment Target. From this drop-down list you can choose the minimum iOS version to support (figure 6.28). Once this is set, your app will only be able to be installed and run on devices running that version of iOS or higher. Users on a lower version won't be able to install your app.

As with Android, APIs don't go away when a new version of the OS SDK is released—they're always available, but they're deprecated when they're no longer supported. Again, as with Android, you can see if you're using a deprecated API by checking for compiler warnings. You can also check the OS version at runtime and call the relevant version of the API depending on what OS version your app is running under, as shown in listing 6.3.

Select the minimum iOS version to target by choosing a Deployment Target.

Figure 6.28 The Deployment Target can be set in the info.plist file.

Listing 6.3 Checking the current iOS SDK

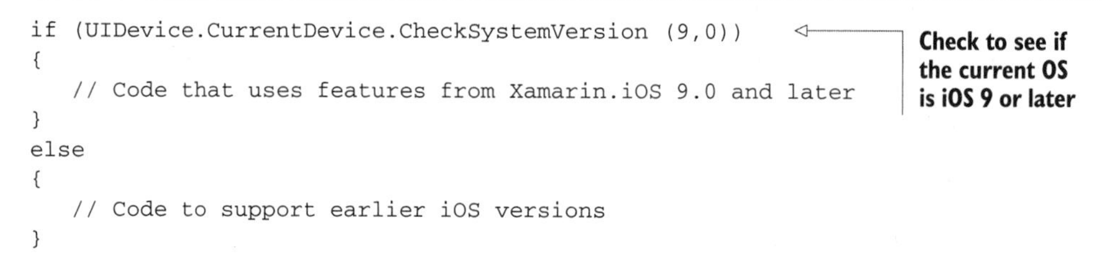

```
if (UIDevice.CurrentDevice.CheckSystemVersion (9,0))
{
   // Code that uses features from Xamarin.iOS 9.0 and later
}
else
{
   // Code to support earlier iOS versions
}
```

Check to see if the current OS is iOS 9 or later

RUNNING AGAINST THE IOS SDK

When you launch your iOS app against the simulator, the simulator will default to using the latest iOS version you have installed. This is because Xcode always installs the latest versions of the SDK only, by default. If you want to test on earlier versions, you can download simulators using Xcode, but you're limited in how far back you can go—at the time of writing, iOS 10 has been out for a couple of months, and the oldest simulator you can install is one running iOS 8.1. To install older versions from Xcode, go to Xcode > Preferences and select the Components tab. This is shown in figure 6.29.

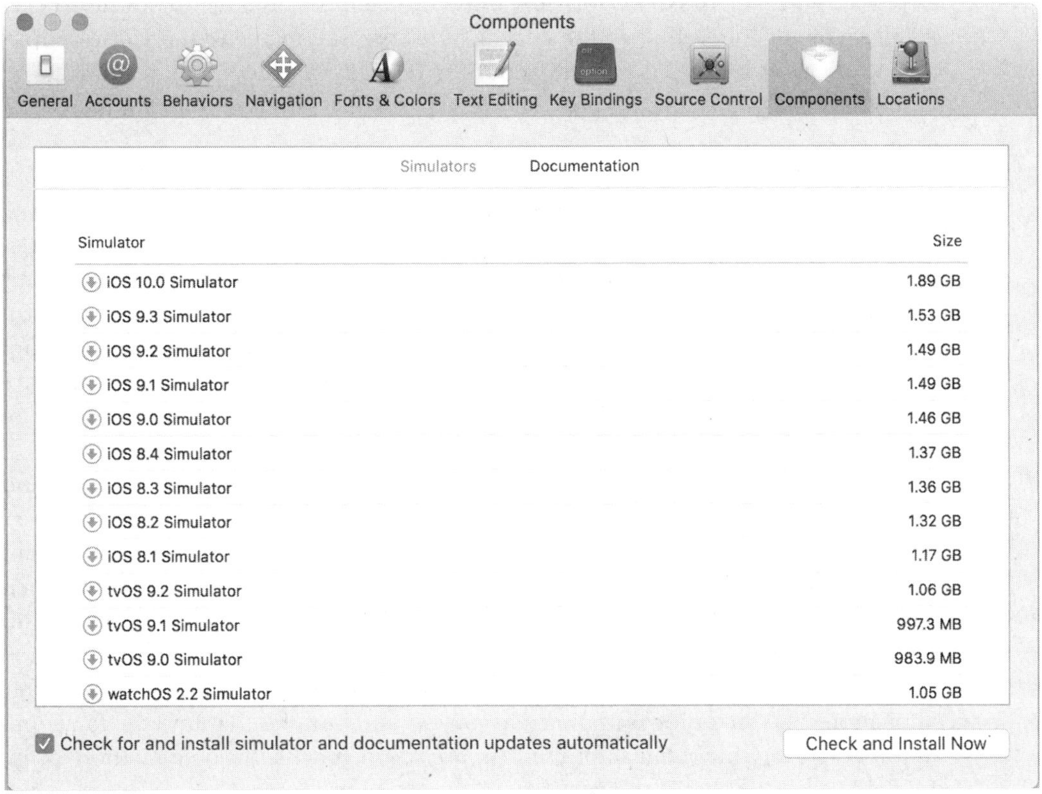

Figure 6.29 Xcode can download and install older versions of the simulator, but only recent versions are available.

You can also test against older versions using physical devices, but you'll need to have these devices already configured with the OS you want to use, as Apple doesn't make older versions of the OS available to download.

6.7 Linking

Mobile apps run on pretty constrained hardware. Mobile devices have less power, less memory, less storage, and unreliable networking. This means your mobile apps need to be optimized for a mobile environment: they need to be small so they don't eat up space (important on a device with only 16 GB of storage) and so they can be downloaded over a cellular connection without eating into users' data plans too much.

For desktop developers, app size isn't normally a consideration, but for mobile it's important, especially as there isn't a .NET Framework available in the OS like there is on Windows. Instead, your apps must ship everything they need to run, all self-contained in one package—be it your code, NuGet packages, or the relevant bits of the .NET Framework. This means your apps could potentially be huge. They could take up a lot of space on the device (which could be a problem with a bottom-of-the-range device with only 8 or 16 GB of storage), and they could be too large to download over a cellular connection, reducing the chance of users installing your app (for example, Apple won't allow users to download apps over 100 MB via cellular connections).

Luckily you can make your apps considerably smaller with the help of linking.

6.7.1 Linking the apps

Our coffee shop, from examples in previous chapters, has been particularly successful, and it's time to move to larger premises. Moving is hard work, so we'll get the professionals involved. When our coffee shop moves, not everything comes with it—we only want to move the things we need to reestablish our coffee shop elsewhere. We can leave behind the blinds, the carpets, and the shelves. We need to decide which things we really need and provide a list to the movers, so they take what's needed and leave the rest behind. This way the moving truck can be smaller, and our moving costs are reduced.

This is something we also want to do to our code. When we build our apps and ship them to our users, such as via an app store, we want our apps to be as small as possible, making them quicker to download and install—something that's very important for users who have expensive mobile data plans with no access to WiFi. Just like when we move our coffee shop, we want to package up what's needed for our app to run and no more. We can do this using the linker.

The Xamarin tooling contains a linker that's run on your code automatically after compilation. The linker looks at the code you use and bundles that into the final app, stripping out everything that's not used (figure 6.30). It does this on a method, property, field, and event basis, so even if you use `string` in multiple places, if you never use the `Substring` method, the linker can strip out that one method and leave the methods you do use.

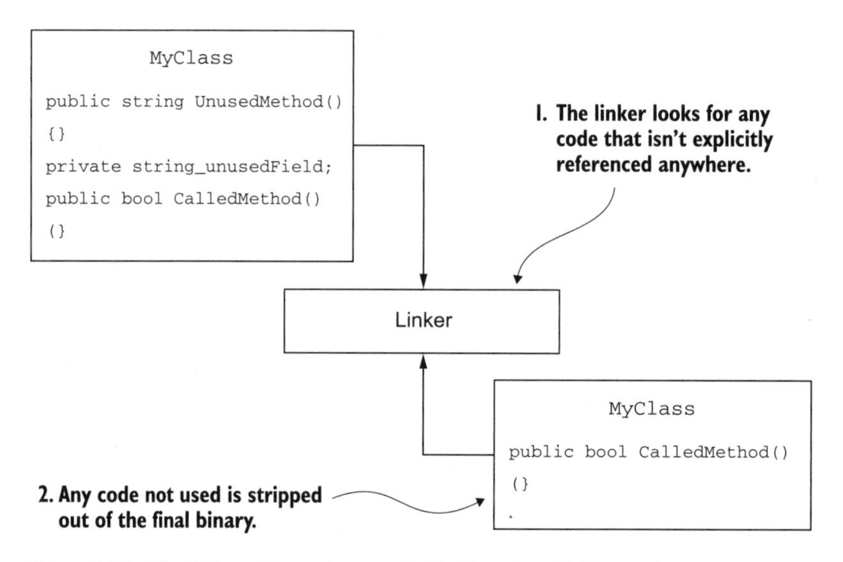

Figure 6.30 The linker strips out any code that's not explicitly used.

Linking is configurable and can be turned off. It can just be used on the SDK to strip out unused code from the OS SDK and relevant .NET Framework, or it can be used everywhere to strip unused code from your assemblies and any NuGet packages.

This is a common concept with languages like C++, but it's not used with C#—there's no SDK to strip out because the .NET Framework is part of the OS, and desktop PCs don't have the hardware constraints of mobile devices.

6.7.2 Linker options

The linker can be configured on the iOS and Android app projects—it's relevant for your final apps, so it's not something that can be configured on class libraries.

For Android, to configure the linker in Visual Studio for Mac, go to the project options by double-clicking the Android app project in the Solution Pad, or by right-clicking it and selecting Options. From there, select the Android Build tab on the left, and then select the Linker tab in the right pane.

On Windows go to the project properties by right-clicking the project in the Solution Explorer and selecting Properties, or by selecting it and pressing Alt-Enter. From the Properties tab, select the Android Options tab on the left, and then select the Linker tab in the right pane (figures 6.31 and 6.32).

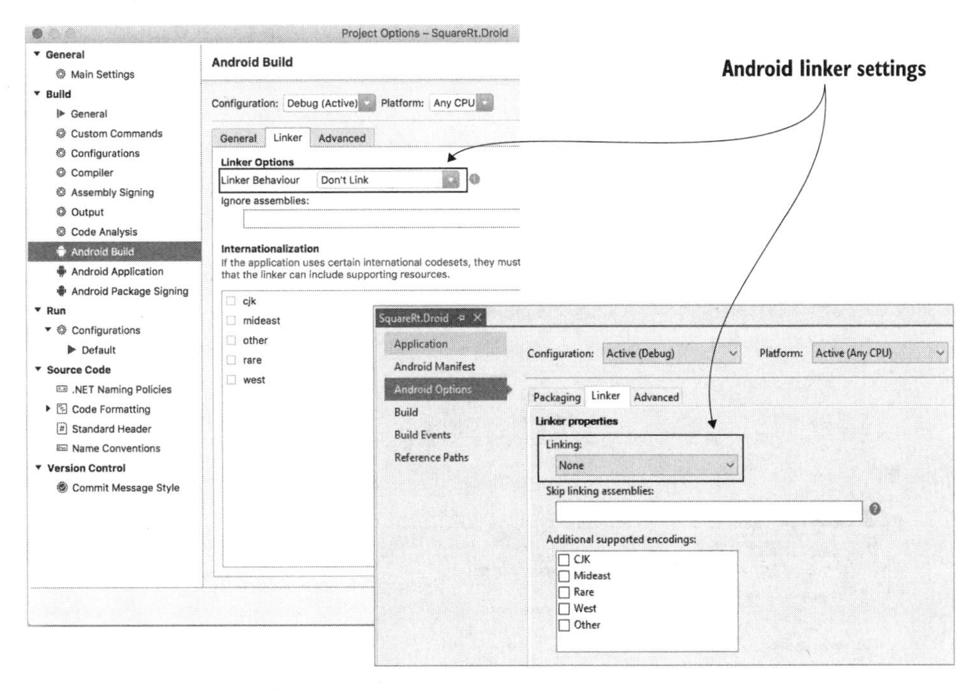

Figure 6.31 The Android linker settings

Figure 6.32 Linker settings, showing the options

For iOS you can configure the linker from the iOS Build tab of the project settings (figure 6.33).

The setting we're interested in here is called Linker Behavior (Mac) or Linking (Windows), and it has three settings, available on a per-configuration (for example, Debug or Release) basis:

- *Don't link*—Don't do any linking, leaving everything in place. This is the default setting for debug builds and it leads to large apps but faster build times. This isn't recommended for release builds.

IF YOUR BREAKPOINTS AREN'T BEING HIT, CHANGE THE LINKER SETTINGS There's a known issue at the time of writing with Xamarin Android apps where if you use Don't Link, sometimes your breakpoints won't get hit when debugging. If this happens to you, change the linker settings to Link Framework SDKs Only.

- *Link Framework SDKs Only (Link SDK Assemblies Only on Visual Studio for Mac)*—This setting will perform linking on all the assemblies provided by the .NET Framework and Xamarin SDKs. It won't link any of your code, or any NuGet packages or external code you use. This is pretty safe, as it's unlikely you'll be

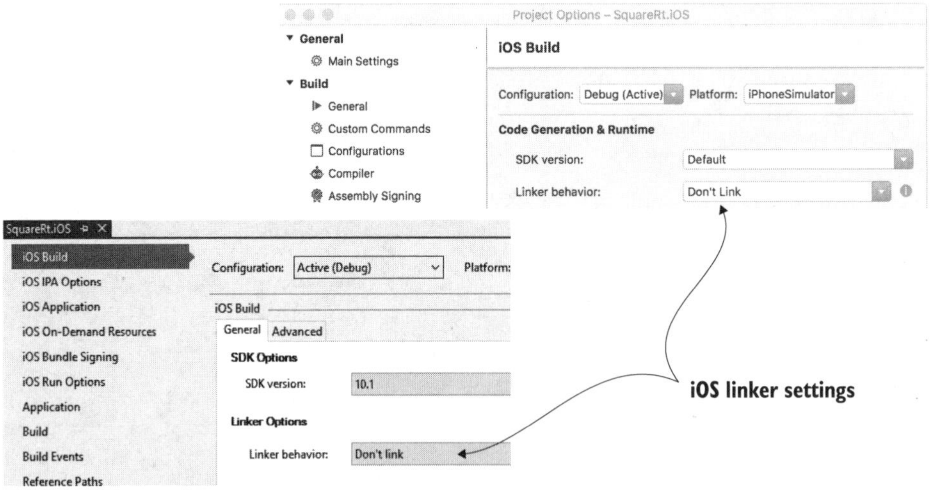

Figure 6.33 The iOS linker settings

accessing framework SDKs via reflection, and it removes most of the code you won't be using, leading to small final app sizes.

- *Link all*—This setting will run the linker over everything—your own code, NuGet packages you use, and all the framework SDKs. This provides the smallest final packages but it risks removing things you'll need if you do any reflection. It's the preferred option for release builds, but you'll need to thoroughly test your app to make sure nothing is stripped out that's needed.

6.7.3 Stopping the linker from doing too much

When our coffee shop moves, we have to tell the movers what to move. When doing this it's easy to miss something—we could tell them to move a coffee machine, but neglect to tell them to move the power leads and pipes. Similarly, when we link, the linker relies on explicit calls to public methods, properties, and events to know what to keep. It's easy to use something without an explicit call, and the linker could strip that out, leading to a crash at runtime. The usual culprit for this is reflection—where we find a property or method based on its name and invoke it. Unfortunately, for developers who use MVVM, reflection is used a lot. You can bind a property by name, and this can be the only reference to it. The linker looks for references, doesn't understand that the `string` representation is a reference to the property, and removes it.

Fortunately you can control the linker using a couple of techniques:

- Explicitly use the public property, method, or event somewhere
- Use the `Preserve` attribute

Explicitly use the public property, method, or event

By explicitly using the property or method, the linker will see the usage and will leave it in. This doesn't have to be functional code, just a reference somewhere. MvvmCross uses this technique. It ensures code isn't stripped out by the linker by using a file called LinkerPleaseInclude.cs containing a class that uses code that would be referenced by reflection. If you look in the root of the iOS and Android projects, you'll see this file (figure 6.34).

Use the Preserve attribute

The `Preserve` attribute can be added to a class, or to the members on a class, to tell the linker to not strip out code. If you set this at the class level, you need to set the `AllMembers` property to `true` to ensure that all members are preserved. The following listing shows this in action.

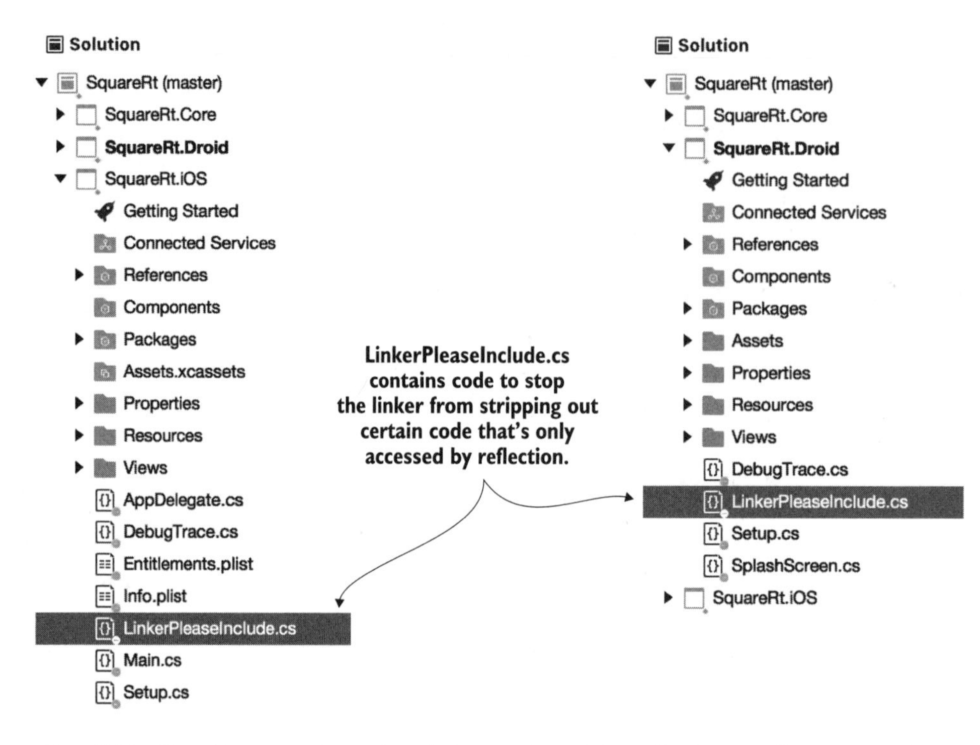

Figure 6.34 MvvmCross provides a class that prevents certain methods, properties, and events from being stripped out by the linker.

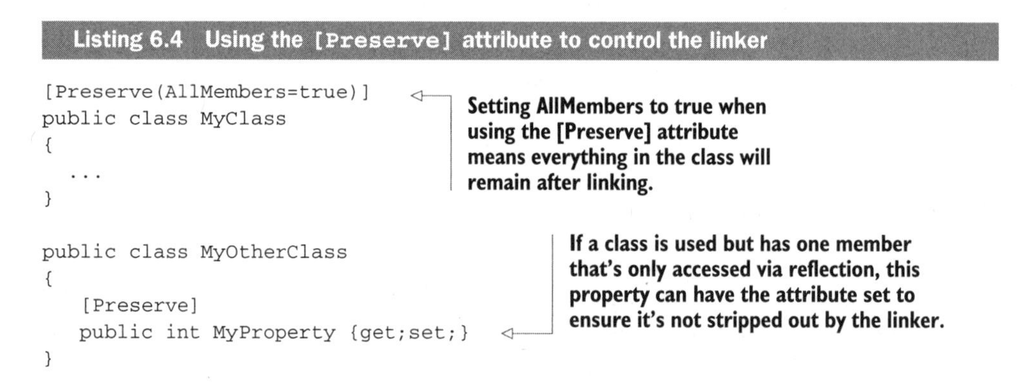

Listing 6.4 Using the `[Preserve]` attribute to control the linker

```
[Preserve(AllMembers=true)]
public class MyClass
{
  ...
}

public class MyOtherClass
{
   [Preserve]
   public int MyProperty {get;set;}
}
```


Unfortunately, this isn't an attribute that's available to .NET Standard libraries. Instead, there are two versions of this attribute—one on iOS (`Xamarin.iOS.Foundation .Preserve`) and one on Android (`Android.Runtime.Preserve`). To use this in a .NET Standard library, you'll need to define the attribute yourself. When you link an iOS app, the linker won't strip out anything with an attribute called `Preserve` on it, regardless of the namespace of that attribute. On Android, it specifically looks for an attribute in the `Android.Runtime` namespace called `Preserve`.

The simplest way to preserve code in a .NET Standard library is to define `Android.Runtime.Preserve` yourself in your core project and use that—the namespace matches, so the Android linker will use it, and the name matches, so the iOS linker will use it. This is, unfortunately, over-complicated, so hopefully Xamarin will improve on this in the future. The following listing shows an example implementation.

Listing 6.5 The `[Preserve]` attribute isn't available in .NET standard

```
namespace Android.Runtime
{
    public sealed class PreserveAttribute : System.Attribute
    {
        public bool AllMembers;
    }
}
```

The attribute should be in the Android.Runtime namespace to ensure it works on Android, which cares about the namespace, and on iOS, which does not.

The AllMembers field can be set to true when using this attribute on a class to ensure all members are preserved.

The attribute class name is PreserveAttribute, so you can reference it just by using [Preserve] without the attribute suffix.

You can find more information about linking in the Xamarin developer docs:

- *Linking on iOS*—http://mng.bz/d55a
- *Linking on Android*—http://mng.bz/v7x1

You now have your solutions at the ready, you've worked out what code you need in which layer and what code should run in the background and UI threads. You've also seen some of the new features of Xamarin iOS and Android apps. Now you're ready to start coding the app proper. In the next chapter we'll dive right into the core project and start writing the cross-platform models and view models.

Summary

In this chapter you learned

- iOS apps are different from Android apps, so you should think about your UI in terms of the platform your app is running on.
- By thinking about the user flows up front, you can start to build up a picture of the classes you'll need and what threads your code can run on.
- Unlike other C# apps, iOS and Android have OSs and SDKs that change regularly, so you need to code for different OS versions if you want to use the latest features.
- iOS users mainly use the latest two OS versions, whereas Android users have a wide range of OS versions.

- Linking reduces your app size, but it can cause problems with code that's not explicitly used but instead is accessed via reflection.
- Mobile apps are shipped with a properties file that provides information on your app to the relevant app store and OS.

You also learned how to

- Map your user flows to the different layers of MVVM.
- Map your user flows to different threads.
- Configure your app's properties.
- Select appropriate SDK versions for compiling and running your app.
- Configure linking to ensure your app is as small as possible, while not removing any code you need.

7 Building cross-platform models

This chapter covers

- Creating simple model layers
- Creating and running unit-test projects to test your models
- Structuring more complex model layers with services, repositories, and data models
- Using an ORM to access SQLite
- What REST services and JSON are
- Accessing web services from .NET Standard libraries

In the last chapter we started planning our mobile apps—we looked at the user flows, thought about the UIs, worked out what code would be in each layer, and thought about the threads our code should run on. Then we created a solution and took a look at some of the options and settings available in mobile apps. We talked about two apps: SquareRt (a simple square-root calculator) and Countr (an app for counting things).

Now we're going to get our hands dirty and write some code. In this chapter we're going to look at the model layer—looking at ways to build simple and more complex cross-platform model layers, thinking about testing our code, and discussing databases and web services. Everything in this chapter is cross-platform—after all, the big reason for using Xamarin is to share code and write all the business and UI logic once. The examples will be relevant to both SquareRt and Countr, so by following these examples you'll be able to build up the model layer of both of these apps.

If you're planing on coding along with this chapter, please make sure you've created the relevant solutions as described in the previous chapter, or use the precreated ones in the Git repository that accompanies this book.

7.1 Building simple model layers

The model layer is a cross-platform layer that represents your data, your business logic, and your access to external resources such as databases or web services (figure 7.1). For some apps, the model layer is pretty thin, with only very basic logic. For others, it's much more in depth. One thing to remember, though, is that this layer should be built in a way that makes sense to your domain—it should use classes, names, and data types that make sense from a business perspective, not ones that necessarily make sense from a UI perspective.

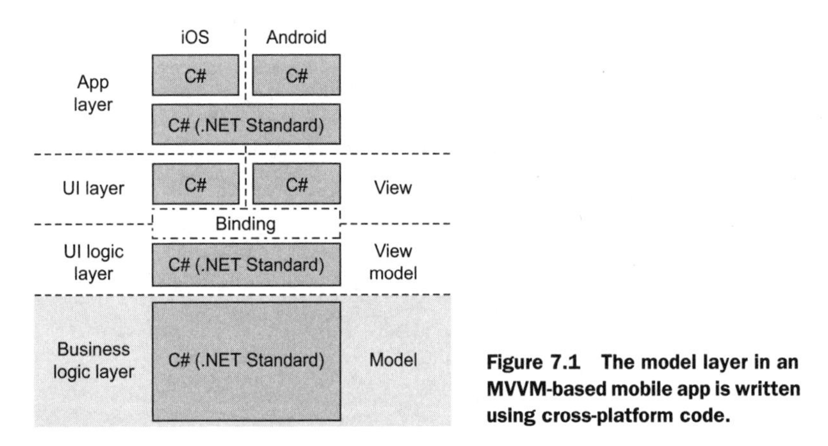

Figure 7.1 The model layer in an MVVM-based mobile app is written using cross-platform code.

As you've already seen, view models map one-to-one with views (so for `FooView` you'd have `FooViewModel`), but they don't have to map one-to-one to a model class (so there's no need to have `FooModel`). Instead, you can create classes in the model that provide data and business logic across multiple views and view models.

In the last chapter we looked at the user flow for the SquareRt app—the app is so simple it only has one. Figure 7.2 shows what we came up with. This app is simple—it only needs one thing in the model layer, the `SquareRtCalculator`. The sole job of this class is to take a number and calculate its square root.

Let's create this class now. Create a new class inside the SquareRt.Core project and call it `SquareRtCalculator`. To do this, right-click the SquareRt.Core project (remember, models are cross-platform, so they'll be in the cross-platform core projects), select Add > New File (for Mac) or Add > New Item (on Windows), select a file type of Class,

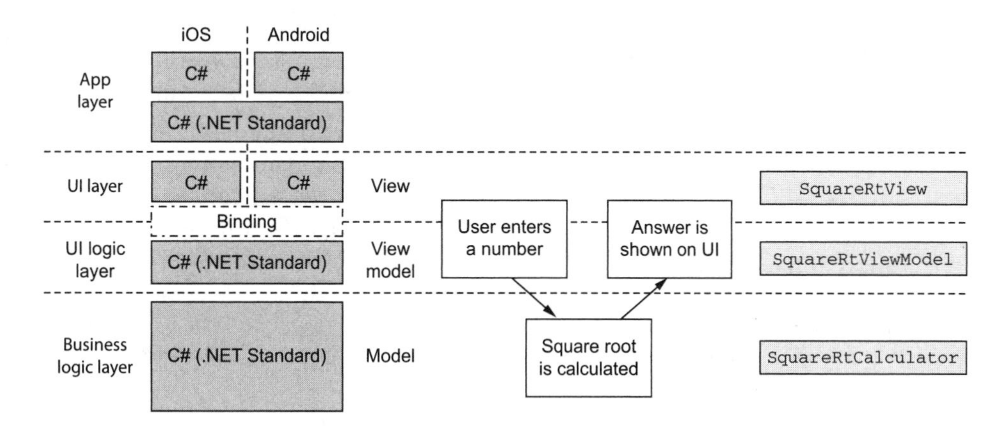

Figure 7.2 The user flow for SquareRt that we mapped to classes in chapter 6

and enter the class name (figure 7.3). As this is a simple project, I won't put this in a folder. I'll just put it in the root of the project.

The following listing shows the simple implementation of this class.

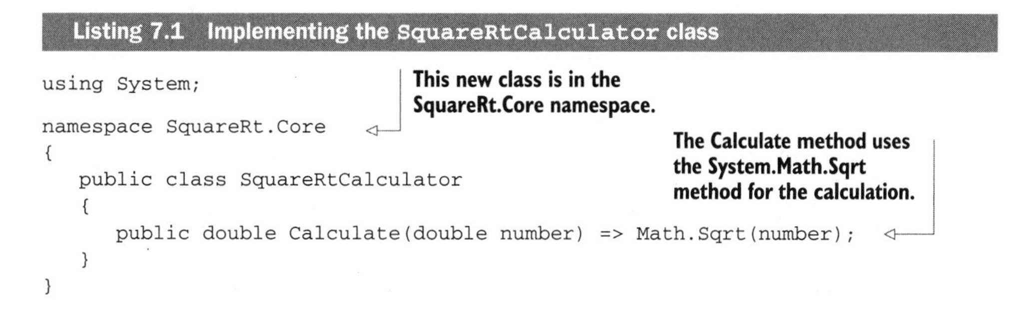

Listing 7.1 Implementing the `SquareRtCalculator` class

```
using System;

namespace SquareRt.Core
{
   public class SquareRtCalculator
   {
      public double Calculate(double number) => Math.Sqrt(number);
   }
}
```

This new class is in the SquareRt.Core namespace.

The Calculate method uses the System.Math.Sqrt method for the calculation.

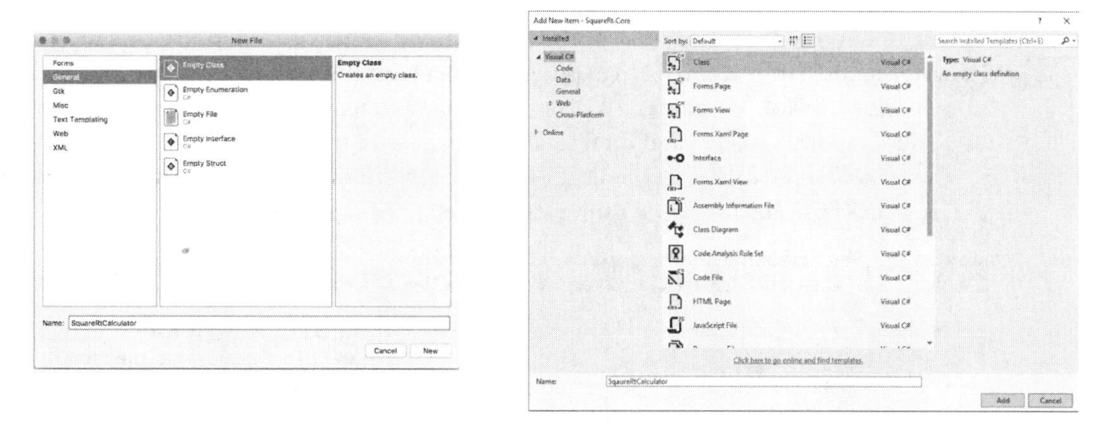

Figure 7.3 Adding the `SquareRtCalculator` class in Visual Studio for Mac (left) and Windows (right)

So far, so simple—we have a class that uses a .NET Framework library to do the calculation for us. But we're not finished here. We have one more thing to do. Back in chapter 4 we discussed testability, including the concept of using interfaces instead of concrete implementations. We looked at IoC containers and saw how we could register classes by interface and then inject those implementations as dependencies in other classes—for example, we could register our `SquareRtCalculator` using an `ISquareRtCalculator` interface and pass that in when constructing a view model, as shown in figure 7.4.

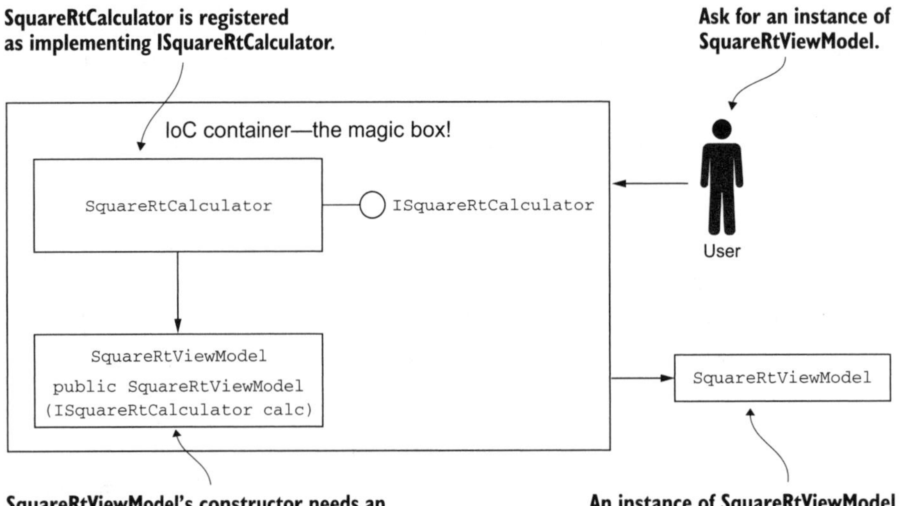

Figure 7.4 Using an IoC container to pass instances of `ISquareRtCalculator` wherever they're needed

This is an important concept and one we shouldn't neglect here, despite the simplicity of our model layer. We need to expose our calculator through an interface and register it with the IoC container. We can start by extracting an interface from our `SquareRtCalculator` class, and then we can register it in the container.

Create a new file called `ISquareRtCalculator` in the same place as the `SquareRtCalculator` class. The following listing shows the code for this.

Listing 7.2 The ISquareRtCalculator interface

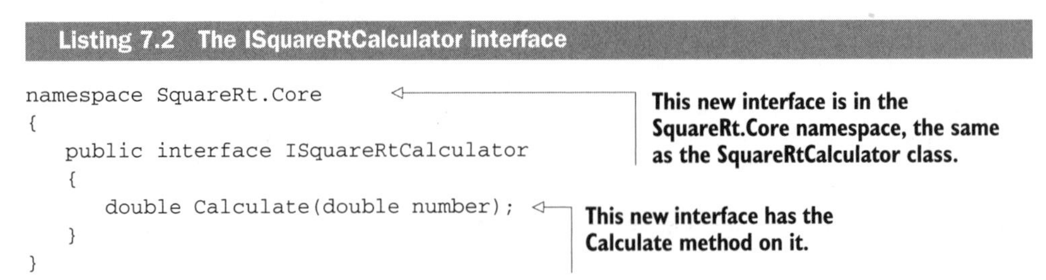

```
namespace SquareRt.Core
{
   public interface ISquareRtCalculator
   {
      double Calculate(double number);
   }
}
```

This new interface is in the SquareRt.Core namespace, the same as the SquareRtCalculator class.
This new interface has the Calculate method on it.

Once the interface is declared, the `SquareRtCalculator` class needs to implement it, as shown in the next listing.

Listing 7.3 `SquareRtCalculator` now implements our new interface

```
public class SquareRtCalculator : ISquareRtCalculator
...
```

SquareRtCalculator now implements ISquareRtCalculator.

The final step is to register this in the IoC container. To do this you need to modify the `App` class in App.cs in the SquareRt.Core project, as shown in the next listing.

Listing 7.4 Adding registration of the `ISquareRtCalculator`

```
using MvvmCross.Platform;
using MvvmCross.Platform.IoC;

namespace SquareRt.Core
{
   public class App : MvvmCross.Core.ViewModels.MvxApplication
   {
      public override void Initialize()
      {
         CreatableTypes()
              .EndingWith("Service")
              .AsInterfaces()
              .RegisterAsLazySingleton();
         Mvx.ConstructAndRegisterSingleton<ISquareRtCalculator,
                                           SquareRtCalculator>();
         RegisterNavigationServiceAppStart<ViewModels.FirstViewModel>();
      }
   }
}
```

A new using directive gives access to the static Mvx IoC container.

A call is made to the Mvx container to construct a new instance of SquareRtCalculator and register it using its ISquareRtCalculator interface.

We now have an interface, a class that implements it, and we've registered it in our container. Although this example is simple, you'll use this basic pattern again and again when constructing your apps, so it's a good habit to get into right off the bat.

When writing code, it's always nice to be able to run it and see what happens. The problem here is that we've written code in the model layer only—it's not wired up to a view model and view, so there's no way to manually test that our code works through a mobile app. We could wait until our app is complete to do our testing, but it would be better to test this code as soon as it's written. What we need is unit testing.

7.2 Unit testing

When making coffee using an industrial coffee machine in a coffee shop, you always need to ensure that your coffee maker is working in tip-top condition. If it's not up to scratch, you could end up with nasty-tasting coffee, or worse, hot steam shooting out at people. This is why you need to test the machine to make sure it's working before you can make the first cup of coffee each day. That's not easy to do manually—testing things like water pressure is hard without special tools. It's a long process to do properly, and being long and boring it's prone to human error.

Luckily, coffee machines have automated tests built in, so when they're first turned on they'll check things like the water pressure, whether they have beans, and anything else they need to ensure they're working correctly. This automated testing is much more reliable than human tests, it happens daily, with some tests, such as checking for beans running continuously, and it allows the baristas to get on with making fantastic hot drinks without worrying. This is something we can also do with our code—instead of waiting until our app is complete to test its functionality manually in a way that's prone to human error, we can use unit testing to write automated tests that can be run on a regular basis, ensuring not only that our code works but that it stays working.

Unit testing is a technique whereby you write some test code to check that your code is working correctly. *Unit* refers to a small runnable unit of code, which is usually taken to mean one public member on a class, such as a method or a property. You want your units to be as small as possible, testing one thing and one thing only. Your tests shouldn't cover more than one unit of code, and they should only validate one or two things—this way, if a test fails, it's immediately obvious which unit of code is failing under what scenario. If you write one huge test that tests a multitude of inputs and outputs, it's hard to spot what the actual problem is.

The purpose of unit testing is to test units of code in isolation with multiple inputs to ensure that they're working as expected, and that they keep working as expected. Not only can you write unit tests to check your code now, but you can run these on a regular basis (manually or, ideally, using a CI server) to ensure that your code continues to work even after other changes are made to the code base. After all, fixing a bug while you're writing your code has a minimal impact on when your code is released or on your customers' opinions of your app. If a bug makes it to your released app, however, it can take much longer to get a fix out to your users, leading to a poor customer experience and bad reviews on app stores.

Unit testing is a huge topic, and one well worth mastering. A full discussion of this topic would take a book in itself, and indeed many good books have been written on this topic, such as *The Art of Unit Testing, Second Edition*, by Roy Osherove (Manning, 2013).

To test the `Calculate` method of our `SquareRtCalculator`, we could wait till we've built the entire app and test it manually, but that's not the best way to do it. By the time the app is built, we could have forgotten how we wrote the code, making it slower to fix any bugs. We could even have handed the app over to another member of the team, who wouldn't know our code. We'd also have to manually test a number of possible calculations to ensure that they were all working, which is time consuming and potentially boring to do manually. And, of course, every time we tweak the app and rerelease it, we'd have to test it all over again. This sounds extreme for a simple calculator, which will probably work the first time, but for more complex apps (the kind you'd be likely to build in the real world), testing all of your code automatically as you're writing it is a huge time saver.

7.2.1 Creating a unit-test project

Before you can write unit tests, you need a new project inside your solution that can contain all your tests. It's common practice to put your tests in a separate project, rather than inside the project you're testing, so that the tests aren't shipped with your final app. A unit-test project is a simple class library—just like the SquareRt.Core project. The only difference is that it uses a unit-testing framework to define code as tests that can be run, either using command-line tools, CI servers, or directly inside Visual Studio.

Unit-testing frameworks are NuGet packages that provide attributes that you can use to indicate that a particular method is a unit test, as well as classes and methods that allow you to validate that your code is correct. They may also include extensions that provide features to your IDE, allowing you to run tests and track passes and failures.

There are a number of popular frameworks (such as xUnit—https://github.com/xunit/xunit), all open source and available for free with their own upsides and downsides. For this book I'll use one called NUnit (https://nunit.org), as it comes built into Visual Studio for Mac and it's easy to use from Visual Studio.

CREATING A UNIT-TEST PROJECT IN VISUAL STUDIO FOR MAC

Visual Studio for Mac works with NUnit support out of the box, and it even ships with a project template you can use to create a unit-test project with NUnit support. To create a unit-test project, right-click the solution and select Add > Add New Project. From the New Project dialog box, select Other > .NET on the left side, select NUnit Library Project from the middle section, and click Next. On the next screen, enter the project name as *SquareRt.Core.Tests* and click Create (figure 7.5). This will create a new project and then automatically download and install the NUnit NuGet package. The project will have a dummy test file in it called Test.cs, which you can delete.

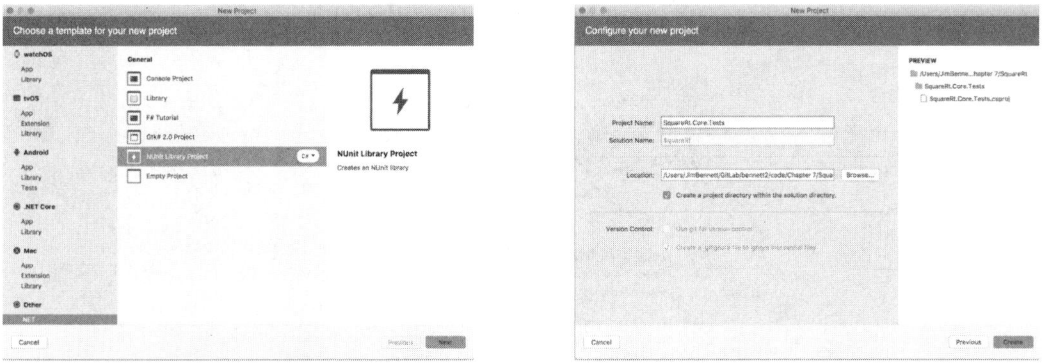

Figure 7.5 Adding a new NUnit library project

This project will need to reference the SquareRt.Core project to be able to test it, so right-click the References folder in the SquareRt.Core.Tests project, select Edit References, and in the Projects tab, check the box next to SquareRt.Core (figure 7.6).

Check the box here to add a reference to the SquareRt.Core project.

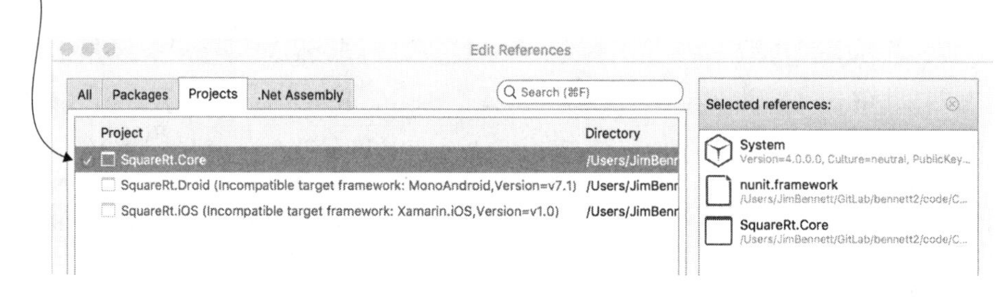

Figure 7.6 Adding a reference to another project

CREATING A UNIT-TEST PROJECT IN VISUAL STUDIO FOR WINDOWS

Getting Visual Studio for Windows to work with NUnit is a little bit more work than for the Mac. By default, it wants to use the Microsoft unit-testing framework, but I prefer to use NUnit, as this is available on both Windows and Mac. To enable NUnit, you'll need to install another extension—go to Tools > Extensions and Updates, select Online in the list on the left, and search for *NUnit*. From the list in the middle, select the NUnit 3 Test Adapter (note the version number 3 in the name) and click the Download button (figure 7.7). Follow the onscreen instructions, and then restart Visual Studio.

Install the NUnit Test Adapter to use the latest version of NUnit (3.x).

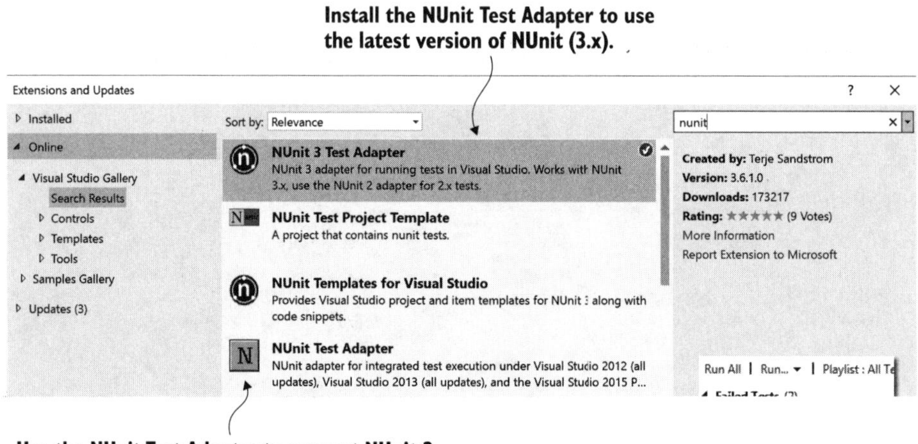

Use the NUnit Test Adapter to support NUnit 2 (the version of Visual Studio for Mac uses).

Figure 7.7 Adding the NUnit 3 extension to Visual Studio. You can also add the NUnit 2 extension to support NUnit projects created by Visual Studio for Mac.

A NUMBER OF POPULAR VISUAL STUDIO EXTENSIONS ALSO PROVIDE WAYS TO RUN TESTS If you use extensions such as ReSharper from JetBrains (www.jetbrains.com/resharper/) or CodeRush from DevExpress (www.devexpress.com/products/coderush/), you already have the ability to run NUnit tests without installing another extension. You'll see all your tests and be able to run them from the relevant ReSharper or CodeRush Test Runner window. See the docs for these extensions for more details.

NUNIT CURRENTLY HAS TWO VERSIONS IN REGULAR USE NUnit has been growing and evolving for a number of years now, and at the time of writing, 3.5 is the latest version. Version 3 has a number of incompatibilities with version 2 in the way the tools that run the tests work. When you create a new unit-test project in Visual Studio for Mac, it will default to using NUnit 2.6.4, which can't be run in Visual Studio using the NUnit 3 test adapter. The "fix" is to either upgrade the NUnit NuGet packages in the test project to the latest version, or to use the NUnit Test Adapter extension (note the lack of NUnit version number in the name), which supports NUnit 2 in Visual Studio.

Once you've added the extension, create a new project by right-clicking the solution and selecting Add > New Project. Select Visual C# from the tree on the left, select Class Library (.NET Framework) from the list in the middle, enter the project name as *SquareRt.Core.Tests*, and click OK (figure 7.8). Although there's a new project type under Visual C# > Tests called NUnit Test Project, it's not advisable to use this, as the resulting project won't work in Visual Studio for Mac. It's always good to create projects that work in both, as you never know what environment other developers in your team might want to use in the future.

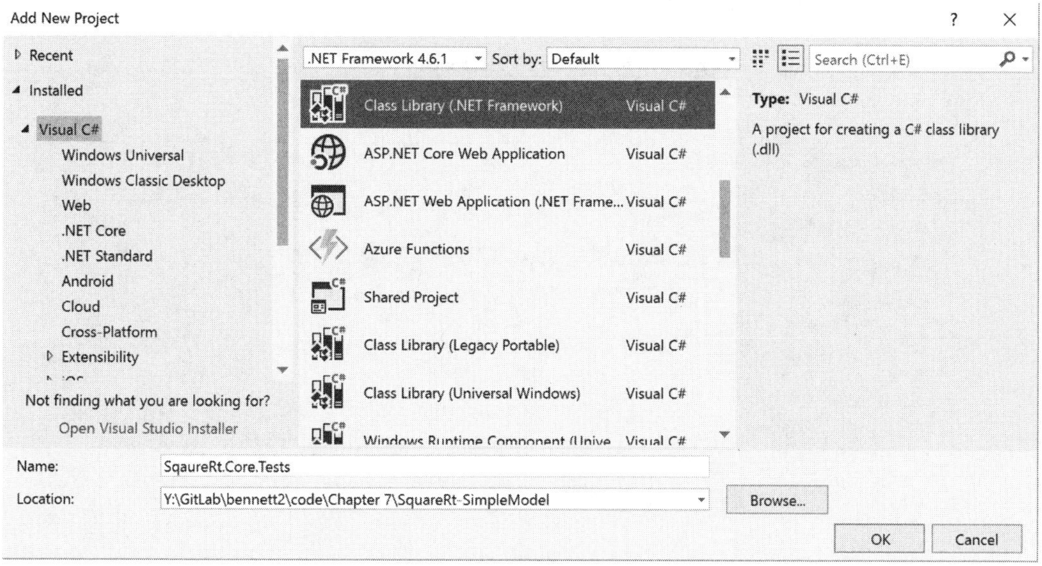

Figure 7.8 Creating a new class library project to put our NUnit tests into

WE'RE CREATING A .NET FRAMEWORK LIBRARY, NOT A .NET STANDARD LIBRARY
This is a .NET Framework library, rather than a .NET Standard library. At the time of writing, .NET Standard is still new and the tooling isn't quite perfect. If you create a .NET Standard library, your tests won't show up in the test explorer, and they won't be able to be run using Visual Studio for Mac. This tooling is constantly being improved, however, so by the time you read this, the .NET Standard unit test libraries may well work fully.

The project will contain a default Class1.cs class file, which you can delete. You'll then need to add the NUnit NuGet packages to this project manually by right-clicking the newly created SquareRt.Core.Tests project and selecting Manage NuGet Packages. Search for *NUnit* in the browse tab and install the latest version (figure 7.9).

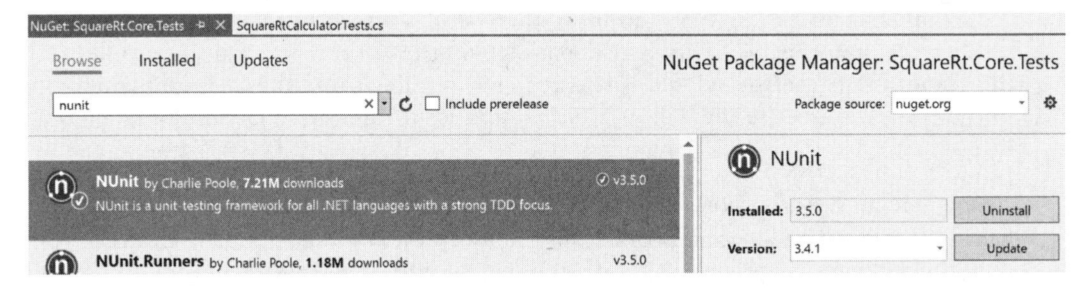

Figure 7.9 Install the NUnit package into your test project.

This project will need to reference the SquareRt.Core project to be able to test it, so right-click the References folder in the SquareRt.Core.Tests project, select Add Reference, and from the Projects tab check the box next to SquareRt.Core (figure 7.10).

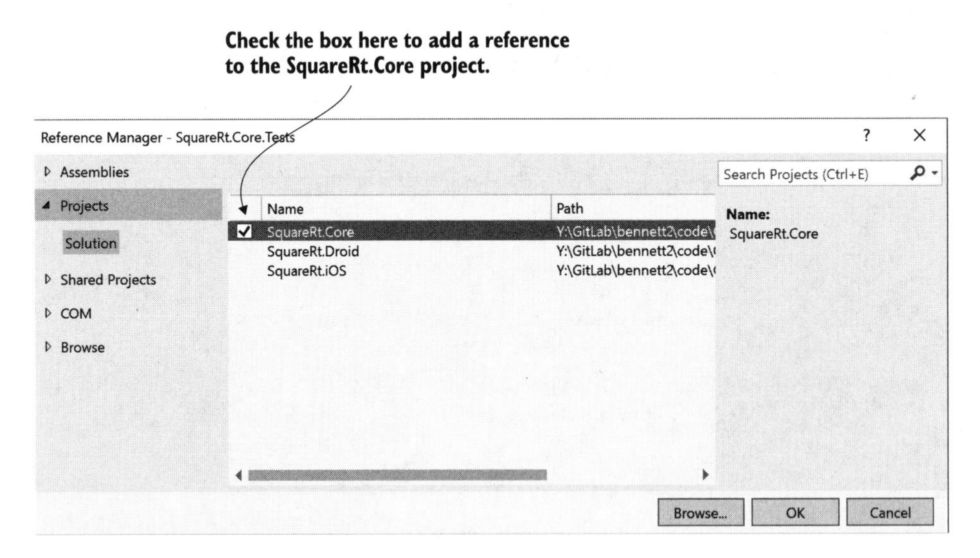

Figure 7.10 Adding a reference to the SquareRt.Core project from the SquareRt.Core.Tests project

7.2.2 Creating your first test

There is a huge range of techniques developers can use to build unit tests, and we're not going to go into too much depth here. Instead we'll focus on a simple way to create tests.

Once you have created the SquareRt.Core.Tests project, it's time to create a first unit-test class to test the calculator. We'll start with a simple test to see if it can correctly calculate the square root of 4. Create a new class in the root of the unit-test project called `SquareRtCalculatorTests`. Add the code in the following listing to this class.

Listing 7.5 A first unit-test class for the square-root calculator

```
using NUnit.Framework;                                  <-- A new using directive to access the NUnit code

namespace SquareRt.Core.Tests
{
    [TestFixture]                                        <-- The TestFixture attribute tells NUnit that this class is a test fixture.
    public class SquareRtCalculatorTests
    {
        ISquareRtCalculator calc;                        <-- An instance of the ISquareRtCalculator

        [SetUp]                                          The SetUp attribute tells NUnit to run
        public void SetUp()                              this method before each and every test.
        {
            // Arrange
            calc = new SquareRtCalculator();             <-- In the SetUp method, the instance of ISquareRtCalculator is set to a new SquareRtCalculator.
        }

        [Test]                                           The Test attribute marks a method
        public void Calculate_4_Returns2()               as a unit test that can be run.
        {
            // Act
            var squareRoot = calc.Calculate(4);          <-- The square root is calculated.
            // Assert
            Assert.AreEqual(2, squareRoot);              <-- Assert.AreEqual is an NUnit static method that will check two values and throw an exception if they're different.
        }
    }
}
```

First you create one-unit test class for each model class that you want to test, usually named something like `ClassNameTests`—in this case we're testing the `SquareRtCalculator` class, so we have a test class called `SquareRtCalculatorTests`. This class is decorated with the `TestFixture` attribute from NUnit, which marks this class as one that contains unit tests (classes that contain unit tests are referred to as *test fixtures*). Visual Studio has test runners that will look for classes in your solution that are marked with this attribute, and will allow you to run the tests defined in these classes.

Second, you need to define any setup or tear-down code. This is code that's run before and after each test and is encapsulated in methods that return `void`, that take no parameters, and that are marked with either the `SetUp` or `TearDown` attributes. In this case you don't need any clean-up code, but you're doing some setup—to save on creating a new instance of the `SquareRtCalculator` in every test method, you're creating it in the setup. This reduces the amount of identical code you'd have to write, and if you ever change the constructor on the `SquareRtCalculator` class, you'd only have to fix up the setup method instead of fixing a multitude of tests. This instance is stored in a field of type `ISquareRtCalculator`—storing this as the interface is intentional. Good unit tests should test the exposed interface of a class because it's this interface that would be passed to other classes (such as a view model), so if you test the interface, you can be sure you're testing all the members exposed to the classes that'll use this.

Finally you need to create the tests themselves. These are methods with a `void` return type (or `async Task` if your test will be testing asynchronous code that you want to `await`), and they don't take any parameters. They're also marked with the `Test` attribute, and it's this that tells the test runner that the method is a unit test. In these methods you write any code that you want to test, and the way to flag a test as failing is by throwing an exception.

This standard structure of a test fixture with multiple tests that are set up, run, and then torn down is shown in figure 7.11.

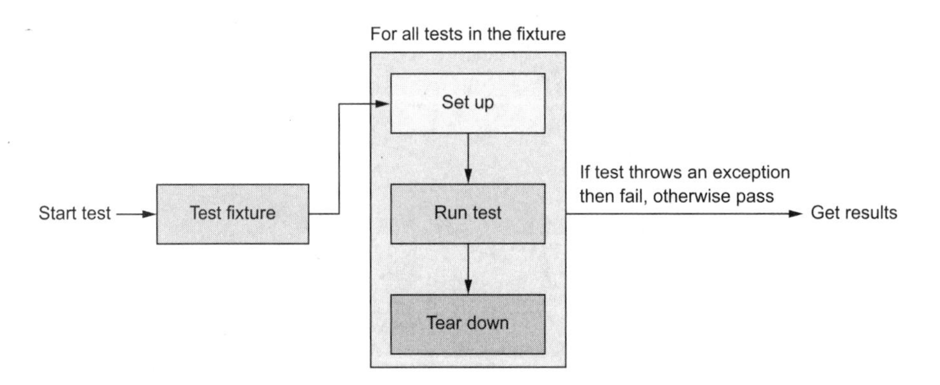

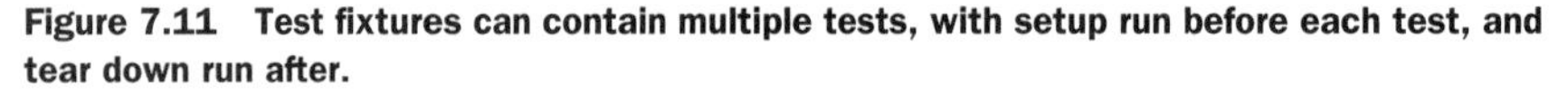

Figure 7.11 Test fixtures can contain multiple tests, with setup run before each test, and tear down run after.

The standard way to write a test is *arrange, act, assert*: set up your code, perform an action, and then verify that the result of the action is correct:

- *Arrange*—This is where you set up your test. This setup includes creating any classes you need and setting a relevant state. In this example, there's minimal setup—just creating a class—but in a lot of tests there might be other setup. For example, if you were testing that a `Name` property correctly concatenates a `FirstName` and `LastName`, your arrange step would be setting the values on the `FirstName` and `LastName` properties.

- *Act*—This is where you perform the action under test, and it should ideally be a single code statement, or, if necessary, the smallest number of statements possible. This is what you're testing, so if this fails you want it to be immediately obvious what has failed, making it easier to debug and fix.
- *Assert*—Once the unit of code has been run, you need to evaluate the results, outputs, or side effects of your code to ensure that the code ran successfully. You assert that what you expect has happened, such as a calculation returning the correct result or correctly modifying an object's state. The way you assert something is to check the relevant condition, and if the condition isn't met, throw an exception. NUnit has a static `Assert` class that can do this for you, with methods to perform various assertions that throw exceptions if the assertions fail.

  A good test will ideally have only one assertion because the test should only check one thing, but sometimes it's more practical to have more than one. For example, if you're testing a `SetName(string firstName, string lastName)` method that sets both the first and last names of an object, you might want to write two assertions: one to assert that the first name is set correctly, and one to assert that the last name is set. These should be kept to a minimum, though, as you want to always be able to link a test failure back to a specific scenario to make debugging easier.

In the case of our test, we're setting up the `SquareRtCalculator` in the setup method (*arrange*), we're calculating the square root of 4 (*act*), and we're verifying that the result is 2 (*assert*). The verification is done using the `Assert` static class that comes from NUnit, using its `AreEqual` method that takes two values and throws an exception if they're different. We can create more tests that follow this pattern to test other values, as shown in table 7.1.

Table 7.1 Our tests follow the pattern of arrange, act, assert

Arrange	Act	Assert
Create `SquareRtCalculator`	`Calculate(0)`	Assert result is 0
Create `SquareRtCalculator`	`Calculate(4)`	Assert result is 2

NAMING YOUR TESTS It's often said that the two hardest things in programming are cache invalidation, naming things, and off-by-one errors. This is true with unit tests, where naming your tests can be hard. Ideally the test name should describe the test and contribute in part to documenting the behavior of the class under test. `TestCalculate` would be a bad name for our test, but `Calculate_4_Returns2` describes the test as using the `Calculate` method and passing in 4 with the expectation that the method will return 2. This is a good patten to follow: `UnitOfWork_StateUnderTest_ExpectedBehavior`. Don't worry about the length of the name—it's better to have a longer, more descriptive test name than a shorter confusing one. You can read more about test naming in Roy Osherove's "Naming standards for unit tests" blog entry at http://mng.bz/qzym.

RUNNING YOUR TESTS IN VISUAL STUDIO FOR MAC

To run your tests, you can do one of two things—run them directly from the file, or run them via the Unit Tests pad.

If you want to run unit tests directly from your code, you need to enable editor–unit-test integration from the application Preferences by going to Visual Studio > Preferences, selecting the Text Editor > Source Analysis tab on the left, and ticking Enable Text Editor Unit Test Integration (figure 7.12).

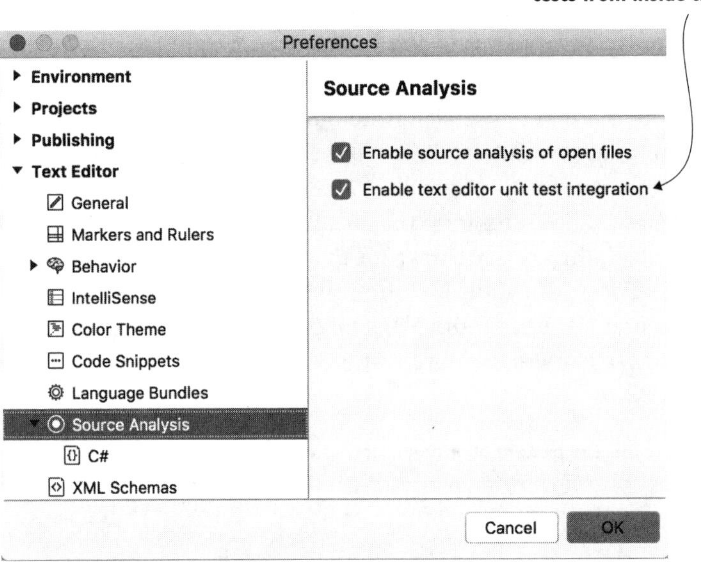

Figure 7.12 To run unit tests from inside the code editor, an option in the preferences needs to be set.

After enabling this, if you look at your test fixture code, you'll notice empty circles in the left margin next to the class declaration for your test fixture, as well as in line with each test method. You can click the circle next to the class declaration to run all the tests in the fixture, or the circle by an individual test to run just that test (figure 7.13). Selecting Run will run the tests and highlight success or failure with either a green circle with a tick in it if the test passes or a red circle with a lightning bolt in it for failure. Selecting Debug will run your test through the debugger, so that you can set breakpoints to debug any issues in your code. Select in Test Pad will open another pad that

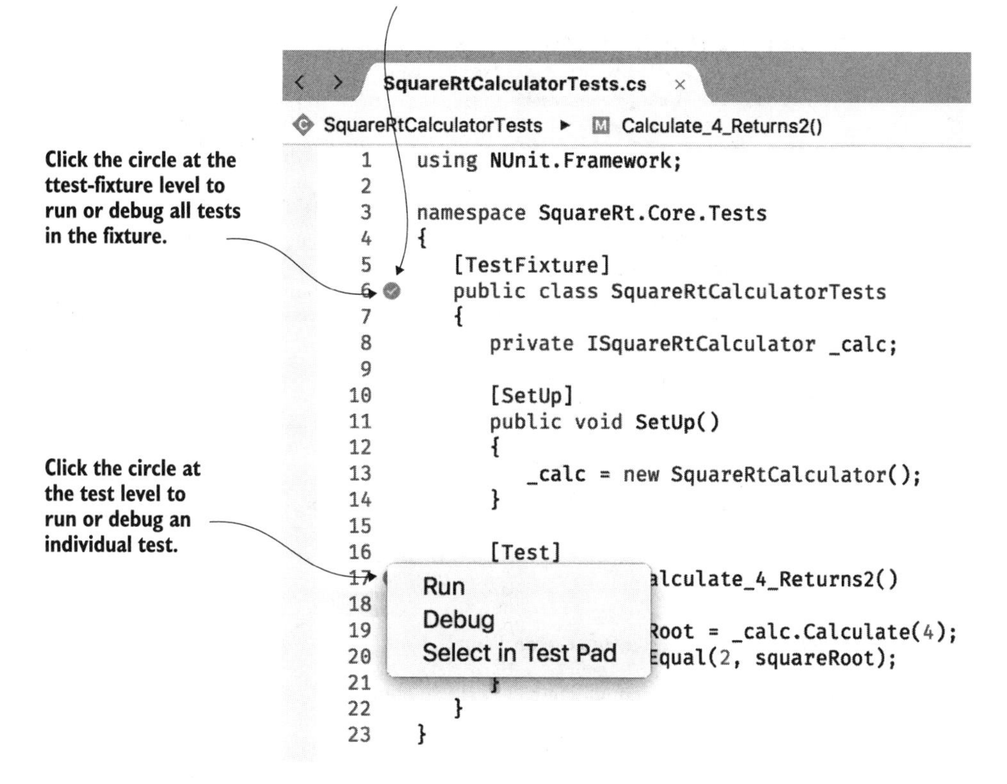
Empty circles indicate a test that hasn't been run. Green means the test passed on the last run, and red means the last run failed.
Click the circle at the ttest-fixture level to run or debug all tests in the fixture.
Click the circle at the test level to run or debug an individual test.
SquareRtCalculatorTests.cs
SquareRtCalculatorTests ▸ Calculate_4_Returns2()
1 using NUnit.Framework;
2
3 namespace SquareRt.Core.Tests
4 {
5 [TestFixture]
6 public class SquareRtCalculatorTests
7 {
8 private ISquareRtCalculator _calc;
9
10 [SetUp]
11 public void SetUp()
12 {
13 _calc = new SquareRtCalculator();
14 }
15
16 [Test]
17 alculate_4_Returns2()
18
19 Root = _calc.Calculate(4);
20 Equal(2, squareRoot);
21 }
22 }
23 }
Run
Debug
Select in Test Pad

Figure 7.13 Unit tests can be run using the circles next to the test classes or methods.

shows all the tests in your solution hierarchically by namespace, so that you can run all tests or any selection you want.

The other option is to run your tests from the Unit Tests pad directly, which you can view by selecting View > Pads > Unit Tests, or by selecting View > Test to have Visual Studio change to a unit-testing layout, with the Unit Tests and Test Results pads showing. You can then run your tests by double-clicking on them in the test pad.

Running your tests in Visual Studio for Windows

To run your tests in Visual Studio, click the Test menu and select Run > All Tests. This will build your solution and then run all the tests it can find in a new Test Explorer window that will appear on the left side. From there you can see all the tests and can run or debug each one by right-clicking it (figure 7.14). If you can't see the Test Explorer, you can show it by selecting Test > Windows > Test Explorer.

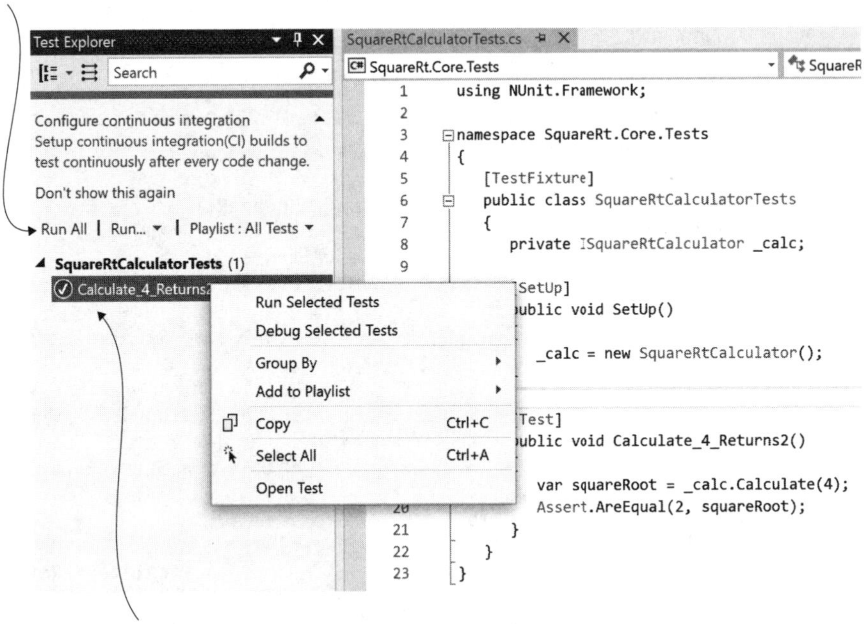

You can run all tests using Run All. Or you can run only failed tests or tests that haven't been run yet, or repeat the last run, using options from the Run dropdown.

Individual tests can be selected and run or debugged.

Figure 7.14 Visual Studio can run tests in Text Explorer.

7.2.3 *What do these tests tell you?*

If you run the `SquareRtCalculatorTests` fixture tests, you should see them all pass—also referred to as *going green*. Unit-test results are often shown using green for pass and red for fail, and you'll often hear the colors used to define pass and fail states. If a developer you're working with tells you your tests are red, it means you have some failures. (If you want to see what a failure looks like, try changing the expected result from 2 to something else, and run the test again.) This test tells you that your calculator can successfully calculate a square root using one input.

It would be easy to add more tests to cover more inputs, to both ensure that your code works, and to explore different inputs. A good example would be to write a unit test for –1. The square root of –1 is *i*, an imaginary number, and this is represented as `double.NaN` in C# (NaN means "not a number"—something that can't be represented by a simple decimal number). By writing a test for this, you could see what the output is and make a decision about how you're going to represent this in your UI—maybe by always showing 0 as the result for negative numbers. Calculating the square root of –1 is the kind of thing a user would do to play with your app, but it's something that, as a developer, it's easy to forget to consider if you were just doing manual testing. By automating testing using unit tests, you're more likely to consider the inputs to your code and cover edge cases.

> **USE TEST CASES TO COVER MULTIPLE INPUTS** You can test multiple inputs and outputs using a single test method by defining multiple test cases. These are test methods that take parameters defining the inputs and expected outputs and then test against these. They have a different attribute on the method—they use multiple `TestCase` attributes, which are created with a list of values that get passed to the method for each test. You can read more on the `TestCase` attribute in the NUnit docs at http://mng.bz/Vj2M.

Unit tests don't just make it easier for you to focus on one method when testing so that you cover the possible inputs and outputs, they give you another very important thing—cross-platform testing of your model layer. You use MVVM to share large amounts of cross-platform code, and by decoupling the UI from the logic, you can write unit tests to test large portions of your code, reducing the amount of slow, laborious manual testing that you'd need to do. This is what you're seeing here—you've written some cross-platform code once, and unit-tested it. You don't have to manually test that the calculations work, just that the UI is wired up correctly. If you hadn't used MVVM and instead had wired up a button directly to the calculation code, you wouldn't have been able to test this except manually. If you'd written your app using Swift on iOS and Java on Android, you'd have had to write this unit test twice.

> **IN REAL APPS THE LOGIC IS MORE COMPLEX THAN A SIMPLE CALL TO MATH.SQRT** This is a simple example of a method that makes a direct call to a system function, but it illustrates the principles. In a real-world app, your logic in the model layer could be more complex, so you'd want to test a variety of inputs and outputs. Thanks to MVVM and Xamarin, you can test complex model-layer logic using unit tests, and test it once.

7.3 Building more complex model layers

The SquareRt app has a simple model layer, but our Countr app needs something a bit more complex—including the ability to store counters somewhere. As a refresher, let's look at the Countr user flows that we discussed in chapter 6. Figure 7.15 shows these.

Let's look at a popular way to structure more complex model layers using services, data models, and repositories.

7.3.1 Services, data models, and repositories

In our hypothetical coffee shop, we have baristas that can turn beans, water, and optionally milk into a delicious beverage. Beans are stored in cupboards behind the counter, milk is in the fridge, and there are taps to provide a good supply of water. If a customer comes in and orders an espresso, a number of things happen:

1. The barista gets some beans out of a bag in a cupboard.
2. The barista puts the beans in a grinder, and takes out ground coffee.

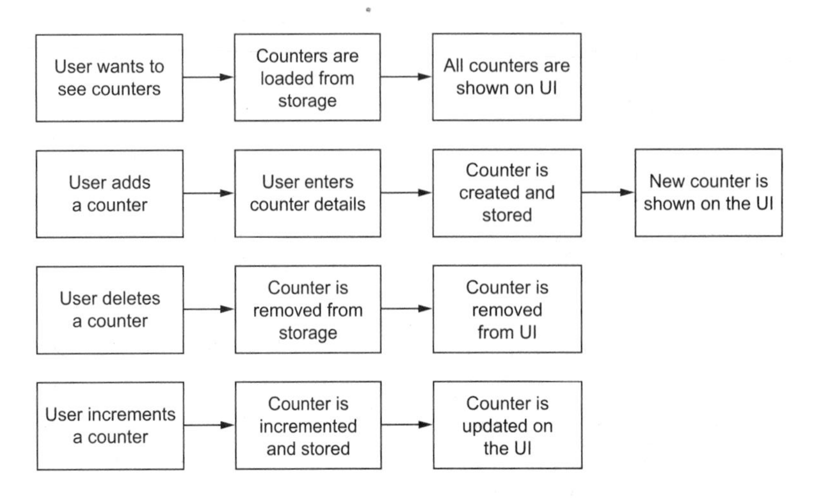

Figure 7.15 The user flows for the Countr app: showing, adding, deleting, and incrementing counters

3. The barista puts the ground coffee into the espresso maker, which is plumbed into the main water supply, puts a cup under the spout, and taps a button.
4. The espresso maker pushes hot water through the grounds and streams coffee into the cup.
5. The barista hands over your coffee.

We can break this down into three categories—entities (coffee beans, cups), places where entities are stored (cupboards), manipulators of entities (barista, espresso machine). These lists are shown in table 7.1.

Table 7.2 Grouping our coffee shop into entities, storage, and manipulators

Entities	Storage	Manipulators
Beans	Cupboard	Grinder
Milk	Fridge	Steamer
Water	Pipes	Barista
Cups		Coffee machine

Let's think about our Countr app in similar terms. We have an entity in the form of a class that represents a counter. We need a place to store the counters, and something to manipulate the counters, such as getting them all, adding new ones, removing them, or incrementing them. A common pattern for doing this is to use a set of data model classes, services, and data repositories:

- *Data models*—Data models are classes for simple data objects—objects that have properties to represent state, but few if any methods. These should map to the real-world entities that your app is concerned with.
- *Services*—Service classes provide the business logic that acts upon those data models, such as creating them from different data, performing calculations, uploading or downloading them from web services, or persisting them to repositories.
- *Repositories*—Repositories are used to persist the data models, usually to a local database such as SQLite.

Table 7.3 Grouping our Countr app into entities, storage, and manipulators

Entities (data models)	Storage (repositories)	Manipulators (services)
`Counter`	`CountersRepository`	`CountersService`

Our MVVM model layer needs to expose state and behavior to the views via the view models. Our services are the entry point into the model layer from the view models. If we have a `CountersViewModel` that shows a list of `Counter` objects on the `CountersView`, it would use `CountersService` to retrieve a list of counters, which would ultimately come from the `CountersRepository`. When a new `Counter` is created, it would be created via the service, which in turn would store the new counter in the repository. Figure 7.16 shows these two flows in action through the layers.

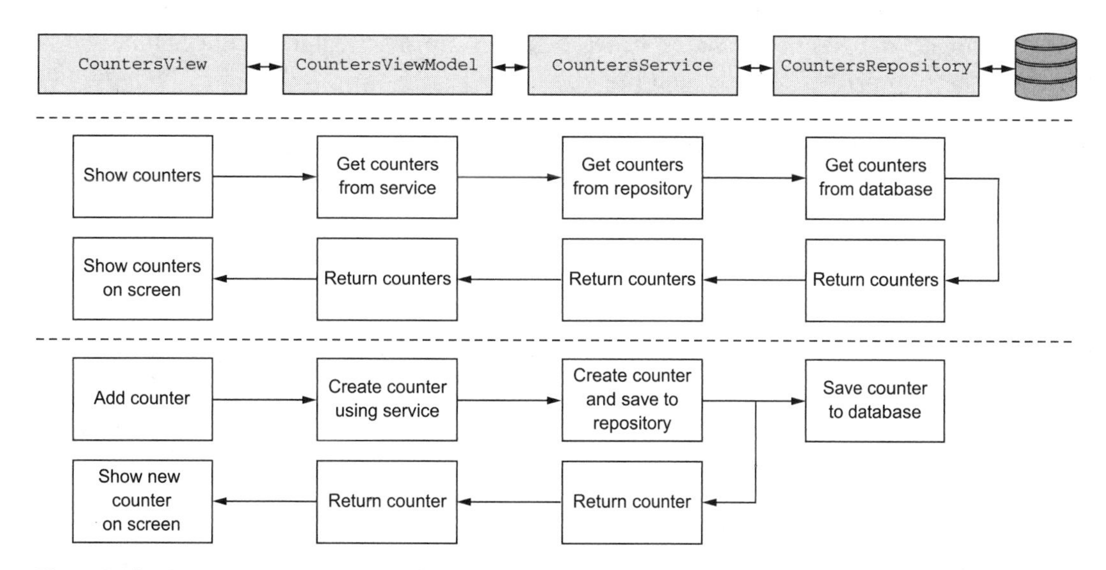

Figure 7.16 The counters view talks to the view model, which in turn talks to the service, which talks to the repository, which stores and retrieves data from a database.

By having separate services and repositories, we get a really good separation in our code, with each layer being relatively thin so it's much, much easier to unit-test. This is one of the key goals of using the MVVM design pattern. It also means that in a larger app you can share services between view models, and share repositories between services.

For example, when creating a new email in an email app, you'd have a view and view model for the new email screen, and this view model would access a service to provide a list of contacts to help the user fill in the To and CC fields. You could also have a service that provides access to the user's photos or other documents for adding attachments. The contacts service could also be used on a screen that shows your inbox, putting pictures beside the sender of each email.

This model also applies to our Countr app—we can use a counters service to not only get the list of counters to display on the main screen, but when the user adds a new counter, the view and view model for an add-counter screen would also use the same service to construct and store the new counter.

Let's now build our service and repository, starting at the bottom with a database and data models, and working our way up through the repository to the service.

7.3.2 Accessing databases

A repository is a class that provides the ability to store and retrieve data from some kind of storage, and the most popular storage mechanism on mobile is a database called SQLite (www.sqlite.org). SQLite is a small, fast, file-based, open source database that has been around for over 15 years, and it comes embedded in iOS and Android. Other databases are available (such as Realm—https://realm.io), but SQLite is the most popular because it's built into the OS. SQLite is very low level with a C API, but there are C# wrappers for this API as well as some really nice open source ORM (object-relational mapping) layers that you can use. ORM is a layer that abstracts database tables, columns, and rows away from you—instead of worrying about how to structure your data in the database, you can create tables based on a class, and perform basic CRUD (create, read, update, and delete) operations just by passing instances of your class around, or by requesting data by class type.

The best ORM for SQLite, by far, is SQLite-Net (not to be confused with SQLite.NET—it has a hyphen in the name instead of a period) from Frank Krueger. It's available in a NuGet package called SQLite-Net-Pcl, which you should add to all the projects in the Countr solution (on Windows you can do this at the solution level, but on Mac you have to add it to the individual projects one by one).

There are many different SQLite packages available, so make sure you install the correct one! Also, be aware that despite the package having PCL in its name, in the latest versions it's a .NET Standard library, not a PCL. This book was written using version 1.4.118, so install that version, although the latest version may also work. In Visual Studio for Mac you can select the version from the drop-down list at the bottom right; on Windows you can select it from the package settings at the right (figure 7.17).

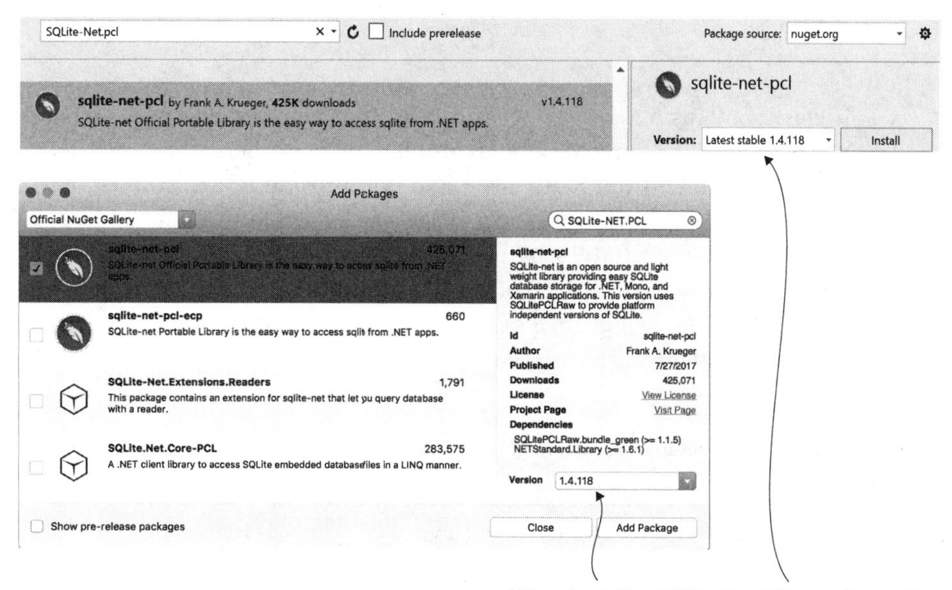

Figure 7.17 The best ORM is SQLite-Net-PCL, but there are a number of NuGet packages available with SQLite in the name, so be sure to install the correct one with the correct version.

We first need to define classes that can store the data we need to persist. Then we'll create a repository that can persist and retrieve those classes. This repository will, in turn, use SQLite-Net to automatically create the relevant tables for us.

STORING MODELS IN THE DATABASE

For the Countr app, you need to be able to store counters and update them when the counter is incremented. To do this, you need a class to represent the counter with a name and a current value. Usually a class like this would be considered a *data model* as it models data (not to be confused with the model layer), so you can create a folder in the Countr.Core project called Models (right-click and select Add > New Folder). Then, add a new class in this folder called `Counter`. The following listing shows the contents of this class.

Listing 7.6 A simple data class to represent a counter

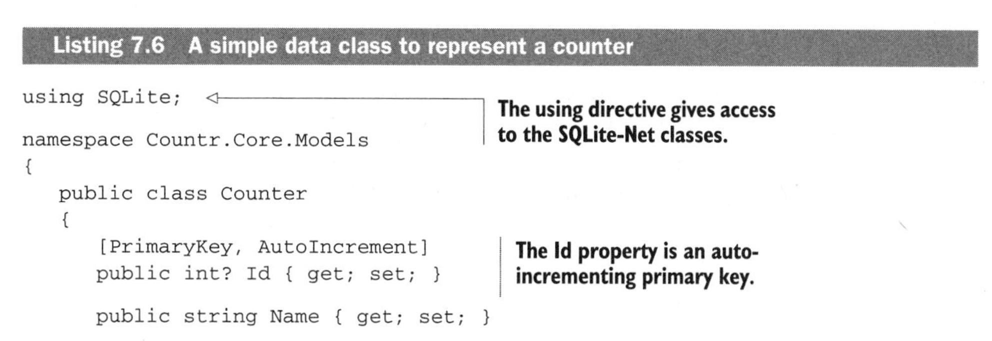

```
using SQLite;

namespace Countr.Core.Models
{
   public class Counter
   {
      [PrimaryKey, AutoIncrement]
      public int? Id { get; set; }

      public string Name { get; set; }
```

```
        public int Count { get; set; }
    }
}
```

This class contains a `Name` property to store the name of the counter, and a `Count` property to store the current value. It also has an `Id` property that's marked with some attributes that come from SQLite-Net and that provide instructions on how the table for this class should be set up. When this class is stored in a SQLite table, it will go into a table called Counter (tables are named by SQLite-Net to match the class name that's stored in them) that has three columns that map one-to-one with the public properties: an `int` column called `Id`, a `string` column called `Name`, and another `int` column called `Count`. Table 7.4 shows the structure of this table with some example counters already added to it.

Table 7.4 The Counter table, showing some example counters that a user might create when they use the app

`Id—int` (primary key)	`Name—string`	`Count—int`
1	"Cups of coffee"	14
2	"Gym sessions"	8
3	"Cakes"	2

You need a primary key column (a column that contains a unique key that you can use to reference each counter), and ideally you don't want to manage this yourself. This is what the attributes on the `Id` property provide. The `PrimaryKey` attribute tells SQLite to make this column the primary key, so it's the unique ID used to reference individual counters, and the `AutoIncrement` attribute tells SQLite to automatically set the value of this ID to the next available value when a new row is added. For example, if you have three counters in the database with IDs 0, 1, and 2, and you add a new counter, it would have its `Id` value automatically set to 3 when it's added to the table. This value is an `int?`—a nullable int. That's because 0, the default value of an `int`, is a valid ID. If the ID was an int and you created and saved a new counter, SQLite wouldn't know if it was a new counter or an update to a counter with an ID of 0. Because you're using an `int?`, the default value is `null`, so SQLite will know to insert the counter.

All these properties have public getters and setters, and this is by design. There's also no constructor, so the compiler automatically creates a default (parameterless) one for you. The way SQLite-Net works when loading data from a table is to construct an object using its default constructor, and then set the properties via reflection using the values from the columns. If you didn't have a default constructor, SQLite-Net couldn't create the object, and if the properties didn't have public setters, the values couldn't be set. When an object is saved, SQLite-Net uses reflection as well—the getters need to be public so that the ORM can get the values to write to the columns in the table. It's fine to add a custom constructor, just as long as you add a parameterless one as well (the compiler won't create a default constructor automatically if another constructor is defined).

CREATING A REPOSITORY

Now that you have a data model, you need to set up a repository to store and retrieve models from a database. By using SQLite-Net, you can deal with your data models directly without having to manually store these objects across different columns in different tables. This makes the repository fairly simple.

Create a Repositories folder in the Countr.Core project, and add a new interface there called `ICountersRepository`. The following listing shows the code for the interface.

Listing 7.7 The interface to the counters repository—simple and easy to understand

```
using System.Collections.Generic;
using System.Threading.Tasks;
using Countr.Core.Models;

namespace Countr.Core.Repositories
{
   public interface ICountersRepository
   {
      Task Save(Counter counter);
      Task<List<Counter>> GetAll();
      Task Delete(Counter counter);
   }
}
```

This is a very simple interface that encapsulates the basic operations you'll want to do to maintain a store of counters—save a counter (either saving a new one or updating an existing one), get them all, or delete one.

But when calling save, how do you know if you're creating a new counter or updating an existing one? The same with delete—how do you know which one to delete? The answer relies on the `Id` field on the `Counter`—the field marked with the `PrimaryKey` attribute. SQLite uses this primary key as the unique identifier of a row in a table, so if you save a counter with an `Id` of 2, it will check for an existing row in the table with the `Id` column set to 2. If it finds one, it will update that row to match the values on the counter being saved; if not, it will create a new row. The same happens with delete: if you delete a counter with an `Id` of 7, it will look for a row in the table with that `Id` to delete; if there isn't one, nothing will happen.

Let's create the `CountersRepository` class now and set up SQLite. Then we'll implement the interface.

SQLite is very easy to set up—you create a connection to a database file by passing it a filename, and the SQLite engine will create a database file if one with that name doesn't exist, or open it if it does. There's a small catch, though—where to store the database file. .NET Standard libraries contain APIs to reference the filesystem, but the filesystem is different on iOS and Android, with different paths for storing local files.

Luckily, there's a Xamarin plugin that gives you a single method to call to get the path for storing local data and that returns the correct value on each platform. To install this plugin, install the PCLStorage NuGet package into all the projects in the solution (figure 7.18). The code in this book was written against version 1.0.2, so use this version if you have any problems.

Figure 7.18 The PCLStorage NuGet package gives access to the filesystem from .NET Standard libraries.

Now that you have this plugin installed, you can use it to provide a path for your SQLite-Net database connection. Create a new class called `CountersRepository` and add the following code.

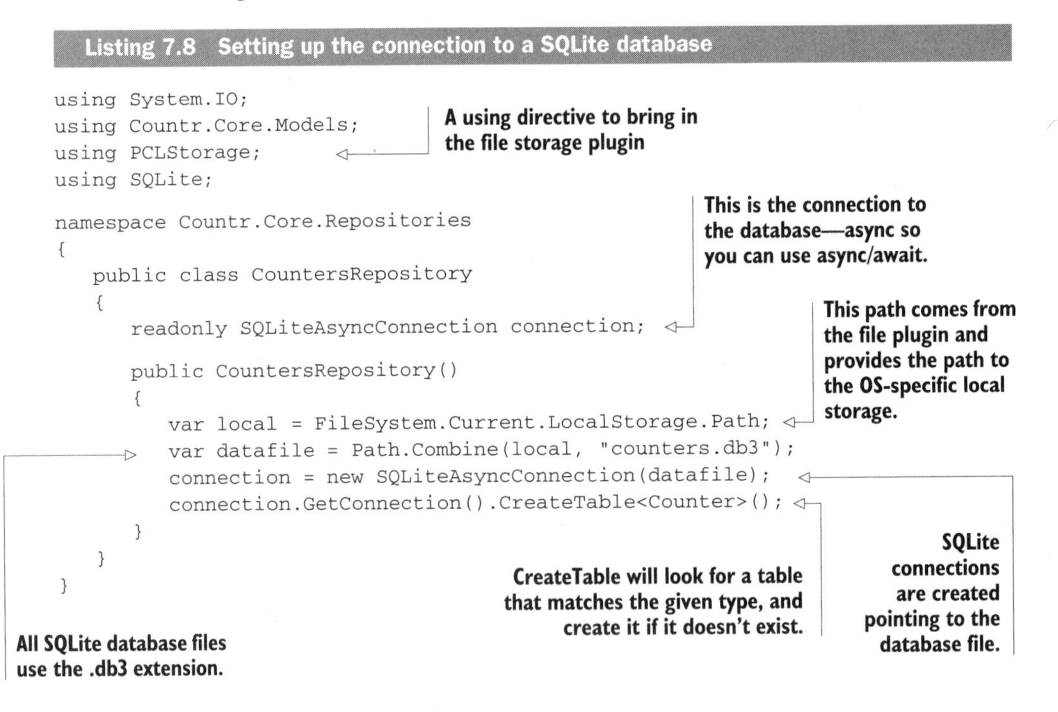

Listing 7.8 Setting up the connection to a SQLite database

```
using System.IO;
using Countr.Core.Models;
using PCLStorage;
using SQLite;

namespace Countr.Core.Repositories
{
   public class CountersRepository
   {
      readonly SQLiteAsyncConnection connection;

      public CountersRepository()
      {
         var local = FileSystem.Current.LocalStorage.Path;
         var datafile = Path.Combine(local, "counters.db3");
         connection = new SQLiteAsyncConnection(datafile);
         connection.GetConnection().CreateTable<Counter>();
      }
   }
}
```

The SQLiteAsyncConnection class gives you an asynchronous connection to the database, allowing you to use async methods that you can await—these methods will handle spawning tasks to run the database interactions from the calling thread. The only downside is that it doesn't provide any synchronous methods—something you need to create the tables in the constructor of this repository. You can get a non-async version of the connection from the async connection using the GetConnection() method, and you can use this to create the table synchronously. This constructor will be called during app startup while the app is on the splash screen, and it will be very fast, so there should be no noticeable app slowdown for the user. Obviously, if you wanted to do more complex database creation work, or migration between different database structures, you should do this on a background thread while displaying something to the user so they don't think their app has locked up—maybe by adding an Init method to the class, which gets called on a background thread during app startup.

Now that you have have your connection, let's implement the repository interface. The following listing shows the implementation. All the async methods call a single async method on the SQLite connection, so instead of marking your methods as async and awaiting the calls, you can just return the tasks directly.

Listing 7.9 The implementation of the ICountersRepository interface

```
using System.Collections.Generic;
using System.Threading.Tasks;
...

public class CountersRepository : ICountersRepository
{
   ...
   public Task Save(Counter counter)
   {
      return connection.InsertOrReplaceAsync(counter);
   }

   public Task<List<Counter>> GetAll()
   {
      return connection.Table<Counter>().ToListAsync();
   }

   public Task Delete(Counter counter)
   {
      return connection.DeleteAsync(counter);
   }
}
```

This class now implements the ICountersRepository interface.

Saves a counter by inserting or updating it based on its Id

Retrieves all the rows from the table and converts them to a list

Deletes the counter with an Id that matches the one passed in

As you can see from this simple implementation, SQLite-Net makes your life really easy when it comes to interacting with databases. This leads to an obvious question—if it's so easy to interact with databases, and each method in the repository is a single SQLite-Net call, then why would you even bother creating a repository in the first place? The answer is, once again, unit testing. You can't easily unit-test code that interacts with a database directly—you'd need a SQLite database. Although you can get implementations of SQLite on Mac and Windows (the platforms that your unit tests run on), they're different from the implementation that runs on a device, and you'd need a lot of setup code to create and configure these databases for each unit test. It's easier to create a very thin repository layer that you can mock out in unit tests. You can't test the repository, but you can mock it to test the services that use it.

> **YOU CAN UNIT-TEST SQLITE BY USING ON-DEVICE UNIT TESTS** Xamarin provides a way to run unit tests on a physical iOS and Android device or emulator. This means you can write unit tests (or, more correctly, *integration tests,* as they test the integration between your app code and the database) against a SQLite database if you want to. You can find more details in the Xamarin iOS unit testing guide at http://mng.bz/0tv6 and the Android troubleshooting guide at http://mng.bz/mMWa.

Now that you have your repository, you need to register it in the IoC container. You've seen already that you can easily register individual classes inside the container, but MvvmCross has a simple way to automatically register multiple classes that are similarly named. If you open App.cs from the Countr.Core project, you'll see the following line.

Listing 7.10 MvvmCross projects register all services into the IoC container by default

```
CreatableTypes()
    .EndingWith("Service")
    .AsInterfaces()
    .RegisterAsLazySingleton();
```

This tells MvvmCross to look inside the current assembly and find all classes with names that end with `Service` and register them as singletons based on their interface (registering them as *lazy singletons* to be precise, meaning they're only constructed the first time they're accessed). Because it's a common pattern to have service class names end in `Service`, MvvmCross projects are set up to automatically register them, by default. You can extend this to include repositories by adding a copy of the same code but with a different name, as follows.

Listing 7.11 Automatically registering all repositories into the IoC container

```
...
CreatableTypes()
    .EndingWith("Repository")
    .AsInterfaces()
    .RegisterAsLazySingleton();
...
```

Once you've added this line, there's no need to explicitly register your `CountersRepository`—MvvmCross will search the assembly, find the repository based on its name ending in `Repository`, get its interface, and register the class against its interface.

7.3.3 Adding a service layer

You have your data model (the `Counter` class) and your repository layer (the `CountersRepository` class). Now you need to add a service layer on top. The view models will interact with the services in this layer, which in turn will use the repositories to store and retrieve data. As a reminder, figure 7.19 shows these layers.

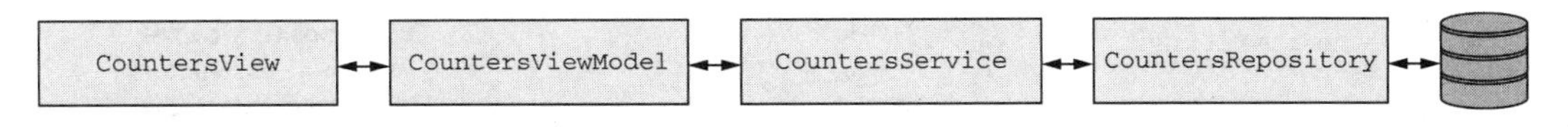

Figure 7.19 The layers in the Countr app

CREATING THE SERVICE

You need to create a new counter service that your view models can interact with, so let's start with the interface, as always. Create a Services folder, and in that folder create a new interface called `ICountersService`, as in the following listing.

Listing 7.12 The interface for the counters service

```
using System.Collections.Generic;
using System.Threading.Tasks;
using Countr.Core.Models;

namespace Countr.Core.Services
{
   public interface ICountersService
   {
      Task<Counter> AddNewCounter(string name);
      Task<List<Counter>> GetAllCounters();
      Task DeleteCounter(Counter counter);
      Task IncrementCounter(Counter counter);
   }
}
```

Methods to create, delete, and get all the counters

A method to increment the counter

The first three methods on this service are fairly self-explanatory—they allow the callers to get, save, and delete counters. The fourth method is a bit different—it increments a counter. It may seem odd to be incrementing a counter from a service when the `Count` value on the counter could be manipulated directly, but there's a good reason for this. If the `Count` property is 0 and is updated directly to 1, then the `Counter` instance is updated, and this new count of 1 is held in memory. If the app dies and is reloaded, what would the counter show? It would show 0 again. You need to persist all changes to the repository to ensure that when the app restarts and all counters are loaded, the correct values are available. By having the service control the incrementing of counters, it can ensure that the new values are always persisted to the database.

Now you have your interface. Let's create the service, and then implement the interface. Create a new class called `CountersService`. The following listing shows the initial code for it.

Listing 7.13 The initial implementation of the counters service

```
using Countr.Core.Repositories;

namespace Countr.Core.Services
{
   public class CountersService
   {
      readonly ICountersRepository repository;

      public CountersService(ICountersRepository repository)
      {
         this.repository = repository;
      }
   }
}
```

The repository comes from a constructor parameter and is stored in a field.

Having the `ICountersRepository` interface as a constructor parameter for `CountersService` tells the MvvmCross IoC container to pass in whatever implementation of the `ICountersRepository` it has to this constructor when the class is created.

Let's wire up the rest of the class now. Add the following code.

Listing 7.14 Implementing the ICountersService interface

```
using System.Collections.Generic;
using System.Threading.Tasks;
using Countr.Core.Models;
...

public class CountersService : ICountersService
{
  ...
  public async Task<Counter> AddNewCounter(string name)
  {
     var counter = new Counter { Name = name };
     await repository.Save(counter).ConfigureAwait(false);
     return counter;
  }

  public Task<List<Counter>> GetAllCounters()
  {
     return repository.GetAll();
  }

  public Task DeleteCounter(Counter counter)
  {
     return repository.Delete(counter);
  }
```

A new counter is created from a name, stored in the repository, then returned.

Getting all counters returns all counters from the repository.

Deleting a counter deletes it from the repository.

```
    public Task IncrementCounter(Counter counter)
    {
       counter.Count += 1;
       return repository.Save(counter);
    }
}
```

Incrementing a counter will increment the Count property and then update the counter in the repository.

Most of this code should be fairly self-explanatory. AddNewCounter constructs a new counter based on the name given, saves it to the repository, and returns it. Increment-Counter increments the Count value on the given counter and saves the incremented version to the repository. GetAllCounters gets all counters from the repository, and DeleteCounter deletes a counter from the repository. IncrementCounter, GetAll-Counters, and DeleteCounter just return the tasks from the async methods they call on the repository. AddNewCounter is marked as async and uses Configure-Await(false) to tell the compiler that after the call to Save, the rest of the code in the method can stay on the same thread that Save used to do its work.

We're done with the model layer now—you have a repository that manages counters using a SQLite database and a service layer that encapsulates all your interactions with counters. But like the model layer for SquareRt, how can you test this? You could wait until the app is built, but it's better to write some unit tests, so that not only can you test the code now, you can test your code again and again and again to ensure you don't break anything in the future. You can't easily unit-test the repository, but you can test your service.

UNIT-TESTING YOUR SERVICE LAYER

Before you can think about unit testing, you need to create a unit-test project. Create a new project called Countr.Core.Tests in the same way as you did the SquareRt.Core.Tests project—either using a new NUnit Library Project in Visual Studio for Mac or by creating a new .NET Framework Class Library in Visual Studio and adding the NUnit NuGet package. Once the project is created, add a reference to the Countr.Core project.

As we've discussed, you can't easily unit-test code that talks to a database, so you can't test your repository. Although the service doesn't interact directly with a database, it does use the repository, which in turn uses a database, so how can you unit-test this?

What you need to do is not use your implementation of the repository. Instead, you need to use a dummy implementation—one that not only doesn't talk to a SQLite database, but ideally one that you can control. For example, to test that the Increment-Counter method on the service is working correctly, you need to ensure that it not only increments the Count property, but that it saves the incremented value to the repository—this checks that you haven't got the save and increment lines the wrong way around. If you have a repository that you can control, you could perform some kind of assertion on the call to Save to ensure that the incremented counter is saved.

There's a great pattern for creating dummy implementations, called *mocking*. In this technique, you create an implementation of an interface and have complete control on

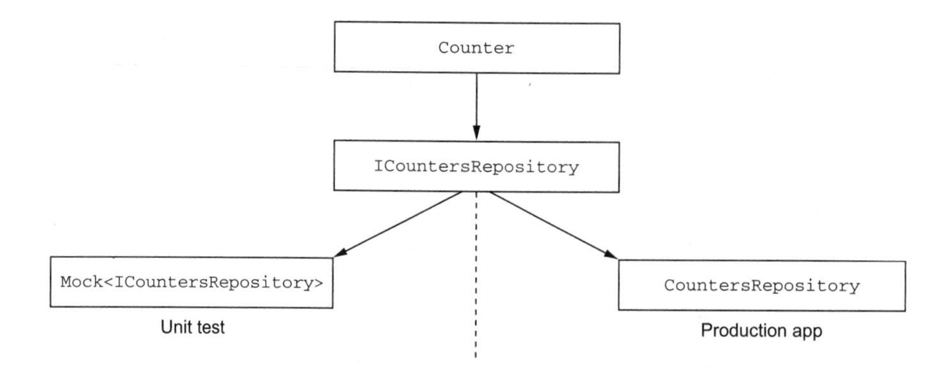

Figure 7.20 Mocking is a simple technique allowing you to unit-test without worrying about dependencies.

a test-by-test basis, allowing you to configure what the methods on the interface do and return, and also verify that the methods are called (figure 7.20).

There are a number of great open source tools to help with this, my favorite being Moq (https://github.com/Moq). To install Moq, add the Moq NuGet package to the Countr.Core.Tests project (figure 7.21).

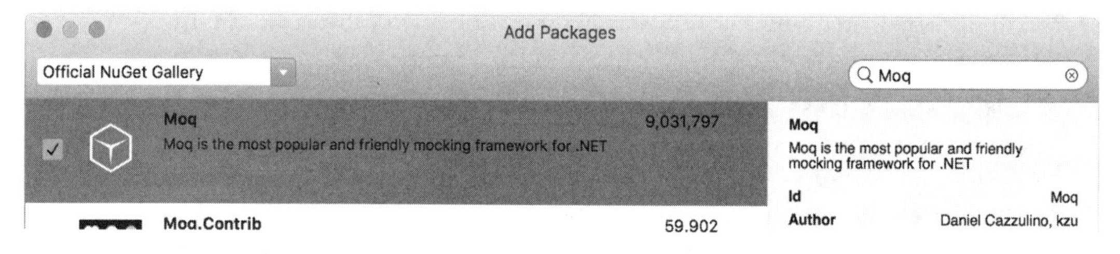

Figure 7.21 Installing the Moq NuGet package gives you a simple way to mock interfaces in your unit tests.

Add a new folder called Services to the test project, and then add a `CountersServiceTests` class. The following listing shows the initial implementation of this class.

Listing 7.15 The initial implementation of the unit tests for the counters service

```
using NUnit.Framework;
using Moq;
using Countr.Core.Repositories;
using Countr.Core.Services;

namespace Countr.Core.Tests.Services
{
   [TestFixture]
   public class CountersServiceTests
   {
      ICountersService service;
      Mock<ICountersRepository>  repo;
```

```
        [SetUp]
        public void SetUp()
        {
           repo = new Mock<ICountersRepository>();
           service = new CountersService(repo.Object);
        }
    }
}
```

In the test fixture setup, a new mock repository is created so that it's ready for each test.

A new instance of the CountersService created using the mock object.

The `Mock<ICountersRepository>` field is a mock of the `ICountersRepository` interface. It has a property called `Object` that's an `ICountersRepository` interface, which you can pass to the constructor of the `CountersService`.

What's powerful about this mock is what happens when you call the methods on the interface. By default, these methods will do nothing and will return the default value for the return type (for example, if you call the `GetAllCounters` method, it will return null), but you can override this behavior. You can set up methods to return whatever you want, perform actions when they're called, or throw exceptions—this can be for all calls to a method, or only when it's called with specific parameters. You can also get a count of how many times a method is called—either the total of all calls, or a count of different calls with different parameters.

Let's start with a simple set of tests for the `IncrementCounter` method. You want to test two things—that the counter is incremented, and that the incremented value is stored. Here's the code for these two tests.

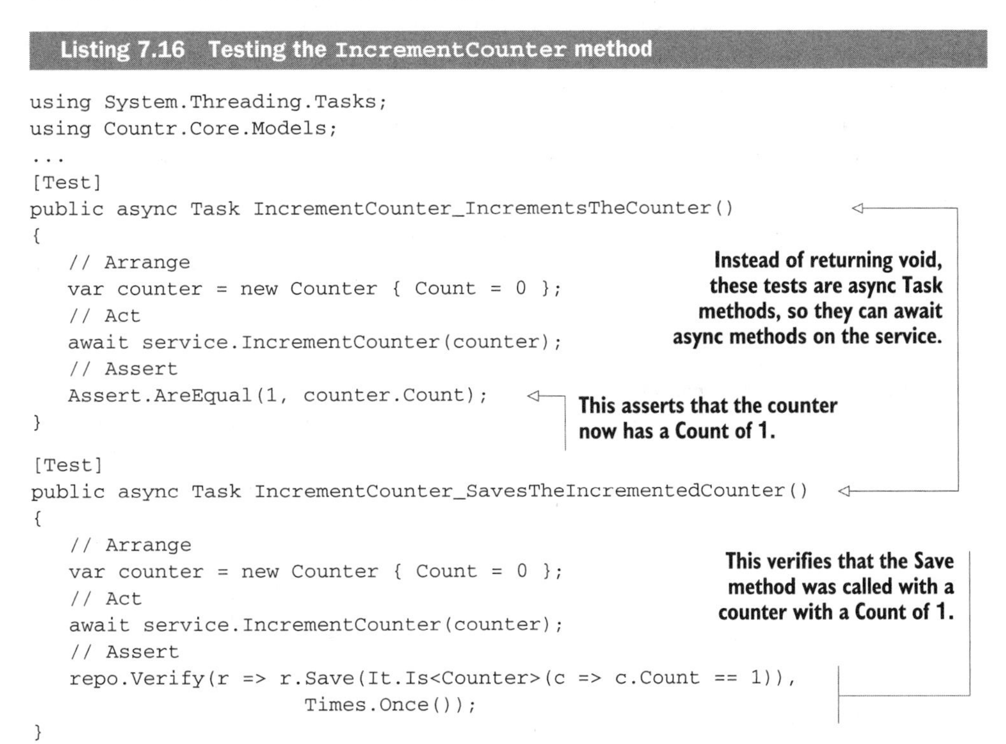

Listing 7.16 Testing the `IncrementCounter` method

```
using System.Threading.Tasks;
using Countr.Core.Models;
...
[Test]
public async Task IncrementCounter_IncrementsTheCounter()
{
   // Arrange
   var counter = new Counter { Count = 0 };
   // Act
   await service.IncrementCounter(counter);
   // Assert
   Assert.AreEqual(1, counter.Count);
}
[Test]
public async Task IncrementCounter_SavesTheIncrementedCounter()
{
   // Arrange
   var counter = new Counter { Count = 0 };
   // Act
   await service.IncrementCounter(counter);
   // Assert
   repo.Verify(r => r.Save(It.Is<Counter>(c => c.Count == 1)),
                       Times.Once());
}
```

Instead of returning void, these tests are async Task methods, so they can await async methods on the service.

This asserts that the counter now has a Count of 1.

This verifies that the Save method was called with a counter with a Count of 1.

These two tests cover the basics of the IncrementCounter method. The Increment-Counter_IncrementsTheCounter test ensures that the counter has an incremented Count after the method has finished—a nice, simple sanity check. The interesting test is the IncrementCounter_SavesTheIncrementedCounter test. This uses a method on the mock repository called Verify that verifies that a method has been called. Let's look at the two arguments passed to Verify.

The first argument, r → r.Save(It.Is<Counter>(c → c.Count == 1)) is used to define which method is being verified. It's a lambda expression where the parameter is the interface for the mock (in this case, the ICountersRepository interface), and you call the method that you want to verify. You then specify what the parameters you're verifying are. They can be fixed values, or you can use the static It class from Moq, which allows you to specify certain conditions about the parameter. You can use It.IsAny<T> to specify any value of type T, or use It.Is<T>(Func<T, bool>) to check for specific properties of the instance of T. In this case we're using It.Is<Counter>(c → c.Count == 1) to say that we want to verify that this method was called using an instance of Counter that has a Count property set to 1. This is a very important part of this test—you need to ensure that the incremented value is saved, and that's what the check for a count of 1 is doing. If the service code saved the counter before incrementing it, this test would fail because the counter passed to Save would have a value of 0.

The second argument, Times.Once(), is the number of times this method was called with the given criteria. You don't have to specify this argument, and if you don't, it verifies that the method was called at least once (with no upper limit on how many times it was called). Here we're saying it should be called only once. After all, there's no point in calling this method more than once. There are a number of alternatives, such as Times.Never, to ensure that the method is never called, or variants that allow you to set the minimum, maximum, or exact number of times the method must be called.

Table 7.5 shows a breakdown of these two tests. They both have the same arrange and act—creating a counter with a count of 0 and incrementing it—but the assertions are different. One test asserts that the count of the counter has incremented, and the other test asserts that the new value has been saved.

Table 7.5 The arrange, act, and assert for the CountersService tests

Arrange	Act	Assert
Create a counter with a count of 0	_service.IncrementCounter(counter)	Assert the counter's count is now 1
Create a counter with a count of 0	_service.IncrementCounter(counter)	Assert a counter with a count of 1 is saved to the repository

This is powerful testing functionality—you can't unit-test the repository, but you can ensure that your services make the correct calls to it.

The other thing you can do is control the return value from the different methods on the interface using the `Setup` method. The following listing shows a test to verify the `GetAllCounters` method on the service.

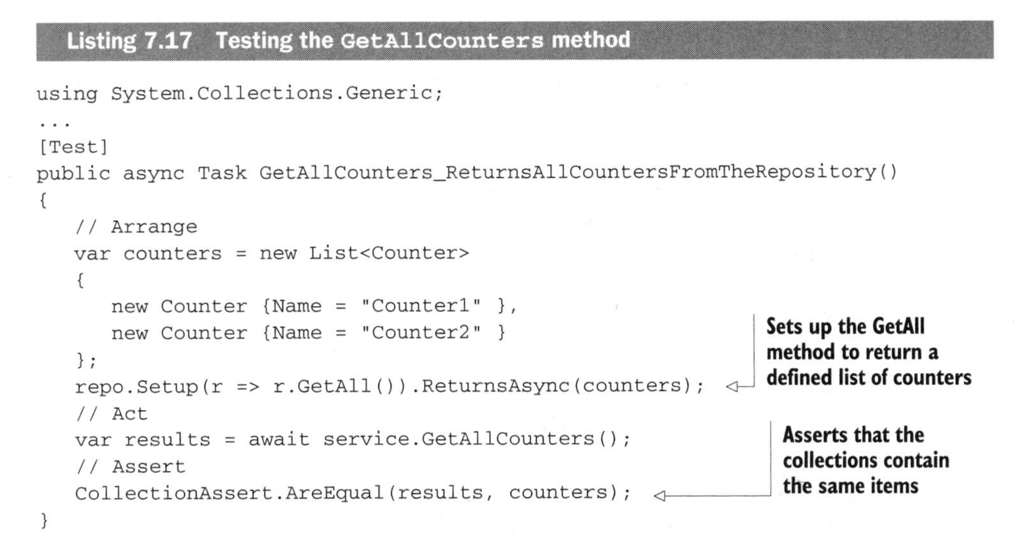

Listing 7.17 Testing the `GetAllCounters` method

```
using System.Collections.Generic;
...
[Test]
public async Task GetAllCounters_ReturnsAllCountersFromTheRepository()
{
   // Arrange
   var counters = new List<Counter>
   {
      new Counter {Name = "Counter1" },
      new Counter {Name = "Counter2" }
   };
   repo.Setup(r => r.GetAll()).ReturnsAsync(counters);
   // Act
   var results = await service.GetAllCounters();
   // Assert
   CollectionAssert.AreEqual(results, counters);
}
```

Sets up the GetAll method to return a defined list of counters
Asserts that the collections contain the same items

The `Setup` method allows you to set up the behavior of a method on the interface. You specify the criteria for the method in the same way as the `Verify` method, and then you can specify callbacks or the value that the method returns. `Returns` specifies the return value of a normal method, and `ReturnsAsync`, which we're using here, specifies the return value of an async method. `CollectionAssert` is an NUnit helper class that can assert on collections, and we're using it here to assert that the results of the call to `GetAllCounters` returns a collection that matches the collection returned from the repository. Table 7.6 shows a breakdown of this test.

Table 7.6 The arrange, act, and assert the Return all counters tests

Arrange	Act	Assert
Set up a list of counters to be returned from `GetAll` on the repository	`_service.GetAllCounters()`	Assert that the counters returned from the service are the same as the counters set up as the return value for the `GetAll` method on the repository

> **MOQ CAN ALSO BE USED TO SET UP PROPERTIES** `Setup` is used to set up methods. For properties there's a pair of similar methods: `SetupGet` and `SetupSet` to set up the getter and setter for a property.

There's plenty more on the service that needs to be tested, and as an exercise you can think up some more tests that would cover all the methods of the service. Run these tests now, though, and enjoy watching them pass.

Once again, we've written one set of unit tests that allow us to test code that will run on both iOS and Android. This is something we couldn't do if we'd just wired up events on the UI to code, or if we wrote our apps using Java and Objective-C/Swift.

7.3.4 Accessing web services

So far we've looked at a simple model layer for our SquareRt app, and a more complex model layer for Countr that uses a SQLite database to save data. Calculations and data persistence are popular things to have in the model layer, but there's one other thing a lot of model layers do that we should look at—making web service calls. Many apps have some kind of service running over the internet to provide data—email apps download and send emails via an email server, and social media apps like Facebook and Twitter download and send posts or tweets over the internet.

By far the most popular way to do this is using REST services over HTTP. These are stateless services whereby different URLs represent resources that you can interact with using CRUD operations. You send HTTP verbs that describe the action you want to do: send a `GET` request to a URL to request data, `POST` to create data, `PUT` to update data, or `DELETE` to delete data. The URL you use describes details about the resource you want to interact with; you can include a body with your request, such as the data to `PUT`; you can use HTTP headers to specify details about the request, such as authorization details; and you can add query parameters to the URL. Query parameters are a way of passing information to a `GET` request using just a URL instead of sending a body of data. You can send information to the HTTP request using JSON (a lightweight way to represent data) or XML, and get results back as JSON or XML. JSON is becoming the most popular as it's simple and lightweight. This is shown in figure 7.22.

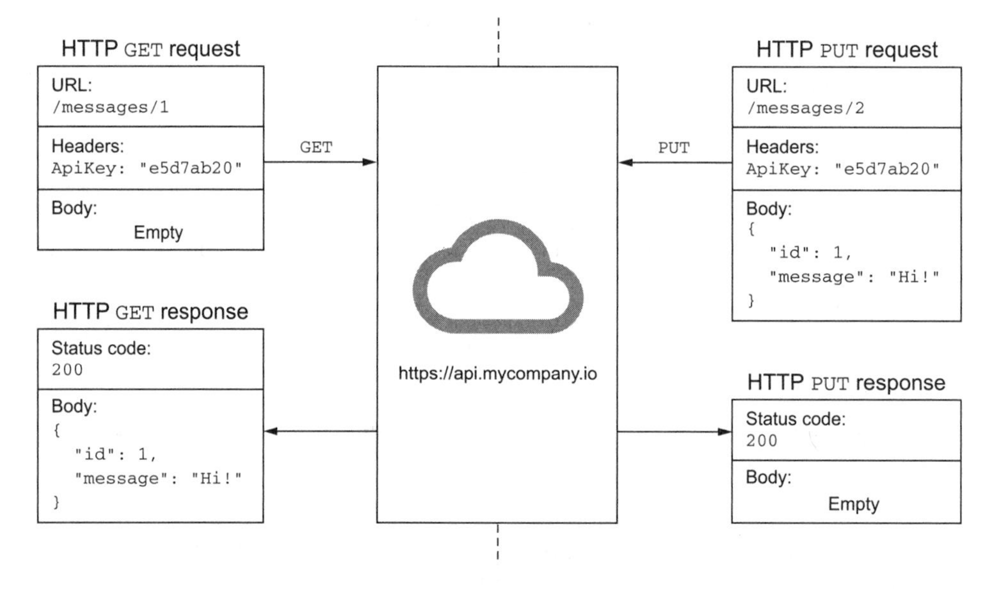

Figure 7.22 REST APIs allow you to send requests to URLs using HTTP verbs, and to get data back.

REST APIs are a huge topic in themselves, and they're outside the scope of this book, but we'll look at how to call a simple REST API and interpret the data from the model layer. For a more detailed look at REST APIs, I recommend *Irresistible APIs* by Kirsten L. Hunter (Manning, 2016).

USING MICROSOFT BING'S SEARCH API TO CALCULATE A SQUARE ROOT

When you're building a commercial app, you may well have a set of REST services provided by your company or client that your app will need to interact with. There are also many third-party APIs that your app can use to incorporate a wide variety of functionality: performing calculations, manipulating images, getting data such as government records, and using artificial intelligence services. One such service is Microsoft Bing—the search engine from Microsoft. Not only can it search the web much like other popular search engines, such as Google, but it can also be used for calculations. You can try this out by going to Bing.com and searching for "square root 4".

Microsoft has made a REST service for Bing available to developers to use inside their apps, allowing a large number of searches per month for only a few dollars (and a lot more searches per month if you're willing to pay more). We can use this API in our SquareRt app to calculate square roots instead of using `System.Math.Sqrt`.

Microsoft has a large number of APIs available to developers as part of its Azure cloud, from simple searches to a whole host of artificial intelligence tools. You can see all of these services from Microsoft's Cognitive Services website at http://mng.bz/B97v. You'll need an Azure account to use these services, so if you don't have one, click Free Account, then Start Free, and follow the instructions to sign up. You'll need a credit card to sign up, but this is only used for verification, and at the time of writing you get $200 worth of credit just for signing up. You can also sign up using Visual Studio Developer Essentials at www.visualstudio.com/dev-essentials/?WT.mc_id=xamarininaction-book-jabenn to get $25 a month in credit for a year.

Once you're signed in, head to the Azure portal at portal.azure.com. Click New on the left side (if the menu on the left is minimized, the New option is a green plus sign), select AI + Cognitive Services in the Azure Marketplace list that appears, and then click Bing Search APIs.

Each thing on Azure that you sign up for (such as access to a cognitive service API, a virtual machine, or a database) is referred to as a *resource*. All resources are part of resource groups—logical groupings of resources that you can manage together. For example, when you're finished using a set of resources, you can delete the resource group to remove all resources in one go. You'll need to configure the Bing Search APIs resource and make it part of a resource group.

Start by entering a name for this resource, such as *SquareRt*, select your Azure subscription, set the pricing tier to S1 (this works out to $3 a month at the time of writing). You'll then need to create a new resource group to put this resource into, so ensure Create New is selected under Resource Group, and enter a name such as *SquareRt* (figure 7.23).

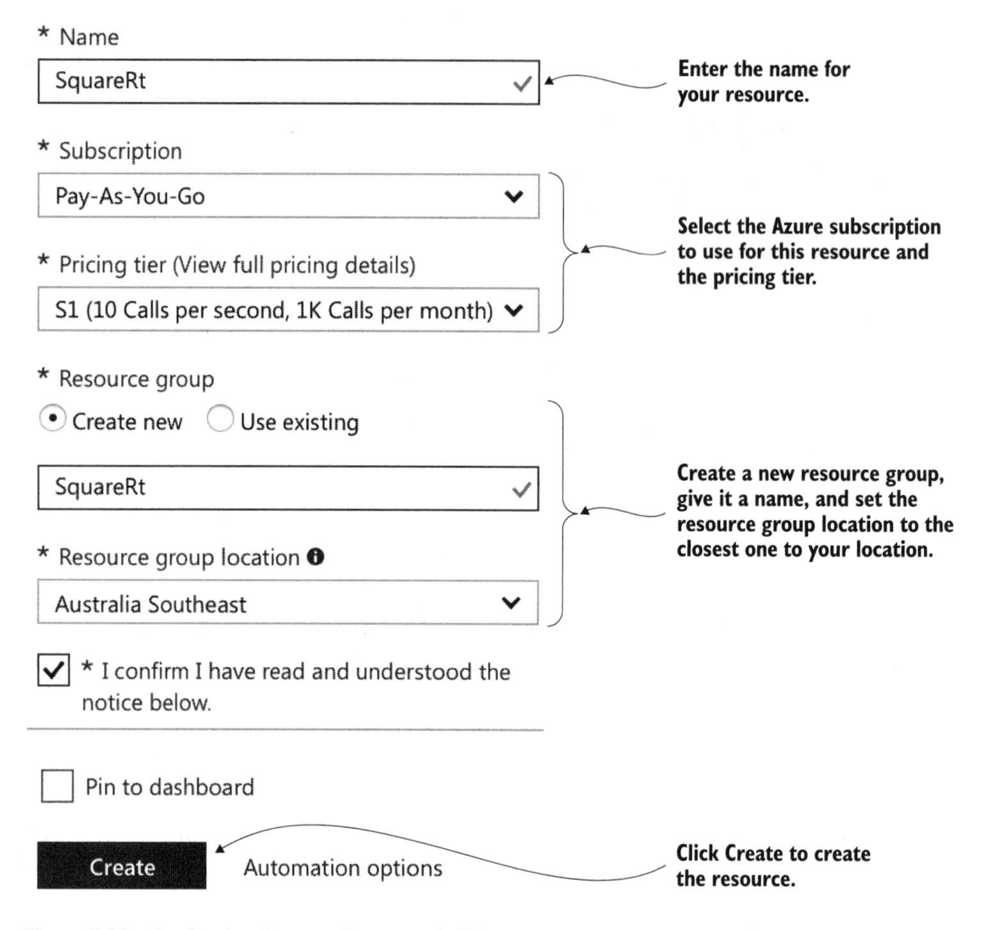

Figure 7.23 Configuring the new Bing search API resource

Each resource group is run from a data center somewhere in the world, and you can configure which data center to use from the Resource Group Location drop-down. Choose the one closest to your physical location, read the terms and conditions at the bottom, and tick the box to confirm you've read them. Finally, click the Create button to create the resource.

Once the resource is created, you'll see an overview page with details about the new SquareRt resource. From here, select Resource Management > Keys on the left to see some API keys that you can use to access these services from your own apps (figure 7.24).

Now that you have your API keys, you can use them to calculate square roots using the Bing web service. When you make a call using this service, you get results back as a JSON object. Because Bing search is a general-purpose API, you don't just get back a single number; instead you get back an object that contains the details of the response, serialized as JSON. I've used the term *JSON* a lot, so who is this Jason fellow?

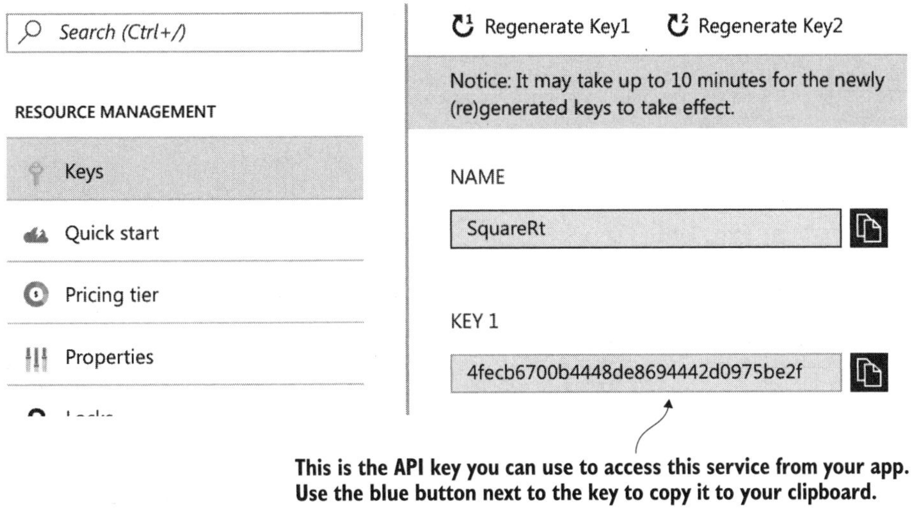

This is the API key you can use to access this service from your app. Use the blue button next to the key to copy it to your clipboard.

Figure 7.24 The Microsoft cognitive service APIs use API keys to control access.

JSON

JSON stands for *JavaScript Object Notation*, and it's a simple, lightweight way of serializing data to a string. You can read more about it at www.json.org, but essentially it's a way of storing data in a string as a set of key-value pairs, and the value can be either a single value such as a string or number, or it can be another set of key-value pairs to represent another object. You can even represent lists of objects. Each string containing an object or an array of similarly typed objects is referred to as a *JSON document* (you may have heard of document databases such as MongoDB—these store JSON documents as indexable and searchable objects).

The following listing shows a JSON representation of an object that would come back from a call to the Bing search API, with figure 7.25 showing a summary of the objects that it represents.

Listing 7.18 A JSON document representing the results of a Bing calculation search

```
{
  "_type": "SearchResponse",
  "computation": {
    "id": "https://api.cognitive.microsoft.com/api/v5/#Computation",
    "expression": "sqrt(40)",
    "value": "6.32455532"
  },
  "rankingResponse": {
    "mainline": {
      "items": [
        {
          "answerType": "Computation",
          "value": {
```

```
                "id": "https://api.cognitive.microsoft.com/api/v5/#Computation"
              }
            }
          ]
        }
      }
    }
```

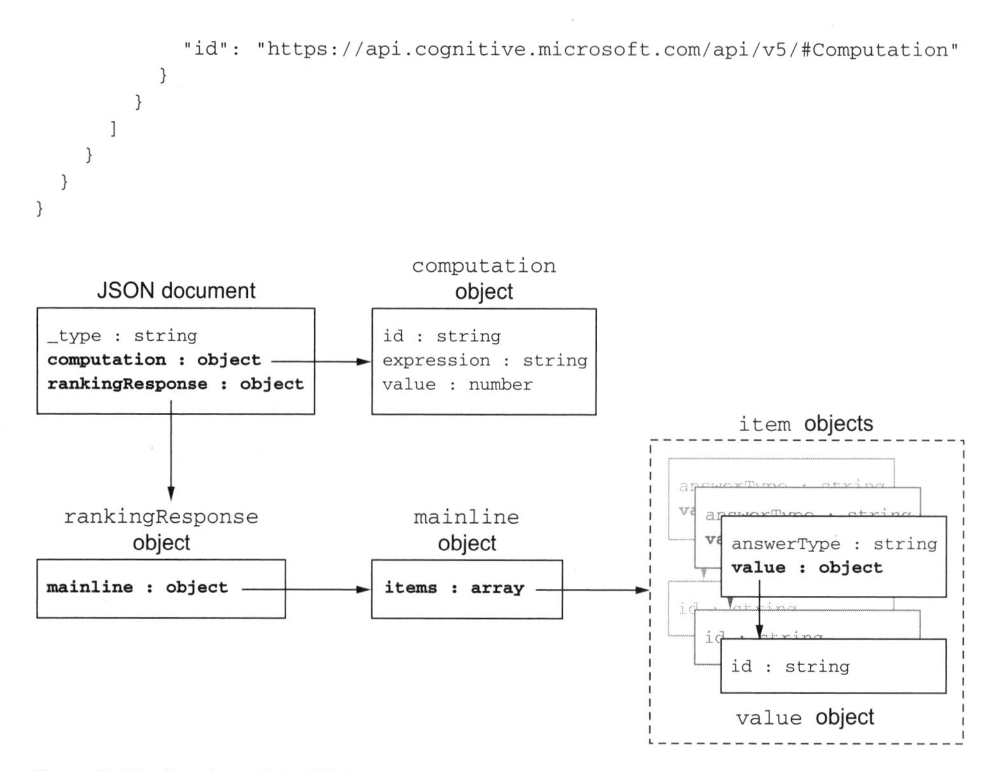

Figure 7.25 Overview of the JSON document returned from the Bing search service

The curly braces (`{` and `}`) represent an object, with the properties of the object defined as a set of key-value pairs. The property name is the key, and it's defined as a string. The value is defined after the colon (`:`) as either a string representation of a value, such as a string or a number, as an object wrapped in braces, or as an array stored inside square brackets (`[` and `]`). The document in listing 7.18 consists of an outer object (in JSON, objects don't have named types) with three properties:

- `_type`—A string
- `computation`—An object with three properties (`id`, `expression`, and `value`)
- `rankingResponse`—An object that has a property called `mainline`, which is an object with a property called `items`, which is an array of objects, each having an `answerType` and `value` property, `value` being another object

JSON seems pretty complex, and parsing a string representation like this is a lot of work. Luckily, once again someone else has done the hard work for us, and you can install a NuGet package to take the complexities away. Newtonsoft.Json, also known as Json.NET, is not only the most installed NuGet package ever (at the time of writing, it has been installed over 42 million times), but it provides a simple way to convert from JSON to C# classes and vice versa. Json.NET can also do value conversions, so if your

C# class has a field of type `double`, it will look at the string value in the JSON and convert it to a decimal number—such as converting `"6.32455532"` in the preceding JSON document to a double value of 6.32455532. If you want to have any interaction with JSON data, I strongly advise you to use Json.NET to make your life much easier.

We'll use it here, so install the Newtonsoft.Json NuGet package. The code in this book was written against version 10.0.3, but later versions should work (figure 7.26).

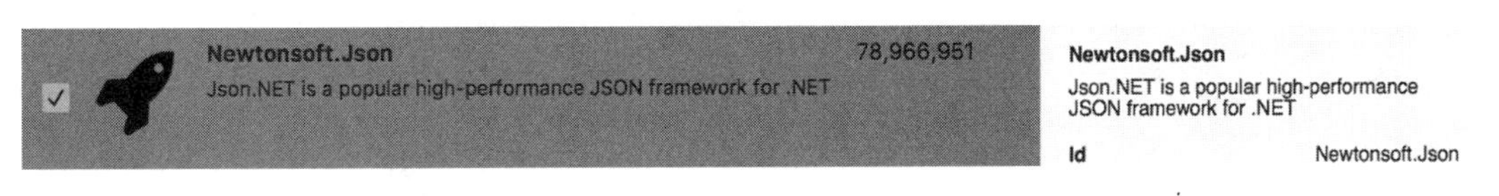

Figure 7.26 Adding the Newtonsoft.Json NuGet package

You saw an example JSON response from the Bing search API in listing 7.18, so let's think about a class that could encapsulate this data. All we really need is the computation's value, so what do we need to do to get this?

We need to define a class hierarchy that matches the JSON document, just focusing on what we need—in this case, a class that has a property called `computation` of a type that has a property called `value`. One good thing Json.NET does is only deserialize the values you have in your classes, ignoring all the others. This is good for us because we only need the `value` property from the `computation` object. It would be a pain to have to implement all the classes and properties in this JSON document just for one field. This also prevents our app from breaking if new fields are added to the JSON, such as if you add extra data that's only used by a later version of your app.

We can define this in code by adding two new classes to the SquareRt project called `Computation` and `SquareRootResponse`. The following listing shows these classes.

Listing 7.19 Classes that represent the JSON response from the Bing search API

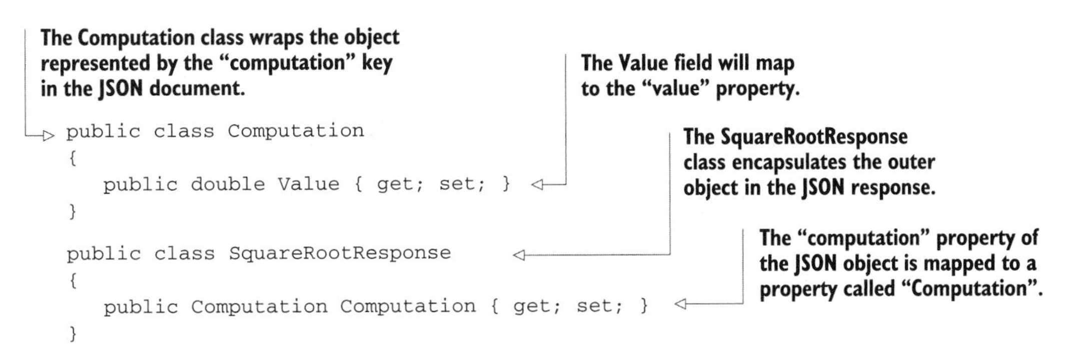


```
public class Computation
{
   public double Value { get; set; }
}

public class SquareRootResponse
{
   public Computation Computation { get; set; }
}
```

Using Json.NET, you can deserialize a string containing a JSON document to a class that you can specify. It will take the properties in the JSON document and map them to properties in the class based on the properties' names. It's also smart enough to ignore case (JSON uses lowercase for the first letter of each property, whereas C# by convention uses uppercase). If you were to deserialize the JSON document in listing 7.18 to a `SquareRootResponse`, it would map the `computation` property in the JSON document to the `Computation` property on the class, and map the properties of the object assigned to the `computation` object to the properties on the `Computation` class. Figure 7.27 shows this mapping.

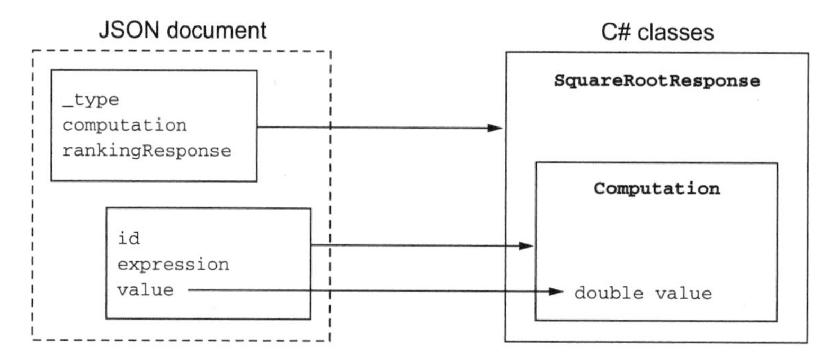

Figure 7.27 The JSON properties are mapped to the properties of C# classes based on their names.

It's fairly simple to map other JSON documents to classes—all you need to do is build a hierarchy of classes with properties that map to the JSON document. These properties don't need to be strings—they can be classes in their own right, as demonstrated by `SquareRootResponse`, or they can be data types such as numbers, like the `Value` property of `Computation`. In the JSON, this is a string, but we're mapping it to a double and Json.NET takes care of the conversion.

Now we have a class that encapsulates what we need from the response. Let's wire this up to an HTTP call.

MAKING WEB SERVICE CALLS

When making a call to a web service, you need to use the device-specific network stack—both iOS and Android have classes that can interact with web services that are specific to the individual OS. The good news for us C# developers is that this is such a normal thing to do that Xamarin and Microsoft have made sure the part of the .NET Framework that allows easy interaction with HTTP endpoints is available in .NET Standard libraries. This means you can hit web services from your core projects.

To make a call to a web service from a .NET Standard library, you can use `HttpClient`—a class that under the hood uses the native network stack to make calls to web services. This class has methods to make all the possible HTTP calls—`GET`, `POST`, `PUT`, and `DELETE`.

To calculate a square root, you need to make a `GET` call to the Bing service. Bing, by default, is a search engine, so you can create a URL that searches for the square root of a particular number, and you can then specify that instead of a simple web search, you're interested in a performing a calculation. There are a whole host of options for this API, and you can read more on it in Microsoft's Web Search API Reference at http://mng.bz/4KQ3.

`HttpClient`, like a lot of modern .NET Framework classes, uses `async` and `await`, so the first thing to do is change our `ISquareRtCalculator` interface to support this. The following listing shows the changes to the interface.

Listing 7.20 Updating the square-root calculator interface to use `async` and `await`

```
using System.Threading.Tasks;

public interface ISquareRtCalculator
{
   Task<double> Calculate(double number);
}
```

You also need to update the implementation of this calculator to not only use `async/await`, but to make a call to the Bing search API to calculate the square root.

Listing 7.21 Making a web service call from the square-root calculator

```
using System.Net.Http;
using System.Threading.Tasks;
using Newtonsoft.Json;
...
public class SquareRtCalculator : ISquareRtCalculator
{
   readonly HttpClient httpClient = new HttpClient();

   public SquareRtCalculator()
   {
      httpClient.DefaultRequestHeaders
         .Add("Ocp-Apim-Subscription-Key",
              "your API key");
   }

   public async Task<double> Calculate(double number)
   {
      var url = "https://api.cognitive.microsoft.com/bing/v5.0/search?" +
                $"q=sqrt({number})&responseFilter=Computation";
      var response = await httpClient.GetAsync(url).ConfigureAwait(false);
      var json = await response.Content.ReadAsStringAsync().ConfigureAwait(false);
      var squareRt =
            JsonConvert.DeserializeObject<SquareRootResponse>(json);
      return squareRt.Computation.Value;
   }
}
```

- **Creates a new instance of HttpClient to interact with web services** (`readonly HttpClient httpClient = new HttpClient();`)
- **Sets the API key on the headers—this would be one of the keys assigned to your Bing search API subscription** (`httpClient.DefaultRequestHeaders`)
- **Specifies the URL of the endpoint to use for the search** (`var url = ...`)
- **Makes an HTTP GET call to get the response** (`var response = ...`)
- **Gets the content of the response as a string containing a JSON document** (`var json = ...`)
- **Converts the JSON document to your new classes** (`JsonConvert.DeserializeObject...`)
- **Returns the value of the calculation from the JSON** (`return squareRt.Computation.Value;`)

This is a complicated set of calls, so let's break it down line by line.

- `readonly HttpClient httpClient = new HttpClient();`

  This creates a new instance of the HTTP client class that you use to interact with web services. You don't need to create a new one for every request—you can reuse the same one.
- _httpClient.DefaultRequestHeaders.Add("Ocp-Apim-Subscription-Key", "<your API key>");`

  This adds a header that includes the API key to all the HTTP requests. You should replace <your API key> with one of the API keys assigned to your account when you set up your Bing search subscription.
- `var url = "https://api.cognitive.microsoft.com/bing/v5.0/search ?q=sqrt({number})&responseFilter=Computation";`

  This is the URL used to perform searches against the Bing API. It sends a request to https://api.cognitive.microsoft.com/bing/v5.0/search using a couple of query parameters. The standard way to send query parameters is using the `?` operator followed by queries in the form of `key=value`, separated using the `&` character. In this example, you're sending a query with the first parameter set to "q=sqrt(<number>)" (where <number> is the number passed in to the `Calculate` method), which is the same as entering a search query of 'sqrt(<number>)', into Bing. The second parameter is `"responseFilter=Computation"`, which tells Bing to run a computation instead of a search. This is broken down in figure 7.28.
- `var response = await httpClient.GetAsync(url).ConfigureAwait(false);`

  This will make the call to the web service and get a response object. This response has a couple of interesting properties: `StatusCode` and `Content`. The status code is the HTTP status code, so 200 for success, 404 if a URL isn't valid, or 418 if the endpoint is a teapot and you've sent a request to brew coffee (yes, really). Anything in the 200 range is success, and anything in the 400 range is an error. You can read more about the possible status codes on Wikipedia

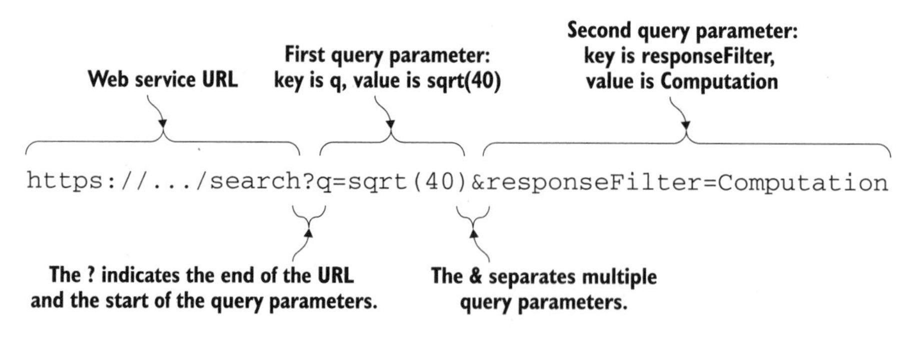

Figure 7.28 HTTP requests can be suffixed with a `?` followed by query parameters as multiple `key=value` pairs separated by an `&`.

(http://mng.bz/dfmF). This call will throw an exception if it times out, or if the status code is in the 400 range. Here we're not handling exceptions for the sake of brevity, but in production code you should handle all possible exceptions from this call.

This is an async method, and the implementation of `HttpClient` will use background threads to do its work. When you call `await httpClient.GetAsync(url)`, a new task is created and run to make the call to the web service on a background thread. `ConfigureAwait(false)` tells the compiler to keep using this background thread to run the rest of the method until the next `await`.

- ```
  var json =
    await response.Content.ReadAsStringAsync().ConfigureAwait(false);
  ```
  The response contains the JSON for the search result, so this call will read the content as a string that you can then deserialize to an object. Again, like `GetAsync`, this will create a task to download the response on a background thread, and the call to `ConfigureAwait(false)` will keep the rest of this method on that background thread.
- ```
  var squareRt =
    JsonConvert.DeserializeObject<SquareRootResponse>(json);
  ```
  Once you have the string response, you can use the static `JsonConvert` class from Json.NET to deserialize the string into an instance of the `SquareRootResponse` class, and you can get the calculated value from there.

The end result of this code is that you've sent a request to the Bing search API to calculate a square root, and you've received a response that you can convert from JSON to a set of C# classes that you can use to get the result as a double. Let's test this out.

TESTING THIS CALL

Our unit tests are designed to test the methods on our classes, so as long as the interface doesn't change, the unit tests should still pass. This is one of the great things about unit testing—you can refactor your implementations, and assuming you haven't made any errors when refactoring, your unit tests should work. We can prove this here—you've changed the implementation of the `Calculate` method, so your tests should still work.

`HttpClient` is implemented in all platforms, including Mac and Windows, so there are no technical problems calling it from a unit test. In the real world you wouldn't necessarily do this in a unit test—instead you'd wrap the web service calls in another class and mock it out (as we did for the database), but we'll do it here as a simple way to call the method and prove that the code works.

You can't just run your test and have it work, though, because you did change the interface slightly. You made the method `async`, so you need to tweak the test to be `async` as well. Make the test return `async Task`, and `await` the `Calculate` call, as shown in the following listing.

Listing 7.22 Making the `Calculate_4_Returns2` test async

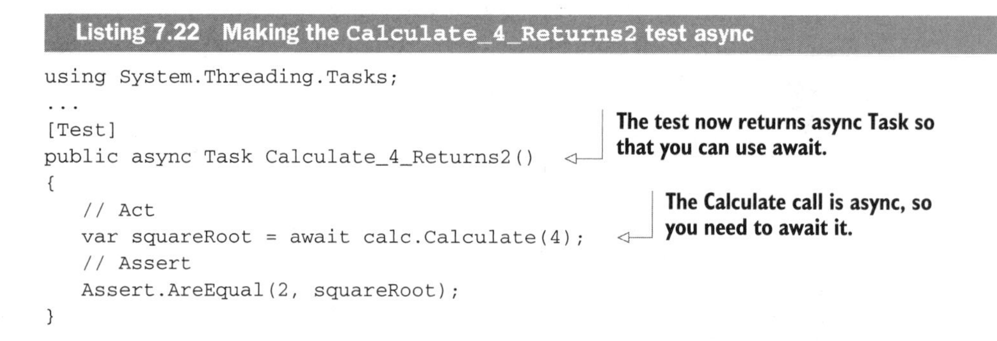

```
using System.Threading.Tasks;
...
[Test]
public async Task Calculate_4_Returns2()
{
   // Act
   var squareRoot = await calc.Calculate(4);
   // Assert
   Assert.AreEqual(2, squareRoot);
}
```

The test now returns async Task so that you can use await.
The Calculate call is async, so you need to await it.

You'll also need to install the Newtonsoft.Json NuGet package into the unit-test project. Once this package is installed, you should be able to run this test and have it work, validating that the Bing API can correctly calculate square roots!

> **THERE'S A LOT OF BOILERPLATE CODE THAT YOU CAN AVOID** When dealing with web services, there's a lot of boilerplate code you end up writing again and again and again. To avoid this, there's a NuGet package that allows you to write a simple interface to your web service, decorating methods with attributes to say which REST calls these methods map to, and the package will build a class to implement the actual HTTP calls. This package is called Refit, and it can be found at https://github.com/paulcbetts/refit. I highly recommend trying this out, as it simplifies your code when dealing with REST APIs.

Now that you've tested your code, it's worth deleting the Bing Search API resource from your Azure account to avoid paying any more than you have to. You can do this in one of two ways: by deleting the resource itself, or by deleting the whole resource group. To delete the resource, select it in the Azure portal and click the Delete button at the top, and then click Yes when asked to confirm. Deleting the entire resource group follows the same process—select it and click the Delete resource group button, but this time you'll need to type in the resource group name to confirm the deleting, making it harder to accidentally delete a resource group.

7.4 A quick recap

We've implemented a couple of different model types in this chapter: a simple one and a more complex one. We've also looked at how you can interact with databases and web services, and we've used a few NuGet packages along the way. Table 7.7 sums up the NuGet packages we've used.

Table 7.7 The NuGet packages used in this chapter

NuGet package	Description
NUnit	Unit-testing framework
SQLite-Net-Pcl	ORM for SQLite databases

Table 7.7 The NuGet packages used in this chapter *(continued)*

NuGet package	Description
PCLStorage	.NET Standard-based filesystem access
Moq	Mocking tools for unit testing
Newtonsoft.Json	Tools for serializing and deserializing C# classes to JSON

We've also created a few interfaces and classes for our SquareRt and Countr apps. Table 7.8 lists them for the SquareRt app, and table 7.9 covers the ones for the Countr app.

Table 7.8 Classes and interfaces we've created for the SquareRt app

Name	Description
`ISquareRtCalculator`	The interface for the calculation logic
`SquareRtCalculator`	The implementation for the square-root calculation logic (either using a direct calculation or the Bing search services)
`SquareRtCalculatorTests`	Unit tests for the square-root calculator
`SquareRootResponse`	Class to represent the JSON response document from the Bing search request
`Computation`	Class to represent the computation section of the JSON response document from the Bing search request

Table 7.9 Classes and interfaces we've created for the Countr app

Name	Description
`Counter`	A data-model class for a counter
`ICountersRepository`	The interface to a repository for storing and retrieving counters
`CountersRepository`	The interface of a repository for storing and retrieving counters from a SQLite database
`ICountersService`	The interface to a service that handles counters, including reading from and writing to the repository and incrementing values
`CountersService`	The implementation of the service that handles counters
`CountersServiceTests`	Unit tests for the counters service

This is our model layer done. In the next chapter we'll move up a layer to the view models.

Summary

In this chapter you learned

- Model layers can be simple or more complex, and they can include any business logic you need, such as calculations.
- Unit tests are a great way to test code without having to build an entire app.
- SQLite provides a simple, file-based database that you can access from a .NET Standard library.
- .NET Standard libraries don't have file access, so you need a plugin to allow you cross-platform access to the filesystem.
- Complex model layers are better split into data models, repositories, and services.
- `HttpClient` provides a nice, cross-platform way to interact with web services.
- If your web service returns a status code of 418, it's actually a teapot.

You also learned how to

- Create a unit-test project and run tests in that project
- Set up a SQLite database, create tables, and set up a class to store inside a table
- Mock interfaces to make it easier to unit-test dependencies between classes
- Use the Bing search API to calculate square roots

8 Building cross-platform view models

> **This chapter covers**
> - Creating simple and master/detail view models
> - Adding state to view models using single-value and collection properties
> - Adding behavior to view models when properties change and using commands
> - Communicating between components using messaging
> - View-model navigation

In the previous chapter we built the cross-platform model layers for our two apps, SquareRt and Countr. We looked at how you can wrap up your model layer in services and repositories that can be shared among different view models. Now it's time to move up a layer and start coding the view models.

8.1 The view-model layer

Like the model layer, the view-model layer is a cross-platform layer (figure 8.1). The difference is that whereas the model layer represents your data and business logic in a way that makes sense to your domain (for example, using services), the view-model layer represents the state and behavior of your UI and is written in a way that makes sense to your view layer.

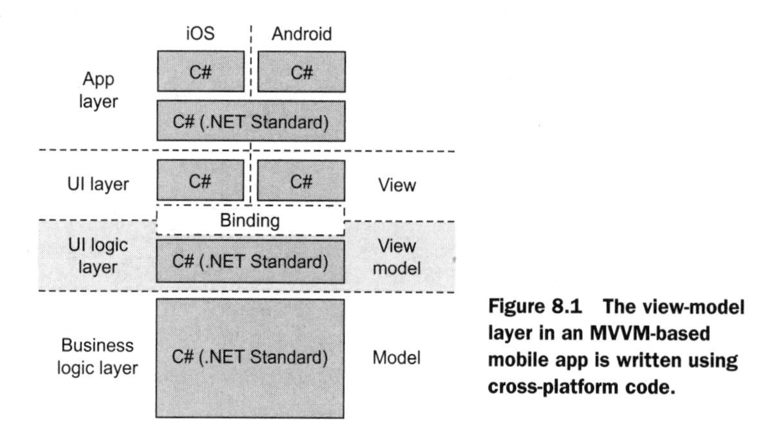

Figure 8.1 The view-model layer in an MVVM-based mobile app is written using cross-platform code.

This means that, in general, you have one view model per view, so for `FooView` you'd have `FooViewModel`, for `BarView` you'd have `BarViewModel`, and so on. This is very different from the model layer, where you have data models that represent the entities in your business layer, and services and repositories to manipulate and store those entities. After all, different views can show or interact with the same entities.

Throughout this chapter, we'll be looking at the responsibilities of the view model, including the following:

- Encapsulating state from the model layer and representing it in a way that makes sense to the view layer
- Providing value conversion between data in the model layer and the view layer
- Providing a way for the view layer to trigger behavior via commands or via properties changing
- Making the behavior in the model layer accessible to the view layer

In chapter 6 we looked at the user flows for our two apps, SquareRt and Countr. Let's review these again, and look at the state and behavior that the different view models need to represent.

8.1.1 The view-model layer inside SquareRt

The SquareRt app is very simple and only has one user flow: a user enters a number, and the square root is calculated. Figure 8.2 shows this flow and the classes you need to implement it.

We've wrapped the calculation code in the model layer in the previous chapter, `SquareRtCalculator`, and we also designed a UI for it. Let's now think about how you can wire this UI up to the model via a view model by looking at state and behavior.

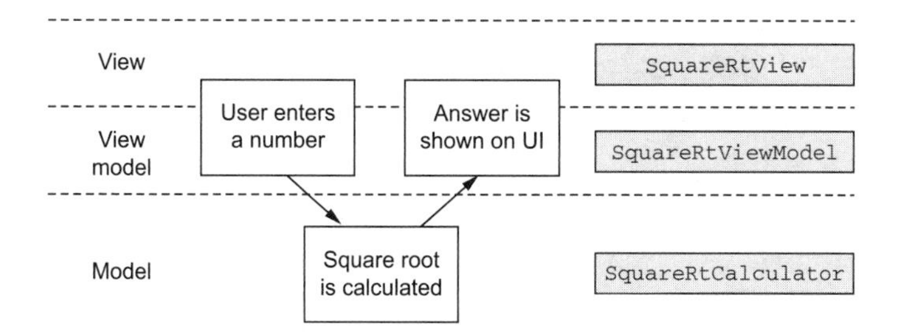

Figure 8.2 The only user flow in SquareRt, and the view, view-model, and calculator classes that you need to implement it

STATE

The first thing to think about is state—what data you show on screen. In this app the state is represented by two numbers: one for input that the user can edit (the number that the square root will be calculated from), and one for output that's read-only (the square root result). It's these two pieces of state that we need to represent in the view model, as shown in figure 8.3.

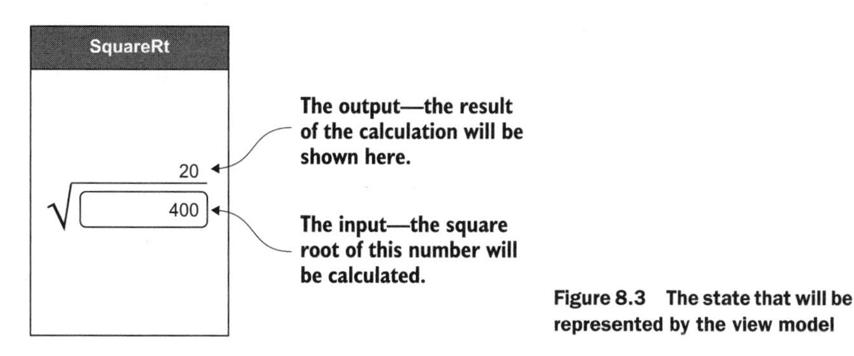

Figure 8.3 The state that will be represented by the view model

One thing to bear in mind is that the values used in the calculations are of type `double`, whereas most text-entry controls deal with raw text and so have `string` values. This means we'll have to perform value conversion in the view-model layer.

BEHAVIOR

Once you have an idea of the state that you need to represent, you need to think about the behavior. The behavior here is also very simple: when the input number is changed, the app needs to calculate the new square root and update the result property on the UI. This is shown in figure 8.4.

Although it's normal to handle behavior using commands, sometimes it's more appropriate to handle simple behavior by using properties, such as when the value of one property is directly dependent on the value of another. In this case, the trigger for the behavior is one property changing, so there's no need to wrap this up in a command.

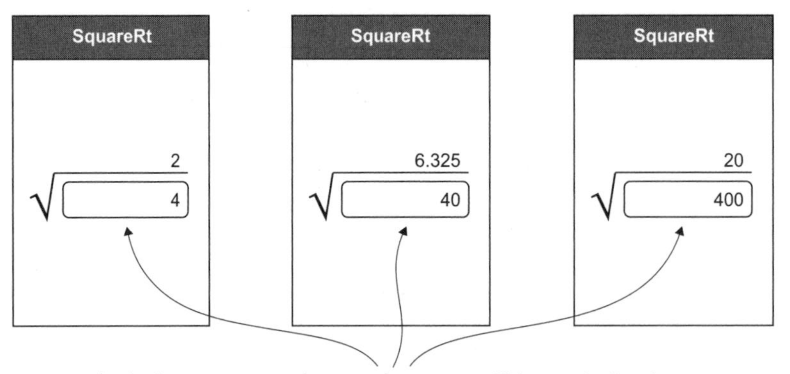

Figure 8.4 The behavior that the view model will need to implement

The simple rule of thumb here is that if one property is dependent on the value of another, it's usually easier to implement the behavior as part of the property change. If the behavior is triggered by an explicit user action, use a command.

8.1.2 The view-model layer inside Countr

SquareRt is a very simple app, but Countr is a bit more complicated. Rather than having one simple user flow, it has four as shown in figure 8.5.

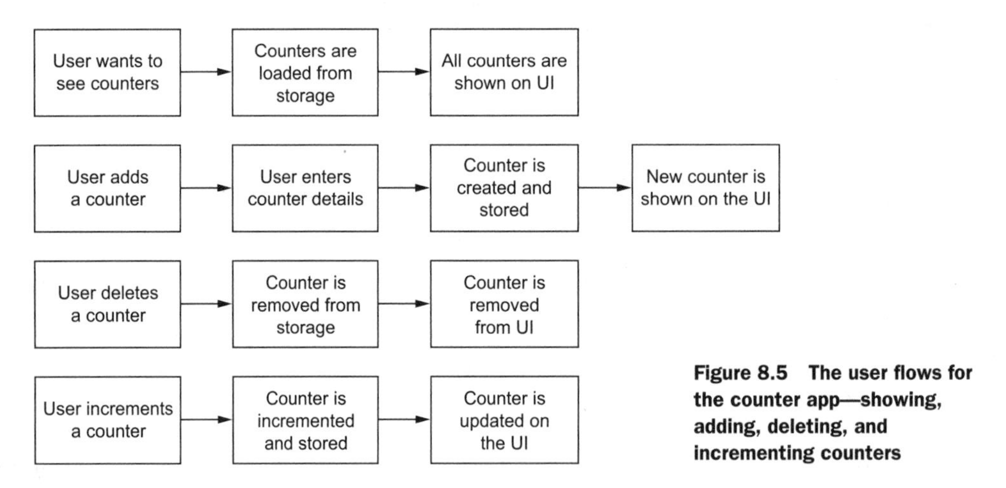

Figure 8.5 The user flows for the counter app—showing, adding, deleting, and incrementing counters

We also have a slightly more complicated UI, with two screens. Following the pattern of one view model per screen, we'll need to have two view models—one for the screen showing the list of counters, and one for the screen to add a new counter (figure 8.6).

You'll probably notice that this app, with one view model (and therefore one view) that shows a list of data, and another view model (and view) for creating, viewing, or editing an item, has a similar pattern to several other apps you use on a regular basis.

View: CountersView, CounterView
View model: CountersViewModel, CounterViewModel
Model: CountersService, Counter

Figure 8.6 The Countr app maps to a set of views, view models, and model-layer classes.

For example, in an email app you'd have one view showing a list of emails in a mailbox, such as your inbox or sent mails. When you tap a button to write a new email, a new screen will appear where you can write your email. Once this email is sent, it'll appear in the list of sent mail. Tapping on an email in the inbox will show a new screen with the contents of that email, as shown in figure 8.7. The same is true in an address book app—these apps normally show a master list of people by name, and when you tap a name it shows the details about that person. If you tap a button to create a new contact, you get a new screen to create the contact, and once you're done, it appears in the master list.

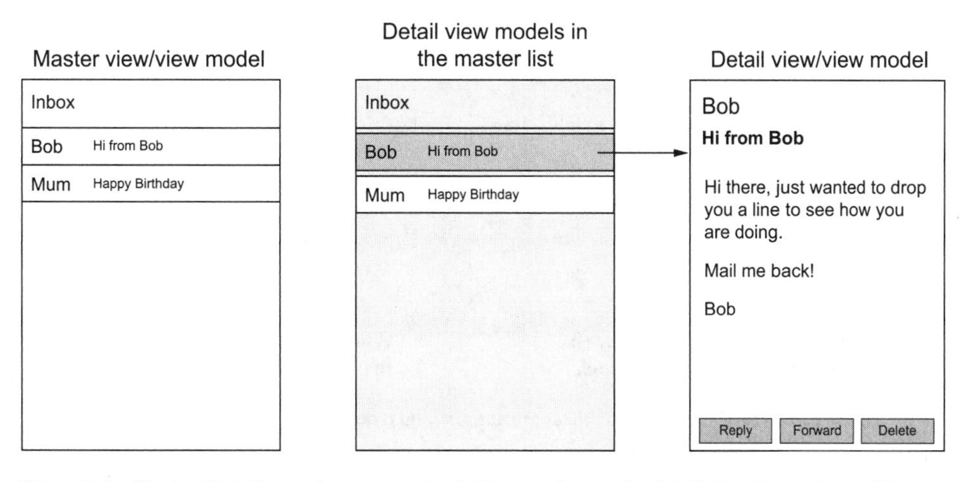

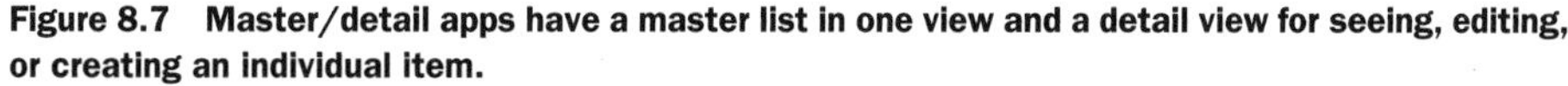

Figure 8.7 Master/detail apps have a master list in one view and a detail view for seeing, editing, or creating an individual item.

Similarly `CountersViewModel` will contain a list of counters, which will each be represented by `CounterViewModel` instances that wrap each counter.

This pattern is called *master/detail*, and it refers to a master list that shows highlights of all the items your app needs to show, and a detail screen that can be used to view or edit the details for a single item, or can be used to add a new item.

The normal navigation pattern for adding new items is via a button (on iOS this is normally on the toolbar; on Android it can be a toolbar button or a floating action button), which displays a blank detail screen where you can enter the details. This detail screen will usually have Save and Cancel buttons in the toolbar. If your app supports viewing more details or editing an item, the normal navigation pattern is to tap on the item in the list, and this will navigate to the detail screen, with a back button at the top left so you can go back to the list. Details usually slide in from right to left on top of the list and slide back out from left to right when done, mimicking papers stacking up and unstacking.

In the Countr app we'll use the master/detail pattern. The master list will show the list of all counters, and the detail screen will be for adding new counters (figure 8.8). If, in the future, we wanted to expand our app to support editing counters (such as changing the name) or viewing more details (viewing when counts were increased, or reports broken down by day, week, month), we could use the same pattern with a detail screen containing all this info.

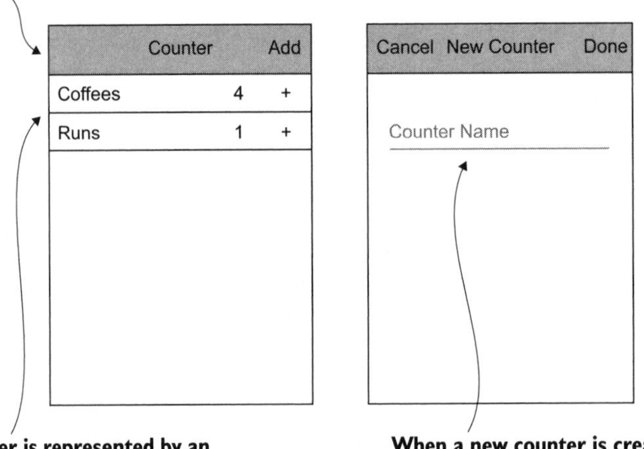
The master list of all the counters stored in the app
Counter
Add
Coffees
4
+
Runs
1
+
Cancel
New Counter
Done
Counter Name
Each counter is represented by an instance of the detail view model.
When a new counter is created, the detail view model is used.

Figure 8.8 The Countr app has a list of counters and a detail screen to add a new counter.

A popular technique for creating the view-model classes for master/detail apps is to stick with two view models—a master view model that contains a list of instances of the detail view model. The detail view model will contain all the state and behavior needed by the detail screen.

STATE

The app will need two view models: `CountersViewModel` and `CounterViewModel`. The state represented by `CountersViewModel` is a collection of counters that will be displayed on screen in a list. Each counter will be represented by an instance of `CounterViewModel`, which has state in the form of the name and current count of the counter. Both of these values will be read-only here, but we can also use `CounterViewModel` for the add-new-counter screen, where the name will be set. This is shown in figure 8.9.

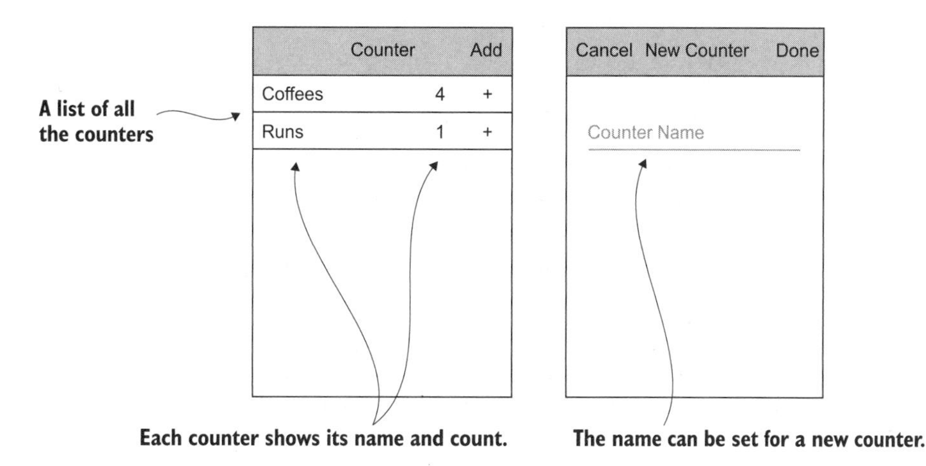

Figure 8.9 The state that will be represented by the two view models: a master view model and a detail view model

BEHAVIOR

The two view models for this app have different behaviors, all triggered by user interactions. This means you can implement behavior via commands, unlike SquareRt, which will use property changes to trigger behavior (figure 8.10).

For `CountersViewModel`, the master view model, you'll need to add behavior for an Add button—this will need to navigate to a new screen so the user can set up a new counter. For `CounterViewModel`, the detail view model, you'll need to add behavior for the Done button, which will navigate back to the master view after creating a new counter, and for a Cancel button, which will navigate back to the master view without

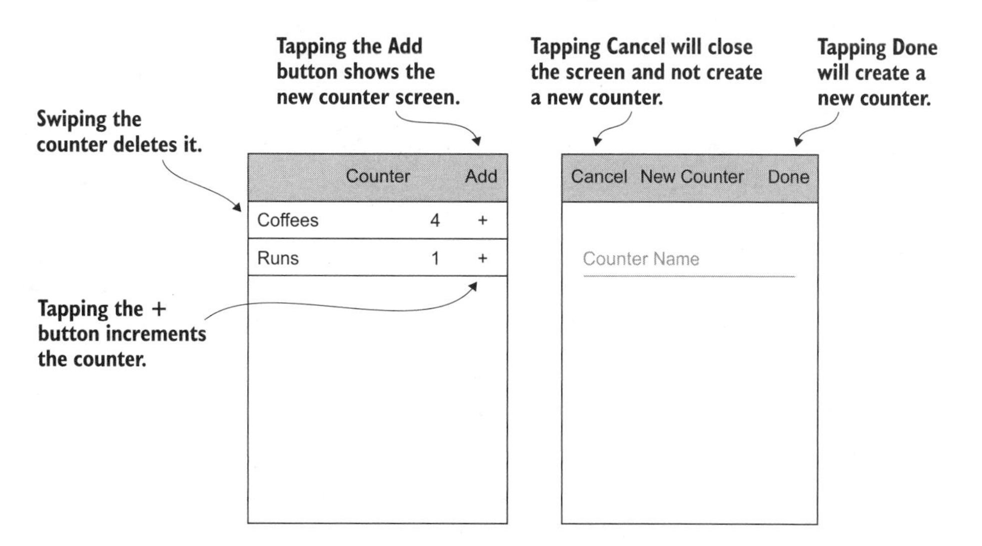

Figure 8.10 The behavior for the master and detail view models

creating a new counter. You'll also need to add behavior that's used by the items in the master list, allowing the user to increment or delete a counter.

8.2 Adding state and behavior to SquareRt

Now that we've reviewed the state and behavior for both of our apps, let's write some code to implement them, starting with the SquareRt app. Launch the SquareRt solution from chapter 7—use the version that does the calculation itself rather than the one that uses the Bing API, because it will be much faster to run.

8.2.1 State inside SquareRt

The first thing we need to do is create the view model for the SquareRt app. Add a new class called `SquareRtViewModel` to the ViewModels folder. The following listing shows the initial code for this class.

Listing 8.1 Taking the `calculator` interface as a constructor parameter

```
using MvvmCross.Core.ViewModels;

namespace SquareRt.Core.ViewModels
{
   public class SquareRtViewModel : MvxViewModel
   {
      readonly ISquareRtCalculator calculator;

      public SquareRtViewModel(ISquareRtCalculator calculator)
      {
         this.calculator = calculator;
      }
   }
}
```

The view model is derived from the MvvmCross base view model.

The constructor takes an instance of the square root calculator.

Once you've added this class, you can delete the `FirstViewModel` class. This class is also referred to in the `App` class, inside the `Initialize` method. Inside this method, a call is made to `RegisterNavigationServiceAppStart` to register the `FirstViewModel` as the startup view model for the app. We'll look at this call in detail later in this chapter, but for now change this call to use the new `SquareRtViewModel` so that the project compiles, as shown in the following listing.

Listing 8.2 Setting the app startup view model to be your new view model

```
public override void Initialize()
{
   ...
   RegisterNavigationServiceAppStart<ViewModels.SquareRtViewModel>();
}
```

This class derives from `MvxViewModel`, the base view-model class from MvvmCross, which provides features such as property-changed notifications.

You need to add a couple of properties to the view model to represent the value you'll calculate the square root of, and the result of the calculation. Although these are simple properties, you do have to put some thought into how to create them. View models are responsible for value conversion, converting values from a format that's relevant to the view to a format that's relevant to the model layer, and vice versa. This model layer deals with `double` values. In contrast, the UI has a text-entry control for entering the input, as well as a label control to show the result, and these kind of UI controls usually deal with `string` values.

You have two choices here—perform the value conversion inside the properties, or do it in a value converter. Let's look at both in turn.

VALUE CONVERSION INSIDE PROPERTIES

You have two properties to consider: one for the input and one for the result. The result will be calculated when you implement the behavior inside the view model, so if you're going to perform value conversion inside the properties, you can also convert the result value to a string as soon as it has been calculated. This means you can make a simple `string` property for the result.

The following listing shows this property, so add this to the view model.

Listing 8.3 `string` property uses a backing field and notifies when the value changes

```
string result;
public string Result
{
   get { return result; }
   private set { SetProperty(ref result, value); }
}
```

Both the backing field and property are of type string.

The getter just returns the value of the backing field.

The setter uses SetProperty to update the field.

This `Result` property is a simple `string` property with a `string` backing field. The getter just returns the field value, so there's nothing too exciting here. The setter is private (after all, you'll be calculating the value inside the view model, so there's no need to make the setter public), and it uses `SetProperty` to update the value. `SetProperty` is a helper method provided by MvvmCross; it will check the existing value against the new value, and if it has changed, it will update the value and raise the property-changed event. If the value hasn't changed, nothing happens.

> **PROPERTY-CHANGED NOTIFICATIONS ARE USED TO UPDATE THE UI** The reason for raising a property-changed notification is to tell the binding layer that the property's value has changed, so the UI should be updated. The binding layer will re-read the property and set the new value on the relevant UI widget.

The `SetProperty` method will also return a Boolean—`true` if the value was different and the property was updated, or `false` if the value was the same, and so wasn't updated. This is helpful if you want to perform other actions when the value changes. For example, in a class with a `Name` property that concatenates `FirstName` and `LastName`, if the call to `SetProperty` inside the `FirstName` or `LastName` properties returns `true`, then your view model can raise a property-changed notification for `Name`.

The result property is easy, but for the input property you actually have to do some conversion. Helpfully, the .NET Framework provides a selection of ways to make this conversion easy. One of these is the `System.Convert` static class, which has methods that perform all kinds of conversions between the different primitive types, such as `double`, `int`, `long`, and `string`. The following listing shows this in action.

Listing 8.4 Converting from a `string` to a `double` and vice versa

```
using System;
...
double number;
public string Number
{
   get { return Convert.ToString(number); }
   set { SetProperty(ref number, Convert.ToDouble(value)); }
}
```

The property is of type string, but the backing field is a double

The property getter converts from a double to a string.

The property setter converts from a string to a double.

This is very much like the `Result` property, except the property is a `string` and converts to and from a `double` backing field, which is of the right type to pass to the calculator in order to calculate the square root. This is shown in figure 8.11.

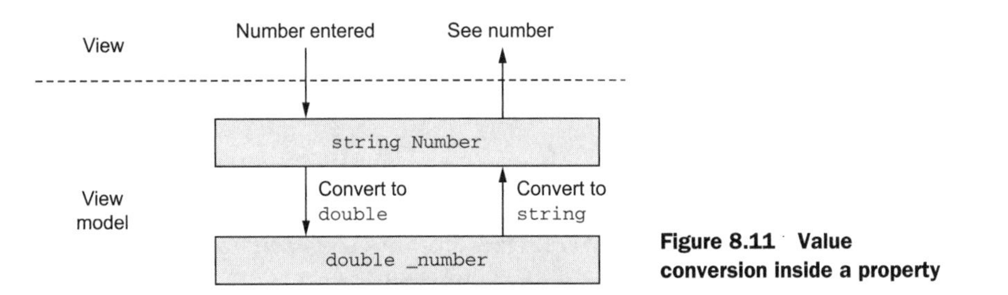

Figure 8.11 Value conversion inside a property

In this example, you're not doing any validation, so if the value passed to `Number` isn't a number, such as the string `"Not a Number"`, then the conversion would throw a `FormatException`. Ideally you should always add validation before converting values, but in this instance it shouldn't be too much of a problem because when we construct the UI in the next couple of chapters, we'll restrict the text-entry controls to only allow numbers.

> **There are many ways to `string` a `double`**
>
> There are many ways to represent a number as a `string`. For example, the number 1,234.56789 can be represented in a number of ways:
>
> - 1,234.56789
> - 1234.56789
> - 1,234.56789000
>
> All of these are valid, but they're not necessarily the format you want. When converting a number to a string, you can use format specifiers to dictate how the number should be represented. Standard format specifiers are available, and you can create custom formats if you need to. You can read all about formatting types in Microsoft's "Formatting Types in .NET" article at http://mng.bz/1ljv.
>
> You should also consider locale. In the U.S., a decimal point is a period (.), whereas in some European countries it's a comma (,). In the U.S., 1,000 means one thousand, but in Denmark it's one. You can read about supporting different locales when converting to strings using the `CultureInfo` class in Microsoft's documentation of the `Double.ToString` method (http://mng.bz/LpJO).

UNIT-TESTING YOUR VALUE CONVERSION

In chapter 7 we discussed how our models couldn't be tested manually because we don't yet have a working app, and the same applies to our view models. We can't test these manually, so we need to write some unit tests.

You can do this now by creating a ViewModels folder in the SquareRt.Core.Tests project and adding a new test fixture class called `SquareRtViewModelTests`. You'll be mocking out the `ISquareRtCalculator` interface, so just like with the `Countr` tests in the previous chapter, you'll need to add the Moq NuGet package (figure 8.12). In addition, your view model derives from an MvvmCross base class, so you'll need to add the MvvmCross NuGet package as well (figure 8.13), making sure that the version of the MvvmCross NuGet package that you add matches the version used in your core project.

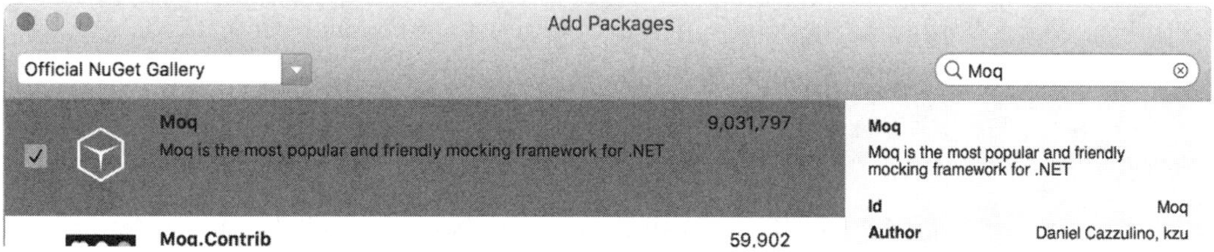

Figure 8.12 Adding the Moq NuGet package to the unit-test project

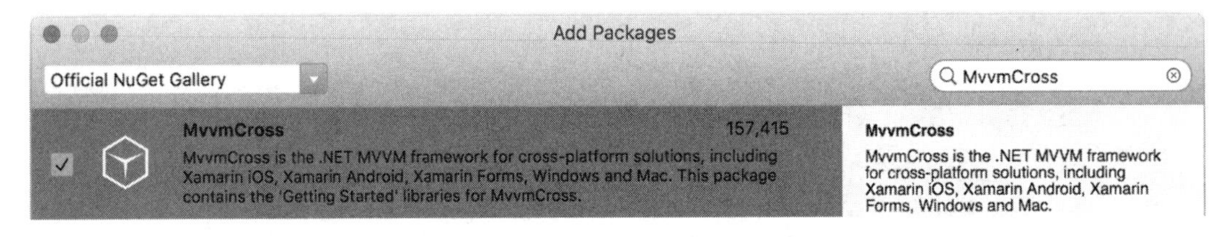

Figure 8.13 Adding the MvvmCross NuGet package to the unit-test project

The following listing shows the initial implementation of this test fixture.

Listing 8.5 Creating a view model from a mock calculator

```
using Moq;
using NUnit.Framework;
using SquareRt.Core.ViewModels;

namespace SquareRt.Core.Tests.ViewModels
{
   [TestFixture]
   public class SquareRtViewModelTests
   {
      Mock<ISquareRtCalculator> calculator;
      SquareRtViewModel viewModel;

      [SetUp]
      public void SetUp()
      {
         calculator = new Mock<ISquareRtCalculator>();
         viewModel = new SquareRtViewModel(calculator.Object);
      }
   }
}
```

A mock calculator is created and used to construct the view model.

In the `SetUp` method of this test fixture class, you initialize a mock `ISquareRtCalculator` and create an instance of the view model using the mock that you can test in your test methods. You can only test the `Number` property at the moment—the `Result` property has a private setter so you can't test it until you add behavior later in this chapter.

The following listing shows an example test to verify that you can get and set a `string` value on the `Number` property correctly.

Listing 8.6 Verifing that the `Number` getter returns same value passed to the setter

```
[Test]
public void Number_ConvertsToAndFromDoubleCorrectly()
{
   // Act
   viewModel.Number = "1234.4321";
   // Assert
   Assert.AreEqual("1234.4321", viewModel.Number);
}
```

This is a simple test, and if you run it, it should pass with no problems. If you want to see what happens if the string isn't a valid number, change the test to pass in a different string that is not a valid number.

Another thing to test here is the property-changed notifications. It's a good sanity check to ensure that the property raises a changed notification if the value changes, so the next listing is a quick test to do this.

Listing 8.7 Verifing a property-changed notification is raised when the number changes

```
[Test]
public void SettingNumber_RaisesPropertyChanged()
{
   // Arrange
   var propertyChangedRaised = false;
   viewModel.PropertyChanged +=
      (s, e) => propertyChangedRaised = (e.PropertyName == "Number");
   // Act
   viewModel.Number = "1";
   // Assert
   Assert.IsTrue(propertyChangedRaised);
}
```

Wires up the PropertyChanged event

Updates the Number property

Checks that the property-changed event was fired

An easy way to test the `PropertyChanged` event is to wire up the event to a handler that sets a `bool` flag to `true` if the event is raised with a property name that matches the property you're interested in. The name of the property that changed comes from the `PropertyName` property of the event args.

If you run this, you'd expect the test to pass. Try it and see what happens. What you'll actually see is that this test fails…

This is a result of the way MvvmCross handles property changes. When you raise a property-changed event, the UI needs to be updated, and as you saw back in chapter 5 this *must* happen on the UI thread. Rather than forcing you to always update properties on the UI thread (something that's hard to do in a view model), most MVVM frameworks help you out by marshaling these events onto the UI thread. This is what's happening here—MvvmCross is helpfully raising the property-changed event on the UI thread using a dispatcher, a class whose sole purpose is to run code for you on the UI thread (figure 8.14). When you run your code inside an app running on iOS or Android, the MvvmCross setup code creates this dispatcher automatically based on your app's UI thread. Inside unit tests there's no UI thread and no dispatcher, so there's nothing to run the code to raise your event.

There are a couple of workarounds. One is to create a mock dispatcher object and set MvvmCross up to use it, but this is too much hard work for our needs right now. Luckily there's a simple shortcut—you can set a flag on your view model to raise the property-changed events on the current thread, rather than using a dispatcher. This is

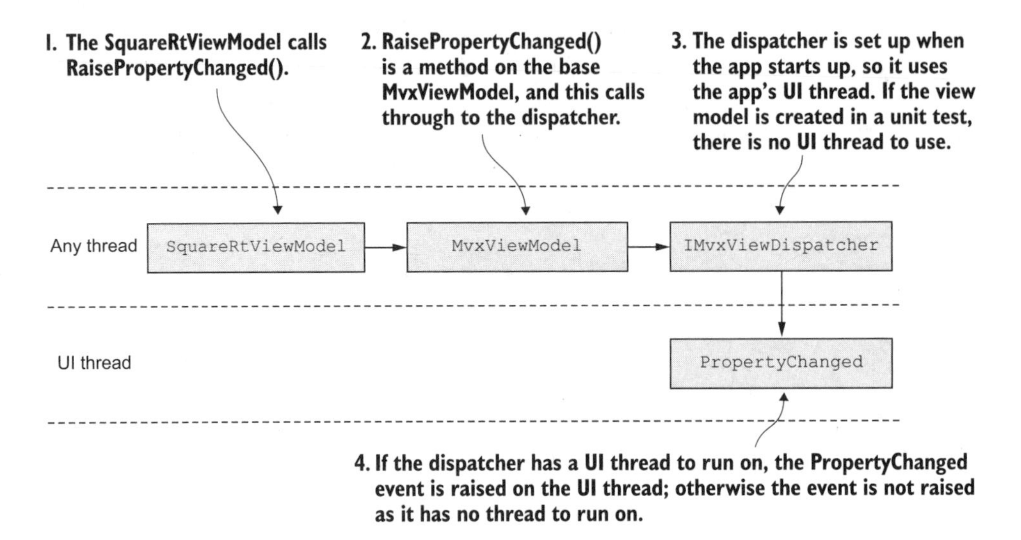

1. The SquareRtViewModel calls RaisePropertyChanged().
2. RaisePropertyChanged() is a method on the base MvxViewModel, and this calls through to the dispatcher.
3. The dispatcher is set up when the app starts up, so it uses the app's UI thread. If the view model is created in a unit test, there is no UI thread to use.
Any thread
SquareRtViewModel
MvxViewModel
IMvxViewDispatcher
UI thread
PropertyChanged
4. If the dispatcher has a UI thread to run on, the PropertyChanged event is raised on the UI thread; otherwise the event is not raised as it has no thread to run on.

Figure 8.14 MvvmCross view models raise property-changed events using a dispatcher.

good enough for our tests, so make the change to the `Setup` method shown in the following listing, and re-run the test.

Listing 8.8 Raising the property-changed events on the current thread

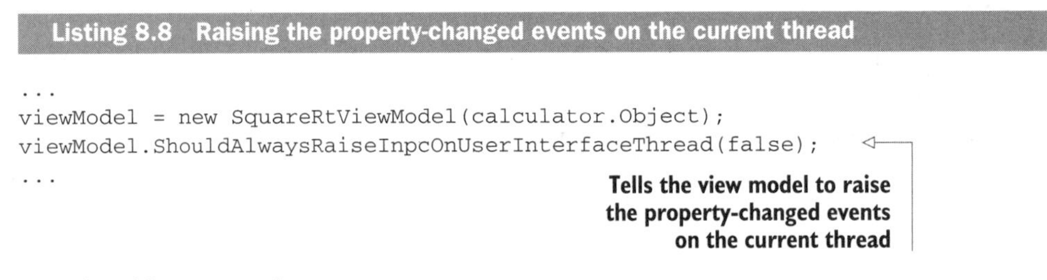

```
...
viewModel = new SquareRtViewModel(calculator.Object);
viewModel.ShouldAlwaysRaiseInpcOnUserInterfaceThread(false);
...
```


You should now see the test pass.

VALUE CONVERSION USING A VALUE CONVERTER

We've looked at value conversion inside a property, and you've seen how you can convert a `string` from the UI to a `double` to use in your calculation. You've also seen that you'll need to convert the result of the calculation to a `string` to set the result property when you implement the behavior inside your view model.

This seems a bit more complicated than we might like, with conversions happening in multiple places. If we extended the app to include more calculations (such as adding a cube-root converter), we'd have to duplicate the conversion code, meaning more places for bugs, and more code to change if we wanted to make any improvements. Ideally, we'd want to do this conversion in one place, and that place is a value converter. We want to maximize code reuse—that's why we're building Xamarin apps using MVVM after all!

We looked at value converters back in chapter 3, but as a recap, a value converter is a class whose sole job is to convert from one type to another. They're used by the binding layer to convert values from the type used by the view model to the type used by the view, and vice versa. They have two methods: `Convert` and `ConvertBack`. `Convert` converts from the view-model type to the view type, whereas `ConvertBack` converts from the view type to the view-model type (figure 8.15). Value converters can use types that are available in .NET Standard libraries, or they can be used for platform-specific types. If they use platform-specific types, they need to live in the relevant iOS and Android app projects, but if they use types available in .NET Standard libraries (such as doubles and strings) they can live in the core project.

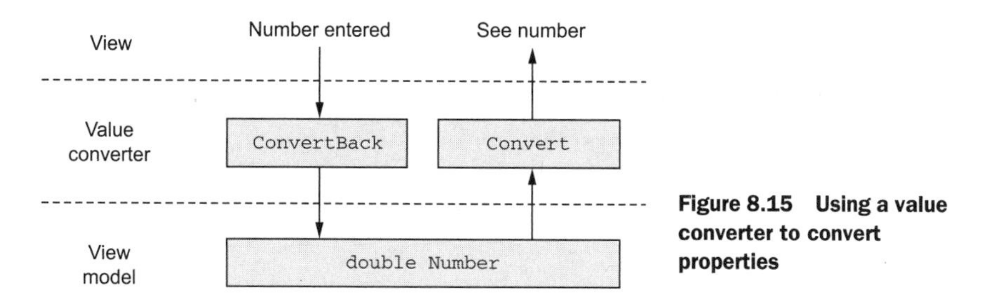

Figure 8.15 Using a value converter to convert properties

Create a folder in the SquareRt.Core project called ValueConverters, and in that folder create a `DoubleToStringValueConverter` class. The following listing shows the code for this converter.

Listing 8.9 A value converter to go from doubles to strings

```
using System;
using System.Globalization;
using MvvmCross.Platform.Converters;

namespace SquareRt.Core.ValueConverters
{
   public class DoubleToStringValueConverter : IMvxValueConverter
   {
      public object Convert(object value, Type targetType,
                            object parameter, CultureInfo culture)
      {
         return System.Convert.ToString(value);
      }

      public object ConvertBack(object value, Type targetType,
                                object parameter, CultureInfo culture)
      {
         return System.Convert.ToDouble(value);
      }
   }
}
```

- There is no standard value-converter interface available to Xamarin apps, so we'll use one provided by MvvmCross.
- Converts the value to a string
- Converts the value back to a double

This converter implements an interface from MvvmCross, `IMvxValueConverter`, which provides the same two methods that most value converters have: `Convert` and `ConvertBack`. The implementation of this converter uses the same logic as you saw earlier when converting values inside the view model itself, using the `System.Convert` static class to perform the conversion.

UNIT-TESTING YOUR VALUE CONVERTER

You can now unit-test this converter to prove it works. Create a ValueConverters folder in the SquareRt.Core.Tests project and add a new test-fixture class `DoubleToStringValueConverterTests`. The following listing shows the code for some tests for converting and converting back.

Listing 8.10 Unit-testing the value converter

```
using NUnit.Framework;
using SquareRt.Core.ValueConverters;

namespace SquareRt.Core.Tests.ValueConverters
{
   [TestFixture]
   public class DoubleToStringValueConverterTests
   {
      [Test]
      public void Convert_ConvertsADoubleToAString()
      {
         // Arrange
         var vc = new DoubleToStringValueConverter();
         // Act
         var converted = vc.Convert(123.456, null, null, null);
         // Assert
         Assert.AreEqual("123.456", converted);
      }

      [Test]
      public void ConvertBack_ConvertsAStringToADouble()
      {
         // Arrange
         var vc = new DoubleToStringValueConverter();
         // Act
         var converted = vc.ConvertBack("123.456", null, null, null);
         // Assert
         Assert.AreEqual(123.456, converted);
      }
   }
}
```

Converts a double to a string and ensures it's converted correctly

Converts a string back to a double and ensures it's converted correctly

If you run these tests, they should all pass.

Before you can use this value converter with your view model, you need to make your view model use doubles only, with no conversion to or from strings. The next listing shows the view-model properties.

Listing 8.11 For a value converter in the binding layer, properties should be doubles

```
double number;
public double Number
{
```

All properties and backing fields are doubles.

```
    get { return number; }
    set { SetProperty(ref number, value); }
}

double result;                    All properties and backing
public double Result              fields are doubles.
{
    get { return result; }
    set { SetProperty(ref result, value); }
}
```

You can also remove the unit tests for the view model that checked the conversion, and change the test for the property changed to use the correct type. Delete the `Number_ConvertsToAndFromDoubleCorrectly` test and change the assignment in `SettingNumber_RaisesPropertyChanged` to set the view model to a double instead of a string. With these changes made, the test should pass.

WHICH ONE TO USE

We've looked at value conversion inside properties and using value converters, so which one should you use? As with all good programming questions, the answer is "it depends." A good rule of thumb is to think about how often this conversion needs to happen, and how complicated it is:

- If it needs to happen for multiple properties across multiple view models, a value converter is the best bet.
- If the conversion is slow (for example, involving a database lookup or a web service call), you need to find a way to make it happen on a background thread, in which case a value converter is out. Value converters are called by the binding layer on the UI thread, so they must be fast. In this situation, it would be better to create a `Task` to convert the value on a background thread when the property to be converted is set.
- If the conversion involves multiple inputs, such as multiple properties, it's easier to do the conversion on the properties inside the view model. Using a value converter would be much more complex, as you'd need to pass multiple properties through.
- If the view type is platform-specific, it has to be in a value converter.

It comes down to whatever fits best for your code. I personally like to do it inside properties where I can. If I find I'm repeating the code, I refactor it into a value converter.

8.2.2 Exposing behavior via property changes

Our SquareRt app is a simple one, with a single user flow. Every time the number is changed, the square root should be calculated, and this behavior is simple enough to execute every time the number changes, rather than waiting for an explicit user action like tapping a Calculate button.

Let's add the code to implement this behavior in the `SquareRtViewModel`. The following listing shows the code you need if you're doing value conversion inside the properties, and listing 8.13 shows the code if you're doing the value conversion in a value converter.

Listing 8.12 Calculating square as a string when Number property changes

```
public string Number
{
   get { return Convert.ToString(number); }
   set
   {
      if (SetProperty(ref number, Convert.ToDouble(value)))
         Result = Convert.ToString(calculator.Calculate(number));
   }
}
```

After the number is set, the result is calculated and converted to a string.

Listing 8.13 Calculating the square root whenever the Number property changes

```
public double Number
{
   get { return number; }
   set
   {
      if (SetProperty(ref number, value))
         Result = calculator.Calculate(number);
   }
}
```

After the number is set, the result is calculated.

In both cases, the result is calculated and the property is updated. When the value is calculated, it's the `Result` property itself that gets updated, not the backing field. This way, a property-changed event is raised, telling the UI to update and show the new value.

Now that we have the behavior defined, let's write a couple of unit tests to verify that the result is calculated and a property-changed event is raised whenever the number changes. The following listing shows these tests, which you can add to `SquareRtViewModelTests`.

Listing 8.14 Ensuring that the result changes when the number is set

```
[Test]
public void SettingNumber_CalculatesResult()
{
   // Act
   viewModel.Number = 4;
   // Assert
   Assert.AreEqual(2, viewModel.Result);
}

[Test]
public void SettingNumber_RaisesPropertyChangedForResult()
{
   // Arrange
   var propertyChangedRaised = false;
```

Tests that the result is calculated from the number

```
    viewModel.PropertyChanged +=
        (s, e) => propertyChangedRaised = (e.PropertyName == "Result");
    // Act
    viewModel.Number = 1;
    // Assert
    Assert.IsTrue(propertyChangedRaised);
}
```

Verifies that a property-changed notification is raised for Result

If you run these tests, surprisingly they fail. That's because we mocked the `ISquareRt-Calculator` interface in the `SetUp` method. Mocks, by default, don't do anything—their properties are all default values for the type (0 for numbers, null for objects), and all methods return the default values. In this case, the `Calculate` method is returning a default value of 0 because we haven't set it up.

Remember, this is a unit test—a test to verify a unit of code in isolation—and we've mocked up the dependencies (in this case, the `ISquareRtCalculator` interface) so that we have control inside our tests. For example, if you were using the version of the square root calculator that used Bing search to calculate the square root instead of a mock object, every unit test would take a while to run as it made a network call, slowing down the tests. Also, running unit tests regularly (something that's very good to do) could easily exceed the number of Bing requests you can make at the lowest price tier, so you'd have to pay more for each test to run. Mocks help eliminate these problems.

What you can do here is set up the mock to act the way you want and simulate the expected behavior. Moq has a simple syntax where you can specify the behavior you want for the methods and properties on your mock objects, either for all calls or for specific calls, based on the parameters provided. This means that for the `Calculate` method you could set it up to always return a specific value, or make it so that if you call it with 4, it returns 2, or if you call it with 9 it returns 3, and so on. You could even have it throw an exception if you call it with –1.

For these tests, we'll set it up to always return 2. The following listing shows the code changes you need to make.

Listing 8.15 Setting up the `Calculate` method to return 2 at the start of each test

```
[Test]
public void SettingNumber_CalculatesResult()
{
    // Arrange
    calculator.Setup(c => c.Calculate(It.IsAny<double>()))
              .Returns(2);
    ...
}

[Test]
public void SettingNumber_RaisesPropertyChangedForResult()
{
    // Arrange
    calculator.Setup(c => c.Calculate(It.IsAny<double>()))
              .Returns(2);
    ...
}
```

The Calculate method is set up so that if it's called with any double value, it will return 2.

If you make these changes and run the tests, they should now pass.

8.3 Adding state and behavior to Countr

SquareRt is now all done, so open the Countr solution and we'll turn our attention to this app.

8.3.1 Single-value properties

Let's start by looking at the `CounterViewModel` for the Countr app. This view model needs to provide state for the name and count of a counter, backed up by an instance of the `Counter` data model from the model layer.

Load up the Countr solution and create a new class in the ViewModels folder of the Countr.Core project. The next listing shows the code for the first part of this class—preparation.

Listing 8.16 The implementation of `CounterViewModel` wraps a `Counter`

```
using Countr.Core.Models;
using MvvmCross.Core.ViewModels;

namespace Countr.Core.ViewModels
{
   public class CounterViewModel : MvxViewModel<Counter>
   {
      Counter counter;

      public override void Prepare(Counter counter)
      {
         this.counter = counter;
      }
   }
}
```

- This view model derives from MvxViewModel.
- The view model uses an instance of Counter to hold the state.
- The Prepare method provides an existing counter as a backing store for this view model.

This view model needs to represent a counter, so it makes sense to use an instance of `Counter` as a backing store to hold this data. `CounterViewModel` has two jobs: in the master list it represents an existing counter, and in the new counter detail view it represents a new counter (figure 8.16). For both jobs it needs to store and expose a counter. Here you can take advantage of a slightly different base view-model class: `MvxViewModel<T>`. This class provides an abstract `Prepare(T parameter)` method that you override to prepare the view model and store the counter, and this method can be called with either an existing counter or a new one.

You might think this is an odd way to do it. After all, for such a class you'd normally have two constructors: a default one that creates a new counter, and one that takes an existing counter as a parameter. You can't do that here, though, because of the way MvvmCross uses view models to navigate between views—something we'll look at in detail later on in this chapter.

Now that you have your `Prepare` method, let's implement the `Name` and `Count` properties using the counter as a backing field. You won't be able to use the `SetProperty`

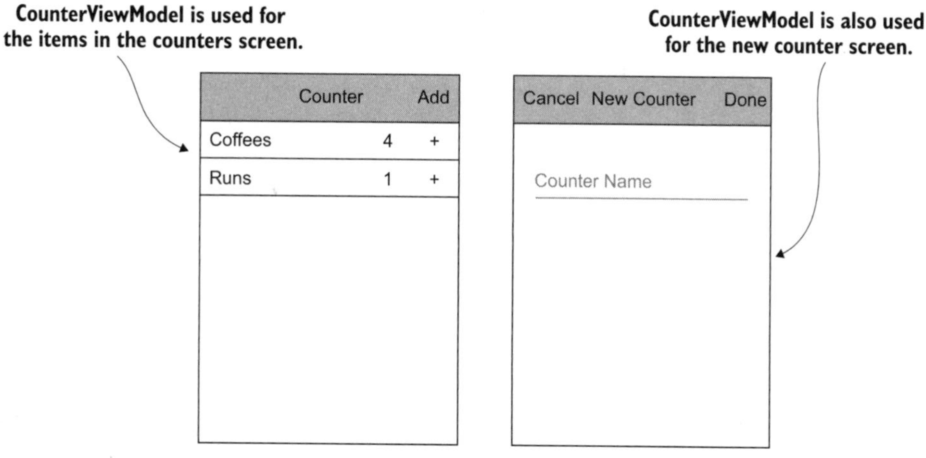

Figure 8.16 The counter view model has two uses—it's an item in the list of counters, and it's the view model for the add-new-counter screen.

helper method here—it needs a reference to the underlying field so that it can both read and write the value. In this case, there's no underlying field, just a property on the backing object that can't be passed by reference. Here's the code for this.

Listing 8.17 Wrapping the properties on the underlying counter

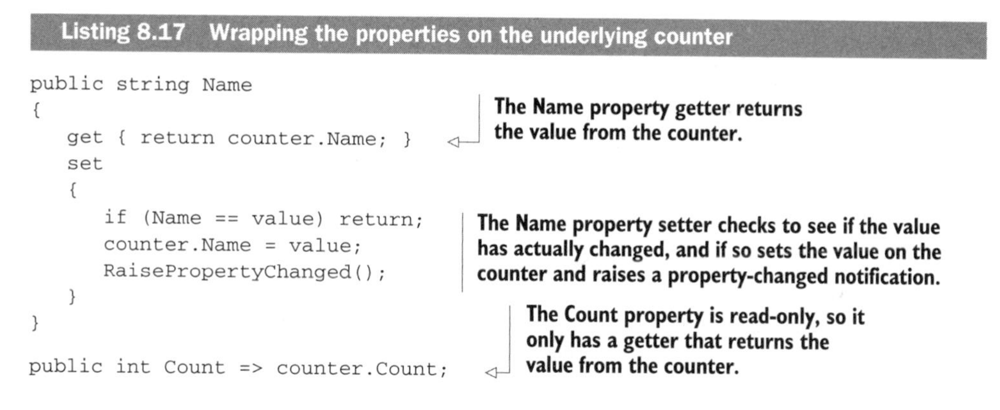

```
public string Name
{
   get { return counter.Name; }
   set
   {
      if (Name == value) return;
      counter.Name = value;
      RaisePropertyChanged();
   }
}

public int Count => counter.Count;
```

The Name property getter returns the value from the counter.
The Name property setter checks to see if the value has actually changed, and if so sets the value on the counter and raises a property-changed notification.
The Count property is read-only, so it only has a getter that returns the value from the counter.

The getters for both the `Name` and `Count` properties are simple pass-through getters—they just return the value on the underlying counter. The `Count` property is read-only (it can only be edited via the + button, so it will be incremented using a command). The `Name` property is not read-only as you'll need to set it when creating a new counter. It follows the standard logic you saw back in chapter 3—if the value hasn't actually changed, do nothing; if it has changed, update the property on the underlying counter and raise a property-changed notification.

Let's now write some unit tests to verify that we haven't made any mistakes with this view model. Create a ViewModels folder in the Countr.Core.Tests project and create a new class in that folder called `CounterViewModelTests`. Once again, you'll need to add the MvvmCross NuGet package, so add this to the tests project now. The following listing shows the the contents of the `CounterViewModelTests` class.

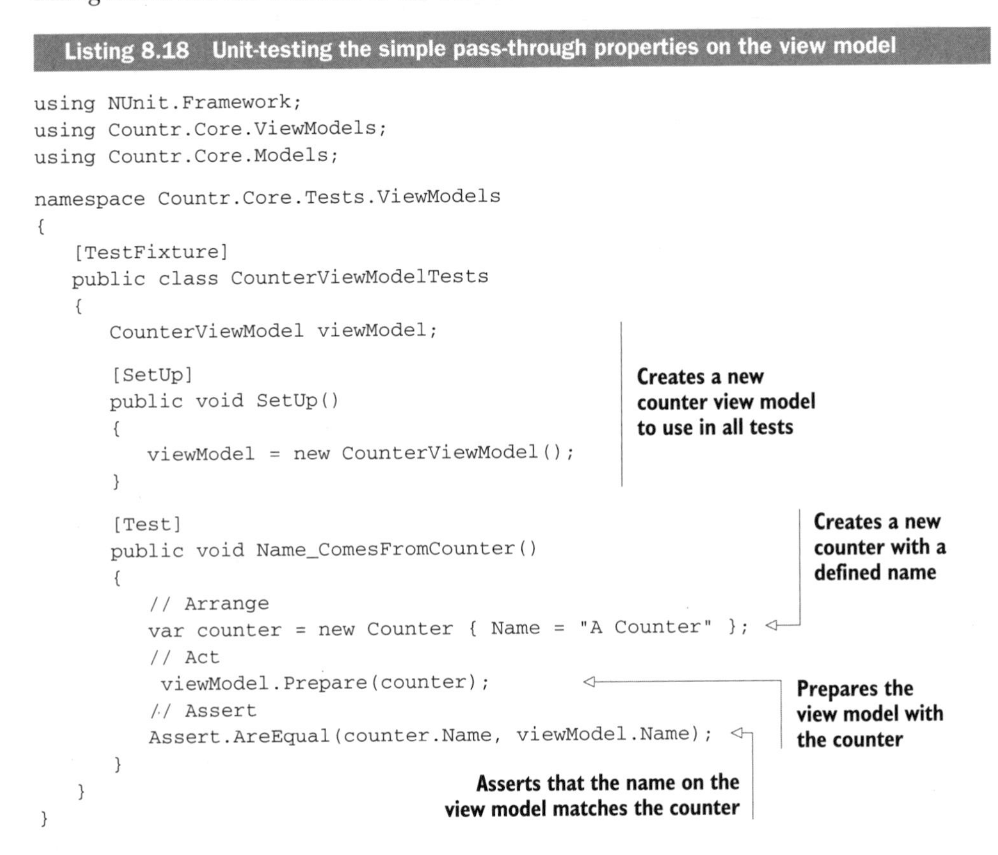

Listing 8.18 Unit-testing the simple pass-through properties on the view model

```
using NUnit.Framework;
using Countr.Core.ViewModels;
using Countr.Core.Models;

namespace Countr.Core.Tests.ViewModels
{
   [TestFixture]
   public class CounterViewModelTests
   {
      CounterViewModel viewModel;

      [SetUp]
      public void SetUp()
      {
         viewModel = new CounterViewModel();
      }

      [Test]
      public void Name_ComesFromCounter()
      {
         // Arrange
         var counter = new Counter { Name = "A Counter" };
         // Act
          viewModel.Prepare(counter);
         // Assert
         Assert.AreEqual(counter.Name, viewModel.Name);
      }
   }
}
```

Creates a new counter view model to use in all tests
Creates a new counter with a defined name
Prepares the view model with the counter
Asserts that the name on the view model matches the counter

This is a simple sanity check to ensure that the counter is wired up correctly, and by running this and watching it pass, you can see that everything is OK. As another sanity check for the `Count` property, you can duplicate this test but verify that the count is correctly passed through. You could also add a test to ensure that the property-changed notification is raised when setting the `Name` property, just as we did for the `Number` property of `SquareRtViewModel`. You can see examples in the source code that accompanies this book.

We now have a working view model for a counter that we can use when creating a new counter, as well as for the items in the list on the main view of the app.

8.3.2 Collections

We've looked at simple, single-value properties on our view model; now let's turn our attention to properties that represent collections of data. You've created one view model to represent a counter, so now you need another view model to represent a list of counters—`CountersViewModel`. Start by creating this class in the ViewModels folder. The following listing shows the initial implementation.

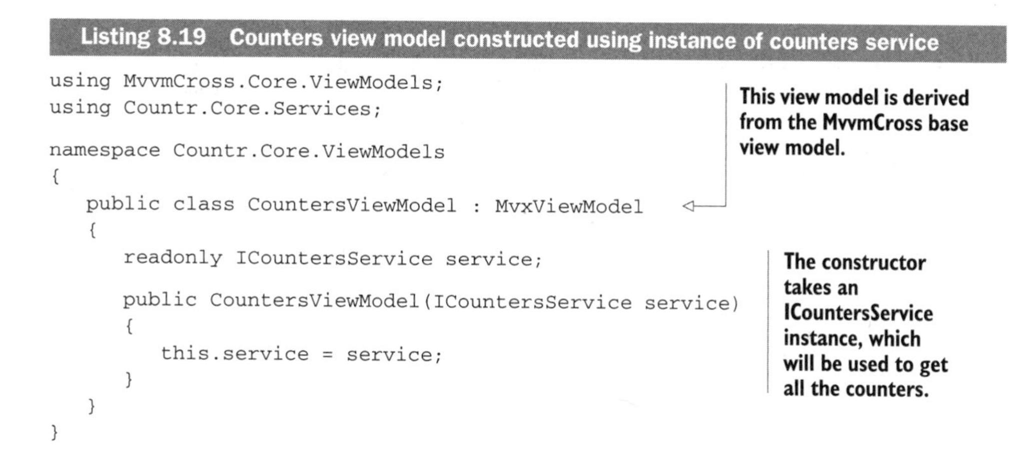

Listing 8.19 Counters view model constructed using instance of counters service

```
using MvvmCross.Core.ViewModels;
using Countr.Core.Services;

namespace Countr.Core.ViewModels
{
   public class CountersViewModel : MvxViewModel
   {
      readonly ICountersService service;

      public CountersViewModel(ICountersService service)
      {
         this.service = service;
      }
   }
}
```

This view model is derived from the MvvmCross base view model.
The constructor takes an ICountersService instance, which will be used to get all the counters.

Again this view model derives from `MvxViewModel`, and the constructor for the view model takes an instance of `ICountersService` (the service in the model layer you created in the last chapter), which it will use to load all the counters.

Now that you have your view model, you need to expose the list of counters. The following listing shows the implementation of this.

Listing 8.20 Exposing counters as observable collection of counter view models

```
using System.Collections.ObjectModel;
...
public class CountersViewModel : MvxViewModel
{
   ...
   public CountersViewModel(ICountersService service)
   {
      ...
      Counters = new ObservableCollection<CounterViewModel>();
   }

   public ObservableCollection<CounterViewModel> Counters { get; }
}
```

The Counters property is an ObservableCollection of CounterViewModel.

This view model exposes a collection of `CounterViewModel` instances. The collection is exposed as an `ObservableCollection`. This is a collection type that implements `INotifyCollectionChanged`, an interface that fires an event whenever the collection is changed. We looked at observable collections in chapter 3, and figure 8.17 recaps how they can be used.

When you create your views, you can bind this collection to some form of list control, and whenever the collection changes (such as when you add or delete counters) the collection-changed event will be fired, causing the binding to update the UI. This is a read-only property, and it's initialized when the view model is created—the instance of `ObservableCollection` won't change, just the contents, so there's no need to ever change the property's value or raise a property-changed event. Observable

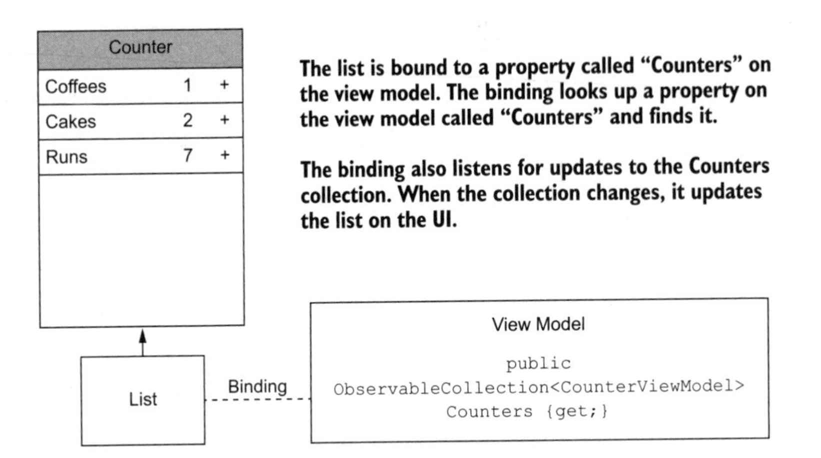
Counter
Coffees 1 +
Cakes 2 +
Runs 7 +
The list is bound to a property called "Counters" on the view model. The binding looks up a property on the view model called "Counters" and finds it.
The binding also listens for updates to the Counters collection. When the collection changes, it updates the list on the UI.
View Model
public ObservableCollection<CounterViewModel> Counters {get;}
List
Binding

Figure 8.17 Collections can be bound to list controls, and when the collection changes, the list control on the UI is updated.

collections are ideal when your collection will change, but they're not necessary if your collection is fixed and will never change. In the latter case you can store the items in any collection, such as a `List<T>`, and expose this property either as a list or as an `IEnumerable<T>`.

This observable collection is exposed as a collection of counter view models. The `ICountersService` exposes a method to get all the counters from the repository, but that returns a collection of `Counter` objects. To make these available as the right type, you can't just expose the counters from the service directly. Instead you need to wrap them in view models. You also need to make a call to the service to load these counters in a background thread and then update the collection back on the UI thread, as shown in figure 8.18. The UI can only be updated on the UI thread, so you should ensure that every update to the observable collection happens on the UI thread.

Ideally, you'd have an `async` method in your view model that's called from the UI thread, and helpfully MvvmCross provides a method you can use, called `Initialize`. The `Initialize` method is a virtual method in the `MvxViewModel` base class that's called by the MvvmCross framework, and it's in overrides of this method that you set up your view model.

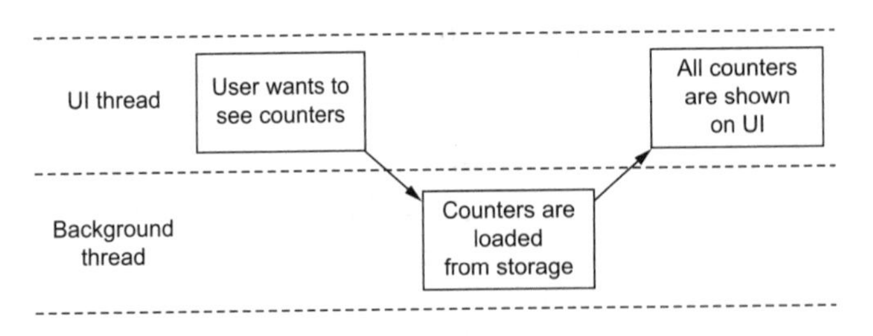
UI thread
User wants to see counters
All counters are shown on UI
Background thread
Counters are loaded from storage

Figure 8.18 You can load counters on a background thread, but you need to show them on the UI thread.

All screens in your app, regardless of platform, will undergo a lifecycle—they're created, shown, hidden, and then destroyed. iOS and Android implement this lifecycle differently, but the basic principle holds true on both platforms. As part of this lifecycle, after the view has been created and shown, MvvmCross will call `Initialize` on the corresponding view model on the UI thread, allowing you to write code to set up the view model (we'll look at this view lifecycle in more detail in chapters 9 and 10). The following listing shows this method and how you can create your view models inside it.

Listing 8.21 Creating counter view models from counters loaded from service

```
using System.Threading.Tasks;
...
public override async Task Initialize()
{
   await LoadCounters();
}

public async Task LoadCounters()
{
   var counters = await service.GetAllCounters();
   foreach (var counter in counters)
   {
      var viewModel = new CounterViewModel();
      viewModel.Prepare(counter);
      Counters.Add(viewModel);
   }
}
```

Initialize comes from the MvxViewModel base class, and it awaits another method.

LoadCounters loads the counters from the service and populates the observable collection with view models prepared with counters.

In the `LoadCounters` method, you can make a call to the counters service to get all the counters. Then, for each counter, you can create an instance of `CounterViewModel`, prepared using that counter, which in turn is added to the observable collection. The `LoadCounters` method will load the counters from a SQLite database (via the service and repository), and this database access will be on a background thread. This means that the UI could be fully visible before you've loaded your counters, but because you're using an observable collection, every time you add a counter view model to the collection, the UI is updated.

The `LoadCounters` method gives us the first of the four user flows we identified for the Countr app. It loads the counters from storage and makes them available to be shown on the UI (figure 8.19).

No view model is complete without a unit test, so let's create the fixture now. Create a class called `CountersViewModelTests` in the ViewModels folder of the Countr.Core.Tests project. The following listing shows the initial implementation of

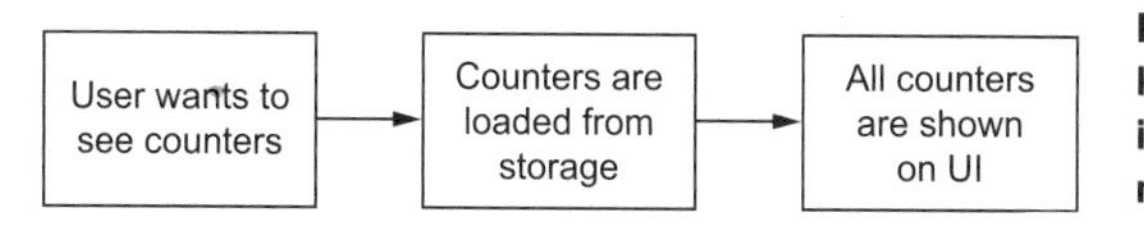

Figure 8.19 The first user flow in Countr, loading and showing counters, is implemented by the `LoadCounters` method on the view model.

this test fixture, creating a mock counters service and using that to create an instance of the view model to test.

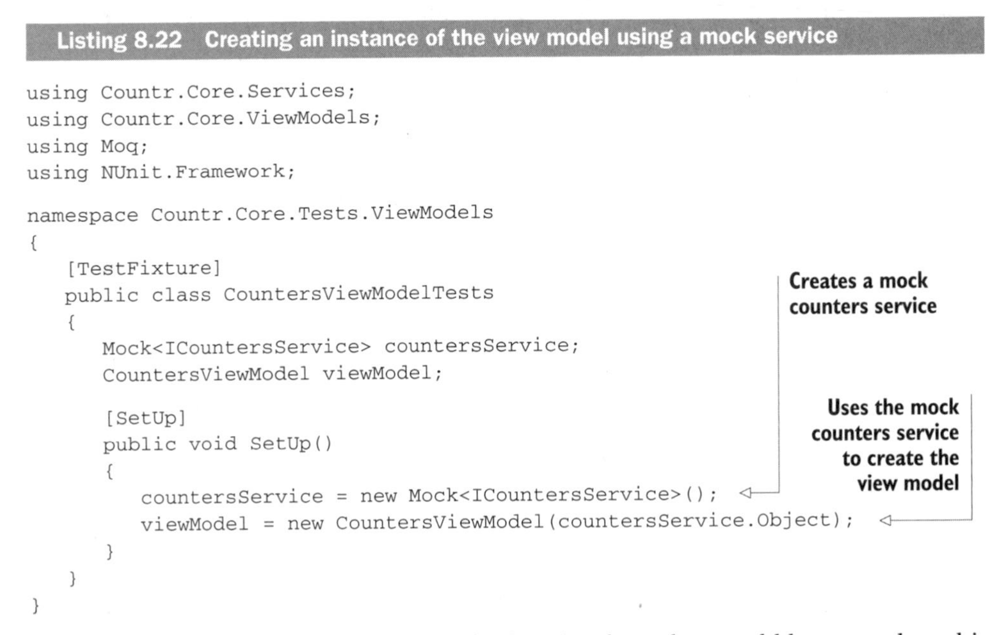

Listing 8.22 Creating an instance of the view model using a mock service

```
using Countr.Core.Services;
using Countr.Core.ViewModels;
using Moq;
using NUnit.Framework;

namespace Countr.Core.Tests.ViewModels
{
   [TestFixture]
   public class CountersViewModelTests
   {
      Mock<ICountersService> countersService;
      CountersViewModel viewModel;

      [SetUp]
      public void SetUp()
      {
         countersService = new Mock<ICountersService>();         // Creates a mock counters service
         viewModel = new CountersViewModel(countersService.Object); // Uses the mock counters service to create the view model
      }
   }
}
```

You can now test the LoadCounters method to simulate what would happen when this view model is created by MvvmCross in the app. The following listing shows an async unit test (which returns async Task instead of void, so that you can await code inside it) to test this method.

Listing 8.23 A test to ensure that the view model wraps the counters correctly

```
using System.Threading.Tasks;
using System.Collections.Generic;
using Countr.Core.Models;
...
[Test]
public async Task LoadCounters_CreatesCounters()
{
   // Arrange
   var counters = new List<Counter>
   {
      new Counter{Name = "Counter1", Count=0},
      new Counter{Name = "Counter2", Count=4},
   };
   countersService.Setup(c => c.GetAllCounters())
                  .ReturnsAsync(counters);    // Sets up the counters service to return some counters
   // Act
   await viewModel.LoadCounters();         // Calls LoadCounters on the view model to create the counter view models
```

```
    // Assert
    Assert.AreEqual(2, viewModel.Counters.Count);
    Assert.AreEqual("Counter1", viewModel.Counters[0].Name);
    Assert.AreEqual(0, viewModel.Counters[0].Count);
    Assert.AreEqual("Counter2", viewModel.Counters[1].Name);
    Assert.AreEqual(4, viewModel.Counters[1].Count);
}
```

Asserts that the counter view models are created correctly

This test starts by creating a list of `Counter` instances with some dummy data. It then sets up the mock counter service to return this list when `GetAllCounters` is called. Finally, it awaits a call to `LoadCounters`, and asserts that the list of `CounterViewModel` instances contains view models that match the canned data. Run this test now, and you should see that it passes.

That's all you need for this view model. This is a standard pattern for master view models when building a master/detail style app. The master view model loads the models for its items from a repository, wraps them all in instances of the detail view model, and exposes them in a collection. If the collection of items can change, they should be exposed in an observable collection so the UI can be notified of any changes. If the collection can't change, a simple `IEnumerable<T>` or `List<T>` is fine.

8.3.3 Exposing behavior using commands

SquareRt has very simplistic behavior that could be implemented inside properties. Countr, on the other hand, has more complex behavior that's triggered by user interactions, and for this we need to use commands. We looked at commands back in chapter 3, so let's have a quick recap now.

Commands are objects that encapsulate the ability to execute a particular action, with optionally the ability to control whether the action can be executed. They implement `ICommand`, an interface with an `Execute` method that executes the action wrapped up in the command and a `CanExecute` method that tells you if the command can be executed or not. You can bind these to user actions on the UI, such as button taps, so that when a button is tapped the command is executed. Commands allow you to provide cross-platform handlers for UI widget events without having to resort to platform-specific event handlers.

You can use commands for the remaining user flows in Countr. Let's start by looking at the simpler ones, beginning with incrementing a counter (figure 8.20). Counters are not incremented directly; instead you use the `CountersService` to ensure the incremented value is persisted to the repository (figure 8.21).

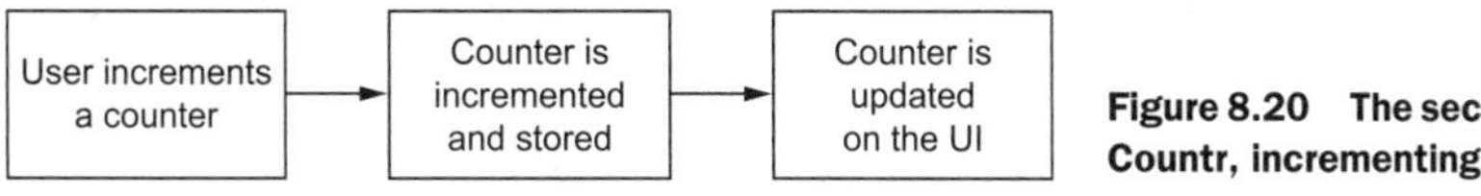

Figure 8.20 The second user flow in Countr, incrementing a counter

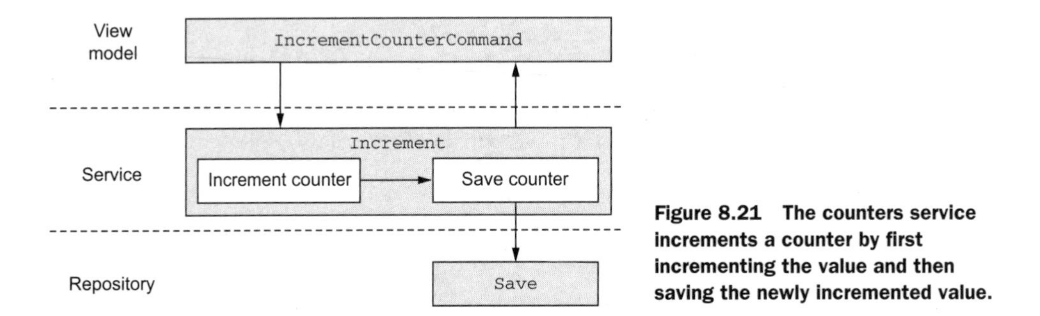

Figure 8.21 The counters service increments a counter by first incrementing the value and then saving the newly incremented value.

The first thing to do is pass an `ICountersService` to the `CounterViewModel`.

Listing 8.24 Passing the counters service to the view model

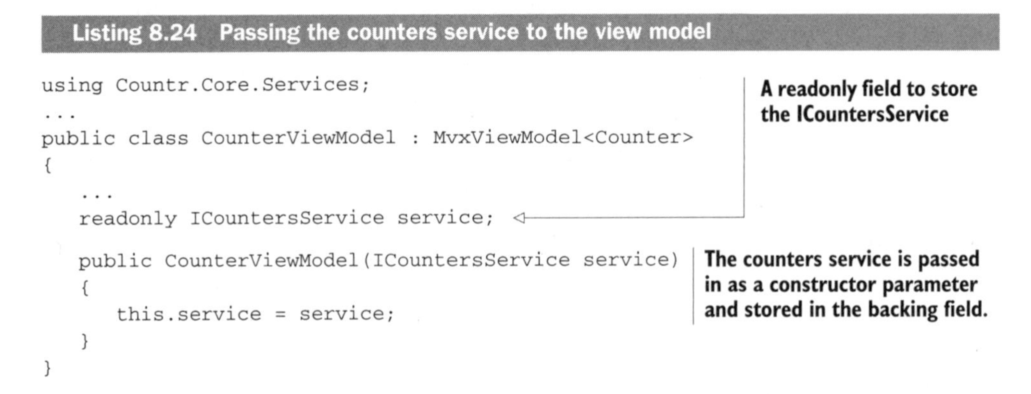

```
using Countr.Core.Services;
...
public class CounterViewModel : MvxViewModel<Counter>
{
   ...
   readonly ICountersService service;

   public CounterViewModel(ICountersService service)
   {
      this.service = service;
   }
}
```

A readonly field to store the ICountersService

The counters service is passed in as a constructor parameter and stored in the backing field.

You've changed the constructor, so you need to update the code that uses it in the `CountersViewModel`, as in the following listing.

Listing 8.25 Counter service needs to be passed to the constructor

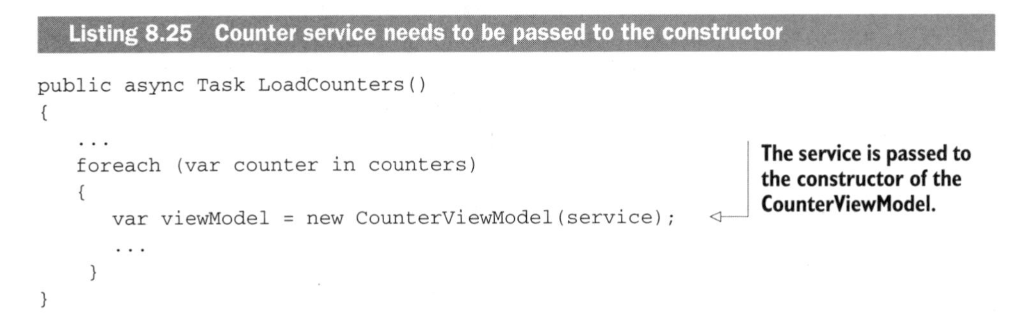

```
public async Task LoadCounters()
{
   ...
   foreach (var counter in counters)
   {
      var viewModel = new CounterViewModel(service);
      ...
    }
}
```

The service is passed to the constructor of the CounterViewModel.

Now you have a service. The next listing creates a command that calls it to increment the counter.

Listing 8.26 Adding a command to the counter view model to increment the counter

```
using System.Threading.Tasks;
...
public CounterViewModel(ICountersService service)
{
```

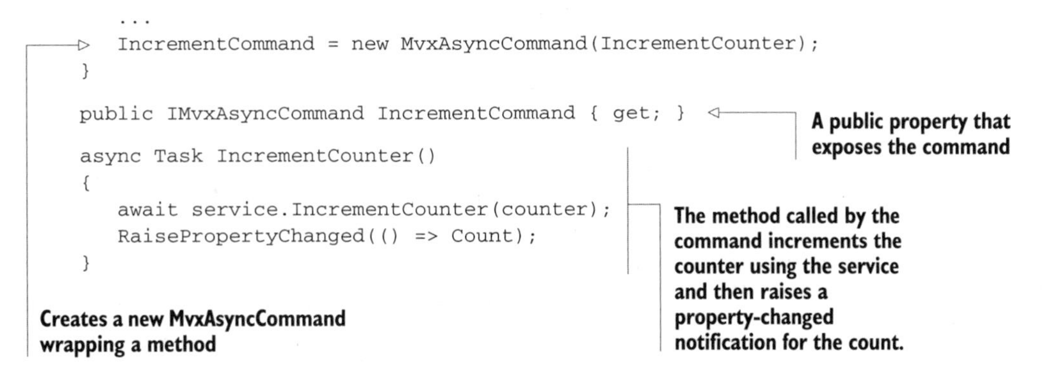

```
    ...
    IncrementCommand = new MvxAsyncCommand(IncrementCounter);
}

public IMvxAsyncCommand IncrementCommand { get; }

async Task IncrementCounter()
{
    await service.IncrementCounter(counter);
    RaisePropertyChanged(() => Count);
}
```

A public property that exposes the command
The method called by the command increments the counter using the service and then raises a property-changed notification for the count.
Creates a new MvxAsyncCommand wrapping a method

This is the first time you've used a command, so let's break down what's happening here, line by line.

- `public IMvxAsyncCommand IncrementCommand { get; }`
  This is a public property exposing the command as an `IMvxAsyncCommand interface` interface. This interface is derived from `ICommand`, the base interface for all commands, but it has extra helper methods on it to run async code. This public property can be bound to a button or similar UI widget.
- `IncrementCommand = new MvxAsyncCommand(IncrementCounter);`
  As we discussed in chapter 3, there's no out-of-the-box implementation of `ICommand` to use, but all MVVM frameworks provide an implementation. In this case, we're using `MvxAsyncCommand`—an implementation of `ICommand` that wraps an async method, and it's this method that's passed in to the constructor. When `Execute` is called on the command, it will call the `IncrementCounter` method on the calling thread (if this command is executed from a button tap, the calling thread will be the UI thread). This command is async, but there's no way button-tap events can await commands, so it's fire-and-forget. It will call the code on the correct thread, but there's no way of knowing when the `Execute` method has finished. This isn't a problem for events, but it's a problem for unit-testing, where you want to know that the command has completed before asserting on anything. Helpfully, `MvxAsyncCommand` also implements `IMvxAsyncCommand` (which derives from `ICommand`) and has async versions of the command methods, such as `ExecuteAsync`, which will execute the command and can be awaited. If you were calling a non-async method instead of an async method for our command's implementation, you could use `MvxCommand`.

  The `Execute` and `CanExecute` methods on `ICommand` take an object parameter, but in a lot of cases this parameter is null. `MvxAsyncCommand` and `MvxCommand` encapsulate this by taking methods as their constructor parameters that have no parameters. If you want to handle a parameter, you can use `MvxAsyncCommand<T>` and `MvxCommand<T>`, where the generic type parameter `T` is the type of the parameter you expect the command to be called with, and where the corresponding actions passed to the command constructor will need to have parameters of type `T`. Using a typed parameter instead of `object` means MvvmCross will handle the conversion for you, throwing an exception if the command is called with the wrong parameter type.

- `async Task IncrementCounter()`
  This is the method called by the command. It's an async method that will use the service to increment the counter and save it to the SQLite database on a background thread (thanks to the SQLite-Net implementation). Then it will raise a property changed for the `Counter` property to tell the binding layer to re-read the value. The value on the underlying counter will be incremented, so the binding layer will read the new, incremented value and update the number displayed on screen.

This command is implemented in our cross-platform view model, and it's crying out for some unit tests, so let's add a couple. The following listing shows the code to add to `CounterViewModelTests`.

Listing 8.27 Testing the increment command

```
using System.Threading.Tasks;
using Moq;
using Countr.Core.Services;
...
Mock<ICountersService> countersService;

[SetUp]
public void SetUp()
{
   countersService = new Mock<ICountersService>();
   viewModel = new CounterViewModel(countersService.Object);
   viewModel.ShouldAlwaysRaiseInpcOnUserInterfaceThread(false);
   ...
}

[Test]
public async Task IncrementCounter_IncrementsTheCounter()
{
   // Act
   await viewModel.IncrementCommand.ExecuteAsync();
   // Assert
   countersService.Verify(s => s.IncrementCounter(It.IsAny<Counter>()));
}

[Test]
public async Task IncrementCounter_RaisesPropertyChanged()
{
   // Arrange
   var propertyChangedRaised = false;
   viewModel.PropertyChanged +=
      (s, e) => propertyChangedRaised = (e.PropertyName == "Count");
```

Defines and creates a mock counters service that's passed to the view-model constructor

Ensures all property-changed events are raised on the current thread

Awaits the call to execute IncrementCommand

Asserts that the counter has been incremented by the service

Listens for property-changed notifications to the Count property

```
    // Act
    await viewModel.IncrementCommand.ExecuteAsync();
    // Assert
    Assert.IsTrue(propertyChangedRaised);
}
```

Awaits the call to execute IncrementCommand

Asserts that the property-changed notification has been raised

These tests take advantage of the `ExecuteAsync` method to await the execution of the command asserting that the counter has been incremented by the service and that the property-changed event has been raised. You don't need to verify that the counter has actually been incremented—you've verified that the increment method on the mock service has been called, and you've also verified in other tests that the actual `IncrementCounter` method on the `CountersService` works, so you can be pretty sure that this code will all work together in your app and increment the counter.

You have your increment command, so the next command to look at is the one to delete a counter (figure 8.22). In a lot of master/detail apps, users can delete items from the list by swiping, so we'll enable the same functionality here. This means you need a command on `CounterViewModel` that allows it to delete itself. You've already got everything you need in your view model, so the command is pretty simple, as shown in the following listing.

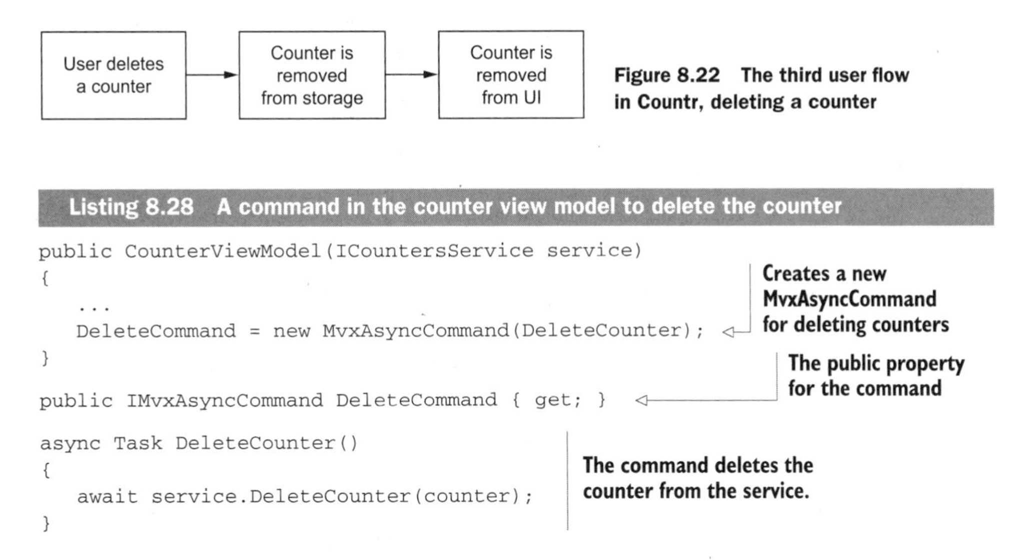

Figure 8.22 The third user flow in Countr, deleting a counter

Listing 8.28 A command in the counter view model to delete the counter

```
public CounterViewModel(ICountersService service)
{
   ...
   DeleteCommand = new MvxAsyncCommand(DeleteCounter);
}

public IMvxAsyncCommand DeleteCommand { get; }

async Task DeleteCounter()
{
   await service.DeleteCounter(counter);
}
```

Creates a new MvxAsyncCommand for deleting counters

The public property for the command

The command deletes the counter from the service.

So far this command is pretty simple, and it's not that different from what you've already seen. It's an async command that calls the counters service to delete the counter. Once you've added this command, add a unit test for it. (If you get stuck, there's an example in the source code that accompanies this book.)

This isn't quite the whole picture, though. This command deletes the counter from the repository, and you know that if the counter is removed from the `ObservableCollection` of counters held by the `CountersViewModel`, the UI will update, but we're missing the bit in between. How does the `CountersViewModel` know to remove the counter from its collection? It doesn't know, so you need to tell it, and the best way to do that is via messaging.

8.3.4 Messaging

In our coffee shop, we have a server who takes coffee orders from customers and writes them on slips of paper, which they pin up somewhere, and we have baristas who pick up these pieces of paper in sequence and make the coffees. This is quite loosely coupled—it doesn't matter who pins the slips of paper up; the baristas just take them and make the drinks, one after the other. As our coffee shop gets more popular, we could employ multiple servers taking orders, or more baristas, and nothing needs to change. We'll just have more people pinning up slips of paper, and more people taking them off. The drinks are still made in order, and we still have a loose coupling between server and barista.

We can follow a similar pattern in our apps by using a publish-subscribe model. In our coffee shop we have servers publishing orders on slips of paper, and baristas subscribing to these slips of paper. We can have parts of our app publishing messages and other parts subscribing to those messages and responding accordingly (figure 8.23).

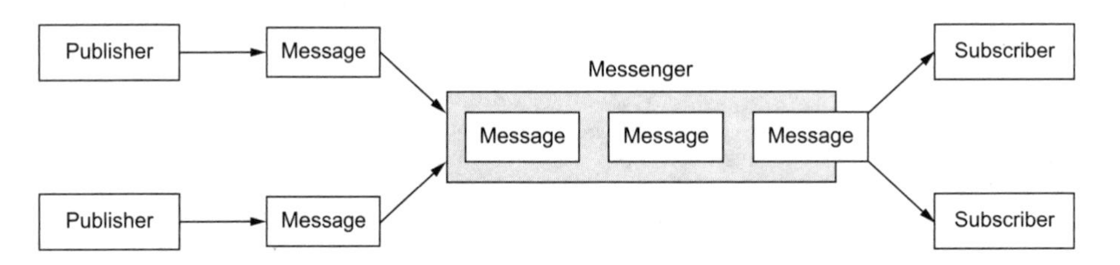

Figure 8.23 A messenger allows different components of an app to publish or subscribe to messages.

We could do exactly this for the delete command—when the counter is deleted, a message could be published to a queue of some description, and the counters view model could subscribe to this queue, get the message that a counter has been deleted, and update its collection accordingly, as shown in figure 8.24.

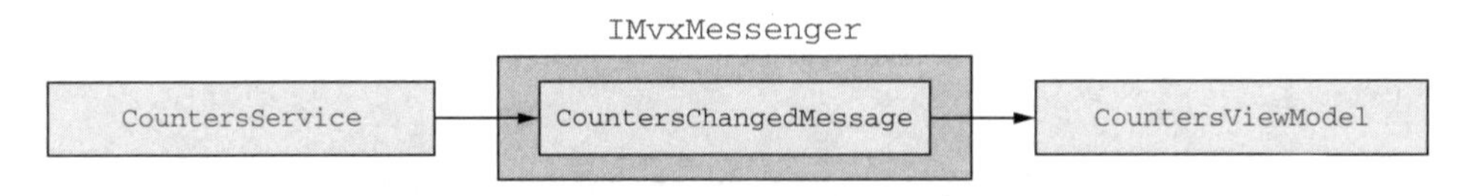

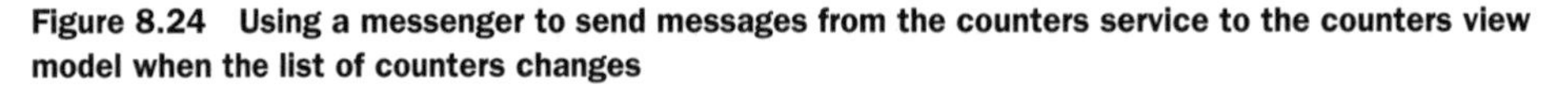

Figure 8.24 Using a messenger to send messages from the counters service to the counters view model when the list of counters changes

Most MVVM frameworks provide a messaging service of some sort—something a class can publish messages to and subscribe to messages from. MvvmCross has one available as another NuGet package, so add the MvvmCross.Plugin.Messenger NuGet package

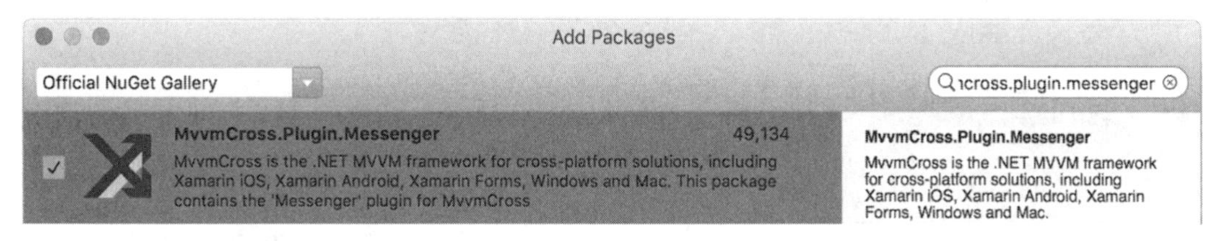

Figure 8.25 Adding the MvvmCross Messenger plugin NuGet package to the Countr.Core project

(figure 8.25) to all the projects in the Countr solution, selecting the same version as the other MvvmCross NuGet packages.

Messenger is an MvvmCross plugin component—an additional component that provides extra useful functionality. Plugins are tightly integrated into MvvmCross; they're even automatically registered in the IoC container just by adding the NuGet package to your app (MvvmCross finds the plugins by using reflection and registers them inside its startup code). You can use this Messenger plugin to publish messages from your counters service when a counter is deleted. You can then subscribe to these messages from the counters view model, and whenever you receive a message, you can reload the counters.

When subscribing to messages, you need to be able to filter them so that you only receive the ones you're interested in, and in the MvvmCross Messenger this is based on the class type of the message. There's a base message type, `MvxMessage`, and you derive from this for each type of message you want to implement. You then publish a message as an instance of your message class. On the subscriber side, you subscribe based on a specific type, and you handle each received message either on the UI thread or on a background thread.

To implement this, you'll need to dip back down to the model layer briefly. Let's start by creating a message type. Add a new class to the Services folder called `CountersChangedMessage`, and add the following code.

Listing 8.29 A message you can publish, telling anyone that the counters have changed

```
using MvvmCross.Plugins.Messenger;

namespace Countr.Core.Services
{
   public class CountersChangedMessage : MvxMessage
   {
      public CountersChangedMessage(object sender)
         : base(sender)
      {}
   }
}
```

This message derives from the MvxMessage base class.

The base class takes the sender of the message as a constructor parameter.

This class defines the message, so you can publish it whenever you delete a counter. The following listing shows the changes to the `CountersService`.

Listing 8.30 Publishing the counters-changed message every time a counter is deleted

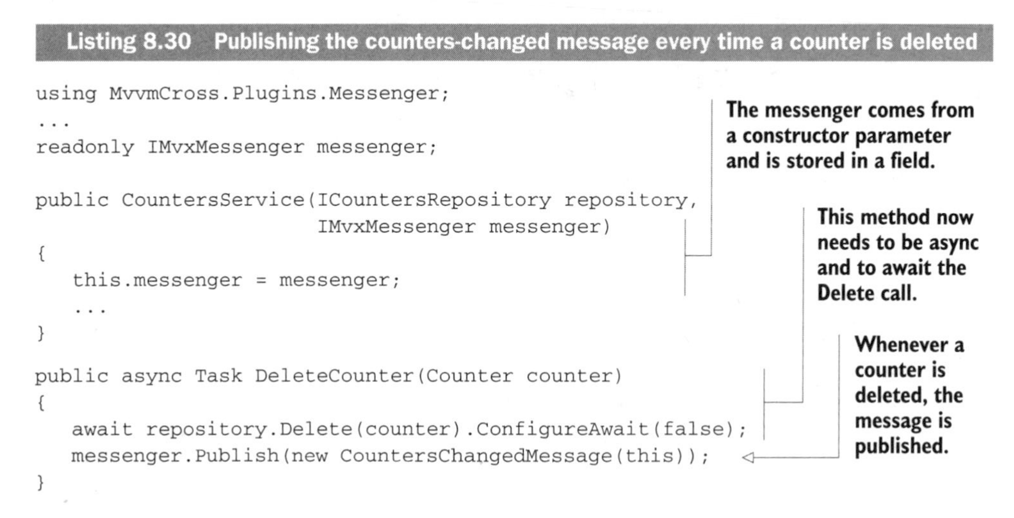

```
using MvvmCross.Plugins.Messenger;
...
readonly IMvxMessenger messenger;

public CountersService(ICountersRepository repository,
                       IMvxMessenger messenger)
{
   this.messenger = messenger;
   ...
}

public async Task DeleteCounter(Counter counter)
{
   await repository.Delete(counter).ConfigureAwait(false);
   messenger.Publish(new CountersChangedMessage(this));
}
```

The messenger comes from a constructor parameter and is stored in a field.
This method now needs to be async and to await the Delete call.
Whenever a counter is deleted, the message is published.

To use the Messenger, just add a constructor parameter of type `IMvxMessenger` to your view model. The plugin is automatically registered in the IoC container, so you can just add it as a constructor parameter, and it'll automatically be populated when the IoC container creates the counters service. Whenever a counter is deleted, the `Publish` method is called with an argument of an instance of this new message type.

The original version of `DeleteCounter` used to just return the `Task` returned from `Delete`, but now that you're doing work after this call, you need to mark the method as `async`, await the call to `Delete`, and use `ConfigureAwait(false)`, because it doesn't matter what thread the rest of the method runs on.

You now need to handle this message in the counters view model, as shown in the next listing.

Listing 8.31 Subscribing to the new message type

```
using MvvmCross.Plugins.Messenger;
...
readonly MvxSubscriptionToken token;

public CountersViewModel(ICountersService service,
                         IMvxMessenger messenger)
{
   token = messenger
      .SubscribeOnMainThread<CountersChangedMessage>
      (async m => await LoadCounters());
   ...
}

public async Task LoadCounters()
{
   Counters.Clear();
   ...
}
```

A field to store a subscription token

The messenger comes from a constructor parameter.

Subscribes to all CountersChangedMessage messages on the UI thread

LoadCounters has been tweaked to clear all counters before reloading.

In `CountersViewModel` you're subscribing on the main thread (the UI thread) for all messages of type `CountersChangedMessage`, and when one is received, the `LoadCounters` method is run. The code for `LoadCounters` has been changed slightly to clear all counters before loading, so that you don't keep adding the same counters to the list again and again. You're not going to have many counters in the list, so clearing and reloading all the counters shouldn't be too slow.

This may seem like overkill, using a Messaging component to detect changes in the counters service, when you could just add an event to the service that the view model subscribes to. But there are advantages to using the Messenger plugin:

- *Weak subscription*—You'll notice that the `SubscribeOnMainThread` method returns a `MvxSubscriptionToken` that you store as a field. Subscribing to messages is a weak subscription, in that the messenger doesn't hold a reference to the subscriber. This means that the garbage collector can collect your view model whenever your code is finished with it; the Messenger won't be holding a reference that keeps the view model alive. If you'd used events, you'd have to manually unsubscribe from the events before the garbage collector could collect the view model, and this is something that's easy to forget to do. The subscription token keeps the subscription alive; as soon as the token is garbage collected, the subscription ends. You can also unsubscribe at any time by disposing of the token using its `Dispose` method.
- *Threading*—When you subscribe to a message, you can choose to handle the messages on the UI thread using `SubscribeOnMainThread` or a background thread using `SubscribeOnThreadPoolThread`. This means you can handle messages using the appropriate thread. With `CountersChangedMessage`, you need to handle it on the UI thread so that you can update the collection. If you'd used an event for this, you'd need to find a way to ensure the event was always handled on the UI thread—that's not easy to do in your view models.
- *Loose coupling*—By using a messenger instead of events, you can loosely couple the publisher to the subscriber. This way, anything can subscribe to the messages and not care where the message came from. You could refactor your code to publish the change messages from the repository instead of the service, and everything would still work. You could add more view models or services that listen to the counters-changed message and respond accordingly, and they wouldn't need to know about the counters service.

Messages let parts of your app communicate without being tightly coupled

Messages are very powerful. You can create as many message types as you need and add properties to them to help you pass data around. In this app there's one message type, and when it's received you clear and reload all counters.

> ***(continued)***
> For an app with only a few counters, this is fine, but for an app with a lot of items in the master list, you'd probably want to be a bit smarter. For example, you could have multiple message types. You could have one message type for a deleted item, with a property on it identifying the item that was deleted. When this is received, just the one item would be removed from the master list. You could then have another message type for when a new item is created, with a property storing the item that was added. When this is received, the new item could be added to the correct position in the master list.

Now that you've added messages, it's time for a unit test. The current unit tests won't compile with the new constructor parameter added to the view models, so you'll need to start by mocking out the messenger in both `CountersViewModelTests` and `CountersServiceTests`. The following listing shows the code for doing this, so make these changes to both unit tests.

Listing 8.32 Mocking out the messenger

```
using MvvmCross.Plugins.Messenger;
...
Mock<IMvxMessenger> messenger;

[SetUp]
public void SetUp()
{
   messenger = new Mock<IMvxMessenger>();
   ...
}
```

After adding this code to both unit-test classes, add the messenger mock to the constructor calls for each view model by passing `messenger.Object` as the required parameter. You can then test that the message is published when a counter is deleted from the service by using the following code in `CountersServiceTests`.

Listing 8.33 Testing that the message is published when a counter is deleted

```
[SetUp]
public void SetUp()
{
   ...
   service = new CountersService(repo.Object,
                                 messenger.Object);     <-- Passes the mock to the service constructor
}

[Test]
public async Task DeleteCounter_PublishesAMessage()
{
   // Act
   await service.DeleteCounter(new Counter());     <-- Deletes a counter from the service
```

```
    // Assert
    messenger.Verify(m => m.Publish
        (It.IsAny<CountersChangedMessage>()));
}
```

Verifies that the messenger publishes a message

You've verified that the service publishes a message, so now let's verify that `CountersViewModel` handles the message correctly. The first thing to do is set this up, as shown in the following listing.

Listing 8.34 Setting up the messenger for unit-testing

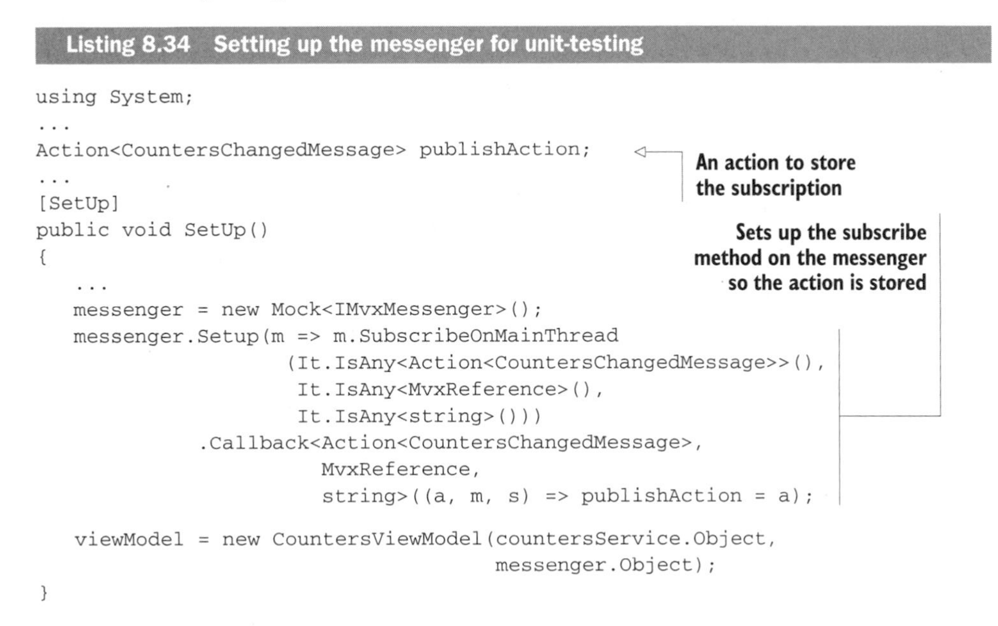

```
using System;
...
Action<CountersChangedMessage> publishAction;
...
[SetUp]
public void SetUp()
{
    ...
    messenger = new Mock<IMvxMessenger>();
    messenger.Setup(m => m.SubscribeOnMainThread
                        (It.IsAny<Action<CountersChangedMessage>>(),
                         It.IsAny<MvxReference>(),
                         It.IsAny<string>()))
                 .Callback<Action<CountersChangedMessage>,
                           MvxReference,
                           string>((a, m, s) => publishAction = a);

    viewModel = new CountersViewModel(countersService.Object,
                                      messenger.Object);
}
```

An action to store the subscription

Sets up the subscribe method on the messenger so the action is stored

When the `SubscribeOnMainThread` method inside the view model is called, it's passed an `Action<CountersChangedMessage>`. In the unit test, you set up this method with a callback that's invoked whenever the `SubscribeOnMainThread` method is called, and in this callback you store the action that's passed to the method. This allows you to simulate the messenger flow.

In the real messenger, the subscription action is stored, and when a message is published, all subscription actions for that message type are called. In the unit test you can simulate this by storing the subscription action and calling it to simulate a message being published. The following listing shows the code for a unit test that uses this approach.

Listing 8.35 Unit-testing that the counters are reloaded when a message is received

```
[Test]
public void ReceivedMessage_LoadsCounters()
{
    // Arrange
    countersService.Setup(s => s.GetAllCounters())
                   .ReturnsAsync(new List<Counter>());
```

Sets up a mock return value from GetAllCounters

```
    // Act
    publishAction.Invoke(new CountersChangedMessage(this));
    // Assert
    countersService.Verify(s => s.GetAllCounters());
}
```

Calls the subscription action to simulate a message being published

Verifies that after the message is published, the counters are reloaded

That's three user flows down, one more to go—adding a new counter. This user flow shows a new screen, so it's time to look into view-model navigation.

8.3.5 Navigation

Back in chapter 3, we looked at two navigation patterns for MVVM: view-first and view-model-first. View-first is where views drive navigation, with each view triggering the loading of its view model, and where navigation consists of one view loading another. View-model-first is where the view models drive navigation, with the view model triggering which view is loaded, and where navigation is one view model showing another.

Like a lot of MVVM frameworks, MvvmCross uses view-model-first navigation. The first screen of the app to be shown is defined by registering the app's start view model. Showing and closing views is controlled by a navigation service that view models can use. MvvmCross has a built-in *presenter* that will find the relevant view for a view model based on its name, so when you show a view model, it will find the relevant view and show that on screen.

You can think of navigating between screens as being like paper stacking up. Each screen is like a sheet of paper, and when you navigate from one screen to another, the new screen is stacked on top, like placing a new piece of paper on top of the stack. When you close a screen, it comes back off the stack of paper, revealing the piece underneath (figure 8.26). You'll have seen this many times over in the apps you use, such as email apps.

When you're using MvvmCross, this is driven via the view models, so you navigate from one view model to another, and the view for the new view model is stacked on top. When you close a view model, the top view is removed from the stack. MvvmCross also allows you to pass data from one view model to the next as they stack up, although it doesn't have anything out of the box for passing data back as you close view models off the top of the stack.

Our last user flow is adding a new counter, and this involves navigating from the counters master list screen to a new counter detail screen at the tap of a button (figure 8.27). From this screen, the user can either cancel adding a new counter and navigate back to the master list, or they can enter the name of the new counter, save it, and navigate back.

Let's start by looking at the MvvmCross navigation service.

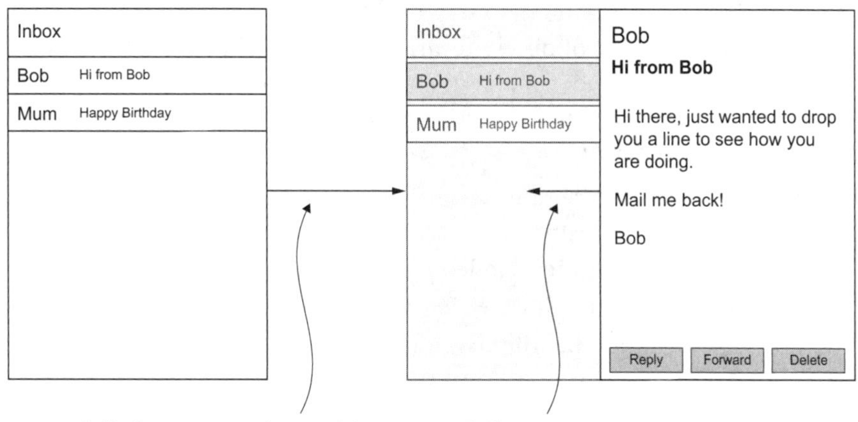

Figure 8.26 Navigation is like sheets of paper being stacked up and unstacked.

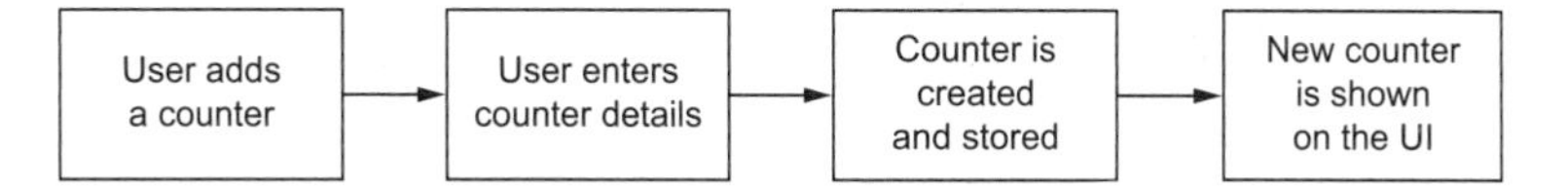

Figure 8.27 The final user flow in Countr, adding a new a counter

NAVIGATION SERVICE

MvvmCross has a built-in navigation service whose sole responsibility is to handle the navigation between view models in your app, providing view-model-first navigation. When you navigate to a view model, it will look up and navigate to the corresponding view inside your platform-specific code based on its name (for example, navigating to `MyViewModel` will cause it to look for a corresponding view called `MyView`). This navigation service is exposed via the `IMvxNavigationService` interface, which is automatically registered inside the IoC container for you by the MvvmCross startup code. This means you can import this interface into your view models and access navigation from your cross-platform code.

This navigation service has a number of capabilities. You can use it to navigate to a view model, navigate and pass data into the target view model, navigate and await a result from the target view model, or close a view model to go back to the previous view. You can also subscribe to events so you're notified when navigation happens. MvvmCross even supports URI-based navigation, so you can create deep navigation stacks with multiple levels (such as long signup flows) and navigate up and down with ease. We're only going to touch on a couple of features of the navigation service here—navigating to a view model passing some data, and closing a view model to navigate back—but you can read more about the MvvmCross navigation service in the MvvmCross documentation at http://mng.bz/tJ7a.

You navigate to a view model using the `Navigate` method on the navigation service. There are a number of different variants of this, but the simplest takes a parameter of the type of view model you want to navigate to. For example, `Navigate(typeof (MySecondViewModel))` would navigate to the `MySecondViewModel` view model. This is an `async` method that you can `await`. When you call this method, it will

1. Create a new instance of the target view model, injecting all constructor parameters using the IoC container.
2. Call `Prepare` on the view model, passing in a parameter if needed.
3. Find the relevant view for the view model and create an instance of that.
4. Show the view, binding the view model to the view.
5. Call `Initialize` on the view model.

One of the other variants of interest to us is `Navigate<TParameter>(Type type, TParameter parameter)`. This will navigate to the view model with the type specified in the first parameter, and prepare it with the parameter passed in. The target view model needs to be derived from `MvxViewModel<TParameter>`, an abstract base class that provides a method you have to override, called `Prepare`, which has a parameter of `TParameter`. It's this method that's called to prepare the view model. This call to `Prepare` happens on the UI thread before the view has been created. After the view is created, another method, `Initialize`, is called, and it's an async method, so it's a great place to load data or perform other asynchronous tasks. You may recognize this base view model—it's the one we used for `CounterViewModel`, meaning you can navigate to this view model and prepare it with a `Counter`.

The final method on the navigation service of interest to us is the `Close` method. This method takes a view model to be closed, and it will close the view that shows the given view model. This is normally called from inside a view model, passing `this` as the parameter to close the current view model, but you can also use it to close other view models if you need to. For example, if you're showing a view model as a progress dialog during a long-running action, you could close it from the calling view model.

SETTING THE STARTUP VIEW MODEL

To get the app navigation working correctly, the first thing you need to do is set up your app start (listing 8.36). When the app is loaded, MvvmCross will first show a splash screen while it's initializing. Then it will find the startup view-model type, and using its built-in presenter it'll find the relevant type for the first view, create the view, create the view model, and show the view.

For Countr, the master list is the first screen that you want to show, so the app should start up using `CountersViewModel`. You can tell MvvmCross to use this view model when the app starts up by registering it as the app start in the `App` class in the core project. Delete the `FirstViewModel` class from the `ViewModels` folder, as you don't need it any more, and make the following change.

Listing 8.36 Setting up the counters view model as the app start

```
public override void Initialize()
{
   ...
   RegisterNavigationServiceAppStart<ViewModels.CountersViewModel>();
}
```

Once you've deleted `FirstViewModel`, the iOS app will no longer compile, which shouldn't be too much of a problem because you're not running the mobile apps at this point, just verifying your code using unit tests. If you want to be able to successfully build everything, just comment out the whole `ViewDidLoad` method in the `FirstView` class in the Views folder of the Countr.iOS app. We'll be working on the view layer for the iOS app in chapter 11.

NAVIGATING TO A NEW VIEW

Next you need to add a command to the master view model in order to show the detail view. MvvmCross has a navigation service that handles the navigation between view models. This service is exposed as the `IMvxNavigationService` interface, and it's automatically registered in the IoC container so you can easily add it as a constructor parameter on the view model. Once you have access to this navigation service, you can use it to show a different view model.

The following listing shows the code you need to add to the `CountersViewModel`.

Listing 8.37 Adding a command to show the counter view model

```
using Countr.Core.Models;
using MvvmCross.Core.Navigation;
...
readonly IMvxNavigationService navigationService;

public CountersViewModel(ICountersService service,
                         IMvxMessenger messenger,
                         IMvxNavigationService navigationService)
{
   ...
   this.navigationService = navigationService;
   ShowAddNewCounterCommand = new MvxAsyncCommand(ShowAddNewCounter);
}

public IMvxAsyncCommand ShowAddNewCounterCommand { get; }

async Task ShowAddNewCounter()
{
   await navigationService.Navigate(typeof(CounterViewModel),
                                    new Counter());
}
```

Injects and stores an instance of the MvvmCross navigation service

A public property for the new command

Shows the counter view model, initialized with a new counter

Creates the new command

This view model now takes an instance of the `IMvxNavigationService` interface as part of its constructor and stores it in a field. This code also adds a new async command that uses the async `Navigate` method on the navigation service to navigate to the `CounterViewModel`, passing a new `Counter` as the preparation parameter.

UNIT-TESTING NAVIGATION TO A NEW VIEW

As well as being a powerful way to navigate between view models, the navigation service also allows for easy unit-testing. It's made available via an interface, so it's trivial to mock out. You can easily verify that your new command shows the relevant view model by adding some more tests to the `CountersViewModelTests` unit-test class, as follows.

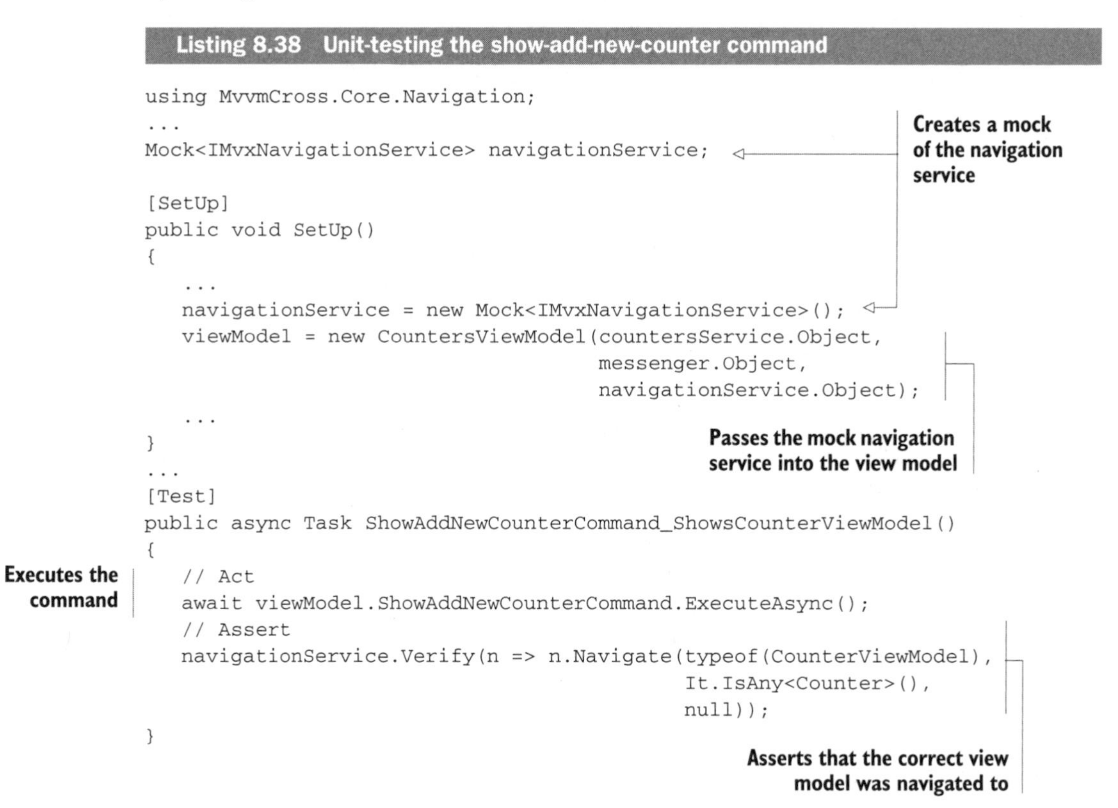
Creates a mock of the navigation service
Passes the mock navigation service into the view model
Executes the command
Asserts that the correct view model was navigated to

Listing 8.38 Unit-testing the show-add-new-counter command

```
using MvvmCross.Core.Navigation;
...
Mock<IMvxNavigationService> navigationService;

[SetUp]
public void SetUp()
{
   ...
   navigationService = new Mock<IMvxNavigationService>();
   viewModel = new CountersViewModel(countersService.Object,
                                     messenger.Object,
                                     navigationService.Object);
   ...
}
...
[Test]
public async Task ShowAddNewCounterCommand_ShowsCounterViewModel()
{
   // Act
   await viewModel.ShowAddNewCounterCommand.ExecuteAsync();
   // Assert
   navigationService.Verify(n => n.Navigate(typeof(CounterViewModel),
                                            It.IsAny<Counter>(),
                                            null));
}
```

For this unit test you need to create a new mock of `IMvxNavigationService`, and once it's created, you pass it into the view model under test. You can then add a test to execute the new command using the `ExecuteAsync` method exposed by `MvxAsyncCommand`, and verify that it calls `Navigate` on the service to prove that the right view model was navigated to. `ExecuteAsync` isn't part of the standard `ICommand` interface; instead, it's a helper method on the MvvmCross commands, and it calls the underlying async method passed to the constructor of the command, allowing you to await the completion of the command.

CLOSING A VIEW AND NAVIGATING BACK

You now have the master view model set up as your app start, and you have a command that navigates to the counter view model using a new instance of `Counter`. The next thing you need is to allow the user to cancel or save the new counter. To do this, you need to add two commands to the counter view model. The following listing shows the code you need to add to `CounterViewModel`.

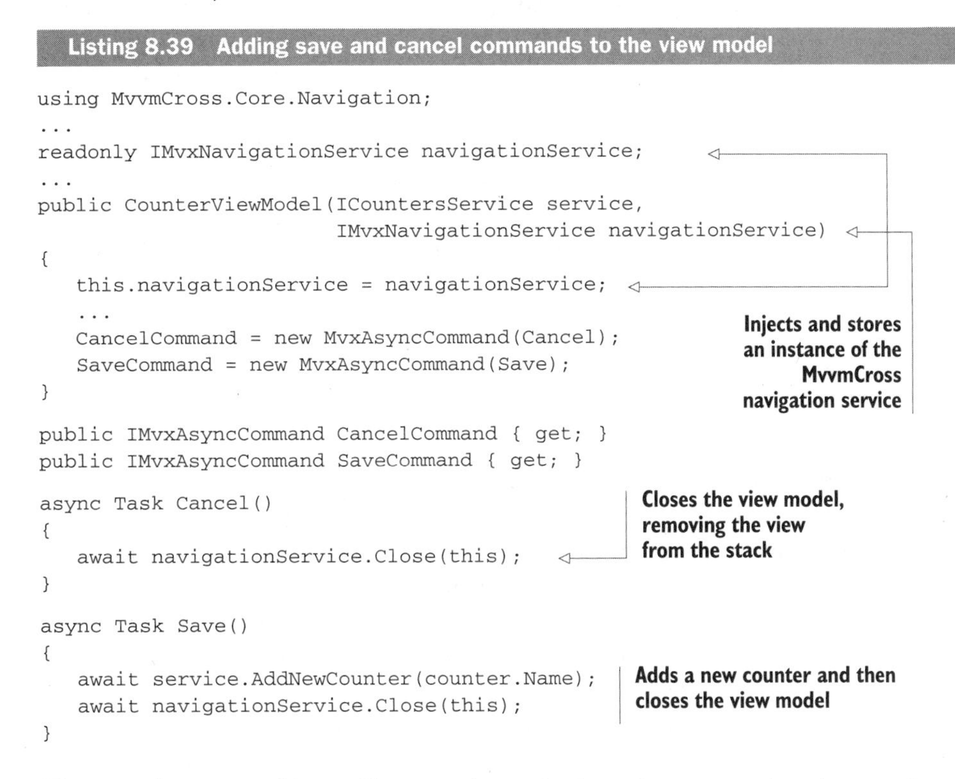

Listing 8.39 Adding save and cancel commands to the view model

```
using MvvmCross.Core.Navigation;
...
readonly IMvxNavigationService navigationService;
...
public CounterViewModel(ICountersService service,
                        IMvxNavigationService navigationService)
{
   this.navigationService = navigationService;
   ...
   CancelCommand = new MvxAsyncCommand(Cancel);
   SaveCommand = new MvxAsyncCommand(Save);
}

public IMvxAsyncCommand CancelCommand { get; }
public IMvxAsyncCommand SaveCommand { get; }

async Task Cancel()
{
   await navigationService.Close(this);
}

async Task Save()
{
   await service.AddNewCounter(counter.Name);
   await navigationService.Close(this);
}
```

Injects and stores an instance of the MvvmCross navigation service
Closes the view model, removing the view from the stack
Adds a new counter and then closes the view model

The cancel command just calls `Close` (a method on the `IMvxNavigationService` that closes a view model) passing in the view model to close (the current view model). This causes the presenter to remove the current view from the stack and show the previous one. The save command uses the counters service to create a new counter, and then closes the view model using the navigation service.

The `CounterViewModel` constructor has changed, so you'll need to add the code in listing 8.40 to pass the navigation service when creating instances of this view model inside `CountersViewModel`.

Listing 8.40 Passing the navigation service to the counter view model

```
public async Task LoadCounters()
{
    ...
    foreach (var counter in counters)
```

```
    {
        var viewModel = new CounterViewModel(service,
                                             navigationService);
        ...
    }
}
```

Passes the navigation service through to the CounterViewModel constructor

This is almost everything you need. The only thing missing is code that shows the new counter on the master view. You don't need to worry about the counter view model telling the counters view model that there's a new counter. Instead you can use the same pattern for adding as you did for deletes. You can change the service to publish a message when a new counter is added, keeping the master list up to date. The following listing shows the code to add to the counters service.

Listing 8.41 The master list will automatically update

```
public async Task<Counter> AddNewCounter(string name)
{
   ...
   messenger.Publish(new CountersChangedMessage(this));
   return counter;
}
```

Once a counter is saved, publish the message

UNIT-TESTING SAVING COUNTERS AND CLOSING VIEWS

You have your commands, so now you need to unit-test them. For the save command you need to verify that the counter is saved to the counters service and that the view model is closed. For the cancel command you need to verify that the counter isn't saved before the view model is closed. You can verify saving using the mock counters service already set up in the unit tests, and you can verify closing the view model using a mock navigation service.

The following code shows the test for the save command, so add it to the `CounterViewModelTests` class.

Listing 8.42 Testing the save command

```
using MvvmCross.Core.Navigation;
...
Mock<IMvxNavigationService> navigationService;
...
[SetUp]
public void SetUp()
{
   ...
   navigationService = new Mock<IMvxNavigationService>();
   viewModel = new CounterViewModel(countersService.Object,
                                    navigationService.Object);
   ...
}
...
[Test]
```

Sets up the mock navigation service

```
public async Task SaveCommand_SavesTheCounter()
{
    // Arrange
    var counter = new Counter { Name = "A Counter" };
    viewModel.Prepare(counter);
    // Act
    await viewModel.SaveCommand.ExecuteAsync();                         <-- Executes the command
    // Assert
    countersService.Verify(c => c.AddNewCounter("A Counter"));          <-- Verifies that the counter was saved
    navigationService.Verify(n => n.Close(viewModel));                  <-- Verifies that the view model was closed
}
```

The code to test the cancel command is nearly identical, except you need to verify that the save wasn't called, as shown in the following listing.

Listing 8.43 Testing the cancel command

```
[Test]
public void CancelCommand_DoesntSaveTheCounter()
{
    // Arrange
    var counter = new Counter { Name = "A Counter" };
    viewModel.Prepare(counter);
    // Act
    viewModel.CancelCommand.Execute();
    // Assert
    countersService.Verify(c => c.AddNewCounter(It.IsAny<string>()),
                                            Times.Never());            <-- Verifies that AddNewCounter was never called
    navigationService.Verify(n => n.Close(viewModel));
}
```

8.4 A quick roundup

This is pretty much everything you need. You've created a number of new classes for the two apps. Table 8.1 shows the classes for the SquareRt app, and table 8.2 shows them for the Countr app.

Table 8.1 The classes and interfaces created for the SquareRt app

Name	Description
SquareRtViewModel	The view model for the square-root app containing the state for the input number, the result, and the behavior for performing the calculation whenever the number changes. This class optionally contains value conversion.
DoubleToStringValueConverter	A value converter that convert from double values in the view model to string values used by the view, and vice versa.
SquareRtViewModelTests	Unit tests for SquareRtViewModel.

Table 8.1 The classes and interfaces created for the SquareRt app *(continued)*

Name	Description
`DoubleToStringValueConverterTests`	Unit tests for `DoubleToStringValueConverter`.

Table 8.2 The classes and interfaces created for the Countr app

Name	Description
`CounterViewModel`	The view model representing an individual counter and the state of the counter, such as its name and count, and encapsulating behavior for incrementing and deleting a counter, as well as saving a counter from a detail view and navigating back to the list view when the user saves the new counter or cancels the creation.
`CountersViewModel`	The view model representing the master list of counters, represented as an observable collection of `CounterViewModel` instances. This observable collection will tell the view to update whenever the list of counters changes. This view model also encapsulates the behavior for navigating to a detail view to add a new counter, as well as detecting changes in the list of counters stored in the repository via a message.
`CountersChangedMessage`	A message that's published over the MvvmCross Messenger whenever the list of messages stored in the repository changes, such as when adding or deleting a counter.
`CounterViewModelTests`	Unit tests for `CounterViewModel`.
`CountersViewModelTests`	Unit tests for `CountersViewModel`.

You now have complete view models for both of the apps, covering the state and behavior needed to implement all the user flows. You've also created unit tests to validate your code.

The unit tests you've built here are not only great validators for your code, they allow you to simulate the UI and verify that your app will work before you've even finished the app. When a property is changed, the binding layer will update the view, so testing that a property-changed event is fired allows you to test that the UI is updated. By testing commands, you can verify what will happen when users tap buttons in the UI. By testing navigation, you can verify that your app will correctly flow from one view to another. You can write unit tests that simulate everything a user can do with your app, and most importantly you can write these tests just once. Xamarin is all about building cross-platform mobile apps with large amounts of code sharing, and that's what you're seeing with these view models—you can write and unit-test the UI logic once, yet still use it to build apps that target both iOS and Android.

In the next chapters we'll start building the platform-specific view layers, starting with Android.

Summary

In this chapter you learned

- State and behavior can be easily unit-tested.
- When the types used by the view are different from the model, you need to provide conversion either inside a property or in a value converter.
- The master/detail pattern is a nice way to show lists of data, with a separate screen that shows more details of an item in the list.
- MvvmCross has lifecycle methods to let you know when your view model is being shown, and it has a way to pass data to a view model before it's shown.
- Messaging is a great way to let parts of your app communicate with each other in a loosely coupled way.
- MvvmCross has a navigation service to handle view-model-first navigation.

You also learned how to

- Add state to a view model
- Convert property values both in place and using value converters
- Unit-test properties and property-changed notifications
- Implement behavior in commands
- Create master and detail view models
- Use messaging to communicate between classes in your apps in a loosely coupled way
- Navigate between view models, passing data using the MvvmCross navigation service
- Unit-test navigation

9 Building simple Android views

This chapter covers

- Android resources
- Creating layout resources in the Designer and by editing the source
- Adding images to support multiple screen densities
- Creating views using activities
- The activity lifecycle

In the previous two chapters we built the model and view-model layers for our two apps. Now it's time to turn our attention to the view layer. This layer uses platform-specific code, so we're going to look at it platform by platform—in this chapter and the next, we'll look at Android (figure 9.1), followed by iOS in chapters 11 and 12.

We'll start here by looking at how to build an Android UI. Then we'll build the UI for SquareRt. In the next chapter we'll look at Countr, and you'll see a slightly more advanced UI that uses recycler views to show lists of data, menus, and navigation.

When building any UI-based app on any platform, you need to understand the concepts behind the app structure. Each platform has a different structure. On Android you structure your apps using *activities*—single screens in your app that each represent a single focused thing that a user would want to do. When building Android apps using MVVM, an activity is the same as a view.

As well as containing code, Android apps also contain resources. These are non-code items, including images and XML files that define things such as constants, UI styling, and the layout of the UIs that can be used by activities to create the screens that users see.

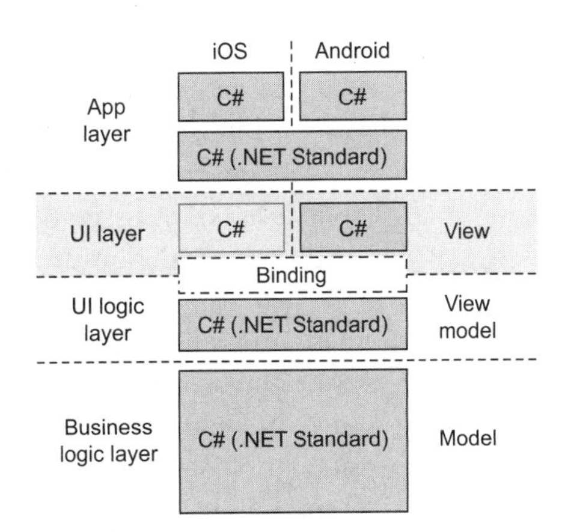

Figure 9.1 The view layer in an MVVM app is written in platform-specific code.

9.1 Building Android UIs

Let's start by thinking about the SquareRt app—an app with a single view. Figure 9.2 shows the UI that we'll build.

When building a view, there are two parts to it: the activity that encapsulates the full screen view, and the actual UI. You can define UIs in code, but that's not the normal way to do it. Instead, the usual and easiest way is by using a layout file—an XML file that defines which controls should be shown on the UI and how they're laid out. These are "inflated" by activities at runtime to create the UI that you see on screen (note that this happens at runtime, not compile time, so if your XML is wrong you may not know it until your app is running and crashes). If you've done any HTML or Windows desktop development using XAML, these layout files should be similar to what you've seen before.

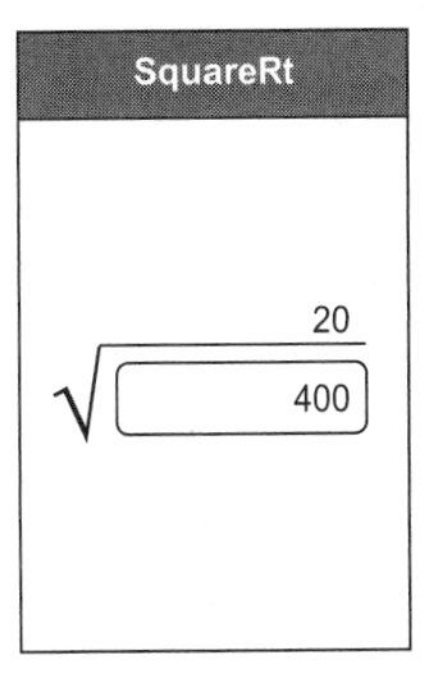

Figure 9.2 The UI for the SquareRt app

9.1.1 Material design

Before we design a UI on Android, it's worth looking into Google's design guidelines—*material design* (https://material.io). These guidelines aren't targeted specifically at mobile apps, but at apps for all screen sizes, be they websites, desktop apps, or mobile apps, both on smaller screens like phones and larger devices like tablets, laptops, desktops, or even TVs. You've probably already seen Google's material design in action—Google uses it for all their mobile apps, like Google Maps or Gmail.

Material design has three key concepts:

- *Material is the metaphor*—When you build your app, you should think about the real-world materials that would be used if your app were a physical thing, and try to emulate that in the way users navigate and the way the app is drawn. The main guideline here is to think in terms of pen and paper, as this is a good metaphor for most apps.

For example, in a mail app, your inbox is like a list on a piece of paper, and when you select an email, another piece of paper would move on top of it containing the mail message (as shown in figure 9.3). By thinking in this way, you can imagine a sense of depth: the mail is on top of the list, so if it's showing full screen, it should appear by sliding over the top; if it's in a pop up, that pop up should have an elevation above the list, shown on the flat screen of your device using a shadow. When you close it, you're pushing the paper away, off the current stack.

Figure 9.3 Use material such as a stack of paper as a metaphor for your design.

- *Bold, graphic, intentional*—Your UI should be crisp and clean, following the principals of print-based design. It should use a well-defined color palette of complementing and contrasting colors, have plenty of white space, and try to provide emphasis for user actions, to help make it obvious to users how they should interact with the app. The meaning of any icons should be clear to the user and should be consistent with other apps or real-world actions.

  A good example is the floating action button, a popular pattern when building Android apps. This is a crisp, round button with a contrasting color and clear icon to make it stand out and indicate its behavior. It's used to provide a quick link to the most popular action a user would want to take during a particular activity. Thinking again about our mail app, a floating Reply button when reading an email provides a quick way for the user to interact with the message they're reading, as shown in figure 9.4.

  Figure 9.4 A distinct floating action button is a clear way to indicate a popular user action.

- *Motion provides meaning*—Your app should use the motion of on-screen components to convey that a user-initiated action is happening, and to convey feedback to the user after the action is complete.

  For example, when you tap an item in the mail app's inbox, the message you've selected could be opened by sliding it in on top of the inbox. This page moving across the screen reflects how you might pull a document from your desk onto the stack of papers you're currently reading. It's a motion that not only indicates to the user that something has happened, but it tries to mimic the real-world behavior of the material—in this case, paper. When the user taps the floating Reply button, it could reduce its elevation as it's being tapped, and then spring back up again, mimicking the real-world behavior of a button (figure 9.5). It could even animate from there by changing from a floating circle to a square that expands to become the reply activity, again using motion to show the user that something has happened, representing the flow from tapping the Reply button to writing a reply.

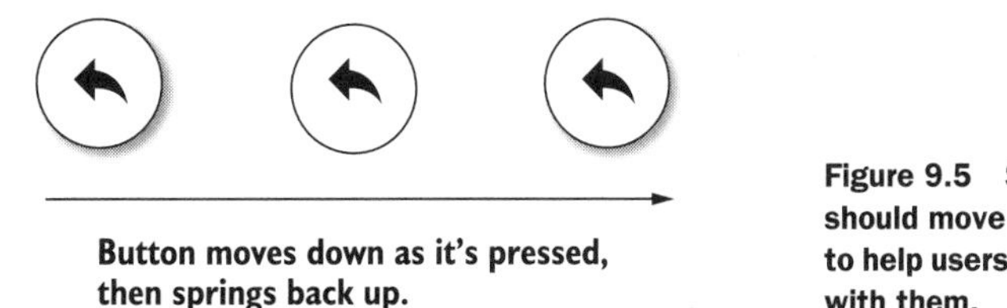

Button moves down as it's pressed, then springs back up.

Figure 9.5 Screen objects should move like real objects to help users feel comfortable with them.

It's highly recommended that you follow Google's material design standards when building an Android app. It makes your app look consistent with other Android apps, and done well it can add an amazing sense of polish to your finished app—thousands of hours of UX research has gone into creating material design. The Android controls are already styled based on this standard, so you can adopt it easily.

9.1.2 *Layout files*

Let's start by defining the UI in a layout file. Open the SquareRt solution from the previous chapter, expand the SquareRt.Droid project, and set it as the startup project. Then delete the dummy first view that was created automatically when you created the new solution by deleting the Views\FirstView.cs, Views\BaseView.cs, and Resources\layout\FirstView.axml files. You won't need them.

To create the layout for your UI, head to the Resources\layout folder and add a new Android layout file called squarert_view.axml—you'll find these under "Android" in the Add New File dialog box.

> **USE LOWERCASE NAMES FOR XML FILES IN ANDROID** The name may seem odd—squarert_view, all in lowercase—but Android prefers lowercase for the filenames of XML files. In some cases, if you refer to one XML resource from another, the reference will fail if the name isn't all in lowercase.

When this file opens up, it will be in a layout editor with two tabs—Designer and Source tabs. The Designer gives you a design surface where you can add layouts and controls from a toolbox and manipulate their properties. The Source code tab shows the raw XML that makes up this layout.

The Designer can be a bit troublesome, giving errors when you try to display the layout and taking a long time to render everything. It depends on the same capabilities as the Google emulators installed with Xamarin—if your emulator works, the Designer should work. Your app will need to build in order for the layouts to render, so if you're having problems with the Designer, make sure you rebuild everything.

Layout files are a type of what Android refers to as *resources*—files that aren't code but are a part of your app.

9.1.3 Resources

Android apps are a mixture of two parts: code and resources. Resources are everything in your app that's not code, including images and XML files for defining layouts, strings, colors, and constants. Resources in Xamarin apps are identical to resources in native Java Android apps—you define them the same way, and you can even reuse the content. For example, if you wanted to port a Java Android app to a Xamarin app, you'd simply copy the entire resource directory over and use the resources as is. The only thing you'd need to change is the file extensions for any layout files. Although these are XML files, in Xamarin apps the file extension .axml is used—this is so that the IDE can distinguish between layout files and normal XML files, and load them in a visual designer instead of a raw XML editor.

9.1.4 Resource locations

All resources live in particular subfolders of the Resources folder, with the subfolder names defining the types of resources. For example, all layout files must live in the Resources\layout folder (or variants thereof); images live in Resources\drawable. Android has a fixed set of resource folders, some of which are listed in table 9.1. You can find the full list in the "App Resources" API guide: http://mng.bz/N41B.

Table 9.1 Available resource folders on Android

Folder	Description
drawable	Images such as .png files or vector images
mipmap	Images used for the launcher icon only (the icon that's shown on the Android home screen). This is optional—you can always use the drawable folder for launcher images. The reason for having a separate folder from drawable is that your launch screen can use higher density images than your device.
layout	UI layouts
menu	XML files that define menus and toolbars
values	XML files containing constant values, including colors, strings, and styles. These files are parsed, and the values defined in them can be retrieved easily in code.

Resources are identified by *resource references*, which are constant values that are available in both C# code and inside XML. In C#, these resource references get converted to constant values in an autogenerated file called Resource.designer.cs, which lives in the root of the Resources folder. (You should never need to touch this file as it's autogenerated from the resources and is rewritten every time resources are changed.) These C# constants are put into a hierarchy of `Resource.<type>.<id>`, whereas in XML files these are named in the format `@<type>\<id>`. For example, if you have an image file in the drawable folder called Line.png, the resource reference for this in C# is `Resource.Drawable.Line`, and in XML it's `@drawable\Line`.

Some resource files are self-contained resources in that the one file contains an entire resource. These include images and layout files—each image is a single image, and each layout file is a single layout. The resource reference for these kinds of files is `@<type>\<filename without extension>` or `Resource.<type>.<filename without extension>` in C# code (so `@drawable\Line` or `Resource.Drawable.Line`).

Other resource files contain multiple resources defined in XML, and the identifiers for these are set based on the type of the resource and the value of a `name` attribute on the resource. For example, if you open the Resources\values\strings.xml file, it will contain the following:

```
<string name="ApplicationName">SquareRt</string>
```

This defines a string resource called `ApplicationName` with the value of `SquareRt`, and the reference for this will be `@string\ApplicationName` or `Resource.String.ApplicationName`.

9.1.5 Editing layout files

You can edit layouts in two ways: using the Designer built into Visual Studio, or by editing the source XML directly.

The *Designer* is a drag-and-drop tool with a toolbox containing all the different controls you can add, as well as a Properties window (referred to as the Properties pad in Visual Studio for Mac) for configuring the views once they're on the layout (figure 9.6). The Designer is based on the layout on a real device, and you can choose the device type you want to use so you can see how your layout looks on various screen sizes and orientations. You can even choose the API level to see how your app would look on older or newer OS versions. The Designer is powerful, making it very easy to build your layouts and see exactly what your app will look like.

If you prefer to edit the source XML by hand, you can use the tabs at the bottom of the Designer to switch to the Source view and code up or tweak your layout manually.

If you look at the app in the Designer, it will seem pretty empty. If you flip to the Source tab, you'll see an XML file with a single element in it, as shown in figure 9.1.

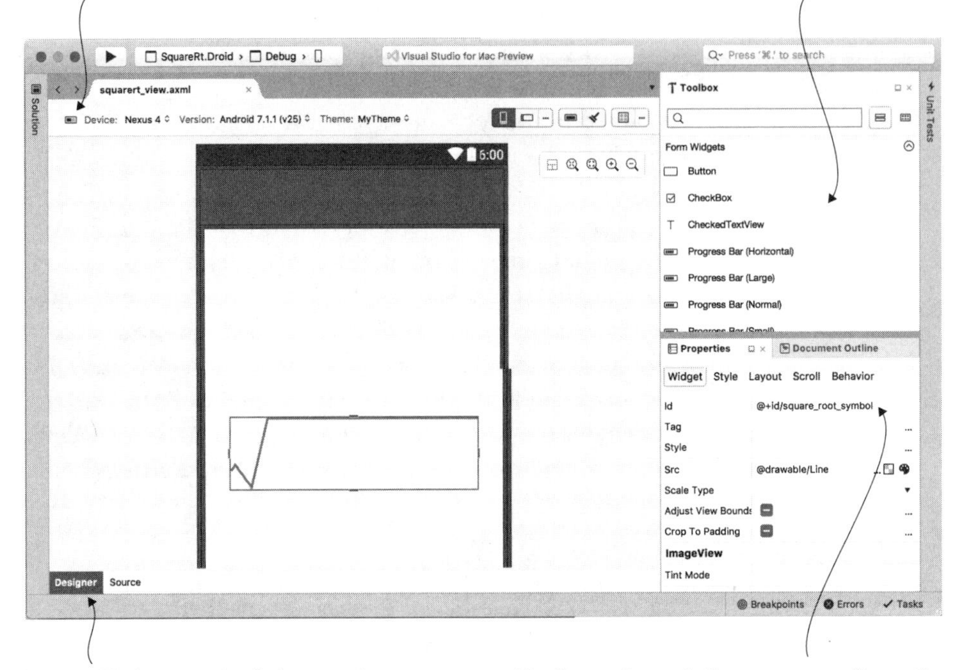

You can choose the device type, OS version, and orientation used to display the layout you're designing.
The toolbox contains all the views and view groups that you can add to your layout.
You can flip between the designer and a source view for editing the raw XML.
The Properties pad allows you to configure the properties on the selected view in the layout.

Figure 9.6 The Designer can be used to visually position and configure the views and view groups in your layout.

Listing 9.1 The contents of a new, blank layout file

```
<?xml version="1.0" encoding="utf-8"?>
<LinearLayout xmlns:android="http://schemas.android.com/apk/res/android"
    android:orientation="vertical"
    android:layout_width="match_parent"
    android:layout_height="match_parent" />
```

This layout file has a single `LinearLayout` element in it with a number of properties from the `android` XML namespace set. This is one of the standard Android UI elements. There are two types of these UI elements:

- *Views* (not to be confused with MVVM views) are controls—UI components that users can interact with, such as buttons and text boxes. These are often referred to as "widgets" in the Android documentation and mostly live in the `Android.Widget` namespace.

- *View groups* are layout controls that contain other views or view groups. The view group is referred to as a *parent*, and the controls inside it are its *children*. Each view group is responsible for laying out its children on screen. How the child controls are laid out is determined by the type of view group used and the layout properties set on the children.

By having view groups contain other view groups and views, you can build up a hierarchy of elements that define your UI (figure 9.7). This hierarchy can be as simple or as complicated as needed, but simple is always better, especially in terms of performance. Each layout file defines one and only one top-level UI element, and this is usually a view group.

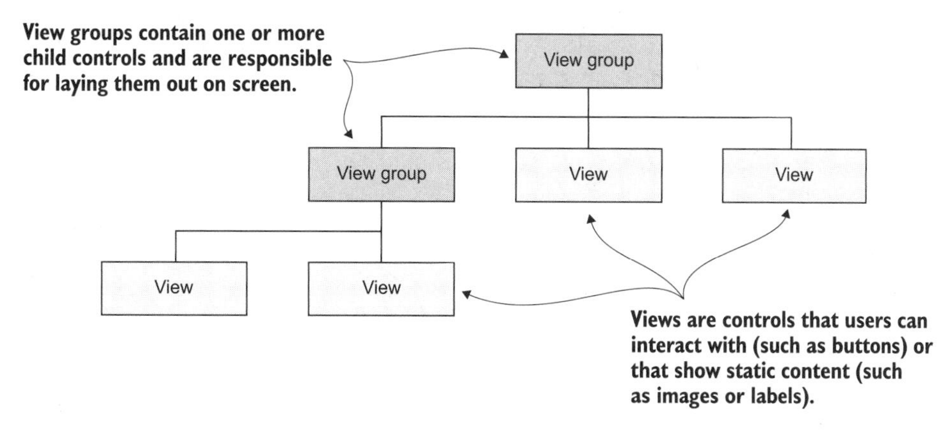

Figure 9.7 Android UIs are a hierarchy of view groups and views.

VIEW GROUPS

Let's take a look at a few of the most used view groups: linear layout, relative layout, and frame layout.

Linear layout

`Android.Widget.LinearLayout` is a view group that lays out its children one after the other in a single direction, either horizontally or vertically (figure 9.8). All children are laid out in the order in which they're added to the layout.

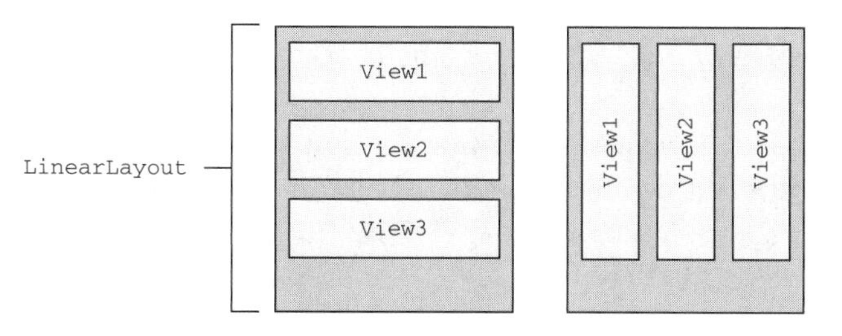

Figure 9.8 Linear layouts lay out their child views in a line, either vertically (left) or horizontally (right).

Relative layout

`Android.Widget.RelativeLayout` is a view group that lays out its children relative to other views—either relative to the view group itself, or to other children. You set properties on each child to specify the layout rules (such as above view *x*, to the right of view *y*, or in the center of the parent), and the relative layout will position everything for you.

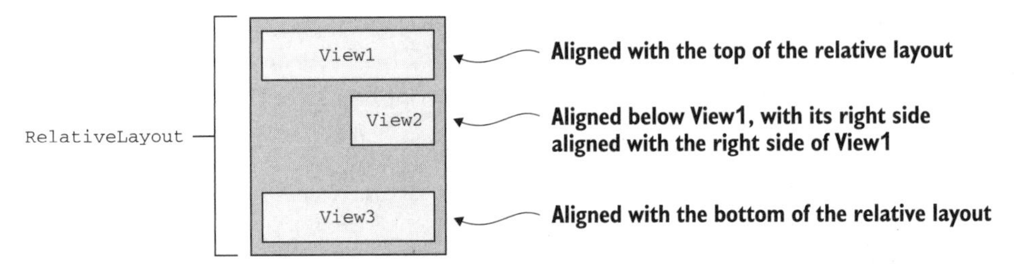

Figure 9.9 Relative layouts lay out their child views based on layout rules.

Table 9.2 shows some of the many properties you can set.

Table 9.2 Some properties for relative layouts

Property	Type	Description
`android:layout_centerInParent`	`bool`	If true, this centers this child horizontally and vertically within its parent.
`android:layout_below`	Resource reference	Positions this child directly below the element with its ID set to the given resource reference.
`android:layout_alignLeft`	Resource reference	Aligns the left side of this child with the left side of the element, with its ID set to the given resource reference.

You can combine properties—such as combining `layout_below` and `layout_alignRight` to put one item directly below another with the right edges of both aligned. You can find a full list of properties in the Android documentation at http://mng.bz/o1VT.

Frame layout

`Android.Widget.FrameLayout` is a view group that's a simple frame for holding one or more children. You add children, and they're laid out on top of each other in the order they're added. You can then position the children inside the frame relative to the frame only, not relative to other controls.

VIEWS

Views are controls that don't contain any children, but provide either controls that users can interact with, or static controls that show something on the UI (figure 9.10).

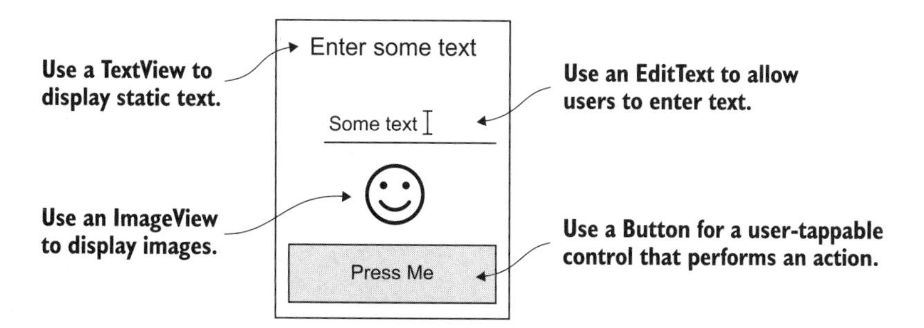

Enter some text
Some text
Press Me
Use a TextView to display static text.
Use an EditText to allow users to enter text.
Use an ImageView to display images.
Use a Button for a user-tappable control that performs an action.

Figure 9.10 Use different views to provide different controls for users to interact with.

- `TextView`—`Android.Widget.TextView` is a static label that shows text that can't be edited.
- `EditText`—`Android.Widget.EditText` is a text-entry control. It's derived from `TextView` but has capabilities to edit text. When a user taps this control, the keyboard pops up, allowing text to be entered. This control can also be configured to limit the values that can be entered, such as just allowing numbers.
- `Button`—`Android.Widget.Button` is a push button that can be tapped by the user to perform an action.
- `ImageView`—`Android.Widget.ImageView` is used to show an image and can scale the image to fit if necessary.

NEWER VIEWS AND VIEW GROUPS USING APPCOMPAT

As you saw back in chapter 6, Android is a horribly fragmented ecosystem. Unlike iOS, where most users are on the latest OS version, most Android users are on older versions—either because they haven't upgraded, or more likely because they can't. Due to the way Google has allowed manufacturers and carriers to modify the version of Android they ship, end users have to rely on both manufacturers and carriers to make Android updates available.

This can be a very slow process. For example, at the time of writing, in New Zealand, Android Nougat has been out for five months, and you can't buy a phone or tablet off the shelf that runs it, except for imported devices. Samsung, which supplies a large percentage of all Android devices, are only just rolling out support for Nougat five months after release, and only for their latest devices. This fragmented ecosystem means developers are unable to implement the latest and greatest Android features because most of their customers won't be able to take advantage of them.

Google is well aware of this problem and has taken steps to work around it. They've done two things: first, they've extracted OS services like location, maps, and game services and put them into separate apps that are installed and updated through the Play store, called Google Play Services. Second, they've back-ported SDKs to earlier versions using a set of support libraries that you can ship with your app, often referred to as AppCompat. These support libraries allow you to use features that were originally written for later OS versions on earlier versions. For example, with Lollipop, Android introduced a new design paradigm called *material design* and shipped updated controls that reflected the new design. To bring this to older OS versions, they released a similar SDK as part of the support libraries, allowing you to create apps that use material design and look the same on OS versions going back to Jelly Bean.

APPCOMPAT TERMINOLOGY The AppCompat library is one of a selection of support libraries available, but the name *AppCompat* is often used to refer to all the support libraries.

These support libraries come from a set of Google Java libraries, and Xamarin has wrapped these as NuGet packages that you can easily add to any Xamarin.Android app. The MvvmCross apps that you've already created reference these NuGet packages, so there's nothing that you need to do to use them, but if you want to use them in other projects, you'll just need to add a couple of packages. (MvvmCross also provides helpers that can take advantage of these packages, or extend them to make them easier to use, as you'll see later in this chapter.) The main package you need to add is Xamarin.Android.Support.v7.AppCompat, as this provides material design to pre-Lollipop devices.

AppCompat provides different classes that implement the standard functionality for Android, such as a different activity base class (one that provides nice colorful toolbars) and different controls. To allow you to support the widest range of OS versions, and to ensure your users get as similar an experience as possible on all devices, it's best to always use AppCompat. You can read more about the support libraries in the Android developer documentation at http://mng.bz/62Gf.

9.1.6 Layout inflation

Layouts contain an XML description of the views and view groups that you want in your UI. To create the UI from a layout file, something needs to read this XML and construct the classes for all the items in it, set the properties, and build the hierarchy of items by setting the children of the view groups. This process is called *inflation*, and it uses an Android class called `LayoutInflater`, which is available as a property on Android activities or can be used behind the scenes by some helper methods on the activity. The term *inflation* is also used when loading other XML resources, such as menus.

9.2 Creating the layout file for the SquareRt UI

To build up the UI for SquareRt, we'll need to put a number of views on the screen. We'll need a toolbar across the top showing the app's name, an `ImageView` showing the square root symbol (√), an `EditText` below the image to allow the user to enter a number, and a `TextView` on top of the image to show the result. We'll also need some view groups to lay these controls out. Figure 9.11 shows the layout of these controls.

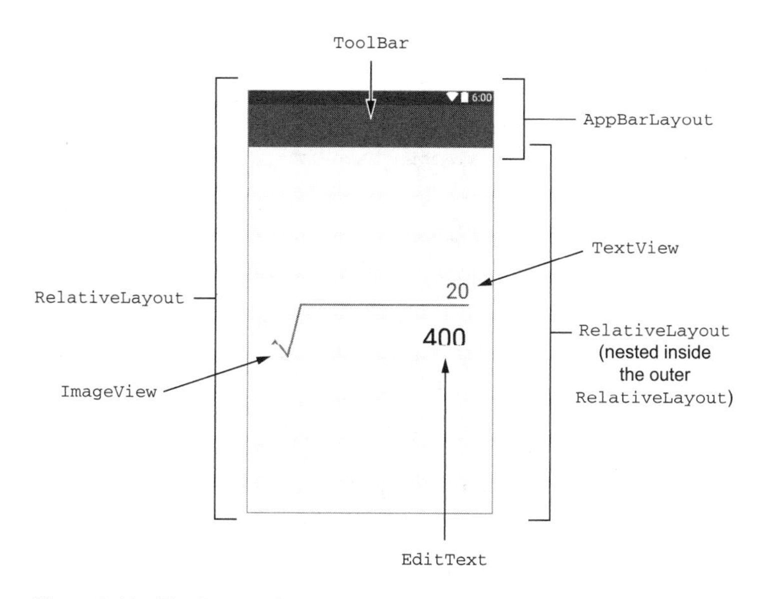

Figure 9.11 The layout of the views and view groups in the SquareRt UI

We're going to build the UI using a mix of both the Designer and the Source editor—both are powerful, so it's good to know how to use both techniques.

9.2.1 Adding a toolbar

The first thing to put on this UI is a toolbar. Modern Android apps follow material design, and part of this is a nice colorful toolbar on the top of every screen showing details about the current task that the user is performing (such as a name), and providing menus and toolbar buttons where necessary. These toolbars are available in the Android SDK on Lollipop and later, and in the support libraries for earlier OS versions. Because we want to support as many versions as possible, we're going to use the version of the toolbar from the support libraries.

Adding the toolbar to the layout

We'll start by adding the toolbar in code (we'll flip over to the Designer later on). The code for this is pretty boilerplate, so switch to the Source view, delete the `LinearLayout`, and add the code in the following listing.

Listing 9.2 Adding a toolbar to the layout

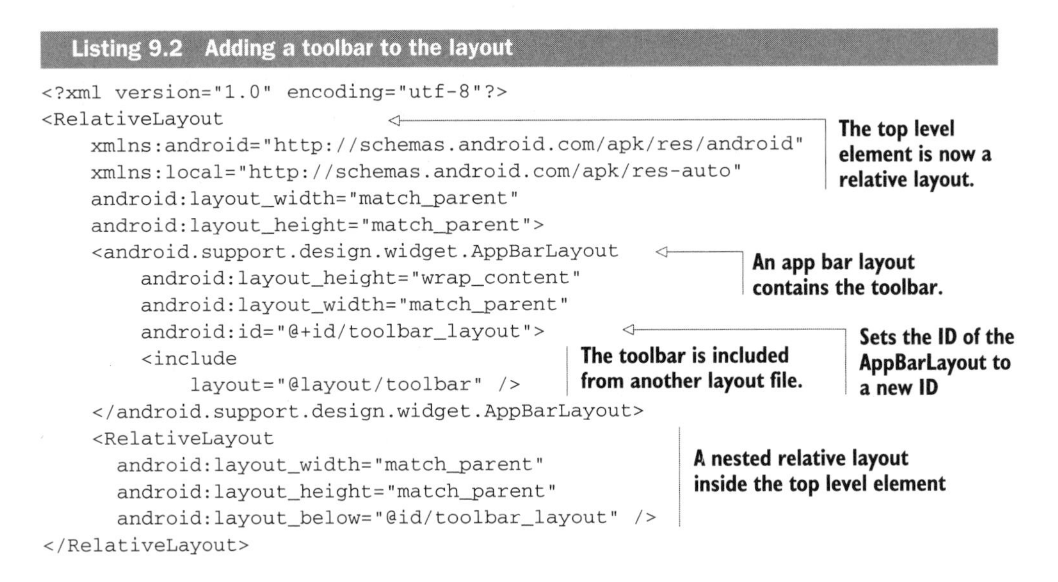

```
<?xml version="1.0" encoding="utf-8"?>
<RelativeLayout
    xmlns:android="http://schemas.android.com/apk/res/android"
    xmlns:local="http://schemas.android.com/apk/res-auto"
    android:layout_width="match_parent"
    android:layout_height="match_parent">
    <android.support.design.widget.AppBarLayout
        android:layout_height="wrap_content"
        android:layout_width="match_parent"
        android:id="@+id/toolbar_layout">
        <include
            layout="@layout/toolbar" />
    </android.support.design.widget.AppBarLayout>
    <RelativeLayout
      android:layout_width="match_parent"
      android:layout_height="match_parent"
      android:layout_below="@id/toolbar_layout" />
</RelativeLayout>
```


In this code you're using a relative layout as the top-level element so that you can lay out everything you need on screen in the way you want. The elements don't need namespaces, but every attribute that's set on each element needs to be a fully qualified name with the namespace as well as the attribute. Two namespaces are defined here: `android`, which references the Android SDK, and `local`, which references the current app (providing access to everything declared in the app and NuGet packages it uses, such as the Android support and MvvmCross libraries).

SETTING THE SIZES

There are two very important attributes on every element: `android:layout_width` and `android:layout_height`. These two attributes come from the base `Android.Views.View` class, which is the base class for all UI components (both views and view groups). They define the size of each view, and they *must* be set for every single element in your layout file. If any items don't have these set, you'll get an exception at runtime.

You can set these to one of three possible values:

- `match_parent`—Make the view as large as possible to fill the available space in the parent. This value was `fill_parent` prior to API 8, and you may see this used in examples online—both will work and will do the same thing.
- `wrap_content`—Make the view as small as possible so it just takes up the space needed by its children.
- A numeric value—Make the view a fixed size.

For the top-level element in a layout file that's used for a full-screen UI, it's pretty standard to use `match_parent` for both width and height to ensure your UI fills the entire screen. For children of the top-level element, you can choose values that make sense for your layout.

If you want to use fixed sizes, you can express the size using different units. Android devices come in all shapes and sizes, with different screen resolutions and densities. These different densities mean you can have two devices the same size, but one can have twice as many pixels each way, with each pixel a quarter of the size. When viewing the same app on these two devices, you'd want them to look the same, with everything on screen being the same physical size—the device with the higher density would just look crisper and sharper. But if you have a view set to 30 pixels high by 30 wide, it would be one quarter of the physical size on the higher density screen.

To get around this problem, Android uses the concept of density-independent pixels called `dp`—virtual pixels that should be the same physical size regardless of screen density (figure 9.12). You can define sizes in your layout files using a numerical size followed by `dp`—such as `30dp` or `100dp`. These map one-to-one with individual pixels on a 160 DPI (dots per inch) screen, so a view with a width of `160dp` would be 160 pixels wide (or one inch). On devices of different densities, the scaling changes, so on a 320 DPI device, each `dp` would be the equivalent of 2 pixels, with the `160dp`-wide view being 320 pixels wide (again, one inch). When you're defining sizing in Android layouts, you should always use `dp` instead of actual pixels.

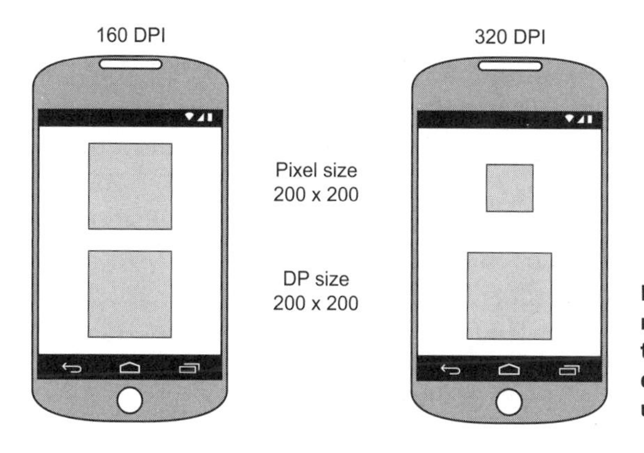

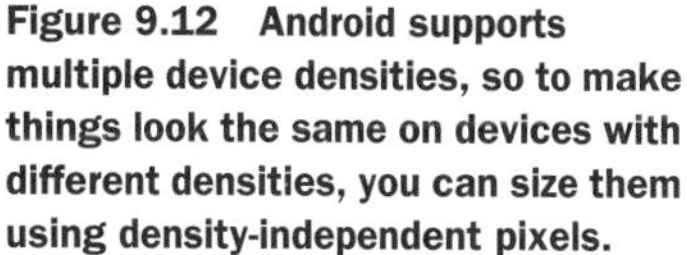
Figure 9.12 Android supports multiple device densities, so to make things look the same on devices with different densities, you can size them using density-independent pixels.

THE ELEMENTS IN THE LAYOUT

This layout file has a `RelativeLayout` as the top-level element, and it currently has two children—an `android.support.design.widget.AppBarLayout` and another relative layout.

The app bar layout is designed to hold toolbars, tab bars, and search controls, and in this case we'll be using it to hold a toolbar (figure 9.13). The app bar layout has the attributes for height and width, with the width set to fill the screen and height set to `wrap_content` to ensure this element is only as tall as need be.

The other attribute that's set on this layout is `android:id`, and it's set to `@+id/toolbar_layout`. This is a special syntax—anything in these files that starts with `@` is a resource reference, and the `+` is indicates that this is a new ID that you're creating. Taken together, `@+id/toolbar_layout syntax` tells the Android code to create a

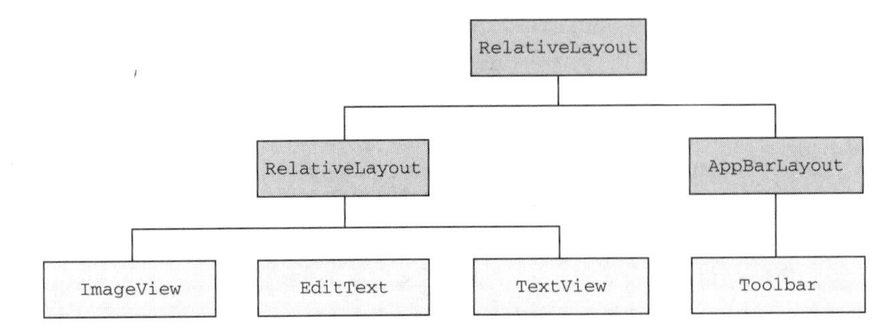

Figure 9.13 The hierarchy of views and view groups in our layout

new ID called `toolbar_layout` and assign that ID to this element. Once this ID is defined, you can use it anywhere in your C# code using `Resource.Id.toolbar_layout` or you can reference it from inside this or any other layout XML file using `@id/toolbar_layout`. The + is only for defining new IDs; you don't use it when referencing the ID or when defining other resource types.

The app bar layout's child—the toolbar—is an element called `include` with one attribute of `layout="@layout/toolbar"`. These `include` elements are a way of including one layout file in another, which is great if you want to share layout code. In the case of toolbars, their layout is usually the same because you'll usually want all toolbars to look and act the same way. In this case, the layout is including the Resources\layout\toolbar.axml file, which contains an AppCompat toolbar. This toolbar layout is pretty boilerplate, so we won't look at it here, but you can read all about toolbars in the Android developer reference documentation: http://mng.bz/0jY8.

The top-level element has a second child, another relative layout, and you can use it to lay out the rest of the UI. This element has an attribute set to position it in its parent—`android:layout_below="@id/toolbar_layout"`. This attribute tells the element to position itself below the element in the parent relative layout with the ID of `toolbar_layout` (the app bar layout). The height and width are set to `match_parent`, but this layout doesn't have a height that matches the parent; instead it has a height that fills up as much space as possible after the other layout rules are applied, so it matches the amount of space left inside the parent container while being below the toolbar layout. This is why `match_parent` is a poor name—the values don't match the parent but rather mean the view will expand to fill the available space after obeying the rest of the layout rules.

Once you have this basic layout in place, you can try flipping to the Designer and seeing what the layout looks like. You'll see a white rectangular screen with a blue toolbar at the top (figure 9.14). We'll now add the rest of the controls to the layout. Figure 9.13 shows the hierarchy we're aiming for.

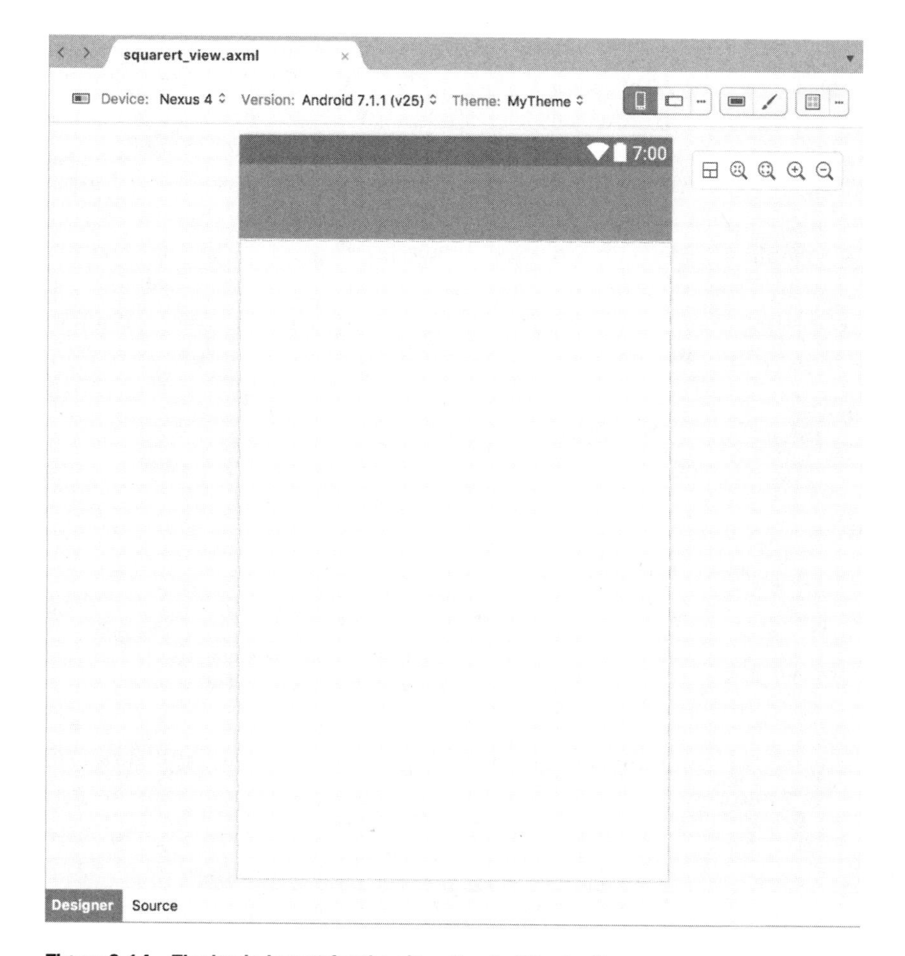

Figure 9.14 The basic layout for the view showing the toolbar

SOMETIMES THE DESIGNER WILL SHOW AN ERROR BUT STILL WORK Sometimes the Designer doesn't quite work properly—instead of seeing a white rectangle with a blue toolbar, you'll see a black rectangle with a black toolbar and a red error bar with a Show Error button that does nothing. This occurs because the Designer fails to use the Android support libraries correctly. If you see this, the Designer will probably still work but just look odd. You may also see a warning in the output along the lines of "The element RelativeLayout has invalid child element android.support.design.widget.AppBarLayout," which you can ignore. Usually a restart of Visual Studio will fix the issue.

9.2.2 Adding an image

You now have a basic layout with a toolbar—let's add the square root symbol (√), and this time we'll do it in the Designer. To add an image, first you need to supply an image file, though to be more correct, you need to supply five image files.

These files are with the code that accompanies this book, in the Images\SquareRt\Droid folder. If you open this folder, you'll see a number of folders with names that start with *drawable*, each containing an image file called Line.png of a particular size. Table 9.3 lists these folders and the resolutions of the images in them. Drag these images to the SquareRt.Droid project, into the matching Resource\drawable folder (so drag from drawable-mdpi to Resource\drawable-mdpi and so on).

Folder	Resolution
drawable	229x65
drawable-mdpi	305x86
drawable-hdpi	458x129
drawable-xhdpi	610x172
drawable-xxhdpi	915x258

Table 9.3 The different versions of the Line.png image added to our app

Why do we need multiple versions of the same image? They will support multiple screen sizes and resolutions—it's the same as using `dp` for sizes instead of pixels.

DRAWABLES

Drawables are a type of resource that's concerned with drawing things on the screen. The most popular type of drawable is a bitmap image (such as a .png file). Android allows you to define multiple versions of each resource, with each version targeting a particular screen size range, resolution, or orientation. Each version is then stored in a resource folder that includes the relevant device details in the name.

All resources are referred to in code by a unique identifier, which is assigned by the compiler to all resources with the same type and name. All the Line.png images you've added will be referred to using the same ID—`Resource.Drawable.Line` in C# code or `@drawable/Line` in XML files. Every time you need to use this image, use the identifier and the OS will pick the relevant version. The OS will check the screen density for the hardware it's running on and load the most appropriate image.

The different image sizes allow your app to look roughly the same on all devices and different densities. These densities are defined using DPI—the number of dots per inch. Table 9.4 shows these densities, along with the name Android uses for devices of that density, and the relative size of the images (when creating your own images, scale them to these relative sizes to size correctly).

Table 9.4 The approximate DPI values for the Android screen densities

Folder	Density	DPI	Relative size
drawable	Low	~120 dpi	0.75x
drawable-mdpi	Medium	~160 dpi	1x
drawable-hdpi	High	~240 dpi	1.5x
drawable-xhdpi	Extra-high	~320 dpi	2x
drawable-xxhdpi	Extra-extra-high	~480 dpi	3x

The OS will fall back to a lower density if the image isn't available, so if there isn't an image in the drawable-xxhdpi folder for an xxhdpi screen, it will use the one from drawable-xhdpi.

This pattern of *<folder name>-<screen resolution>* can be used in any of the resource folders, and you're not limited to screen densities. For example, layout files are used to define the UI, and you might want one UI for your app when running with the screen in portrait orientation, and a different one when running in landscape—you can define these in layout folders suffixed with *-port* or *-land*. You can also have different UIs for larger or smaller screens (for example, you might want your app to look different on a tablet than on a phone), and you can do this by specifying different resources for screens with different sizes.

You can read more about this, including the huge range of possible folders for different resource variations in the "Providing Alternative Resources" section of the Android documentation: http://mng.bz/d0M9.

ADDING AN IMAGEVIEW CONTROL

Now you have our image resource, so let's show it in the layout. From the Designer tab, locate ImageView in the toolbox (you can type the name in the toolbox search box to filter the list) and drag this onto the layout in the Designer below the toolbar.

On Visual Studio for Mac, you should be able to find the toolbox on the right side of the Designer. If you can't see it, you can show it by selecting View > Pads > Toolbox from the menu. On Windows, it's usually docked and hidden on the left. You can show by selecting View > Toolbox from the menu.

Once that's done, you need to set the image and position the view by setting its properties, which can be done using the Properties window. In Visual Studio for Mac, these properties are grouped into tabs and are named with easy-to-read English versions of the XML attribute names. On Windows, all the properties are in a long list and have the same names as the attributes in the XML.

Ensure the `ImageView` is selected in the Designer, and then find the `src` property in the Properties window (in Visual Studio for Mac you'll need to be on the Widget tab to see it, and it's called Src). It will have a default value set, and to the right of the default value will be an ellipsis icon (...). Click this icon to launch the resource

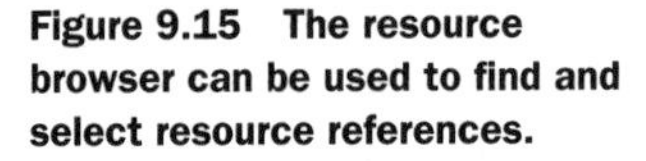

Figure 9.15 The resource browser can be used to find and select resource references.

browser, which will show a window with all the resource references available in your app (figure 9.15). Search for the `line` drawable resource, select it, and click OK. This will update the image in the Designer to show the square-root symbol's image.

Now that you have your image, you need to position it in the center of the space below the toolbar. The `ImageView` is sitting inside a relative layout, so all you have to do is set a property to position the `ImageView` inside it. Find the `layout_centerInParent` property (in Visual Studio for Mac, it'll be in the Layout tab and be called Center in Parent), and tick it. You don't need to manually set the `layout_width` and `layout_height` parameters yourself (in Visual Studio for Mac, these are called Width and Height and are in the Layout tab). When this control was dragged onto the toolbox, these were both automatically set to `wrap_content`, and this will size the view to match the size of the image.

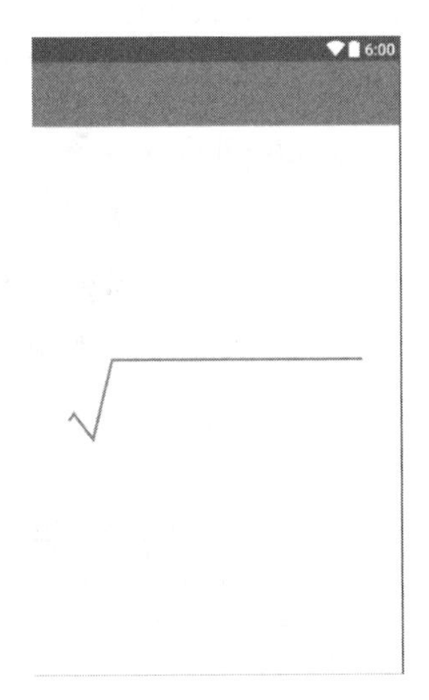

Figure 9.16 The app with the `ImageView` centered in the area below the toolbar

The `ImageView` will also have its `id` property set to a default value of `@+id/imageView1`. You'll be using this ID later to position other views, so change it to a more friendly name of `@+id/square_root_symbol` using the Properties window (in Visual Studio for Mac you'll find the ID property in the Widget tab). Figure 9.16 shows what the layout should now look like.

9.2.3 *Adding an EditText control*

Next up is adding a text-entry control so the user can enter a number to calculate the square root from. For this, we'll mainly use the Designer, but you'll have to switch to the Source to add the finishing touches.

ADDING THE EDITTEXT CONTROL TO THE LAYOUT FILE

The control you need to use here is an `EditText`, but you won't find it if you look in the toolbox. Instead, there's a whole section in the toolbox called Text Fields that contains different preconfigured text-entry controls based on the type of data you want your users to be able to enter. For example, you can drag a `Date` text field onto the layout and have the control configured so you can only enter valid dates, or you can drag a `Password` field on and have a control that masks the user input.

In our case, we're dealing with numbers, so you need to drag a `Number (Decimal)` text field from the toolbox over the image on the layout (which will be surrounded by a green line when your mouse is over it), and drop it on the green line on the top. The Designer is a bit flaky when dealing with relative layouts, so unless you drop it just right, it may not add the control at all. Figure 9.17 shows where to drag it to.

If you're having trouble, you can open the Document Outline pad (on Visual Studio for Mac it's below the toolbox by default, behind the Properties pad; on Windows

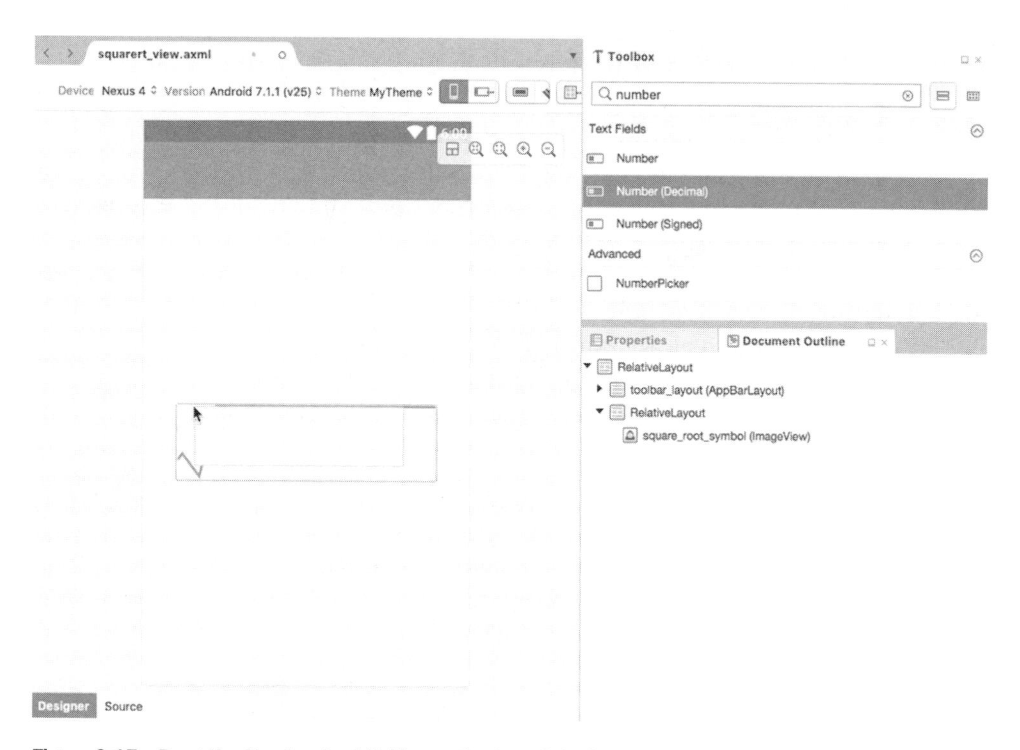

Figure 9.17 Drag the Number text field over the top of the image.

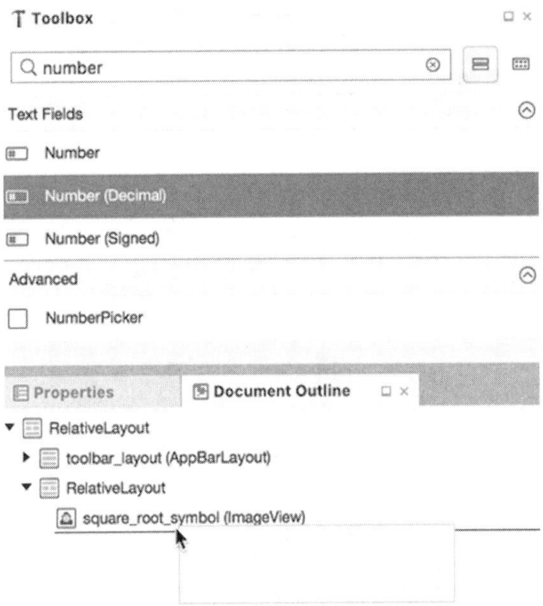

Figure 9.18 Drag the Number text field to the relative layout using the document outline.

you can show it using View > Other Windows > Document Outline). Expand everything and drag the text field into there, dropping it on the inner relative layout, as shown in figure 9.18.

Once your control is added, you'll see it with a blue border indicating that it's selected. Be careful not to click off it, as the empty white `EditText` control will disappear into the white background of the layout. If you do click elsewhere and unselect it, open up the document outline and click the control in there to select it again.

If you now look at the properties for this `EditText` control, you'll see that the `inputType` property (Input Type in Visual Studio for Mac in the Widget tab) is set to `numberDecimal`. This will limit the keys on the keyboard so that users can only enter numeric values and decimal points. You can also see this if you flip to the Source view, where the `android:inputType` attribute is set to the same value.

POSITIONING THE EDITTEXT CONTROL

Now you need to position this control. You want it tall enough to show the text inside it, and for it to be positioned over the top of the image, lining up with the bottom and right side, with the left side being slightly indented to fit in the correct place. You can configure all of this using the properties made available by the parent relative layout. Figure 9.19 shows what we want to achieve.

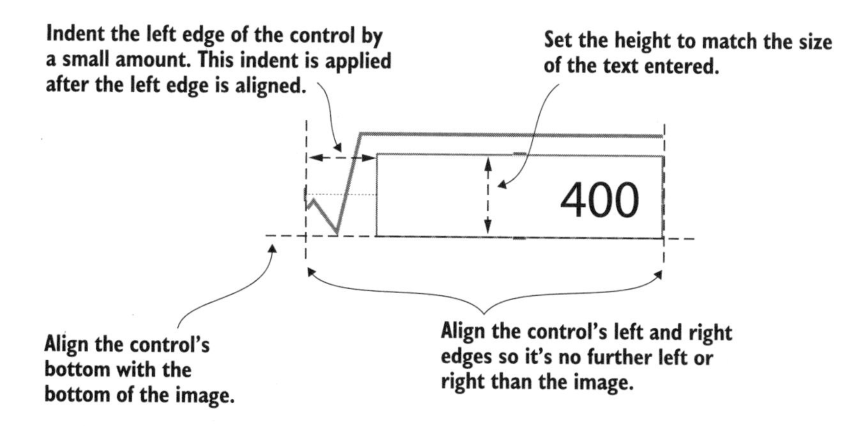

Indent the left edge of the control by a small amount. This indent is applied after the left edge is aligned.
Set the height to match the size of the text entered.
400
Align the control's bottom with the bottom of the image.
Align the control's left and right edges so it's no further left or right than the image.

Figure 9.19 The alignments you need to lay out the `EditText` control in the right position relative to the image

The properties you'll need to set are shown in table 9.5, with their names in Visual Studio on Mac and Windows listed. In Visual Studio for Mac, these are all in the Layout tab.

Table 9.5 The properties to set to position the `EditText` control inside the image

Property (Windows)	Property (Mac)	Value	Description
`layout_width`	Width	`match_parent`	Makes the control as wide as possible—not necessarily as wide as the parent, but as wide as possible based on the other layout constraints
`layout_height`	Height	`wrap_content`	Makes the control only as tall as it needs to be to show the text
`layout_alignBottom`	Align Bottom	`@id/square_root_symbol`	Aligns the bottom edge of this control with the bottom edge of the `ImageView`
`layout_alignRight`	Align Right	`@id/square_root_symbol`	Aligns the right edge of this control with the right edge of the `ImageView`
`layout_alignLeft`	Align Left	`@id/square_root_symbol`	Aligns the left edge of this control with the left edge of the `ImageView`
`layout_marginLeft`	Margin Left	`60dp`	Adds 60dp of space to the left edge

MARGINS AND PADDING When laying out controls, you can set the margin or padding to add spacing between controls. *Margins* are space added outside a control; for example, a left margin of `60dp` means the control is sized and laid out to ensure that there's always a gap of `60dp` on the left of the given control. *Padding* is inside the control and is used for view groups or similar containers. It means that all the children of the control should be sized and laid out to ensure there's the given padding is always included between the outer edges of the child controls and the edges of the parent.

Some of these properties may seem to conflict with each other, but the layout engine (the code built into Android that looks at your views, and sizes and positions them on screen correctly) applies these in a priority order that makes your layout work. For example, when aligning the left edge of the `EditText` control with the left edge of the `ImageView`, the layout engine knows that you want a `60dp` margin, so it positions the left edge of the control `60dp` to the right of the left edge of the `ImageView`.

You now have your `EditText` control in the right place, so you can now configure the text properties to make the text in the control look nice. Ideally you'll want the text aligned to the right side, as this is the way numbers are normally aligned, and the font should be large enough to be easily read.

Aligning the text is easy, using the Gravity property (in Visual Studio for Mac, this is in the Widget tab). The Gravity property is used in a number of views to position the contents of that view, and for text controls like `EditText` and `TextView` it positions the text. By default, text is positioned on the left and centered vertically, but you can change this using the various Gravity options. These options are a flags enum, so you can do a binary `OR` on them to use multiple values at the same time, using the | operator. For example, if you wanted to position the text on the bottom right, you could set it to `bottom|right`. In this example, we'll set the gravity to `right`.

GRAVITY ALSO HAS START AND END `Left` and `right` will align the content of a view to the left or the right, which is fine for languages that are read from left to right, but for right-to-left languages such as Arabic or Hebrew this may put things in the wrong place. Instead it's better when building apps that will be localized to support multiple languages to use `start` and `end`. In left-to-right languages such as English, `start` is aligned left and `end` is aligned right; in right-to-left languages, `start` is aligned right and `end` is aligned left.

The default text size for an `EditText` control is probably a bit small for what we need, so you can make it larger. A size of about `40dp` will give a nice text size, using the density-independent pixels you saw earlier in the chapter. But although this will work, and do a fine job, we can do better.

On Android devices there are options to increase or decrease font sizes to suit the user's accessibility needs—for example, making the default fonts larger for users with visual impairments. If you set the font size using `dp` units, it won't change based on the user's settings. If you want it to change, you can use `sp` (scalable pixels) instead of `dp`. If the font size of the device is set to normal, the size in `sp` maps one-to-one with the `dp` value (so `40sp` is the same size as `40dp`), but if the device's font size is changed, the `sp` size will be larger or smaller. Ideally you should always use `sp` for font sizes so that they're always sized according to the user's preference. Let's set the `EditText` control to have a `textSize` property of `40sp` (in Visual Studio for Mac, this property is in the Style tab and is called "Text Size").

BINDING

You have your `EditText` control styled now, so the last thing to do is bind it to the view model. For this, flip to the Source view, as you'll need to use a custom property provided by MvvmCross. Add the following line of code to the source.

Listing 9.3 Adding binding code to view to bind `Number` property on view model

```
...
<EditText
   ...
   local:MvxBind="Text Number, Converter=DoubleToString"/>
...
```

Bind the Text property to the Number property on the view model

This is a simple line of code, but it's very important. This is our first binding, and it binds the `Text` property of the `EditText` to the `Number` property of the view model, using a converter. Let's break this line down:

- `local:MvxBind`—The `MvxBind` attribute is defined inside the MvvmCross libraries and is used to create a binding on the view. When the layout is inflated in an activity (which we'll wire up later in this chapter) a binding will be created.
- `Text Number`—This tells the binding to bind the `Text` property on the `EditText` to the `Number` property on the view model.
- `Converter=DoubleToString`—This tells the binding to use a converter. MvvmCross does a lot based on names (such as determining which view is used for which view model based on the class names), so the binding layer is smart enough to look in your code for a converter called `DoubleToStringValueConverter`.

You can use this syntax any time you want to bind anything using MvvmCross inside a layout XML file: to bind properties, or to bind events to commands (something we'll do when we look at Countr). You can even bind multiple things in the same statement by separating them with a semicolon followed by a space. For example, if you wanted to bind the text on a button to a property called `Title`, and the click handler to a command called `GoCommand`, you could write the following line: `local:MvxBind="Text Title; Click GoCommand"`.

This is all you have to do to wire up the view model to this UI control, and this is what makes the MVVM pattern so powerful. One line of platform-specific code interacts with many lines of cross-platform code.

9.2.4 Adding a result TextView control

The final control you need to add is the result. This is a `TextView`, a control that shows static text, so find Text View in the toolbox and drag it to the UI, dropping it over the line at the top of the `ImageView`. Set the properties to position and style this control as shown in table 9.6. There's nothing new here; these are similar properties to those for the `EditText` control.

Table 9.6 The properties to set on the `TextView`

Property (Windows)	Property (Mac)	Value	Description
`textSize`	Text Size	`32sp`	Sets the font size for the text in scalable pixels
`gravity`	Gravity	`right`	Aligns the text of this text view to the right
`layout_width`	Width	`match_parent`	Makes the control as wide as possible—not necessarily as wide as the parent, but as wide as possible based on the other layout constraints
`layout_height`	Height	`wrap_content`	Makes the control only as tall as it needs to be to show the text
`layout_above`	Above	`@id/square_root_symbol`	Positions this control above the `ImageView`
`layout_alignLeft`	Align Left	`@id/square_root_symbol`	Aligns the left edge of this control with the left edge of the `ImageView`
`layout_alignRight`	Align Right	`@id/square_root_symbol`	Aligns the right edge of this control with the right edge of the `ImageView`

The final thing to set up is the binding for the value, so flip to the Source tab and add the following code.

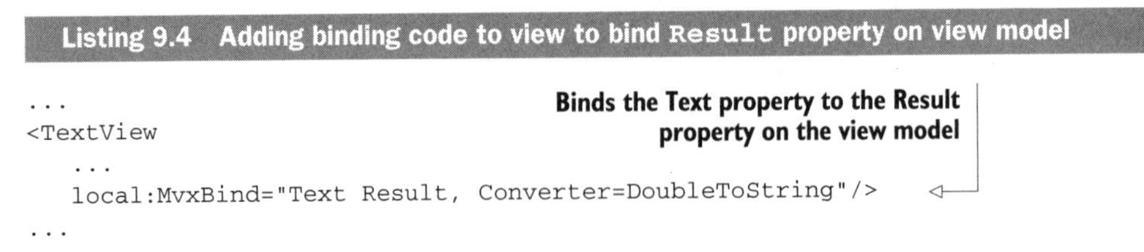

Listing 9.4 Adding binding code to view to bind `Result` property on view model

```
...
<TextView
  ...
  local:MvxBind="Text Result, Converter=DoubleToString"/>
...
```

Binds the Text property to the Result property on the view model

That's it—your layout is now done. Now it's time to turn our attention to the view class itself.

9.3 Building the SquareRt view

We've defined the layout resource that defines the UI for the SquareRt view, so now it's time to build the UI itself, by defining an activity.

9.3.1 What is an activity?

In Android, an *activity* represents a single screen in your app, and it's equivalent to an MVVM view. The name is suggestive of the intention. It should be the place a user performs an activity of some sort—a task or group of related tasks so that it represents a real-world activity that the user would want to do. For example, in Countr we have two screens: one for viewing multiple counters and performing actions on items in the list, and one for creating a new counter. These screens are distinct activities, and each would be modeled by an instance of the `Activity` class. In our SquareRt app, we only have one task that the user will want to do—calculating the square root—so this app will only require one activity.

An activity is a class derived from `Android.App.Activity`, which is a class in the Android SDK. This class is responsible for everything to do with the screen that it shows. AppCompat also has a base activity derived from this activity class called `Android.Support.V7.App.AppCompatActivity`, which provides an activity that uses material design. The activity is responsible for creating the view, including constructing all the UI components, and it manages the lifecycle of the screen, including tracking when the activity is created, visible, hidden, or destroyed. All Android apps have one main launcher activity, and this is the activity that's loaded and shown when your app first starts up.

When your app is packaged, installed, and run, the Android OS looks at the manifest file to see what activities it has, including seeing what the main launcher activity is, so all activities *must* be declared in the manifest. As Xamarin developers, we don't need to define all the activities in the manifest file manually. All we need to do is add the `[Activity]` attribute to our activities, and the Xamarin tooling will add these to the manifest for us. You can define your main launcher activity by setting the `MainLauncher` property on this attribute to `true` (something that's already done for us on the splash screen activity from MvvmCross). You can also set other properties about your activity on this attribute, including its icon and title.

Most apps will start with a splash screen activity that shows a simple image while the app is starting up, and this is such a popular thing to do that MvvmCross gives you a splash screen out of the box using a class called `MvxSplashScreenActivity`. Our app was configured to use this as the base class of the `SplashScreen` class when we created it. The important thing to be aware of with this activity is that it starts up the MvvmCross framework, including launching the view for the view model that you've registered as your app start.

9.3.2 The activity lifecycle

Each activity has a lifecycle, a set of methods that get called during the lifetime of that activity, depending on whether the activity is being created, destroyed, shown, or hidden. These are all called on the UI thread. Figure 9.20 shows this lifecycle.

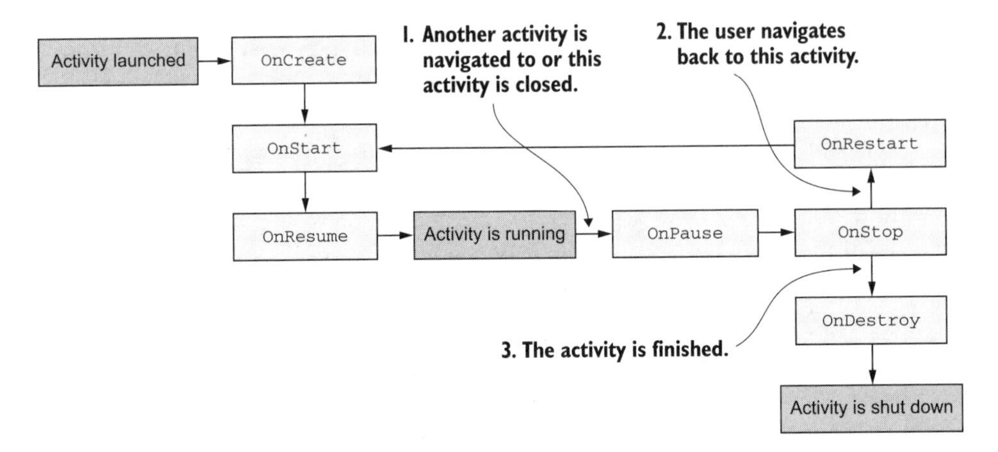

Figure 9.20 Each activity goes through a lifecycle as it's shown, hidden, reshown, or destroyed.

These lifecycle methods are all virtual methods on the `Activity` class, so you can override them as needed. For example, `OnStart` is called every time an activity becomes the current activity and is visible to the user, so in an app that shows data from a web service (such as a social media app) this would be a good place to kick off a background task to reload any data. The most important one to override is `OnCreate`—this method is called when an activity is first created but before it's shown on the UI, so it's here that you should build up your actual user interface by inflating a layout file.

By default, activities are recreated when the screen gets rotated. This means the current activity is destroyed and goes through the destruction part of the lifecycle (`OnPause`, `OnStop`, and `OnDestroy` are all called in order) and a brand new instance of the class is constructed and goes through the creation lifecycle (`OnCreate` is called followed by `OnStart`). The biggest upside of this is that it allows full support for different layouts for landscape and portrait orientations. As mentioned earlier in this chapter, resources can be loaded from different folders based on the device setup, so you can create two different layouts with the same name, but one in the Resources\layout-land folder and another in the Resources\layout-port folder, and every time the activity is recreated as it's rotated, the correct layout file will be loaded. MvvmCross handles this activity recreation for you, so when a new activity is created it re-uses the same instance of the view model. You don't need to do anything to persist state in the view between rotations—the view model handles it all for you.

9.3.3 Creating an activity for the view

Android uses activities to define each screen, and these are analogous to MVVM views, so to create the view for your app, you need to create an activity. In the Views folder, add a new class called `SquareRtView` and add the code from the following listing.

Listing 9.5 The code for the square root view

```
using Android.App;

using Android.OS;
using MvvmCross.Droid.Support.V7.AppCompat;

namespace SquareRt.Droid.Views
{
   [Activity(Label = "@string/ApplicationName")]
   public class SquareRtView : MvxAppCompatActivity
   {
      protected override void OnCreate(Bundle bundle)
      {
         base.OnCreate(bundle);
      }
   }
}
```

An attribute to mark this class as an activity

The view derives from a base MvvmCross activity.

Overrides the OnCreate method and calls the base

This is the basic structure of our activity class. The base class is `MvxAppCompatActivity`, an MvvmCross class that derives from `AppCompatActivity` (the base activity class for screens that use AppCompat to support material design on pre-Lollipop devices), and it comes with support for view models, including automatically setting the view model when you navigate to this view.

> **FOR ACCESS TO UNDERLYING VIEW MODELS, A GENERIC VERSION CAN HELP** `MvxAppCompatActivity` has a property called `ViewModel` with the type of `IMvx-ViewModel`, which is the base interface on the `MvxViewModel` base view-model class. This way you can access your view model by its base interface and cast it to the type you need. If you prefer to avoid the cast, you can use `MvxAppCompat-Activity<T>`, where `T` is your view-model type. This provides a `ViewModel` property of type `T` instead of `IMvxViewModel`, so you don't have to cast it.

This activity is decorated with the `[Activity]` attribute, which tells the tooling to automatically add your activity to the manifest when the app is compiled. This won't add the activity to the manifest in the `Properties` folder of your project, but it adds it to the version that's output at compile time. You can see this in action yourself by compiling the app and looking at the AndroidManifest.xml file in the Obj\Debug\android folder. You'll see that the activity has been added, albeit with a strange name that starts with `md5<something>`. This is the magic that Xamarin has to do to avoid packaging errors, and it's probably nothing you'll ever need to worry about. You can read more about it under the heading "Android Callable Wrappers" in the Xamarin documentation: http://mng.bz/4G4C.

The Label property is one of a number of properties you can set on the [Activity] attribute, and it's used to configure the title that appears in the toolbar (toolbars, by default, show the activity's label, but this can be changed if you want). You're not defining a specific name here though; instead you're using another resource reference to the ApplicationName string. Normally you can't use resource references inside strings—only in XML files—but the values you're setting here are used to populate the AndroidManifest.xml file. This means setting Label = "@string/ApplicationName" will add an entry to the manifest that looks something like this:

```
<activity android:label="@string/ApplicationName"
   android:name="md5b1836f203309c9917b270ff5361286e3.SquareRtView" />
```

Seeing as this is in an XML file, Android will be able to resolve the resource reference.

There are a number of other properties you can set to configure your activity (such as setting the icon on the toolbar). You can read more on these in the Android "App Manifest" API guide: http://mng.bz/bCXA.

SHOWING THE LAYOUT

You have an activity now, but it doesn't do much. The next thing to do is to load the layout so it shows on the UI. Each activity has a single content view—an instance of Android.Views.View that is the top-level element to show on screen (and this is usually a view group containing other views). Activity comes with a helper function that can take a layout resource, inflate it (constructing and configuring all the views and view groups defined inside it), and set the result as the content view for the activity. The following listing shows the code change to do this, so make this change to SquareRtView.

Listing 9.6 The content view of an activity can be loaded from a resource

```
protected override void OnCreate(Bundle bundle)
{
   ...
   SetContentView(Resource.Layout.squarert_view);   <-- Sets the content view to load from a resource
}
```

This code uses a resource reference to find the layout, inflate it, and set it as the content view. This SetContentView method exists on the base Activity class and uses a layout inflater that comes as part of the Android SDK, but MvxAppCompatActivity has its own implementation of this method that uses a custom layout inflator provided by MvvmCross. The MvvmCross layout inflater uses the Android implementation to construct the views, but it also reads the MvxBind attributes and builds up the bindings for you automatically.

The last thing to do is to set up the toolbar. Each AppCompat activity has an action bar that can show the title or provide navigation between activities (we'll look at navigation a bit more in the next chapter, with the Countr app). This action bar can be set up to use any toolbar control. You have a Toolbar defined in your layout, so you can set this up as the action bar using the following code.

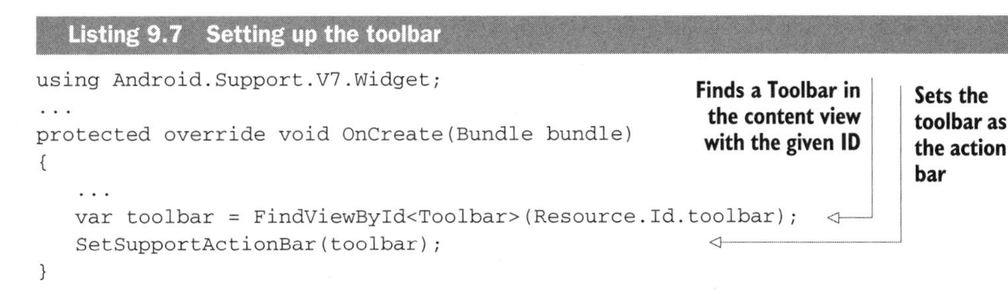

Listing 9.7 Setting up the toolbar

```
using Android.Support.V7.Widget;
...
protected override void OnCreate(Bundle bundle)
{
   ...
   var toolbar = FindViewById<Toolbar>(Resource.Id.toolbar);   // Finds a Toolbar in the content view with the given ID
   SetSupportActionBar(toolbar);                               // Sets the toolbar as the action bar
}
```

FindViewById will walk the UI looking for any view that has an ID set to the given value, and will return the base `Android.Views.View` or null if it's not found. The generic version, `FindViewById<T>`, will look for a view with the given ID of type `T` and return it as an instance of `T` if it's found, return null if it's not found, or throw an exception if it's found but is a different type. This is a relatively expensive call, especially if you have a complex UI, so if you need to access views in multiple places, you should cache them in a field or property in the `OnCreate` method.

Once the toolbar is found, it's set as the support action bar. The "support" part of the name refers to using AppCompat, and it's used when setting AppCompat toolbars. There's a `SetActionBar` method that's used when you're not using AppCompat toolbars, but ideally you should always use AppCompat to support as wide a range of Android OS versions as possible.

9.3.4 Running the app

You're done. This is all you need to do to create your view. You should now be able to build and run the app using one of the preconfigured emulators and calculate some square roots (figure 9.21).

When you run the app, the following things will happen:

1. The Android OS looks at the manifest, finds the activity that's set as the main launcher (the splash screen that was auto-created for you and that can be found in SplashScreen.cs in the root of the project), and starts it.
2. The splash screen uses the MVVMCross framework code to find the view model registered as the app start in the `App` class in the SquareRt.Core project—in our case this is `SquareRtViewModel`.
3. Based on the name of the view model that's set as the app start, it finds the `SquareRtView` activity and launches it.
4. As the activity runs, the `OnCreate` method is called by the Android OS as part of the activity lifecycle.

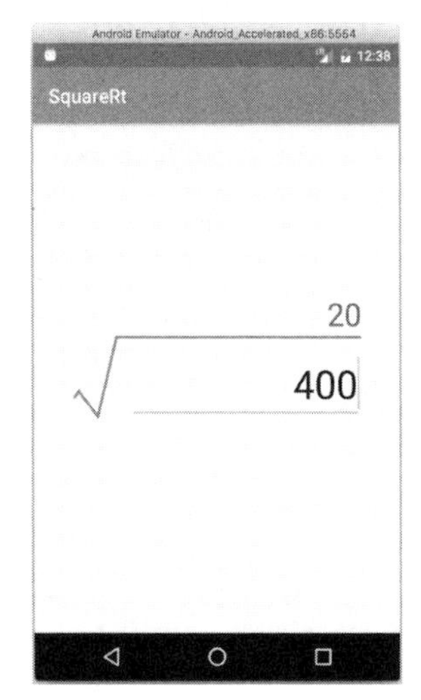

Figure 9.21 The working SquareRt app

5. In OnCreate, the layout file with the ID of squarert_view is inflated, creating all the views and view groups defined in the file, and setting all the relevant properties.
6. The MvvmCross framework finds all the MvxBind attributes that are set and creates the bindings so that every time the number in the EditText control changes, the view model is updated, and every time the result on the view model changes, the TextView control is updated.
7. The MvvmCross framework detects the Converter=DoubleToString on the binding, looks for the first class in the assembly that implements IMvxValueConverter that has a name starting with DoubleToString, finds DoubleToStringValueConverter in the SquareRt.Core project, creates an instance of it, and uses it as a value converter on the binding.

You've now finished the simple view layer for SquareRt, so in the next chapter we'll take a look at Countr, and we'll tidy up both our apps by improving their icons and splash screens.

Summary

In this chapter you learned

- Google has guidelines, called *material design*, for building mobile apps.
- Android uses resources for non-code assets, and these can be made available in different versions for devices of different sizes, orientations, or screen densities.
- Layouts are defined in XML and are used to define the controls on the UI.
- You can bind controls to properties and commands from inside the layout XML, or in code if necessary (for example, when handling menu items).
- Android has layout controls that can position child controls inside them.
- Views are derived from activities, and these load their UIs from layout resources.

You also learned how to

- Create layout resources using the Designer and by editing the source
- Add multiple images to support different screen densities

10 Building more advanced Android views

This chapter covers

- Using recycler views
- Configuring and handling menus
- Activity navigation and the Back button
- Setting app icons
- Styles, themes, and XML drawables
- MvvmCross application lifecycle and launch screens

In chapter 9 we looked at the basics of creating an Android UI, including layout files, images, and activities, and we ended up by building the complete UI for SquareRt. In this chapter we'll be looking at some more advanced Android UI topics so we can build the UI for Countr: using recycler views to show lists of data, and adding menu items to the Android toolbar, for example. We'll then look at improving our apps' icons and launch screens.

10.1 Building the UI for Countr

SquareRt is done, so let's move on to Countr. Start by launching the Countr solution from chapter 8 and the dummy first view activity and layout, just as you did for SquareRt. This is a more complicated UI that has two screens, so you'll need two activities and two layouts. I'll be showing you how to create these UIs in code as it's easier to show in a book, but feel free to try to achieve the same results using the Designer (keeping in mind that you'll have to switch back to the Source view to set up the MvvmCross bindings).

Figure 10.1 shows the UI we want to create.

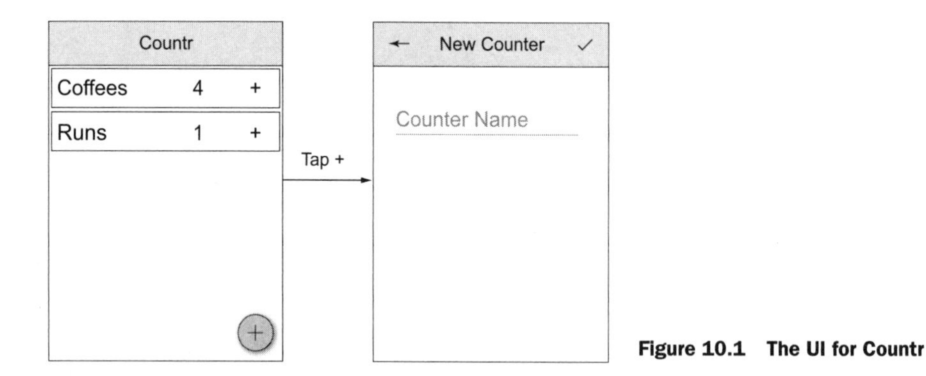

Figure 10.1 The UI for Countr

10.1.1 Creating the UI for the master view

The first view we'll create for the Countr app is the master view, using the layout shown in figure 10.2. It will have the same toolbar as the `squarert_view` layout, and it will need to contain a widget for showing a list of counters, as well as a floating button for adding a new counter.

Create a new layout resource called `counters_view` and add the following code to it.

Listing 10.1 The basic outline of the counters view layout

```
<?xml version="1.0" encoding="utf-8"?>
<RelativeLayout
   xmlns:android="http://schemas.android.com/apk/res/android"
   xmlns:local="http://schemas.android.com/apk/res-auto"
   android:layout_width="match_parent"
   android:layout_height="match_parent">
   <android.support.design.widget.AppBarLayout
      android:layout_height="wrap_content"
      android:layout_width="match_parent"
      android:id="@+id/toolbar_layout">
      <include
         android:id="@+id/toolbar"
         layout="@layout/toolbar"
         local:layout_scrollFlags="scroll|enterAlways" />
   </android.support.design.widget.AppBarLayout>
```

```
    <FrameLayout
       android:layout_below="@id/toolbar_layout"
       android:layout_width="match_parent"
       android:layout_height="match_parent">
    </FrameLayout>
</RelativeLayout>
```

Below the toolbar layout is a frame layout.

This is the same as the initial view code we wrote for the SquareRt layout file, except here we're using a `FrameLayout` below the toolbar layout instead of a relative layout. We don't need to position the other items on-screen relative to each other, so there's no need to use a relative layout.

The children of a frame layout are laid out on top of each other in the order they're added, so the first child is on the bottom, the next child is on top of the first child, and so on (if you have two views of the same size in the same position, the second will hide the first). Our frame layout needs two children to match the UI we're aiming for: a view that shows a list of counters, and a floating button that floats over the list to add a new counter.

We need to start with the list of counters, and for this we need to add a recycler view.

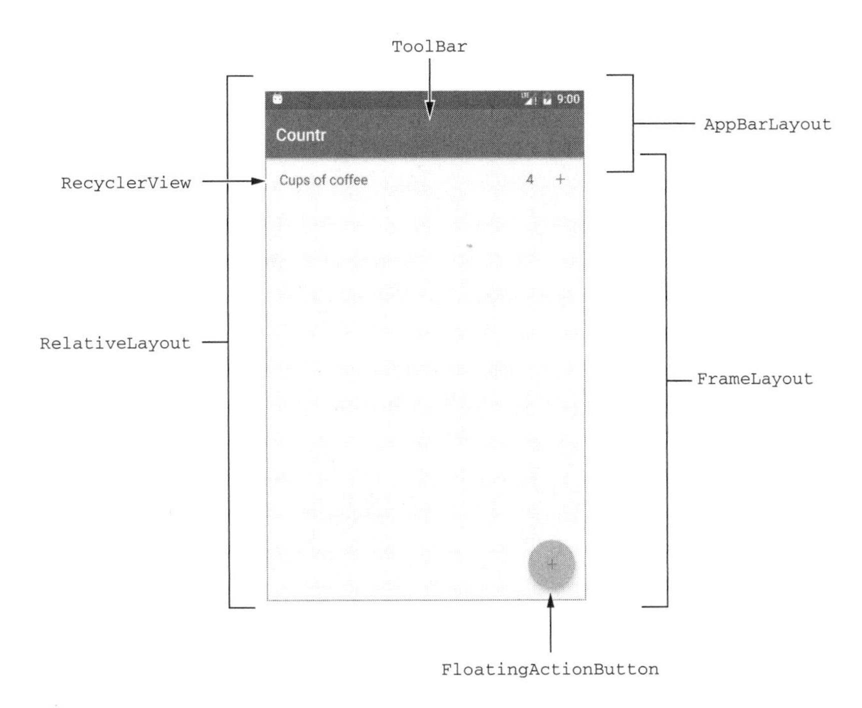

Figure 10.2 The layout of the views and view groups in the master Countr UI

10.1.2 Recycler views

A lot of apps need to show data as some form of list, and Android has a widget called `ListView` that contains a scrollable list of views representing all the items in the list. This is highly inefficient—if you have one thousand items in your list, the list view will contain one thousand views, one for each item. Most of them won't be visible on-screen, but they'll take up memory as well as UI thread time to draw and position them.

To improve on this, Android added a widget called `RecyclerView` as part of its support library. It works the same way as far as the user is concerned, but it's implemented in a much more efficient way by recycling views. It creates only enough views to cover what can be shown on the UI, and as the user scrolls, views that are no longer visible are recycled and are moved to the other end of the list (figure 10.3).

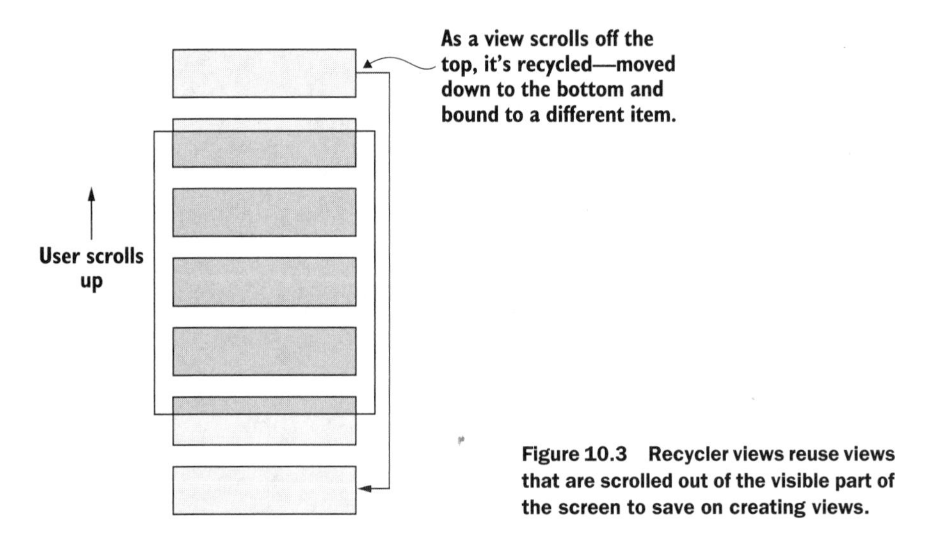

As a view scrolls off the top, it's recycled—moved down to the bottom and bound to a different item.
User scrolls up

Figure 10.3 Recycler views reuse views that are scrolled out of the visible part of the screen to save on creating views.

Recycler views have a number of components that need to be set up. As well as creating the recycler view on the layout, you also need to set up a layout manager, an adapter, and a view holder. The layout manager is responsible for laying out the items in the recycler view, and Android supplies two out of the box for laying items out in a vertical list or a grid (you can create your own layout manager if you need a different layout). The adapter needs to know about the list of items that you want to show in the recycler view, and it's responsible for creating and updating the views that are shown in the list, including updating them when the data changes. The view holder is a wrapper that stores the view for each item (usually loaded from a layout file) in the list, allowing it to be recycled.

Recycler views take a bit of work to get working well, but luckily MvvmCross takes some of the hard work out of the process by providing its own recycler view implementation. This `MvxRecyclerView` view derives from `RecyclerView` but it has its own adapter that knows about observable collections. It can automatically create the views needed to show the items, binding them to the items in the observable collection to be handled. It also creates and manages view holders for you—you just need to specify the layout file to use, and it creates all the view holders, inflating the layout you give it and creating any bindings in that layout file to bind to each item in the collection that's used as the item source of the recycler view. The only thing you need to set up manually is the layout manager.

If you want to set up your own recycler view, there's some great `RecyclerView` documentation in the Xamarin documentation: http://mng.bz/79CO.

To add the MvvmCross recycler view to the UI, add the code in the following listing to the `counters_view` layout.

Listing 10.2 Adding an MvvmCross recycler view to the layout

```
<FrameLayout
   ...>
   <mvvmcross.droid.support.v7.recyclerview.MvxRecyclerView
      android:layout_width="match_parent"
      android:layout_height="match_parent"
      android:id="@+id/recycler_view"
      local:MvxBind="ItemsSource Counters" />
...
```

Creates a recycler view that fills the available space and sets its ID

Binds the items source to the Counters property of the view model

This adds a recycler view to your layout, sets it to fill all the available space inside the frame layout, and gives it the ID of `@+id/recycler_view`. It then binds the `ItemsSource` on the `MvxRecyclerView` to the `Counters` property on the view model—a property of type `ObservableCollection<CounterViewModel>` that exposes all the counters stored in the database.

You also need to tell the recycler view how to show the `CounterViewModel` instances, and to do this you need to define another layout that you set as the item template for the recycler view—*item template* is the MvvmCross terminology for the layout resource that describes how to show and bind each item. Let's now look at creating the UI for the item templates.

10.1.3 Creating the UI for the recycler view items

You now have the recycler view set up in your layout, but you haven't defined the layout for the items that are shown in the list—the `CounterViewModel` instances. You need to define how they're going to be shown, and this is done by creating a new layout file. The layout needs to have a text view for the counter's name, another text view that shows the current count, and a button that the user can tap to increment the counter (figure 10.4). This layout is used one per counter in the list, and when they're created, they are bound to the instance of the `CounterViewModel` that they're showing.

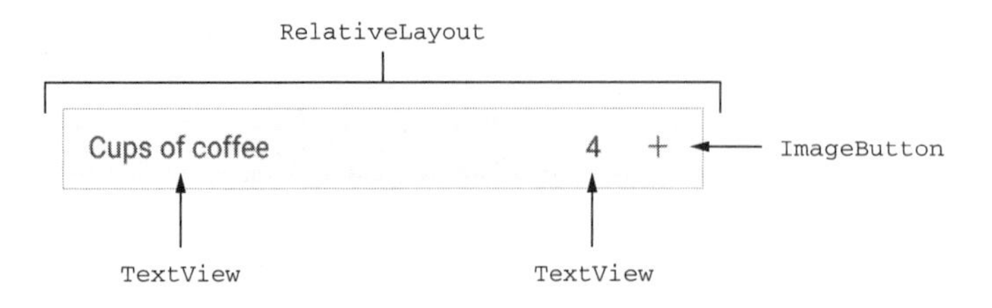

Figure 10.4 The layout of the views and view groups for each item in the recycler view

The layouts for individual items are once again defined in layout XML files, so add one called `counter_recycler_view` and start by adding the following code.

Listing 10.3 The initial layout for the individual items in the recycler view

```
<?xml version="1.0" encoding="utf-8"?>
<RelativeLayout
    xmlns:android="http://schemas.android.com/apk/res/android"
    xmlns:local="http://schemas.android.com/apk/res-auto"
    android:orientation="vertical"
    android:layout_width="match_parent"
    android:layout_height="50dp">
</RelativeLayout>
```

This is a simple relative layout for an item that's as wide as the available space on the screen but that's only `50dp` high, as this is all you'll need to show the content.

You can now add the button to increment the counter. For this, you need an image for a plus symbol. If you look in the images folder in the Git repository for this book's source, you'll see an image called plus.png. Copy this from the various size folders to the relevant folders in the app. Then add the code in the following listing to the relative layout.

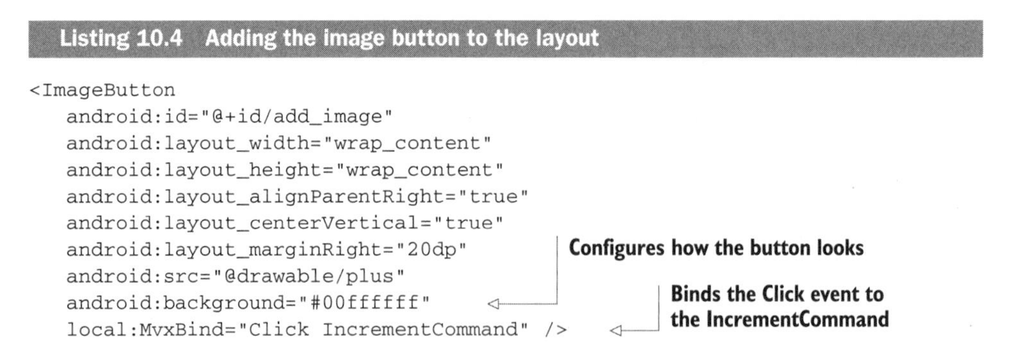

Listing 10.4 Adding the image button to the layout

```
<ImageButton
    android:id="@+id/add_image"
    android:layout_width="wrap_content"
    android:layout_height="wrap_content"
    android:layout_alignParentRight="true"
    android:layout_centerVertical="true"
    android:layout_marginRight="20dp"
    android:src="@drawable/plus"
    android:background="#00ffffff"
    local:MvxBind="Click IncrementCommand" />
```


`ImageButton` is a widget that's pretty much identical to a `Button`, except that it shows an image instead of just showing text, and this image is set using the `src` property the same way an `ImageView` does.

Most of the layout should be pretty familiar: the image button is laid out in the vertical center of the parent relative layout, on the right side with a right margin of `20dp`. The ID is also set so that you can position another text view relative to it. The only new property here is `background`. Buttons are normally styled using Android styles, and the default style for buttons is to have a background color. You don't want this background color—you want the plus symbol to be on a white background—so the background is set to `#00ffffff`, the hexadecimal representation of transparent white.

> **COLORS ARE DEFINED USING ARGB VALUES IN HEX** When specifying colors in Android resources, you use aRGB values defined using hexadecimal numbers, which are always prefixed with a `#`. The four bytes represent values for the alpha (how transparent the color is, with 0 being transparent and FF being opaque), red, green, and blue components. The alpha value is optional, and if it's not set, an alpha of FF is assumed. The values are set in this order: `<alpha><red><green><blue>`.

This is also the first time we've bound an event to a command. It's pretty simple—you specify the name of the event on the control and the name of the command to bind to. In this case, you're binding the `Click` event of the `ImageButton` to the `IncrementCommand` command on the counter view model.

The next thing you need to add are some text views to show the name and count of the counter. The following listing shows the code to add inside the relative layout.

Listing 10.5 Adding text views for the name of the counter and its count

```
<TextView
   android:layout_width="wrap_content"
   android:layout_height="wrap_content"
   android:layout_centerVertical="true"
   android:layout_alignParentLeft="true"
   android:layout_marginLeft="20dp"
   android:textSize="16sp"
   local:MvxBind="Text Name"/>
<TextView
   android:layout_width="wrap_content"
   android:layout_height="wrap_content"
   android:layout_centerVertical="true"
   android:layout_toLeftOf="@id/add_image"
   android:layout_marginRight="20dp"
   android:textSize="16sp"
   local:MvxBind="Text Count"/>
```

You now have your layout defined, so the last thing to do is to tell the recycler view to use it to show the counters. To do this, flip back to the `counters_view` and add the attribute in the following listing to the recycler view.

Listing 10.6 The recycler view needs to be told what layout to use to show items

```
local:MvxItemTemplate="@layout/counter_recycler_view"
```

This attribute tells the recycler view that every time it needs to create a new view for an item, it should inflate the `counter_recycler_view` layout and bind it to the counter view model. This is a recycler view, so only as many instances of the view as you need are created. When a view is recycled, the view model that's bound to it is changed, and the binding layer will re-evaluate the properties and update the UI to reflect the new view model.

> **ADDING UI AWESOMENESS WITH COORDINATOR LAYOUTS** Android has another layout called `CoordinatorLayout` that's able to coordinate its behavior based on other controls on the screen. For example, you can use a coordinator layout as the top-level layout control for your activity, and set it up so that as you scroll the recycler view, the toolbar disappears, only reappearing as you scroll back to the top. You can read more about this in the Base Lab Blog's "Nested Scrolling with CoordinatorLayout on Android" entry: http://mng.bz/Anun.

10.1.4 Floating action buttons

The final thing to add to the counters UI is a floating action button. These are reasonably new UI components, and they're designed to provide access to a common action that a user wants to do on a screen. In the counters app, we'll use this to create a new counter, in the same way that Google's Gmail app uses a floating action button to create a new email. These floating buttons are a part of Google's material design standard, and as such are available in the Android support libraries.

Add the following code to the frame layout in the `counters_view` layout, below the recycler view.

Listing 10.7 Adding a floating action button to the counters screen

```
<android.support.design.widget.FloatingActionButton
   android:layout_width="wrap_content"
   android:layout_height="wrap_content"
   android:layout_gravity="bottom|right"
   android:layout_margin="16dp"
   android:src="@drawable/plus"
   local:MvxBind="Click ShowAddNewCounterCommand" />    <-- Binds the click event
```

This floating action button reuses the plus image that you've used in the recycler view item layouts. It also binds the `Click` event to `ShowAddNewCounterCommand` on the counters view model.

That's everything for the master counters view.

10.1.5 Creating the UI for the detail view

Now let's turn our attention to the detail screen, which needs to show an `EditText` control where the user can enter the name of a new counter. It also needs Done and Back buttons on the toolbar so the user can either save the counter or go back and not add a counter. The layout for this is shown in figure 10.5.

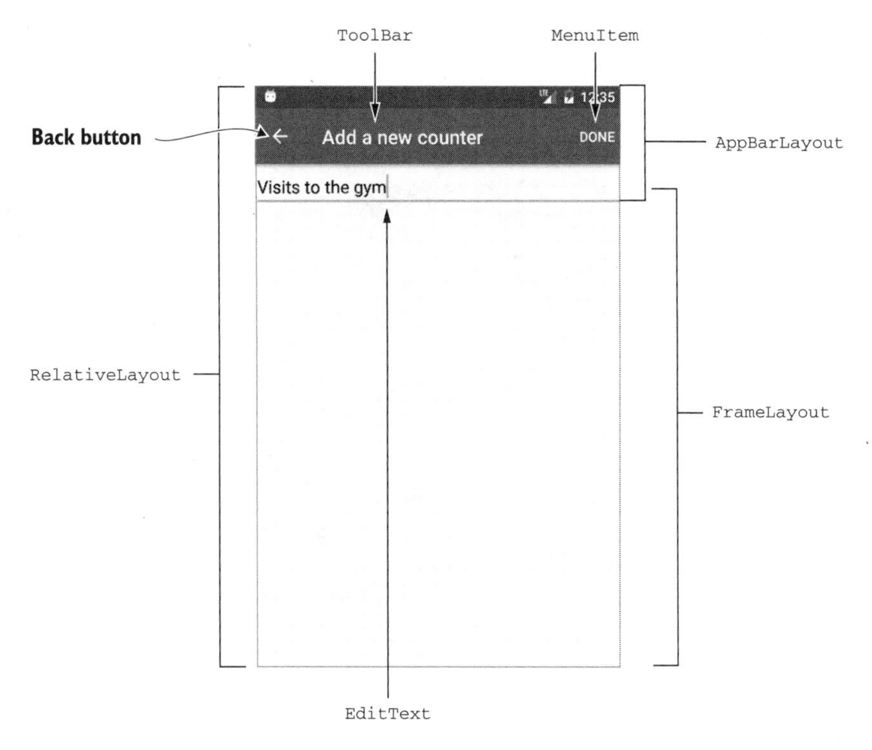

Figure 10.5 The layout of the views and view groups in the detail counter UI

You can start building the counter detail view by creating a new layout called `counter_view`. Then copy the outline structure defined earlier in listing 10.1 into this layout file: the outer relative layout, app bar layout, toolbar include, and frame layout. Then add the following code to the frame layout. This code should look familiar by now.

Listing 10.8 Adding an `EditText` control for the counter name

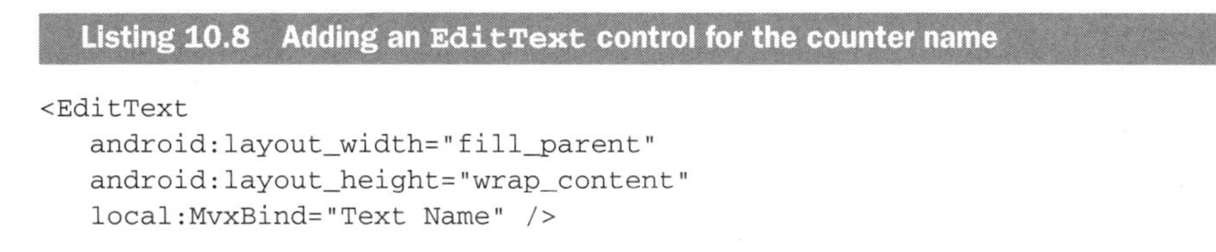

```
<EditText
   android:layout_width="fill_parent"
   android:layout_height="wrap_content"
   local:MvxBind="Text Name" />
```

That's the layout done. Now you need to define a menu to add the Done button to the toolbar. You don't have to define the Back button in a layout; this is something you can add in code later, as it's a standard activity feature.

10.1.6 Menu items

Menus are defined in resources that are stored in the menu folder. They're XML files that contain a list of menu items and their configurations.

You need to add a menu to add the Done button to the toolbar, so create a folder called menu in the Resources folder and add an XML file to that folder called new_counter_menu.xml containing the following code.

Listing 10.9 Menus are defined in XML

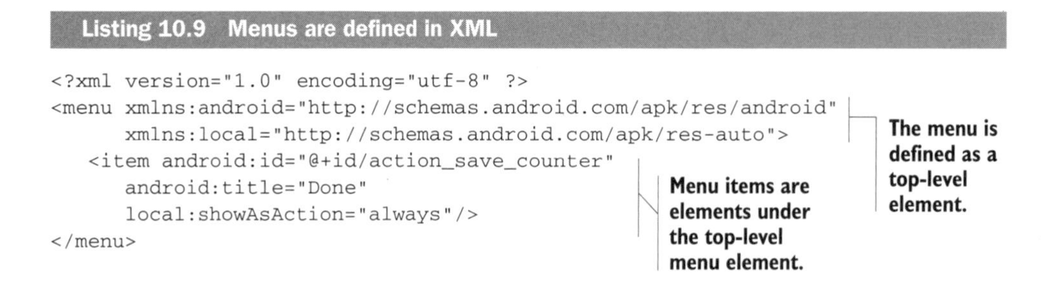

```
<?xml version="1.0" encoding="utf-8" ?>
<menu xmlns:android="http://schemas.android.com/apk/res/android"
      xmlns:local="http://schemas.android.com/apk/res-auto">
   <item android:id="@+id/action_save_counter"
      android:title="Done"
      local:showAsAction="always"/>
</menu>
```

The menu is defined as a top-level element.
Menu items are elements under the top-level menu element.

These menu resources consist of a top-level menu element that contains one or more item elements that define the menu. As you'll see later in this chapter, you can inflate one of these menu resources into a toolbar to get items on the menu. When these items are inflated, the OS will work out how much space you have and show only as many items as it can, with the rest being in an overflow menu that's shown using vertical ellipses (three vertical dots). Against each menu item, you can specify the text or icon to show, and you can set whether you always want it on the menu, always want it on the overflow, or want it wherever it fits best.

In this case, you just have text for the menu, and this is set with the `android:title="Done"` property. This will be a popular option for the user to select, so you'll want this to always be on the menu instead in an overflow menu. This is set using `local:showAsAction="always"`. This menu also has an ID (`android:id="@+id/action_save_counter"`), and it's very important that this is set. There's no direct way to wire up code to a menu, either via Android or using MvvmCross. Instead, when a menu item is tapped, a method in the `Activity` class is called with the ID of the menu item that was tapped. By setting the ID, you can identify which menu item was tapped inside the `Activity`.

That's it for resources. Now it's time to start on the view code itself.

10.2 Building the Countr activities

You have your layouts, so it's time to work on the activities. You need to create two activities: one for the master view and one for the detail view.

Create two activities in the Views folder: one called `CountersView` and one called `CounterView`. Add the following code to the `CountersView`.

Listing 10.10 The counters master view

```
using Android.App;
using Android.OS;
using Android.Support.V7.Widget;
using Countr.Core.ViewModels;
using MvvmCross.Droid.Support.V7.AppCompat;

namespace Countr.Droid.Views
{
   [Activity(Label = "@string/ApplicationName")]
   public class CountersView : MvxAppCompatActivity<CountersViewModel>
   {
      protected override void OnCreate(Bundle bundle)
      {
         base.OnCreate(bundle);

         SetContentView(Resource.Layout.counters_view);

         var toolbar = FindViewById<Toolbar>(Resource.Id.toolbar);
         SetSupportActionBar(toolbar);
      }
   }
}
```

Uses the generic version of the MvvmCross activity

Uses the counters_view layout

This code is the same as for the SquareRt activity, except that it uses a different layout resource, and it uses the generic version of `MvxAppCompatActivity` so that the `ViewModel` property is of the correct type (you'll be using it later).

Now add the same code to the `CounterView` activity, except using `CounterViewModel` and the `counter_view` layout, and change the activity label to be "Add new counter", as shown in the following listing.

Listing 10.11 The counter detail view

```
...
[Activity(Label = "Add a new counter")]
public class CounterView : MvxAppCompatActivity<CounterViewModel>
{
   protected override void OnCreate(Bundle bundle)
   {
      ...
      SetContentView(Resource.Layout.counter_view);
   }
}
```

As an exercise, you can try moving the "Add a new counter" label to a resource (the source code that accompanies this book has it as a resource).

10.2.1 Setting up master recycler views

Recycler views take a little bit of setup in the activities that use them. Recycler views use layout managers to determine how to lay out the items that they're showing, and there's no default for this, so you always need to set it up.

To set up the recycler view, add the following code to the `CountersView` activity.

Listing 10.12 Setting up the recycler view to use a linear layout manager

```
using MvvmCross.Droid.Support.V7.RecyclerView;
...
protected override void OnCreate(Bundle bundle)
{
   ...
   var recyclerView = FindViewById<MvxRecyclerView>(Resource.Id.recycler_view);
   recyclerView.SetLayoutManager(new LinearLayoutManager(this));
}
```

Finds the recycler view in the UI, and sets its layout manager

This code finds the recycler view based on its ID, and then sets the layout manager for it. This layout manager arranges items in a vertical list.

You also want to support swipe-to-delete. This is a nice feature to have, but it's not the easiest to set up. There's no out-of-the-box swipe handling for recycler views. Instead you have to write your own using a class called `ItemTouchHelper` from the support library.

First, you define a callback class—a class that derives from the `ItemTouchHelper.Callback` class, which has a set of abstract methods to implement touch callbacks. Then you construct an `ItemTouchHelper` using the callback and attach this to the recycler view. This is quite a standard pattern on a lot of Android SDK classes—Java (the language used for the underlying Android SDK) doesn't have events, so unlike C#, where you can wire behavior up to events, Java relies on callback classes with methods that are called when things happen. When Xamarin bound the Android SDKs, they converted some callbacks to events to make it easier for C# programmers to use them, but not all, and this is one they haven't provided events for.

To create the callback, create a new class in the Views folder called `SwipeItemTouchHelperCallback`, and add the following code.

Listing 10.13 Creating the callback for swiping on the recycler views

```
using Android.Support.V7.Widget;
using Android.Support.V7.Widget.Helper;
using Countr.Core.ViewModels;

namespace Countr.Droid.Views
{
   public class SwipeItemTouchHelperCallback
    : ItemTouchHelper.SimpleCallback
   {
      readonly CountersViewModel viewModel;

      public SwipeItemTouchHelperCallback(CountersViewModel viewModel)
         : base(0, ItemTouchHelper.Start)
```

This derives from ItemTouchHelper.Callback, the base callback class.

Stores an instance of the CountersViewModel that you can use to delete a counter

Specifies the supported swipe directions

```
        {
            this.viewModel = viewModel;
        }
    }
}
```

When the callback is constructed, it needs to call the base class constructor specifying the drag and swipe operations you want to support. Drag-and-drop is useful if you want to support rearranging items, but we don't need it here. We just want to support swiping from end to start (from right to left), and this is what you're specifying by passing `0` as the first argument to the base class constructor (meaning no drag support) and `ItemTouchHelper.Start` as the second parameter (meaning you're supporting swiping toward the start).

The base callback class is an abstract class, so you have to implement a couple of methods, as shown in the following listing.

Listing 10.14 Implementing the required callback methods

```
public override bool OnMove(RecyclerView recyclerView,
                            RecyclerView.ViewHolder viewHolder,
                            RecyclerView.ViewHolder target)
{
   return true;
}

public override void OnSwiped(RecyclerView.ViewHolder viewHolder,
                              int direction)
{
   viewModel.Counters[viewHolder.AdapterPosition]     When an item is
      .DeleteCommand.Execute();                        swiped, delete it.
}
```

These two methods are abstract in the base class, so they have to be implemented. `OnMove` is called whenever drag-and-drop takes place, and as this is something you're not supporting, you can just return `true`. `OnSwiped` is the interesting one—it's called whenever an item is swiped, and the parameters include an instance of the `ViewHolder` class. `ViewHolder` is a backing class used to store data for each of the items in the recycler view, and it has an `AdapterPosition` property that tells you the position of the item that was swiped in the list—this position maps to the position of the `CounterViewModel` inside the collection on the `CountersViewModel`. When a swipe is detected, you can retrieve the counter view model from the counters view model stored in the `viewModel` backing field, and execute `DeleteCommand` on it. This will then delete the counter, which in turn will remove it from the observable collection in the view model, which will cause the UI to update to show the collection minus the deleted item.

IT'S ALWAYS GOOD TO PROVIDE FEEDBACK TO THE USER When users are swiping, it's good to provide feedback as to what is happening, and a usual way to do this is to have some kind of delete indicator with a red background under the item as it's swiped away. The callback has a method you can override called `OnChildDraw`, which is called every time an item needs to be drawn, such as when it's swiped. You can override this method to add something behind the item as it's swiped away. The sample code that accompanies this book does this, showing a red background as you swipe the item away.

Now that you have your callback, it's time to wire it up to the recycler view in `CountersView` via a touch helper. Add the following code to the bottom of the `OnCreate` method.

Listing 10.15 Wiring up the callback to the recycler view

```
using Android.Support.V7.Widget.Helper;
...
protected override void OnCreate(Bundle bundle)
{
   ...
   var callback = new SwipeItemTouchHelperCallback(ViewModel);
   var touchHelper = new ItemTouchHelper(callback);
   touchHelper.AttachToRecyclerView(recyclerView);
}
```

Creates the callback and uses it to construct a touch helper and then attach it to the recycler view

That's the master view finished, so let's move on to the detail view.

10.2.2 The detail view

You've already created the basic shell of your `CounterView`, which provides most of what you need, except for the toolbar and menu. You now need to provide a Back button so that the user can navigate back to the master view without adding a counter (referred to as an Up button in Android), and you need to wire up the menu resource for the Done button.

ADDING THE BACK BUTTON

The Back button is easy—toolbars have one built in, but it's not shown by default. You can show it by adding the following code to the `OnCreate` method.

Listing 10.16 Showing the Back button on the toolbar

```
protected override void OnCreate(Bundle bundle)
{
   ...
   SupportActionBar.SetDisplayHomeAsUpEnabled(true);
}
```

Shows the Up button

This method turns on the Up button in the toolbar—the Back arrow on the left side pointing left. This button doesn't do the navigation by itself; instead you need to handle it when it's tapped manually.

All buttons and menu items in the toolbar are referred to as *options* in Android, and you can create options either by turning them on in the toolbar (as you just did) or by adding more menu options (as you'll see later in this chapter). When any menu item is tapped, the `OnOptionsItemSelected` method on the activity is called, with the menu item that was tapped being passed as a parameter. To handle any toolbar menu, you need to override this method, check the ID for the item that was tapped, and respond accordingly. The following listing shows the code to handle the Up button.

Listing 10.17 Handling the up button

```
using Android.Views;
...
public override bool OnOptionsItemSelected(IMenuItem item)
{
   switch (item.ItemId)
   {
      case Android.Resource.Id.Home:
         ViewModel.CancelCommand.Execute(null);
         return true;
      default:
         return base.OnOptionsItemSelected(item);
   }
}
```

Overrides the OnOptionsItemSelected method

ItemId is the ID of the menu item.

Android.Resource.Id.Home is the ID of the Up button, and it comes from the Android SDK.

The Up button has a hard-coded ID that comes from the Android SDK. If the options item that's selected has this ID, you can execute `CancelCommand` on the view model to navigate back to the master view model, therefore closing the detail view and showing the master view.

Android devices have hardware Back buttons

Instead of using the Up button, the user could also tap the hardware Back button (all Android devices have a Back button, either a physical button or a software button that's pretty much always visible). This will bypass the `OnOptionsItemSelected` method and just close the current activity, removing it from the navigation stack and going back to the previous activity. This isn't a problem for us, as this will stop the new counter activity and not save the counter, so it will be the same as tapping the Up button.

If you don't want the activity to close when the user taps the Back button, and instead to perform some action (such as stopping the button from working or doing some kind of cleanup or saving some data) you could override the `OnBackPressed` method on the activity, and not call the base version.

ADDING THE DONE MENU ITEM

We've handled the Up button, so now we need to add the Done button to save the new counter. You've already defined a menu resource for this, so you need to add it to the toolbar.

As part of the activity's creation, the virtual activity method `OnCreateOptionsMenu` is called by the Android OS to configure the toolbar, and you can override this to configure your own toolbar menu items. Add the following code to the view to do this.

Listing 10.18 Inflating menu items into the toolbar

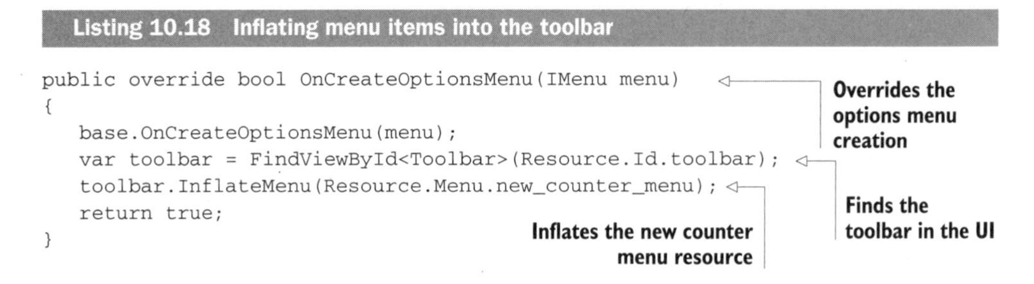

```
public override bool OnCreateOptionsMenu(IMenu menu)
{
   base.OnCreateOptionsMenu(menu);
   var toolbar = FindViewById<Toolbar>(Resource.Id.toolbar);
   toolbar.InflateMenu(Resource.Menu.new_counter_menu);
   return true;
}
```

Overrides the options menu creation
Finds the toolbar in the UI
Inflates the new counter menu resource

As with layouts, the term for reading the menu XML and creating the menu items is *inflating*. The toolbar can inflate the menu resource, adding the menu items to it.

You can now wire up this new menu item in the same way as the Up button: add another `case` statement for the ID of the Done button to the `OnOptionsItemSelected` method that executes `SaveCommand` on the view model. The following listing shows this.

Listing 10.19 Adding the Done button to the options menu handling

```
switch (item.ItemId)
{
   case Resource.Id.action_save_counter:
      ViewModel.SaveCommand.Execute(null);
      return true;
   ...
}
```

If the Done menu item is tapped, execute the save command

10.2.3 Running the app

Your app is now fully implemented, so launch it in the default emulator and try creating some counters, incrementing them, and deleting them. Figure 10.6 shows the two screens in the working app. You can also kill and relaunch the app, and see that the counters have been persisted.

If you have any issues running the app, such as crashes or hangs, they may be caused by known issues in different versions of Xamarin or MvvmCross. Check out the Troubleshooting thread on the *Xamarin In Action* forum on the book's website for more details: http://mng.bz/9JAY.

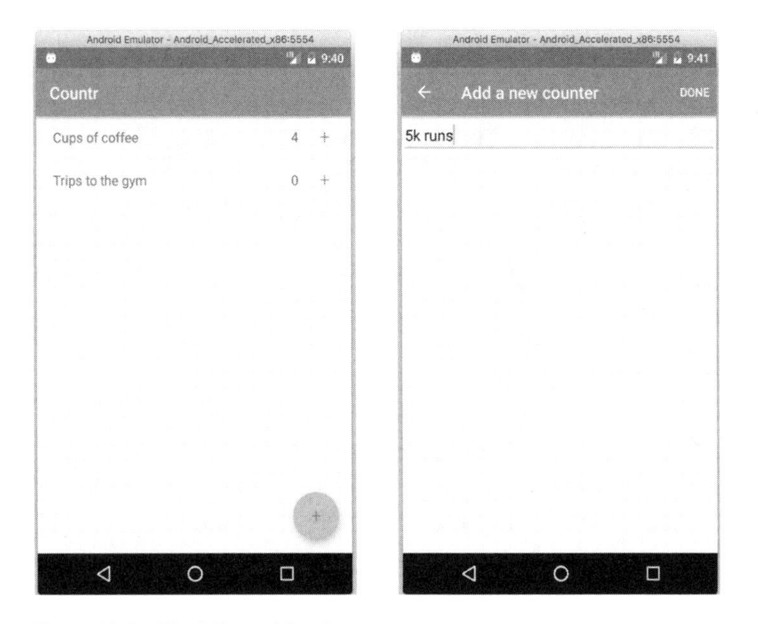

Figure 10.6 The fully working Countr app

When you run the app, the following things will happen:

1. The Android OS looks at the manifest, finds the activity that's set as the main launcher, and starts it (the splash screen that was automatically created for you and that can be found in SplashScreen.cs in the root of the project).
2. The splash screen uses MvvmCross framework code to find the view model registered as the app start in the `App` class in the `Countr.Core` project—in this case, it's `CountersViewModel`.
3. Based on the name of the view model that's set as the app start (`CountersViewModel`), it finds the `CountersView` activity and launches it.
4. As part of the activity lifecycle, the `OnCreate` method is called by the Android OS.
5. In `OnCreate`, the layout file with the ID of `counters_view` is inflated, creating all the views and view groups defined in the file and setting all the relevant properties. This method also wires up the layout manager for the recycler view and sets the touch handler to support swipe-to-delete.
6. The MvvmCross framework finds all the `MvxBind` attributes that are set and creates the bindings, wiring up the counters observable collection in the view model as the source for the items in the recycler view, and connects the click event of the floating action button to the relevant command.
7. When a user swipes on a counter, the touch handler callback's `OnSwiped` method is called, and the code manually executes the delete command.

8 When a user taps the floating action button, the command is executed, which navigates to the `CounterViewModel`. The MvvmCross framework finds the `CounterView` based on the name of the view model and shows this view. During the inflation of the layout for this view, the MvvmCross layout inflater looks for the `MxBind` attributes and binds the `EditText` to the name property on the view model.

9 In the counter view, if the user taps the Up button, the cancel command is executed. If they tap the Done button, the save command is executed. Both commands tell MvvmCross to close the current view model, which closes the view and navigates back to the master view.

10.3 App icons and launch screens

You've completed both the SquareRt and Countr Android apps, but they still need a bit of improvement. If you look at the Android launch screen, you'll see that both apps have a default MvvmCross icon, and if you launch either one of the apps, you'll see an MvvmCross launch screen. Let's now improve these both.

10.3.1 App icons

The first thing to update is the app icon. Here I'll only show you how to update the icon for Countr, but the same principle applies for all Android apps, so feel free to update the SquareRt icon too.

GENERATING APP ICON IMAGES

As with image resources, Android app icons come in different sizes so that they can look the same on devices with different screen densities. This means that you'll need to generate multiple versions of the same icon. Table 10.1 shows the sizes you'll need.

Density	Size (pixels)
mdpi	48 × 48
hdpi	72 × 72
xhdpi	96 × 96
xxhdpi	144 × 144
xxxhdpi	192 × 192

Table 10.1 Sizes of Android launcher images for different screen resolutions

You could do this manually, but it's a lot of work and not really necessary, as you'll usually want an identical icon on all platforms and screen sizes. Luckily there are a plethora of tools and websites that can help by taking a large image and creating scaled-down versions for the image sizes you'll need. These are two of my favorites:

- *MakeAppIcon* (https://makeappicon.com)—On this website, you provide a large image, and they email you a zip file containing all the icons you'll need. It's free to use, but they also have Mac and Windows apps you can buy to do conversions on the desktop. They recommend providing an image at 1536 × 1536 pixels, and they support Photoshop, JPEG, and PNG files. In the Images\Countr\AppIcons folder in the source code that accompanies this book, you'll find an image called CountrIconSource.png. Upload this image (or create your own image in your favorite drawing tool) to https://makeappicon.com. You'll need to give them your email address, and they do tick a "Subscribe to our newsletter" checkbox by default, so uncheck this if you don't want their newsletter. After a couple of minutes, you'll receive an email with a zip file of icons.

- *Sketch* (https://sketchapp.com—Mac only)—Sketch is an amazing vector-based drawing tool, and it's one of the best tools on a Mac for designing your app and any app assets, like icons. There are a number of great templates available that do the same thing as MakeAppIcon—you give it one image, and it creates all the different sizes for you. You can find a lot of these templates on www.sketchappsources.com. The one I use is App Icon Template: http://mng .bz/NOxV.

Create some icons using whatever method you prefer, or you can find some in the Images\Countr\AppIcons folder in the source code that accompanies this book.

UPDATING THE APP ICONS

Android icons can be treated like any Android image resource and be added to the `drawable` resource folders, but this isn't the recommended way. It's better to put them in the `mipmap` resource folders—these are special `drawable` folders that follow the same naming convention for different screen densities (for example, `mipmap-hdpi`, `mipmap-xhdpi`, and so on) but they're only used for launcher images. Some devices have launchers that display larger images than normal for their screen density, so they need access to different image densities. By default, all launcher images are called ic_launcher.png (Google seems to like to start all icon names with `ic_` to distinguish icons used for the launcher, toolbars, and menus from other image assets).

To update the launcher images, copy yours (either created or downloaded) into the relevant `mipmap` folders. If you used MakeAppIcon, the Sketch template mentioned previously, or the icons from the book's source code, they'll already be in the correctly named `mipmap` folders, so just copy them over. Once they're there, rebuild the app and redeploy it to see the new icon. You may need to delete it from your emulator to see the change.

The app icon is set inside the Android manifest file, so if you want to change it to a different icon filename, you can do that there (figure 10.7).

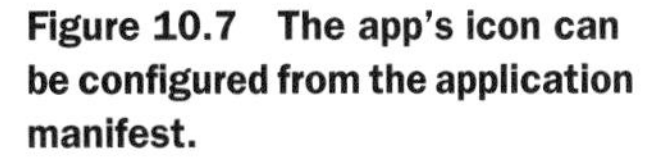

Figure 10.7 The app's icon can be configured from the application manifest.

10.3.2 Launch screens

You've fixed your icon, so now let's fix up the launch screen. Again I'll focus on Countr here, but you can follow the same steps to update SquareRt. Launch screens are also referred to as *splash screens* (a term that MvvmCross seems to prefer and that's more popular with desktop apps), but *launch screen* seems to be the term preferred by Google and Apple.

Out of the box, there's nothing in Android to create explicit launch screens. In fact, Google has been against launch screens in the past, calling them a UX anti-pattern, but now they're a part of the material design spec. The standard pattern for them is to have the initial activity act as a launch screen, and this launch screen activity should then load the main app activity.

ANDROID APPLICATION LIFECYCLE AND THE MAIN LAUNCHER ACTIVITY

All Android apps have a main application class derived from `Android.App.Application` that defines the application name, icon, and theme, and that on startup will launch your main launcher activity. You don't need to have the application class explicitly defined in your project—if no application class is found when your app is compiled, one will be created for you automatically using the values defined in the application manifest.

When this application class starts, it will look for an activity with the `MainLauncher` property set to `true`, construct it, show it, and then start the activity lifecycle. For MvvmCross apps, the main launcher is an activity derived from `MvxSplashScreen-Activity`, and there's one called `SplashScreen` in the root of Android projects. If you look at the source for this activity, you'll see that its constructor calls the base class constructor, passing a layout resource ID:

```
public SplashScreen() : base(Resource.Layout.SplashScreen)
```

If you look at the SplashScreen.axml layout file, you'll see that it contains only a single text view with the text "Loading…" and nothing else. If you run your app and watch it load, you'll see more on the launch screen—it will start with a black screen with `Mvvm-Cross` written across it in white letters, and then a few seconds later the text "Loading…" will appear at the top left (figure 10.8).

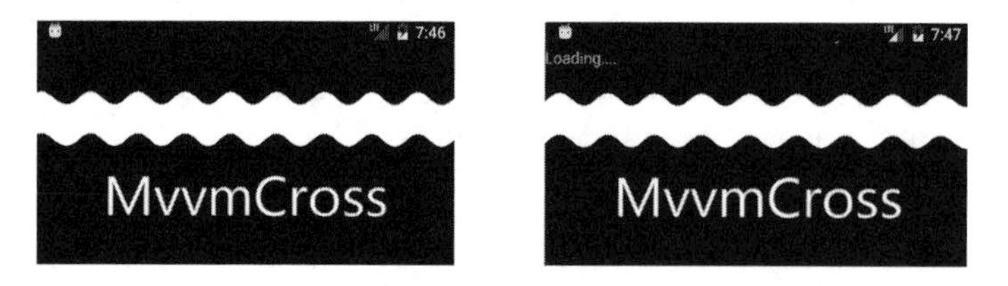

Figure 10.8 The launch screen shows a black screen with white text for a few seconds (left) before showing the "Loading..." text (right).

The black screen with the `MvvmCross` text doesn't come from the layout resource; instead it comes from the activity's style. All Android UI components, be they activities or widgets, can be styled, and a style defines how the widget or activity looks on-screen, including colors, fonts, layouts, and even what's shown as the background.

When the Android application starts up, it launches the main launcher activity, showing it on-screen. As soon as the activity is shown, it's rendered using its style, and then the activity lifecycle kicks off, calling the `OnCreate` method (figure 10.9). In this method, MvvmCross sets up everything it needs to run the app—it initializes all its internals, loads everything into the IoC container, and works out the views for the view models. Once everything is loaded, it loads the layout resource and updates the UI to show the `Loading...` message.

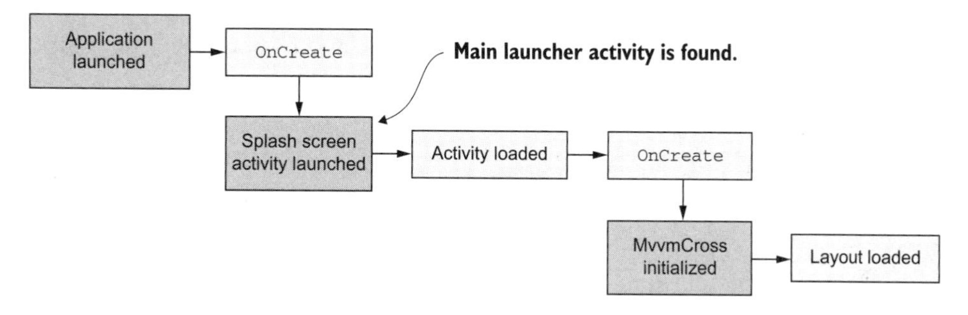

Figure 10.9 When your app starts up, it loads the splash screen activity marked as the main launcher, and this initializes MvvmCross before loading a layout.

If you want to personalize the launch screen for your app, you'll need to change the splash screen activity's style.

STYLES

Styles are defined in XML resources in the values folder. Usually styles are defined in a file called styles.xml, but they can be defined in any XML file in that folder. Each style is an XML `style` node with a `name` attribute that defines the name of the style. Styles can also have parents, defined using the `parent` attribute, and they'll inherit all the style settings from the parent. (For example, if style A sets a font to bold, and style B uses style A as its parent, anything styled with style B will also have its font set to bold.) This style node then contains one or more `item` elements that define the values in the style.

Widget styles are outside the scope of this book. I'll just be focusing here on application and activity styles. You can read more on styling in the Android "Look and Feel" API guide: http://mng.bz/l1TV.

If you open the SplashScreen.cs file and look at the `Activity` attribute on the class, you'll see the activity's theme set using `Theme="@style/Theme.Splash"`. The term *theme* seems to be used interchangeably with *style*, but a theme is something you set for the whole application in the application manifest or on an activity using the `Theme` property in the `Activity` attribute. Themes can also be used to link styles together. For example, as a part of setting the application theme, you can set individual styles to apply to different types of widgets. All activities have a theme, either set explicitly as in the `SplashScreen` activity, or set on the application in the manifest. If you don't set a theme in the manifest, and you don't set one on your activity, your app will crash when it tries to load the activity.

If you open the SplashStyle.xml file in the values folder, you'll see the Theme.Splash style, shown in the following listing.

Listing 10.20 The style for the splash screen

```
<style name="Theme.Splash" parent="android:Theme">
   <item name="android:windowBackground">@drawable/splash</item>
   <item name="android:windowNoTitle">true</item>
</style>
```

This style element has the name `Theme.Splash`, and it inherits all the values from the Android-supplied `Theme` style. It defines two elements:

- `windowBackground`—Identifies the drawable to show as the background for the activity when it's loaded
- `windowNoTitle`—Specifies whether the window should be shown without a title bar

When this style is applied to the splash screen activity, it sets the value of these two properties on the activity as it's loaded and before it's shown on screen. This means that the activity is fully styled before the user sees it, showing `@drawable/splash` as the activity's background as soon as it's loaded. This is shown while the activity is created, and then the layout resource is loaded over the top. If you look at the Splash.png file in the drawable folder, you'll see a black background with the `MvvmCross` text on it—this is what you'll see when you launch the app, and it's shown in figure 10.10.

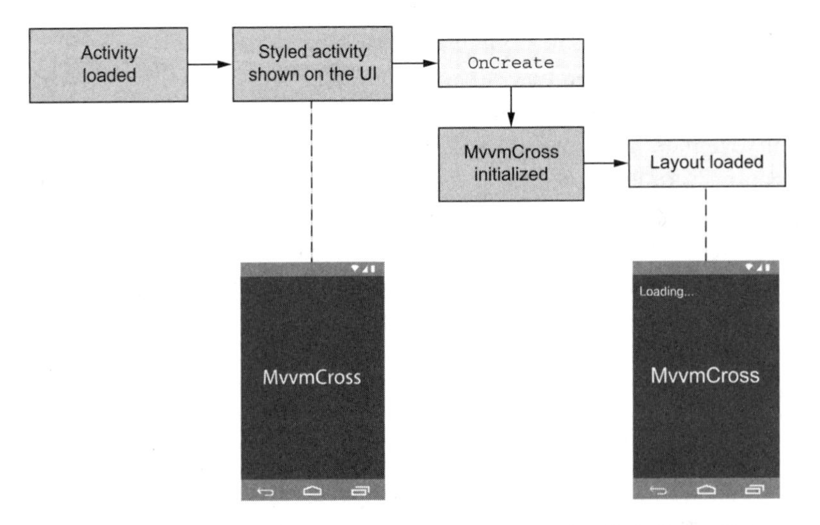

Figure 10.10 When activities are shown, they're drawn using their theme. This happens before the activity lifecycle is run, `OnCreate` is called, and layouts are loaded.

STYLES FOR ANDROID V21 AND ABOVE In the resources folder, you'll see two "values" folders: values and values-v21. The values folder contains values that apply to all devices and OS versions, whereas the values-v21 folder contains styles for devices running API level 21 and higher, essentially allowing you to style material design properties that aren't available on older devices. You can read more about this in the Android "Look and Feel" API guide: http://mng.bz/X0vg.

If you want to update the launch screen, the simplest thing to do would be to change the image. This would work, but it wouldn't be ideal as these images are made to fit on whatever device your app runs on, so depending on the aspect ratio or orientation, the image could be distorted. Instead you can use an XML drawable.

XML DRAWABLES

On Android, drawables can be bitmap-based image files, such as PNG files, or they can be XML files that have drawing instructions (similar to vector-based image formats, such as SVG). Having a bitmap for a launch screen is no good, because it doesn't scale correctly for different aspect ratios. Although you can provide different bitmaps for different screen densities, multiple devices with the same density might have different aspect ratios, leading to the bitmap being stretched differently. Using an XML drawable allows you to define a background once that scales correctly for any aspect ratio or orientation.

We'll only look at a simple drawable here that allows us to show a bitmap without scaling, but there's a lot you can do with XML drawables. You can read more on them in the Android "Resource Types" API guide: http://mng.bz/qQMU.

Let's start by creating a new XML file called splashscreen.xml in the drawable folder. You can also delete the Splash.png image file, as we won't be using it anymore. For our new splash screen, we'll have an image in the center with a colored background, so that it looks just like the app icon (figure 10.11).

The first step is to define the colored background. Listing 10.21 shows the code to add to the splashscreen.xml file to do this.

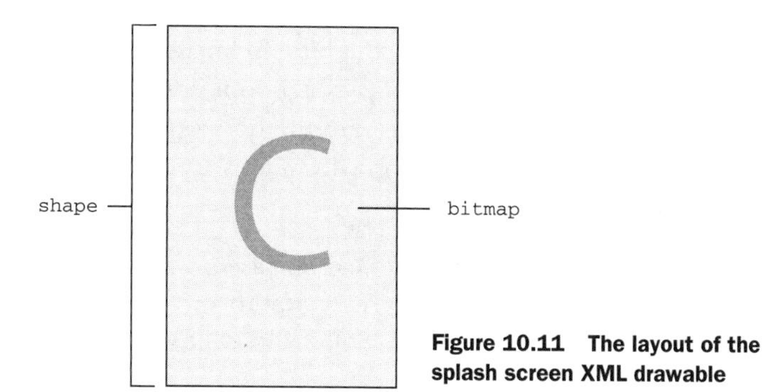

Figure 10.11 The layout of the splash screen XML drawable

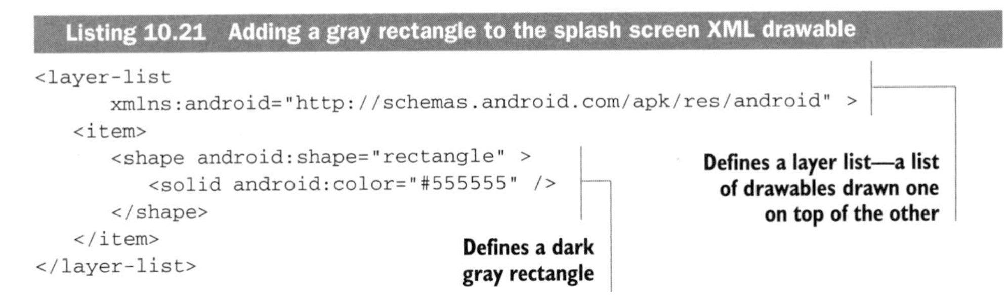
Defines a layer list—a list of drawables drawn one on top of the other
Defines a dark gray rectangle

Listing 10.21 Adding a gray rectangle to the splash screen XML drawable

```
<layer-list
      xmlns:android="http://schemas.android.com/apk/res/android" >
   <item>
      <shape android:shape="rectangle" >
         <solid android:color="#555555" />
      </shape>
   </item>
</layer-list>
```

For this drawable we need a background and an image, so we can use a *layer list*—this is a drawable element that contains other elements, and it draws them one on top of the other with the first item in the list drawn first, the second on top of that, and so on. Our layer list only has a single item, defined by the `item` node and containing a `shape`. Shapes can be `rectangle`, `oval`, `line`, or `ring`, and by default they scale to fill the available space—so our rectangle will scale to fill the entire screen. This shape is filled with a solid color of `#555555`, a nice dark gray.

The next thing to add is a bitmap in the middle. You can find the bitmap to use in the images in the book's source code. Copy the launch_image.png file from the various Android drawable folders in the source code into the same drawable folders in your app. Once the image is there, add it as a bitmap item to the bottom of the layer list in the XML drawable.

Listing 10.22 Adding a bitmap to the splash screen XML drawable

```
<layer-list
      xmlns:android="http://schemas.android.com/apk/res/android" >
   ...
   <item>
      <bitmap
         android:gravity="center"
         android:src="@drawable/launch_image" />
   </item>
</layer-list>
```

Adds a bitmap item to show a bitmap in the drawable

This adds a new item to the layer list containing the bitmap image you've just copied. When adding bitmaps, you can specify the `gravity`—the layout positioning. A `gravity` of `center` maintains the image size and positions it in the horizontal and vertical center. You can use any of the standard Android gravity values to position the bitmap wherever you want, or resize it to fill the screen.

YOU CAN'T HAVE TEXT IN AN XML DRAWABLE One surprising omission from XML drawables is text—there's no way to render any form of text in your drawable. The only way to include text is to create a bitmap containing the text you want, and then use that.

The splash screen is now complete, so you need to tell your app to use it. Open the SplashStyle.xml file from the values folder, and update the window background to be the new drawable, as shown in the following listing.

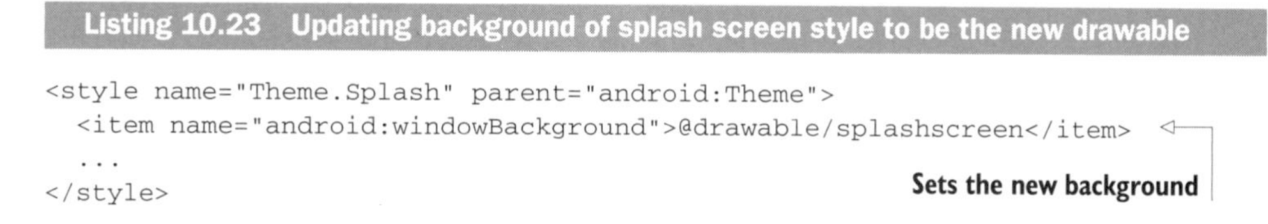

Listing 10.23 Updating background of splash screen style to be the new drawable

```
<style name="Theme.Splash" parent="android:Theme">
  <item name="android:windowBackground">@drawable/splashscreen</item>   <-- Sets the new background
  ...
</style>
```

If you build and run the app, you'll now see the nice new splash screen.

STYLING OUR APP

There is a huge array of things you can style in your apps—probably enough to warrant a separate book—but one simple one that's worth looking at is colors. The built-in Android styles have a set of named colors that are used for different parts of the UI, and it's really easy to override these to make your app look totally different. Figure 10.12 shows some of these named colors and how they're used.

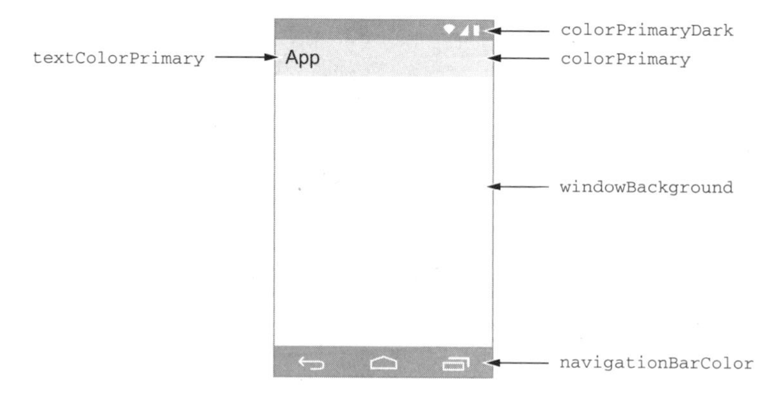

Figure 10.12 Some of the standard named colors used in an Android app

The colors for an app are defined as named color resources in a resource file called colors.xml that lives in the values folder, and these are applied to the named colors used in the styles.xml file. To change the color of your app, all you need to do is change these values depending on your preferred app color scheme. Google has a material design color tool to help you define your app color schemes: https://material.io/color/.

Let's change the default blue toolbar of the app to a much nicer orange color. Make the following changes to the colors.xml file.

Listing 10.24 Updating some of the app colors

```
...
<color name="primary">#FF9800</color>
<color name="primaryDark">#F57C00</color>
...
```

Updates the primary and primaryDark colors

Make this change, and build and run the app—you'll see that the app now has a nice orange toolbar.

We're now done with our Android apps. Over the last chapter and this one, you've built two apps, one with a simple UI and another with a more complicated multiscreen UI with a recycler view. You've set up app icons and a launch screen. In the next two chapters we'll do the same thing, but on iOS.

> **Be wary of poor Android performance**
>
> Android apps can suffer badly from poor performance, and this isn't helped by the "race to the bottom" for some Android device manufacturers focused on making the cheapest devices possible by using older and slower hardware. When building complicated Android apps, it's worth trying to reduce the number of views in your layout, as well as avoiding overdraw—the drawing of the same pixel multiple times with the same color. For example, if your style has a red background, and you put a layout with a red background on top, the OS has to draw each red pixel twice—once for the background and again for the layout. If your layout doesn't have a background set, it will still appear red (due to the red background underneath), but only one red pixel will be drawn, improving performance.
>
> You can read about improving performance in Android apps in Tomasz Cielecki's "Improving layout performance on Android" blog entry: http://mng.bz/r7MU.

Summary

In this chapter you learned

- Recycler views can be used to show lists of items.
- Menu items can be added to the toolbar.
- App icons come in different resolutions to support different screen densities.
- Activities can be styled, and their background drawable is shown while the activity is loading.

You also learned how to

- Configure a recycler view to bind to an items collection in a view model, and to show these items using a custom layout.
- Add menus and handle when the user taps on them.
- Handle the toolbar Up button.
- Create XML drawables.
- Change app colors.

11 Building simple iOS views

This chapter covers

- iOS storyboard resources
- Laying out controls using auto layout and constraints
- Supporting multiple screen sizes using size classes
- Adding images to support multiple screen sizes using asset catalogs
- Creating view controllers
- The view controller lifecycle

In the last two chapters we built the UIs for SquareRt and Countr on Android. In this chapter and the next, we'll build these view layers on iOS (figure 11.1). We'll start here by looking at how to build an iOS UI and then build the UI for SquareRt. In the next chapter we'll look at Countr, and you'll see some slightly more advanced UI techniques, including using table views to show lists of data, menus, and navigation.

The iOS SDK is different from that of Android, but the basic principles for UIs are the same—a UI layout is defined in an XML file, and there's a class that loads this layout and provides access to the layout's UI components. Where on Android we used `Activity` for the views, on iOS we use `UIViewController` (iOS, like macOS, has MVC built in). Android uses layout XML files, and iOS uses storyboards.

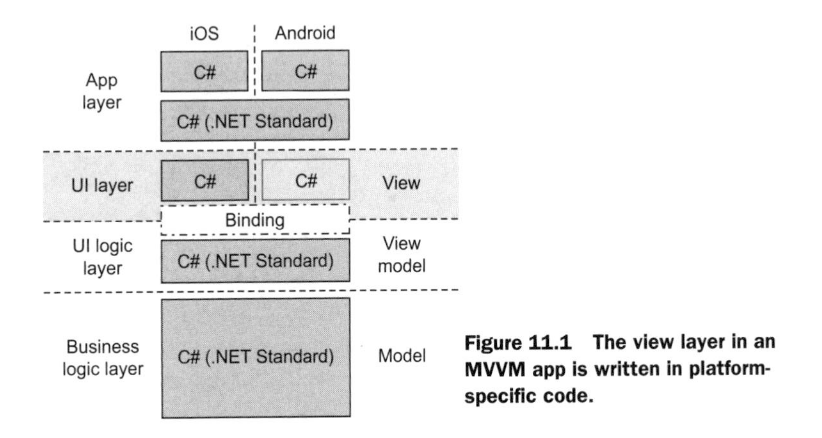

Figure 11.1 The view layer in an MVVM app is written in platform-specific code.

11.1 Building iOS UIs

Let's start by thinking about our SquareRt app, which has a single view. Figure 11.2 shows the UI that we want to build.

As in Android, we have to build two things to make this UI: a layout file called a *storyboard*, and a code-behind view controller class. We'll look at what storyboards are and at the different components that go into a UI, including some examples of controls we can use. Then we'll look at how iOS handles different screen resolutions using auto layout, and we'll wrap up with images. Before we get started building the UI, though, it's worth taking a brief moment to consider design and to look at the iOS human interface guidelines.

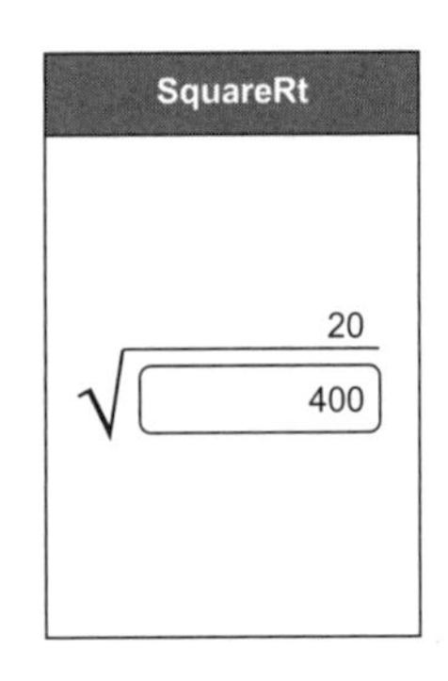

Figure 11.2 The UI for the SquareRt app

11.1.1 iOS human interface guidelines

Apple has put a huge amount of work into, and emphasis on, its human interface guidelines. Not only does Apple strongly encourage developers to follow them, it will even reject an app submission if it breaks some of the rules. For example, if you use standard icons for the wrong actions, your app will be rejected.

These concepts are behind the guidelines:

- *Deference*—The UI should play second fiddle to the content. It should enhance the content and provide an easy way to interact with it, but it should never get in the way of or distract from the content.

  A good example is a weather app, with a full-screen image behind the weather details that can be associated with the current weather. This can enhance the content by conveying the main theme (the current weather) without distracting from the data, as shown in figure 11.3.
- *Clarity*—Your UI should be kept clear and simple. Use negative space (or whitespace) to help your app look calm and clean. By including space around

the content, you can help focus the user's attention on what's important, rather than making them look though a lot of noise to find what they're looking for. *Where's Waldo* might be a fun book, but a confusing UI that forces the user to search for content doesn't make for a good experience. Your content should also be limited to a small amount of data, with easy navigation to more data that the user can use when they're ready. You should also ensure legibility by using the standard system fonts, which are designed to look good at all sizes, and chose your colors carefully to highlight and enhance content.

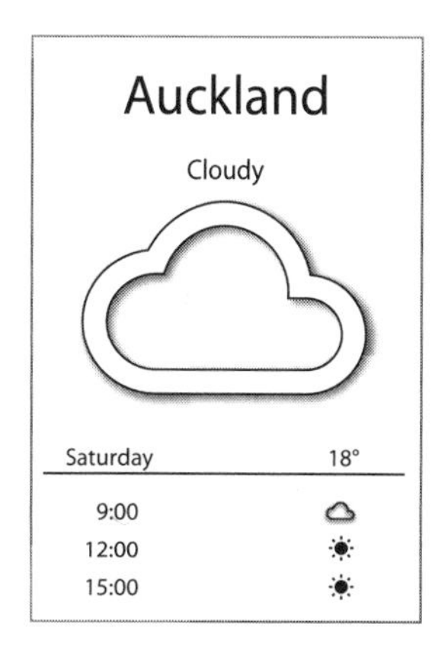

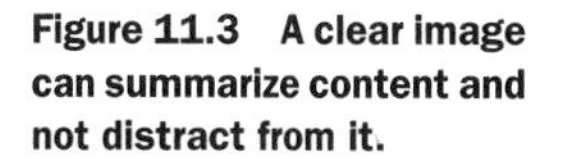

Figure 11.3 A clear image can summarize content and not distract from it.

The weather app in figure 11.3 is a good demonstration of this. It keeps the content minimal and it uses crisp, clear text with good spacing between the content (figure 11.4).

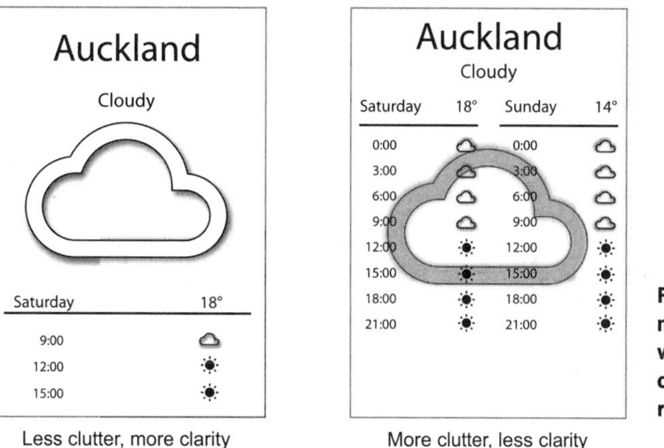

Figure 11.4 Lots of negative space (or whitespace) can enhance clarity by helping to reduce clutter.

- *Depth*—By displaying content in different layers, you can establish a hierarchy of information. The more important information can be on top, to guide the user's focus, and the less important information can be hidden below, keeping it from being a distraction. This can be accomplished by using translucency to make a layer above very obvious (such as the folders on the iOS springboard), or by using a transition that zooms down to more granular data or up to less granular data (such as the iOS Calendar app that zooms in from year to month to day and back out).

  For example, our weather app could show an overview of the weather for each day of the week, and tapping on a day could zoom in to show a more detailed breakdown. This is shown in figure 11.5.

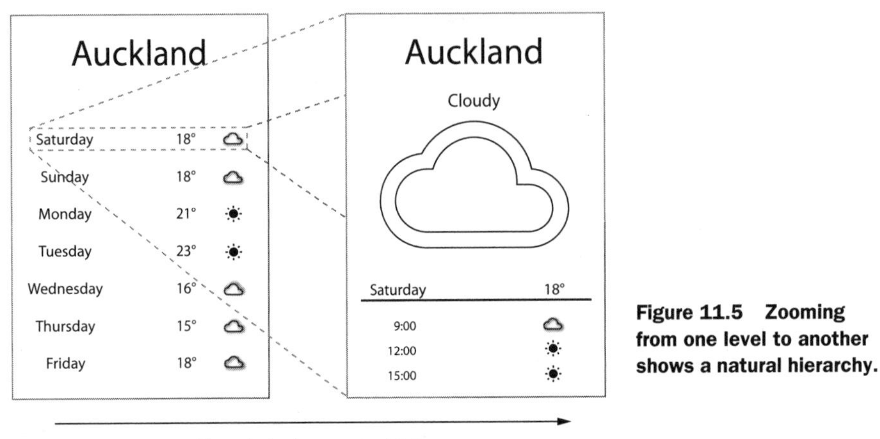

Figure 11.5 Zooming from one level to another shows a natural hierarchy.

By following Apple's human interface guidelines, you can make your app match the experience that an iOS user expects and ensure that once you submit it to the app store, your app won't be rejected for breaching these guidelines.

You can read more on these guidelines on Apple's Developer website: http://mng.bz/GI7e.

11.1.2 Storyboards

Storyboards are XML files that allow you to define the layout of controls for one or more screens in a single file. You can use them to create a whole application in one layout file and visualize the flow from one screen to another to another, all the way through your app. Each screen on the storyboard is backed by a view controller (a class derived from `UIViewController`), and each view controller contains a single view (referred to as the *superview*), which can contain multiple controls. This is shown in figure 11.6.

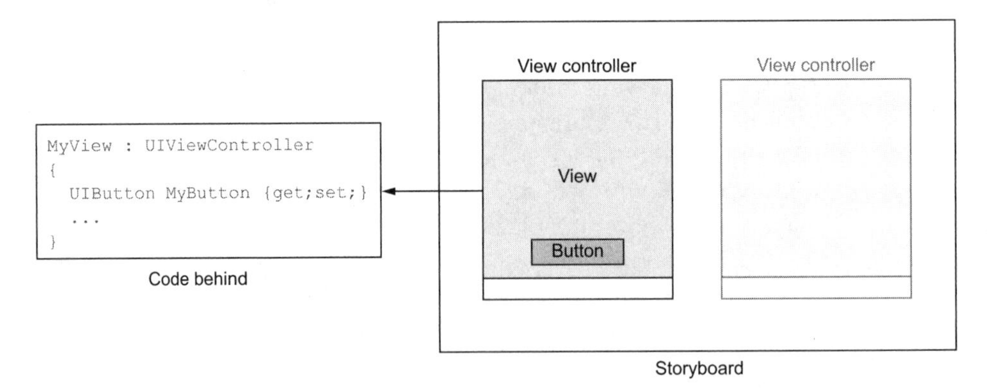

Figure 11.6 Storyboards can contain multiple view controllers, and each view controller has a single view inside it that can contain one or more controls, as well as a backing class.

Storyboards can also define transitions between screens that can be triggered by UI elements, and the Apple term for these is *segues*. For example, you can wire up a button to trigger a segue to another view controller inside the layout file. We won't be using segues here, as these are a pure iOS concept. Instead we'll be using view-model navigation to show different screens.

> **THE IOS SDK HAS SOME ODD-LOOKING CLASS NAME PREFIXES** The SDKs for iOS are built using Objective-C, a nearly 40-year-old language that doesn't have namespaces. This means that to avoid the possibility of name collisions (multiple classes with the same name), class names are prefixed with an identifier to group them, based on their functionality. The iOS SDKs mostly use two-character identifiers, such as `UI` for any class that's used for the UI (a group of classes that are referred to as `UIKit`). The Xamarin wrappers keep these two-character prefixes to make it easier to see which SDK class is being used, but it also puts these classes into namespaces. For example, `UIViewController` is part of `UIKit`, so in the Xamarin wrapper it's `UIKit.UIViewController`.

Although storyboards are XML, they're not really designed to be human-readable, so unlike with Android, we'll be doing everything inside a designer (figure 11.7). Also, because they're complex XML files, there's an ongoing debate about how to best build storyboards—you can create one storyboard that contains all your view controllers for your entire app, or you can create one storyboard per view controller. The

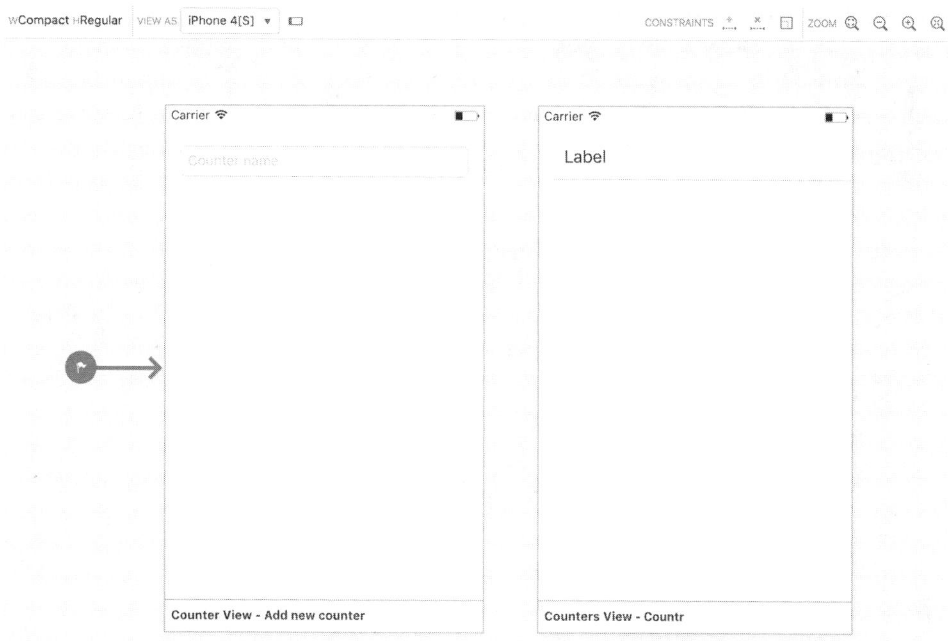

Figure 11.7 The storyboard designer in Visual Studio showing two view controllers

downside to one storyboard per controller is that you can't define and use segues in your layout files (not a problem for us, as we'll be using view-model navigation), but the upside is that it's much easier when you have multiple developers working on the same app. If multiple developers change the storyboard and commit to source, you're asking for a world of pain, and merge conflicts that are hard to fix, as the XML isn't particularly human-readable. Having one storyboard per screen reduces the chance of multiple developers changing the same storyboard.

> **NIBS AND XIBS** Storyboards were added to iOS 5; before that Apple used Nibs and Xibs (layout files that define a single screen, as opposed to storyboards where you can define multiple screens). Nibs were the original layout files and contain binary data. Xibs are XML versions of Nibs, so they're much better for source code control. You can still use Nibs and Xibs if you want, but storyboards are now preferred.

Storyboards in Xamarin apps are identical to the storyboards you'd use in a native Objective-C or Swift iOS app (just like Android layout files). If you want to reuse a storyboard from an existing iOS app, you can just copy it in and it will work.

> **YOU CAN USE XCODE TO EDIT STORYBOARDS** If you're using Visual Studio for Mac, you can also edit storyboards using Xcode if you want. Visual Studio will create a dummy Xcode project with your storyboard, and any other resources it needs (such as images). Any edits you make in Xcode are automatically synchronized back to Visual Studio.

On Android, you design for multiple screen sizes and orientations by putting different layout files in different folders in the Resources folder. iOS, in contrast, doesn't have different storyboards for different screen sizes. Instead you design one screen that will resize and adjust itself to all the different supported screen sizes. When you size and position controls on screen, you don't do it based on pixels; instead you define a set of rules (called *constraints*) against each control to say how it should be drawn. This is very similar to the way relative layouts work on Android. You can, for example, say that a text box should be centered horizontally and vertically in the screen and have a button below it. All the supported devices and orientations are grouped into separate "size classes" based on their sizes. You can then configure the layout rules differently for different size classes.

Once you've defined your layout in the storyboard designer, you can view it as if you were using different devices to see how it would look on all possible screen sizes and orientations. This allows you to design your screens for all available iOS devices. The limited number of iOS device sizes makes it really easy to design an app that looks amazing for all your users, unlike on Android, where there's a huge range of screen sizes.

11.1.3 Controls

Back in chapter 9, we defined a layout for SquareRt on Android, and now we'll create a similar layout on iOS. Unlike Android, iOS doesn't have a relative layout control that we can use to position everything. Instead we have to add all the controls to the view, and then create constraints between them to position everything. Android has a few layout controls for positioning controls, but iOS doesn't really have these layout controls—it has a stack layout that arranges items horizontally or vertically, but that's it. Constraints are the usual way to lay everything out.

iOS has all the standard user interaction controls, such as buttons, labels, and text boxes that you'd want to use for most apps. These controls are sometimes referred to as widgets, as they are for Android. Let's look at a few of them, shown in figure 11.8:

- *Label*—`UIKit.UILabel` is a static label that shows text that can't be edited.
- *Text field*—`UIKit.UITextField` is a text-entry control. When the user taps this control, the keyboard pops up, allowing text to be entered. This control can also be configured to limit the values that can be entered, such as just allowing numbers.
- *Button*—`UIKit.UIButton` is a push button that can be tapped by the user to perform an action.
- *Image view*—`UIKit.UIImageView` is used to show an image, and it can scale the image to fit, if necessary.

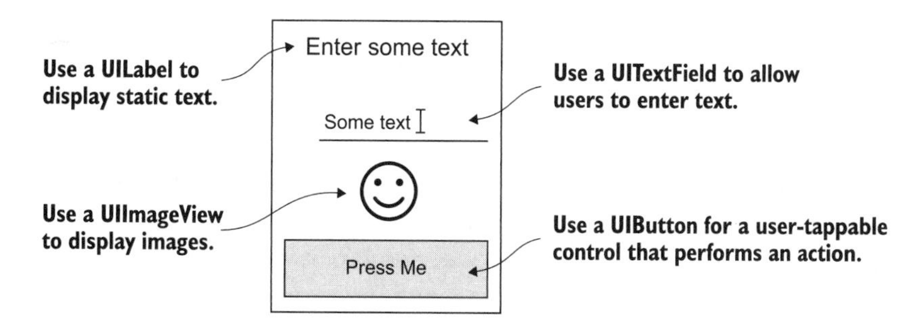
Use a UILabel to display static text.
Enter some text
Use a UITextField to allow users to enter text.
Some text
Use a UIImageView to display images.
Use a UIButton for a user-tappable control that performs an action.
Press Me

Figure 11.8 Some of the controls available to iOS developers

11.1.4 Different screen resolutions

Just like Android, iOS has support for different screen resolutions, but unlike Android, iOS has a small number of device sizes, and Apple was very smart about how it supports different screen resolutions, making things a lot simpler.

When the first iPhone came out 10 years ago, it had a 320 × 480 resolution—the screen was 320 pixels wide by 480 pixels high. Images were drawn with the correct pixel size, so to display an image that took up exactly half the screen, you'd draw an image that was 180 × 240 pixels. When controls were laid out on layout files, this was done using pixel positions and sizes, such as putting a button 100 pixels from the left and 40 from the top, and sizing it to 120 pixels wide by 40 pixels high. This was set inside the layout file or set programmatically in the view controller code.

After the iPhone, Apple released the iPad with a resolution of 768 × 1024 pixels (figure 11.9). This meant that apps needed to be rewritten to handle the new screen size (although you could just ignore iPads, and your app would be scaled up to not quite fit on the screen). To make it easier to write apps, developers could create different layout files for iPhones and iPads, or just handle the different layouts programmatically in their view controllers.

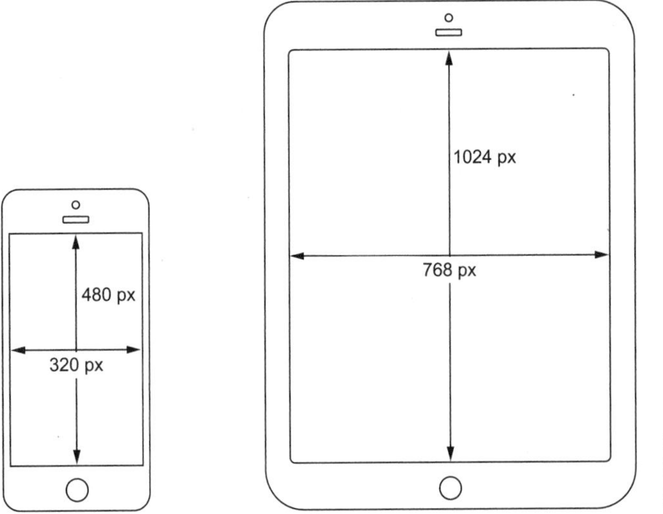

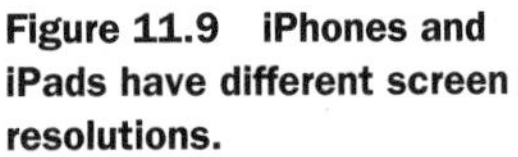
Figure 11.9 iPhones and iPads have different screen resolutions.

The screen size for the iPhone stayed the same until the iPhone 4 came along with its *retina* resolution. Retina resolution was simply double the resolution in each direction, so 640 × 960 pixels (figure 11.10). As an app developer, you wouldn't want your app to be suddenly half the size—you'd want it to look the same on retina devices as it did on non-retina devices, just taking advantage of the higher resolution to make fonts look smoother and images sharper. Apple made everything just work by changing the layout positioning to use *points*—a virtual measurement system (similar to Android's display-independent pixels) that treated each iPhone screen as being 320 points by 480 points (and iPads as 768 points by 1024 points). These points mapped one point to one pixel on the original iPhones, and one point to two pixels on the retina iPhones. This meant everything just worked—your apps would look the same on all devices, retina and non-retina. A button that was 100 pixels wide on the first iPhone would be 100 points wide in the retina iPhone, so 200 pixels, making it the same physical size on screen, just rendered at a higher resolution.

Over time, the array of iPhones and iPads has grown to include retina iPads with double the resolution of the original iPad and larger phones, such as the iPhone 5 with its taller display and the phablet iPhone 7 Plus with its much larger screen. For these larger screens, iOS still uses the idea of points rather than pixels. Table 11.1 shows the physical and logical resolutions of the currently available IOS devices.

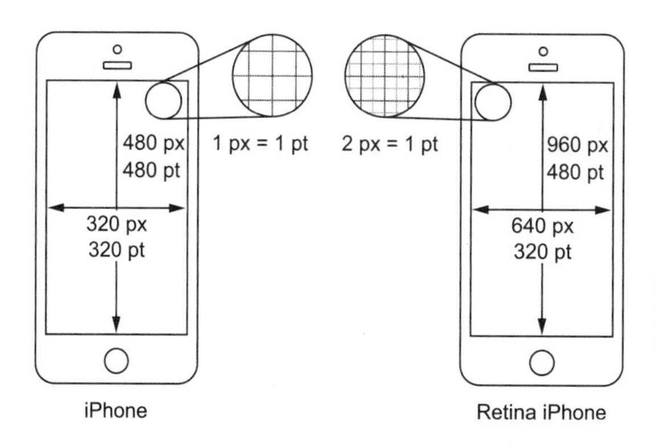

Figure 11.10 Retina devices have double the pixel resolution of non-retina devices.

Table 11.1 Resolutions of current iOS devices

Device	Screen resolution	Points
iPhone Se	640 x 1136	320 x 568
iPhone6s	750 x 1334	375 x 667
iPhone 6s Plus	1080 x 1920	414 x 736
iPhone 7	750 x 1334	375 x 667
iPhone 7 Plus	1080 x 1920	414 x 736
iPad Mini	1356 x 2048	1024 x 768
iPad Air	1356 x 2048	1024 x 768
iPad Pro (9.7")	1356 x 2048	1024 x 768
iPad Pro (12.9")	2048 x 2732	1024 x 1366

With this increase in the number of devices, Apple chose not to define different layouts for all the devices, as this would be complicated and lead to developers not always supporting all devices (especially when new devices are released). Handling all this in code would also be too difficult. Instead, with iOS 6, Apple introduced a new way of laying out controls: auto layout using constraints.

11.1.5 Auto layout with constraints

If you've ever been to a classical concert, ballet, or opera, you may have noticed that the orchestra always seems to be arranged the same way. There's a stage at the front, the conductor stands in the middle with their back to the audience, the first violins are on the conductor's left, and the rest are laid out in a semicircle from left to right—second violins, then violas, then cellos. Woodwinds are behind the violas, percussion at the back (figure 11.11). This layout is consistent, regardless of the size or shape of

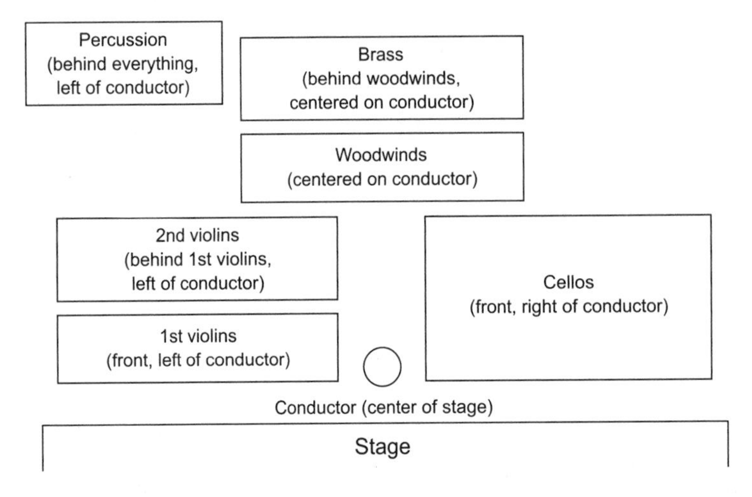

Figure 11.11 Orchestras are laid out relative to the conductor.

the concert hall or theater. Essentially, there are rules that determine how the orchestra should be laid out so that it looks the same in all concert halls.

With auto layout, instead of sizing and positioning controls exactly using points, you create layout rules (called *constraints*) that size or position controls relative to other controls or the parent view. At runtime, the specific positions are calculated by considering all these rules, and the controls are laid out accordingly. This way, your UI looks the same, regardless of the size or shape of your device, just like an orchestra looks the same regardless of the size or shape of the concert hall they're playing in.

Imagine you have an app that needs a button in the center of the screen. Laying this out using point-based positioning in a layout file would be impossible—your button might be centered on an iPhone 6 but be off-center on an iPhone SE or 6 Plus or iPad (figure 11.12). You could do it in code, but you'd need to write the code once for each device size and orientation (remember, some apps work with the device in landscape as well as portrait orientation), and if a new device was released, your code might not work.

With auto layout, you can create a constraint that centers the button horizontally and vertically in its parent view. At runtime, the OS will do all the math for you and put the button in the correct place. Regardless of what device you run it on or the screen's orientation, the button will be in the middle. You can also define off-

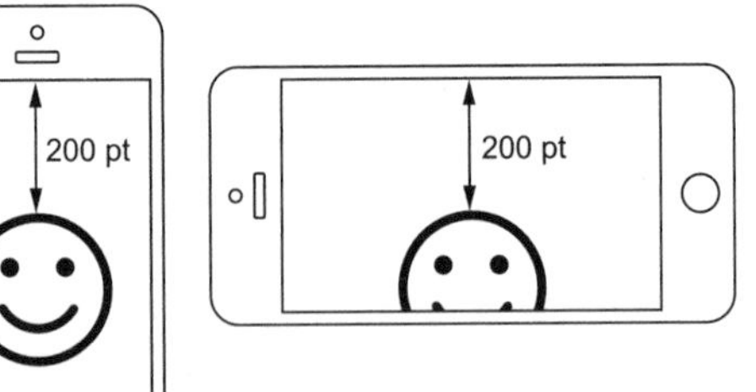

Figure 11.12 Positioning using explicit values leads to bad layouts when changing screen sizes or orientations.

sets using points—for example, you could put a button 50 points below the vertical center.

To lay out a UI, you have to provide enough constraints that the layout engine can work out where to put everything. Too few constraints and the layout can't be calculated, too many and there won't be a single layout that satisfies them all.

ANATOMY OF A CONSTRAINT

A constraint is a relationship between the sizes or positions of two components of the view, such as controls or the parent view. Constraints can be used to define the top, bottom, leading, or trailing edge positions, the position of the horizontal or vertical centers, and the height and width (figure 11.13).

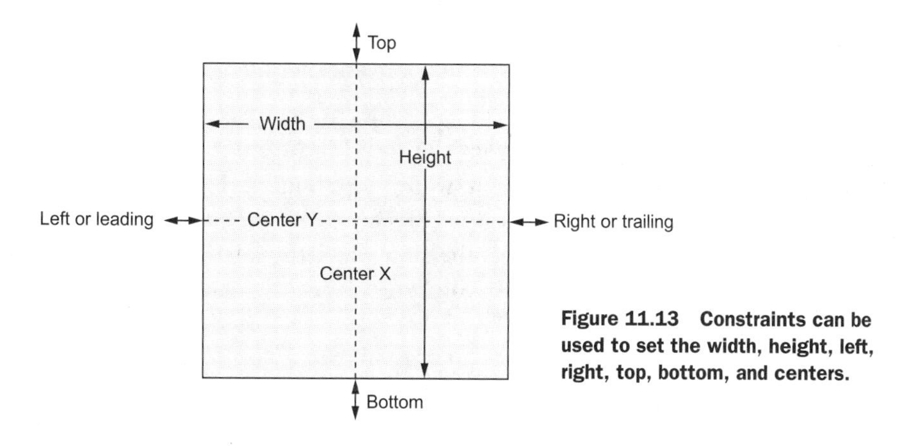

Figure 11.13 Constraints can be used to set the width, height, left, right, top, bottom, and centers.

> **LEADING AND TRAILING EDGES** Rather than use "left" and "right," iOS uses "leading" and "trailing" edges to support both left-to-right and right-to-left languages. If the device is set up for a left-to-right language such as English or Spanish, the leading edge is the left side and the trailing edge is the right. For right-to-left languages such as Arabic or Hebrew, the leading edge is the right and the trailing edge is the left.

Constraints are described as equations showing the relationship between two values, and iOS does a whole lot of algebra to satisfy all the equations. Let's look at a simple example of positioning a button 20 points below a label, as shown in figure 11.14. The equation for this is shown in figure 11.15.

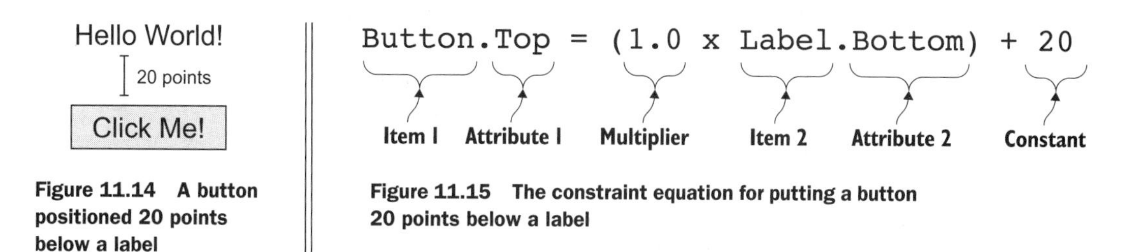

Figure 11.14 A button positioned 20 points below a label

Figure 11.15 The constraint equation for putting a button 20 points below a label

COORDINATES ARE BASED ON THE TOP LEFT Like most UI systems, the top-left coordinate is 0,0, with horizontal values increasing as you move right and vertical values increasing as you move down. A label positioned at 0,100 would be above a button positioned at 0,120.

This constraint tells the iOS auto layout engine that the top of the button should be set to the value of the bottom of the label multiplied by 1, plus 20. This means that if the bottom of the label was 120 points from the top of the screen, the top of the button would be (1 x 120) + 20 = 140 points from the top. This constraint sets the top of the button based on the label, but it could also be defined the other way around, setting the bottom of the label as the top of the button minus 20. Either way will work just as well.

Each constraint describes the relationship between at least one attribute on a control or superview and either an attribute on another item, a constant value, or a combination of the two:

- *Items*—These are controls or views in your layout.
- *Attributes*—These are the height, width, top, bottom, left, right, horizontal center, or vertical center of the control or view. Views have margins that default to 8 points, so if one of the items is the superview, the attributes can use these margins if you want. For example, you can constrain to the leading margin rather than the leading edge.

  The parent view in a view controller sits at the top of the screen with the status bar overlapping it, so if you want to position something below the status bar so that it's not overlapped, you can use the top layout guide attribute instead of the top. This is only available on the top-level view in a view controller.

  You can apply a multiplier to an attribute, so if you want a button to be twice as wide as a label, you can set the multiplier to be 2.0.
- *Constants*—You can set a constant in points, and this is used as is, or it's added (or subtracted if you use a negative constant) to the attribute value if the constraint has two items. With a single item in the constraint, a top attribute with a constant of 20 sets the top to 20. If there are two items, having a top attribute on the first item with a constant of 20 and a second item with a bottom attribute will put the first item 20 points below the bottom of the second.

Constraints are used to set position and size, but for some controls, such as image views, buttons, and labels, you don't need to set the size yourself. These controls have what's known as an *intrinsic size*, so rather than sizing them yourself, they're automatically sized to their contents—for example, image views will resize themselves to fit the image inside them unless you tell them otherwise. Labels are the same—they have an intrinsic size based on the length of the text inside them.

By using a combination of attributes and constants, you can define pretty much any rule you need.

For auto layout to work successfully, every control must be fully constrained; there must be enough constraints defined to position and size everything. It's all well and good saying that the button should be 20 points below the label, but if there are no constraints to set the position of the label (so the button can be positioned below it) or to set the position of the button (so the label can be positioned above it), the auto layout will fail, causing a crash at runtime.

The easiest way to get a working layout is to start with an anchor point—somewhere on the screen you can anchor one control to—and then to lay out all the rest of your controls based on that one control. For example, in our SquareRt UI we want the square root symbol in the center of the screen, so when we create this view and set the constraints, we'll position this first, and then lay out all other controls based on it.

You don't have to use constraints to lay out your controls—you can use point-based sizes and positions, but if you do, your app won't look right on all devices unless you write a lot of code to lay out your app for all possible screen sizes and orientations. We'll be using constraints for our app, as this is the easiest and recommended way to build UIs.

You can read more about auto layout and constraints in Apple's Auto Layout Guide at http://mng.bz/SVKv.

11.1.6 Image resources and asset catalogs

When Apple introduced the retina iPhone 4, it mapped pixels to points to allow your apps to work without any changes, with one pixel in an image taking up four pixels on a retina screen—two pixels in each direction. This was great for making your app look and work the same, but you could also take advantage of the higher resolution screen by providing higher resolution images that would be rendered with one pixel in the image taking up one pixel on the retina screen. These images have the same names, but the higher resolution version has a suffix of *@2x*. For example, if you had a PNG image called Face.png to display on the screen, you would create two images—one with a pixel resolution of 180 × 240 for non-retina iPhones called Face.png, and one with a resolution of 360 × 480 for retina iPhones called Face@2x.png (figure 11.16).

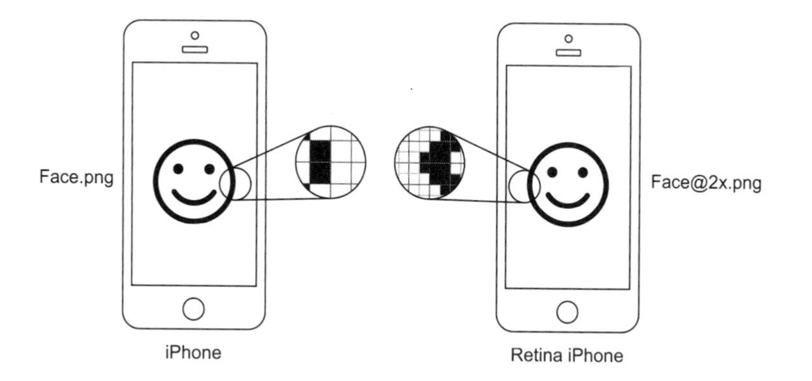

Figure 11.16 @2x images are twice the resolution, but they're the same size on screen.

In your code, you'd refer to the image by the name `Face`, and the OS would automatically load the correct version depending on the screen resolution—both images would take up the same physical size on screen. If the higher resolution image wasn't there, the OS would just use the lower one and render it at the correct point size (figure 11.17).

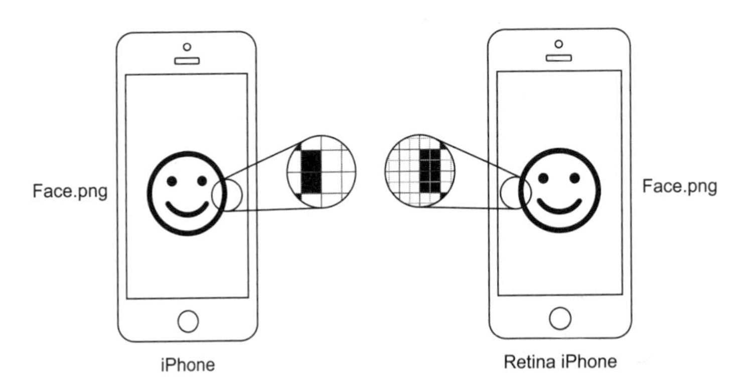

Figure 11.17 If no @2x image is available, images are rendered at twice the pixel size on retina devices, with one image pixel taking up 4 pixels on screen.

With the iPhone 6 Plus, Apple needed to handle an even higher screen resolution, so for this device (as well as the newer iPhone 7 Plus) it introduced @3x images—three times the resolution of non-retina images. Again, you can just use a non-retina version or a @2x image, and the OS will scale it to fit, but by using @3x you get a better-looking image. Currently, you can't buy a non-retina iPhone, and since iOS 9 there hasn't been a version of iOS that runs on non-retina devices, so there's no need to provide the non-retina version of an image in any apps you write unless you want to target older phones (remember, unlike Android, iOS users update, and 95% of users are on iOS 9 or 10). Instead, you should always provide the @2x and @3x versions.

Images can live in one of two places. First, there's a Resources folder where you can put all your images, including different size variations. Unlike Android, the different sized images have different filenames, so they can live in the same folder. This is not the ideal place to keep images, particularly if you have lots of images.

In iOS 7, Apple introduced a better place to put images, called *asset catalogs*, as shown in figure 11.18. Asset catalogs contain image sets—named collections that store images of all supported resolutions. You can provide your @2x and @3x images inside an image set, and even provide separate iPhone and iPad images or images for Apple watch apps. Each named image set is treated as a named image, so if you have an image set called `Face`, you can use it as if it were an image in the Resources folder called `Face`—the right size for the device will be used. Each asset catalog can contain multiple image sets, and you can have multiple asset catalogs, allowing you to organize your images however you want.

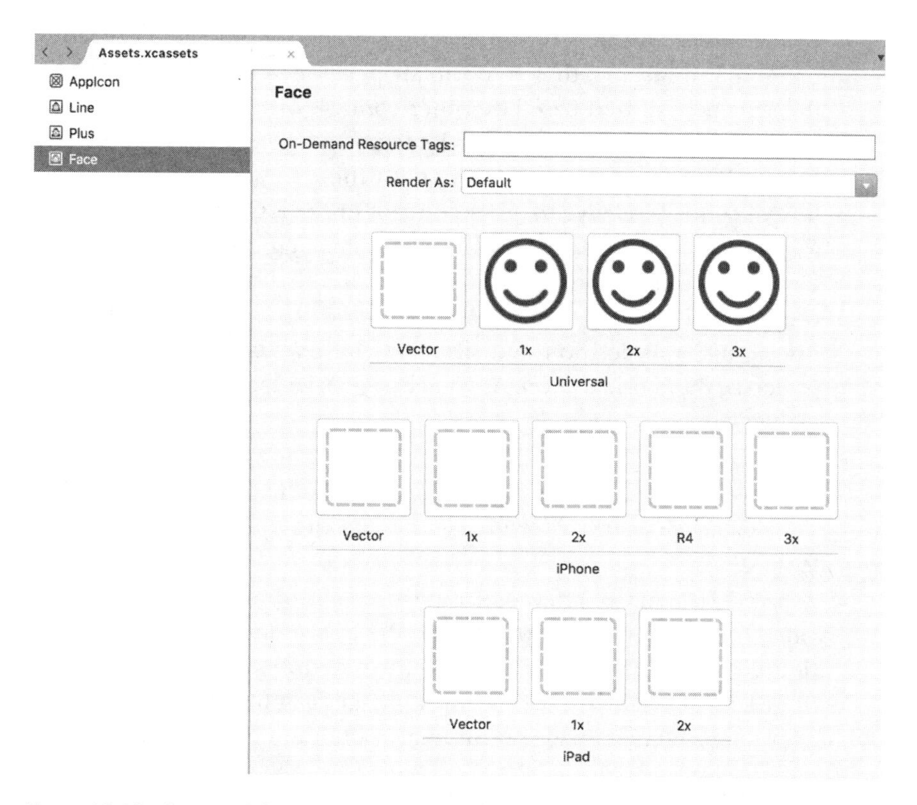

Figure 11.18 Asset catalogs make organizing your images easier. They can include images for all resolutions of iPhones and iPads or images that work on both.

Asset catalogs can also be used for your app icon, allowing you to provide the many versions needed for different devices and for searching (iOS uses a different icon size for search results). These catalogs can also support other file types, including videos, audio files, and binary data. You can even have some resources download on demand, rather than being part of the initial app download. This is useful for large media such as large game maps or videos.

11.1.7 A quick recap

Before we create our first storyboard, let's quickly recap what we've covered:

- *Storyboards*—A storyboard is a way to visually define the UI for one or more screens. On a storyboard you can add one or more view controllers to represent the UI for each screen, and you can drag controls onto them from the toolbox to create their views.
- *Screen resolutions*—Different devices have different screen resolutions, and iOS makes this easier by dealing with screen sizes using points, which are virtual pixels. Points were designed with the aim that controls or images with the same point size will look the same on all devices.

- *Constraints*—Controls on the UI aren't sized and positioned based on precise pixel values. Instead, they're normally positioned relative to other controls on the screen, and sized based on other controls or their intrinsic size (the size of their content, such as the size of the text in a label, given its font type and size). Constraints provide rules for laying out the UI by specifying the size and position of controls relative to other controls or the parent view, such as positioning a control in the center of the screen, or making two controls the same width. You can set offsets to other controls, such as the distance between the bottom of one control and the top of the one below it, using points. When the UI is drawn, iOS will position and size everything automatically depending on the screen size and orientation. As you change orientation, the screen layout will be recalculated.
- *Anchor points*—When working out what constraints you need to design your UI, it's easiest to start with an anchor point—a control that's in a fixed position in the view (such as in the center)—that you can position other controls relative to.
- *Images*—To handle different screen sizes and resolutions, images can be provided in different resolutions so that the images look sharper on higher resolution devices. If different sizes aren't provided, smaller images are scaled up to fit or larger images are scaled down. Images can be defined in an asset catalog, providing a named image set for images of different resolutions.

11.2 Creating the SquareRt storyboard

Let's start by creating a storyboard for the SquareRt app. Open the SquareRt solution and head to the SquareRt.iOS app. Expand the Views folder and delete the FirstView.cs and FirstView.Storyboard files—you won't be using them. Then add a new storyboard called SquareRtView.storyboard (figure 11.19).

This should open the storyboard up in the designer, but if not, double-click it to open it. The storyboard designer works by connecting to a Mac build agent, so if you're using Visual Studio on Windows, you'll need to have an active and connected Mac build agent.

> **IF NOTHING SHOWS UP, TRY BUILDING THE APP** Sometimes nothing will show up in the storyboard designer in Visual Studio. If this happens, try rebuilding your app—this usually fixes it.

On Visual Studio for Mac, when you open the storyboard designer, the toolbox, Properties, and Document Outline pads will open up. If you can't see these, you can open them from the View > Pads menu. On Visual Studio on Windows, the same windows may not be visible, and if not they can be opened from the View menu.

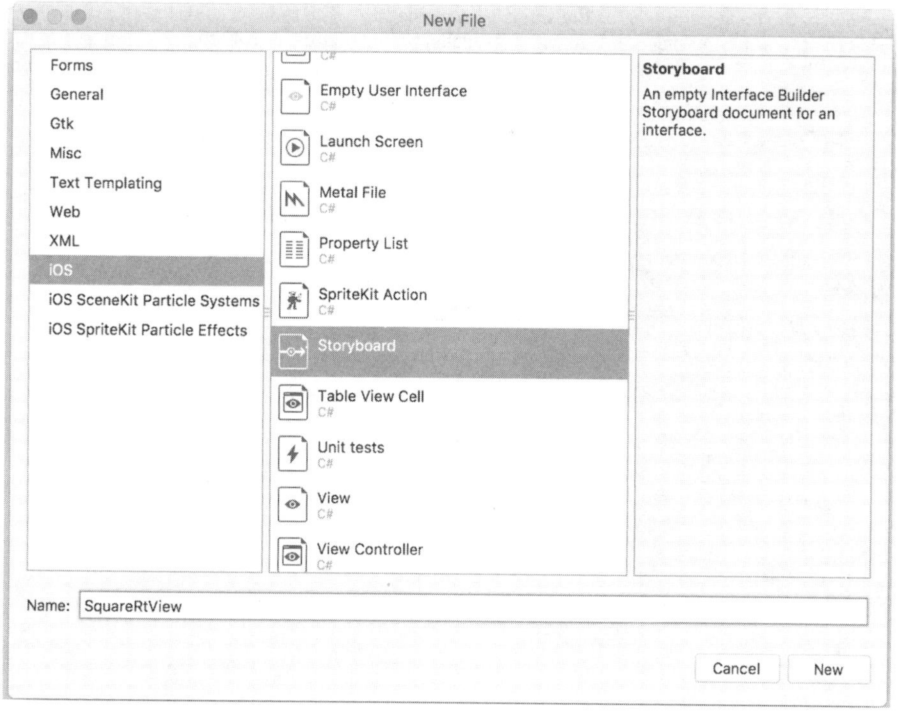

Figure 11.19 Adding a new storyboard

11.2.1 *Adding our first view controller*

When you create a storyboard, it's empty. The first thing you need to add to it is a view controller. View controllers are full screens—they contain a single *view* (an iOS UI layout control that contains other views or controls) that fills the screen, and it's that view that you add your controls to. You must have a view controller to design anything. For example, you can't just add a button to a storyboard.

View controllers come in different types, but they all derive from the `UIViewController` class, which you can use for a basic, empty screen. There are also view controllers for things like tabbed screens or lists. You just need a basic view controller for the SquareRt app because it's a simple single-screen app, so drag a view controller from the toolbox to the designer (figure 11.20).

The view controller you've created isn't an instance of a `UIViewController`; instead, it's just the UI that will be applied to a view controller. Later in this chapter, after we've designed the UI, we'll create the view controller backing class and wire it up to the view controller on the storyboard.

The view controller is shown in the designer as a large white rectangle with a slightly shorter rectangle inside it. The outer rectangle is the view controller, and the inner one is the single view that the view controller contains. If you click the view, it

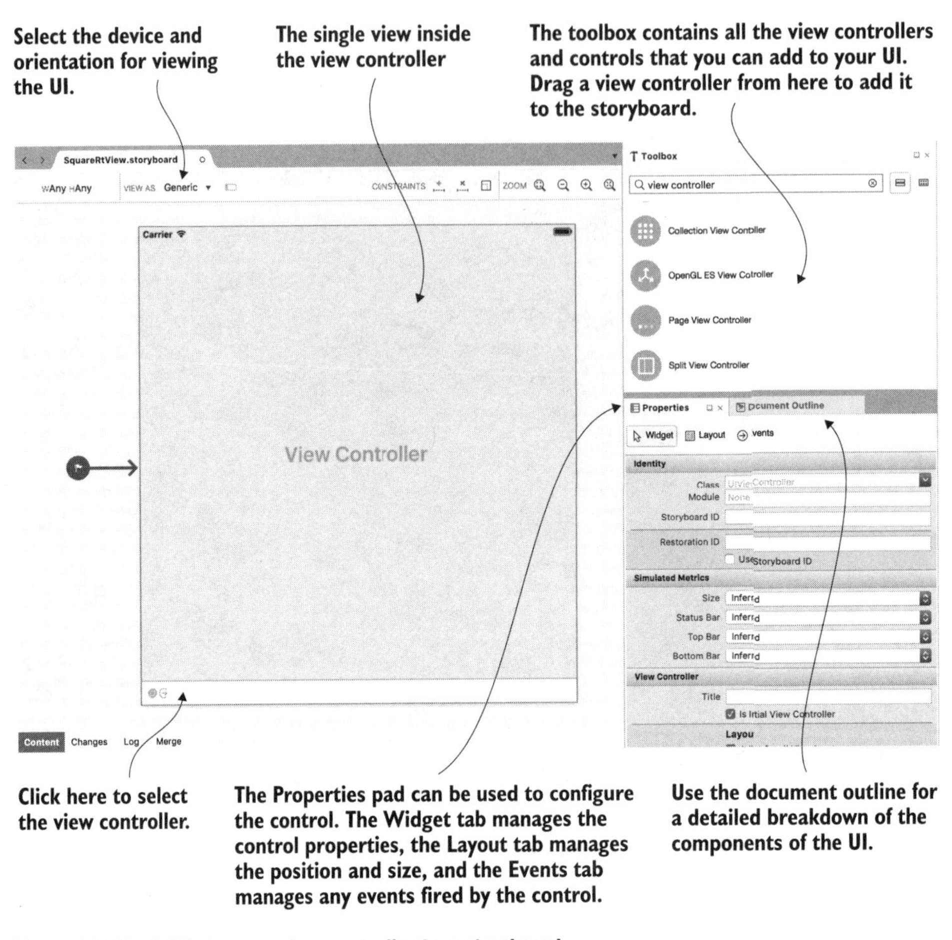
Select the device and orientation for viewing the UI.
The single view inside the view controller
The toolbox contains all the view controllers and controls that you can add to your UI. Drag a view controller from here to add it to the storyboard.
SquareRtView.storyboard
Toolbox
view controller
Collection View Controller
OpenGL ES View Cotroller
Page View Controller
Split View Controller
View Controller
Properties
Document Outline
Widget
Layout
Events
Identity
Class
Module
Storyboard ID
Restoration ID
Simulated Metrics
Size
Status Bar
Top Bar
Bottom Bar
View Controller
Title
Is Initial View Controller
Content
Changes
Log
Merge
Click here to select the view controller.
The Properties pad can be used to configure the control. The Widget tab manages the control properties, the Layout tab manages the position and size, and the Events tab manages any events fired by the control.
Use the document outline for a detailed breakdown of the components of the UI.

Figure 11.20 Adding a new view controller to a storyboard

will be highlighted, showing that it's filling the whole screen. The default view is a simple view with a few properties you can configure, such as the background color. This is good enough for what we need, but you can delete that view and replace with another if you need anything specific, such as a scroll view allowing you to scroll through content that's too large for the screen, or a web view to display full-screen web content.

> **SELECTING A VIEW CONTROLLER** To select a view controller in a storyboard, you have to click the outer rectangle at the bottom of the designer. If you click in the middle, it will select the superview.

The Properties pad for the view, and for any control you add to it, shows three tabs: Widget, Layout, and Events. The Widget tab shows the properties of the control or view, such as its name, coloring, font size, source image, or whatever is relevant to the particular control. The Layout tab defines the layout of the control inside its parent view, and this is where you can edit any constraints you define to position the control.

The Events tab is used to wire up events against the control, such as button clicks. We won't be using the Events tab; after all, we're using MVVM, so things like click events will be bound to commands!

We want the app to have a visible title, so set the Title property on the view controller to be SquareRt.

11.2.2 *Adding an image*

Let's add a first control to the UI. We want to start with an image showing the square root symbol (√) in the center of the screen, and then position the rest of the controls around it.

ADDING THE IMAGE FILE

Before you can create the control, you need to add the image file you'll use. We'll add this to an asset catalog, and by default iOS apps come with an asset catalog called Assets.xcasset you can use. Asset catalogs are shown as a special folder inside your iOS project, just like NuGet packages or project references (figure 11.21).

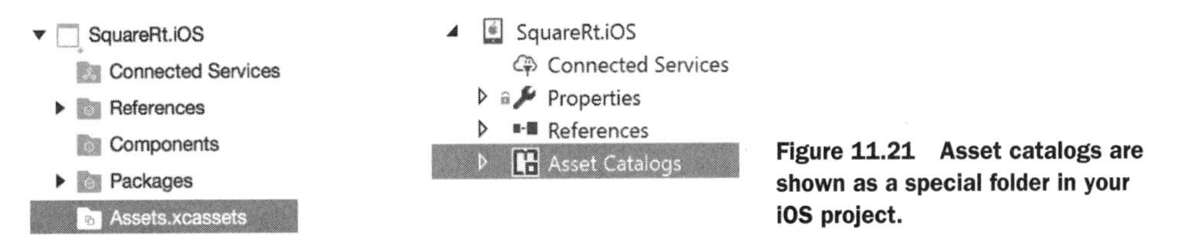

Figure 11.21 Asset catalogs are shown as a special folder in your iOS project.

If you double-click the asset catalog, it will open in an editor that allows you to create new image sets and assign the images. On the left is a list of image sets, and on the right are the contents of the selected image set.

To add the image you want, right-click the list of image sets on the left and select New Image Set (figure 11.22). This will create a new image set called `Image`. You can double-click it to change the name, so do this and rename it to `Line`. On the right you can assign images for the different resolutions (@2x, @3x, and so on) for different devices. We want to set universal images—images that will be used for both iPhone and iPad. Click the box above 2x in the Universal section, and select the Line@2x.png image from the images\SquareRt\iOS folder from the book's source code. Do the same for the 3x image.

> **USING VECTOR IMAGES** If you don't want to create multiple sizes of each image, you can create vector images as PDFs and put them into the Vector box on the image set. These images will be scaled to fit at compile time, automatically generating the relevant sizes for you. It may sound weird to use PDFs, because these are usually associated with documents (you might even be reading this book as a PDF), but they're vector-based files just like other more popular formats, such as SVG, and they can be exported using tools like Sketch and Adobe Illustrator. You can read more about this in Xamarin's "Application Fundamentals" guide, at http://mng.bz/Krwf.

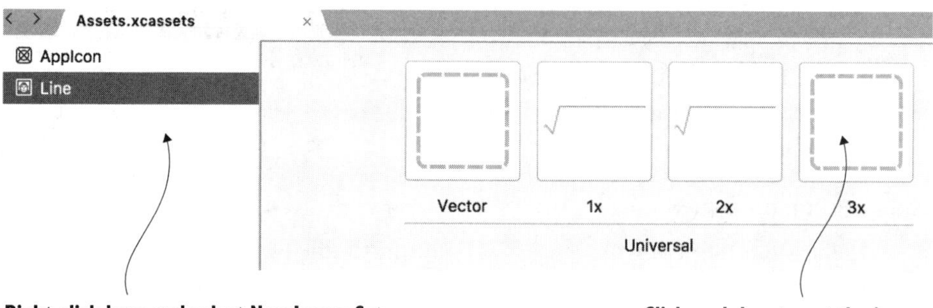
Assets.xcassets
AppIcon
Line
Vector
1x
2x
3x
Universal
Right-click here and select New Image Set to add a new image set.
Click each box to set the image.

Figure 11.22 New image sets are added from the asset catalog, and images can be added to each image set for the different resolutions.

Adding the control

Now that you have your image file, it's time to put it on the screen. Open up the storyboard and drag an image view from the toolbox to the view controller. When you add the image view, it should be highlighted in blue to show that it's selected, and the Properties pad will show its properties.

On the Widget tab of the Properties pad, there's a property called Image with a drop-down list of all the images that have been added to the app. From that list, choose Line, the image you just added, and you should see it rendered inside the image view, albeit sized weirdly. By default, image views are added to storyboards at a fixed size of 240 × 128, and they're positioned wherever you drop them.

Laying out the control

All controls must be fully constrained—they must have enough constraints defined to size and position everything. You could set the size, but that's not necessary here because image views default to the size of the image inside them if no other size rules are defined. For this image view, you just need to set the position.

To create a constraint, you need to set the image view to layout mode and use the constraint drag handles. When you dragged the image view onto the view controller, it was highlighted and circular handles were displayed on each corner and in the middle of each edge. You can use these handles to set a fixed size if you want to, but we want to set constraints. If you click the Constraint editing mode button, it will change to show the constraint handles. You saw these handles in chapter 4; figure 11.23 shows these handles.

We want to position the image in the center of the screen, and to do this we'll need two constraints: one for the horizontal center and one for the vertical.

Drag the square center drag handle over the center of the superview in the view controller, as shown in figure 11.24. You'll see two green dashed lines appear at the horizontal and vertical centers of the superview. First drag to the left-to-right centerline, and you'll see it turn blue. Drop the handle here to set the vertical center constraint. Then do the same using the top-to-bottom line to set the horizontal center constraint.

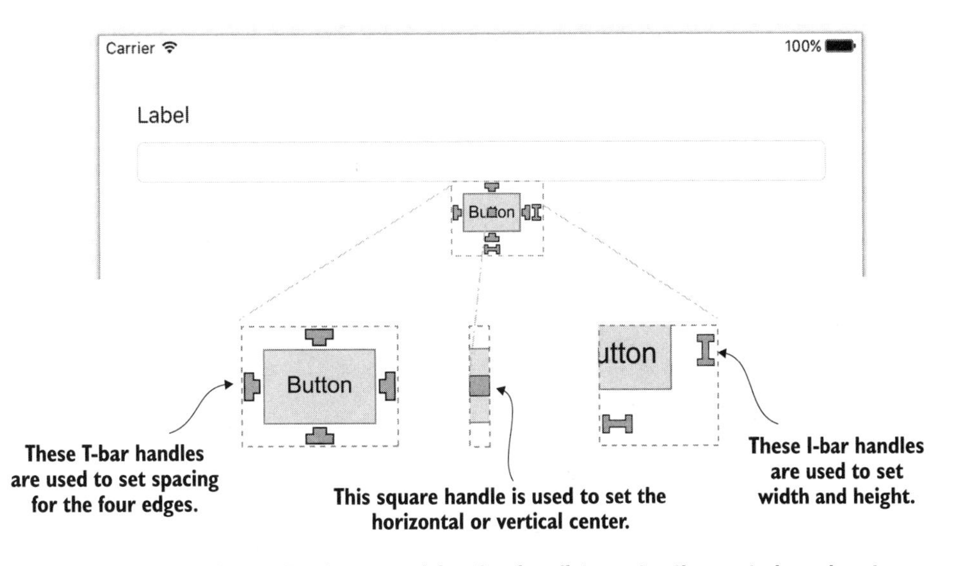

Figure 11.23 Constraint handles for constraining the size, distance to other controls, and center alignment

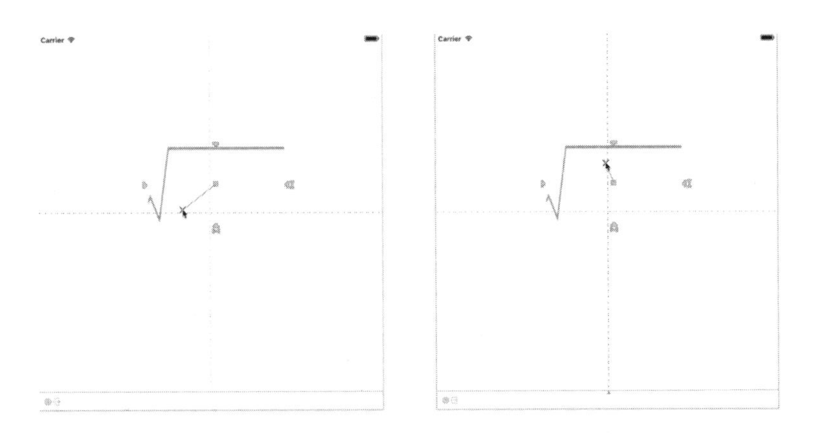

Figure 11.24 To create the center constraints, first drag the center constraint handle and drop it on the horizontal dashed guideline. Then drag and drop it onto the vertical one.

You can look at these constraints in two places. With the image view selected, select the Layout tab in the Properties pad and you'll see these constraints listed. You can also look at the Document Outline pad, where you'll see them as children of the superview, not the image view (figure 11.25).

Constraints are children of the superview because they're rules that are used to lay out everything; they're not specific to one control. For example, if you created a constraint to position a button under a label, this constraint could also be thought of as

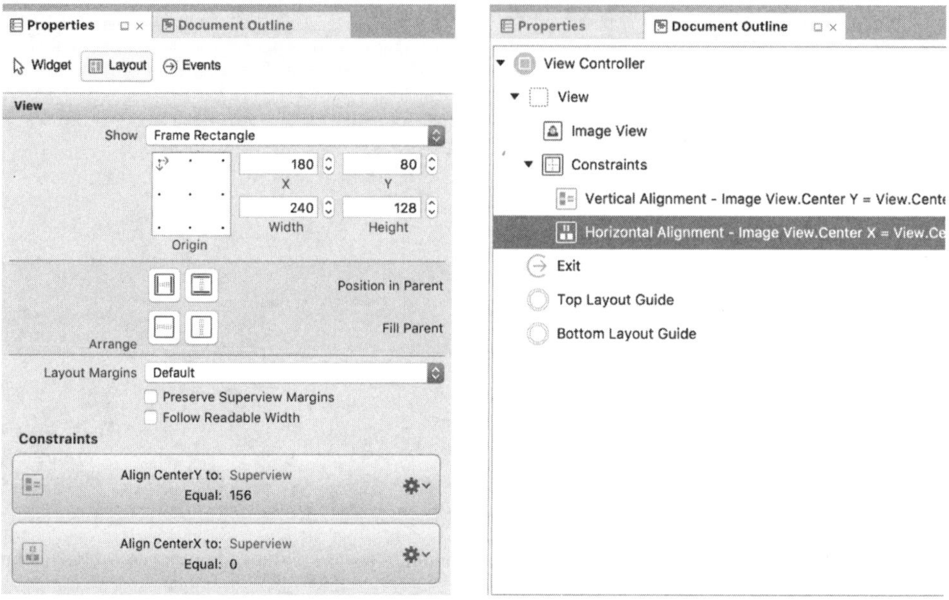

Figure 11.25 Constraints are visible in the Layout tab of the Properties pad, or in the Document Outline pad.

positioning the label on top of the button, so it wouldn't make sense for this constraint to be a child of the button or the label.

When these constraints are created, the designer assumes the position of the image view on-screen is where you want it to sit relative to the center of the superview. In my case, the image view was slightly above and to the left of the center when I dragged the handles, so the constant values set on the constraints put my image 11 points to the left of center and 46 points above. We want the image to be in the center, so we need to set the constants to be 0.

To do this, you need to open the constraints in the Properties pad and edit the values. You can select the constraints in two ways: select the image view and find them in the Layout tab of the Properties pad, click on the cog at the left, and choose the Select and Edit option (figure 11.26). Or find them in the Document Outline pad and double-click them. Either approach will select the constraint in the Properties pad.

Once the constraint is selected in the Properties pad, go to the Widget tab to see its settings: items, attributes, multiplier, and constants. In my case, I had the following:

- ImageView.CenterX = (1.0 x View.CenterX) + 0*
- ImageView.CenterY = (1.0 x View.CenterY) + 156*

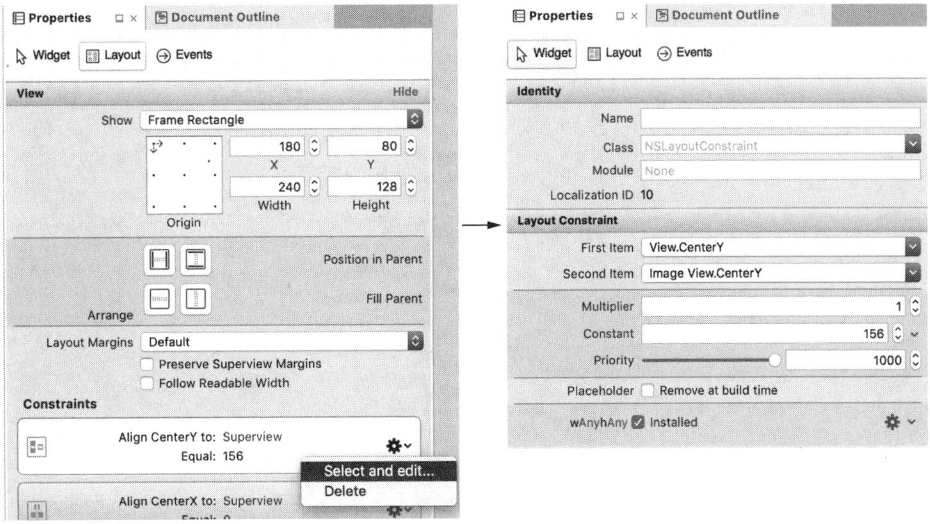

Figure 11.26 Constraints can be selected from the Layout tab of the Properties pad (or by double-clicking the Document Outline pad), and their properties can be edited in the Properties pad.

Your values will probably be different, depending on where on the screen you dropped the image view. To position the image in the dead center of the image view, change the value of the constants to 0, either by typing in a new value or by using the up/down spinners next to the value.

Once the constraints are set, you'll notice that the image view doesn't move to its new position. Instead, you'll see the highlight change from blue to orange when the image view is selected. This indicates that the location and size of the control in the designer isn't where the control will be when you run the app. You'll also see a rectangle with a dashed orange outline. This indicates where the control will be positioned and how large it will be. If you select the image view and click the Update Frames button in the designer toolbar, the image view will move and be resized to reflect the layout at runtime—sizing itself to the size of the image in the view, and positioning itself at the center of the superview (figure 11.27).

Now you have your image in the center. Let's put a text-entry control below it so the user can enter a number that you can calculate the square root from.

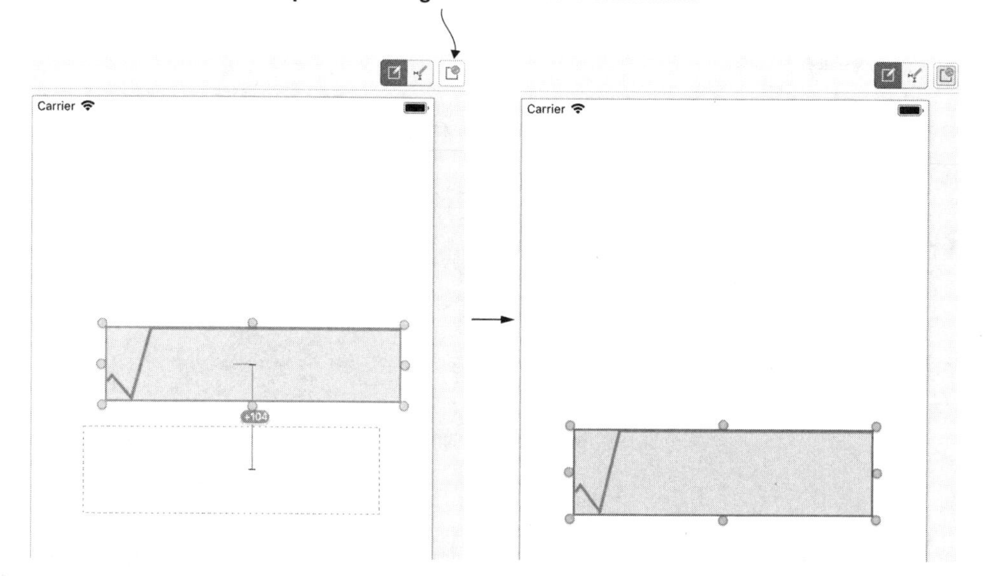
Click here to update the designer to match the constraints.
Carrier
Carrier

Figure 11.27 Once the constraints are set, you can update the designer to show what the UI will look like at runtime.

11.2.3 Adding a text field

The control for allowing a user to enter text is `UITextField`, called Text Field in the toolbox. Drag one of these onto the view controller. The default font is a bit small, and users can enter any values they want into it, so we'll increase the font size and limit it to numbers. Both these changes can be made in the Properties pad. We'll also add some placeholder text to guide the user as to what they should do, and we'll align the text to the right as numbers are usually aligned. By default, text fields also have a border with rounded corners that doesn't resize when the font size is increased, so we'll change this to no border by setting the border style. These changes are shown in figure 11.28.

To change the font, click the T on the right edge of the Font setting and select a size of 40 in the popup. This will set it to use the default system font, but sized at 40 points. As on Android, these font sizes are based on a virtual size so that they look the same on all devices—a font with a size of 40 will look the same on retina and non-retina devices, or on larger devices like iPads or iPhone Pluses.

IOS SUPPORTS DYNAMIC TYPE SIZES BASED ON USER SETTINGS As well as being able to set a fixed size font, you can set a named font size. In the font settings popup under the font drop-down, you'll see some named text styles. These map to different font sizes depending on the user's text preferences, set for the device in the Settings app. If you use these sizes, the fonts in your app will resize to respect the user's settings. You can read more about this in Apple's Human Interface Guidelines, at http://mng.bz/6M4B.

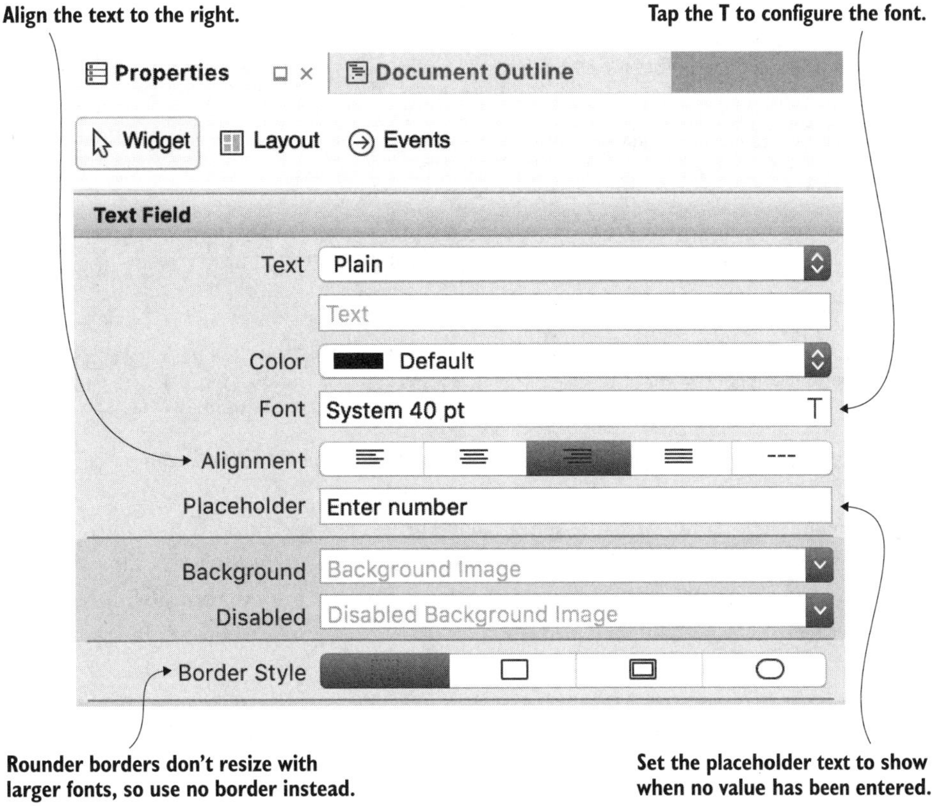

Figure 11.28 Setting the properties for the text field from the Properties pad

To limit the user to only being able to enter numbers, set the Keyboard Type property to Decimal Pad. To set the placeholder text, update the Placeholder property value to "Enter number". To set the alignment, click the right-align button in the Alignment section. To remove the border, click the first button for the Border Style property—the one with the picture of a dashed-line border. The text will also default to "Text," so clear the Text property.

Next up are the constraints. As on Android, you need to position this text field relative to the image. You need to align the right edges, inset the left edge of the text field from the left edge of the image view, and align the bottom of the text field with the bottom of the image (figure 11.29). We'll be setting the width based on the left and right constraints, but like image views, text fields have intrinsic sizing so you don't need to set the height—it will be set automatically from the font size.

To set the bottom constraint, select the text field, click the Constraint editing mode button, and then drag the bottom T-bar handle (it will be an upside-down T). You'll see dashed horizontal green lines showing what you can constrain the bottom edge to, including the edges of the superview and the top, middle, and bottom of the

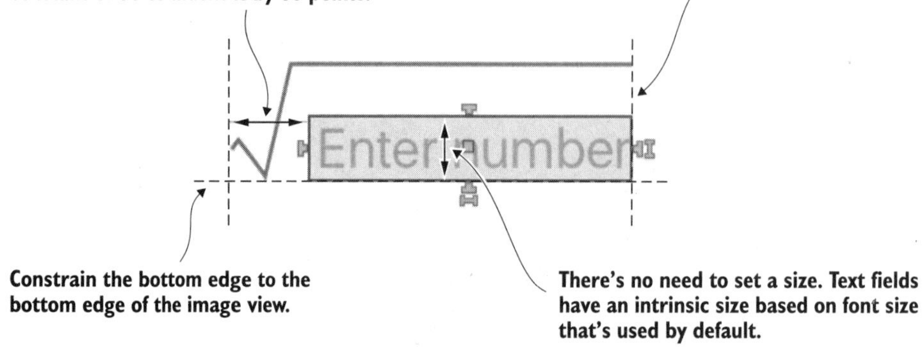
Constrain the leading (left-hand) edge to the leading edge of the image view. Use a constant of 60 to indent it by 60 points.
Constrain the trailing (right-hand) edge to the trailing edge of the image view.
Enter number
Constrain the bottom edge to the bottom edge of the image view.
There's no need to set a size. Text fields have an intrinsic size based on font size that's used by default.

Figure 11.29 The constraints to position the text field, relative to the image

image view (figure 11.30). Drag the handle over the dashed line at the bottom of the image view, which will turn blue, and drop it. Just like when you placed the image view, the constraint that's created will assume that the current position of the text field is where you want it, so it will set a constant that you'll need to change to 0.

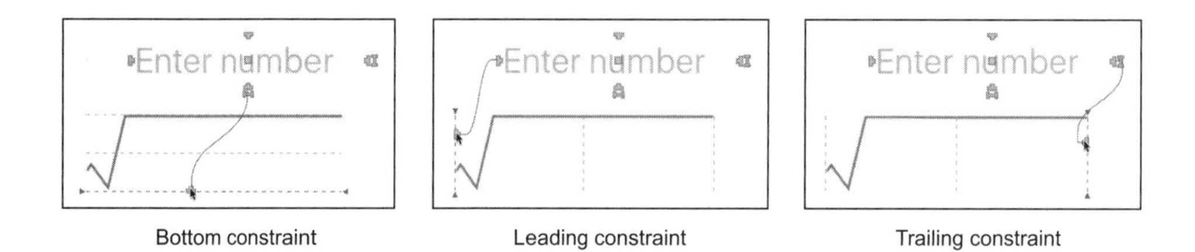
Enter number
Enter number
Enter number
Bottom constraint
Leading constraint
Trailing constraint

Figure 11.30 Set the constraints by dragging the T-bar handles to the dashed lines displaying the edges of the image view.

To set the left and right constraints, do the same with the T-bar handles on the left and right sides, dragging them over the green dashed lines on the left and right sides of the image view. For the right side, set the constant to 0, and on the left set the constant to 60. Once you're done, click the Update Frames button to position the text field.

This will provide enough constraints to position the text field relative to the image view. If you select the text field and look at the Layout tab in the Property pad, you'll see the three constraints (shown in figure 11.31). You can also look at the layout of the image view and see five constraints—the two to position the image view, and the three that position the text field relative to the image view.

That's two out of three controls done. Now it's time to position the result.

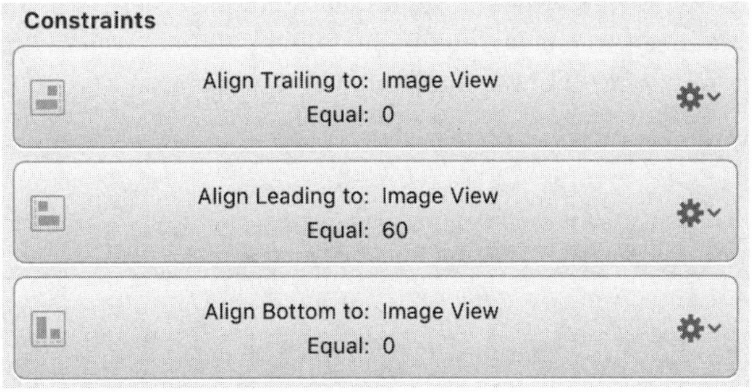

Figure 11.31 The constraints for the text field

11.2.4 Adding the result label

The result is just static text, so we can use a `UILabel`, called Label in the toolbox. Drag one of these above the image view. We'll make the font the same size as that in the text-entry control, and we'll right-align the text. Set the properties in the same way as you did for the text field.

For the constraints, constrain the bottom of the label to the top of the image view and add a bit of spacing by setting the constant to 15. Then constrain the left and right edges of the label to the left and right edges of the image view (figure 11.32).

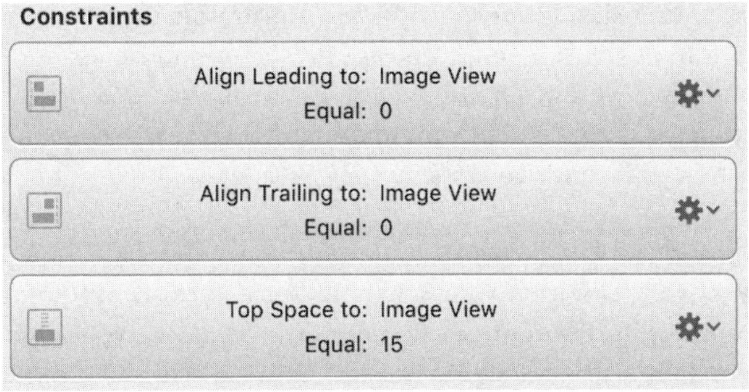

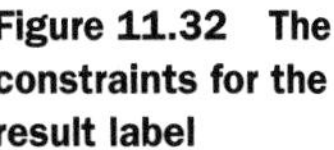

Figure 11.32 The constraints for the result label

11.2.5 Seeing the layout on different devices

By default, the storyboard designer shows how your app will look on a generic device—essentially a square device. This isn't a real-world representation, as no iPhones or iPads are square, but it's ideal for creating an initial layout. Once your view is laid out, you can see how it looks on different devices and orientations by selecting from the View As options in the storyboard toolbar.

These options allow you to view your app as it would appear on the currently available device sizes, as shown in figure 11.33. It doesn't list all devices—just one of each of the possible sizes. For example, at the time of writing I can select iPhone 6 Plus but not iPhone 6s Plus or iPhone 7 Plus—these devices are all the same size and resolution, so there's no real need to have them all available in the menu. You can also use the orientation button to toggle between portrait and landscape.

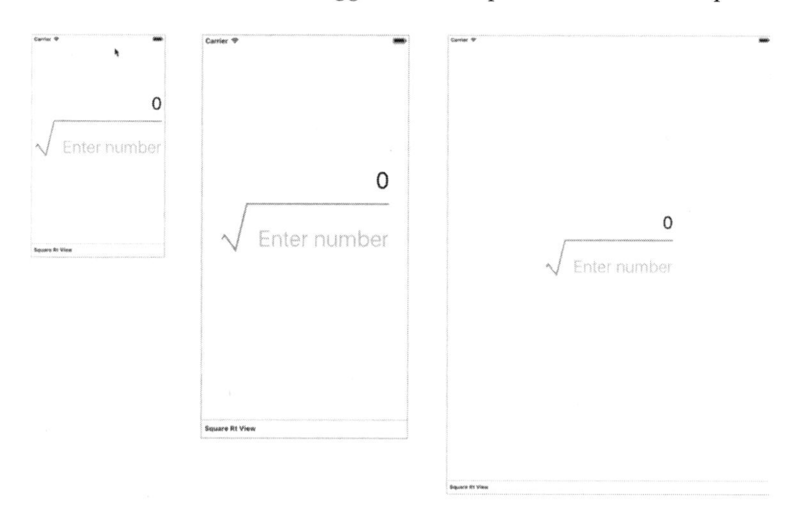

Figure 11.33 The SquareRt view on an iPhone 4s, iPhone 6, and iPad

If you play with these options, you'll see the storyboard update for each device and orientation, and everything should look good—the constraints we set will always put the image in the middle of the screen and position everything else around it, so the UI should work on all sizes and orientations. You'll also notice as you change these options that the button on the far left of the storyboard toolbar will change. This button sets the view to show different size classes.

11.2.6 Size classes

Sometimes you'll want to tweak what your UI shows for devices of different sizes, or when your app is running in different orientations. For example, you might want to increase a font size on larger devices, or you may want to lay things out differently for an app running in landscape. To help with this, Apple introduced the concept of *size classes.*

WHAT ARE SIZE CLASSES?

Size classes are the way the iOS SDK groups different device sizes and orientations together, based on similarities between screen size or aspect ratio. You can use these different size classes to provide support for configuring certain controls or constraints differently, depending on the size or aspect ratio. When viewing your UI in the storyboard designer, you can select the generic device and choose a size class to see how it would look on a range of devices (that's instead of selecting a specific device in the storyboard). Table 11.2 shows the size classes for the currently available devices.

Table 11.2 The size classes for the currently available iOS devices

Device	Portrait (width/height)	Landscape (width/height)
iPad (Air, Mini, Pro)	Regular/regular	Regular/regular
iPhone Plus (6 Plus/7 Plus)	Compact/regular	Regular/compact
iPhone 7/6s/SE	Compact/regular	Compact/compact

CONFIGURING CONTROLS BASED ON SIZE CLASSES

Some apps look different in portrait and landscape orientations, with their UIs restructured to take advantage of the available space. For example, when viewing a photo in the iOS Photos app in portrait mode, the app takes advantage of the tall aspect to put a toolbar with some editing buttons on the bottom of the screen. In landscape orientation, there's less height, so to show as much of the photo as possible, the toolbar buttons are moved to the top navigation bar—this bar is now wider, so it has more room for buttons. You can see this in figure 11.34.

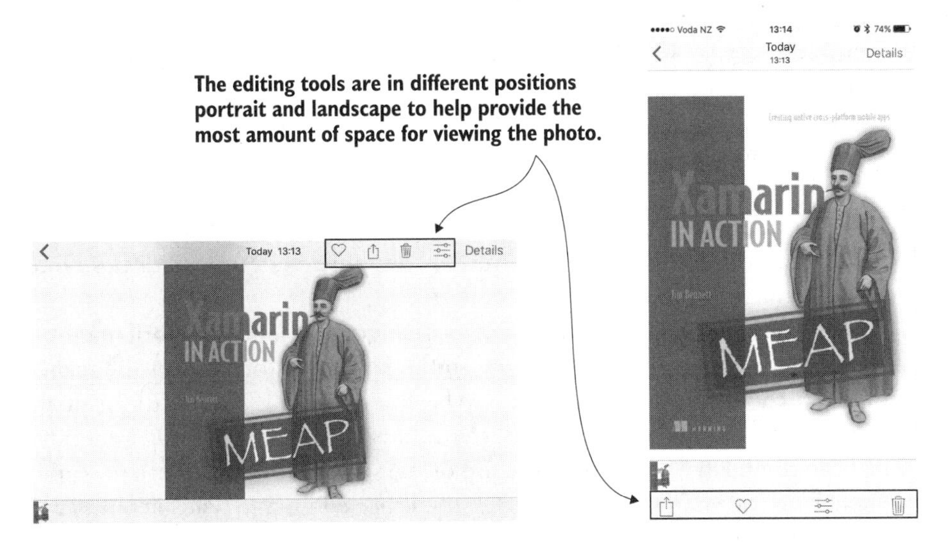

Figure 11.34 The iOS Photos app has a different UI for landscape and portrait orientations.

You can configure controls differently for different size classes. For example, you can show or hide controls based on whether the app is in portrait or landscape orientation. You can also configure constraints based on size classes, so you could set an image view to be in the center for portrait and bottom for landscape. When you configure controls, you can choose which range of size classes to use in each direction, so you can choose any, compact, or regular for both the height and width. For example, you could have a control that's visible for any height and compact width, which would only show on non-Plus iPhones in landscape and portrait, on iPhone Plus in portrait only, and not on iPads.

In the Widget tab of the Properties pad for controls, there's a Views section, at the bottom of which is the configuration for size classes. By default, you'll see "**w** Any **h** Any" with a ticked checkbox marked Installed next to it. This shows that the control is available for all size classes—in Apple's terminology *installed* means a control is available for a particular size class, and *Any* refers to both regular and compact sizes (figure 11.35).

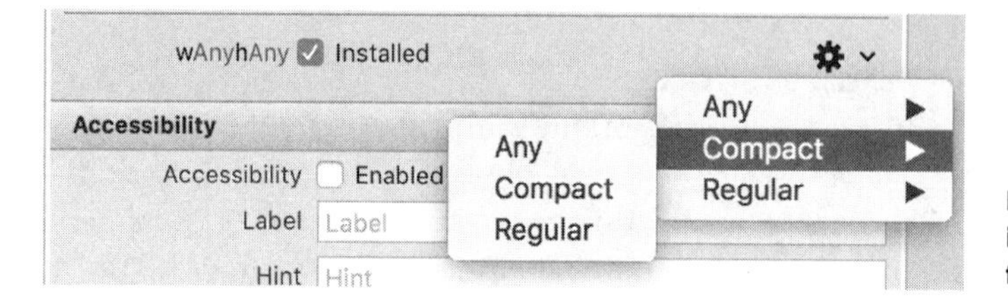

Figure 11.35 The installed size classes for a view

To set the size classes for a control, click the cog and choose the size class that you want the control installed for. You can choose multiple options, and you'll see Regular represented by an R and Compact by a C (for example, "**w** C **h** R" means compact width and regular height). You need to make sure that only the ones you want are ticked, so untick "**w** Any **h** Any" (this is usually unticked when you add a new size class). You can also use the – button on the left to remove size classes.

Constraints can be configured the same way. If you select a control, head to the Layout tab in the Properties pad, find a constraint, and edit it using the Select and Edit option from the cog, you'll see that the constraint also has size classes at the bottom of the Widget tab. This allows you to configure a control so it's positioned differently for different orientations.

For example, SquareRt might not look so good in landscape orientation—it has a text field in the middle of the screen, so the keyboard would cover the text-entry control on the iPhone. Ideally we'd want to lay the screen out differently for small iPhones in landscape, so that everything fits. It would be better if everything were moved up so that the result label was right at the top of the screen—but only for landscape on small phones (as shown in figure 11.36). On the iPhone Plus and iPads in landscape, having everything in the vertical center is fine, as it is for all devices in portrait.

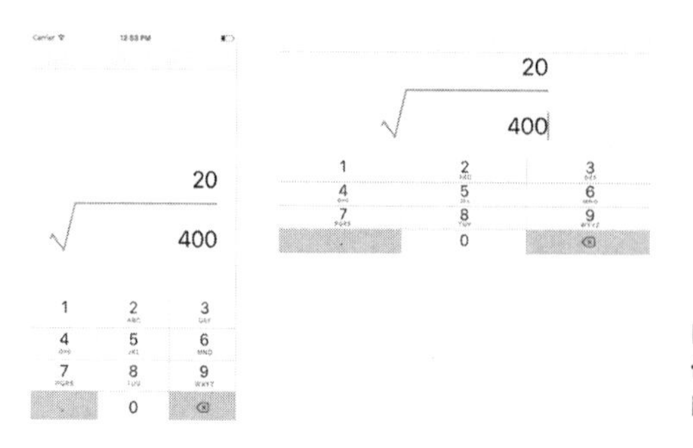

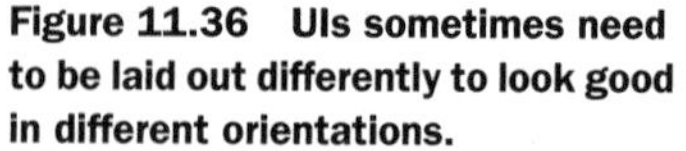

Figure 11.36 UIs sometimes need to be laid out differently to look good in different orientations.

To make this change to SquareRt, you need to configure the CenterY constraint on the image view to apply to everything except iPhones in landscape, and then create a new constraint on the result label to put it at the top just for landscape iPhones. Remember, the layout engine will look at all constraints to work out where it should put everything, so constraining the top of the result label to the top of the screen will be enough for the layout engine to determine where to put everything: the result label goes at the top, the image view goes underneath, and the number entry aligns its bottom to the image view.

Small iPhones in landscape use the compact width and compact height size classes, so you'll need a constraint just for this one size class to fix the label to the top. Add a new top constraint by selecting the result label, clicking it again so the constraint handles are visible, dragging the top T-bar handle to the top of the superview, and setting the constant to 0. Then install the Compact/Compact size class by clicking the cog next to "**w** Any **h** Any" and selecting Compact > Compact. This will add a new entry of "**w** C **h** C". Then untick "**w** Any **h** Any."

This adds your new constraint, but you have a conflict—for landscape iPhones the result label should be at the top, but you still have the constraint putting the image in the center. You need to configure that center constraint to only apply when the size class is not Compact/Compact. To do this, you need to uninstall the Any/Any size class and add Regular/Any and Any/Regular—this covers any device or orientation where either the width or height is not compact. Select the CenterY constraint from the Document Outline or the Layout tab of the properties for the image view and add Regular > Any and Any > Regular from the cog menu (figure 11.37).

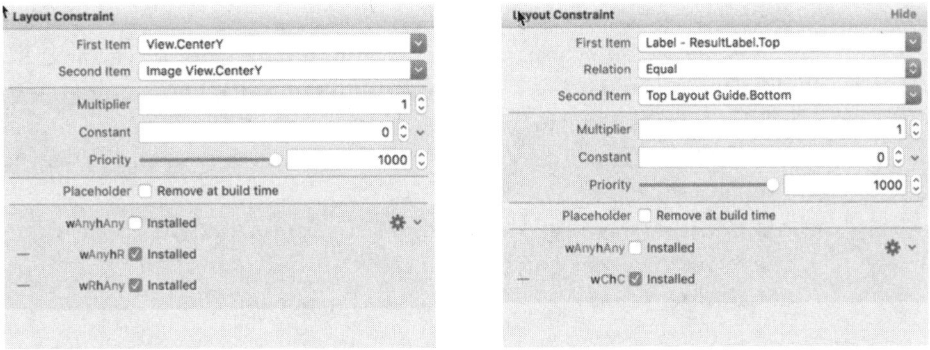

Figure 11.37 Configuring constraints to only be installed for specific size classes

This will position everything at the center or top depending on the device, as shown in table 11.3.

Table 11.3 The location of the controls on different iOS devices and orientations

Device	Portrait	Landscape
iPad (Air, Mini, Pro)	Center	Center
iPhone Plus (6 Plus/7 Plus)	Center	Center
iPhone 7/6s/SE	Center	Top

If you want to learn more about what you can do with size classes, there's a great tutorial, "Adaptive Layout Tutorial in iOS 11: Getting Started," available at http://mng.bz/5cah.

Once you've set this all up, you should be able to change the selected device, orientation, or size class and see the UI update to match. Play with the different sizes and orientations and see what happens. See how the different constraints cause the UI to update in different ways, depending on the size and orientation. Now is also a good time to play with different layouts and see if you can lay out the controls differently.

11.2.7 A quick recap

We've covered a lot so far, so let's quickly recap before moving on to the code behind:

- *View controllers*—When building storyboards, you can add view controllers by dragging them from the toolbox. Each view controller has a single child view referred to as the *superview*, and you add controls to this view.
- *Controls*—To add controls such as labels, images, or text fields, drag them from the toolbox. You can configure their properties from the Widget tab of the Properties pad.
- *Constraints*—You can set constraints from the designer by clicking the controls until the constraint handles appear, and then dragging them to the other item in the constraint relationship, such as another control or the superview. You can then configure the constraints more accurately in the Layout tab of the Properties pad.
- *Size classes*—iOS groups devices into size classes based on similar size characteristics. You can tweak controls and constraints so that they're only applicable for certain size classes.

11.3 Building the SquareRt view

When you created the view controller in the storyboard, you weren't creating a class. Instead you were defining a UI that can be used by an instance of a view controller. Now that you have the UI defined, it's time to create the view controller proper and wire up the storyboard.

11.3.1 What is a view controller?

A *view controller* is an object derived from `UIViewController` that manages a set of views and controls that make up part of your application's user interface. Usually a view controller is an entire screen, but it can also be a part of the screen. For example, tab controls are view controllers, with each tab being its own view controller. Each view controller has a single root view that fills the entire space on screen, and this is often referred to as the *superview*. From an MVVM perspective, a view controller is a view, and it will have a corresponding view model.

A view controller is analogous to an Android activity—it represents a full-screen task that the user is doing. When you navigate to another task using another screen, your app will load a new view controller. The SquareRt app is a single-screen app, so it only needs one view controller.

In non-MVVM apps, you'd define a startup storyboard in the info.plist file, and when your app starts up, it would load this storyboard, find the view controller that's marked as the initial view controller, create the relevant view controller class for it, and launch it. This happens behind the scenes in your app, and you configure it simply by setting the startup storyboard. For our MvvmCross apps, we don't need to do this. Instead, when the app starts up, the MvvmCross code will find the startup view model, then find the relevant view based on its name, and launch the view controller.

11.3.2 View lifecycle

Each view controller has a *lifecycle*—a set of methods that are called as the view is loaded, it appears on screens, it disappears, and it unloads. These are methods in the base `UIViewController` class that you can override, and they're always called on the UI thread. Figure 11.38 shows this lifecycle.

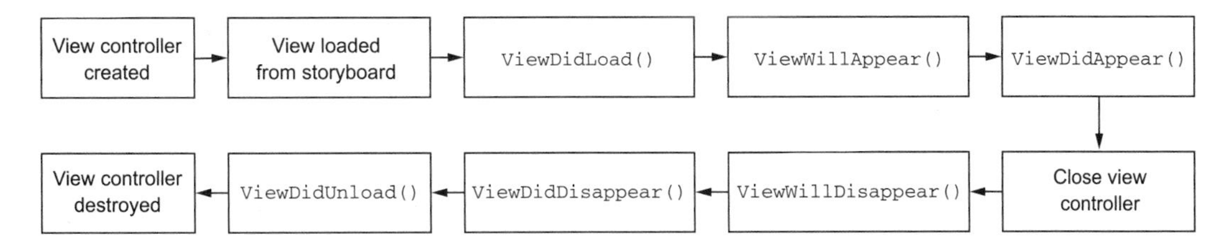

Figure 11.38 The lifecycle of a view controller from being created and loading the view to closing the view controller and unloading the view.

The most used method in this lifecycle is `ViewDidLoad`, which is called after the view has been loaded from a storyboard or Nib file. At this point the UI will be fully created, and any properties that are wired up to controls (you'll see these later in this chapter) are fully set and available for use. If you need to do any configuration of the UI in code, this is the method to do it in.

Unlike Android, view controllers aren't recreated when you rotate the screen. There's nothing you have to do manually—the view will readjust itself automatically based on the constraints you set. If there's anything you need to do in code when the screen rotates, you can override the `ViewWillTransitionToSize` method.

11.3.3 Creating the view controller

The first thing to do when creating a view controller is create the class itself, so in the Views folder create a new view controller called `SquareRtView` (the view controller option will be in the iOS section of the New File dialog box). This will create two code files, SquareRtView.cs and SquareRtView.designer.cs, with the designer file nested underneath the view. These files both contain a single `SquareRtView` class, with partial class definitions in each file. The designer file is autogenerated, so if you make any manual changes to it, they'll be lost. A Xib file will also be created, in this case called SquareRtView.xib, which can be deleted, because you'll be using the storyboard you've already created instead a Xib file.

Because we're using MvvCross, you'll need to make a couple of small changes to the view controller code.

The first thing you need to do is change the base class to one that comes from MvvmCross, to provide some basic MVVM functionality.

Second, you need to tell MvvmCross that your view controller will load its UI from a storyboard—using both an attribute and by changing the constructor. Traditional iOS apps start from a storyboard that will create the view controller backing class, and you navigate to another view controller in the storyboard using a segue—it's essentially view-first navigation. We're using view-model–first navigation, so you need to tell the MvvmCross framework how to load the view from the view model.

Listing 11.1 shows the code changes you need to make in SquareRtView.cs.

Listing 11.1 Setting up the view controller for MvvmCross

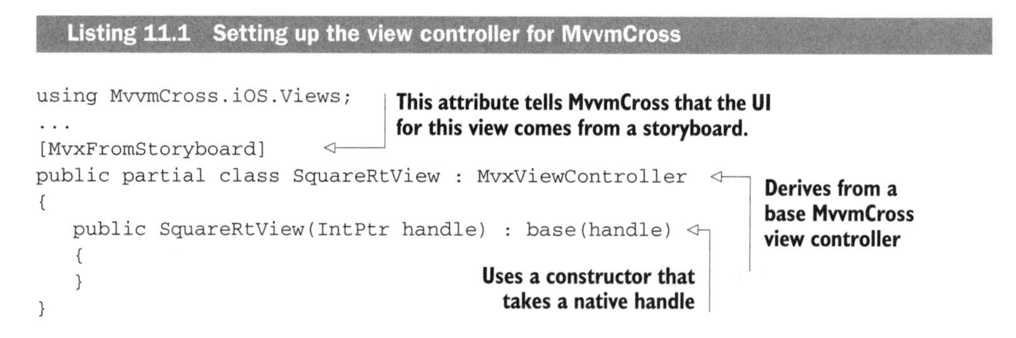

using MvvmCross.iOS.Views;
...
[MvxFromStoryboard]
public partial class SquareRtView : MvxViewController
{
public SquareRtView(IntPtr handle) : base(handle)
{
}
}
This attribute tells MvvmCross that the UI for this view comes from a storyboard.
Derives from a base MvvmCross view controller
Uses a constructor that takes a native handle

The `MvxFromStoryboard` attribute tells MvvmCross that the view controller needs to load its view from a storyboard (as opposed to loading it from a Nib or creating it manually).

The `MvxViewController` base class derives from `UIViewController` but provides MVVM functionality, such as having a property called `ViewModel` that provides access to the view model for the view. The `ViewModel` property is of type `IMvxViewModel`, the base interface for MvvmCross view models. There's also a generic version of `MvxView-Controller`, which takes a type derived from `IMvxViewModel` as its type argument, and if you use this the `ViewModel` property will be of the right type. For example, if you use `MvxViewController<SquareRtViewModel>`, the view-model property will be of type `SquareRtViewModel`.

The constructor that was provided when the file was generated can be deleted—it was for view controllers that use Xib files, and it passes the name of the Xib file to the base `UIViewController` so that it can create the UI. You're using a storyboard here, so this constructor is redundant. Instead you need to add a constructor that takes an `IntPtr` and passes this to the base class. This `IntPtr` parameter is a native handle to the native view controller class and is outside the scope of this book—we just need to define this constructor to allow our app to work.

Once your view controller class is defined, you need to wire it up to the view controller on the storyboard.

11.3.4 Wiring up controls to the view controller

To wire up the `SquareRtView` view controller to the storyboard, open up the storyboard and select the view controller in it (remembering to click the bottom rectangle). In the Widget tab of the Properties pad, there will be a Class drop-down showing all the view controller classes available in your app. Select SquareRtView (figure 11.39). This tells the storyboard that `SquareRtView` is the backing class to use, but this is a one-way thing—the storyboard knows about the view controller, but the rest of the app doesn't know about this link.

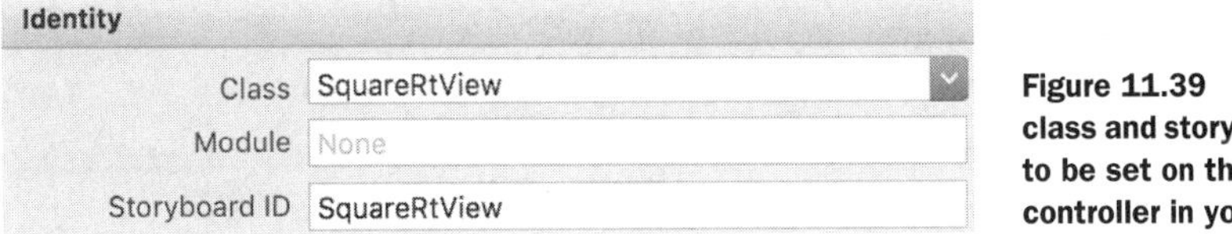

Figure 11.39 The backing class and storyboard ID needs to be set on the view controller in your storyboard.

When you navigate to the `SquareRtViewModel`, the MvvmCross framework needs to know which view to load. It could find the view controller by name, but then it wouldn't know which storyboard to use to load the UI. Instead, what you need to do is set an ID on the view controller in the storyboard so that when you navigate, Mvvm-Cross knows which view controller to use from the storyboard, and therefore which backing view-model class to load. To set this ID you need to set the value of the Story-board ID on the Widget tab of the Properties pad to SquareRtView.

Next up, you need to wire up your controls. In the Android version of this app, you bound the controls inside the .axml file, but you can't do this with storyboards as there's no way to define any custom properties. Instead, you need to bind in code, and to do that you need access to the controls that you've added. This is easy enough to do—the Widget tab on the Properties pad for controls has a Name field, and setting this will create a property inside the view controller backing class for that control with the name you enter. Set the name for the text field to be NumberEntry and for the label to be ResultLabel.

If you open up the SquareRtView.cs file, you won't see these properties. Instead, open the SquareRtView.designer.cs file and you'll see them there. This is the purpose of the designer file—when you give controls names, properties for them are created in this file (figure 11.40). The following listing shows the contents of the file after setting the name on the text field.

Identity	Hide
Name	NumberEntry → `UIKit.UITextField NumberEntry { get; set; }`
Class	UITextField

Identity	
Name	ResultLabel → `UIKit.UILabel ResultLabel { get; set; }`
Class	UILabel

Figure 11.40 Setting the name on the controls adds a property with that name to the designer file.

Listing 11.2 Designer files contain properties for named controls on the storyboard

```
[Register ("SquareRtView")]
partial class SquareRtView
{
   [Outlet]
   [GeneratedCode ("iOS Designer", "1.0")]
   UIKit.UITextField NumberEntry { get; set; }

   void ReleaseDesignerOutlets ()
   {
      if (NumberEntry != null)
      {
         NumberEntry.Dispose ();
         NumberEntry = null;
      }
   }
}
```

- This attribute registers this class with the iOS runtime.
- The property for the control
- Cleanup code to dispose of the control after the storyboard closes

The code in this file is autogenerated, so if you make any changes, they will be lost. The `Register` attribute tells the compiler to register this class with the iOS runtime—that's way outside of the scope of this book, but doing so allows the iOS runtime to interact directly with the class, which is needed so that this class can be used by the storyboard designer.

The property that's created for the number entry control is private and is of type `UITextField`. This designer file contains a part of the `SquareRtView` class, so you can access this property in the SquareRtView.cs file. The `Outlet` attribute is used to define a property that's set from a control on the storyboard—the term iOS uses for controls in the view controller that are on the storyboard is *outlets*, and this property tells the

Xamarin runtime to use the property as the outlet for the storyboard control. These properties are set once the storyboard is loaded.

The `ReleaseDesignerOutlets` method is called automatically by iOS when the view controller closes, and the generated code inside it calls `Dispose` on the controls and marks them as null so that the garbage collector can clean them up.

The SquareRtView.designer.cs is an autogenerated file, so for the purposes of this book we can just accept that it has some magic and use its properties. The magic, though, is all based on how Xamarin apps talk to the native SDKs. Xamarin apps have two objects for each control: an instance of the underlying native iOS control, and an instance of a .NET wrapper object. The wrapper exposes the same properties and methods as the underlying native class, and these are implemented by calling the property or method on the native object. This is a very advanced topic, so if you want more information, check out Xamarin's iOS guide: http://mng.bz/f5q4.

11.3.5 Binding the view controller

Once your view has been loaded from the storyboard, you need to bind the controls to your view model. You can do this in `ViewDidLoad`, the lifecycle method that's called after your view has been loaded from a storyboard. At the time this is called, all the properties for your controls will have been set. If you open `SquareRtView`, you'll see that this method was created for you when the new view controller class was added.

To bind your view model to the view in code, you start by creating a *binding set*—this is a collection of bindings used by MvvmCross. In the set you add bindings for the relevant controls and then you apply the binding set, which binds the controls. The following listing shows the code you need to add to the bottom of the `ViewDidLoad` method.

Listing 11.3 Creating the binding set for SquareRtView

```
using MvvmCross.Binding.BindingContext;
using SquareRt.Core.ViewModels;
using SquareRt.Core.ValueConverters;
...
public override void ViewDidLoad()
{
   base.ViewDidLoad();

   var set = this.CreateBindingSet<SquareRtView, SquareRtViewModel>();
   set.Bind(ResultLabel)
      .To(vm => vm.Result)
      .WithConversion<DoubleToStringValueConverter>();
   set.Bind(NumberEntry)
      .To(vm => vm.Number)
      .WithConversion<DoubleToStringValueConverter>();
   set.Apply();
}
```

Annotations:
- Creates the binding set
- Binds the result label to the result property on the view model
- Binds the number entry to the number property on the view model
- Applies the binding set

This code starts by creating a binding set between the `SquareRtView` and the `SquareRtViewModel`. This is strongly typed so that you can easily bind properties on the view model directly, rather than using string names. It then binds the `ResultLabel` label control to the `Result` property on the view model, using `DoubleToStringValueConverter` from the core project. The same is done for the `NumberEntry` control, binding it to the `Number` property. Finally, the binding set is applied, and this will read the values from the view model, update the view, and listen for changes to both the view-model properties and the UI controls.

11.3.6 Another quick recap

Before we run the app, let's have another recap:

- *View controllers*—The `UIViewController` class is the base class for all view controllers. On storyboards you define the layout for a view controller, and in code you define the actual backing class.
- *MvvmCross has a view controller base class*—MvvmCross provides `MvxViewController` as a backing class for a view controller that supports binding. You can wire this up to a storyboard by setting the `MvxFromStoryboard` attribute and setting the storyboard ID on the view controller on the storyboard.
- *Named controls become properties*—If you name a control on a storyboard, a corresponding property is created in the designer file for the view controller class.
- *Binding*—Controls can be bound to properties on the view model, using converters if required.

EVERYTHING YOU DO WITH A STORYBOARD YOU CAN ALSO DO IN CODE You don't have to use storyboards if you don't want to—you can just create a `UIViewController` and build the UI in code, adding a parent view and controls, and setting up constraints. Some developers prefer this as they find it easier to set up constraints either by writing them manually, or by using helper libraries such as Fluent Layout (https://github.com/FluentLayout/Cirrious.FluentLayout). The big downside to coding your UIs is that you lose the ability to visualize your layout at design time, which can be painful if you're iterating a UI with a designer. The upside is that storyboards can add extra views to your UI, which may slow down a very complicated UI—something you can optimize by hand when creating your views in code.

11.3.7 Running the app

Everything is now done for SquareRt—your UI has been created and bound to the view model. It's time to try it out, so select an appropriate simulator and run the app. Try it on an iPhone as well as an iPad to see how the auto layout makes it look awesome on all devices. Also try rotating the simulators using the Rotate Left and Rotate Right options in the Hardware menu (or by using the shortcut keys ⌘-← or →-⌘) to see that it looks great in both landscape and portrait orientations (figure 11.41).

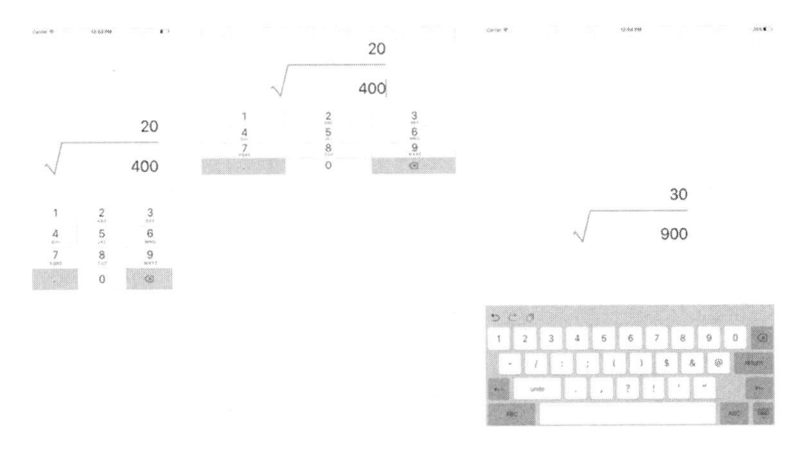

Figure 11.41 SquareRt running on an iPhone in portrait and landscape, and on an iPad

> **IPADS DON'T HAVE A DECIMAL KEYBOARD** If you try the app on an iPad simulator, you'll notice that the keyboard shows everything, not just numbers. This is a limitation of iPads. I guess Apple thought that having only a tiny keyboard wouldn't look as good. For our purposes, it's not a problem, but in a real-world app you'd want to do something to work around this, such as by building a custom keyboard-like control for number entry.

> **SCALING THE SIMULATOR** If the simulator is too large to fit on screen, you can change the scale using the Scale option in the Window menu.

When you run the app, the following things will happen:

1. iOS will start your app and start the MvvmCross framework, which finds the view model registered as the app start in the `App` class in the SquareRt.Core project—in our case, `SquareRtViewModel`.
2. The MvvmCross framework will find the storyboard and view controller with the ID of `SquareRtView`, finding it in the SquareRtView.storyboard file.
3. The storyboard will be launched, which in turn will create an instance of the `SquareRtView` view controller.
4. The view controller will start its lifecycle and load the UI from the storyboard, laying out all the controls using the constraints specified for the current device and orientation.
5. The `ViewDidLoad` method will be called, and the view controller will bind the controls to the view model.
6. The binding will use `DoubleToStringValueConverter` in the SquareRt.Core project, creating an instance of it and using it as a value converter on the binding.
7. If the screen is rotated, the layout engine will re-evaluate all the constraints and lay out the screen again.

Summary

In this chapter you learned

- Apple defined how best to design iOS apps in its Human Interface Guidelines.
- iOS defines user interfaces using storyboards.
- UI controls are positioned using constraints that define relationships between the positions of controls, and these are resolved at runtime to absolute positions based on the screen size and orientation.
- Different size classes can be used to configure screens differently for different device sizes and orientations.
- Views are derived from view controllers, which are loaded from storyboards.
- MvvmCross can bind controls to view models in code after the UI has been loaded.

You also learned how to

- Create images that support multiple screen sizes using asset catalogs.
- Lay out controls by defining constraints in the storyboard designer.
- Configure constraints based on size classes.
- Bind controls in view controllers.

12 Building more advanced iOS views

> **This chapter covers**
> - Creating table views
> - Navigation bar buttons
> - Setting app icons
> - Launch screens
> - The Appearance API

In the last chapter you built the UI for SquareRt on iOS, using storyboards, view controllers, images, some controls, and constraints. In this chapter we'll look at some more advanced iOS UI topics and build the UI for Countr, using table views to show lists of data, and adding menu items to the navigation bar. We'll then look at our app's splash screen and improve that, before finally tweaking our app icons.

12.1 Building the UI and view controllers for Countr

Let's start working on Countr. Open the Counter.iOS project and delete the dummy FirstView.cs, FirstView.designer.cs, and FirstView.storyboard files from the

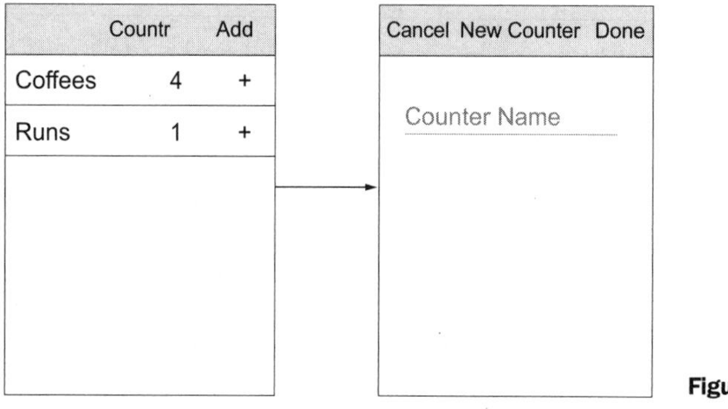

Figure 12.1 The UI for Countr

Views folder, as these won't be needed. For Countr, you need to create two views: the master view showing all counters, and the detail view for adding a new counter. Figure 12.1 shows the UI we want to create.

On Android, when you have an app with multiple screens, every screen is generally an activity, and you use the toolbar's Back button to navigate back, closing the current activity. On iOS it's different—you have multiple view controllers, one for each screen, and these live inside a parent navigation view controller. This navigation view controller provides a toolbar at the top that shows the current view controller's title, and when you navigate to a new view controller, it shows a Back button with the title of the previous view controller in it.

When using MvvmCross, you don't need to explicitly add a navigation view controller, as the framework adds it for you and uses it to navigate between screens. That means you just need to create view controllers for the two screens in the Countr app, and let MvvmCross handle the navigation.

12.1.1 Creating the UI for the master view

For the master view you'll be creating the storyboard at the same time as the view controller. Start by creating a new view controller in the Views folder called CountersView (and delete the CountersView.xib file that's automatically created), and add a storyboard called CountersView.storyboard.

TABLE VIEWS

For the master view, you need a full-screen list of all the counters and a toolbar button for adding a new counter. Like Android, iOS has a control designed to show lists of data, called `UITableView`. This control has a data source that provides the list of items to show, and it will create only enough rows to show the visible data, reusing them as you scroll. Each row uses a control called a *cell*, derived from `UITableViewCell`, to show the data.

TABLE VIEW CONTROLLERS

Screens whose only jobs are to show lists of data are popular, so iOS has a `UITableView-Controller`—a view controller that comes preconfigured with a full-screen

UITableView, accessible through a property called TableView. In addition, MvvmCross has its own implementation of UITableViewController that supports binding, which can make your life easier.

To create a table view controller, you have to add one to your storyboard and then wire it up to code behind. Start by opening the storyboard, finding Table View Controller in the toolbox, and dragging it to the designer. You want to set the class for this view controller to CounterView, but if you look in the Class drop-down in the Properties pad, you won't see this view listed. That's because the designer is smart enough to only allow you to use view controllers derived from UITableViewController as the backing class for a table view. Open up the CountersView.cs file and make this a table view controller. The following listing shows the code you need to add for this.

Listing 12.1 CountersView needs to be a table view controller

```
using MvvmCross.iOS.Views;
...
[MvxFromStoryboard]
public partial class CountersView : MvxTableViewController
{
   public CountersView(IntPtr handle) : base(handle)
   {
   }
}
```

Tells MvvmCross this comes from a storyboard — annotates [MvxFromStoryboard]

Derives from the MvvmCross table view controller — annotates the class declaration

Uses a constructor that takes a native handle — annotates the constructor

Once this class derives from MvxTableViewController (which in turn derives from UITableViewController) you can update the class in the properties for the storyboard to be CountersView, and you can also set the Storyboard ID to CountersView so that MvvmCross knows which storyboard to navigate to when the app starts up. The Title property should also be set to Countr as well, so the app name appears at the top of the app when it's running.

TABLE VIEW DATA SOURCES

Table views build rows using a table view source—a class that derives from UITableViewSource. This class provides information to the table view about how many rows of data there are, and what cell needs to be used for each row. When you implement a data source, you need to provide it with two things: information about the actual source data and details on which cells to use.

The data for the table view will come from the view model, in the form of an ObservableCollection<CounterViewModel>, so you need to create a data source that you can wire up to this observable collection. MvvmCross comes to your aid here—it has its own data source that can be bound to an observable collection, and it will wrap it in a way that provides all the data the table view needs, including telling the table view when the collection is updated so that it can update the rows. To use the MvvmCross data source, the first thing to do is to create a new class called `CountersTableViewSource` in the Views folder. The following listing shows the code for this.

Listing 12.2 The table view data source for the counters table

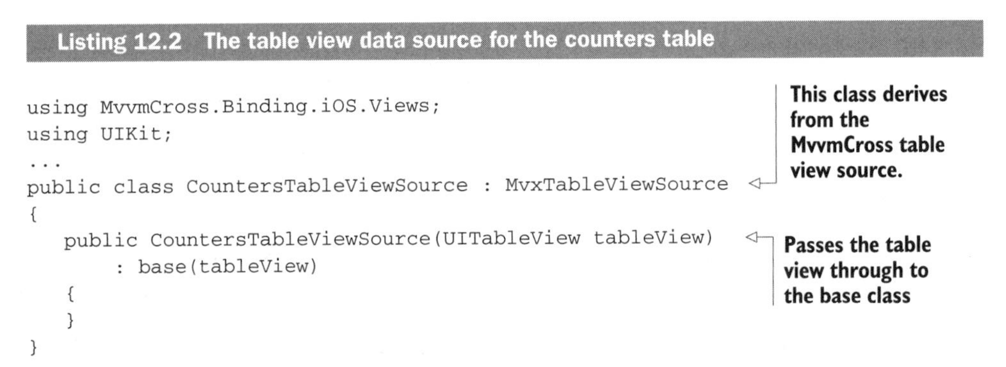
This class derives from the MvvmCross table view source.
Passes the table view through to the base class

```
using MvvmCross.Binding.iOS.Views;
using UIKit;
...
public class CountersTableViewSource : MvxTableViewSource
{
   public CountersTableViewSource(UITableView tableView)
       : base(tableView)
   {
   }
}
```

`CountersTableViewSource` derives from `MvxTableViewSource`, an implementation of `UITableViewSource` that can be bound to a collection. The constructor for this class needs the table view itself, so that it knows which table view to update when the collection changes. To use this table view source, you need to create it and pass it to your table view. Add the following code to `CountersView` to wire this up.

Listing 12.3 Creating a table view source

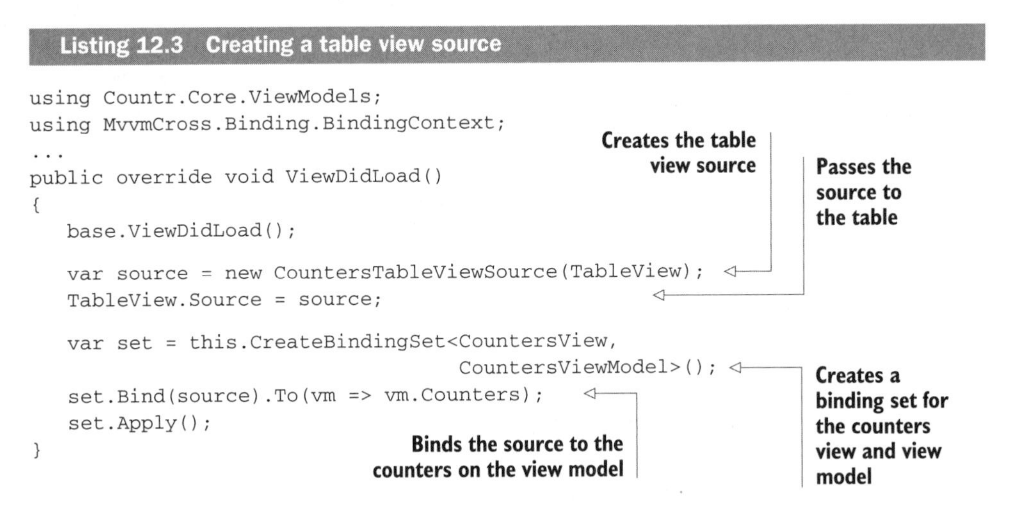
Creates the table view source
Passes the source to the table
Creates a binding set for the counters view and view model
Binds the source to the counters on the view model

```
using Countr.Core.ViewModels;
using MvvmCross.Binding.BindingContext;
...
public override void ViewDidLoad()
{
   base.ViewDidLoad();

   var source = new CountersTableViewSource(TableView);
   TableView.Source = source;

   var set = this.CreateBindingSet<CountersView,
                                  CountersViewModel>();
   set.Bind(source).To(vm => vm.Counters);
   set.Apply();
}
```

Once the table view source has been created, you can create a binding set, just as you did when binding the number and result properties in SquareRt to controls, and you can use it to bind the counters to the table view source. This binding keeps everything in sync—the table view is initialized with any counters already in the view model, and when the collection changes, the table is updated automatically.

You have your data, so now you need a cell to show it.

TABLE VIEW CELLS

Despite the name *table view*, these views aren't really tables—they have multiple rows but only one column, so they're essentially simple lists. Even so, they're called table views, and just like in a data table, each element is referred to as a *cell*. Because there's only one column, each row is represented by a single cell.

For Countr, we need one cell for each counter in the app, and because we're using MVVM, we want to bind each counter to a row. A cell isn't like a cell in an Excel spreadsheet, which only contains a single value. Here a cell is like the view inside a view controller—it can contain any number of controls, all laid out using constraints.

Every row in the table is an instance of `UITableViewCell` or a derived class. `UITableViewCell` provides a basic UI for a row, with two labels for a title and subtitle, an image, and an accessory indicator (used to indicate that something can happen, such as an arrow to indicate that a new screen will be shown by tapping the item). This is good enough for some simple tables, but if you want to customize it, you can do so by deriving a class from `UITableViewCell`, with a UI defined in the storyboard.

Table views are like Android's recycler view in that they recycle cells—they only create enough cells to fill the screen, and as cells are scrolled off the screen, they're reused at the other end with new data (in our case, bound to a different counter). You can mix and match cells in a table view, so when you create one, you give it an identifier based on the type of cell. This identifier is a simple string and is a fixed value for each type of cell. Table views get their cells from the table view source. In the table view source, when you need to provide a cell to the table view, you start by asking the table view to provide a cell for a given identifier, and if it has one available that's been scrolled off the UI, you'll get that. Otherwise you'll get a new instance of the cell. Either way, you then configure the cell to show the data you want, and you return it to the table view. This is shown in figure 12.2.

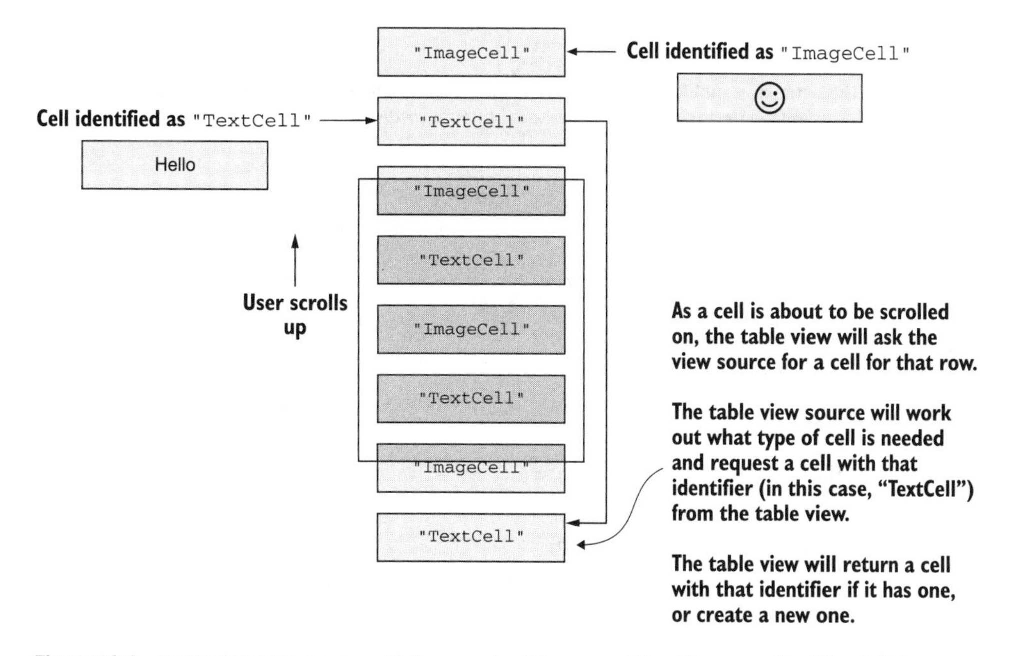

Figure 12.2 Table views can have multiple named cell types, and they'll reuse cells of the right types as needed.

You need a custom cell to show your counter, so let's start by creating one. The first thing to do is create a new table view cell called `CounterTableViewCell` (Table View Cell is an option in the Add New File dialog in iOS). This will create three files: CounterTableViewCell.cs, CounterTableViewCell.designer.cs for the class itself (once again, the .designer file is autogenerated), and CounterTableViewCell.Xib. The Xib file can be deleted, as you'll be designing your cell using a storyboard (unfortunately there isn't an easy way to create just the cell and designer files without the Xib).

Once you have the class, you can design the cell. You can do this in the storyboard for the counters view. When you design a table view controller in a storyboard, you can also add what are called *cell prototypes*—layouts for cells that you can give an identifier to. When your table view source requests a cell from the table using that identifier, the table view knows to use this layout for the cell. These layouts have backing classes defined, just like view controllers, and when the layout is used, it's the backing class that's created. Figure 12.3 shows the prototype for a cell you can use to show a counter.

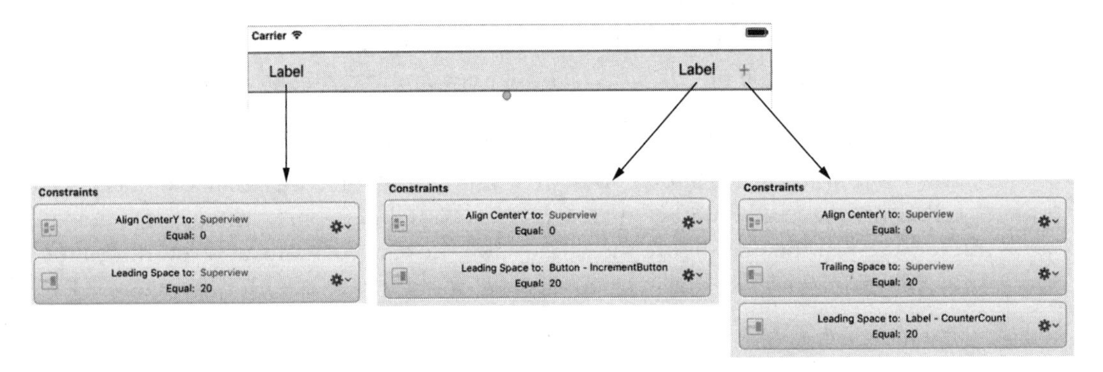

Figure 12.3 The prototype cell for a counter containing two labels and a button, laid out with one label on the left of the cell, the button on the right, and the second label to the left of the button

Open the CountersView.storyboard and look at the view controller. You'll see a white box at the top of the table view inside the view controller. This is a prototype cell, and it's this you need to configure for your counter cell. (If you look at the properties of the table view, you'll see a property called Prototype Cells set to 1, which means the table has one cell prototype—you can increase this if you need more.)

Click the prototype cell to see its properties, and set the Class drop-down to CounterTableViewCell and the Identifier to CounterCell. This identifier is what you use in your table view data source to get a new `CounterTableViewCell`. For this UI, you need two labels, one to show the counter name and one to show the count, and a plus button. For the plus button, add a new image set to the asset catalog called Plus, and add the different sized plus images from the images\Countr\iOS folder in the source code that accompanies this book.

Once the images have been added, drag the following controls to the cell prototype:

- A label called `CounterName`, centered vertically and left-constrained to the left side of the superview with a constant of 20 to give it some space.
- A button called `IncrementButton`, centered vertically and right-constrained to the right side of the superview with a constant of 20 to give it some space. Set the image to be `Plus`.
- Another label called `CounterCount`, centered vertically and right-constrained to the left side of the button with a constant of 20.

Once these controls are added, you'll be able to see them in the CounterTableView-Cell.designer.cs file.

Next up is to use this cell, so you need to change your table view source to generate one and return it. Open CountersTableViewSource.cs and add the following code.

Listing 12.4 Returning the new cell from the table view source

```
using Foundation;
...
protected override UITableViewCell GetOrCreateCellFor(UITableView tableView,
                                                      NSIndexPath indexPath,
                                                      object item)
{
    return (CounterTableViewCell)tableView
           .DequeueReusableCell("CounterCell");    <-- Gets or creates a cell for the identifier "CounterCell"
}
```

The `GetOrCreateCellFor` method is called by the MvvmCross table view source to get the cell for a particular row. This code will ask the table view for a cell with the identifier of `"CounterCell"` using the `DequeueReusableCell` method (often referred to as *dequeuing the cell*), which will return one that has been scrolled out of view or create a new one. The prototype cell you created had an identifier of `"CounterCell"`, so the table view will use this prototype to create the new cell, constructing an instance of `CounterTableViewCell` and setting its UI to match the one defined in the storyboard. The MvvmCross table view will then bind the item at the given position to the cell.

INDEX PATHS Rather than use a simple integer value for row numbers, iOS uses `NSIndexPath`. This does more than hold a simple row number, it also handles sections. You can structure your table to group rows into sections. For example, a contacts app might group by the first letter of the contacts' names. If you had two sections in your table, and the first section had five rows and the second had three, you wouldn't refer to the last row in the second section as row eight. Instead, it would have an `NSIndexPath` with a section of two and a row of three. You can read more about grouping rows in the Apple Developer Documentation at http://mng.bz/6lKR.

You've created your cells, defined their UI, and set up your view source to construct them—the last thing you need to do is add code to bind everything. Each cell needs to be bound to an instance of `CounterViewModel` (because the source data for the table is an `ObservableCollection<CounterViewModel>` from the counters view model). To do this, you need to add some binding code to the `CounterTableViewCell` class.

Start by deleting the provided constructors and fields, and add the code in the following listing.

Listing 12.5 Binding the table view cell to a counter

```
using System;
using Countr.Core.ViewModels;
using MvvmCross.Binding.BindingContext;
using MvvmCross.Binding.iOS.Views;
...
public partial class CounterTableViewCell : MvxTableViewCell
{
   public CounterTableViewCell(IntPtr handle) : base(handle)
   {
      this.DelayBind(() =>
      {
         var set = this.CreateBindingSet<CounterTableViewCell,
                                         CounterViewModel>();
         set.Bind(CounterName).To(vm => vm.Name);
         set.Bind(CounterCount).To(vm => vm.Count);
         set.Bind(IncrementButton).To(vm => vm.IncrementCommand);
         set.Apply();
      });
   }
}
```

Derives this cell from the MvvmCross cell base type

Binds the controls to the view model

Most of this code is the same as you've seen before, binding properties or a command to controls. The only new thing is `DelayBind`. Unlike view controllers where you can bind when the view is loaded, you don't have a way to know when cells are fully set up with all the controls created, ready to bind. Delayed bindings are run when the data context is set for the first time. The data context is set in the MvvmCross table view source after the cell has been dequeued—you can be sure at this point that it has been fully constructed and the UI set.

In general, if you don't know when the UI will be set and the controls will be ready, you can use a delayed binding, and you define this in the constructor. Otherwise, you can bind in a method such as `ViewDidLoad`.

SWIPE TO DELETE

Unlike Android, swipe-to-delete is baked into iOS and is really easy to implement. This is implemented in the table data source, this time by overriding the `CommitEditingStyle` method. By default, swiping on a table view does nothing, but as soon as you override this method, swipe-to-delete is magically turned on. The following listing shows the code for adding this to `CountersTableViewSource`.

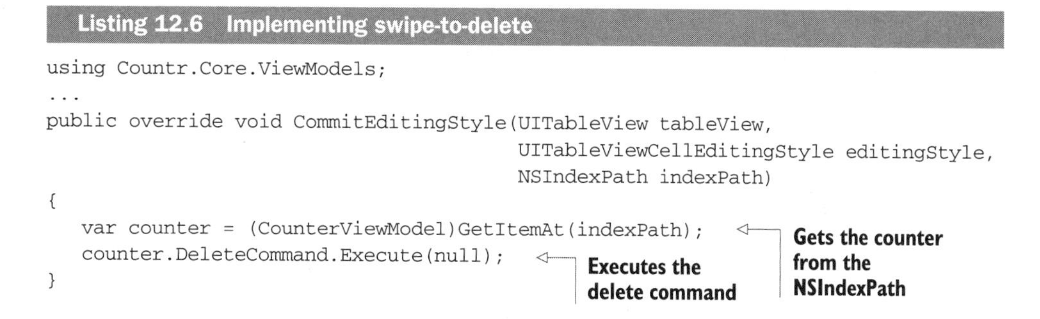

Listing 12.6 Implementing swipe-to-delete

```
using Countr.Core.ViewModels;
...
public override void CommitEditingStyle(UITableView tableView,
                                        UITableViewCellEditingStyle editingStyle,
                                        NSIndexPath indexPath)
{
   var counter = (CounterViewModel)GetItemAt(indexPath);
   counter.DeleteCommand.Execute(null);
}
```


This method is called by iOS when you swipe the cell from right to left and tap the Delete button that appears. `GetItemAt` is a method on `MvxTableViewSource` that will look in the underlying collection for the object that's at the given `NSIndexPath`, and once you have this object, you can cast it to a `CounterViewModel` and execute `DeleteCommand`. This command, behind the scenes, will cause the collection to be updated, raising a collection-changed event that will be picked up by `MvxTableViewSource`. This data source in turn will tell the table view to update, removing the row from the table.

12.1.2 Navigation bars and buttons

When building iOS apps that have multiple screens, you need a way of indicating to the user what screen they're on, and of showing a way to get back to the previous screen. On Android you do this using the toolbar that's included in the layout, and which is used to navigate to another activity. iOS has a different way of doing this—it uses navigation controllers.

Navigation controllers are a type of container view controller. They are view controllers (and derive from `UIViewController`), but they don't have much of a UI themselves. Instead they're used to hold other view controllers and provide a way to navigate between them. Each contained view controller can be thought of as a screen, with the navigation controller providing a toolbar at the top and handling navigation between them (figure 12.4).

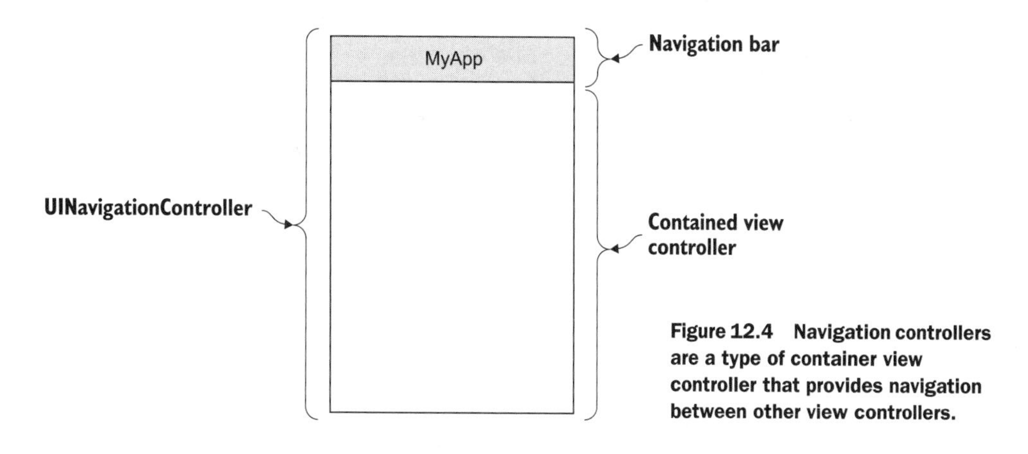

Figure 12.4 Navigation controllers are a type of container view controller that provides navigation between other view controllers.

Navigation view controllers are instances of `UINavigationController` and provide a toolbar at the top of the screen that shows the title. Underneath this toolbar, they show the view controller for the current screen. When you navigate to another screen, a new view controller is created and is shown inside the navigation controller, updating the navigation bar to show the title of the new screen. The navigation bar also provides a Back button that shows the name of the previous screen, so that users know where they're navigating back to. This is shown in figure 12.5.

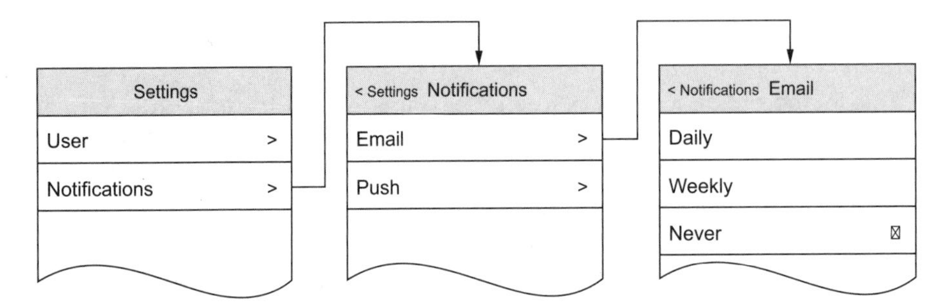

Figure 12.5 Out of the box, iOS handles navigating forwards and backwards, including updating the navigation bar to show the previous page name.

MvvmCross uses a navigation controller, but it does so behind the scenes, creating one that's used to show the startup screen and handle navigation to new pages. When you call `ShowViewModel` inside your view model, the view controller that's created for the relevant view is hosted inside the same navigation view controller.

You can also use the navigation bar as a toolbar—it can have buttons on the left and right and can host a control in the middle. By default, the left button is a Back button, and it's only used if you've navigated to the current page from another page (the first page of your app won't have a left button, and the second page will have a Back button showing the name of the first page). The middle section by default shows a static label with the title of the view controller, but this can be changed to any control, such as showing an image instead of a title. The right button provides a single toolbar button, usually for the most popular creative action (similar to the floating action button in Android). This is shown in figure 12.6.

> **LEFT AND RIGHT ARE FLIPPED FOR RTL LANGUAGES** For right-to-left languages like Hebrew and Persian, the left bar button item is on the right, and the right bar button item is on the left.

The left and right buttons are of type `UIBarButtonItem`, which is a control that's designed to put buttons on navigation bars. These buttons can be configured with any text or an image, but iOS also provides a set of standard buttons (called *system buttons* because they're defined in the `UIBarButtonSystemItem` enum) for the most common tasks, such as Refresh, Add, and Done.

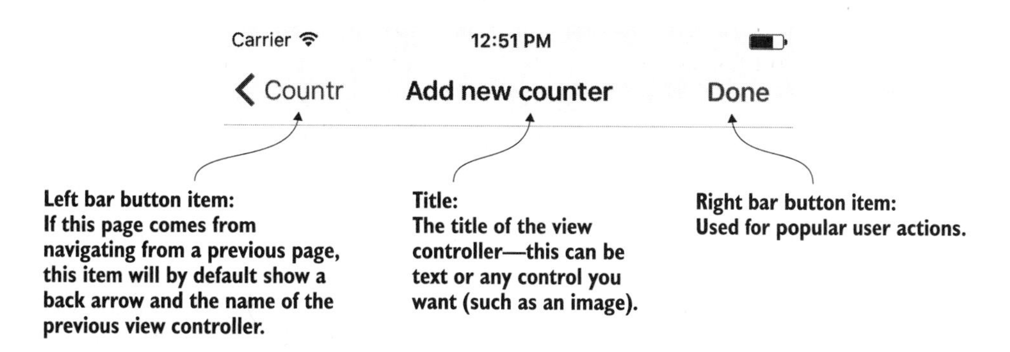
Carrier
12:51 PM
Countr
Add new counter
Done
Left bar button item: If this page comes from navigating from a previous page, this item will by default show a back arrow and the name of the previous view controller.
Title: The title of the view controller—this can be text or any control you want (such as an image).
Right bar button item: Used for popular user actions.

Figure 12.6 Navigation bars have buttons on the left and right with a title in the middle.

You can use the standard Add button in your master page. To add this button to the navigation bar and bind it to your view model, add the following code to `CountersView`.

Listing 12.7 Adding a bar button item to the navigation bar and binding it to a command

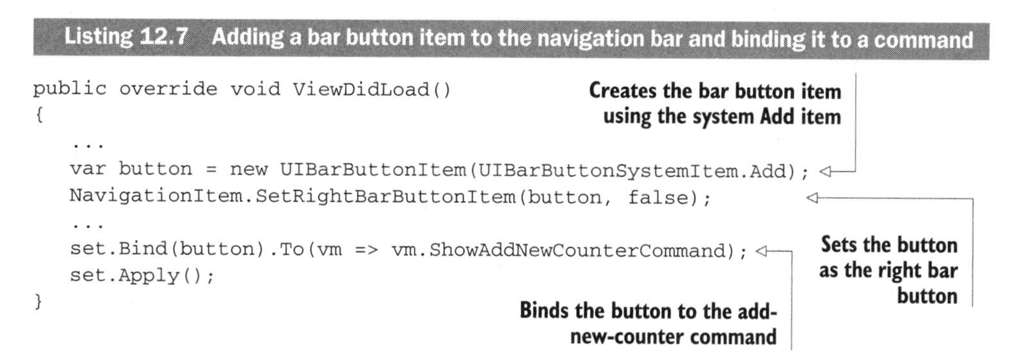

```
public override void ViewDidLoad()
{
    ...
    var button = new UIBarButtonItem(UIBarButtonSystemItem.Add);
    NavigationItem.SetRightBarButtonItem(button, false);
    ...
    set.Bind(button).To(vm => vm.ShowAddNewCounterCommand);
    set.Apply();
}
```

Creates the bar button item using the system Add item
Sets the button as the right bar button
Binds the button to the add-new-counter command

This code will create the bar button as the system-provided Add button, add it to the right side of the navigation bar, and bind it to the add-new-counter command on the view model. This button will navigate to the add counter screen, so let's now implement that screen.

> **DON'T MISUSE SYSTEM BUTTONS** If you plan on using system buttons, make sure you only use them for their intended purposes. For example, if you want a Delete button, don't use the Stop button (an X). Apple *will* reject your app for misuse of the system buttons. You can see the system buttons in Apple's UIKit documentation at http://mng.bz/4741.

12.1.3 Creating the UI for the detail view

The counter detail view is a very simple screen, with a text field for entering the name of the new counter, and a Done button to save it. To create this view, start by creating the relevant files in the Views folder: a new view controller called `CounterView` (don't forget to delete the `CounterView.Xib` file that's created automatically when you add a new view controller), and a storyboard called CounterView.storyboard.

For the UI, drag a new view controller onto the storyboard, set its class to `Counter-View`, and set the storyboard ID to `CounterView`. Drag a text field onto this view controller, set its name to be `CounterName`, clear the text property and set the placeholder text to be `"Counter name"`. Because this is a text field, you don't need to set the size (remember, it has an intrinsic size based on its content), but you do need to set the position. Constrain the top to the top layout guide (when you drag the top T-bar handle, the superview will have a big green box at the top labeled "Top layout guide"), and constrain the left and right sides to the left and right sides of the superview. Ideally, the text field should be indented a bit instead of being hard up against all edges, so set the constant for each constraint to 20. Figure 12.7 shows these properties and constraints.

Figure 12.7 The properties and constraints for the counter name text field

Once the UI is created, open the view controller and add the following code to set the right base class and tell MvvmCross that this view controller comes from a storyboard. This code is the same as you've used for other view controllers.

Listing 12.8 Setting the counter view to use the MvvmCross base view controller

```
using MvvmCross.iOS.Views;
...
[MvxFromStoryboard]
public partial class CounterView : MvxViewController
{
   public CounterView(IntPtr handle) : base(handle)
   {
   }
}
```

Next you need to override the `ViewDidLoad` method and create the navigation bar item to save the counter (we'll use the system-provided Done item for this). Then you need to bind this button and the counter name text field to the view model. The following listing shows this code, which again is similar to code you've already written.

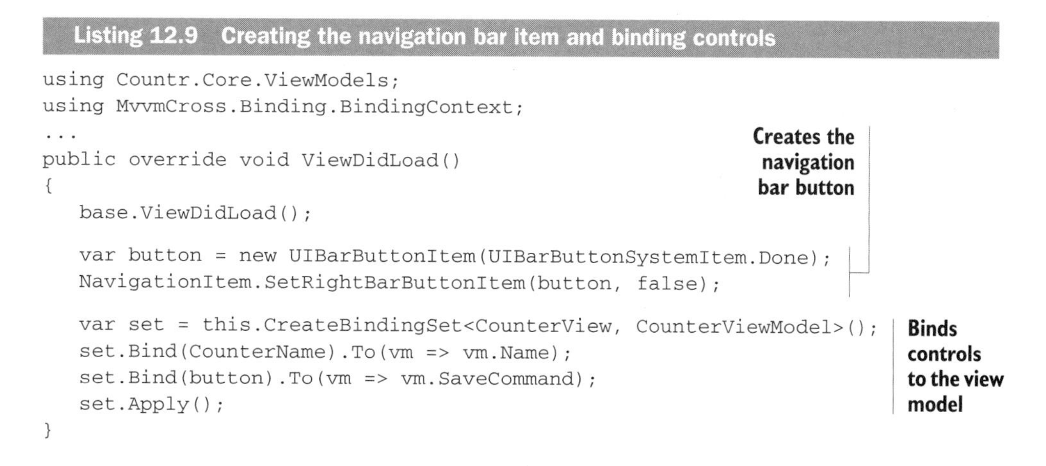
Creates the navigation bar button
Binds controls to the view model

Listing 12.9 Creating the navigation bar item and binding controls

```
using Countr.Core.ViewModels;
using MvvmCross.Binding.BindingContext;
...
public override void ViewDidLoad()
{
   base.ViewDidLoad();

   var button = new UIBarButtonItem(UIBarButtonSystemItem.Done);
   NavigationItem.SetRightBarButtonItem(button, false);

   var set = this.CreateBindingSet<CounterView, CounterViewModel>();
   set.Bind(CounterName).To(vm => vm.Name);
   set.Bind(button).To(vm => vm.SaveCommand);
   set.Apply();
}
```

That's all you have to do for the detail view. You don't need to wire up the Back button to anything—the navigation controller will detect the Back button being tapped and will close the view controller for you.

12.1.4 A quick recap

Before you run Countr, let's have a quick recap:

- *Table views*—iOS uses table views to display lists of data—these are single-column tables showing data in rows called cells. You can add table views in the same way as any other control, but if you want to have a full-screen table view, it's easier to use a table view controller—a view controller that has a full-screen table view as its superview. Table views use cell recycling, so they only create enough cells to fill the UI, and as cells are scrolled off the top they're reused on the bottom.
- *Table views data sources*—Table views have data sources that map the source data to cells. They're responsible for providing cells populated with data on demand, and they update the table view when the source data changes. Table view data sources can also be used to implement swipe-to-delete.
- *Table view cells*—Rows in table views are cells, and they're defined using cell prototypes—reusable views that are used to display each row.
- *MvvmCross table view helpers*—MvvmCross has its own table view controller and data source that supports binding.
- *Navigation*—iOS provides navigation controllers—container view controllers that provide navigation among other view controllers and that automatically add a toolbar at the top that has a Back button. You can also add buttons to this navigation bar.

12.1.5 Running the app

The Countr app is now fully implemented, so launch it in one of the simulators and play at creating counters, incrementing them, and deleting them. You can also kill and relaunch the app and see that the counters have been persisted. Figure 12.8 shows what the two screens in the app should look like.

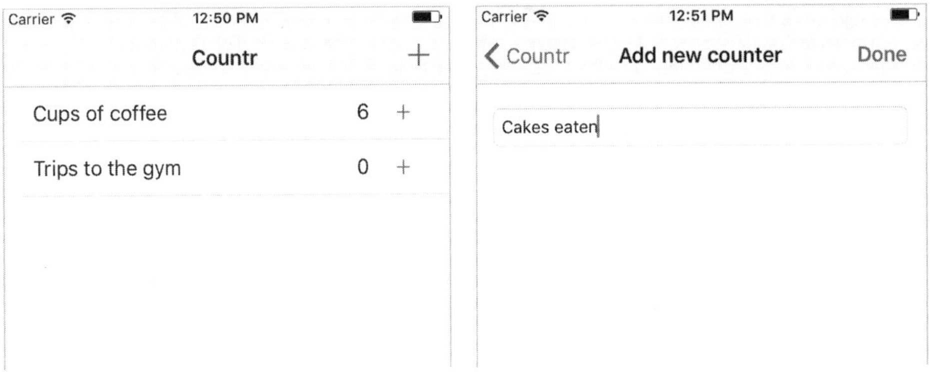

Figure 12.8 The fully working Countr app

If you have any issues running the app, such as crashes or hangs, they may be caused by known issues in different versions of Xamarin or MvvmCross. Check out the troubleshooting thread on the *Xamarin In Action* forum at http://mng.bz/9JAY for more details.

When you run the app, the following things will happen:

1. iOS will start your app and start the MvvmCross framework, which creates a navigation controller to host the app and then finds the view model registered as the app start in the `App` class in the Countr.Core project—in this case, `CountersViewModel`.
2. The MvvmCross framework finds the storyboard and view controller with the ID of `CountersView`, finding it in the CountersView.storyboard file.
3. This storyboard is launched, which in turn creates an instance of the `CountersView` view controller. This view controller is hosted inside a navigation view controller.
4. The view controller starts its lifecycle and loads the UI from the storyboard, laying out all the controls using the constraints specified for the current device and orientation.
5. The `ViewDidLoad` method is called, and the view controller binds the controls to the view model.
6. The table view data source is created and bound to the `Counters` property on the view model. This is passed to the table view and updates the rows on screen. Each row is created using the `CounterCell` prototype, and the counter view

model is bound to this cell using a delayed binding, so that it only binds after the UI is fully constructed.

7 The navigation bar button is created and bound to a command on the view model.

8 When a user taps the Add toolbar button, the command is executed, which navigates to the `CounterViewModel`. The MvvmCross framework finds the `CounterView` based on the name of the view model, finds the storyboard based on the storyboard ID of `CounterView`, and launches this storyboard, which in turn creates the `CounterView` view controller, binding all the controls and creating another navigation bar button.

9 In the counter view, if the user taps the Back button, the view controller is closed and the previous view controller (the counters screen) is shown. If they tap the Done button, the save command is executed, and this closes the current view model, which closes the view controller and navigates back to the master view.

10 If a counter is added or removed, the table view data source detects these changes and tells the table view to update its rows.

11 When a user swipes on a counter, the table view source's `CommitEditingStyle` method is called, and the code manually executes the delete command.

12.2 App icons and launch screens

We've completed both our iOS apps, but they still need a bit of improvement. If you look at the iOS home screen, you'll see that both of our apps have a default MvvmCross icon, and when you launch the apps you'll see MvvmCross launch screens. Let's improve these both.

As we did for Android in chapter 10, we'll only look at Countr here, but the same principles apply to all apps, so feel free to update SquareRt too.

12.2.1 App icons

In chapter 10 we generated app icons for our Android apps. Whichever method you used would also produce iOS app icons as an image set ready to be added to an asset catalog. MakeAppIcon will provide icons for both platforms, and most Sketch app icon templates also export icons for iOS and Android.

Android needed five app icons, which may seem like a lot, but it's nothing compared to iOS—Apple went icon-crazy with iOS, and you need to provide icons for a whole range of devices at different resolutions, as well as a different icon for when users search for your app, another one if you integrate with the iOS settings app, and different sizes for older OS versions if you support them. To cover all iPhones and iPads, you need 20 icons, and for most apps these will be 20 identical icons at different sizes. Figure 12.9 shows all these different icons.

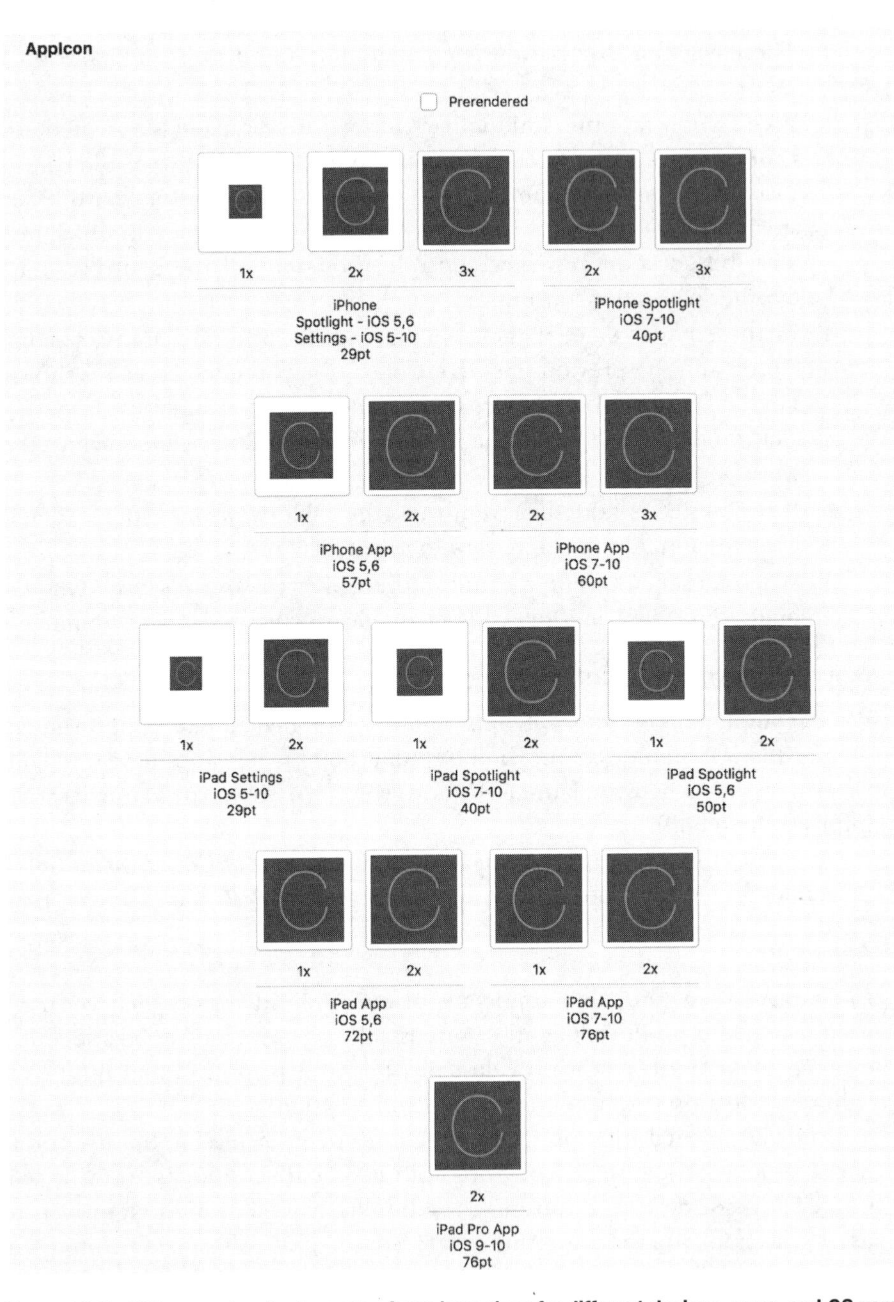

Figure 12.9 iOS supports a huge range of app icon sizes for different devices, uses, and OS versions. These are the possible icons for iOS devices; you can also configure different icons for Apple Watch apps.

You can see all the icons in your asset catalog. By default, apps have a special image set in their asset catalog called `AppIcon`, and this is for app icons. It's not like the image sets for normal images, with normal, @2x, and @3x icons for universal, iPad, or iPhone. Instead it has images for all possible iOS, macOS, and watchOS screen sizes and usages. Table 10.2 lists some of these sizes. Although this is a lot of icons, you'll usually want to use the same base icon for everything, so tools like MakeAppIcon really help.

Table 12.1 Image sizes of iOS icons for different uses

Size	Filename	Used for
120 x 120	Icon-60@2x.png	Home screen on retina iPhone
180 x 180	Icon-60@3x.png	Home screen on retina HD iPhones (the "Plus" phones: 6s Plus and 7 Plus)
76 x 76	Icon-76.png	Home screen on non-retina iPads
152 x 152	Icon-76@2x.png	Home screen on retina iPads
167 x 167	Icon-83.5@2x.png	Home screen on iPad Pros
40 x 40	Icon-Small-40.png	Spotlight (searching for apps)
80 x 80	Icon-Small-40@2x.png	Spotlight on retina devices
120 x 120	Icon-Small-40@3x.png	Spotlight on retina HD devices
29 x 29	Icon-Small.png	Settings
58 x 58	Icon-Small@2x.png	Settings on retina devices
87 x 87	Icon-Small@3x.png	Settings on retina HD devices

Once you generate your icons, you can update them in one of two ways: by manually using the asset catalog or by copying the files in. To update using the asset catalog, open the `AppIcon` image set and then either drag the image with the right resolution onto the relevant image (for example, drag an image at 120 × 120 onto the 2x image labelled iPhone App iOS 7-10 60pt), or click on the image in the image set and select the file.

Once you generate your icons, you can update them in one of two ways: manually using the asset catalog, or by copying the files in.

To update using the asset catalog, open the `AppIcon` image set, and then either drag the image with the right resolution onto the relevant image (for example, drag an image at 120 × 120 onto the 2x image labelled iPhone App iOS 7-10 60pt), or click the image in the image set and select the file. This is rather painful, as there are a lot of images to update, so it's easier to copy the files in.

To copy the files in, open Explorer or Finder and open the Countr.iOS folder. Then open the Assets.xcassets folder. In there will be a set of folders for each image set, named <ImageSetName>.imageset. There will also be a slightly different one for the app icons called AppIcon.appiconset. Open the AppIcon.appiconset folder and you'll see some images as well as a JSON file called Contents.json. These are the different images in the image set, and the JSON file is used to specify which image is used for each purpose. You'd normally never edit this JSON file—it's created and updated by the asset catalog editor when you add or change image sets. If you replace the images, you must keep the names the same or they won't match what's in the JSON file, but if you use a tool like MakeAppIcon, you won't only get the images, but also a new Contents.json file, so you can just replace the entire folder.

To update your app icon, open the Images\Countr\AppIcons\iOS folder from this book's source code, and copy the entire contents of AppIcon.appiconset into the asset catalog folder in your app. Rebuild and rerun your app, and you'll see that the icon has been updated on both the home screen and the search screen. If the icon doesn't update, you'll need to delete the app from your device or simulator, do a full rebuild, and try again.

12.2.2 Launch screens

Our app now has a nice icon, but we still need to fix up the launch screen. The default launch screen shows the app's title along with a copyright message, so it would be good to show something a bit nicer. Unlike on Android, launch screens on iOS aren't views. Instead they're baked into the OS and are shown while the application itself is starting up.

iOS APPLICATION LIFECYCLE

You saw in the last chapter that iOS view controllers have a lifecycle—a set of methods that are called as the view controller is created, shown, hidden, and destroyed. The same is true for the underlying application. When your app is run, an application class is created automatically for you, and as the application goes through its lifecycle, it will make callbacks to a delegate class (a class that implements a particular interface that's used to handle callbacks, because Objective-C doesn't have events). This class is referred to as your application delegate, and it derives from `UIApplicationDelegate`.

All iOS apps have an application delegate class in the root of the project, and it's usually called AppDelegate.cs. The following listing shows the class declaration.

Listing 12.10 The application delegate class derives from an MvvmCross base class

```
[Register("AppDelegate")]
public partial class AppDelegate :
      MvxApplicationDelegate
{
   ...
}
```

The app delegate has a Register attribute on it.

The app delegate derives from an MvvmCross class.

This class derives from `MvxApplicationDelegate`, which in turn derives from `UIApplicationDelegate`, and it provides some lifecycle handling that MvvmCross uses internally. It also has a `Register` attribute that's used to tell the Xamarin tooling that this class should be exposed to the underlying iOS runtime so that it can be accessed by core SDK classes. This allows the main iOS application class to use this delegate for its lifecycle.

The app delegate overrides one method, `FinishedLaunching`, and this is called when the application has finished launching and is ready for user code to be run. By default, this code shows a `Window`, which is the UI container for the app itself. In MvvmCross apps there's also some setup code to ensure that the IoC container is initialized and that the initial view model is set and started.

There are other methods on this delegate that you can override to handle launch options if you want to implement 3D touch or handle notifications. You can read more about app delegates in Xamarin's API documentation at http://mng.bz/K01c.

> **DON'T CALL THE BASE METHODS** Delegates are based on an Objective-C principle called *protocols*. These are like interfaces, but you only implement the methods you want, not everything. The base delegate classes don't do anything at all, so you shouldn't call the base methods when overriding. In fact, the Xamarin iOS SDK will throw an exception if you do.

When your app starts up, it will immediately show the launch screen. It will then work through the application lifecycle (shown in figure 12.10), calling methods on the application delegate, before finally calling `FinishedLaunching`, in which MvvmCross will initialize everything and load the first view. This means your launch screen will be shown throughout the startup process, unlike in Android where you need to show an activity while initializing everything.

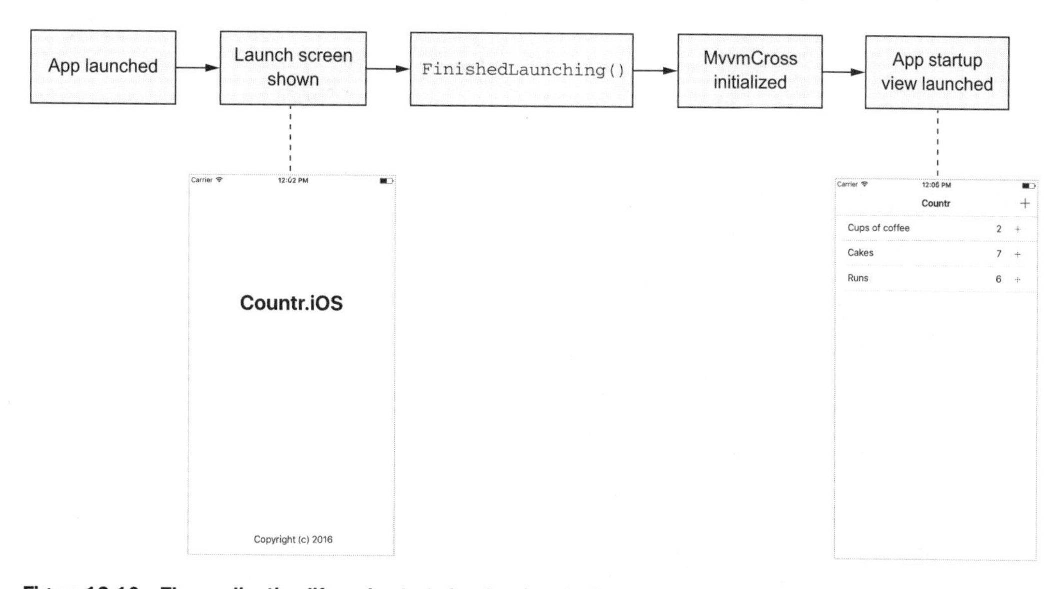

Figure 12.10 The application lifecycle starts by showing the launch screen. Then the app delegate methods are called, and this loads the first view.

UPDATING THE LAUNCH SCREENS

iOS launch screens can be a static image, a storyboard, or a Xib. Storyboards and Xibs are preferred over static images as they can be sized for different screen sizes, orientations, and resolutions. Images are a hangover from before iPads when there were only one or two screen sizes to support. Although storyboards are the preferred way of defining UIs from the views in your app, you can still use a Xib for a launch screen if you want. After all, Xibs are for defining single screens, and a launch screen will only ever be a single screen.

The default MvvmCross apps have a launchscreen.xib file in the Resources folder that's used, so you can edit this. Xib files are edited the same way as storyboards, the only difference being that they only have a single view in them and don't need a view controller.

If you open the launchscreen.xib file in a designer, you'll see some static controls on it—two labels, with one showing the name of the iOS project (such as SquareRt .iOS) and the other showing a copyright message. This isn't great, so let's make it look like the provided icon by doing the following:

1. Delete the two labels.
2. Set the background color of the view by selecting it, and then in the Property pad open the Background drop-down in the Layout tab, and select `Dark Gray Color`.
3. Add a new image set to the asset catalog called AppLaunchImage, and add the three `AppLaunchImage` images from the Images\Countr\iOS source code folder to the 1x, 2x, and 3x universal images.
4. Drag a new image view from the toolbar to the view, and constrain it to the center of the view. Set the Image property in the Property pad to be `AppLaunchImage`.

Figure 12.11 shows what the launch screen should look like when you're done.

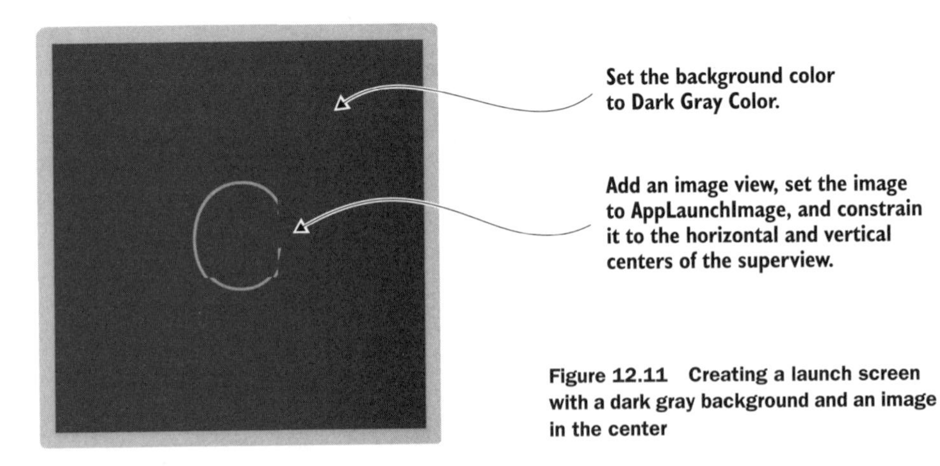

Set the background color to Dark Gray Color.
Add an image view, set the image to AppLaunchImage, and constrain it to the horizontal and vertical centers of the superview.

Figure 12.11 Creating a launch screen with a dark gray background and an image in the center

LAUNCH SCREENS ARE CONFIGURED IN INFO.PLIST The launch screen is configured in the info.plist file, so if you want to delete the Xib and replace it with a storyboard or a static image, you can configure this by opening the plist and updating the Launch Images section.

Build and run your app, and you'll see that you now have a nice shiny splash screen to go with your nice shiny icon. If the splash screen doesn't update, you'll need to delete the app from your device or simulator, do a full rebuild, and try again.

STYLING THE APP

We have a nice icon and a nice launch screen, but the app is still a bit plain, with a white title bar, white background, and black text. It would be good to add a splash of color, such as making the title bar orange like we did for the Android app. Unlike Android, iOS doesn't have XML-based styles. Instead it has an Appearance API where you can set in code the default colors for various UI widgets. In your app delegate you can set these defaults, and they'll be applied everywhere in your app. Note that these are defaults that you'll be setting—you can still override them explicitly on an individual basis.

Open AppDelegate.cs and add the following code to the start of the `FinishedLaunching` method.

Listing 12.11 Setting the default appearance for the navigation bar

```
public override bool FinishedLaunching(UIApplication app,
                                       NSDictionary options)
{
   UINavigationBar.Appearance.BarTintColor = UIColor.Orange;
   UINavigationBar.Appearance.TintColor = UIColor.DarkGray;
   var attrs = new NSDictionary(UIStringAttributeKey.ForegroundColor,
                                UIColor.DarkGray);
   UINavigationBar.Appearance.TitleTextAttributes
     new UIStringAttributes (attrs);
   ...
}
```

On the `UINavigationBar` class is a static property called `Appearance` of type `UINavigationBarAppearance`. It contains a set of properties that define the look and feel of the UI. These properties also exist on `UINavigationBar`—if you set them on an instance of `UINavigationBar`, they will apply to that single instance, but if you set them on the Appearance, they'll apply to all navigation bars. This is a nice way of doing it because you can play with the look and feel of a control on a storyboard, and once you're happy with the way it looks, set the properties using the Appearance API and have that look and feel apply everywhere.

The preceding listing sets the `BarTintColor` on the `Appearance` property to orange, which sets the background color for the navigation bar. You also set the `TintColor`, which sets the tint that's applied to any buttons on the navigation bar. When you ran the app earlier, you may have noticed that the plus button was blue, despite the image being dark gray. This is because iOS applies a tint to all buttons so that they look the same, and this tint defaults to blue. By setting the bar tint color, you can change this for all buttons on the navigation bar.

The last thing you set is the appearance attributes of the title. When dealing with labels, there are a number of things that can be configured, such as the text color, font, and font size, so you need to set attributes to specify which property you want to override. In this case you just want to override the text color, so you need a set of string attributes that just contains a single entry for the foreground color. You do this by creating a `NSDictionary` (a dictionary class like `Dictionary` from the .NET Framework, but from the underlying iOS SDK) containing a key-value pair with the key as `UIStringAttributeKey.ForegroundColor`, a string constant for the foreground color, and the value as the color dark grey. You could configure other attributes by adding more entries to this dictionary.

If you build and run the app now, it should look nicer, with an orange navigation bar. You can configure pretty much anything on the UI by using the Appearance API, so try it out and see what other improvements you can make to your apps.

12.3 Making the apps production-ready

Congratulations—you've built two cross-platform native apps using Xamarin and the MVVM design pattern!

In the first part of this book, you learned how you could use the MVVM design pattern to build cross-platform native apps, and in this part you got your hands dirty with some code and built two apps. Each app has a cross-platform model layer containing business logic, and a cross-platform view-model layer containing UI logic. You've also built platform-specific view layers so that your apps have native UIs and look and act like the platform on which they run.

This isn't the end of our apps' stories. The next step is to release the apps to the stores, ready for users to download them and enjoy the fruits of your labor. Before you can do this, you need to make sure your apps are production-ready, and the next part of this book will focus on achieving this. We'll look at how you can sign your apps so that they can run on physical devices, how to test your UIs on local devices and using Xamarin's Test Cloud, how you can automate builds and instrument your apps to get crash reports and usage information using Visual Studio App Center, and how you can distribute your apps to beta testers and then the actual Google and Apple stores.

Summary

In this chapter you learned

- Table views are used to show lists of data.
- App icons come from asset catalogs.

You also learned how to

- Configure a table view using a table view source and prototype cells, and then bind this to a collection.
- Add toolbar buttons to the navigation bar and bind these to commands.
- Update the launch screen.
- Use the Appearance API to configure the colors on the UI.

Part 3

From working code to the store

Once your app builds and runs, there's still a ways to go to get a production-quality app on the iOS and Android stores. In this part of the book, you'll take one of the example apps from the previous chapters and work through the steps to get it running on real devices, test the UI, add analytics to ensure it works once deployed, and then roll it out to the stores.

Chapter 13 looks at how to run apps on real devices (which is harder than you might think), including setting up Android devices for developers, configuring iOS devices, and generating iOS provisioning profiles.

Chapter 14 covers UI testing—the ability to write and run automated tests that interact with your app the way a real person would.

Chapter 15 introduces Visual Studio App Center and shows how it can be used to build your apps, run the UI tests from chapter 14 against devices in the cloud, and set up your apps to track usage information and crashes.

Finally, chapter 16 covers the final stage in your app's journey: delivery to users. It looks at using App Center to provide beta-test builds to select users, and then it shows how to finally publish apps to the Google Play store and Apple App Store.

13 Running mobile apps on physical devices

This chapter covers

- Setting up Android devices for debugging apps
- Signing Android apps
- Creating iOS provisioning profiles
- Debugging on iOS devices

In part 2 of this book we built two apps for iOS and Android using the MVMM design pattern. In this part, we're going to look at how to take our apps from working code to production-ready apps released to the Apple App Store and Google Play store. We'll start in this chapter by looking at how to sign our apps so that we can run them on real devices. Then, over the next three chapters, we'll look at writing automated UI tests to validate that our apps work, look at using Visual Studio App Center to build our apps, run our UI tests in the cloud, monitor for crashes, and provide analytics to trace how how users are using our apps, and finish up by deploying to beta testers and the Google Play and Apple App stores.

So far, we've tested our apps by running them on Android emulators and iOS simulators. These virtual devices are good enough for simple testing purposes, but we really need to run our apps on physical devices—after all, the end goal is to have an app we can sell in the store to people using phones and tablets, not emulators and simulators.

When Apple designed iOS, it wanted to protect users from malicious apps that could steal your data or run up huge phone bills by calling premium-rate telephone numbers. Apple made sure all apps are sandboxed, and only apps approved by Apple and published in their App Store could be run on any device. That's great for end users, but not so great for developers. As developers, we can get around this a little bit, but only by configuring our apps to run on one or more specific devices. With Android, Google hasn't provided the same level of safety, but it does have some options turned on by default to stop apps from unknown sources being run (for example, apps that were downloaded from the internet directly instead of from the Play store), and you need to do some device setup before you can debug an app.

We'll start this chapter by setting up an Android device for debugging and run our apps on it. Then we'll look in more detail at how we can sign our Android apps so they're ready for distribution via the Play store. We'll see a quick, dirty, and free way to debug your app on an iOS device, and then we'll look in more detail at how you can sign your iOS apps using an Apple Developer account and run them on a selection of real devices.

Parts of this chapter deal with running on actual devices, so you'll need a real Android device and a real iOS device to test on. If you don't have one or both of these, feel free to skip the relevant sections, but as you start developing real-world apps, it will be worth getting some real devices to test on, even if they're cheap second-hand phones or tablets. After all, real devices are much less performant than an emulator running on top of desktop hardware, and emulators won't have some of the features of real devices that you many want to use in your apps, such as cameras, accelerometers, and Bluetooth.

13.1 Running Android apps on a real device

We'll start by looking at Android—first at how to run apps on a real device, and then at signing apps to prove to Google and the world that they really came from us and haven't been manipulated by third parties.

The easiest way to run your apps on your Android device is to put the device in developer mode, plug it into your PC or Mac, and run your apps on it using the debugger. To put your device in developer mode, find the build number in the Settings app and tap it seven times (figure 13.1). Yup, really, seven times—not a joke.

The location of the build number varies, depending on the manufacturer, but it's easy enough to find. Open the Settings app, find the About Device tab (on older Android versions, this will be under the General tab). Look for a field called Build Number, or Software Information, and tap that. Then look for Build Number. Once

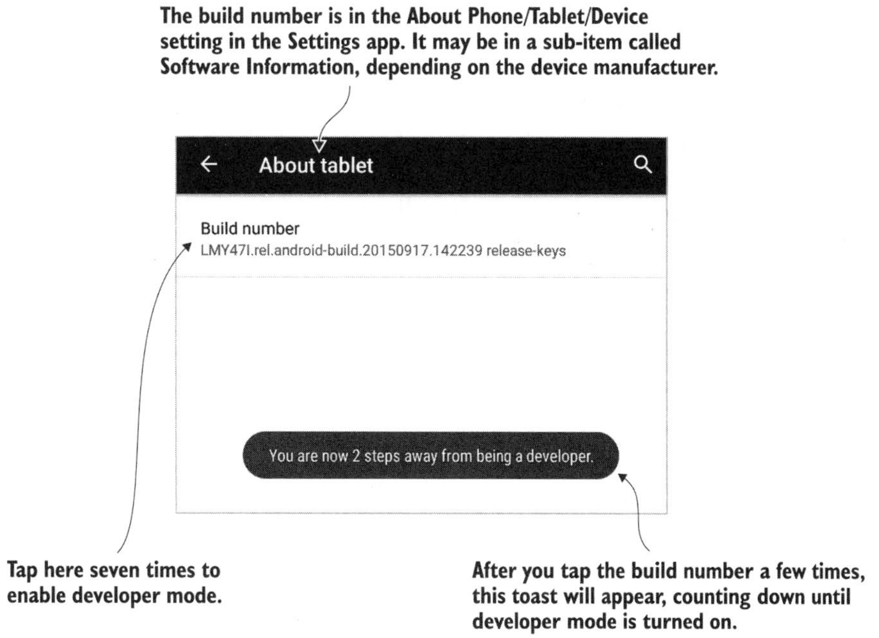

The build number is in the About Phone/Tablet/Device setting in the Settings app. It may be in a sub-item called Software Information, depending on the device manufacturer.

Tap here seven times to enable developer mode.

After you tap the build number a few times, this toast will appear, counting down until developer mode is turned on.

Figure 13.1 Tap the build number seven times to enable developer mode.

you've found this, tap it seven times. After a few taps, you'll see a toast saying something like "You're now 2 steps away from being a developer," with a number that counts down as you tap. After seven taps, a toast will appear saying that you're in developer mode, and a new Developer Options menu will appear under Settings.

Once your device is in developer mode, turn on USB debugging. This is a two-step process:

- *Turn on USB debugging*—Tap the Back button to go back to the main Settings menu, and then tap Developer Options. There are a huge number of developer options you can tweak, but we're only interested in the Debugging section, where you'll see an option called USB Debugging. Turn this on, and then tap OK when you're asked if you want to allow USB debugging (figure 13.2).

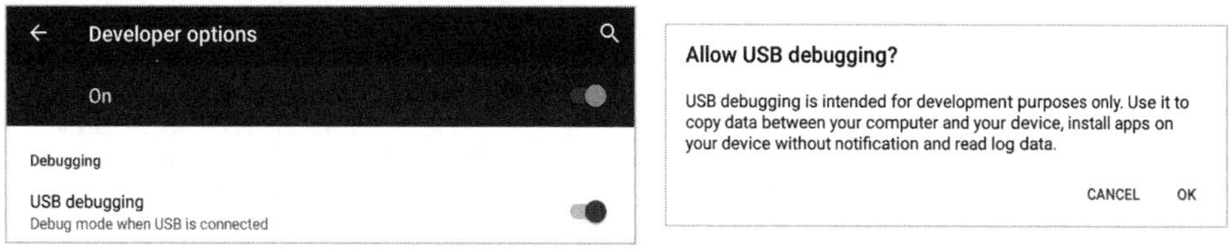

Figure 13.2 Turn on USB debugging and tap OK at the prompt.

- *Allow USB debugging from a particular PC or Mac*—Once USB debugging is turned on, connect your Android device to your Mac or PC with a USB cable. Once you do this, you should see a popup on the device asking for permission to allow USB debugging from your PC (although you've turned USB debugging on from the device, you still have to allow it for each connected PC or Mac). This is shown in figure 13.3.

  When the box pops up, check the Always Allow From This Computer check box to avoid having to accept it every time, and then tap OK. If you don't see this box, unplug your device, make sure Visual Studio is running, and then plug it back in again. This setting is on a per PC or Mac basis, so if you use multiple developer machines, allow it on each one that you use.

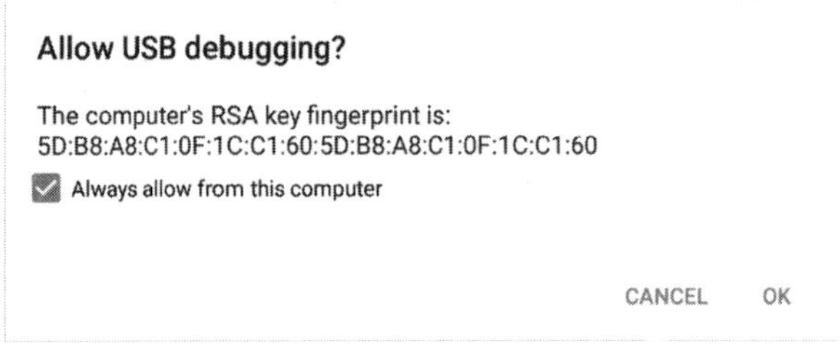

Figure 13.3 Once USB debugging is turned on, you need to allow individual computers to connect and debug.

Once USB debugging has been enabled, you'll be able to select your device in the drop-down just as you selected emulators, as shown in figure 13.4. Give it a try now by opening up either the SquareRt or Countr solution, setting the Droid app as the startup project, selecting your device, and clicking the Run button. Your app will build, and it should launch on your device. You should be able to debug it in the same way as when it runs on an emulator.

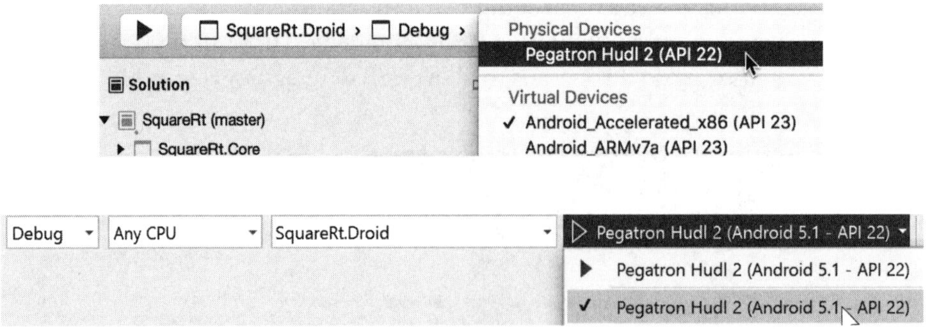

Figure 13.4 When you have a device configured and plugged in, you can select it for debugging.

13.2 Signing Android apps for publishing

The end goal with our Android apps is to have something up on the Google Play store that users can download and use. This means our users need to be able to not only install our apps, but also be able to install any updates we release with new features or bug fixes. For this store flow to work, we need a unique way of identifying our apps so that the Play store can know which apps a user has purchased or downloaded, and what versions they have on their devices, so that the store can update older versions to the latest release. This identity is made up of three parts: the package name, version number, and signing keystore. Version number was discussed in chapter 6, so here we'll only look at the package name and keystore.

13.2.1 Setting the package name

We looked at the package name and version number back in chapter 6, but to recap, the package name is the unique identifier for an app, and it's usually a reverse domain name suffixed with the app name (such as io.jimbobbennett.countr). The version number is an integer that defines the build for an app. When you publish an app to the store (something we'll look at in chapter 16), Google will use the package name to uniquely identify the app and the version number to manage updates. When you publish a new version of an app, you increment the version number so that Google knows there's an update.

As this will be the first build of our apps, we don't need to worry about the version number, but now would be a good time to set the package name. This defaults to com.companyname.<app name>, so for Countr this will be set to com.companyname.Countr, and for SquareRt it would be com.companyname.SquareRt. When you package up your app to run it on an emulator or device, or when you're preparing for a store release, an Android package (APK) file is created. This package contains your app code and all your resources, and it's named <package name>.apk, so for Countr it would be com.companyname.Countr.apk. You can see this in the output folder of the Droid project (for example, Countr.Droid\bin\Debug) after you deploy to a device or emulator by running the app (packages aren't created when you compile, just when you deploy).

The package name is set in the application manifest, accessible on Windows in the project properties and on Visual Studio for Mac by double-clicking the AndroidManifest.xml file in the Properties folder. Update this to a suitable reverse domain name (your domain if you own one, or a suitable unique name, suffixed with the app name). For example, I'd use io.jimbobbennett.countr. This is essentially the same as the iOS bundle identifier, so you can set it to the same value you used for that. Once it's set, redeploy the app and take a look in the output folder—you'll see the APK with the new name.

13.2.2 Keystores

This leads to the obvious question—if your app is uniquely identified by its package name and version number, what's to stop someone else from releasing an app with the same package name that contains malicious code? The answer is the *keystore*. When you package up your apps, sign them with a keystore file that contains one or more private keys that are yours and yours alone. When you update an app on the Google Play store, if the update isn't signed with the same key, it will be rejected.

Whenever you run an app on an Android device, it must be signed with a keystore—even when you're debugging. Xamarin makes this part pretty easy—it creates a default keystore that's used to sign your apps. This is ideal for debugging, but when you want to release your app to the store, you have to sign with your own keystore file (we'll look at how to create one in the next section). The Xamarin default keystore is created every time you install Xamarin and will be different for different developers, and it will change if you need to reinstall the Xamarin tools. When you publish to the Google Play store, you have to sign all releases of your app with the same key, or Google won't know that the releases all come from you—it will reject updates signed with a different key.

Keystores can be reused across multiple apps. This means you can have one keystore and use it to sign all your apps, if you want. By doing this, you lose a bit of security—if someone gets hold of your keystore and password, they have control of all your apps, but you also make your life easier because you only have one keystore and password to manage. It's up to you which you prefer—some developers use a single keystore for all apps and some use multiple keystores. Do what works for you.

13.2.3 Creating keystores and signing builds

When you're ready to publish your app for other people to use, package it up and sign it with your keystore—a process known as *archiving*. This is essentially the same as what happens under the hood when you run your app on a device or emulator—an APK file is created and signed, except in this case you're specifying a particular keystore to use rather than using the default one that Xamarin creates for you. As a part of this process, you can create a new keystore file if necessary.

To start the process, set your Droid app as your startup project, and from Visual Studio for Mac select Build > Archive For Publishing, or from Windows select Build > Archive. This will compile your app, create an unsigned APK file, and open up the Archive Manager, shown in figure 13.5. The Archive Manager shows all the archives you've created for your project, and from there you can sign them. Select the newly created archive for your app and click Sign and Distribute in Visual Studio for Mac, or Distribute on Windows.

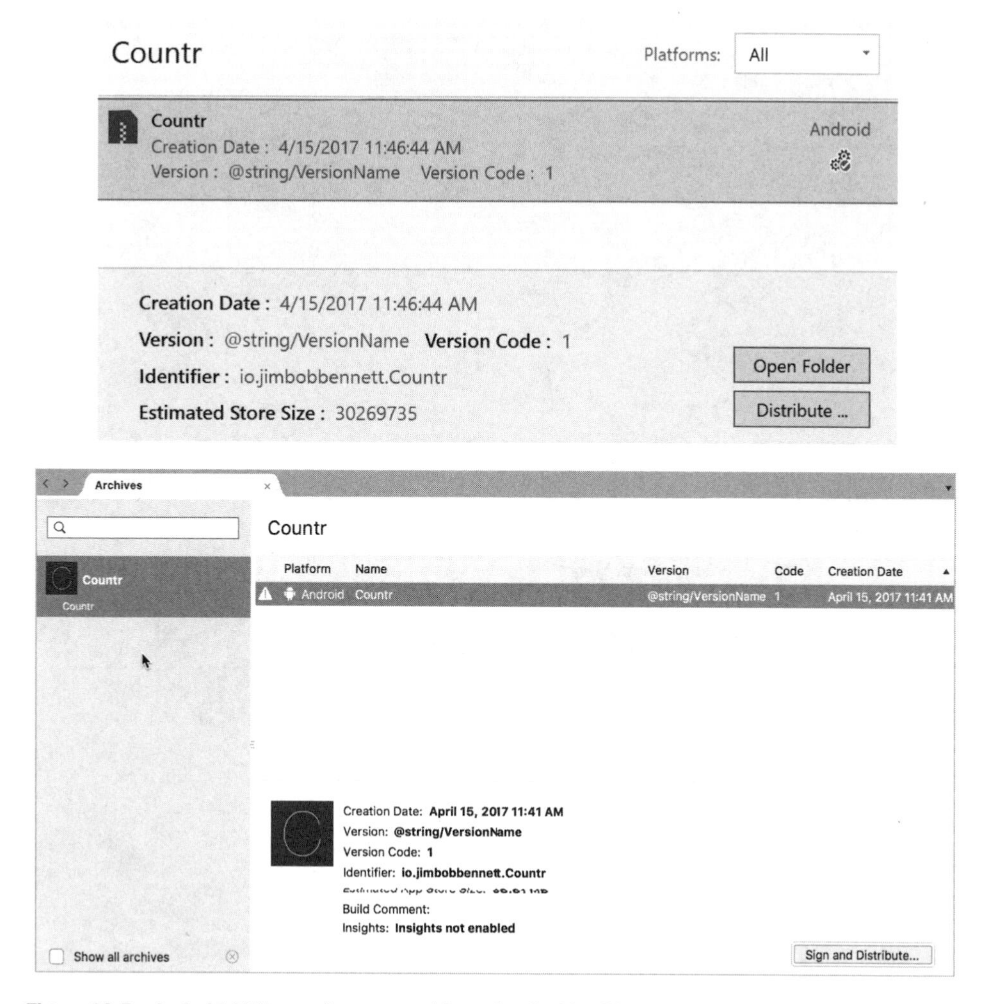

Figure 13.5 Android APKs can be managed from the Archive Manager.

A dialog will pop up, allowing you to select how you want to distribute your build—either as an ad hoc build or directly to the Google Play store (figure 13.6). We're not planning to release to the store yet, so select Ad Hoc to create an APK that's saved locally. The next step is to select the keystore you want to use to sign the app, and it's here that you can create a new keystore. Click Create a New Key in Visual Studio for Mac, or the big green plus button on Windows.

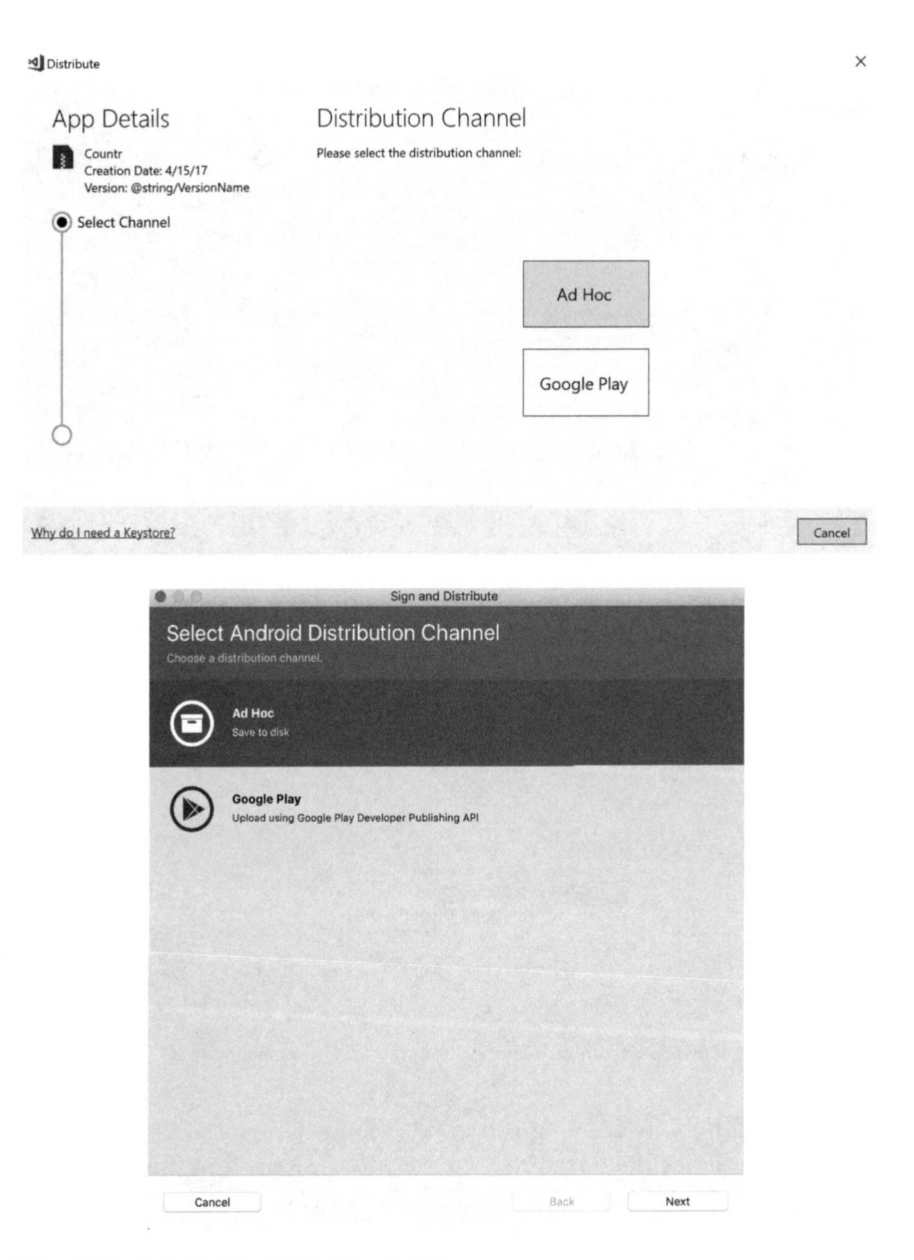

Figure 13.6 Selecting the distribution channel

In the dialog that pops up (figure 13.7), enter an alias for the keystore (this will become the filename), add a password, and then set at least one piece of information in the personal information section. Click OK. This will generate your keystore, containing a private key protected by your password. On Windows, these keys are created in your home directory under <home>\AppData\Local\Xamarin\Mono for Android\Keystore\<alias>\<alias>.keystore. On Mac, they're created in ~/Library/Developer/Xamarin/Keystore/<alias>/<alias>.keystore, where <alias> is the alias you gave it when creating it. Keep this file, alias, and password safe—back it up, ideally to a secure cloud store, and back up your password using a cloud-based password manager. If you lose this keystore, you won't be able to publish updates to your app.

Figure 13.7 Creating a keystore file involves giving it a name, a password, and one piece of personal information.

KEEP YOUR KEYSTORE SAFE You *must* keep your keystore and its password safe. Make sure it's secure and backed up, preferably to a secure cloud service. If your key is stolen, the thieves could use it to sign malicious versions of your app. If it's lost or you forget your password, you won't be able to update your app on the store.

After creating (and backing up) the keystore, select it, and click Save As in Visual Studio on Windows, or Next and then Publish on Mac. Choose a destination to save the archive to, and enter your keystore password when prompted. Your APK will then be signed and saved. This APK is the end result of all your hard work so far—you now have an Android app designed, built, and archived, ready for distribution. You can send this APK to beta testers or distribute it to the Google Play store.

That's Android done, so let's move on to iOS.

13.3 Running iOS apps on a real device

It's pretty easy to get debugging working on an Android device. On iOS it's not so easy and involves something that iOS developers dread—*provisioning profiles* (figure 13.8).

I Am Devloper
@iamdevloper
The new Apple ad should show a developer crying whilst trying to complete the Provisioning Profile process. That's real life.

Figure 13.8 Provisioning profiles aren't the most popular thing with developers...

13.3.1 What is a provisioning profile?

Provisioning profiles are used to tie up three things:

- *A signing certificate*—Signing certificates are used to verify that your app really does come from you and not from an imposter.
- *An app ID*—App IDs identify one or more apps and matches the bundle identifier in your app's info.plist. Bundle identifiers are usually reverse domain names suffixed with the name of your app (for example, I'd use io.jimbobbennett.countr for Countr), so app IDs will either match this or use a wildcard for the app names (such as io.jimbobbennett.*).
- *Device UDIDs (or store release)*—All iOS devices have a *unique device ID* (UDID). When you create a provisioning profile, you can create one of two types of profiles—a development or ad hoc profile that you can run on test devices, or a store profile for when your app is released to the App Store. Development and ad hoc provisioning profiles need a list of UDIDs for the devices they can be run on, and once this list is set, you can only use this profile to run on those devices (to change this list, regenerate the profile). For store profiles, you don't need to set a UDID list, but these profiles can only be used to sign builds that will be deployed to the store and can't be used for local testing.

Your provisioning profile is embedded into your app package when you compile for devices. The build step that does this first verifies that the certificate used in the profile is yours and that it's in your keychain. Then it verifies that the app ID matches. When you run your app on a device, the device itself will refuse to allow the app to be installed if the UDID isn't in the profile. This is just for physical device builds—simulators don't need provisioning profiles.

You used to need a paid Apple Developer account to create a provisioning profile and run on a physical device, but Apple recently relaxed that requirement and will allow you to use Xcode (Apple's IDE) to generate a temporary profile for your device for development and testing purposes. This profile only lasts a week and needs to be regenerated every time it expires.

Later in this chapter we'll look at profiles in more detail (and you'll need a paid Developer account for this), but to start with, let's just use Xcode to create a profile. Xcode is only available on Macs, and you should already have it installed or you wouldn't have been able to build iOS apps with Xamarin. If you're on a Mac, launch it (it should be in your Applications folder). If you're using Windows with a remote Mac build host, you'll need to log in to your Mac, either directly or remotely.

13.3.2 Bundle identifiers

Xcode doesn't know anything about Xamarin and can't be used to load your Xamarin app, but you can trick it a bit. All apps are identified by their bundle identifier in their info.plist, and if you have multiple apps with the same bundle identifier, you can reuse the provisioning profile for both of them. When you submit an app to the store, the bundle identifier needs to be unique, so you can't use the same ID for multiple apps that you want to put on the store, but there's nothing stopping you from creating a dummy app with the same bundle ID just to get a profile. You can create this dummy app by creating an app in Xcode with a bundle identifier that matches your apps, letting Xcode create the profile, and then using it in your Xamarin app.

The first thing to do is get your bundle identifier. Open the SquareRt solution (or Countr—it doesn't matter, as the steps are pretty much the same), and then open the info.plist file in the SquareRt.iOS project. In the Identity section there should be a Bundle Identifier that defaults to com.companyname.SquareRt (figure 13.9).

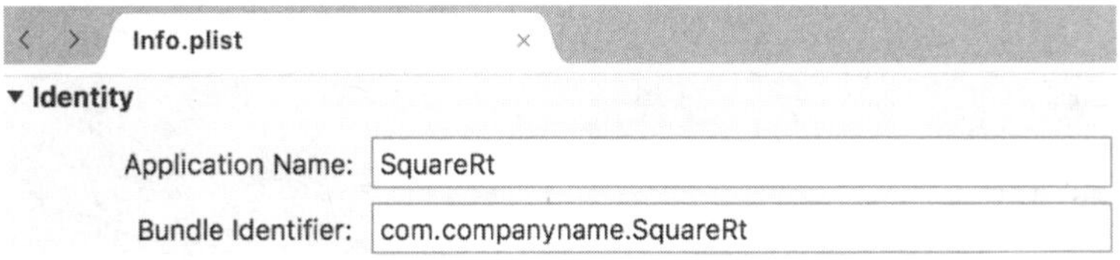

Figure 13.9 The bundle identifier is set in the info.plist file.

This is a two-part thing made up of an organization identifier and a product name, the organization identifier being com.companyname in this example, and the product name being SquareRt. When creating multiple apps, you should follow the same convention using the same organization identifier but different product names. Choose a suitable identifier, such as a reverse domain name if you have your own domain, or something with your own or your company name in it, suffixed with the product name, .SquareRt (for example, I use io.jimbobbennett.SquareRt).

13.3.3 Creating a dummy app in Xcode

To create a dummy app, open up Xcode and create a new project by selecting File > New > Project. Select Single View Application from the iOS tab and then click Next. In the next screen, set the Product Name to SquareRt and the Organization Identifier to whatever you set as the first part of the bundle identifier in your info.plist. The end result should be that the read-only Bundle Identifier field matches the bundle identifier in your Xamarin app, so if you used com.companyname.SquareRt, the product name should be SquareRt, the organization identifier should be com .companyname, and you should see the bundle identifier showing com.companyname .SquareRt. This is shown in figure 13.10.

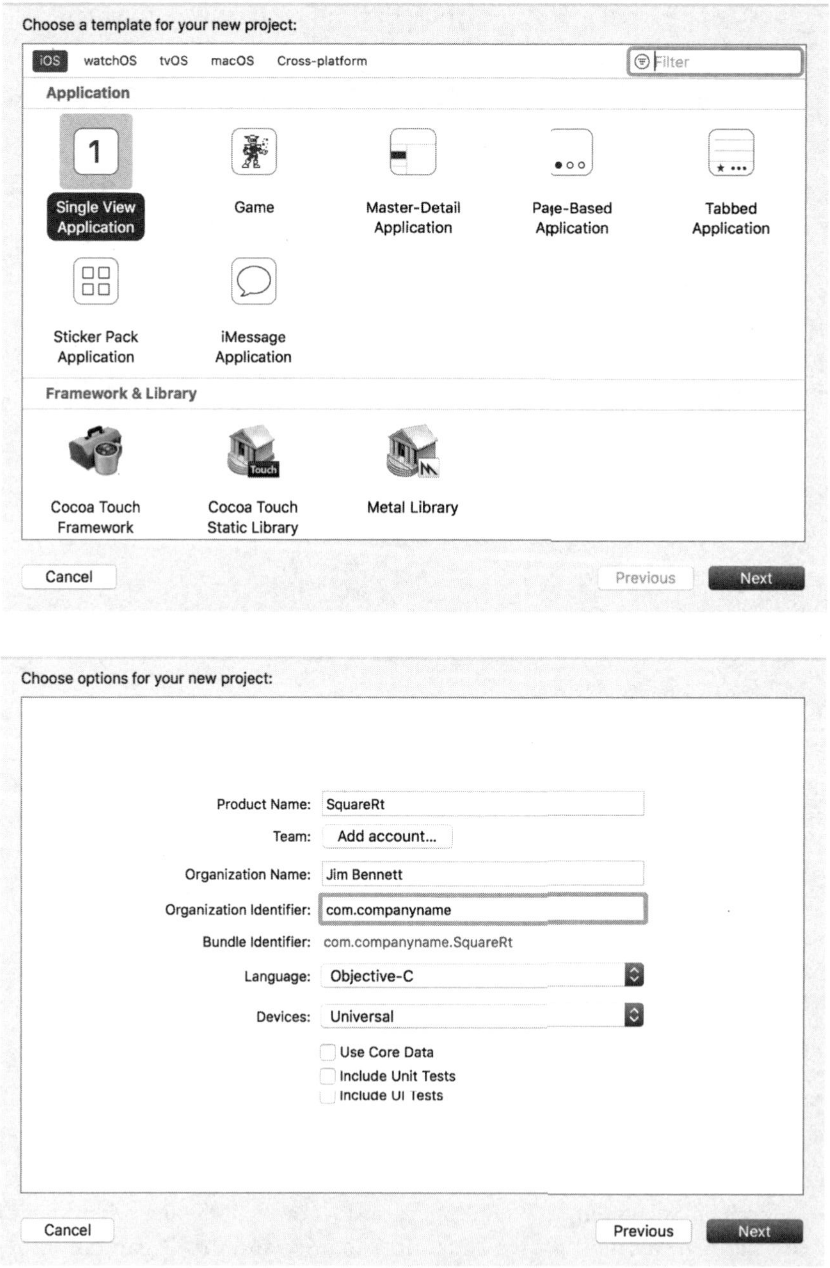

Figure 13.10 Create a new iOS Single View app with a bundle identifier that matches your Xamarin app.

Next, add an account—Xcode will only create profiles for valid Apple IDs. Click the Add Account button and log in with a valid Apple ID (or use Create Apple ID if you don't have one). This can be any Apple ID, including the account you use with iTunes to buy songs and apps. Once you've logged in with your Apple ID, you can close the dialog that popped up (figure 13.11).

Figure 13.11 Xcode needs a valid Apple ID to create profiles, and it will automatically create a default team for you from your Apple ID.

The Add Account button will be replaced with a drop-down where you can select your team—rather than have individual profiles for single developers, Apple thinks of profiles as belonging to teams, so that everyone developing an app can share the same profile. If you've logged into Xcode before, the Add Account button won't show and it will display the team drop-down straight away. A default team is created for you, called <Your Name> (Personal Team), so select this from the drop-down and click Next, select a folder to save your app to, and click Create.

Once your app is created, connect your device using a USB cable and then select it as the active device in the drop-down at the top left (figure 13.12). When it's selected, Xcode will automatically generate a provisioning profile for you that lasts seven days.

Once this profile has been created, switch back to Visual Studio. You should then be able to select your device, ready to run your app. Visual Studio for Mac usually shows the device the first time. If you don't see your device straight away on Windows, try unplugging it and plugging it back in, or restarting Visual Studio.

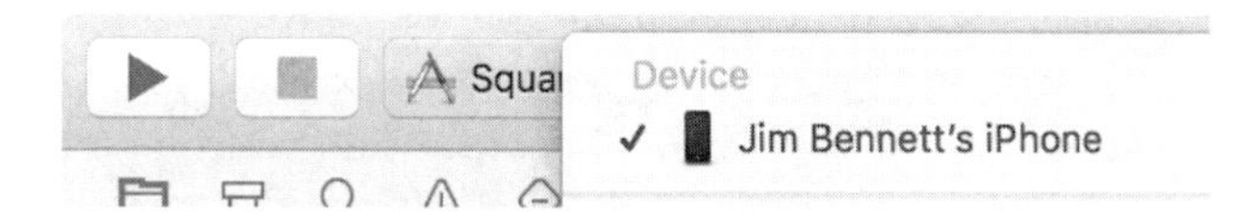

Figure 13.12 Once your device is plugged in, select it from the drop-down in the top left.

13.3.4 Running your app on a physical device

Once you're ready to run your app, there's one more step. If you try to run the app, it will install on your device but not start up. Instead, if you launch it, it will show an error like the one in figure 13.13.

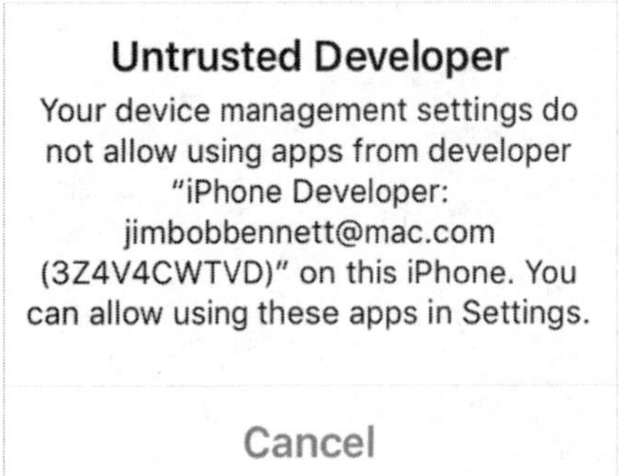

Untrusted Developer

Your device management settings do not allow using apps from developer "iPhone Developer: jimbobbennett@mac.com (3Z4V4CWTVD)" on this iPhone. You can allow using these apps in Settings.

Cancel

Figure 13.13 The first time you install an app using a provisioning profile from Xcode, you need to trust it.

This is because Apple likes to be really secure. Not only do you need to set up the temporary provisioning profile on your Mac, you also need to allow it on your device. If you try to run the app manually, you'll be presented with an alert telling you it's from an untrusted developer. Open the Settings app, go to General > Device Management, select your Apple ID, and tap the Trust <your Apple ID> button. Then tap Trust on the dialog that pops up.

Once that's done, you can launch the app in a debugger, and you should see it run on your device. You can now run and debug your app on the device as you would in the simulator—setting breakpoints, evaluating variables, and stepping through code.

> **TRUST LASTS ONLY WHILE YOU HAVE AN APP FROM THAT APPLE ID INSTALLED** When you trust the Apple ID, your phone will allow all apps from that Apple ID to run. If you installed Countr and SquareRt using provisioning profiles based on the same Apple ID, you'll only need to trust it once and both apps will work.
>
> This trust only lasts as long as you have at least one app installed. Once you have no more apps installed from a particular Apple ID, the trust is revoked and you have to trust it again the next time you install one of your apps.

13.4 Creating iOS provisioning profiles

As you might expect, iOS signing is completely different from signing for Android—the biggest difference being cost. Anyone can create signed APKs for free. You only need to pay if you want to distribute via the Google Play store, and it's a one-time cost of $25 (at the time of writing). For iOS, when you want to sign your apps to run on devices other than your own, or you want to avoid re-signing via Xcode every seven days, or you want to publish to the store, you must be a fully paid-up member of the Apple Developer program. This currently costs $99 every year.

To sign up, head to https://developer.apple.com, sign in with your Apple ID, and follow the instructions to purchase a Developer account. The Apple Developer site is pretty helpful and it changes frequently, so I won't cover the specific steps here. Be aware, though, that Developer accounts are tied to either an individual developer or to a business, and each account only lets you publish under the account owner. If you have an account at work as part of a business membership, you won't be able to use that account to publish your personal apps.

iOS signing is based on provisioning profiles—you provision your app to run as an ad hoc build on a fixed set of devices or to run on any device when distributed via the store. As you've already seen, a provisioning profile ties a certificate to an app ID and optionally to one or more devices, so let's create a provisioning profile for debugging using a real device, similar to what we created with Xcode earlier, but one that won't expire every seven days. We'll start by looking at certificates.

13.4.1 Certificates

A certificate is used to sign your apps to certify that they're from you. They can be thought of as similar to Android keystores, but with a few important differences. You need different certificates for different things, so you create one certificate for debugging your app on devices, a different one for distribution via the store, and perhaps others for using push notifications, using Apple Pay, or building VoIP apps. The other big difference from Android is that your certificates are stored in the Apple Developer portal, so Apple keeps copies of all your certificates—eliminating the worry about losing them.

You can create certificates in one of three ways—from the Apple Developer portal, using Xcode from your development Mac or Mac build host, or by using Visual Studio for Mac and a tool called Fastlane.

Creating certificates using Xcode

Launch Xcode and ensure you've signed in using the Apple ID you used to sign up with the Apple Developer Program. Click Xcode > Preferences, select the Accounts tab in the dialog box that appears, and then select your Apple ID on the left side. You'll see the details of your Apple ID on the right. Click the Manage Certificates button at the bottom.

This will open another dialog showing all your installed certificates (which will probably be empty). Click the plus button at the bottom and select iOS Development (figure 13.14). This will create a certificate for you, install it in your macOS keychain, and upload it to the Apple Developer portal.

Creating certificates using Visual Studio for Mac and Fastlane

To help with automating the whole Apple app maintenance process, an open source set of tools called Fastlane was created (Fastlane is now maintained by Google). It provides a whole range of tools that connect to Apple's Developer services, allowing you to manage certificates, app IDs, and provisioning profiles, and even upload apps to the store with screenshots and metadata. Fastlane isn't officially supported by Apple,

Figure 13.14 You can manage iOS certificates from Xcode.

but it's used by a huge number of developers and works really well. Fastlane's full capabilities are outside the scope of this book, but you can use it via Visual Studio for Mac to create certificates. You can read more about Fastlane at https://fastlane.tools.

The first step is to install Fastlane. You can find instructions on Fastlane's Docs page about how to install it via Homebrew, Ruby, or downloading a zip file (https://docs.fastlane.tools). Pick your favorite method and install it (I prefer to download the zip file and run the installer, as there are no other dependencies).

Next, launch Visual Studio for Mac, select Visual Studio > Preferences, and then select Publishing > Apple Developer Accounts from the left side. To add a new Developer account, click the green plus button under Apple IDs. You'll see a dialog box telling you that you'll be redirected to Fastlane to log in (figure 13.15), so click OK and enter your Apple ID and password in the terminal that will appear. Your credentials will be stored in your Apple keychain, not uploaded to Fastlane or Xamarin.

You may then see a dialog from macOS asking for permission for Visual Studio to access the new credentials in the keychain—if this pops up, click Always Allow.

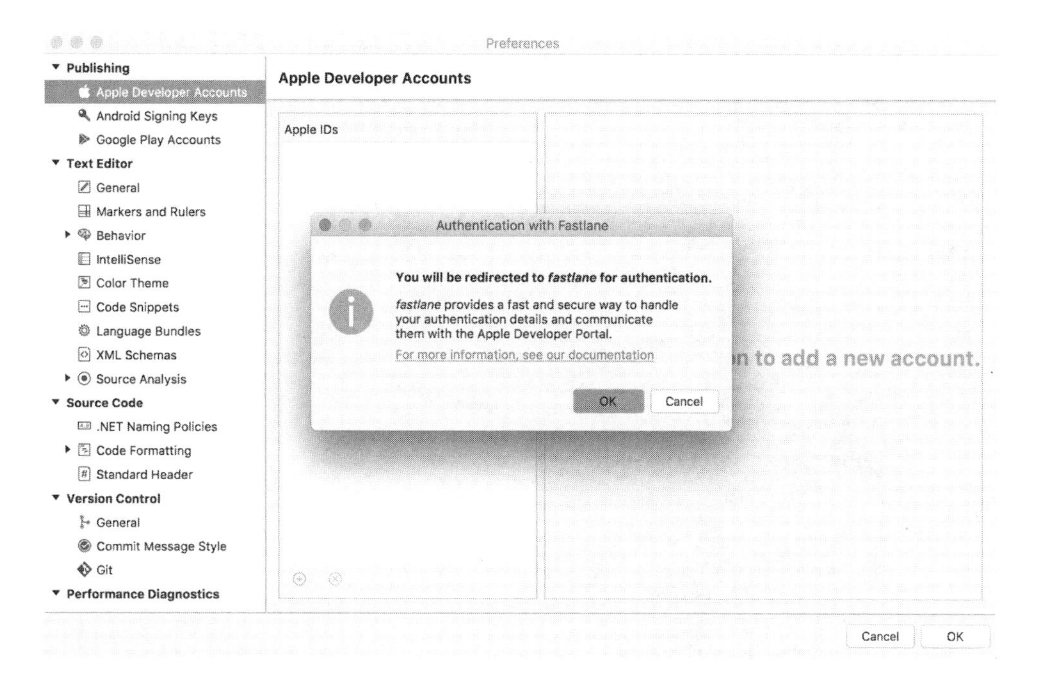

Figure 13.15 You can add an Apple Developer account from the Visual Studio for Mac preferences.

Once your Apple ID has been added, click View Details and you'll see another dialog box showing your certificates and provisioning profiles. From here, click Create Certificate > iOS Development (figure 13.16). This will create your certificate, install it in your macOS keychain, and upload it to the Apple Developer portal.

CREATING CERTIFICATES USING THE APPLE DEVELOPER PORTAL

You can create certificates from the Apple Developer portal, but I highly recommend using Xcode or Visual Studio for Mac, as these are much easier.

To create a certificate from the Developer portal, follow these steps:

1. Log in to https://developer.apple.com, and in the menu click Account > Certificates, Identifiers, and Profiles.
2. Select Certificates > All on the left side, and click the plus button at the top right.
3. Choose iOS App Development, and click Continue.
4. Follow the on-screen instructions to create a certificate-signing-request file using Keychain Access on your Mac. Then click Continue.
5. Click Choose File and select the CertificateSigningRequest.certSigningRequest file that was created by Keychain Access. Then click Continue.
6. Click the Download button to download the certificate. Then double-click the downloaded file to install it in your keychain.
7. Click Done to return to the list of certificates (figure 13.17).

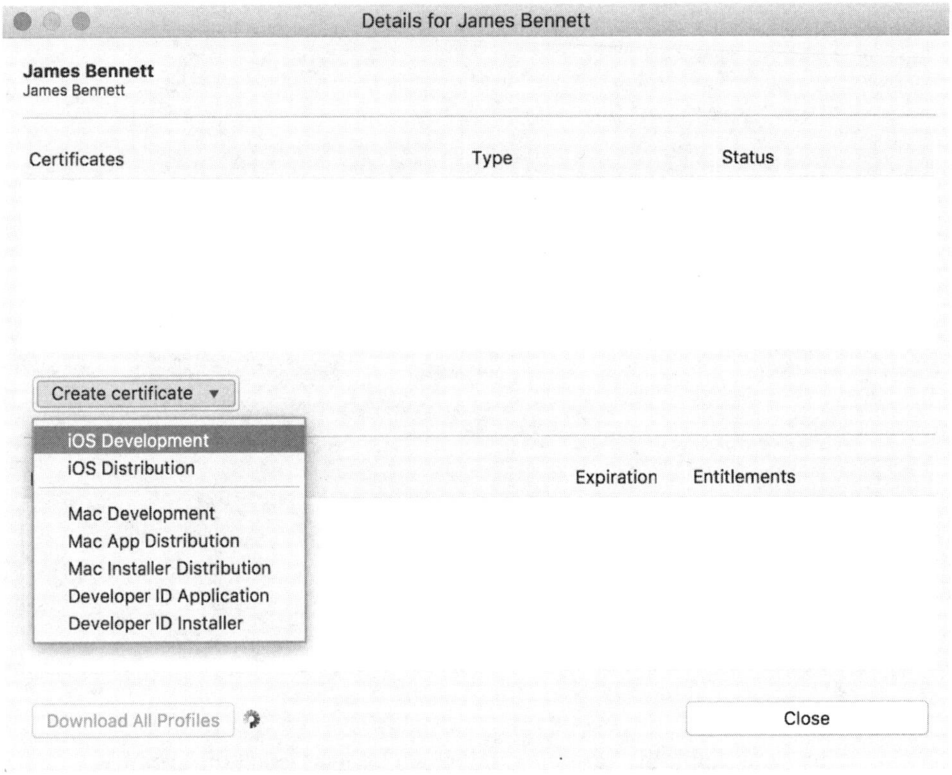

Figure 13.16 Visual Studio for Mac can be used to create new certificates.

Figure 13.17 You can also manage iOS certificates from the Apple Developer portal.

Once that's done, you'll see your newly created certificate. From here you'll also see any certificates that you create using Xcode or Visual Studio for Mac. By clicking a certificate, you can download it (for example, if you need to set up a new Mac developer machine, or you want to use the same certificate for multiple Macs) or you can revoke the certificate so that it can no longer be used.

13.4.2 App IDs

Once you have a signing certificate, you can sign any of your apps to verify that they're yours, so the next step is to create an App ID to identify each of your apps. These are identifiers for one or more apps, and they're used to tie your certificate to those apps. App IDs also allow you to specify certain services that your app can support, such as iCloud access, push notifications, or Siri (these are outside the scope of this book). App IDs have to be created from the Apple Developer portal, and there are two types of App ID you can create: explicit or wildcard.

- *Explicit App IDs*—Explicit App IDs are based on a reverse domain name, which should be the same as the bundle identifier in your app (for example, com.companyname.Countr). These IDs can be used to tie a provisioning profile to a single app and must be used if you want to include certain services in your app, such as push notifications or Apple Pay.
- *Wildcard App IDs*—Wildcard App IDs contain a wildcard and so can be used for multiple apps. For example, an App ID of com.companyname.* could be used for any app with a bundle ID that starts with com.companyname, so com.companyname.Countr as well as com.companyname.SquareRt. Wildcard App IDs can't be used with most Apple services, such as push notifications.

We'll use a wildcard App ID for now as we don't need any of those services for our two apps.

App IDs can only be created from the Apple Developer portal, so log on to https://developer.apple.com and in the menu select Account > Certificates, Identifiers and Profiles. Choose Identifiers > App IDs on the left side and then click the plus button on the right.

Enter a description for your App ID, such as *Xamarin In Action apps*, and then select Wildcard App ID in the App ID Suffix section (figure 13.18). Enter a wildcard bundle ID using the same format that you used when setting the bundle ID for your apps, but use * instead of the app name. For example, if the bundle IDs you've used for your two apps are com.companyname.Countr and com.companyname.SquareRt, you'd set your wildcard bundle ID as com.companyname.*. You don't need any app services for these apps, so leave those all unchecked and click Continue. Check the values in the next screen and then click Register to create your App ID.

13.4.3 Devices

Provisioning profiles can either be linked to one or more devices that can be used for debugging or for distribution to beta test users (we'll look at distribution in more detail in chapter 16), or they can be set up for store builds and be used for any device, as long as your app is distributed via the store.

To create a provisioning profile linked to devices, you have to first register those devices on the Apple Developer portal, and Apple has some hard limits on these devices. You're limited to 100 devices of each product family (so 100 iPhones, 100

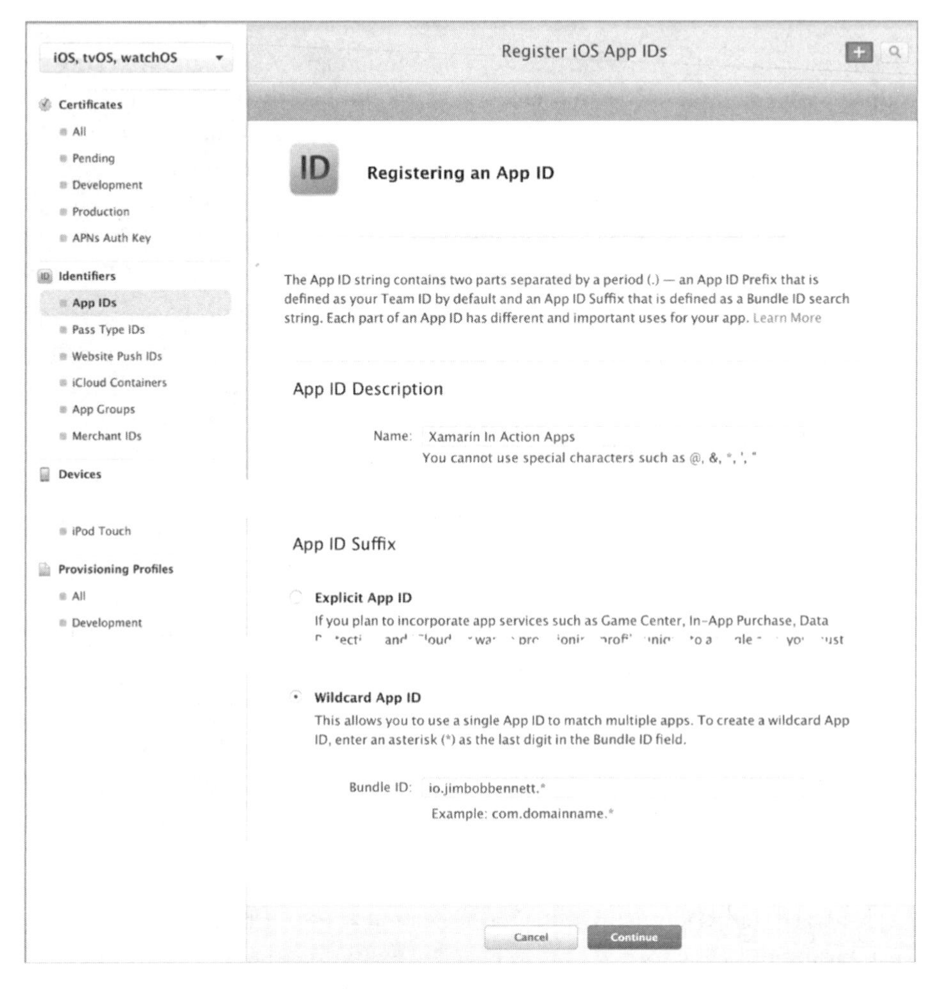

Figure 13.18 App IDs are created from the Apple Developer portal (some parts of the form have been removed to save space).

iPads, 100 Apple Watches, and so on) per membership year. This means you can add up to 100 of each device and no more, and then you can't register any more for a year, even if you unregister these devices.

To register a device, you first need its UDID, which you can easily get from Xcode. Plug your device in, open Xcode, and select Window > Devices. From here you'll see all connected devices as well as all simulators that Xcode has installed for you, as shown in figure 13.19. Select your device from the list on the left, and you'll see all the details about it on the right. Under Device Information you'll see the Identifier. Double-click this value and copy it to the clipboard.

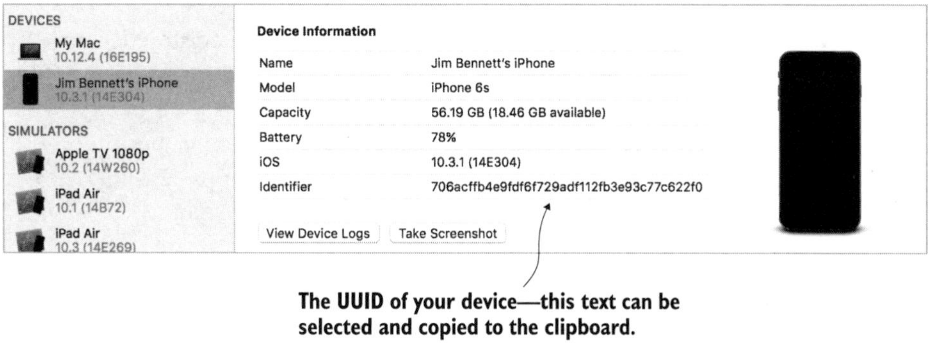

DEVICES
My Mac
10.12.4 (16E195)
Jim Bennett's iPhone
10.3.1 (14E304)
SIMULATORS
Apple TV 1080p
10.2 (14W260)
iPad Air
10.1 (14B72)
iPad Air
10.3 (14E269)

Device Information

Name	Jim Bennett's iPhone
Model	iPhone 6s
Capacity	56.19 GB (18.46 GB available)
Battery	78%
iOS	10.3.1 (14E304)
Identifier	706acffb4e9fdf6f729adf112fb3e93c77c622f0

View Device Logs | Take Screenshot

The UUID of your device—this text can be selected and copied to the clipboard.

Figure 13.19 You can find device identifiers for plugged-in devices using Xcode.

Once you have your device ID, head to the Certificates, Identifiers and Profiles section of the Apple Developer portal, select Devices > All on the left, and click the plus button on the right. Enter a name for your device and the identifier from Xcode, click Continue, and then click Register (figure 13.20). You can also upload a tab-separated file from here with multiple device IDs if you want.

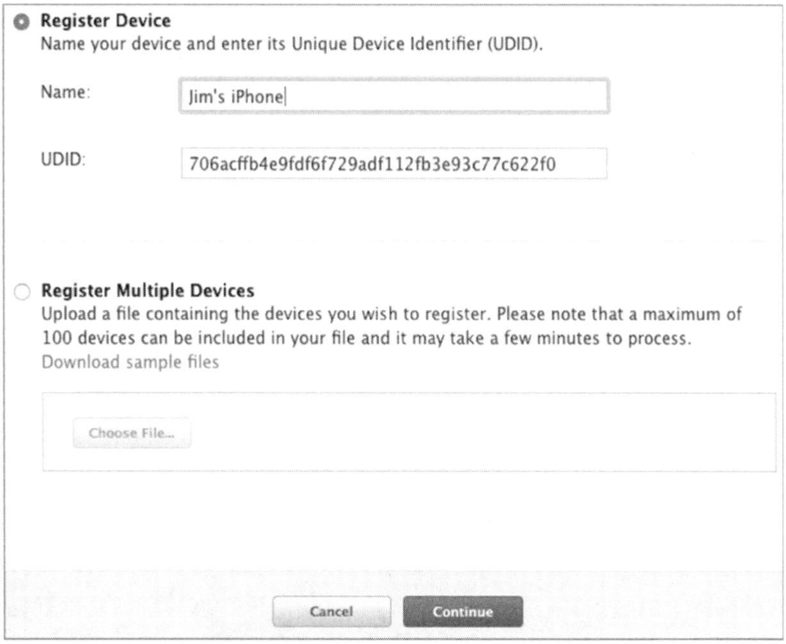

Register Device
Name your device and enter its Unique Device Identifier (UDID).

Name: Jim's iPhone

UDID: 706acffb4e9fdf6f729adf112fb3e93c77c622f0

Register Multiple Devices
Upload a file containing the devices you wish to register. Please note that a maximum of 100 devices can be included in your file and it may take a few minutes to process.
Download sample files

Choose File...

Cancel | Continue

Figure 13.20 From the Apple Developer portal you can register individual devices or upload a file with multiple devices.

13.4.4 Provisioning profiles

You have an iOS development certificate and you've registered your App IDs and device, so now now you can create a profile. Once again, you have to do this from the Certificates, Identifiers and Profiles section of the Apple Developer site, so from there select Provisioning Profiles > All on the left and click the plus button on the right.

From here you can create profiles for iOS and tvOS apps, and there are three types of profiles you can create:

- *App development*—Use this to debug your app on real devices.
- *Ad hoc*—These profiles are used to distribute your app to a limited number of devices for beta testing.
- *App Store*—Use this when you're ready to distribute your app to the store.

We'll be looking at distributing your app with ad hoc and store profiles later in this book, so for now select iOS App Development and click Continue. In the next screen, select the App ID you created earlier in the drop-down and click Continue. Next, check the certificate you created and click Continue. Then select your device and click Continue. Finally, give your profile a name, such as Development, and click Continue. This will create the provisioning profile. Just like certificates, these are stored on the Apple Developer portal, so there's no need to keep backup copies.

Once your profile is created, install it on your Mac. You can do that in one of three ways: you can download it from the Developer portal using the Download button (figure 13.21) and then double-click it in the Finder to install it, or you can download it using Xcode or Visual Studio for Mac.

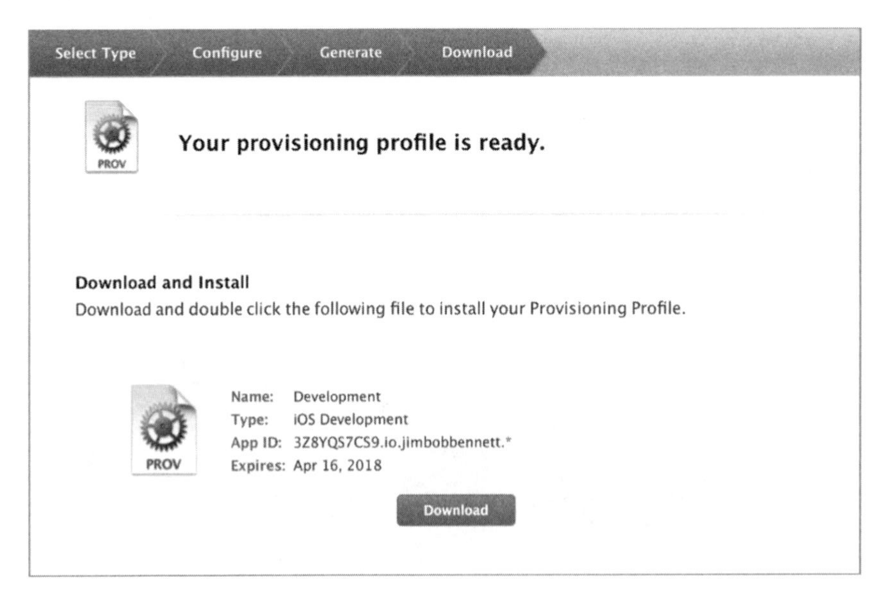

Figure 13.21 After creating a provisioning profile, you can download and install it from the Developer portal.

To install from Xcode, go to Xcode > Preferences, click the Accounts tab, select your Apple ID, and click the Download All Profiles button. From Visual Studio for Mac, click Visual Studio > Preferences, select Publishing > Apple Developer Accounts on the left side, select your Apple ID, click the View Details button, and then click the Download All Profiles button. This is shown in figure 13.22.

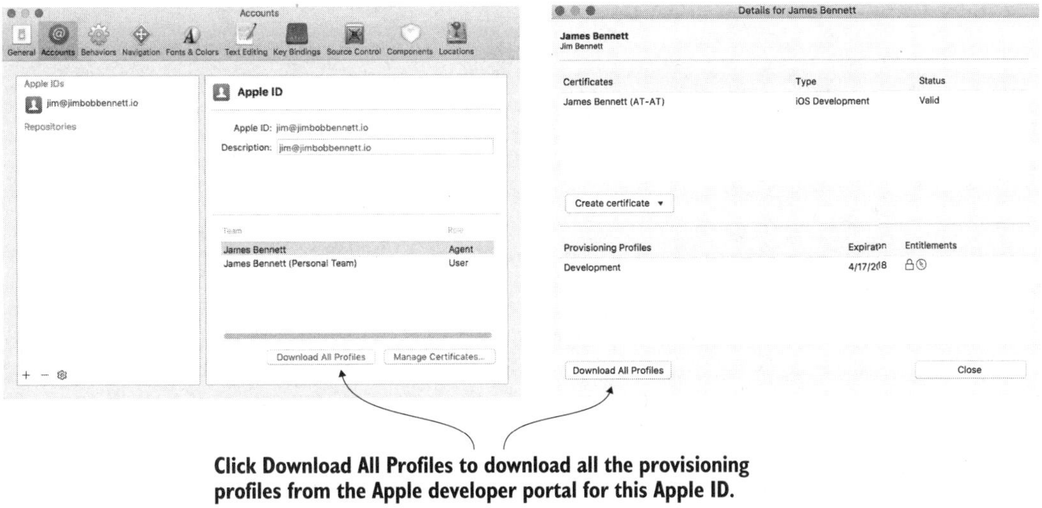

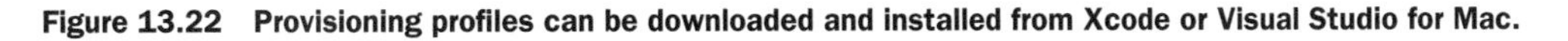

Figure 13.22 Provisioning profiles can be downloaded and installed from Xcode or Visual Studio for Mac.

13.4.5 Running your app using the new provisioning profile

Now that you have a provisioning profile created, you can use it when debugging your app. If you're using Visual Studio for Mac for your development, restart it if you downloaded and installed the profile manually or downloaded it using Xcode. If you're using Visual Studio on Windows, restart it regardless of how you installed the provisioning profile. Once you've restarted Visual Studio (if needed), you should be able to plug your device in, select it, and run your apps on it.

By default, when you build an iOS app, Xamarin is smart enough to choose a provisioning profile automatically, based on the bundle ID of your app and the UDID of the device you're trying to run on. If you need to manually select a different profile, you can do that from the iOS Bundle Signing section of the iOS app properties (figure 13.23). Most of the time, though, these should be left at their default setting of Automatic.

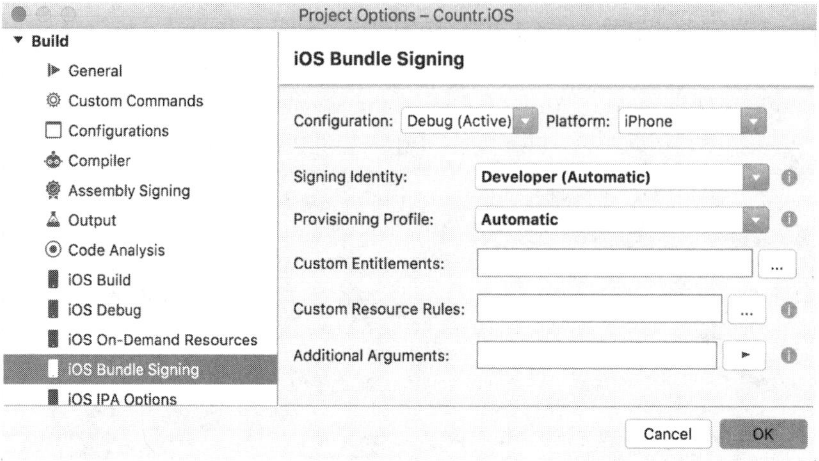

Figure 13.23 You can change the Provisioning Profile in the iOS bundle settings of the project properties, but it's best left on Automatic.

13.4.6 Troubleshooting

When you run your app on your device, if something isn't configured correctly, you'll get the following compiler error when you try to run your app:

"Error: No installed provisioning profiles match the installed iOS signing identities."

This means that the provisioning profiles that Xamarin knows about don't tie up with the device you're trying to run on. There are a number of steps you can take to find out what's wrong:

- *Make sure your app is set to use the automatic profiles*—In the iOS app properties, head to the iOS Bundle Signing tab and ensure that Automatic is selected for Signing Identity and Provisioning Profiles.
- *Make sure the certificate is installed on your Mac*—If you created your certificate using the Apple Developer portal instead of using Visual Studio for Mac or Xcode, make sure you've downloaded it and installed it on your Mac.
- *Make sure the App IDs match*—Double-check your bundle identifiers in your app and the App ID used to create the provisioning profile to make sure they match and that there are no spelling mistakes. If you made a mistake on the Apple Developer site, delete and recreate the App ID, which will invalidate the provisioning profile that uses it, so this will need to be re-created and re-downloaded.
- *Make sure the device UDID is correct*—Double-check the device UDID shown in Xcode against the one in the Developer portal. Again, if this needs to be changed in the Developer portal, you'll need to recreate your provisioning profile.

- *Ensure that the profile has been downloaded and installed*—Make sure that the provisioning profile has been downloaded by either re-downloading it manually from the Apple Developer site and double-clicking it to install it, or by clicking the Download All Profiles button from the details dialog of the Apple Developer Accounts tab of the Visual Studio for Mac preferences, or by clicking the Download All Profiles button on the Accounts tab in the Xcode preferences.
- *Restart Visual Studio*—Profiles are only loaded when the IDE starts up, so make sure you restart Visual Studio.

You've now signed iOS and Android apps. In the next chapter we'll take these apps and create some automated UI tests for them, to validate that everything works.

Summary

In this chapter you learned

- Android and iOS have security around apps to ensure you only run approved apps on your devices.
- Android apps are signed with a keystore that you must keep safe.
- Android apps are identified by a package name. iOS apps are identified by a bundle identifier, and these are normally both reverse domain names suffixed with the app name.
- To run iOS apps on devices, you need a provisioning profile, which links a signing certificate with an App ID and optionally one or more devices.
- You can create temporary provisioning profiles using Xcode.

You also learned how to

- Turn on developer mode on an Android device and enable USB debugging.
- Create a new keystore and use it to sign an Android APK.
- Create a temporary provisioning profile using Xcode.
- Create an iOS signing certificate using Xcode, Visual Studio for Mac, and the Apple Developer portal.
- Register an App ID and iOS devices in the Apple Developer portal.
- Create and use provisioning profiles.

14 Testing mobile apps using Xamarin UITest

This chapter covers
- What UI testing is
- Using Xamarin UITest to do UI testing
- Using the REPL
- Interacting with controls
- Asserting that the UI is correct

As we've built our apps, we've written a lot of unit tests to verify the model and view-model layers, but we've written nothing to test the view layer. Although this layer is small, there could still be issues that aren't spotted until the app is out in the wild. Fortunately, we can write automated tests to help catch such bugs before users see them, causing them to uninstall our apps and move to a competitor's offerings.

14.1 Introduction to UI testing

One of the great things about the MVVM design pattern is that it allows us to maximize the code in our cross-platform model and view-model layers. Not only have we written the bulk of our code just once, but we've managed to write unit tests for it, so we have some degree of confidence that the code works. These unit tests are great, but they don't cover two important questions: have we used the correct controls on our view and bound them correctly, and does our app actually run on the device?

It's great to have a property on a view model that's bound to a text field so that the user can enter the name of a counter, but what if we accidentally used the wrong control, such as a label instead of a text box? Or maybe we used the right control but forgot to add the binding code? What if in our app we used a feature that was only added to the Android SDK in API 21, but our app manifest shows that our app will run on API 19 and higher? This is where UI testing comes in—it allows us to run our apps on emulators, simulators, and devices and write automated tests in code against it.

The concept behind UI testing is simple: you run your app and have something interact with it as if it were a user by using the user interface components (such as tapping buttons or entering text in text boxes), and you validate that everything is working by ensuring the app doesn't crash and that the results of the user's actions are shown on the UI as expected. This kind of testing was first used with desktop apps, where the aim was to make testing more reliable and cheaper—after all, humans are expensive, and they can get bored and make mistakes or miss problems after testing the same screen many, many times. Automated UI testing also allowed for better time usage, with tests being run overnight and developers discovering whether they'd broken anything the next morning.

For desktop apps, UI testing was reasonably simple—launch the app and test it, maybe testing on a few different screen sizes but always on one OS with maybe one or two different versions, because desktop OSs don't change very often. With mobile, things have become more complicated. There are two major OSs that you'll want to support with your cross-platform apps, and there are multiple versions of these OSs available. You also have different hardware with different screen sizes. On iOS this isn't too bad—you only need to support a small number of OS versions (maybe just the current and previous one) and a small number of different devices. On Android, however, as you've already seen, it's a mess with multiple OS versions in regular use, a huge range of screen sizes available, and worst of all, customizations to the OS from both the hardware manufacturers and carriers.

This is why UI testing is hugely important for mobile apps. There's no way a human could test on a wide range of devices without needing a lot of time or lots of humans involved in the process (expensive) and without them all going mad as they install the app on yet another device and run the same test for the millionth time.

14.1.1 Writing UI tests using Xamarin UITest

You write UI tests in essentially the same way that you'd write a unit test: you decide what you want to test and then write some code to create the test. This code will use some kind of framework that can launch your app and interact with it as if it were a real user.

There are a number of different frameworks for testing, and table 14.1 lists some of these.

Table 14.1 UI testing frameworks

Framework	Platforms	Language	Description
Espresso	Android	Java	This is Google's testing framework for Android apps, so it has deep integration with Android: https://google.github.io/android-testing-support-library/docs/espresso/.
XCTest	iOS	Objective-C/Swift	This is Apple's UI testing framework, so it has deep integration with iOS: https://developer.apple.com/reference/xctest.
Appium	iOS/Android	Any (Java/C#/PHP/Ruby, and so on)	An open source cross-platform testing framework based on Selenium, a web UI testing framework: http://appium.io.
UITest	iOS/Android	C#/F#	This is Xamarin's testing framework, which is heavily integrated into Visual Studio for Windows (Android) and Mac (iOS and Android): https://docs.microsoft.com/en-us/appcenter/test-cloud/uitest/?WT.mc_id=xamarininaction-book-jabenn.

In this book we'll be focusing on Xamarin UITest because it's very well integrated into Visual Studio. For testing Android apps, you can use either Windows or Mac, but for testing iOS apps you'll need to use a Mac—iOS testing isn't supported on Windows at the moment.

Xamarin UITest is based on a testing framework called Calabash that was written in Ruby and is fully open source and maintained by Xamarin. UITest is a layer on top of Calabash that allows you to write your tests in C# and run them using NUnit. These tests are written in the same way as unit tests using the arrange, act, assert pattern (shown in figure 14.1), with the arrange part launching the app and getting it to the relevant state for testing, the act part interacting with the UI as if it were a user, and the assert part querying the UI to ensure it's in the correct state.

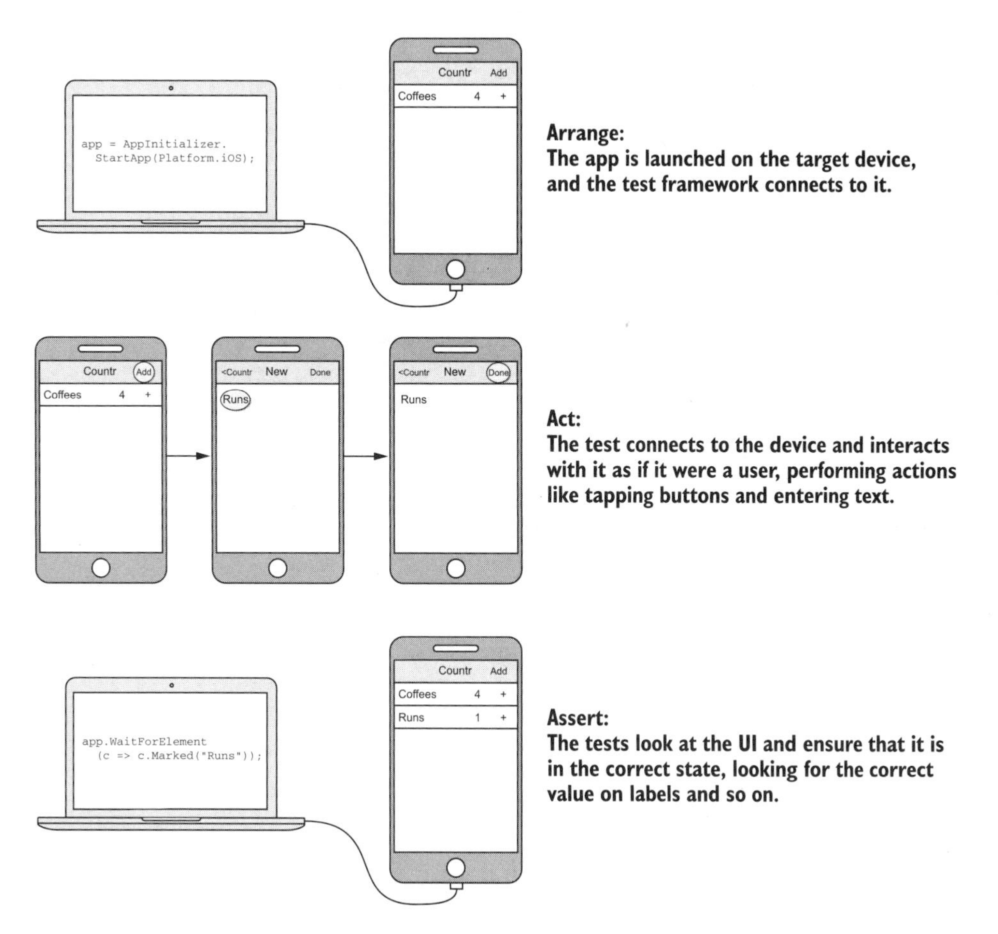
app = AppInitializer.
StartApp(Platform.iOS);
Countr Add
Coffees 4 +
Arrange:
The app is launched on the target device, and the test framework connects to it.
Countr Add
Coffees 4 +
<Countr New Done
Runs
<Countr New Done
Runs
Act:
The test connects to the device and interacts with it as if it were a user, performing actions like tapping buttons and entering text.
app.WaitForElement
(c => c.Marked("Runs"));
Countr Add
Coffees 4 +
Runs 1 +
Assert:
The tests look at the UI and ensure that it is in the correct state, looking for the correct value on labels and so on.

Figure 14.1 UI tests, like unit tests, follow the arrange, act, assert pattern.

14.1.2 Setting up your app for UI testing

In this chapter we'll just be focusing on the Countr app, as there's more to test there, so you can open the completed Countr solution from the previous chapter.

When you built the model layer in the app you added a new unit test project that tested both the model and view-model layers. For our UI tests, we'll need a new project that will contain and run the UI tests.

CREATING THE UI TEST PROJECT

Add a new UITest project to the Countr solution: On Visual Studio for Windows, right-click the solution, select Add > New Project, and from the Add New Project dialog box select Visual C# > Cross-Platform on the left, and select UI Test App in the middle (figure 14.2). On Mac, right-click the solution, select Add > Add New Project, and select Multiplatform > Tests on the left and UI Test App in the middle, and then click Next. Name your project Countr.UITests and click OK (on Windows) or Create (on Mac).

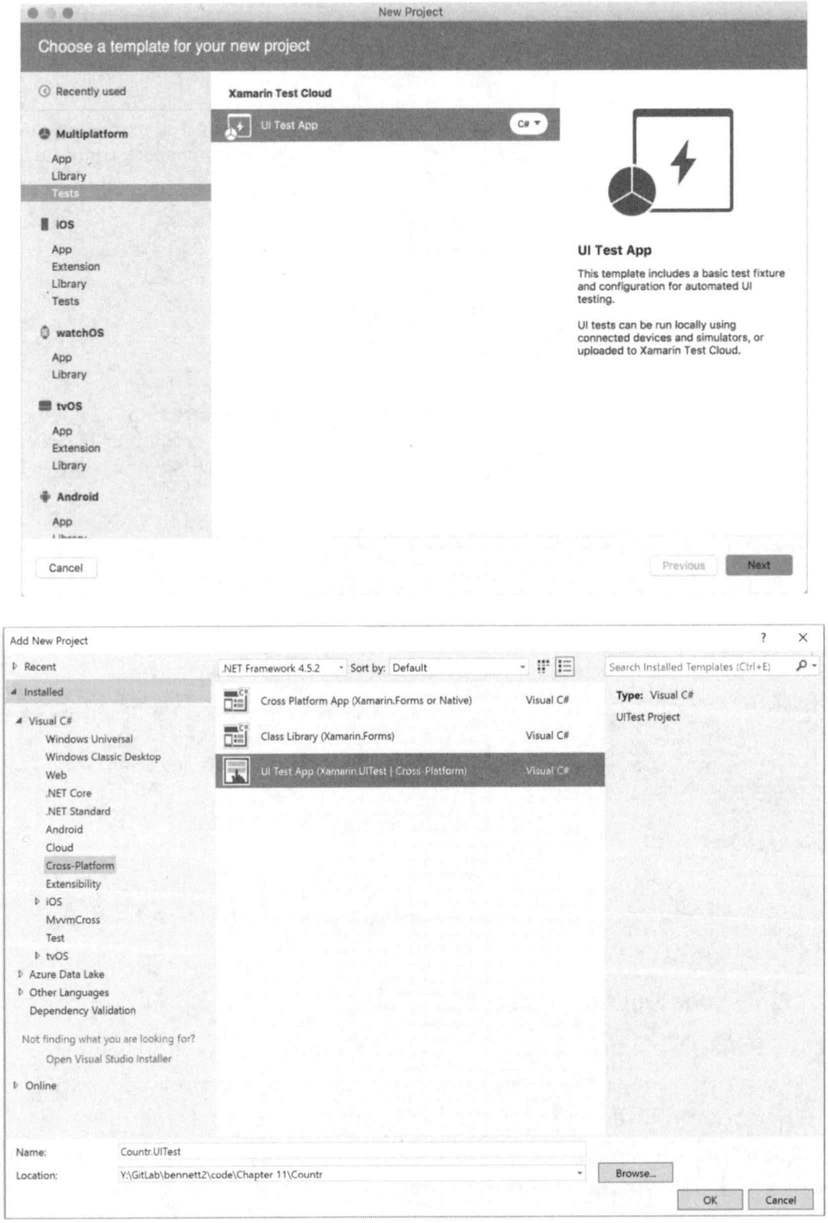

Figure 14.2 Adding a new UITest project using Visual Studio for Mac (left) and Windows (right)

Once the test project has been added, it will install two NuGet packages that UITest needs: NUnit and Xamarin.UITest. It's worth at this point updating the Xamarin.UITest NuGet package to the latest version, as they often push out bug fixes to ensure it works on the latest mobile OS versions. Do *not*, however, update NUnit. UITest will only work with NUnit 2, not NUnit 3, so if you update this package, your tests won't work and you'll need to remove the package and re-install NUnit 2.

The UI test project has two files autogenerated for you: AppInitializer.cs and Tests.cs:

- *AppInitializer.cs*—This is a static helper class with a single static method that's used to start your app. UITest has an `IApp` interface that represents your running app, and this interface has methods on it for interacting with the UI elements in your app or, to a limited extent, the device hardware (for example, rotating the device). The `StartApp` method in the `AppInitializer` class returns an instance of `IApp` that your tests can use. This method uses a helper class from UITest called `ConfigureApp` to start the app, and this helper class has a fluent API that allows you to configure and run your app. The autogenerated code in the app initializer doesn't do much to configure the app; it just specifies the app's type (Android or iOS) based on the platform passed in to the method.
- *Tests.cs*—This file contains a UI test fixture that you can run. This test fixture class has a parameterized constructor that takes the platform to run the tests on as one of the values from the `Platform` enum, either `Platform.iOS` or `Platform.Android`. It also has two `TestFixture` attributes, one for each platform. This means that you really have two test fixtures—one Android and one iOS. This fixture has a setup method that uses `AppInitializer` to start the app before each test and a single test that calls the `Screenshot` method on the `IApp` instance, which is returned from the app initializer, to take a screenshot.

SETTING UP YOUR ANDROID APPS FOR UI TESTING

By default, Xamarin Android apps are configured in debug builds to use the shared mono runtime (mono being the cross-platform version of .NET that Xamarin is based on). When you deploy your app to a device or emulator, it takes time to copy the code over, so anything that can make your app smaller reduces install time, which is good.

Xamarin Android apps use a mono runtime to provide the .NET Framework, and this is a large piece of the code bundled in your app. Rather than bundling it in, you can use a shared version that is installed separately for debug builds, making your app smaller. Unfortunately, when doing UI tests, you can't use the shared runtime, so you have two options:

- *Don't use the shared runtime*—You can turn off the shared mono runtime from the project properties. In Visual Studio for Windows, you'll find it in the Android Options tab at the top of the Packaging page. On Mac, it's on the Android Build tab at the top of the General page. Untick the Use Shared Mono Runtime box to turn this off, but be aware that this will increase your build times.

- *Release builds*—Release builds don't have the shared mono runtime turned on. After all, when you build a release version, it's usually for deployment, such as to the store, and your users won't have the shared mono runtime installed. The downside to using a release build is that you need to grant your app permission to access the internet so that it can talk to UITest. This isn't a problem if your app already accesses the internet, but if it doesn't, you many not want to ask your users for this extra permission, as they might not want to grant it. If you want to use a release build, you can grant this permission in Visual Studio by opening the project properties, heading to the Android Manifest tab, and finding the Internet permission in the Required Permissions list and ticking it. On Mac, double-click the AndroidManifest.xml file in the Properties folder and tick the permission (figure 14.3).

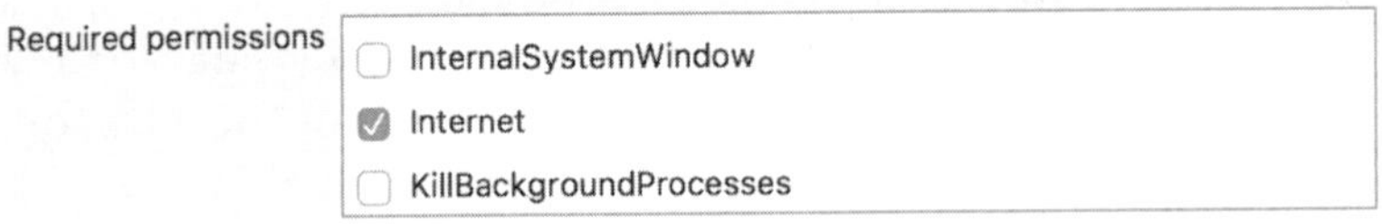

Required permissions

- [ ] InternalSystemWindow
- [x] Internet
- [ ] KillBackgroundProcesses

Figure 14.3 Adding the internet permission to AndroidManifest.xml

For the purposes of this book, we'll use release builds for Android, so open the Android manifest and add the Internet permission.

SETTING UP YOUR IOS APPS FOR UI TESTING

Apart from the issue of the shared mono runtime, UITest just works with Android out of the box—UITest can connect to your running Android app on a device or an emulator and interact with it. iOS, on the other hand, isn't quite as simple. Due to the stricter security on iOS, you can't simply have anything connect to a simulator or device and interact with the app. Instead you need to install an extra component into your iOS apps that you initialize before your UI tests can run. To do this, add the Xamarin .TestCloud.Agent NuGet package (figure 14.4) to the Countr iOS app (Test Cloud is the Xamarin cloud-based testing service that we'll look at in the next chapter, and you'll see the name used in a few places with UITest).

Once this NuGet package is installed, you'll need to add a single line of code to initialize it. Open AppDelegate.cs and add the code in the following listing.

Listing 14.1 Enabling the Calabash server for debug builds only

```
public override bool FinishedLaunching(UIApplication app,
                                        NSDictionary options)
{
   #if DEBUG
   Xamarin.Calabash.Start();
   #endif
   ...
}
```

For debug builds, start the Calabash server

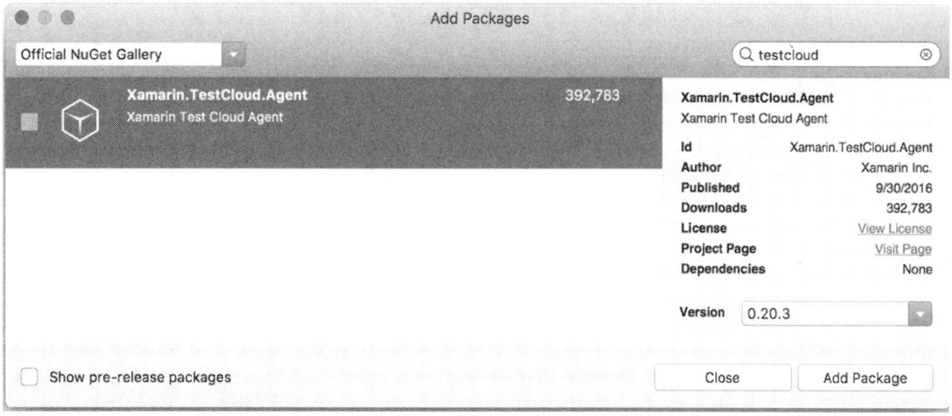

Figure 14.4 Adding the Xamarin Test Cloud Agent NuGet package

This code starts the Calabash server for debug builds only. The Calabash server is an HTTP server that runs inside your app, and the UITest framework connects to it so it can interact with your app. Apple is very strict about security in its apps and would never allow an app with an open HTTP port like this on the App Store. To avoid this, the Calabash server is only enabled for debug builds—for release builds this code won't get run, the linker will strip it out, and your app won't be rejected from the App Store (at least not due to the Calabash server).

14.1.3 Running the auto-generated tests

UI tests are run in the same way as any other unit tests—you can run them from the Test Explorer (Windows) or Test pad (Mac).

UI tests rely on having a compiled and packaged app to run, so the first step is to build and either deploy to a device, emulator, or simulator or run the app you want to test. Note that just doing a build isn't enough for Android—a build compiles the code, but it doesn't package it up. The easiest way to ensure you have a compiled and packaged app is to run it once.

On Android, create a release build; for iOS use a debug build to enable the Calabash server. You also need to set what device, emulator, or simulator you want to run your tests on in the same way that you'd select the target for debugging.

GETTING READY TO RUN THE TESTS

If you open the Test pad or Test Explorer, you may not see the UI tests if the project hasn't been built (figure 14.5). If you don't see the tests, build the UITest project, and the tests should appear.

If you expand the test tree in Visual Studio for Mac, you'll see two fixtures: Tests(Android) and Tests(iOS). These are the two fixtures declared with the two `TestFixture` attributes on the `Tests` class. When you run the tests from `Tests(Android)`, it will construct the test fixture by passing `Platform.Android` to the constructor, which in

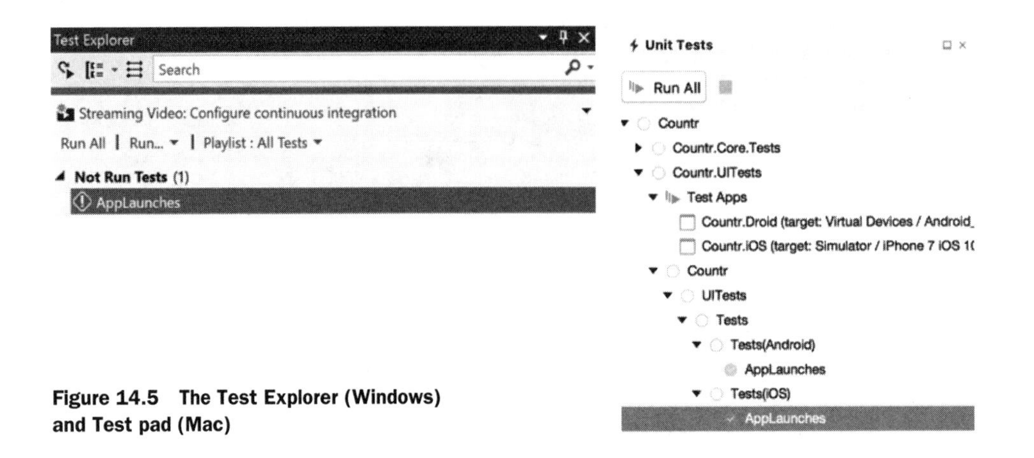

Figure 14.5 The Test Explorer (Windows) and Test pad (Mac)

turn will use the `AppInitializer` to start the Android app. `Tests(iOS)` is the same, but for the iOS app. Under each fixture you'll see the same test, called `AppLaunches`.

In Visual Studio, you won't see the same hierarchy out of the box, so drop down the Group By box and select Class to see the tests grouped by test fixture (figure 14.6). You can only test Android apps with Visual Studio, so feel free to comment out the `[TestFixture(Platform.iOS)]` attribute in the `Tests` class to remove these tests from the Test Explorer.

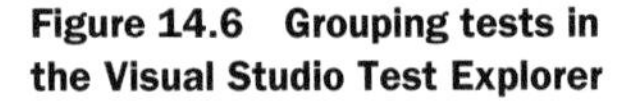

Figure 14.6 Grouping tests in the Visual Studio Test Explorer

Before you can run the test, make a small tweak. Despite the fact that the test calls `app.Screenshot`, this test won't spit out a screenshot. For some reason, UITest is configured to only create screenshots if the tests are run on Xamarin's Test Cloud, so you need to change this configuration to always generate screenshots. To do so, add the following code to AppInitializer.cs.

Listing 14.2 Enabling local screenshots for UI tests

```
public static IApp StartApp(Platform platform)
{
   if (platform == Platform.Android)
   {
```

```
        return ConfigureApp
            .Android
            .EnableLocalScreenshots()     <-- Calls EnableLocalScreenshots
            .StartApp();                       on the fluent configuration
    }                                          API to turn on screenshots

    return ConfigureApp
        .iOS
        .EnableLocalScreenshots()        <--
        .StartApp();
}
```

By default, the `StartApp` method doesn't do anything to configure the app that's being tested, which means that it expects that the app to be tested is a part of the current solution. You also need to configure UITest so it knows which apps in the solution it should use, as there could be multiple apps.

SETTING THE APP TO TEST IN VISUAL STUDIO FOR MAC

Open the Test pad and expand the Countr.UITests node. Under this you'll see the test fixtures, as well as a node called Test Apps, shown next to a stack of green arrows. Right-click this and select Add App Project. In the dialog box that appears, tick Countr.Droid and Countr.iOS, and then click OK. You'll see these two apps appear under the Test Apps node.

If you right-click one of them, you'll see a number of options, including a list of possible target devices to run against, with Current Device ticked. This list is used to set which device the UI tests should be run against when you run them from the pad. If you leave Current Device selected, it will use whatever target is set from the main toolbar, but if you always want the tests to run against a particular emulator, simulator, or device, you can select it from here.

> **YOU CAN ALSO CONFIGURE THE APP IN CODE** If you want to run an app outside the solution, or run the tests outside the IDE (such as from a CI server), you can configure which app to run and which device to run it on using the Configure App fluent API. See the Xamarin developer docs at http://mng.bz/fE5S for more information on how to do this.

SETTING THE APP TO TEST IN VISUAL STUDIO

UITest uses NUnit to run tests, so you need to ensure Visual Studio is configured to run NUnit tests. Back in chapter 7 we installed the NUnit 3 test adapter, but to use UITest you'll also need to install the NUnit 2 adapter. Select Tools > Extensions and Updates, and then select the Online tab on the left and search for *NUnit 2*. Select NUnit 2 Test Adapter in the list in the middle and click the Download button (figure 14.7). You'll need to close Visual Studio for this to be installed, so relaunch it after the install and reload the Countr solution.

Visual Studio only supports testing Android, so delete the `[TestFixture(Platform.iOS)]` attribute from the `Tests` class. This will stop iOS tests from showing up in the Test Explorer.

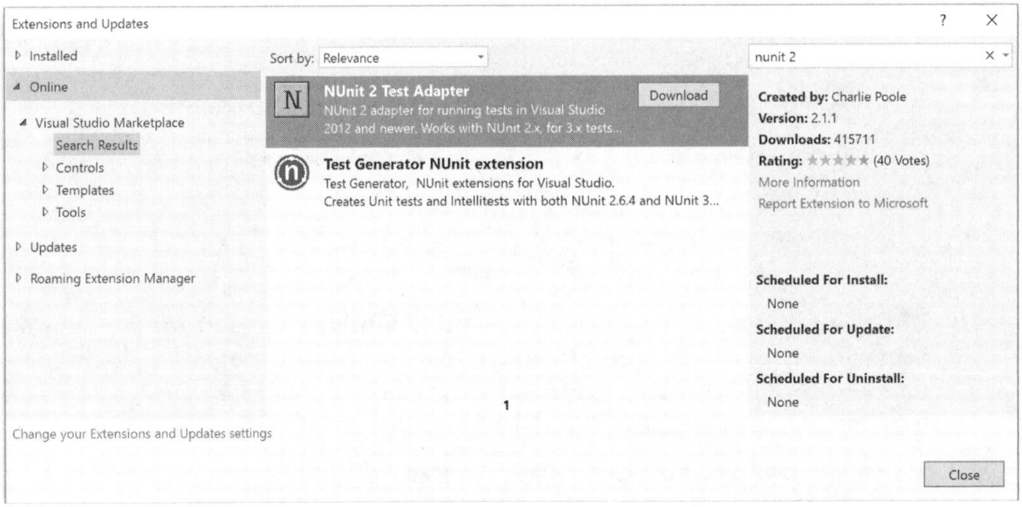

Figure 14.7 Installing the NUnit 2 test adapter

Unlike Visual Studio for Mac, there's no way on Windows to set the test apps. Instead you need to configure this in code by giving it the path to the Android APK, which is in the output folder and is named based on the Android package name with the .apk file extension. Release builds also have a suffix of *-Signed* to indicate that they've been signed with your keystore. You set the package name in the Android manifest in the last chapter, based on a reverse domain name (mine was set to io.jimbobbennett.Countr), and you can find this file in Countr.Droid\bin\Release if you've built using the release configuration or Countr.Droid\bin\Debug for the debug configuration. We'll be using release Android builds for the purposes of this book, so add the following code to point UITest to the right APK, substituting in your package name.

Listing 14.3 Configuring UITest to use the Countr.Droid APK file

```
if (platform == Platform.Android)
{
   return ConfigureApp
       .Android
       .EnableLocalScreenshots()
       .ApkFile ("../../../Countr.Droid/bin/Release/
        <your package name>-Signed.apk")
       .StartApp();
}
```

Configures the app to use the release APK

Replace `<your package name>` in this code with the name of your package (for example, I'd use `io.jimbobbennett.Countr`). This assumes your UI test project has been created in the same directory as all the other projects, so the folder for Countr.UITests is at the same level as the folder for Countr.Droid. If not, change the path in this code to match your folder structure.

When tests are run, they'll be run on the device or emulator that you've selected for the build configuration, just as for debugging your apps. This makes it easy to change the device that tests are run on by changing the drop-down in the toolbar, just as you'd change the target for debugging, as shown in figure 14.8.

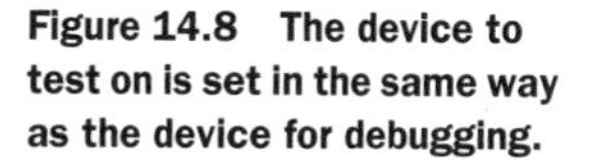

Figure 14.8 The device to test on is set in the same way as the device for debugging.

RUNNING THE TEST

Once the test apps have been configured, you can run the tests by double-clicking them in the Test pad in Visual Studio for Mac, or by right-clicking them in the Visual Studio for Windows Test Explorer and selecting Run Selected Tests. If you're testing Android, set the build configuration to release, and for iOS set it to debug.

Request for network access on iOS

When you run Countr or the UI tests on iOS, you may get a dialog box popping up asking if Countr.iOS.app can accept incoming connections, as shown below. This is the macOS firewall detecting the Calabash HTTP server running in your app, so if you see this, click Allow.

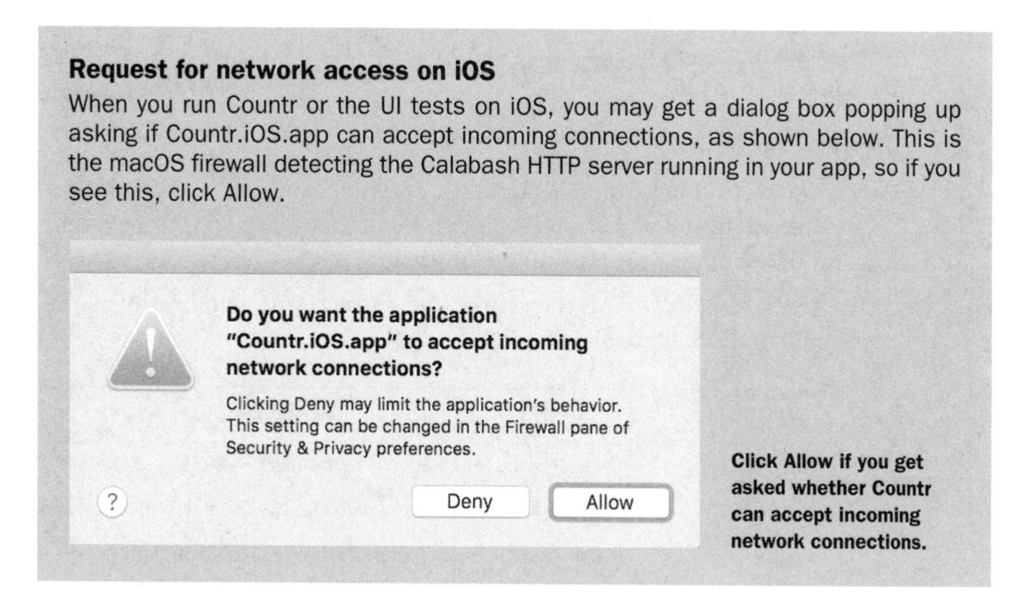

Click Allow if you get asked whether Countr can accept incoming network connections.

When the test is run, the following things happen:

1. The unit test runner loads the test fixture, passing the relevant platform to the constructor.
2. Before each test, the `BeforeEachTest` method marked with the `SetUp` attribute is called, and this in turn calls the `StartApp` method on `AppInitializer`. This will configure the app for the relevant platform, enable screenshots, and launch the app, returning an `IApp` instance that's stored in the `app` field on the test class and that can be used to interact with the app.
3. UITest knows which app to start and what device to launch it on based on the `TestApps` setting or the configured APK, so it will launch the relevant emulator, simulator, or device and start the app.
4. On iOS, before the app is launched, another app will be installed on the simulator or device, called "Device Agent". This is part of the iOS XCTest framework, which UITest uses under the hood and is needed to control your app. You can just ignore this app; if you delete it, it will be reinstalled next time the test is run.
5. The test case is run—in our case, a test called `AppLaunches`, which calls the `Screenshot` method to capture a screenshot.
6. The screenshot is captured and placed in the output directory of the UI test project. This screenshot can be found at Countr.UITests/bin/Debug/screenshot-1.png.
7. The test will pass, as nothing went wrong.

As a first test this is OK, but not great. It shows that the app launched, which in itself is a valuable test, but it doesn't tell us much more than that. The screenshot is not of much use either—on iOS it will be the first screen, but on Android it might just be the splash screen, depending on how long the app takes to launch. Let's now look at writing some proper tests.

14.2 Writing tests

Our apps are running inside a simple UI test, but how can we take this further and write some useful tests? First, let's define a couple of tests that we want to run, and then we'll look at how we can implement them:

- *Adding a counter*—This test should add a new counter and verify that it has been added. It would involve the following steps:

Step	Description
Arrange	Start the app (this happens in the `BeforeEachTest` method).
Act	Tap the Add button, add a name for the counter, and tap the Done button.
Assert	Verify that the new counter is visible with a count of 0.

- *Incrementing a counter*—This test should take an existing counter, increment it, and verify that the count has gone up by one. It would follow these steps:

Step	Description
Arrange	Start the app (this happens in the `BeforeEachTest` method) and add a new counter.
Act	Tap the Increment button for the new counter.
Assert	Verify that the new counter has a count of 1.

These are simple tests. We'll start by building the structure of the test methods, and then we'll look at how we can fill in the tests. Add the following code to Tests.cs.

Listing 14.4 Test methods ready for implementing our UI tests

```
[Test]
public void AddingACounterAddsItToTheCountersScreen()
{
    // Arrange
    // Act
    // Assert
}

[Test]
public void IncrementingACounterAddsOneToItsCount()
{
    // Arrange
    // Act
    // Assert
}
```

14.2.1 The visual tree

UITest views your app as a visual tree. This concept should be familiar to you if you've done UI development before with WPF or HTML, but essentially it's a hierarchical representation of everything that's visible on the screen, and it should map to the UI that you've designed in your storyboard or Android layout file. For example, for the counters screen in Countr, the visual tree on Android when showing two counters would be something like the tree shown in figure 14.9.

This tree is a hierarchy, so there are parent/child and sibling relationships. The `RelativeLayout` has a `TextView` as one of its children, a `RecyclerView` as its parent, and another `RelativeLayout` as its sibling.

UITest has a number of methods on the `IApp` interface that interact with your app, and they know which controls to use based on an app query. App queries are functions that look inside the visual tree of your app for a control that matches a specific thing—this can be based on some kind of identifier, text inside the control, or its class type. You can also query based on relationships, such as finding parent, child, or sibling controls. When you write a UITest test, you use app queries to find the controls

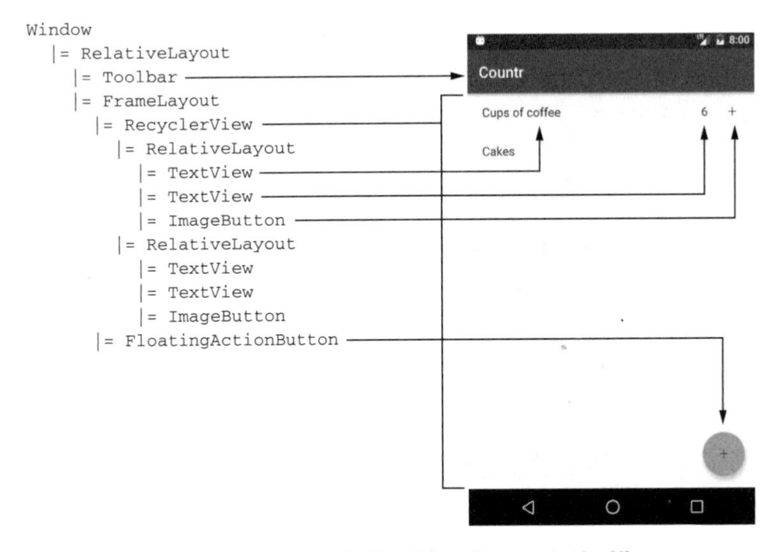

Figure 14.9 The visual tree on Android and how it maps to the UI

that you want to interact with. Working out exactly what app query to write can be easy when you know the visual tree for your app, but sometimes it's more difficult and requires writing complicated queries. Luckily, there's a REPL that makes it easy to see your app's visual tree and try out queries while your app is running.

14.2.2 The REPL

A Read-Evaluate-Print loop (REPL) is a command-line tool that allows you to execute commands inside some kind of context. You may have used something similar before, such as the Interactive window in Visual Studio, where you can run C# code that has access to the current application stack while debugging.

You can launch the UITest REPL by using the `IApp.Repl()` method, so update one of the new tests to call this method with the following code.

Listing 14.5 Launching the REPL from a UI test

```
[Test]
public void AddingACounterAddsItToTheCountersScreen()
{
   app.Repl();   <-- Adds a call to launch the REPL
   ...
}
```

Once this code has been added, run the test. It will hit this line, launch the REPL in a terminal or command-line window, and wait (figure 14.10). The `Repl()` method will only return once the REPL has closed, either by closing the command-line window or using the `exit` command, so you should only use this method when building your tests. You should remove it once your tests are written, or your tests will never finish.

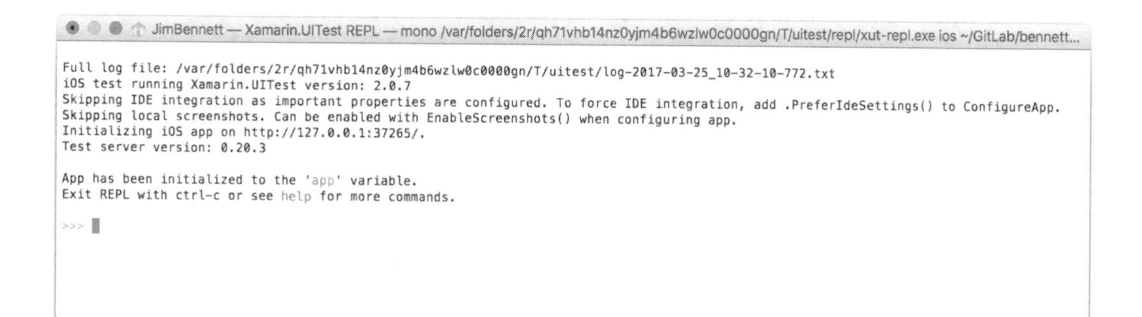

Figure 14.10 The REPL running in a command-line window

You may also find that you can't stop your tests from inside Visual Studio while the REPL is running, so if you need to stop your tests, you'll need to manually close the REPL.

Once you're in the REPL, the most useful command is `tree`, which shows the visual tree. Type this and press Enter. Figure 14.11 shows the visual tree on iOS, and figure 14.12 shows the visual tree on Android.

```
App has been initialized to the 'app' variable.
Exit REPL with ctrl-c or see help for more commands.

>>> tree
[CalabashRootView > ... > UILayoutContainerView]
  [UINavigationTransitionView > UIViewControllerWrapperView]
    [UITableView] label: "Empty list"
      [UITableViewWrapperView]
      [UIView]
  [UINavigationBar] id: "Countr"
    [_UIBarBackground]
      [UIImageView]
      [UIVisualEffectView]
        [_UIVisualEffectBackdropView]
        [_UIVisualEffectFilterView]
        [_UIVisualEffectFilterView]
    [UINavigationItemView] label: "Countr"
      [UILabel] label: "Countr",  text: "Countr"
    [UINavigationButton > UIImageView] id: "add_counter_button",  label: "Add"
>>>
```

Figure 14.11 The visual tree for Countr on iOS inside the REPL

```
App has been initialized to the 'app' variable.
Exit REPL with ctrl-c or see help for more commands.

>>> tree

[[object CalabashRootView] > ... > FrameLayout]

  [FitWindowsLinearLayout] id: "action_bar_root"
    [ContentFrameLayout > RelativeLayout] id: "content"
      [AppBarLayout] id: "toolbar_layout"
        [Toolbar] id: "toolbar"
          [AppCompatTextView] text: "Countr"
      [FrameLayout]
        [MvxRecyclerView] id: "recycler_view"
        [FloatingActionButton] id: "add_counter_button"
>>>
```

Figure 14.12 The visual tree for Countr on Android in the REPL

This visual tree is a representation of the visual tree inside your app, flattened a bit to be more useful. It shows the controls using the underlying types from the OS, and it shows some string-based properties on the controls, such as the text of a button. The tree will look different on iOS and Android because the controls are different on each platform.

> **THE REPL IS A FULL-FEATURED C# REPL AS WELL** UITest app queries are written in C#, so to make the REPL work, Xamarin had to provide full C# capabilities inside it, with a field called `app` pointing to your `IApp` instance. This means you can run other C# code if you want, just as in the Immediate window in Visual Studio, and if you call a variable by its name with no operators or methods, the value will be printed to the console.

The first step of our first test involves tapping the Add button to add a new counter, so we need to write a query for this.

14.2.3 Identifying controls

There are a number of different ways to query for a control, such as based on the class or the text inside it, but for our Add counter button, this might be problematic. On iOS, it's a text-based button showing the text *Add*, but on Android it's a floating action button with an image inside it and no text. We could write different queries for different platforms, but this isn't ideal—we want to have as much cross-platform code as possible, both in our apps and our tests.

The easiest thing to do is to assign some kind of unique ID to the navigation bar button on iOS and the floating action button on Android, and use this to identify the control. That way we can use this identifier in the test, and it will work on both platforms. Identifiers are easy to add—on Android you can use the `id` property in the layout AXML file, and on iOS you can add an `AccessibilityIdentifier` property.

Let's start with Android. Open the counters_view.axml layout file and add the following code.

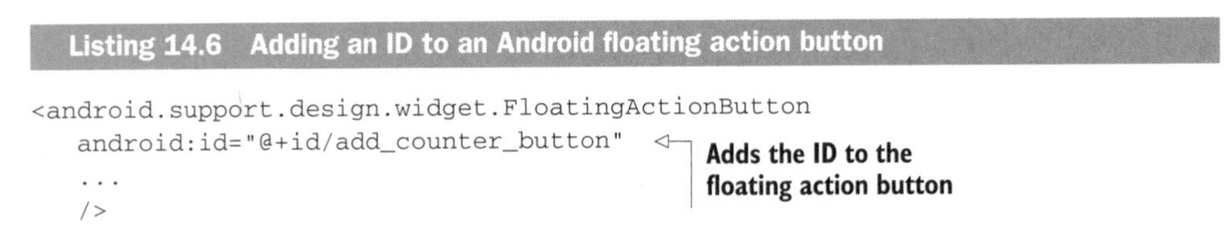

Listing 14.6 Adding an ID to an Android floating action button

```
<android.support.design.widget.FloatingActionButton
    android:id="@+id/add_counter_button"
    ...
    />
```

Adds the ID to the floating action button

On iOS, open the CountersView.cs file and add the following code. We're doing this in code because the navigation bar button is created in code, but for controls on a storyboard, this can be set using the Properties pad.

Listing 14.7 Adding an ID to an iOS navigation bar button

```
public override void ViewDidLoad()
{
   ...
   var button = new UIBarButtonItem(UIBarButtonSystemItem.Add);
   button.AccessibilityIdentifier = "add_counter_button";     <-
   ...
}
```

Sets the accessibility identifier on the navigation bar button

CASING FOR ID NAMES In this example I've used lowercase names with underscores for the IDs simply because this matches the Android standard, and it means we can stay consistent with the standard for IDs used for identifying controls in UI tests, as well as for relative layout references and other uses. It's up to you what naming convention you use, but you must use the same value on iOS and Android for the UI tests to work.

After making these changes, build and deploy the app, and then rerun the UI tests and look at the tree in the REPL. In the Android tree you'll see this:

```
[FloatingActionButton] id: "add_counter_button"
```

On iOS, you'll see this:

```
[UINavigationButton > UIImageView] id: "add_counter_button", label: "Add"
```

Now that you have your IDs set, it's time to write your first query. In the REPL, type `app.` and you'll see a load of autocomplete options identifying the methods on the `IApp` instance. `app` is an instance of `IApp` pointing to your app, and it's the same as the `app` field in the `Tests` class. That means everything you write in your REPL can be used in your tests. One of the auto-complete options is `Query`, which can be used to perform an app query and return all the controls that match the query.

App queries are lambda functions using the same syntax as C#, so start by typing *app.Query(c => c.*. The parameter to the function, `c` in this case, is of type `AppQuery`, which has a stack of methods that can be used to run different queries. All methods return the `AppQuery` instance, so you can chain multiple calls if needed.

After typing the period (`.`), you'll see an autocomplete list showing all the possible methods, such as `Child`, `Id`, `Marked`, and `Text`. You need to use the `Id` method, passing the ID you've just set as the parameter. Run the command `app.Query(c => c.Id("add_counter_button"))` and look at the results. Queries return a list of all items that match the query, and in this case there's a single item: the floating action button or navigation bar button (depending on platform). This query and its result is shown in figure 14.13. We'll look at a whole range of different app queries you can run later in this chapter.

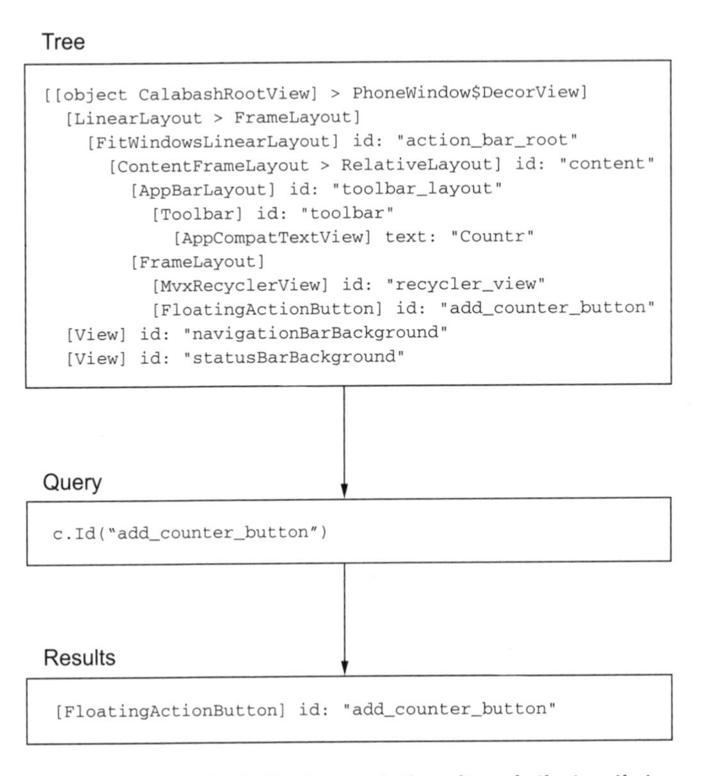

Tree
[[object CalabashRootView] > PhoneWindow$DecorView]
[LinearLayout > FrameLayout]
[FitWindowsLinearLayout] id: "action_bar_root"
[ContentFrameLayout > RelativeLayout] id: "content"
[AppBarLayout] id: "toolbar_layout"
[Toolbar] id: "toolbar"
[AppCompatTextView] text: "Countr"
[FrameLayout]
[MvxRecyclerView] id: "recycler_view"
[FloatingActionButton] id: "add_counter_button"
[View] id: "navigationBarBackground"
[View] id: "statusBarBackground"
Query
c.Id("add_counter_button")
Results
[FloatingActionButton] id: "add_counter_button"

Figure 14.13 Querying by ID returns only those items in the tree that match the ID.

14.2.4 Tapping the Add button

Once you've found the Add counter button, you can tap it easily. In the app field, there's a method called `Tap` that takes an app query. This will run the query and tap the first item it finds that matches the query. If nothing matches the query, it will throw an exception.

If you type *app.* again, you'll see `Tap` in the autocomplete list. Run the `Tap` command using the same app query as before: `app.Tap(c => c.Id("add_counter_button"))`. The REPL has a command history, so you can always just tap the Up arrow to see the query again and edit the command to use `Tap` instead of `Query`. If you watch your app while this command is running, you'll see the new counter screen appear. We'll look at some of the other methods on `IApp` later in this chapter.

This gives you the first part of the Act step of your add new counter test, so let's add this to the test. Add the following code to tap the button before the REPL is shown.

Listing 14.8 Tapping the add new counter button from the test

```
[Test]
public void AddingACounterAddsItToTheCountersScreen()
{
   // Arrange
   // Act
   app.Tap(c => c.Id("add_counter_button"));    <-- Taps the add counter button
   app.Repl();
   // Assert
}
```

THE REPL HAS A COPY COMMAND The REPL has a `copy` command that copies the entire command history to the clipboard. This is useful for writing tests in the REPL and then copying them to the clipboard to paste into your own tests.

The next step is to enter the counter name into the text box.

14.2.5 Entering text

Entering text is as simple as tapping buttons—there's an `EnterText` method on the `IApp` interface that takes an app query and a string containing the text you want to add. Once again, though, how do you know which control to enter the text into. If you run the `tree` command again, you'll see a different tree—after all, the app has navigated to the add new counter screen, but there's nothing in common between the iOS `UITextField` and Android `AppCompatEditText`. As before, you need to add some IDs.

Add the following code to the counter_view.axml layout file in the Android project to add the Android IDs.

Listing 14.9 Add an ID to the Android text-entry field

```
<EditText
   android:id="@+id/new_counter_name"    <-- Adds an ID to the text-entry field
   ...
   />
```

On iOS, this time you can do it from the storyboard instead of the code. Open CounterView.storyboard, select the counter name text field, and set the `Identifier` property in the Accessibility section of the Widget tab to be `new_counter_name`, as shown in figure 14.14.

Now if you build, deploy, and run the UI test to tap the Add button, and you launch the REPL and look at the tree, you'll see that the text box has an identifier of `new_counter_name`. You can now use the `EnterText` method to set the text by running `app.EnterText(c => c.Id("new_counter_name"), "My Counter")`. This will find the first element matching the query, and enter the text, character by character, simulating what would happen when a user types the text.

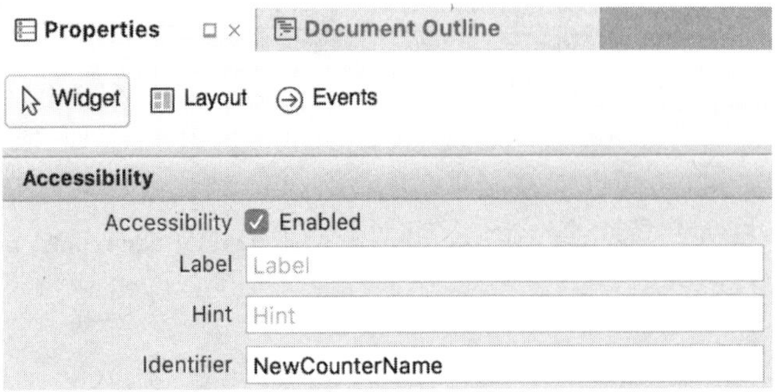

Properties | Document Outline

Widget | Layout | Events

Accessibility

Accessibility: Enabled
Label: Label
Hint: Hint
Identifier: NewCounterName

Figure 14.14 Setting the Accessibility Identifier from a storyboard

Add the following code to the test before the REPL.

Listing 14.10 Entering text from the test

```
[Test]
public void AddingACounterAddsItToTheCountersScreen()
{
   // Arrange
   // Act
   app.Tap(c => c.Id("add_counter_button"));
   app.EnterText(c => c.Id("new_counter_name"), "My Counter");
   app.Repl();
   // Assert
}
```

Enters text into the counter name text box

> **DISCONNECT THE HARDWARE KEYBOARD** On iOS, text is entered by tapping the keys on the software keyboard. This means that if you're using a simulator to run your tests, you'll need to disable the hardware keyboard from inside the simulator by ensuring Hardware > Keyboard > Connect Hardware Keyboard is unchecked. If you don't, any UI test that enters text will fail with "Timed out waiting for keyboard."

14.2.6 Finding controls based on their text

After setting the name, you need to tap the Done button to add the counter. This time there's a similarity between the button on both platforms—they both have a button with the text set to "Done." This means that rather than having to set an identifier, you can query for the text directly. From the REPL, query for this using `app.Query(c => c.Text("Done"))`, and you'll see the Done button.

If you do this on Android, you might notice something interesting—the text of the button is "Done" in the tree, but on screen it's "DONE", all in capitals. This is because the default button style on Android capitalizes the text, but just the text on the display, not on the underlying control. This is very helpful, as text queries are case sensitive: querying for "Done" gives one result, but querying for "DONE" gives none. When building your app, you can set the text for controls using normal casing on both iOS and Android, you can query for it in the same way on both platforms, but you can still have Android buttons automatically show on screen in uppercase.

Text queries can query for any text on a control—so for labels it will match the static text that's showing, for text boxes it will match the text entered by the user, and for buttons it will match the button text. If you use this query with the `Tap` command, it will tap the Done button and add the counter, navigating back to the counters screen.

Try it out and then add it to the unit test so it matches the following listing.

Listing 14.11 Tapping the Done button

```
[Test]
public void AddingACounterAddsItToTheCountersScreen()
{
   // Arrange
   // Act
   app.Tap(c => c.Id("add_counter_button"));
   app.EnterText(c => c.Id("new_counter_name"), "My Counter");
   app.Tap(c => c.Text("Done"));      <-- Taps the button with the text "Done"
   app.Repl();
   // Assert
}
```

14.2.7 Assertions

The Arrange (handled by the `BeforeEachTest` setup method) and Act steps are done. Now it's time to move on to Assert, where you assert that you can see a new counter with the name of `My Counter` and a count of 0.

The easiest way to do asserts is to use an app query for what you're looking for, and assert the results of the query by using some helper methods on the `IApp` interface. `IApp` has two useful methods for this: `WaitForElement` and `WaitForNoElement`. Both take an app query. The first will wait for at least one element that matches the query, timing out if nothing is found after 10 seconds and throwing an exception. The other will wait until no elements match the query, and again will throw an exception if there are elements that match the query after 10 seconds. The 10-second timeout is configurable, so it can be made longer if needed (such as if your app is running a slow action).

For this assertion, ensure that you can see the new counter with the name of `My Counter` on the counters screen. If you look at the tree in the REPL, you'll see there's a label with the text "My Counter" as part of the tree view or recycler view, but if you do a text query for "My Counter" you wouldn't be able to distinguish between the counter showing on the counters screen or the text box on the add new counter screen showing the same text. Essentially, the test couldn't assert that the Done button had actually done anything. What you want is to verify that you can see the text in the right place, and you can do this by using multiple app queries.

The first thing to do is to add some more IDs so you can identify the labels in the table view or recycler view that show the name and count. To do this on Android, add the code in the following listing to the counter_recycler_view.axml layout file to add the ID of "counter_name" to the name label and "counter_count" to the count label.

Listing 14.12 Adding IDs to the counter view used by the recycler view

```
<TextView
    ...
    local:MvxBind="Text Name"
    android:id="@+id/counter_name"/>     <-- Sets the counter name label ID
<TextView
    ...
    local:MvxBind="Text Count"
    android:id="@+id/counter_count"/>    <-- Sets the counter count label ID
```

For iOS, once again you can do this from the storyboard by selecting the labels in the cell prototype in the CountersView.storyboard file and setting the Identifier properties in the Accessibility section. Select the counter name label and set the identifier to be "counter_name"; then select the counter count label and set the identifier to be "counter_count".

Once you have these identifiers in place, rebuild and redeploy the apps, and then rerun the UI test. Once the REPL loads, run the `tree` command and you'll see that the two labels now have their IDs set. You now have two ways to query the counter name: you can query based on the ID (but that doesn't tell you what text is showing), or you can query based on the text (but that won't tell you if the text is on the counters screen, or if you're still on the add new counter screen and the text is in the text box).

To solve this problem, you can combine the queries. The app query methods are part of a fluent interface—one that returns the same object that the method was called on, allowing you to essentially chain methods. This means you can combine queries for the ID and the text. Try it out by running the command `app.Query(c => c.Id("counter_name").Text("My Counter"))`. This will search for all items that have an ID of `counter_name`, and from those results will return only the ones with the text set to `My Counter` (figure 14.15). You can chain as many queries as you like—the first query in the chain queries the entire visual tree, and each subsequent query queries the result of the previous query.

You'll see that this query will return a single result, the label showing the new counter in the list, and you can write an identical query to prove that the count is 0 by querying for the ID "counter_count" and the text "0". You can turn these queries into assertions in your test by using the `WaitForElement` method, as shown in listing 14.13. Also, you can remove the `Repl` call, because you don't need it for this test anymore.

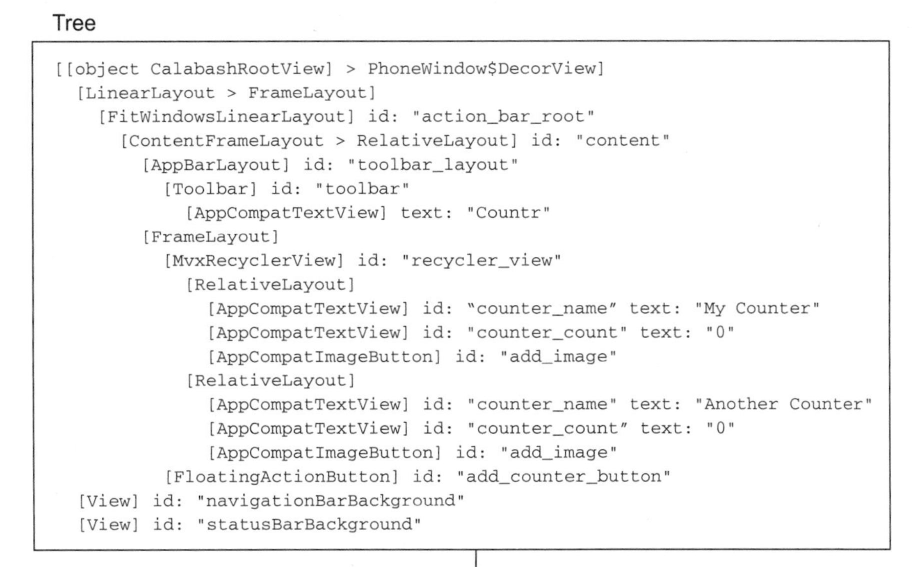


```
[[object CalabashRootView] > PhoneWindow$DecorView]
  [LinearLayout > FrameLayout]
    [FitWindowsLinearLayout] id: "action_bar_root"
      [ContentFrameLayout > RelativeLayout] id: "content"
        [AppBarLayout] id: "toolbar_layout"
          [Toolbar] id: "toolbar"
            [AppCompatTextView] text: "Countr"
        [FrameLayout]
          [MvxRecyclerView] id: "recycler_view"
            [RelativeLayout]
              [AppCompatTextView] id: "counter_name" text: "My Counter"
              [AppCompatTextView] id: "counter_count" text: "0"
              [AppCompatImageButton] id: "add_image"
            [RelativeLayout]
              [AppCompatTextView] id: "counter_name" text: "Another Counter"
              [AppCompatTextView] id: "counter_count" text: "0"
              [AppCompatImageButton] id: "add_image"
          [FloatingActionButton] id: "add_counter_button"
  [View] id: "navigationBarBackground"
  [View] id: "statusBarBackground"
```

ID query

```
c.Id("counter_name"))
```

Results

```
[AppCompatTextView] id: "counter_name" text: "My Counter"
[AppCompatTextView] id: "counter_name" text: "Another Counter"
```

Text query

```
.Text("My Counter")
```

Results

```
[AppCompatTextView] id: "counter_name" text: "My Counter"
```

Figure 14.15 Querying by ID and text returns only those items in the tree that match the ID and text.

Listing 14.13 The complete test, asserting that the new counter has been found

```
[Test]
public void AddingACounterAddsItToTheCountersScreen()
{
   // Arrange
   // Act
   app.Tap(c => c.Id("add_counter_button"));
   app.EnterText(c => c.Id("new_counter_name"), "My Counter");
   app.Tap(c => c.Text("Done"));
   // Assert
   app.WaitForElement(c => c.Id("counter_name").Text("My Counter"));
   app.WaitForElement(c => c.Id("counter_count").Text("0"));
}
```

The assertions, verifying the text is correct for the new counter

After making this change, run the test, and you'll see it pass.

14.2.8 Proving your test by breaking things

You now have a test that passes, but ideally you should make your test fail at least once, just to be sure that the test is working as expected. There are many ways to break the app, but a simple way would be to comment out one of the bindings (to simulate what would happen if you had a bug in your code due to forgetting a binding). Try commenting out the bindings in `CountersView`, as follows.

Listing 14.14 Commenting out some bindings to simulate a bug in the code

```
public override void ViewDidLoad()
{
   ...
   //var set = this.CreateBindingSet<CountersView, CountersViewModel>();
   //set.Bind(source).To(vm => vm.Counters);
   //set.Bind(button).To(vm => vm.AddNewCounterCommand);
   //set.Apply();
}
```

Comments out the bindings

If you make this change, build and deploy the app, and re-run the test, you'll see it fail. If you look in the output, you'll see the error shown in figure 14.16.

This error shows you that the query for the control with the ID of "new_counter_name" didn't find anything, and the stack trace points to the call to `EnterText` in the `AddingACounterAddsItToTheCountersScreen` test. This tells you that when the query was run, the new counter name text box wasn't showing, so now you need to find out why.

There are multiple ways to debug a UI test. By *debug*, I mean see what's happening on screen when your test runs. When a UI test is running through the debugger, you can only debug the test itself. You can't step into the app or attach the debugger to the app, so if you need to debug a problem inside your app, you'll need to run it and manually work through the tests steps to get there.

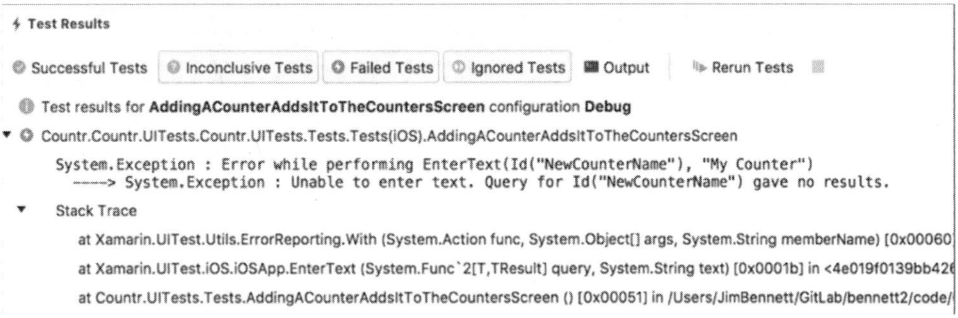

Test Results

Successful Tests | Inconclusive Tests | Failed Tests | Ignored Tests | Output | Rerun Tests

Test results for **AddingACounterAddsItToTheCountersScreen** configuration **Debug**

Countr.Countr.UITests.Countr.UITests.Tests.Tests(iOS).AddingACounterAddsItToTheCountersScreen

```
System.Exception : Error while performing EnterText(Id("NewCounterName"), "My Counter")
  ----> System.Exception : Unable to enter text. Query for Id("NewCounterName") gave no results.
```

Stack Trace

at Xamarin.UITest.Utils.ErrorReporting.With (System.Action func, System.Object[] args, System.String memberName) [0x00060

at Xamarin.UITest.iOS.iOSApp.EnterText (System.Func`2[T,TResult] query, System.String text) [0x0001b] in <4e019f0139bb42

at Countr.UITests.Tests.AddingACounterAddsItToTheCountersScreen () [0x00051] in /Users/JimBennett/GitLab/bennett2/code/

Figure 14.16 The output of a test failure, showing that the query for "new_counter_name" didn't give any results

To see what's happening when the test runs, you can do one of the following:

- *Debug the UI test*—UI tests can be debugged just like any other unit test. You can set breakpoints, step through, evaluate variables, and do anything else you'd normally do in a debugger. The usual way to debug a UI test is to set a breakpoint on the line that fails, then debug the test by right-clicking it in the Test Explorer or Test pad and selecting Debug Test. This will launch the test in a debugger and break on the breakpoint.

  To do this for your test, set a breakpoint on the call to `app.EnterText(c => c.Id("new_counter_name"), "My Counter")`, and debug the test. When the breakpoint is hit, take a look at the app and you'll see that it's still on the counters screen, not the add new counter screen. This suggests that tapping `add_counter_button` didn't work, and you can test this theory by manually tapping the button and seeing what happens. When you run a UI test, it's the same as if you manually followed all the steps, so you can interact with the app yourself at any time to try things out. (Some developers even use UI tests to get their app to a known state that takes multiple steps, saving themselves the boring repetition of getting there manually.)
- *Use the REPL*—The REPL is a great way to investigate issues. Debugging can help find the line that failed, but sometimes the REPL can help you find out why it failed. For example, if an automation ID was missing, you could see this from the tree (a regular scenario, especially when using multiple layout files on Android to support multiple screens). You can launch the REPL from any point in your test by making a call to `app.Repl()`, either by adding this manually to the code or by breaking on a breakpoint and calling it from the Immediate window.

  If you want to try the REPL as a debugging tool, try uncommenting the binding code in `CountersView` so that the add new counter button works again, but remove the ID from the add new counter button in the iOS CountersView or Android counters_view.axml. Build and deploy the app, and put a breakpoint on the call to `EnterText`. When the app breaks on this breakpoint, open the

Immediate window (View > Debug Pads > Immediate in Visual Studio for Mac, or Debug > Windows > Immediate in Visual Studio) and run `app.Repl()`. You can then call `tree` to see that the Add button doesn't have an ID set.

- *Take screenshots*—At each step in your test, you can save a screenshot by making a call to `app.Screenshot("<name>")`. The name you pass should be an identifier for where in the test the screenshot was taken—these names aren't used for local screenshots, but if you use Test Cloud (we'll look at it in the next chapter), these names will be shown against each screenshot. Screenshots are a great way to see the state of the app as the test is run, and they can be especially useful if you have a flappy test—one that passes most of the time but fails occasionally (for example, a test that relies on an external resource, such as a web service that's sometimes not available or a network that times out or loses connection).

  To debug your issue using screenshots, add the following code to your test fixture.

Listing 14.15 Taking a screenshot of the test as it runs

```
[Test]
public void AddingACounterAddsItToTheCountersScreen()
{
   ...
   app.Tap(c => c.Id("add_counter_button"));
   app.Screenshot("About to enter text");        <-- Take a screenshot
   app.EnterText(c => c.Id("new_counter_name"), "My Counter");
```

  If you look in the output folder of the UI tests, which will be Countr.UITests/bin/Debug if you run your tests as a debug build, you'll see a screenshot called screenshot-1.png. This is the state of the app before the `EnterText` method was called, so if your app was working you'd see the add new counter screen. You can see main counters screen instead, so it's obvious that something isn't working when the Add button is tapped.

- *App Center crash reports*—If your app crashes during a UI test, you won't be able to see, in a debugger, which line of code is causing the crash. If you wired up your app to App Center crash analytics, you would be able to see the crash details in App Center.

Once you're done, revert all changes to the bindings and IDs, rebuild and redeploy the app, and re-run the test to ensure it passes.

14.3 Testing incrementing a counter

Time to finish the tests by adding the last one—testing incrementing a counter. This test increments a counter and ensures that the count has been correctly incremented, so as part of the Arrange step you'll need to create a new counter. You can do this by reusing the test code from the previous test, as follows.

Listing 14.16 Creating a new counter in the Arrange step of the test

```
[Test]
public void IncrementingACounterAddsOneToItsCount()
{
    // Arrange
    app.Tap(c => c.Id("add_counter_button"));
    app.Screenshot("About to enter text");
    app.EnterText(c => c.Id("new_counter_name"), "My Counter");
    app.Tap(c => c.Text("Done"));
    // Act
    // Assert
}
```

Creates a new counter

For the Act step, you need to tap the Increment button. Once again, this is different on iOS and Android, so you need to set an ID. On Android, the ID for the image button in the counter_recycler_view.axml layout file has already been set to `add_image`, so that the count label could be positioned to the left of it, so you can reuse this ID on iOS. Open CountersView.storyboard and set the accessibility identifier for the Increment button to be "add_image". Once this ID is set, you can add a call to tap the button, and an assert that the count text is now "1", as shown in the following listing.

Listing 14.17 Tapping the Increment button and asserting on the new value

```
[Test]
public void IncrementingACounterAddsOneToItsCount()
{
    ...
    // Act
    app.Tap(c => c.Id("add_image"));
    // Assert
    app.WaitForElement(c => c.Id("counter_count").Text("1"));
}
```

Taps the Increment counter button

Asserts that the counter count is now 1

Run this test, and it should be a nice green color. You now have two UI tests that ensure you can add counters and increment them, and you have some confidence that you've built an app that works.

UI tests should not be the only tests you run. They're a great way to ensure that your view is bound correctly and that all the parts of your app work together, but they should always be used in conjunction with thorough unit testing.

14.4 The app interface and app queries

Let's take some time to recap the `IApp` interface and look at what else is available on this interface. We'll also look in more detail at app queries.

14.4.1 The IApp interface

The `IApp` interface has a number of methods that can interact with your app. Some take app queries and interact with the controls that match the query, and others act on the app as a whole. Table 14.2 shows some of the general methods on this interface.

Table 14.2 `IApp` interface methods

Method	Description
`Back`	Navigates back using the iOS navigation bar or Android Back button. On Android, this uses the hardware Back button, so if the keyboard is showing, this will dismiss the keyboard rather than going back. If your screen has any text-input controls that would show the keyboard, you should dismiss the keyboard first.
`DismissKeyboard`	Hides the keyboard if it's visible.
`Repl`	Shows the REPL.
`SetOrientationLandscape` and `SetOrientationPortrait`	Changes the orientation of the device.
`Screenshot`	Takes a screenshot (only works in Test Cloud unless the app is configured to allow local screenshots).
`Invoke`	Invokes a backdoor method, allowing you to interact with hidden features in your app. You can read more about these in Xamarin's documentation at http://mng.bz/MSXX.

Table 14.3 shows some of the methods that take app queries.

Table 14.3 `IApp` interface methods that take app queries

Method	Description
`Query`	Returns all the items in the visual tree that match the query.
`Tap` and `DoubleTap`	Taps (or double-taps) the first item in the visual tree that matches the query (if there are multiple matches, only the first is tapped), and throws an exception if none is found.
`EnterText` and `ClearText`	Enters text into or clears all text from the first item that can accept text and matches the query. If there are multiple matches, the text is only entered into the first one. If there are no matches, an exception is thrown.
`Flash`	Makes all controls that match the query flash. This is useful when writing complicated queries and you want to test them out.
`ScrollDownTo` and `ScrollUpTo`	These methods take two queries: one for a scrollable container, and one for an item to find. They scroll up or down inside the control that matches the scrollable container query for an item that matches the item query.
`WaitForElement`	Waits for an element that matches the query and throws an exception if none are found in a certain period of time (defaults to 10 seconds).

Table 14.3 `IApp` interface methods that take app queries *(continued)*

Method	Description
`WaitForNoElement`	Waits for no elements that match the query and throws an exception if any is found after a certain period of time (defaults to 10 seconds).

You can read more about this interface and about how the different methods work in Xamarin's documentation at http://mng.bz/J9co.

14.4.2 Queries

An app query defines the criteria used to find items in the visual tree. App queries have a fluent interface, with methods you call to define criteria that all return another app query instance, which you can then call another method on to build up more detailed criteria. Some of these methods are shown in table 14.4.

Table 14.4 AppQuery methods

Method	Description
`Id`	Finds controls that have an Android resource ID or iOS accessibility identifier set to the specified ID.
`Text`	Finds controls that have text that matches the query, such as the text on labels, text boxes, or buttons.
`Marked`	This is a combination of `Id` and `Text`, so finds anything that has an ID or text matching the given string.
`Button`	The same as `Marked`, but only for buttons.
`Switch`	The same as `Marked`, but only for switches.
`TextField`	The same as `Marked`, but only for text fields.

You can also query using strings instead of app query objects, and this is the same as using `Marked`. For example `app.Tap("FooBar")` is the same as `app.Tap(c => c.Marked ("FooBar"))`.

App queries can also be used to find parents, children, and siblings, so they can be used to walk around the tree if necessary. You can find more information on building up app queries in the Xamarin documentation at http://mng.bz/kyx0.

THERE'S A LOT MORE YOU CAN DO WITH APP QUERIES AND UITEST In this chapter I've only lightly touched on app queries and the capabilities of UITest. You can write some pretty advanced queries, including walking the visual tree based on parent, child, and sibling relationships and even invoking iOS or Android methods on controls and querying based on the results (such as finding all switches that are on). You can also expose methods inside your app (called backdoors) that you can call from the `IApp` instance, or invoke native methods on existing controls. This invoking of native methods can be useful when UI testing components that draw on the screen, such as chart or graphing controls—you can't check what's drawn using a UI test, but you can expose data through a native method that you can call and verify. You can read more about the capabilities of UITest in the Xamarin developer docs at http://mng.bz/cpM5.

Your app is now well tested and well on the way to being production-ready. In the next chapter we'll look at setting up Visual Studio App Center to automatically build your apps, run your UI tests on a range of real devices in the cloud, and set up user analytics and crash reporting so that you can track how your users use the apps and what issues they have once you release them to your beta and production users.

Summary

In this chapter you learned

- Xamarin UITest allows you to write automated UI tests in C#.
- UITest can be used to interact with controls, including tapping buttons or reading values.
- Apps have a visual tree made up of a hierarchy of controls.
- You can write tests against the visual tree.

You also learned how to

- Use the REPL to query your app's visual tree and interact with it.
- Use app queries to find controls on screen.
- Write UI tests using the same arrange, act, assert pattern you've already used for unit tests.

15 *Using App Center to build, test, and monitor apps*

This chapter covers

- Getting started with Visual Studio App Center
- Setting up app builds in App Center
- Running UI tests on real devices in the cloud using App Center
- Capturing and analyzing user data including analytics, behavior, and crash reports

Back in chapter 1 we discussed the mobile-optimized development lifecycle that's ingrained in all the mobile tools offered by Xamarin and Microsoft. It's shown again in figure 15.1.

In previous chapters we've looked at the first couple of steps in this lifecycle: develop and test. We've written apps and built unit tests and UI tests. Now we need to consider the remainder of this lifecycle, and to do this we need to take advantage of another tool from Microsoft and Xamarin called *Visual Studio App Center*. If you're excited about DevOps (and I hope you are) then this chapter is for you. If not, this chapter should be relaxing after the intense learning of the previous chapters—it's more about learning how to configure and use App Center than about learning new

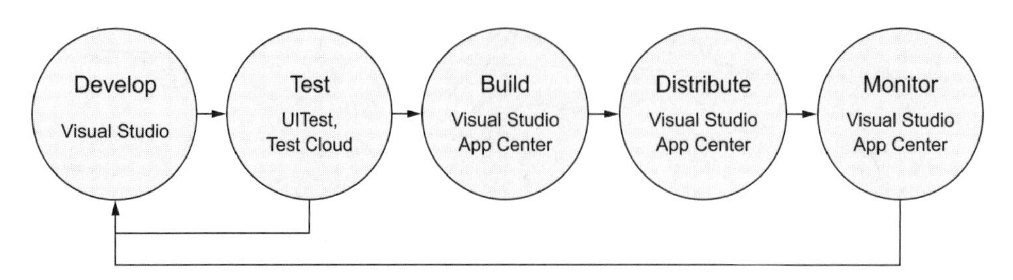

Figure 15.1 The mobile-optimized development lifecycle is a continuously iterating cycle of develop, test, build, distribute, and monitor.

concepts. The end product should be worthwhile—a built and tested app set up for crash reporting and user analytics, ready to be released to users in the next chapter.

15.1 Introducing Visual Studio App Center

Visual Studio App Center is billed as "Mission Control for apps," and it provides a one-stop shop for managing the mobile-optimized development lifecycle in your mobile apps, covering part of test as well as build, distribute, and monitor:

- *Test*—App Center integrates with Test Cloud, which allows you to take the UI tests you wrote in the last chapter and run them on real devices in the cloud. (In this case, the "cloud" is a warehouse in Denmark with racks and racks of phones and tablets.)
- *Build*—App Center has tools that can take your code and build it either on demand or when you push to source code control.
- *Distribute*—From App Center you can distribute your builds to beta testers, including adding notifications inside your app when an update is available. In an upcoming release you'll also be able distribute to the Google Play and Apple App Stores.
- *Monitor*—Using App Center you can not only get analytics about the users who are using your apps, you can also get automatically uploaded crash reports if your app crashes for your users.

In this chapter and the next we'll be looking at using App Center to perform all these steps in the lifecycle, starting in this chapter with build, test, and monitor, and looking at distribution in the next chapter. This is slightly out of order in terms of the lifecycle, but it makes sense to developers—we need to set up the build before we can test it, and we need to add analytics before we distribute so that we can see the results as soon as possible.

You can access App Center at https://appcenter.ms (figure 15.2). At the time of writing, it's free for light usage, with paid plans if you need more features. You can log in by clicking the Get Started button, and then create an account using either a Microsoft account (you probably set one of these up when installing Xamarin, if you didn't already have one), or by connecting it to your GitHub, Facebook, or Google account.

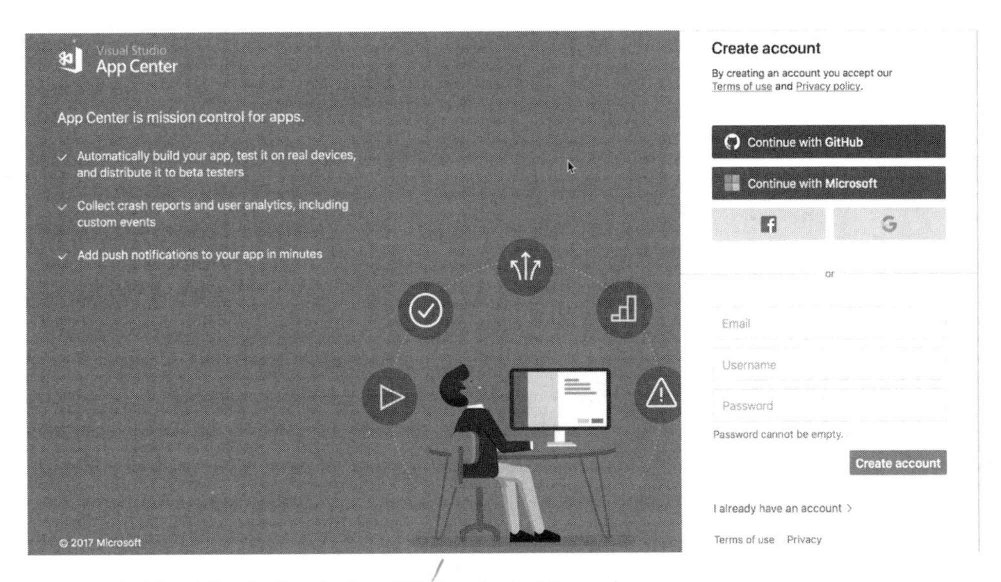

Figure 15.2 Visual Studio App Center—Mission Control for apps

Once you've connected to App Center, it's worth setting up an App Center password associated with the email address used by the service you connected with. This will allow you to log in from the command line later, which is necessary for running UI tests. To do this, click the cog icon next to your name to see the user settings, go to the Password tab, and click the Send Set Password Email button. You'll receive an email with a link to follow to set a password. Click this link and set a password.

15.1.1 Apps

App Center is built on the concept of *apps*, with each app being a single, releasable app for a single platform. Although you may think of Countr as a single app available on iOS and Android, from the perspective of App Center it's actually two apps, one Android and one iOS.

APP CENTER COVERS MORE THAN JUST MICROSOFT PRODUCTS As part of the new "Any developer, any platform" approach, Microsoft has made sure that App Center works for all mobile developers, not just Xamarin developers. App Center supports native iOS and Android apps built using Objective-C, Swift and Java, Xamarin, Windows UWP, and React Native—and it actually supported native iOS and Android before Xamarin. This means that if you work with a mixture of app technologies, you can still use App Center to manage everything.

For each app, App Center provides a number of services:

- *Build*—App Center can connect to a source code repository (currently GitHub, VSTS, and BitBucket are supported). For each branch in your repo you can create a build to compile your solution or an individual project using any available build configuration either on demand or whenever the code is updated in the repo. You can sign your build using an Android keystore or iOS provisioning profile and even launch it on a real device, using Test Cloud as a sanity check to ensure that your app runs and doesn't crash on startup.
- *Test*—Xamarin has a huge data center in Denmark with thousands of real devices that you can run your app on using automated UI testing. App Center can be used to configure, start, and display the results of these test runs.
- *Distribute*—App Center can distribute your app, as soon as it's built, to beta testers or to the Google Play or Apple App Stores. Beta test users will get an email with a link to download your app so that they can test it, and they can even get notifications inside their apps that an update is available. I'll cover distribution in chapter 16.
- *Crashes*—Most apps will crash at some point, and App Center has an SDK you can add to your apps to track crashes. If your app crashes, the App Center SDK will track this, and the next time your app is run and is online, it will upload the crash details, including the stack trace, to App Center.
- *Analytics*—It's always good to know how your users are using your app, so that you can track pain points and see what features are popular or are not being used, so you know which areas to work on. It also helps to see user demographics—if your app is in English but is popular in Italy, you might want to offer it in Italian, for example. The App Center SDK can help to track this kind of information.

15.1.2 Users and organizations

When you log in to App Center, you're logged in as a user, and you can have apps assigned to you as an individual. Users can also be part of an organization—essentially a named group of users with different permissions. You can be an *admin* user and have full control over the organization, or a *collaborator* who can just create and manage apps inside the organization. You can read more on organizations in Microsoft's documentation at http://mng.bz/ge1o.

15.1.3 API

App Center was written API-first—that is, the development team at Microsoft created public APIs for managing your apps, and then the web portal was written to use these APIs. This means that anything you can do in the App Center web portal, you can also do using a public REST API. You can easily integrate App Center into any existing build or CI tools that you already use. For example, if you already have an automated build and release process using a tool like Jenkins, you can replace the steps for building your app with calls to App Center, and use that to run your builds. Microsoft's API documentation is available at http://mng.bz/szn6.

15.1.4 CLI

App Center also has a command-line interface that you can use to do everything App Center can do from a command line. Microsoft's App Center docs have more information on the CLI, covering the huge range of features it offers: http://mng.bz/Bkin. We'll get this set up and use it later in this chapter to run automated tests.

15.1.5 Getting help

App Center has excellent documentation. Just click your name at the bottom of the menu and select Docs & APIs (or you can find it at http://mng.bz/fS43). You can also interact directly with the App Center team at Microsoft if you get stuck, find bugs, or have feature suggestions—just click the blue and white speech-bubble button. From there you can start conversations with the team, see their responses, and see messages about new features.

15.2 Setting up builds

App Center apps are based on code for a mobile app from a source control repository, so before you can set up a build, you need to put the source code for your app into a repository that App Center can access. At the time of writing, App Center supports three providers: Git repos in GitHub (https://github.com) and BitBucket (https://bitbucket.org), and Git or TFS repos in Visual Studio Team Services (https://www.visualstudio.com/team-services/). Source code control is outside the scope of this book, so if Git is new to you, I recommend *Learn Git in a Month of Lunches* by Rick Umali (Manning, 2015). For the rest of this section, you'll need to have a basic understanding of Git, including being aware of branches, commits, and pushes.

In this chapter and the next, we'll just be looking at setting up Countr, but feel free to set up SquareRt as well, for practice. You'll need to add your Countr code to one of the three source code repository providers. Each one has comprehensive documentation to get you started. I personally use GitHub, because you can use a GitHub account to log into App Center, and this automatically gives App Center access to your repos, but use whichever you feel most comfortable with.

IDEALLY YOU NEED A PRIVATE REPO The different source code repository providers have both private and public repositories available. Later in this chapter we'll be adding an app secret to our app to wire up analytics and crash detection, and ideally this value should be kept private. This means it's worth creating a private repo to put your code into.

15.2.1 Creating your first App Center app

Once your code is in source control, the next step is to create an app in App Center. We'll begin by creating an Android app, then create the iOS one.

From the App Center landing page, click the Add New App button at the top right.

A panel will slide out on the right where you can enter details for your app (figure 15.3). Set the name as *Countr - Android*, add a description, set the OS to Android and the Platform to Xamarin, and then click Add New App. This will create the app and show a Getting Started page with details on how to set up the App Center SDK for crash reporting and analytics (we'll look at that later in this chapter).

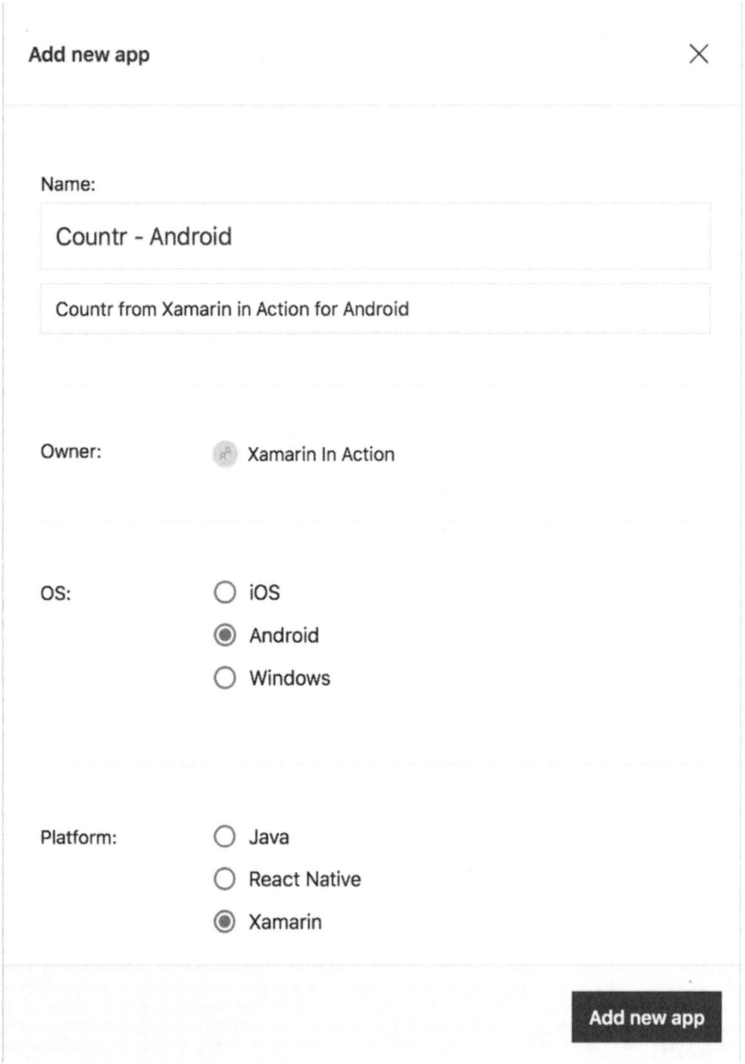

Figure 15.3 Setting up your app in App Center

The next step is to configure a build, and to do this you need to connect App Center to your source code repository. Click the Build tab on the menu on the left, select your repository provider of choice (figure 15.4), and follow the instructions to connect it to App Center. Once it's connected, choose the repo that you put the source code for Countr into.

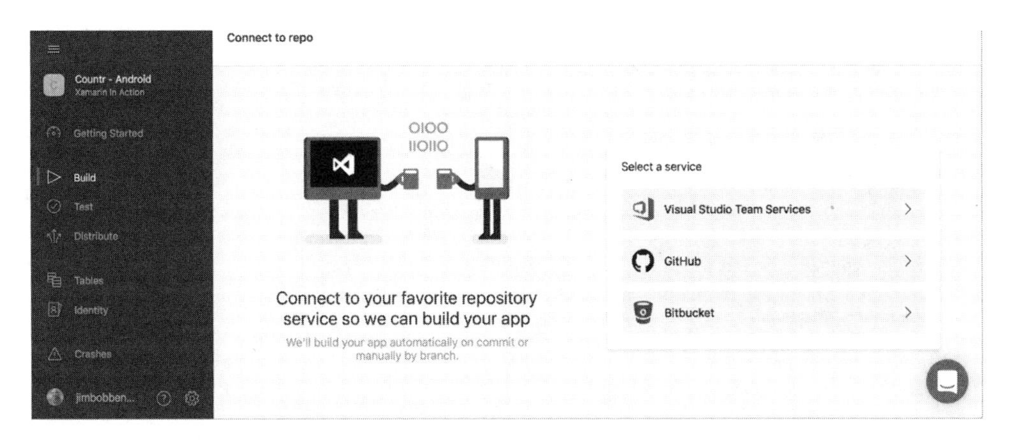

Figure 15.4 To create a build, you first need to connect App Center to your source code repository.

15.2.2 Configuring the Android build

Once you've set up your repo, the Build tab will show all available branches in that repo, so if you set up a new Git repo you'll probably only see one branch called "master". Click the master branch, and then click Set Up Branch. A panel will slide out with options to configure your branch, as shown in figure 15.5.

This configuration is divided into four sections:

- *Build App*—In this section you can configure how your app should be built.
  - *Project*—The first option is the project to build—your solution could contain multiple Android apps, so here you can select the one to build. Our solution only has one Android app, so Counter.Droid should be selected.
  - *Configuration*—From here you can set the build configuration you want to compile with: either Debug or Release (or any others if you have more set up). You'll need a release build for running UI tests later (to avoid having to uncheck the Shared Mono Runtime option in your Android project), so set this to Release.
  - *Mono Version*—Here you can select which version of Mono (the open source version of the .NET Framework that runs on macOS) to use when compiling your app. At the time of writing, Mono 5 has been released with a whole swath of improvements and new features, but there have also been some bugs. You can choose to use the latest version (currently Mono 5) or use Mono 4.

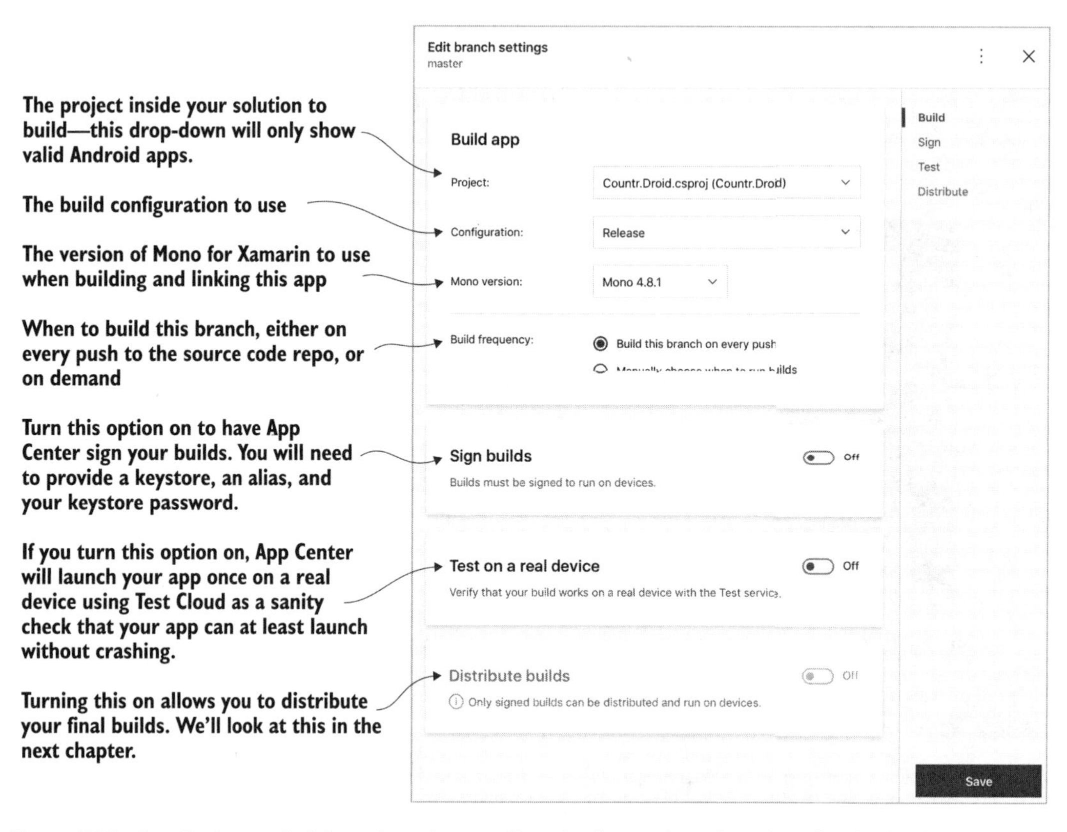
The project inside your solution to build—this drop-down will only show valid Android apps.
The build configuration to use
The version of Mono for Xamarin to use when building and linking this app
When to build this branch, either on every push to the source code repo, or on demand
Turn this option on to have App Center sign your builds. You will need to provide a keystore, an alias, and your keystore password.
If you turn this option on, App Center will launch your app once on a real device using Test Cloud as a sanity check that your app can at least launch without crashing.
Turning this on allows you to distribute your final builds. We'll look at this in the next chapter.
Edit branch settings
master
Build app
Project:
Countr.Droid.csproj (Countr.Droid)
Configuration:
Release
Mono version:
Mono 4.8.1
Build frequency:
Build this branch on every push
Sign builds
Off
Builds must be signed to run on devices.
Test on a real device
Off
Verify that your build works on a real device with the Test service.
Distribute builds
Off
Only signed builds can be distributed and run on devices.
Build
Sign
Test
Distribute
Save

Figure 15.5 App Center can build your branch, as well as sign it, test it, and set it up for distribution.

- *Build Frequency*—The build frequency can be set to either on every push to this branch, or manually, on demand. Leave this set to Build This Branch on Every Push—this way every time you push one or more commits to your repository, the app will be rebuilt.

- *Sign Builds*—App Center can sign your builds using your Android keystore. You can take advantage of this to sign your build using the keystore you created back in chapter 13. Turn on Sign Builds, upload your keystore from the very safe place where you keep it, enter the alias you used when creating it in the `KEY_ALIAS`, and then enter your keystore password into both the `KEYSTORE_-PASSWORD` and `KEY_PASSWORD` fields (when you set up a keystore using Xamarin, it uses the same password for the keystore as for the signing key inside it).
- *Test on a Real Device*—By turning this option on, your app will be launched on a real device inside App Center's Test Cloud service, and the test will verify that your app launched successfully. It won't run the UI tests you wrote in the previous chapter; it will just launch the app and check for a crash (we'll look at running UI tests in Test Cloud later in this chapter). This is a great sanity check

that your build has worked and that your app at least starts up. You have no control over which device it will run on—it will be a compatible one with at least your app's minimum SDK installed, but other than that you have no control. It will also make your build take longer, as you'll have to wait for an available device. This runs using UITest, so use a release build so the shared Mono runtime isn't used, as discussed in chapter 13.

You'll need a valid Test Cloud subscription for this to work, but as part of your App Center free trial, you'll get a valid subscription; turn this option on.

- *Distribute Builds*—These options allow you to distribute final builds to either beta testers or the store. We'll look at this in chapter 16, so leave this off for now.

Once your build is configured, click Save. This will queue up a first build under the master branch, as shown in figure 15.6.

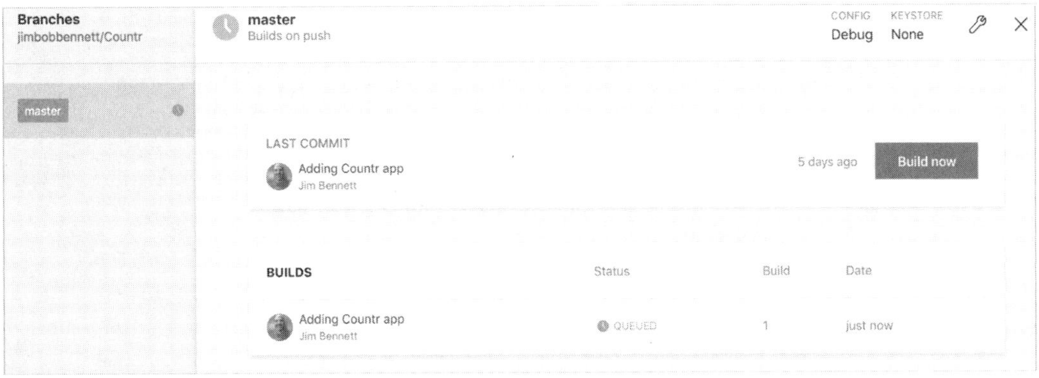

Figure 15.6 All builds for a branch can be seen by clicking on the branch.

Under each branch is a list of all the builds for that branch, and this will only have one entry so far—the build that was kicked off by setting up the branch. If you click the build, you can see more information about it, including a full build log. Figure 15.7 shows the bottom of the build log.

Once your app has built, you'll see the build marked as a success, as well as how long the build took and logs detailing everything that happened. The build has taken your code from your source code repository, restored the NuGet packages you use, compiled your Android app, signed the APK using your keystore, installed it on a device, and launched it to verify that everything has worked. You'll also have an option to download the Android APK and build logs if you want to. If your app didn't build, check the build output and fix up whatever is causing the issue.

This is your Android app set up and built. Now let's set up the iOS app.

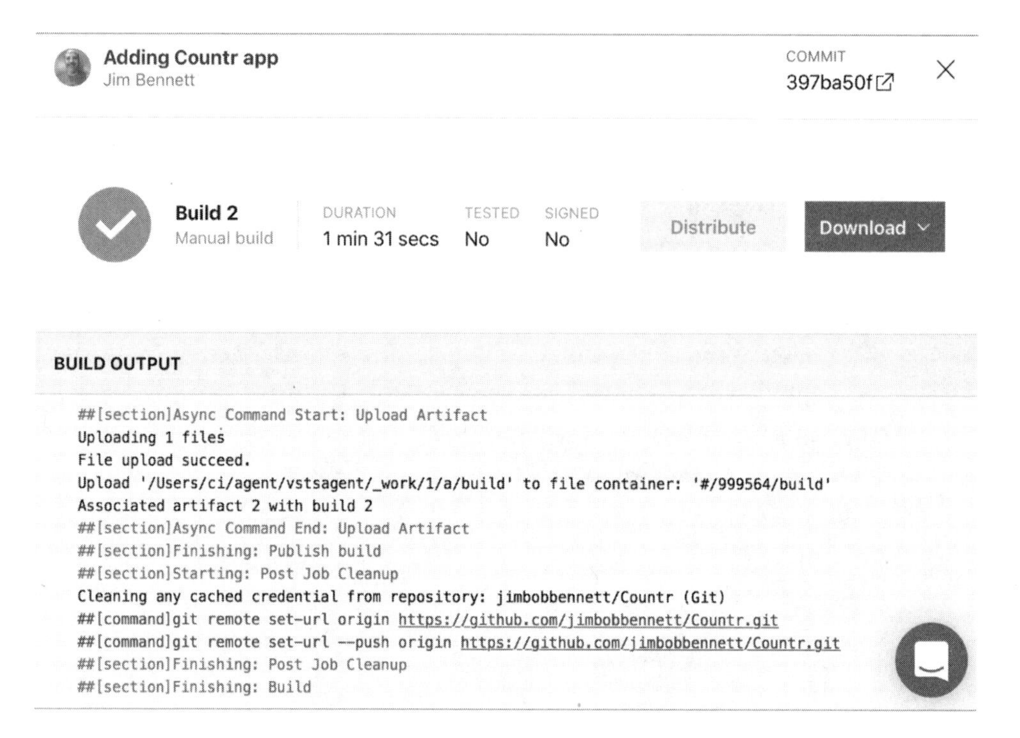

Figure 15.7 Your Android app should build successfully.

15.2.3 Configuring the iOS build

Although you're building a cross-platform Xamarin app, you're really building two apps, one iOS and one Android. This means you have to set up your iOS app as a separate app in App Center. Repeat the same steps as for the Android app, but call the app Countr - iOS and set the OS to iOS.

As before, select the master branch to set up the build. The Build App section has a few different options than the Android version, as shown in figure 15.8:

- *Build app*
  - *Project*—Unlike Android, you can only select the solution you want to build here, not the project. This means you should only have one iOS app in your solution, to avoid confusion—if you have more than one, it might be worth breaking them out into separate solutions. This setting should default to Countr.sln.
  - *Configuration*—This is the same as the Android configuration section. To be able to run a launch test on your builds using UITest, you need to use the Debug configuration, so set this to Debug instead of Release.
  - *Mono Version*—Here you can select which version of Mono to use when compiling your app. At the time of writing, Mono 5 has been released with a

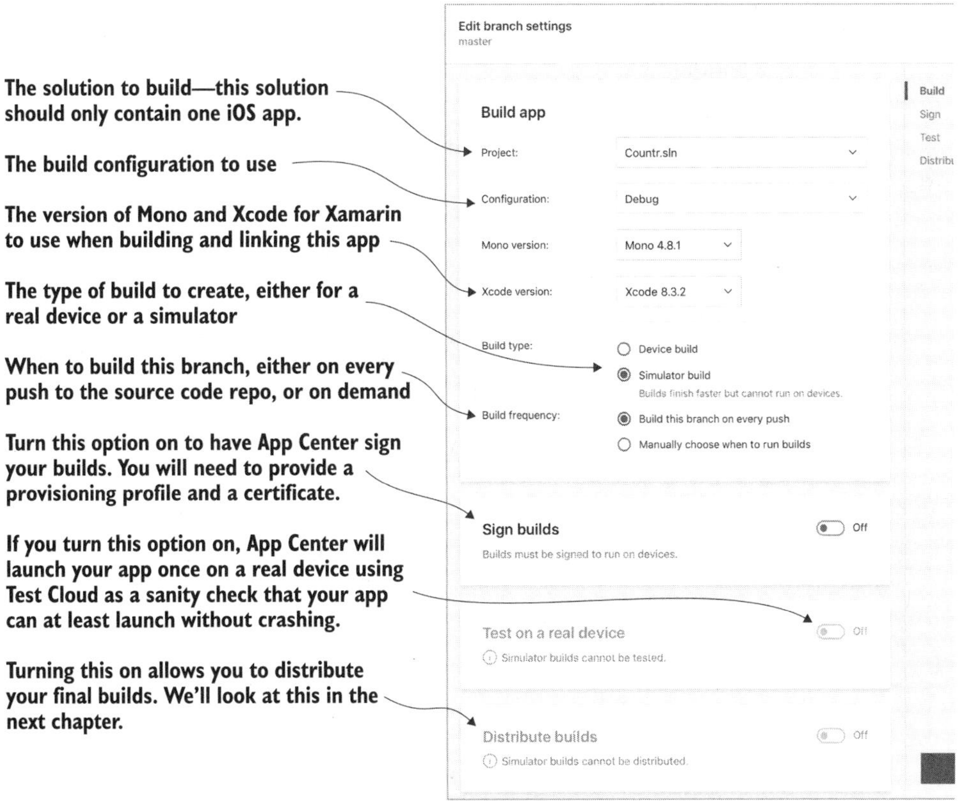

The solution to build—this solution should only contain one iOS app.

The build configuration to use

The version of Mono and Xcode for Xamarin to use when building and linking this app

The type of build to create, either for a real device or a simulator

When to build this branch, either on every push to the source code repo, or on demand

Turn this option on to have App Center sign your builds. You will need to provide a provisioning profile and a certificate.

If you turn this option on, App Center will launch your app once on a real device using Test Cloud as a sanity check that your app can at least launch without crashing.

Turning this on allows you to distribute your final builds. We'll look at this in the next chapter.

Figure 15.8 iOS builds have a few more options than Android builds.

whole swath of improvements and new features, but also some bugs. Here you can choose to use the latest version (currently Mono 5) or to use Mono 4.

- *Xcode Version*—You can configure which version of Xcode to use when building. Only recent versions are available (for example, at the time of writing 8.3.2 is the latest, and you can only select versions starting at 8.0), but this is useful if you need an earlier version. You can just leave the default setting, which will be the latest released version.
- *Build Type*—Unlike Android, iOS builds come in two types—simulator and device builds. Set this to Device Build so that you can run a launch test on a real device (launch tests aren't available on simulators).
- *Build Frequency*—Leave this set to Build This Branch on Every Push.

- *Sign Builds*—App Center can sign your iOS builds using your certificate and provisioning profile.
  - *Provisioning Profile*—The easiest way to set the provisioning profile is to head to the Apple Developer site (https://developer.apple.com), log in, go to the

provisioning profiles section of Certificates, Identifiers and Profiles, and download your developer profile. Once it's downloaded, upload it to App Center.

- *Certificate*—App Center needs your signing certificate as a .p12 file. You can't download this from the Apple Developer website; instead you need to export it from your keychain. Open Keychain Access on your Mac and search for a certificate whose name starts with *iPhone Developer* (figure 15.9). Select this certificate and click File > Export Items, enter a name, select a sensible location, and click Save. When you're prompted, enter a password to use to encrypt this certificate.

  From App Center, upload this .p12 file and enter the password you used.

- *Test on a Real Device*—Turn this option on to sanity check your app on a real iOS device.
- *Distribute Builds*—Leave this off for now.

Once your build is set up, click Save and watch the logs to see it build and run the launch test. Again, if the build fails, check the build output and fix up any issues.

Figure 15.9 Use Keychain Access to export your certificate.

15.3 Testing your apps using Test Cloud

When your apps were built, App Center uploaded them to a real device for a simple launch test. When you write your own UI tests and run them locally, you can run them against simulators or actual devices, but there's a limit to how many devices you can feasibly own and use. When running UI tests from the IDE, you can only target one device at a time, and although there are ways to run tests on multiple devices at the same time, this requires complicated configuration for Android and a lot of Mac build servers for iOS. Ideally, you'll want to test on a wide range of devices of all configurations running all manner of OS versions, but this means a massive hardware spend and a long time to run all the tests. Fortunately, *Test Cloud* offers an alternative.

15.3.1 What is Test Cloud?

Test Cloud is a cloud-based device lab containing many thousands of real Android and iOS devices that you can run your UI tests on, and it's available as part of App Center. You can create a test session with a selection of devices, submit your tests to it, and it will wait for those devices to become available, install your app on them, and run your UI tests.

You can then see the results in a dashboard, where you can break them down by OS, device type, device manufacturer, OS version, or whatever you need to analyze any test failures. You can also see screenshots of your app running, track memory usage, and even download the device log.

This is a paid service (with a 30-day free trial, of course, to lure you in), but it removes the cost of buying and maintaining your own devices, plus the time of setting up and running tests manually.

15.3.2 Preparing your apps to be tested

Test Cloud runs UI tests against a signed and packaged application: an APK (Android package) for Android or an IPA (iOS application archive) for iOS. Android apps should be release builds, but iOS apps should be debug builds so that the Calabash server is enabled.

There are two ways to get this package: downloading the build from App Center, or building locally. At the time of writing you can't automatically test a build inside App Center (apart from the launch test). You have to run tests from your local dev box.

Downloading packages from App Center

When App Center builds and signs your app, it creates an app package—an IPA on iOS and an APK on Android. If you select an individual build for a branch, you'll see a Download button at the top right (figure 15.10). Click this and select Download Build to download the APK or IPA.

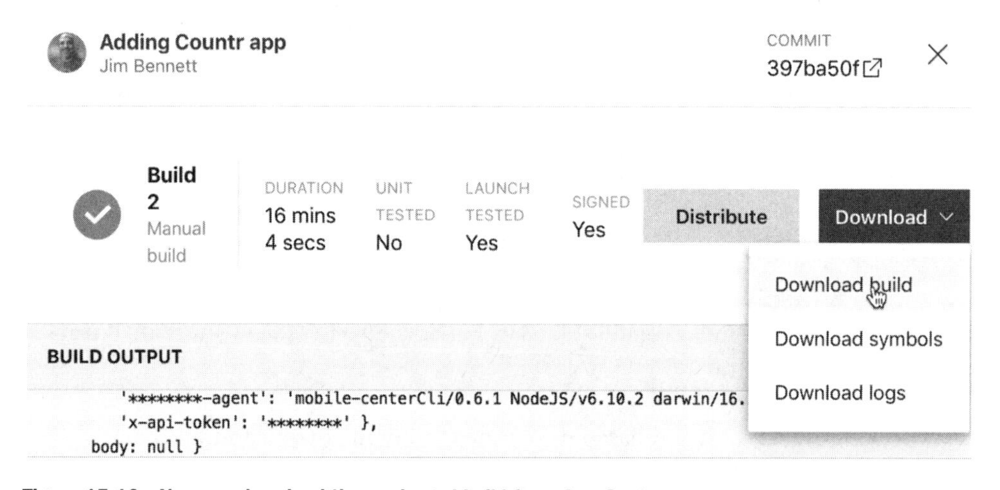

Figure 15.10 You can download the packaged build from App Center.

BUILDING LOCALLY

To generate the Android APK locally, set the build configuration in Visual Studio to release and run your app on a device or emulator—this will compile your app and package it as an APK.

For iOS, IPAs aren't built by default for debug builds in Visual Studio, so you need to configure your builds to generate them by checking the Build iTunes Package Archive (IPA) option in the iOS IPA Options section of the project properties (figure 15.11). With this option ticked, you'll get an IPA every time you build your app, so tick it, set the configuration to debug (remember that you need debug to have the Calabash server enabled), and rebuild. Your IPA needs to be a device build, so make sure it's built against a physical device (simulator builds won't work on Test Cloud), and if you don't have a device at hand, select Generic Device. Don't worry about which provisioning profile is used for the device build; Test Cloud will re-sign it with their provisioning profile.

COMPILING THE UI TESTS

You'll need to make sure your UI test project has been built from Visual Studio. The configuration doesn't matter. You just need to remember which configuration you used, because you'll need the path to it later when you run the tests.

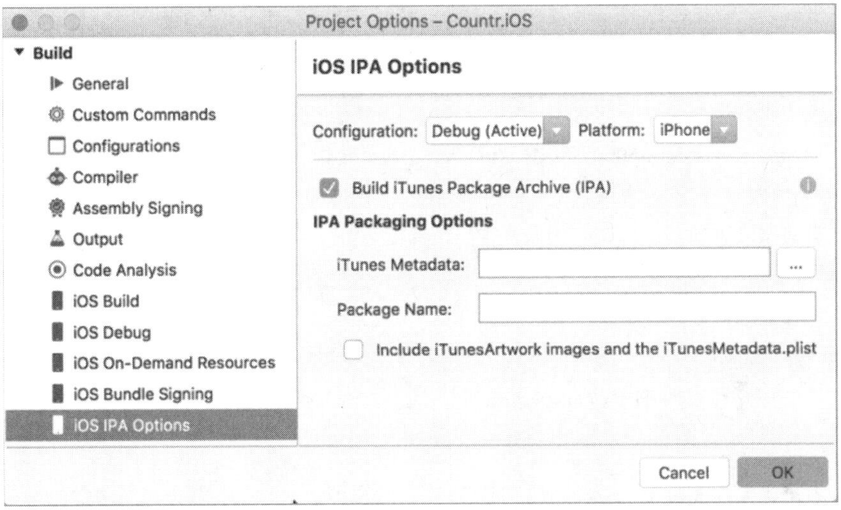

Figure 15.11 To create an IPA file with every build, turn on Build iTunes Package Archive.

15.3.3 Creating a test run configuration

When you want to use Test Cloud, you start by creating a test run configuration, and this configures which OS your app supports and what devices you want your test to be run on. You can then assign tests to a series, allowing you to group multiple test run configurations. For each run configuration, you're given the command that you can run locally to upload your app to Test Cloud and start the test run.

You can access Test Cloud from the Test tab in App Center for one of your apps. Select this tab, and then click the New Test Run button at the top of the screen. Once you click this, you'll be presented with a panel containing a wizard that will allow you to configure the test run.

The first panel allows you to select the devices you want to run your UI tests on. This includes a range of devices and OS versions (for example, on iOS there are 160 different combinations ranging from iPhones to iPads and OS versions from 8 up), and you can search this list to find the device and OS configurations you want to run on. You can type in the search box to filter by name, or click the funnel icon to filter by device type, OS, CPU, or other values. If you click the information icon to the right, you'll see a popup giving detailed device information. For now, just select a couple of devices—any device will do.

Once you've selected your devices, you can save your selection using the Save Set button, and you'll be prompted to enter a name for the device set. This device set will be remembered, and the next time you create a test, you'll be able to reuse this set or create a new configuration.

After selecting the devices you want, click the Select <x> Devices button (figure 15.12).

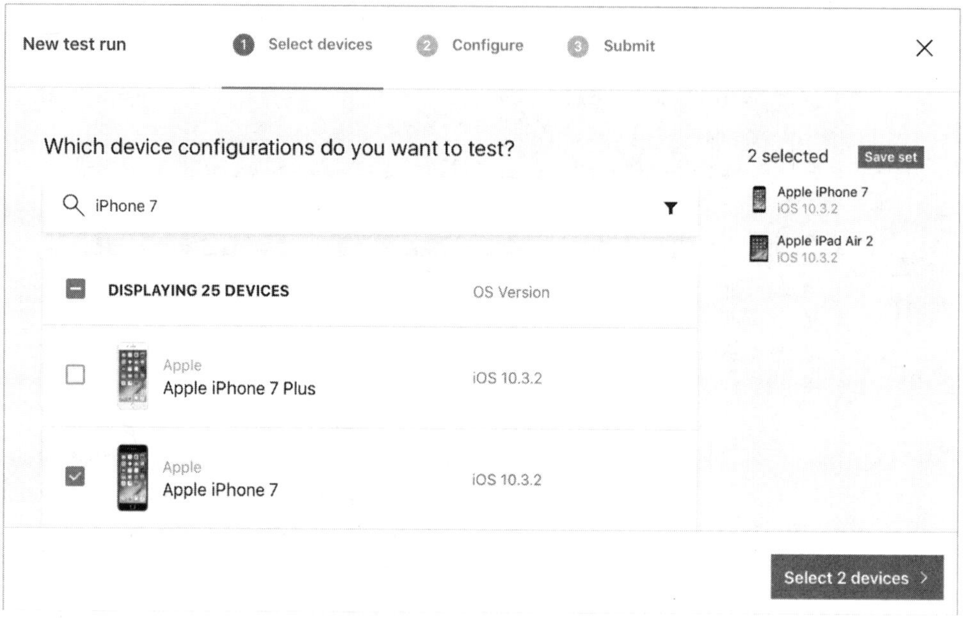
New test run
1 Select devices
2 Configure
3 Submit
Which device configurations do you want to test?
iPhone 7
DISPLAYING 25 DEVICES
OS Version
Apple
Apple iPhone 7 Plus
iOS 10.3.2
Apple
Apple iPhone 7
iOS 10.3.2
2 selected
Save set
Apple iPhone 7
iOS 10.3.2
Apple iPad Air 2
iOS 10.3.2
Select 2 devices

Figure 15.12 Selecting the devices to test on

In the next panel (figure 15.13) you can configure the test run details.

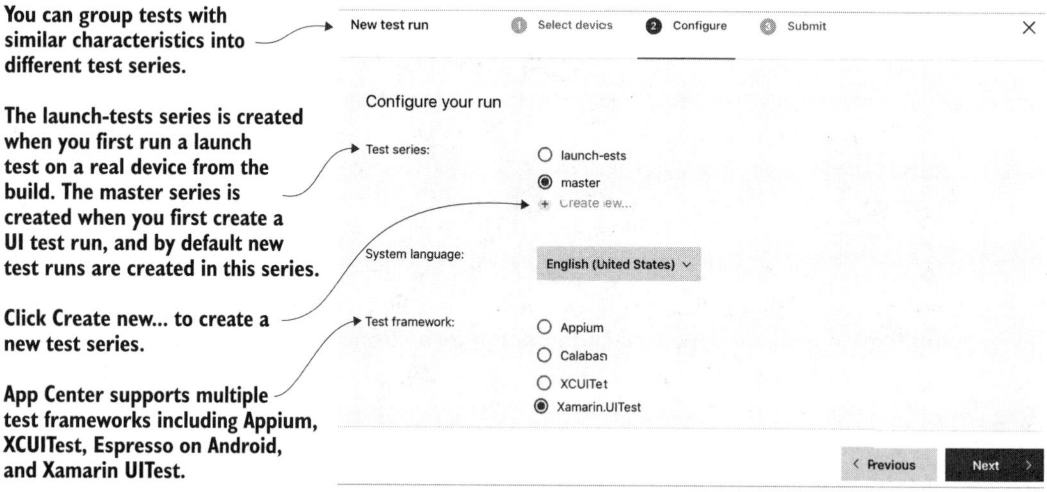
You can group tests with similar characteristics into different test series.
The launch-tests series is created when you first run a launch test on a real device from the build. The master series is created when you first create a UI test run, and by default new test runs are created in this series.
Click Create new... to create a new test series.
App Center supports multiple test frameworks including Appium, XCUITest, Espresso on Android, and Xamarin UITest.
New test run
Select devics
Configure
Submit
Configure your run
Test series:
launch-ests
master
System language:
English (United States)
Test framework:
Appium
XCUITet
Xamarin.UITest
Previous
Next

Figure 15.13 Configuring the test series and testing framework

- *Test Series*—Test series are named groups for grouping tests based on whatever criteria you want. You should see two test series: `launch-test` was created when you selected to run a launch test for your app at build time, and `master` is a default test series created for you. Select `master` for now.
- *System Language*—Your tests can be run on devices configured with one of a small selection of system languages, so if you need your devices to run in a different language, select it here.
- *Test Framework*—Test Cloud supports a number of frameworks, including the native Apple and Google frameworks, Appium, and UITest. Your tests were written using UITest, so select this option.

When you click Next, you'll be presented with a final panel with details about your test run and instructions on how to run it (figure 15.14). At the moment, you can't launch a test run from App Center. Instead, you have to run it from the command line. Don't click the Done button yet, as the contents of this panel are necessary to run the tests.

New test run
1 Select devices 2 Configure 3 Submit

Submit your tests to finish

Prerequisites

In order to submit tests, you need to install App Center Command Line Interface (CLI), version 0.2.1 or later.

1. Install Node.js, version 6.3 or later.
2. Install the `appcenter-cli` NPM package:

Copy to clipboard
```
npm install -g appcenter-cli
```

You must also have Xamarin.UITest installed via the NuGet package **Xamarin.UITest**. For more details, please also read Adding Xamarin.UITest to your solution.

Running tests

Do not use personal data in your tests. Learn more.

To run the tests in App Center, run the following commands from the directory that contains the NuGet **packages** directory.

Copy to clipboard
```
appcenter test run uitest --app "Xamarin-In-Action/Countr-Android" --devices
"Xamarin-In-Action/pixels" --app-path pathToFile.apk --test-series "launch-tests" -
-locale "en_US" --build-dir pathToUITestBuildDir
```

Figure 15.14 The last panel shows commands to run to execute the test series.

15.3.4 Running tests from the command line

To run your tests, you'll need to have Node.js installed—the App Center command-line tools are implemented as a Node.js JavaScript package that can be run from the command line. If you haven't heard of Node.js before, it's a JavaScript runtime that can run JavaScript libraries such as the App Center tools, among others. Head to https://nodejs.org and install Node.js before continuing.

Once Node.js is installed, install the App Center tools using the Node.js package manager.

For macOS, launch a Terminal window and run this command:

```
sudo npm install -g appcenter-cli
```

On Windows, launch a command prompt as an administrator and run this command:

```
npm install -g appcenter-cli
```

Once Node.js is set up, navigate to the root of the Countr solution using the Windows command prompt or macOS terminal.

If you've never used the App Center command-line interface (CLI) before, you'll need to log in. Enter the following command:

```
appcenter login
```

This will launch a browser window where you'll need to log in to App Center. Once you've logged in, you'll be given an access code that you'll need to copy and paste into the command prompt or terminal to complete the log in.

Once you're logged in, it's time to run the tests. On the last panel, you'd have seen a command to run:

```
appcenter test run uitest --app "Countr-iOS" --devices <your devices>
➥ --app-path
pathToFile.ipa  --test-series "master" --locale "en_US"
➥ --build-dir pathToUITestBuildDir
```

The `<your devices>` part will be a short hex string showing a unique identifier for the devices you selected, or the name used if you saved the device set. A couple of values in this command need to be replaced before you can run it:

- `pathToFile.ipa` *or* `pathToFile.apk`—This is the IPA or APK to upload and test against. If you downloaded the build from App Center, set this value to be the path to the downloaded build. If you built it locally, set this to the local package—for example, Countr.iOS/bin/iPhone/Debug/Countr.iOS.ipa would point to your Countr iOS debug IPA, or Countr.Droid/bin/Debug/io.jimbobbennett.Countr-Signed.apk for the Android version.
- `pathToUITestBuildDir`—This is the path to a folder containing the assemblies that contain the actual UI tests. This should be set to the output directory of the UI test project, so use Countr.UITests\bin\Debug.

Make these changes to the command, and then run it. It'll take a few minutes to run, so while it's running, let's look in more detail at what we have run.

> **YOU MAY BE ASKED FOR TELEMETRY INFORMATION** The first time you run an App Center command from the command line, you might be asked if you want to enable *telemetry*—analytics around how you use the CLI tools that Microsoft is gathering to help improve the user experience. Enter `y` to enable telemetry, `n` to disable it.

BREAKDOWN OF THE COMMAND

Let's take a look at the command and its parameters in more detail. The `appcenter` command is used to interact with all the available functionality in App Center. Table 15.1 shows the different parameters used to submit tests.

Table 15.1 The parameters for the App Center command

Part	Description
`test run uitest`	Tells App Center you want to run some Xamarin UI tests.
`--app "<app name>"`	Sets the app name for the test you want to run. App names on their own refer to apps owned just by you. For an app owned by an organization, use the format `"Organization name/app name"`—for example, `"Xamarin-In-Action/Countr-Android"`. The name should be in quotes because app names can have spaces in them.
`--devices <your devices>`	A unique ID defining what devices to use. If you saved your device set, it will be the name you set when saving (prefixed with your organization name if your app is part of an organization). Otherwise it will be a unique ID generated by Test Cloud that references your devices.
`--app-path pathToFile.ipa/apk`	The path to the IPA or APK for your app. If you used the one built by App Center, this is the path to wherever you downloaded it. If you built it locally, this will be under the current folder, so Countr.iOS/bin/iPhone/Debug/Countr.iOS.ipa to point to your Countr iOS debug IPA or Countr.Droid/bin/Release/io.jimbobbennett.Countr-Signed.apk for Android.
`--test-series "master"`	The series to run your test under. Tests can be grouped by series so you can compare different test runs or builds. For example, you could have a `develop` series for builds that you're actively working on that just tests recent changes, and a `release` series for your release candidates that tests everything.

Table 15.1 The parameters for the App Center command *(continued)*

Part	Description
`--locale "en_US"`	The device language to use, which is useful if you want to test your app with multiple languages. Test Cloud only supports a limited set of languages at the moment, but this list should grow over time as Microsoft has always been superb at supporting multiple languages.
`--build-dir pathToUITestBuildDir`	The path to the folder containing the assemblies that have your UI tests. These need to be compiled assemblies, so make sure it points to an output path and that your tests are built (for example, `Countr.UITests\bin\Debug`).

WHAT HAPPENS WHEN YOU RUN THIS COMMAND

When you run this command, it will start by uploading your IPA or APK and tests to Test Cloud. It will then validate that your app package will work on the devices you've selected (for example, checking that it supports the OS version on the device). Once that's validated, it will wait for the devices to be ready. When one is ready, it will start the test on that device, and as the others become available, the tests will start on those devices. If you use a popular device, you could be waiting a while—Xamarin is adding more devices all the time, but there can still be a wait. Once the tests are run, you'll see the pass and fail counts in the command-line window. Figure 15.15 shows this process.

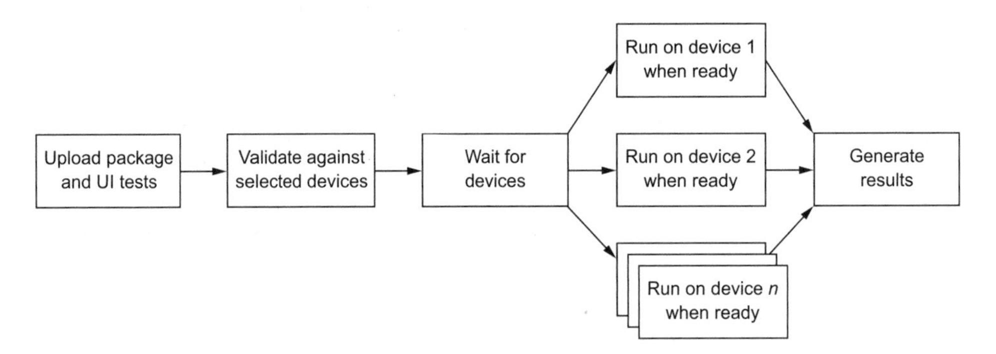

Figure 15.15 The App Center CLI uploads your binaries, validates them, and then runs the tests on the selected devices.

How long this takes depends on the speed of your network connection (after all, you have to upload a multi-megabyte package) and the availability of the devices. My last run, for example, took 10 minutes. The output follows (with repeated lines replaced with ellipses to make the output much shorter):

```
Preparing tests... done.
Validating arguments... done.
```

```
Creating new test run... done.
Validating application file... done.
Uploading files... done.
Starting test run... done.
Test run id: "865a554c-5d0d-45d4-b748-5c15b8bec2ce"
Accepted devices:
  - Apple iPad Air 2 (10.3.2)
  - Apple iPhone 7 (10.3.2)
Current test status: Validating
...
Current test status: Running on 2 devices (0 / 2 completed, 0 pending)
...
Current test status: Running on 1 device (1 / 2 completed, 0 pending)
...
Current test status: Tests completed. Processing data.
Current test status: Done!
Total scenarios: 3
3 passed
0 failed
Total steps: 10
```

This shows that the three tests ran and passed. You'll also receive an email from App Center with the test results.

Now let's open up App Center to see more details.

15.3.5 Viewing the test results on App Center

To see the results of your tests, open up App Center for your app and select the Test tab. In there you'll see a summary of all your test runs (figure 15.16).

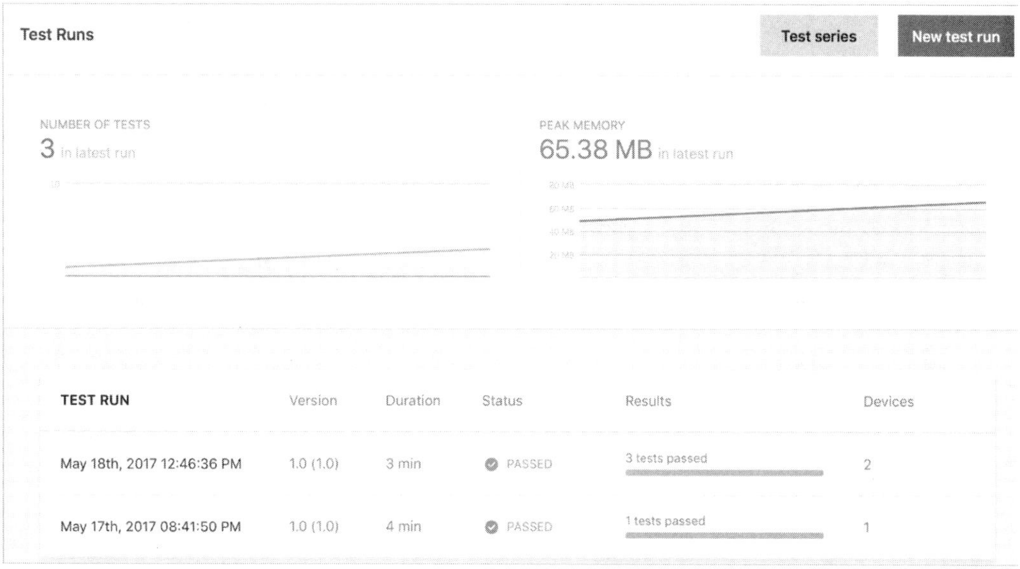

Test Runs

Test series

New test run

NUMBER OF TESTS

3 in latest run

PEAK MEMORY

65.38 MB in latest run

TEST RUN	Version	Duration	Status	Results	Devices
May 18th, 2017 12:46:36 PM	1.0 (1.0)	3 min	PASSED	3 tests passed	2
May 17th, 2017 08:41:50 PM	1.0 (1.0)	4 min	PASSED	1 tests passed	1

Figure 15.16 The Test dashboard gives an overview of all your tests runs for your app.

This shows the number of tests over time and the peak memory usage of your app as line charts. Underneath these charts is a list of all the test runs in chronological order, with the most recent at the top. As you move your mouse over the lines in the charts, the corresponding test runs for that point will be highlighted. You can click the lines or the test runs in the list to see the details of an individual run.

Even though you've only run your tests once, you'll see two tests showing: the test run you just did with three tests in it, and a run with a single test. The single test run was the launch test performed by your build, so not only can you tell from the build tab that it was successful, you can also see more details on it in here.

Click the test run you've just done to see a dashboard showing more details. This dashboard shows a summary of the run, with the date and time, the time taken, the version of your app, how long the test took, charts showing the success and failure breakdown by test and device, and a list of all the tests run. The list of tests includes the peak duration and memory usage, as well as the status. This is shown in figure 15.17.

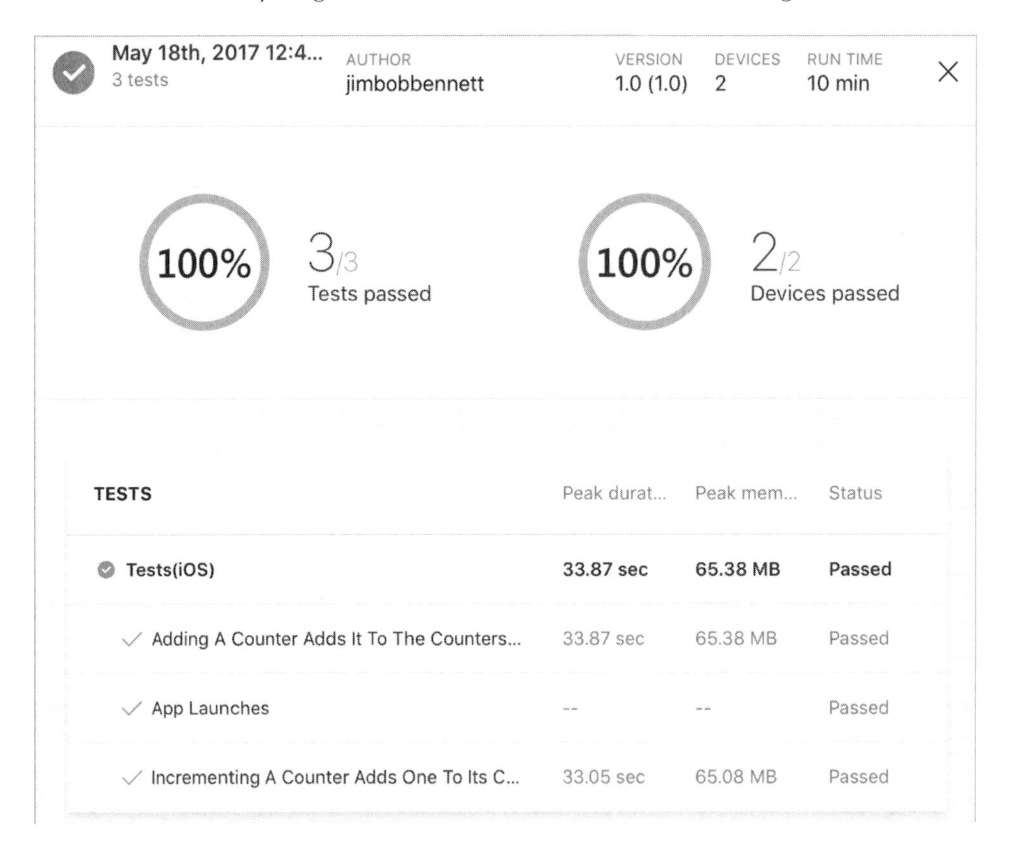

Figure 15.17 The Test dashboard, giving an overview of the latest test run

You shouldn't see any failures for your tests, but to see what failures look like, try breaking the app (just as we did back in chapter 14 to show UI test failures) and rerun the tests—not forgetting to revert the breaking code once the tests are done. Figure 15.18 shows what a test run with a failing test looks like.

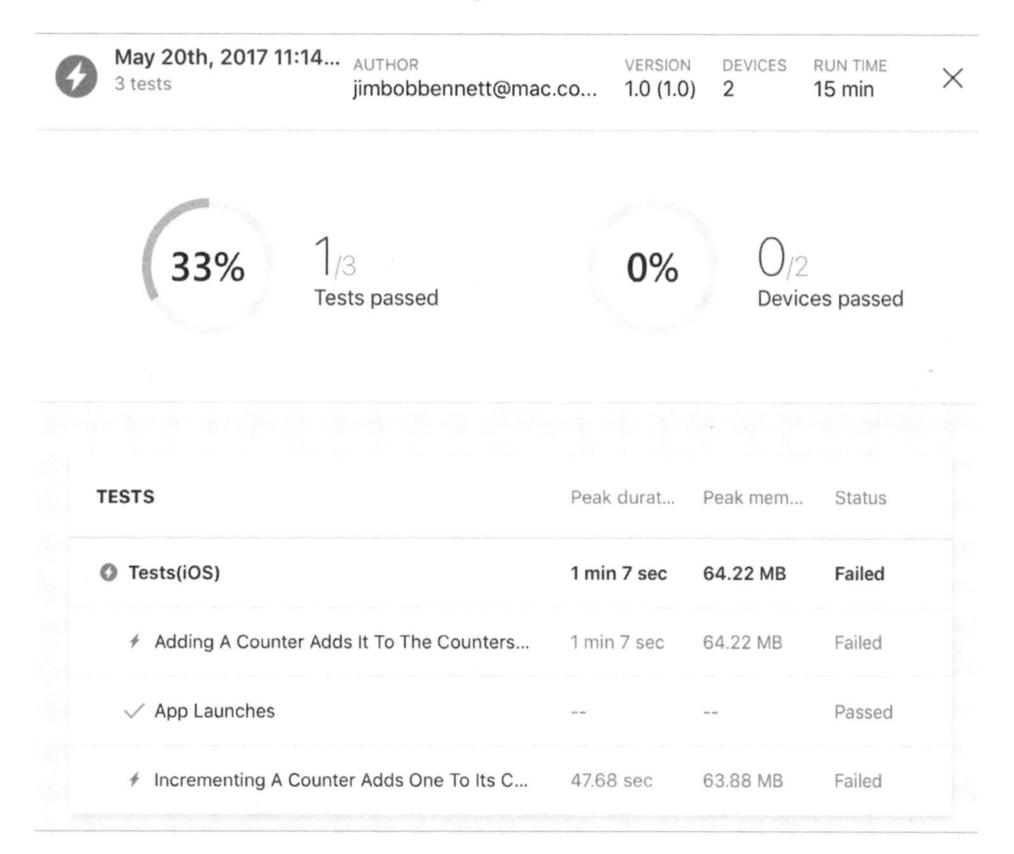

Figure 15.18 The Test Cloud dashboard showing a failing test

When you click a test in the list, you'll be shown a breakdown of that test (figure 15.19). The left panel will show a tree of all the tests in the run, with the test you clicked expanded. It will show a list of steps that match up to the calls to `IApp.Screenshot()` that you added to your UI tests back in chapter 14 to capture named screenshots at various points in the test. As you click each step, you'll see the screenshot that was captured for each of the devices in your test run, and this screenshot will be updated as you click into the different steps. You can then click an individual device to see more details, such as the test duration, memory usage, and CPU usage at each screenshot. You can also access device information and even the system log (useful sometimes for debugging test failures). This is shown in figure 15.20.

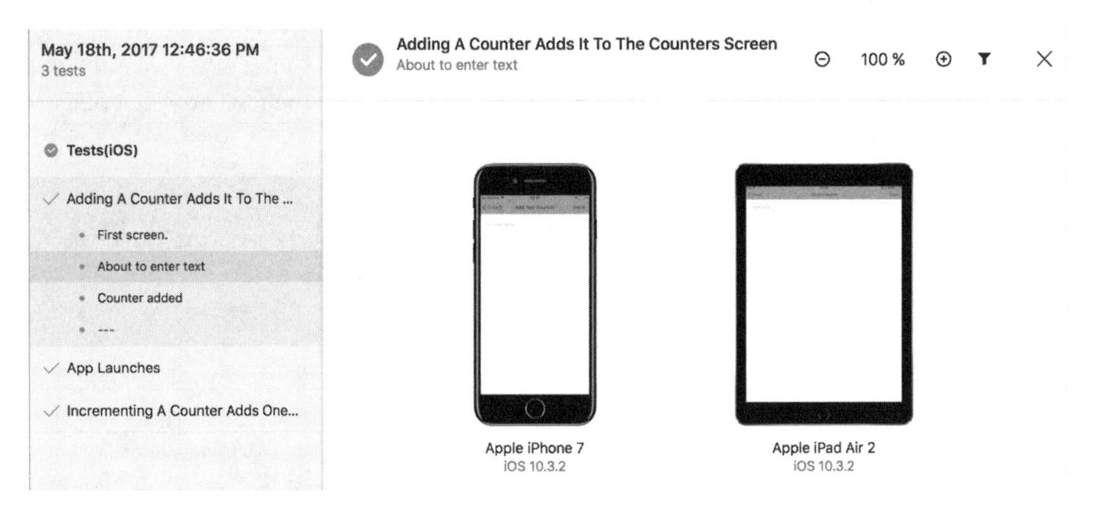

Figure 15.19 The details of a test run

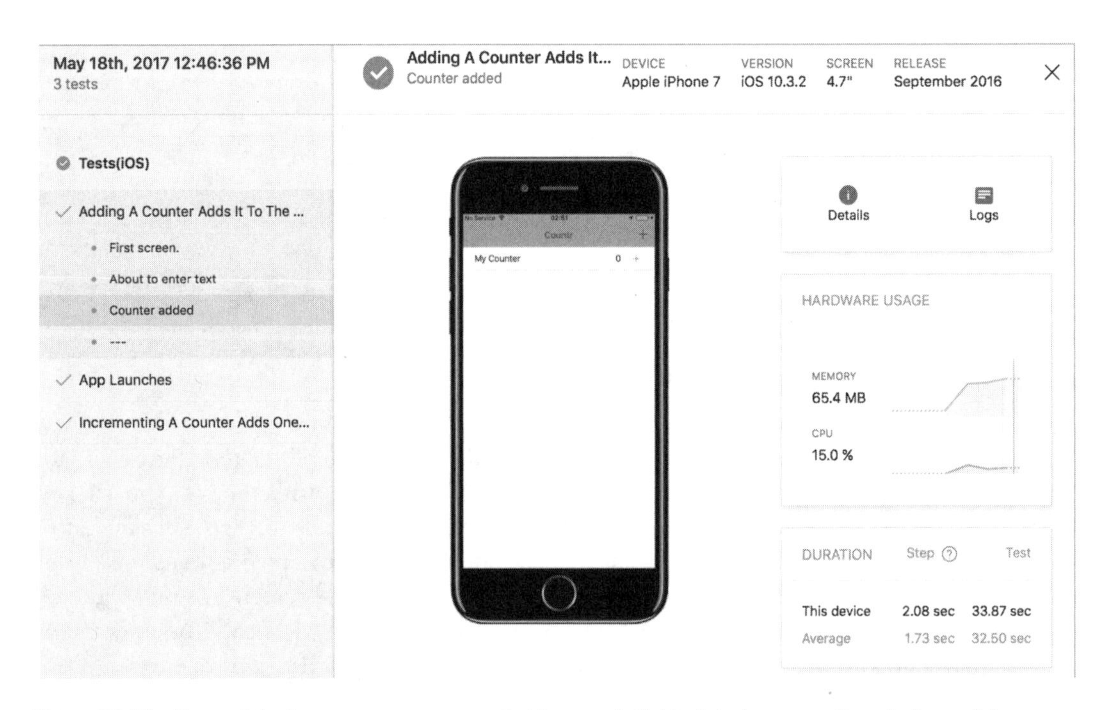

Figure 15.20 For each test you can see a screenshot from an individual device, as well as device metrics.

The ability to see screenshots can be an incredibly powerful tool. When you design your app, it's hard to know how it will look on all devices. You can use simulators to test all available iOS devices, but this is time consuming. Testing all possible Android devices manually would take a huge amount of time and require a lot of configured emulators or a large pile of physical devices. By using Test Cloud inside App Center and capturing screenshots, you can build up UI tests that work through your app, capturing screenshot after screenshot from all the screens in your app. You can then use the App Center dashboard to review these screenshots and quickly compare multiple devices. This is a fast way of seeing how your app looks, and it's a great way to justify the expense of App Center—the cost of paying developers to check apps on multiple devices is way higher than the cost of App Center!

You've now got your app building on iOS and Android and tested in the cloud. The next step in preparing for release is to set up analytics and crash reporting, so that once your beta test and production users have your app, you can not only analyze how the app is used, but also monitor for any crashes in order to fix them as soon as possible.

15.4 Analytics and crash reporting

When you finally release your app to your users, you want them to have the best experience possible. Good experiences lead to repeated use, good reviews, and recommendations; bad experiences lead to users deleting your app and giving bad reviews (with bad reviews leading to potential users skipping your app for a competitor's). One way to guarantee a bad experience is to have an app that crashes. You can test your app to reduce the chance of crashes, but they're a fact of life—users always seem to end up doing something developers didn't expect, causing a crash. Even extensive unit and UI testing can't cover everything.

You may not be able to prevent your app from crashing, but you can monitor for crashes, find out what causes them, and fix it as soon as possible. Your users may well forgive a crash if they get a fix pretty swiftly, and this is where crash monitoring comes in. App Center has an API you can add to your app that will monitor for crashes, and once the app is restarted it will upload a crash report so that you, as the developer, can see what caused the crash and fix it.

To help give users the best experience possible, you should also take time to understand your audience—to see what type of devices or OS versions they use, see what parts of the world they live in, and discover what languages they speak. You can use this information to tailor your app to give your users a five-star experience. App Center also has an API to help with this.

15.4.1 Adding the App Center SDKs

To enable crash reporting and analytics, the first thing you need to do is install the App Center NuGet packages, so head back to Visual Studio and load your app. Install Microsoft.AppCenter.Crashes and Microsoft.AppCenter.Analytics into the Countr.Core, Countr.Core.Tests, Countr.iOS, and Countr.Droid projects (figure 15.21).

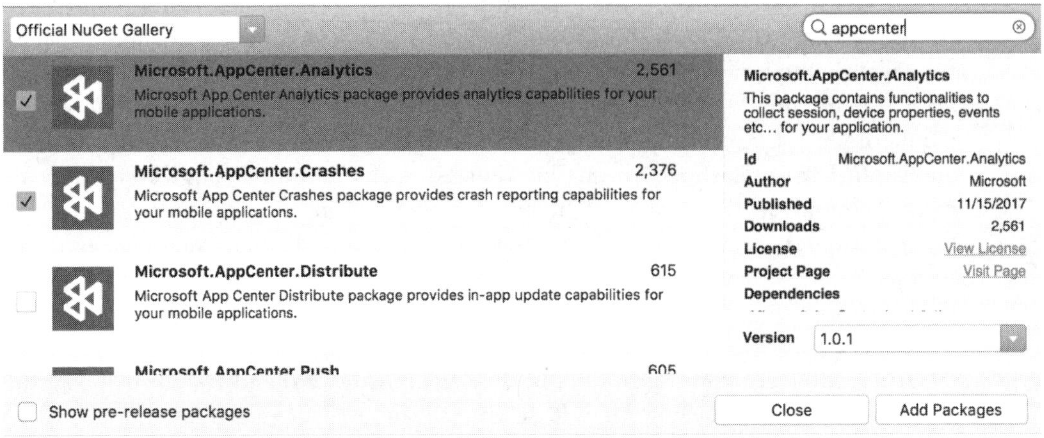

Figure 15.21 Adding the App Center NuGet packages

Once the NuGet packages are added, configure the SDK inside each project. Part of this configuration is to connect the SDK with the particular app inside App Center, so that it knows where to send the crashes and analytics. This connection is configured using an app secret that's generated for you when you create your app—this secret is a GUID that's unique to your app and can be found by selecting Settings from the menu. On the Settings tab, you'll see the app secret at the top right.

SETTING UP THE SDK ON ANDROID

The SDK needs to be configured as early on in your app's lifecycle as possible, so the easiest place to do this is inside the splash screen. This way everything is configured as soon as the app starts up, and any crashes that happen during startup can be caught.

Add the following code to the `SplashScreen` class in the Droid project.

Listing 15.1 Adding App Center to Countr.Droid

```
using Microsoft.AppCenter;
using Microsoft.AppCenter.Analytics;
using Microsoft.AppCenter.Crashes;
...
protected override void OnCreate(Android.OS.Bundle bundle)
{
   base.OnCreate(bundle);

   AppCenter.Start("<your app secret>",
                   typeof(Analytics),
                   typeof(Crashes));
}
```

Adds an override for the OnCreate method

Starts App Center using your app's secret

Replace `<your app secret>` with the value of the app secret for your Android app. Remember, the iOS and Android versions are different apps in App Center, and they have different app secrets, so make sure you use the right one. This line tells App Center to start both analytics and crash reporting.

App Center requires three permissions: `ACCESS_NETWORK_STATE`, `INTERNET`, and `READ_EXTERNAL_STORAGE`. The SDK will automatically add these permissions for you when you compile your app, so you don't need to add them manually and you won't see them ticked in the Android manifest file.

SETTING UP THE SDK ON IOS

On iOS, the best place to configure App Center is in `AppDelegate`, so add the following code to the `FinishedLaunching` method override, again replacing `<your app secret>` with the value of the app secret for your iOS app.

Listing 15.2 Adding App Center to Countr.iOS

```
using Microsoft.AppCenter;
using Microsoft.AppCenter.Analytics;
using Microsoft.AppCenter.Crashes;
...
public override bool FinishedLaunching(UIApplication app,
                                       NSDictionary options)
{
   AppCenter.Start("<your app secret>",
                   typeof(Analytics),
                   typeof(Crashes));
   ...
}
```

15.4.2 *Understanding your audience*

Audience data is invaluable in enabling you to make decisions about your app. If you have a large number of customers in certain countries using languages that your app is not available in, then perhaps it's time to add translations for that language. If users are on old OS versions, you may need to perform extra testing or support. If you've targeted your UI toward phones, but most users are on tablets, maybe you need to rethink your UI. All this information can be found in App Center's analytics.

Once you've added the App Center SDK to your apps, fire one of them up and play with it for a while. Then open App Center for the app you've been using and head to the Audience page under the Analytics tab in the menu. It make take a minute or two for this information to update, but when it does you'll see a breakdown of the usage for your app.

At the top of this page are a couple of filters, allowing you to filter the information you see based on app versions or date ranges. The preview version of App Center only supports 90 days of data, but once it's fully released you should be able to pay more to access more data if needed. From here you can see how many users use your app daily, how long they spend in your app, which versions of your app they use, their device types, OSs, languages, and locations.

- *Active Users*—This panel shows a graph with three lines, giving the number of unique devices that have used your app over the past day, week (seven days), and month (30 days)—the day starts at midnight UTC, so it may not reflect a local "day" for you (figure 15.22). This panel can give you a great indication about the increase in app users, and by looking for sudden peaks, you can see when larger numbers of people started using your app—maybe you can tie it back to a marketing push or a new app version. If you see this number trailing off, maybe it's time to add new features and do a marketing push to highlight these to your users, to keep them coming back.

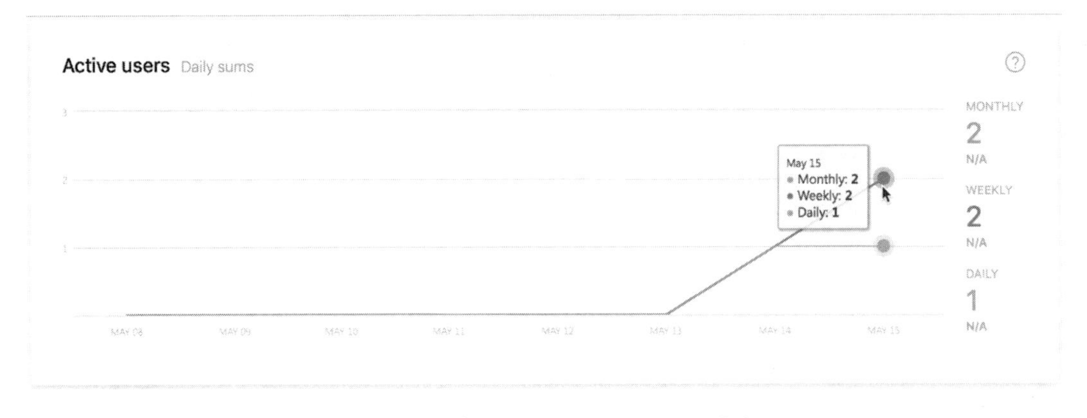

Figure 15.22 Active users shows how many unique users use your app each day.

- *Engagement*—It's all well and good seeing that new users are signing up for your app, but you also need to consider how engaged they are. Are they regularly coming back as opposed to using it once and deleting it, and are they spending enough time in your app to get the most from it? The Engagement tab can give you this information (figure 15.23). The Daily Sessions Per User shows how many times per day your app is run on each unique device, displaying a graph with a count against dates; the Session Duration shows how many users are using your app for a certain period of time, split into buckets ranging from a few seconds to over an hour.
- *Devices*—The Devices section shows the top four devices that your users have used, the number of users on each device type, and a percentage breakdown (figure 15.24). It also shows the top four OS versions, and what percentage of the users on those versions are on each.

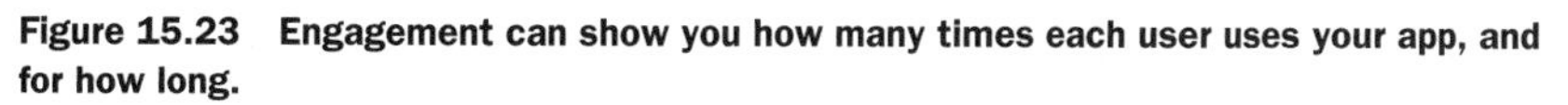

Figure 15.23 Engagement can show you how many times each user uses your app, and for how long.

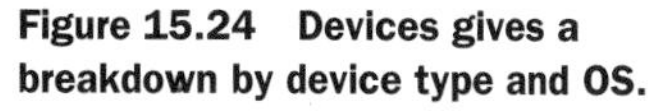

Figure 15.24 Devices gives a breakdown by device type and OS.

- *Country/Region and Languages*—This section gives a breakdown by country, showing a map identifying the countries your users are based in. Darker shading of a country means a higher percentage of users. This country data is taken from the country of the mobile carrier, so it's only available on devices with a SIM card—most of the data will come from phones, with much less from tablets because a lot of tablets don't have cellular connectivity. This section also shows the name and percentage of users in the top seven countries. The language data shows the top seven major language settings from the device. English would include British users, along with New Zealand English, Australian English, and US English. This is shown in figure 15.25.

Countries

none	1	N/A
New Zealand	1	N/A

Languages

English	2	N/A

Figure 15.25 Breakdown by country and language

- *Versions*—The versions section shows the top 20 app versions that your users are using (figure 15.26).

Figure 15.26 Versions breaks down your app usage by app version.

15.4.3 *Adding event tracking*

Just by adding the App Center SDKs and calling the `Start` method, you get user analytics, and this is useful for understanding more about your users. The next thing you want to learn is what your users are doing with your app, what steps they take, or how often they use certain features. You can use this information to understand what users do most often and how they do it, and maybe this can help you improve your app. For example, in the Countr app, if users are deleting counters a lot and immediately adding new ones with the same names, they're probably trying to reset the counter to 0. This would suggest you should add a "reset count" option.

As well as tracking what users do, you can also attach information to these events, so that you can learn more about their behavior. For example, in a news app you could track not only that a user wants to see the entire story behind a headline, but also what story they tap on, to determine what stories are more popular. In a camera app you could track not only that the user has shared a photo, but where they shared it to.

MONITORING AND PRIVACY If you're monitoring users, you need to consider their privacy. These analytics don't capture any personally identifiable information by default, but you could easily add user-identifiable data, such as tracking a login with the username they've used. It's good practice to have a privacy policy, so that users know that you're capturing data, what data you're capturing, and what you plan to do with it. Also check the laws in the countries in which you operate, as there may be legal considerations.

SIMPLE EVENT TRACKING

The simplest event tracking is to track a named event. In Countr, a good event to track would be the user tapping the plus button to add a new counter. The App Center SDK works in cross-platform code as well as in platform-specific app projects, so you can add the event tracking to your view model.

Open `CountersViewModel` in the Countr.Core project, and add the following code.

Listing 15.3 Tracking when the user shows the add new counter screen

```
using Microsoft.AppCenter.Analytics;
...
void ShowAddNewCounter()
{
   Analytics.TrackEvent("Show add new counter");   <-- Tracks the event
   ...
}
```

You can use this to track an event with any name you want, within limits—you can only have 200 distinct event names in use, and each name must be less than 256 characters in length.

When you call `TrackEvent`, the data is queued up and sent in the background, usually pretty instantly. This means the thread isn't blocked. If the device is offline, this data is persisted and sent the next time the device is connected to the internet. This data is also persisted between sessions, so if the device is offline and the app is terminated, the data will be sent the next time the app is run with the device online.

ADDING DATA TO EVENTS

Events can have properties attached as key-value pairs in a `Dictionary<string, string>`, allowing you to provide custom data to your events. Again, as with events, there are some limits to the data you can provide—each key and value is limited to 64 characters, and you can only add up to five properties to each event.

You can use this to track when the user saves a new counter, tracking not only the event but the name the user has assigned to the counter. This information could be useful. For example, if certain counter names are used a lot, you could offer that name as a predefined default somehow.

To add data to an event, add the following code to the `CountersService` in the `Countr.Core` project.

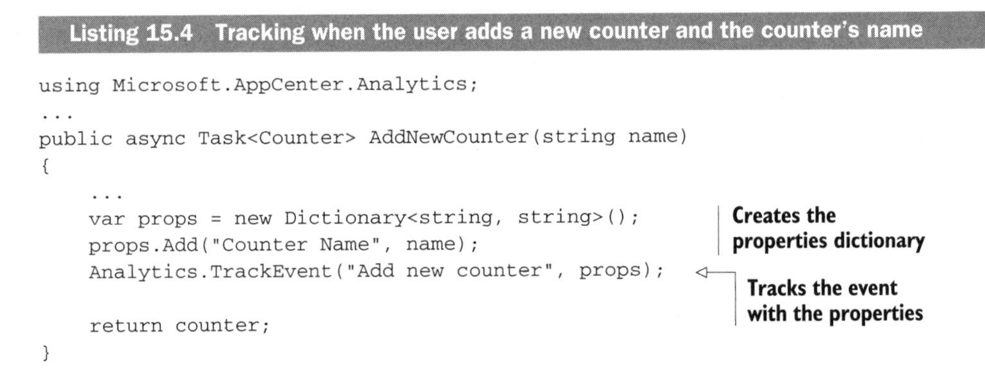

Listing 15.4 Tracking when the user adds a new counter and the counter's name

```
using Microsoft.AppCenter.Analytics;
...
public async Task<Counter> AddNewCounter(string name)
{
    ...
    var props = new Dictionary<string, string>();
    props.Add("Counter Name", name);
    Analytics.TrackEvent("Add new counter", props);

    return counter;
}
```


You can repeat this same pattern to track when the user deletes or increments a counter.

SEEING THE EVENTS

Once you've started collecting data, you can see it in App Center in the Events page under the Analytics tab. Again, like analytics, you can filter based on time periods or particular app versions (figure 15.27).

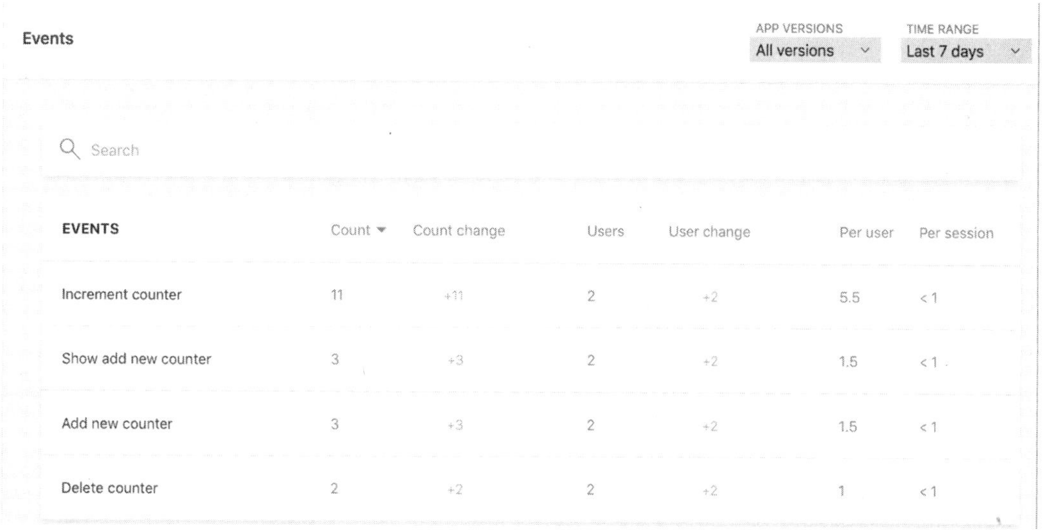

Events

APP VERSIONS: All versions | TIME RANGE: Last 7 days

Search

EVENTS	Count	Count change	Users	User change	Per user	Per session
Increment counter	11	+11	2	+2	5.5	< 1
Show add new counter	3	+3	2	+2	1.5	< 1
Add new counter	3	+3	2	+2	1.5	< 1
Delete counter	2	+2	2	+2	1	< 1

Figure 15.27 App Center shows you all events, including the total count and for how many users this event was tracked.

For each event, you can see how many times it was tracked (including a delta since the previous time period), for how many users it was tracked, and an average number of times the event was tracked per user and per session. This gives a great overview of the popularity of a feature. You might hope that for Countr you'd see an increment counter event tracked for most of your users for each session, meaning that the app was being used on a regular basis for its intended purpose of counting things.

You can click an event to drill down into more information. When you do, it shows a breakdown over time of that event:

- *Counts*—Three panels provide the counts for the events—how many times the event was raised (figure 15.28). You can view a graph that shows on a day-by-day basis how many users executed the code that raised this event and the total number of times the event happened. You can also see the average count per user and per session.

Figure 15.28 You can see the number of users who raised an event, and the total number of times the event was raised.

- *Event properties*—For events with properties, App Center will show all the properties that have been sent against this event (remember, you can only send five unique properties against each named event). For each of these properties, it will show the top 10 values with a count of how many times the event was raised with that value, and the change in that count over time. This is shown in figure 15.29.

15.4.4 Crash reporting

App Center is able to provide crash reporting for your app. If your app crashes, the SDK can detect details about the crash and upload this information to App Center the next time the app is started. Once you have a crash report, you can fix the bug that caused it and hopefully get a fix to your customers before they uninstall your app and leave a bad review.

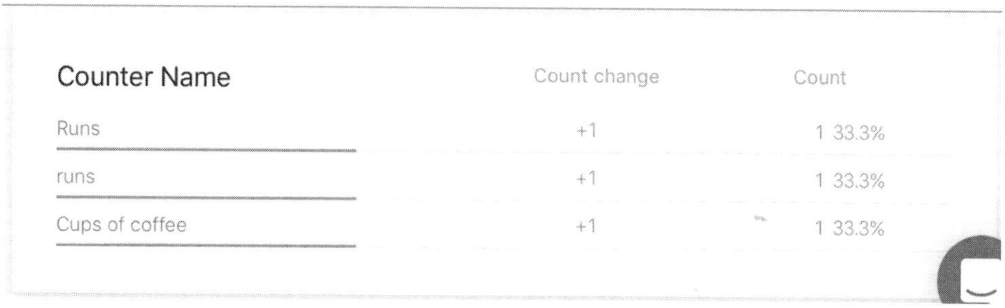

Counter Name	Count change	Count
Runs	+1	1 33.3%
runs	+1	1 33.3%
Cups of coffee	+1	1 33.3%

Figure 15.29 For events with properties, you can see the number of times the event was raised with specific values.

The App Center SDK does this by hooking into the .NET unhandled exception handler, as well as the OS-specific unhandled exception mechanisms. This means any exception that's unhandled, be it in .NET code or native code, will be caught and sent up to App Center. When a crash does happen, there's no guarantee that anything in your app will actually be working for the remainder of its life, so the exception details will be saved locally, and when your app is restarted the crash data will be sent.

NOT ALL EXCEPTIONS WILL BE CAUGHT App Center can catch most exceptions, but not all. Out-of-memory exceptions won't be caught because there's no memory left to catch them with. Also, due to a limitation with the Xamarin runtimes, stack overflow exceptions won't be caught.

To see this in action, you can create a fake crash and see the report in App Center. To create an exception, you can add a `throw` statement to throw a new exception. Add the following code to the `CountersService` in the `Countr.Core` project.

Listing 15.5 Crashing your app when you increment a counter

```
public Task IncrementCounter(Counter counter)
{
    throw new System.Exception("Crash");    <-- Throws an exception
    ...
}
```

Make this change and then run the app. When you increment a counter, it will crash. Relaunch the app so that the crash report can be uploaded, and then head to App Center and open the Crashes tab (figure 15.30). As with the analytics and events, you can filter this data by date range or version.

Figure 15.30 The Crashes tab shows crash-free users per day and a list of the crashes received.

The first part of this tab shows two graphs. The first shows the percentage of users per day that are crash-free—those who managed to use your app for the day without experiencing any crashes. The second shows a total count of crashes each day in the selected time period. This allows you to make a decision about how important a crash fix is—if you have 100 users and 50 of them get a crash each day, then it's pretty important. But if you have millions of users and only one or two get a crash, maybe it can wait for your next scheduled release.

The second part shows a list of crash groups—groups of crashes that are the same. For example, if in one version of your app 100 users got the same crash in the same place, you wouldn't see 100 rows here. Instead you'd see one row for that crash showing it happened to 100 users. This makes it easier to manage crashes.

If you click a crash group, you can see more details of the crash (figure 15.31). You can see details of the affected users, including how many users got the crash and how many times, and which devices it occurred on. This is useful information. For example, you might only get a crash on a particular OS version or a particular device, meaning you need to source a device or simulator matching those characteristics for testing your fix.

The stack trace gives you a breakdown of where the crash happened. In the example in figure 15.31, you can see it happened in `IncrementCounter`, which is expected,

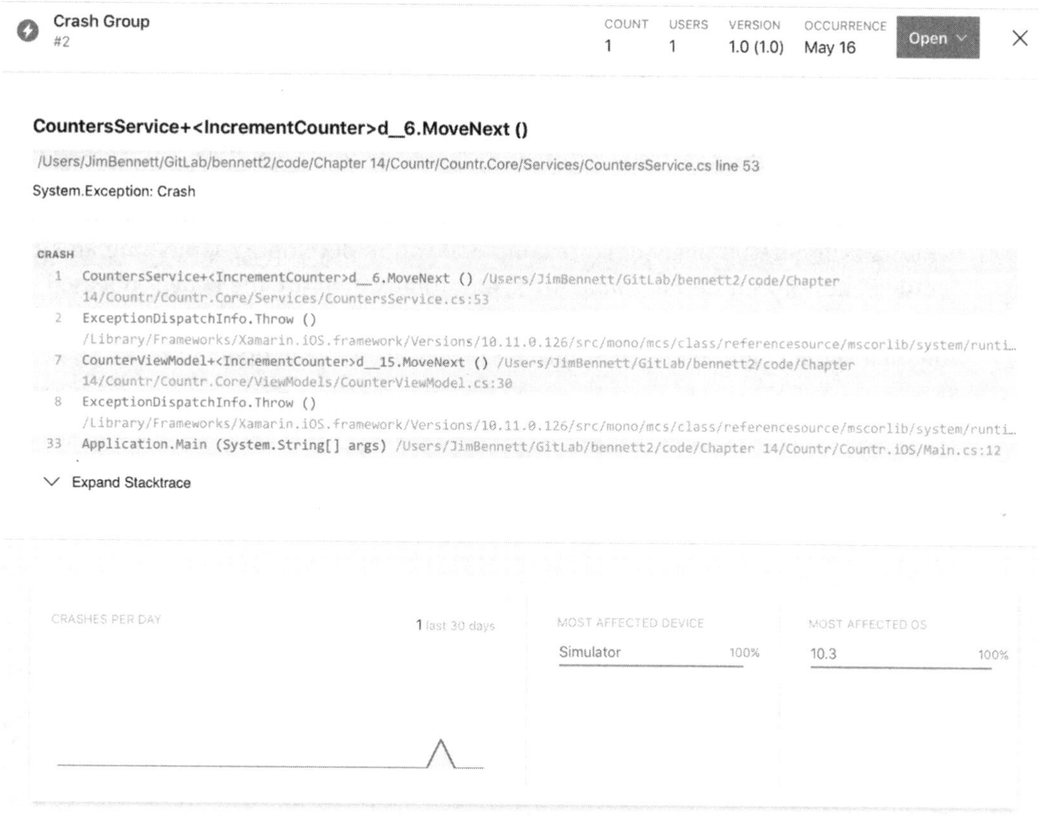

Crash Group
#2

COUNT 1 | USERS 1 | VERSION 1.0 (1.0) | OCCURRENCE May 16 | Open

CountersService+<IncrementCounter>d__6.MoveNext ()

/Users/JimBennett/GitLab/bennett2/code/Chapter 14/Countr/Countr.Core/Services/CountersService.cs line 53

System.Exception: Crash

```
CRASH
 1  CountersService+<IncrementCounter>d__6.MoveNext () /Users/JimBennett/GitLab/bennett2/code/Chapter
    14/Countr/Countr.Core/Services/CountersService.cs:53
 2  ExceptionDispatchInfo.Throw ()
    /Library/Frameworks/Xamarin.iOS.framework/Versions/10.11.0.126/src/mono/mcs/class/referencesource/mscorlib/system/runti…
 7  CounterViewModel+<IncrementCounter>d__15.MoveNext () /Users/JimBennett/GitLab/bennett2/code/Chapter
    14/Countr/Countr.Core/ViewModels/CounterViewModel.cs:30
 8  ExceptionDispatchInfo.Throw ()
    /Library/Frameworks/Xamarin.iOS.framework/Versions/10.11.0.126/src/mono/mcs/class/referencesource/mscorlib/system/runti…
33  Application.Main (System.String[] args) /Users/JimBennett/GitLab/bennett2/code/Chapter 14/Countr/Countr.iOS/Main.cs:12
```

Expand Stacktrace

CRASHES PER DAY 1 last 30 days

MOST AFFECTED DEVICE
Simulator 100%

MOST AFFECTED OS
10.3 100%

Figure 15.31 Crash groups show details on affected users and the stack trace of the crash.

as this is where you put the `throw`. The stack trace looks a little weird, with the exception actually happening in `CountersService+<IncrementCounter>d__6.MoveNext ()`, a method that doesn't exist. This is one of the downsides to async/await—the compiler creates some magic behind the scenes to handle the thread-switching, and this appears in the stack trace. You have to look at the created method names and look for things that match your code, such as the `IncrementCounter` buried inside the compiler-created method name.

The default stack trace tries to only show you relevant code, and it highlights what it thinks are methods from your code, not the SDKs. You can expand the stack trace to see the full trace, including all SDK methods, if you need to.

The stack trace information is created using symbol information—data that links the calls inside your binary to the source code. For Android, this is stored inside the app package, but for iOS this isn't available. This means that you'll need to provide a symbol file in order to see a stack trace on iOS. If you built your app using App Center, it will automatically get the symbol file from the build, but if you built locally you may need to provide the symbol file. The Symbols tab under Crashes will show you if there are crashes with missing symbols, and from there you can upload your symbol files. These files are created at the same time as the IPA when you compile your app, and they're output to the same place and have the file extension .dsym.

Crash groups have a status—Open, Closed, or Ignored. All new crashes default to Open, and you can change the status as needed. Once you fix a crash, you can mark it as Closed to show it's no longer an issue and can be ignored. You can also mark crashes as Ignored if needed. For example, if you're developing something and get a crash as part of your development work, and you fix it before the code is released, you can mark that crash group as Ignored. You can filter crashes on the dashboard based on their status, and the filter defaults to Open, only showing open crashes.

> **REVERT THE THROW!** Once you've played with the crash reports, don't forget to remove the `throw`!

You've built your app, tested it on real devices in the cloud, and set it up to track your users and report crashes. You're finally ready to put it in the hands of your users. In the next chapter we'll look at using App Center to distribute your app to beta test users, before finally uploading it to the store.

Summary

In this chapter you learned

- App Center is "Mission Control for apps" and provides services for the mobile-optimized development lifecycle.
- You can use App Center to build and test your apps as well as viewing analytics, user events, and crash reports.

You also learned how to

- Set up apps and builds in App Center.
- Run UI tests on real devices in the cloud using Test Cloud from inside App Center.
- Add the SDKs to your apps to capture analytics, user events, and crash reports.
- View analytics on your apps and see what steps users are taking inside your apps.
- See crash reports and use them to manage app crashes.

16 Deploying apps to beta testers and the stores

This chapter covers

- Using App Center to distribute apps to beta testers
- Publishing Android apps to the Google Play Store
- Publishing iOS apps to the iOS App Store

In the previous chapter you added some final release prep to your app—you turned on analytics and crash reporting, set up builds in App Center, and ran some UI tests on a range of devices in the cloud. You're finally ready to put your app into the hands of your users, starting with beta test users and then finally releasing to the stores.

In this chapter you'll see how to use App Center to distribute your apps to beta testers, including automatically updating these installs whenever you push out a new release. We'll then follow up by looking at how you can actually release your apps to the stores, including what information you need to provide with your apps. As in the previous chapters, we'll only be focusing on Countr here. We'll also be looking at one OS at a time, starting with Android.

16.1 Distributing Android apps to beta testers

Before you think about a final, production release of your app to the app stores, it's worth putting it in the hands of some beta testers first. This way you can get real-world feedback, address usability issues, and find and fix bugs. If you just put it out to the stores immediately, you'd risk bad reviews. It would be a shame for your app to fail because of one-star reviews that could have easily been avoided with a little beta testing. Ideally you want to allow beta test users to play with your app as soon as possible, even before the app is finished—the quicker you get feedback, the sooner you can change your app.

Visual Studio App Center makes it easy to distribute apps to beta testers. From App Center you can register test users via email and notify them every time a new build is ready. You can even set your app to check for updates every time it's launched, and, if an update is available, to automatically update itself.

16.1.1 Enabling app distribution

Enabling app distribution is incredibly easy on Android. You set up the users you want to test your app, and they make a small settings tweak on their devices. Then you either automatically distribute your app on every build, or distribute manually whenever you want to release an update.

REGISTERING USERS

App Center has the concept of *collaborators*—people who are collaborating on your app or are part of your organization in various capacities. Each app collaborator is registered by an email address and has one of three possible roles:

- *Manager*—This role has complete control over an app, including managing all settings, adding collaborators, and configuring services like testing, distribution, and analytics.
- *Developer*—Developers can create builds against branches and run them, or run UI tests.
- *Viewer*—This role is for app users only—they can see and download builds. This is the role you need for your beta testers.

To create a collaborator, head to the Settings tab for your Android app inside App Center, click the Edit button in the Collaborators section (it looks like a pencil), and then add your collaborators' email addresses (figure 16.1). For beta test users, you'll set the role to be Viewer.

Once you assign a collaborator, they'll receive an email inviting them to collaborate on your app. They'll need to click the Accept Invitation link in the email, which will open a web page where they can accept the invitation and create an App Center account if they don't already have one (using a username and password, or by connecting via Facebook, Google, GitHub, or a Microsoft account).

Once they've accepted the invitation and created an account, there's one last thing they'll need to do—allow apps from unknown sources. Although Android has minimal security, later versions will by default block the installation of apps from outside of

Enter an email address and click Return to add a collaborator.

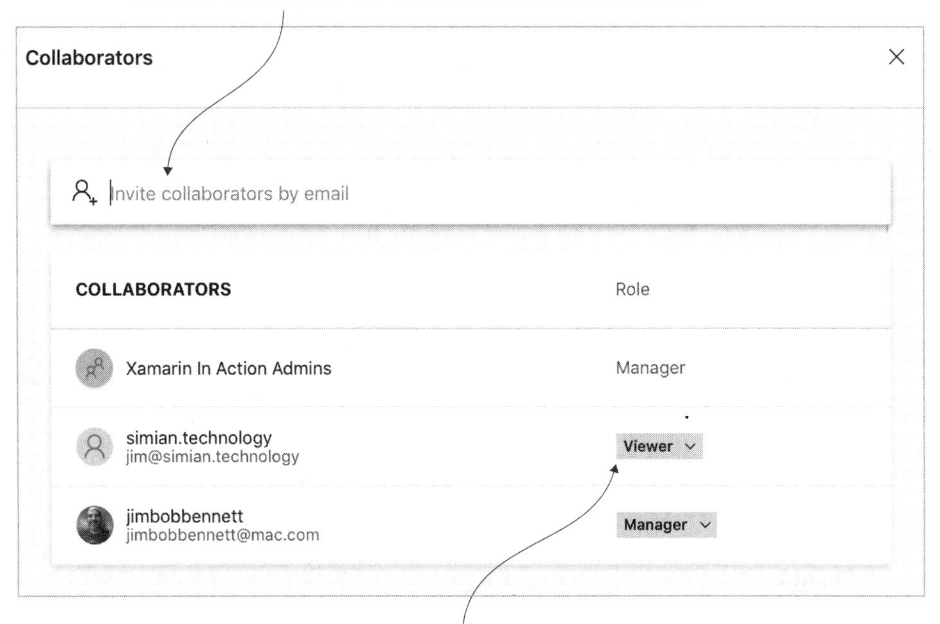

Use this dropdown to select the collaborator's role.

Figure 16.1 You add and configure app collaborators from the Settings tab.

the Google Play store. This block is easy to turn off from the Settings app—head to Personal > Security, and then under Device Administration turn on the Unknown Sources option (figure 16.2). Be aware that some device manufacturers like to tweak the Settings app, so this option may be in a different place in the settings.

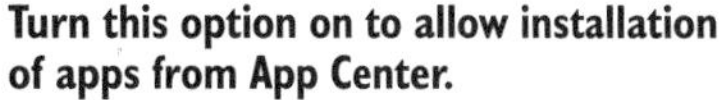

Figure 16.2 Allow apps to be installed from unknown sources.

Be warned, turning the Unknown Sources setting on allows apps to be installed from any unknown source—both your apps from App Center and more nefarious apps from other places. The user will still need to explicitly tap an Install button to install an app, but less technically savvy users may need a bit of security training before turning this option on.

CREATING DISTRIBUTION GROUPS

App Center allows you to group and manage collaborators by adding them to *distribution groups*, which are named groups of collaborators. These distribution groups allow you to distribute different builds to different people. For example, you could have a QA group that gets every build of your app for thorough testing and a Beta Testers group that only gets manually distributed builds at major milestones. Collaborators on your app can belong to multiple groups. When you create users, they are all by default added to a distribution group called Collaborators that's created for you when you first create your app.

You can manage these groups by selecting Distribute > Groups from your app in App Center. To add a new distribution group, click the New Group button at the top right, enter a group name, and enter the collaborators to add to the group, as shown in figure 16.3. You can start entering the names of users who are already set up for your app, and you'll see an autocomplete box with their details that you can select from. Or you can enter an email address to add new users, and they'll be invited to sign up with App Center and become a collaborator.

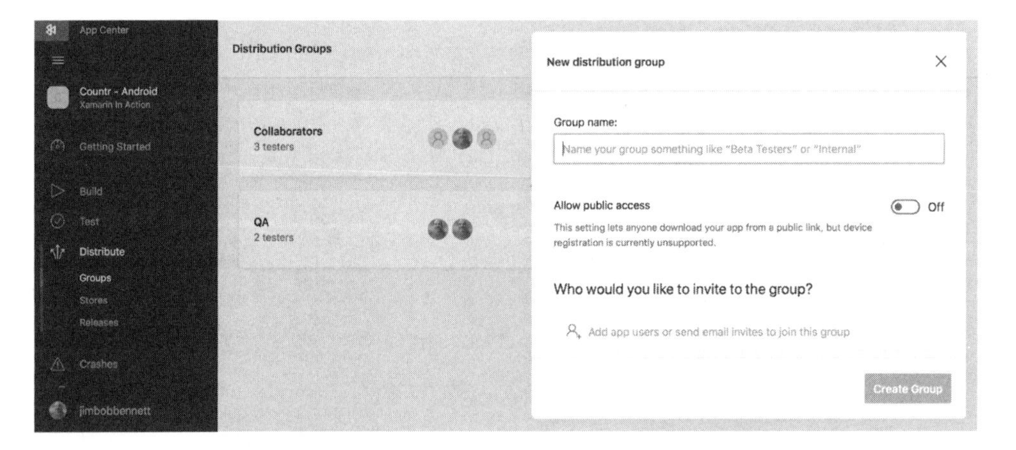

Figure 16.3 Add distribution groups to allow you to distribute different builds of your app to different users.

DISTRIBUTING BUILDS

Once you have your collaborators, you can distribute your app to them in one of two ways: automatic distribution on every build, or manual distribution.

Automatic distribution is the simplest way to provide updated builds. Every time your app is built (either manually or by pushing code to a branch set up to build on every push), your users get notified about it and can install or update your app. This is great for pushing bug fixes and new functionality to your test group. It also ensures that your app builds successfully inside App Center, including passing a launch test, before it's distributed.

To turn automatic distribution on, head to the Build tab for your Android app, select the master branch, click the spanner button to configure the branch, scroll to the bottom, and check the Distribute Builds option (figure 16.4). If you've set up multiple distribution groups, you'll be able to select one of those groups here, and the app will only be automatically distributed to the group you select. This defaults to the Collaborators group.

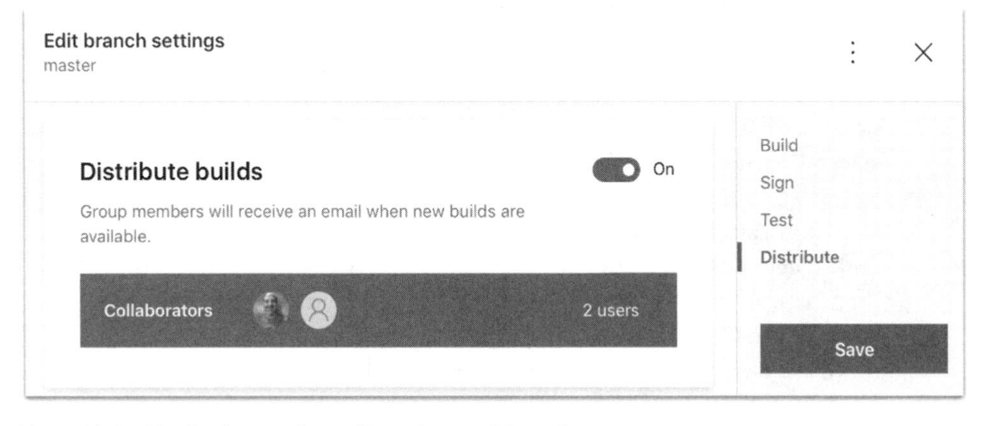

Figure 16.4 Distribution can be configured on each branch.

Once you click Done, your branch will be built and an email will be sent to all collaborators in the selected distribution groups, letting them know there's a new version of your app available. They'll need to open this email on their Android device and follow the link provided to install your app. This is shown in figure 16.5

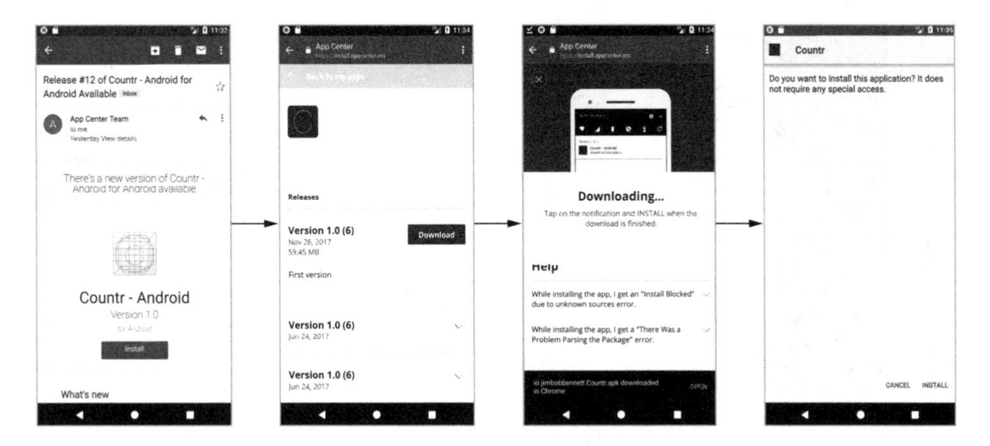

Figure 16.5 After each build, users will get an email with a link to download and install your app from App Center.

Once users receive the email, they can tap the Install button on the email which will take them to a web page inside App Center where they can download your app. This page shows some details about the version they're installing, such as the version number and release notes, and it has a Download button that downloads the APK to their device. Once it's downloaded, they'll be able to open the downloaded APK to install it.

To manually distribute an APK, you'll need to build it yourself and then upload it to App Center for distribution to your users. Although this is less convenient than the automatic distribution, it does give you more control over your releases. For example, if one user has a particular issue on their device, you could create a new distribution group just for that one user, create a possible fix or add more logging to your local source code, create a local build, and manually distribute it just to the affected user. If your code changes fix their issue, you can then push them to your source code repo and redistribute to everyone.

To manually deploy your app, create an archive signed with your app's keystore—we looked at the process for doing this back in chapter 13. Once you have your APK, select Distribute > Releases inside App Center and then click the Distribute New Release button at the top right. A panel will slide out (figure 16.6) with a number of steps you can follow to distribute your app. Start by clicking the Upload APK button and select your APK, or drag and drop your APK file over the button. Your APK will then be uploaded, which may take a while depending on the speed of your internet connection. Once your release is uploaded, click the Next button.

In the next panel, you can optionally add release notes describing your changes. In the third panel, you choose which distribution group to send the release to. Clicking Distribute in the final panel will distribute your release. All the users in your distribution group will receive an email with a link to download the new release, in the same way as with automatic releases.

Figure 16.6 To distribute your app manually, you start by uploading the APK.

MANAGING RELEASES

The Releases section of the Distribute tab also allows you to manage your releases. From here you can see all the releases of your app, with details against each including the APK size, version number, and which distribution group it went to (figure 16.7).

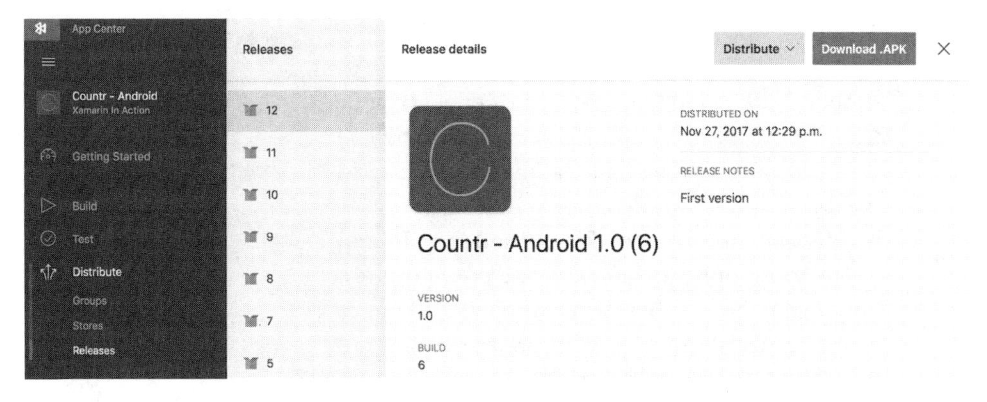

Figure 16.7 Manage releases from the Releases section of the Distribute tab.

You can also use this tab to download releases, which is useful if you deleted the email with the app link, if you want to install an older version for upgrade testing (to make sure you have no data loss when upgrading from an older version of your app to a newer one), if you want to install on a device that doesn't have email set up on it, or if you want to get someone outside of the release's distribution group to install that release. If you don't want anyone installing a particular release you can also delete it.

16.1.2 Auto updates

It's pretty good to notify users with an email and have them click a couple of links to download an update. But what would be much better is if your app were able to detect that an update was available and could allow users to update from inside the app. Happily for us, this is something that App Center supports, and it's really easy to implement.

To make auto updates work, enable this feature inside your app. Open the Countr solution and add the Microsoft.AppCenter.Distribute NuGet package to the Countr.Droid app. Then enable it by adding distribution to the call to AppCenter.Start in the splash screen. Open SplashScreen.cs and add the following code.

Listing 16.1 Adding App Center distribution to Countr.Droid

```
using Microsoft.AppCenter.Distribute;
...
protected override void OnCreate(Android.OS.Bundle bundle)
{
   base.OnCreate(bundle);
```

```
    AppCenter.Start("<your app secret>",
                    typeof(Analytics),
                    typeof(Crashes),
                    typeof(Distribute));
}
```

Adds distribution to the App Center startup

This tells App Center that as well as supporting analytics and crash reporting, you also want to support auto updates. As you'd expect, your users will need to install this version first before they can auto update—just adding this code to the latest builds won't auto update any earlier builds that don't have this turned on. In-app updates also only work for Release configuration builds, not Debug builds. Commit the changes enabling distribution to your source code control so that your app builds, and install this version on your device using App Center.

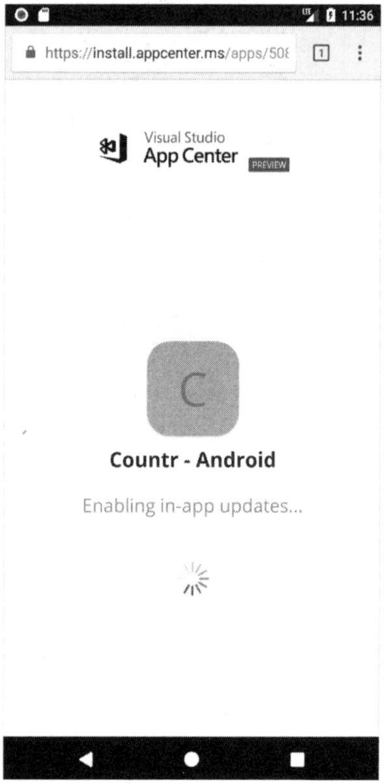

Once your app starts up for the first time after enabling in-app updates, it will need to quickly connect to App Center to register the installation (figure 16.8). Your app will launch, then switch to a web browser, then back to your app.

Figure 16.8 When you launch your app for the first time, it will connect to App Center to enable in-app updates.

Once distribution has been enabled, the app will check on every startup to see if an update is available, and if there is one, it will tell the user and prompt them to install the update. What defines whether an update is available? Just running another build with the same or updated source code isn't enough; instead you need to increment the version number. Back in chapter 6 you saw that Android defines two versions: a version number (or code) and a version name. The version name is your internal way of representing the version as a string; here the version number is what we're interested in. This is a numerical value that's used to tell Android, App Center, and (as you'll see later) the Play store that there's an update to the app.

Every time you want an update to be made available to users, you need to increment this version number. For now you can manually increment it inside the application manifest. App Center does offer a way to auto increment this as part of your builds, but that's outside the scope of this book.

To see this in action, you'll need to update the version number. You can do this in Visual Studio for Mac by double-clicking the AndroidManifest.xml file in the Properties folder and incrementing the Version Number field in the manifest editor (figure 16.9). In Visual Studio on Windows, right-click on the Countr.Droid project file, select Properties, select the Android Manifest tab, and increment the Version Number. If you prefer editing XML files manually, it's the `android:versionCode` attribute on the `manifest` node that you need to increment. It doesn't matter how much you increment this value—all that matters is that the new value is higher. Once you've updated the version, commit the change and push it to your source code repository. App Center will then build your changes and make the update available.

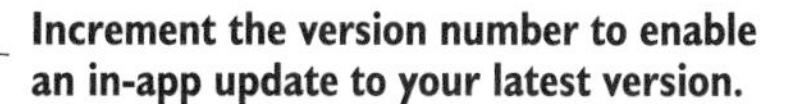

Figure 16.9 To indicate that a new version of your Android app is available, increment the version number in the manifest.

Once the code has been built, restart your app on your Android device. Update checks are only run when your app starts up from being terminated, not when it is restored to the foreground, so you may need to explicitly kill your app before relaunching it. This check will connect to App Center and check for an updated version, and when it finds one a dialog will be shown asking if you want to download the update now or delay for a day (figure 16.10). Tap Download and the app update will download in the background. Once the app has downloaded, a dialog will pop up to install it, so tap Install and your app will be updated.

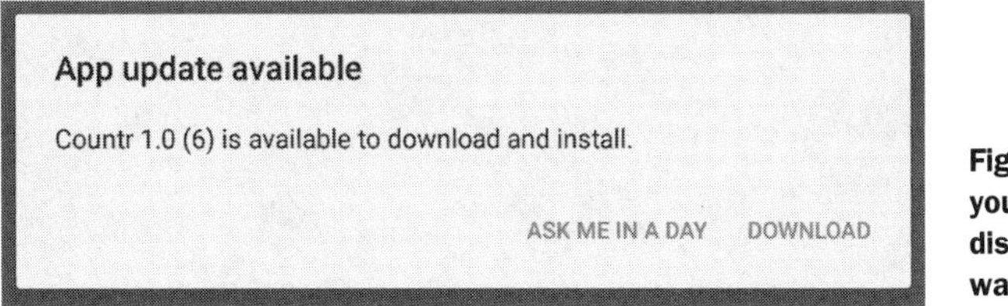

Figure 16.10 Upon launching your app after an update has been distributed, you'll be asked if you want to update.

16.2 Publishing Android apps on the Google Play store

Once you've sent your app to your beta testers, they've given feedback, and you've used this feedback to make your app ready for release, the next step is to publish your app to a store so users can download and install it. Google has an app store that's baked into Android, called the Google Play store. You can publish your apps to this store, and any Android user will be able to open the store app on their device and discover and download your app. This store also manages updates, so if you release an updated version to the store, users will be able to easily install the update. Depending on their settings, your app may even be updated automatically with no user intervention required.

16.2.1 Setting up your account

Before you can publish to the Google Play store, you need to set up an account and pay a registration fee. Start by heading to http://play.google.com/apps/publish/ and then sign in with a valid Google account. You'll then be presented with a few steps to work through to sign up for a developer account. These steps should be self explanatory, and I won't go into details here as they do change on a regular basis and vary from country to country, and depending on whether you want to charge for your app. The main thing to be aware of is the fee—you'll need to pay a U.S. $25 registration fee to create an account. The good news is that unlike Apple, this is a one-time charge, not a yearly fee. Once you've signed up, you'll be logged into the Google Play console.

16.2.2 Creating your app

Once you have your account set up, the next step is to create your app. From the Google Play console, click the Publish an Android App on Google Play button (figure 16.11).

The first step in publishing an app is giving it a name. Your name can be up to 50 characters in length and doesn't have to be unique, although if you use the name of another app, you may run into problems. If you try to call your app Facebook, for example, you'll probably be kicked off the store. Google also requires all names to be

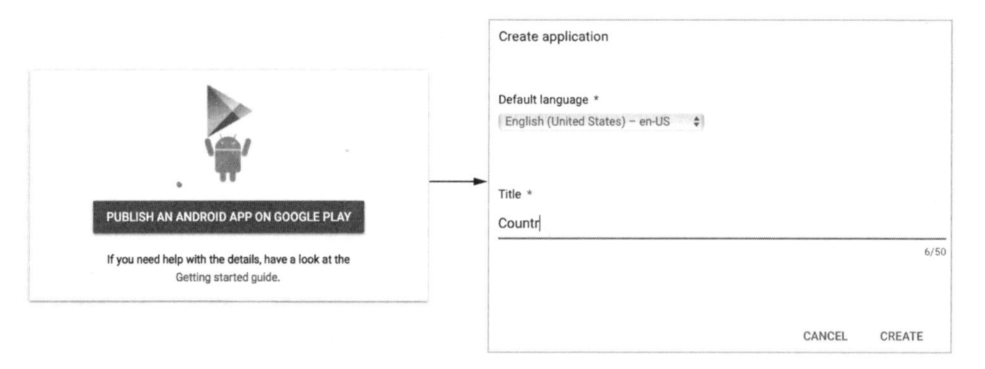

Figure 16.11 Click the Publish an Android App button to create a new app on the Play Store and then enter the app's name.

suitable for all store users of all ages, so if you use profanity or a title that's not appropriate for all ages, your app will not make it to the store. Enter the app name you want to use into the Create Application dialog box and click Create.

UPLOADING YOUR APK

Once you've created your app, upload your APK to the Play store. You can't set your app's content rating (the appropriate-age rating for your app) until you've uploaded an APK.

The first step is to download the APK from App Center. You can download the APK you want to publish by selecting the Build tab, clicking the master branch, selecting the most recent build, and clicking Download > Download Build.

> **YOUR APP WILL SHARE ITS ANALYTICS ACROSS DEVELOPMENT, BETA TESTING, AND THE STORE** You'll notice we're using the same App Center app for development, beta testers, and the store. This means that crashes and app analytics that come from debugging the app will be mixed in with those from the beta testers and the final users who get the app from the store. This isn't ideal. In a production app you'd set up multiple apps with different app secrets for development, beta testing, and production, and set these using compiler flags with multiple build configurations. That's outside the scope of this book, but you can read more about build configurations in Jon Goldberger's "Demystifying Build Configurations" article on Xamarin's blog at http://mng.bz/40uO.

The second step is to upload the APK that was built by App Center to the Play store. From the Google Play console, select App Releases from the menu on the left. From the app releases page, you can manage alpha, beta, and production releases. We're only going to create a production release, as we've used App Center to manage our beta already, so click the Manage Production button and then Create Release on the next page.

> **GOOGLE PLAY APP SIGNING** Google recently added the ability to store and manage your keystores inside their developer console. By using this, you can upload your keystore to Google and have them manage your app signing for you. You download a new keystore that Google creates and use this to sign your apps for publishing to Google; then Google re-signs them with their stored keys. This topic is outside the scope of this book, but you can read more about it in Google's documentation at http://mng.bz/RWTt.

You should now see a screen allowing you to configure a new production release. If you see an option to sign up for Google Play App Signing, click Not Now to continue. Click the Upload APK button and select the APK you downloaded from App Center. After the APK has been uploaded, click the Save Draft button.

Once your APK has been uploaded, you'll see it appear in the APKs to Add section, showing the version code from the application manifest. You can also add a release name here—this is an internal name you can use to identify releases, and it defaults to the version name of your app. You can change this name to help track your releases, such as setting it to an internal code name for a particular release based on the features of that release, or to anything that makes sense to you. This name only appears in the Play console, not on the store. You can also add release notes detailing what's new in this version—that's not much use for the first version of your app, but as you add updates you can detail them here. Once you've filled this all in, click the Save button.

SETTING THE CONTENT RATING

Every app published on the store needs to have a content rating. This defines the age your app is suitable for and it covers the content of your app, so consumers can decide if it's appropriate for them. This content rating can also limit in which countries your app can be published—some local laws prohibit certain content.

To set your content rating, head to the Content Rating tab, and from here you can fill out a questionnaire that'll be used to automatically set your content rating. Start by clicking the Continue button.

On the first page of the questionnaire, enter your email address and select the type of app you're publishing. For Countr this is "Utilities, productivity, communication or other". Work through the questions—the answers should all be No—and then click Save. Once it's saved you can click Calculate Rating to calculate the rating for your app—this should be suitable for everyone. Once it's calculated, click Apply Rating to set this rating for your app. When you finally publish your app, you'll be emailed a content-rating certificate as part of Google's app review process.

ADDING PRODUCT DETAILS

Once you've uploaded your APK, add a range of details about your app that will appear on the store listing. These include text descriptions of your app, screenshots, and information about what type of app you've submitted. Just like with the app's name, this content will be available to everyone, so it needs to be suitable for all ages regardless of the app type. If you include a screenshot containing nudity, your app won't be published (even if you're publishing an adult content app or a medical/ educational app). You can read Google's policy on this content in the Google Play Developer Policy Center, at http://mng.bz/6Kn2.

Head to the Store Listing tab to enter this information. These fields are required:

- *Title*—This is the app name you entered when creating your app—you can change it from here if you need to.
- *Short description*—This is a single-line description of your app that's used on the store as a tagline. This should be a short, snappy sentence to entice users into reading more about your app or installing it. It can be up to 80 characters.
- *Full description*—This is where you can enter a more detailed description about your app, covering its features, how it can help users achieve their goals or solve their problems, or anything else that explains your app to your target audience. You can enter up to 4000 characters here.
- *Screenshots*—You can attach screenshots to your store listing, either as JPEGs or PNGs. The minimum length of any side is 340 px, and the maximum is 3840 px.

You have to attach at least two, and you can add phone screenshots or tablet screenshots. Although these images are called "screenshots," you aren't limited to screenshots. Some developers like to attach images containing screenshots with annotations around them, highlighting the features of their app. If you want to capture a screenshot from your device, you'll need to determine the combination of keys that captures one—usually it's pressing the volume-down button and the power button at the same time, but it varies from device to device.

It can be a pain regenerating simple screenshots from your app for phones and tablets every time you prepare a release, so what some developers do is create UI tests that put the app in a state that looks good and then capture a screenshot. They can then run these tests in Test Cloud against a phone and a tablet and download the resulting images.

- *High res icon*—This is a version of your app icon that's shown on the store listing, so it needs to be larger than the icons that go with your app. It has a required size of 512 × 512 pixels. It also needs to be a PNG file. If you used MakeAppIcon back in chapter 10, you would have received a high res icon as part of the zip file you downloaded. If not, there's one you can use in the source code that accompanies this book, called playstore-icon.png, in the Images\Countr\AppIcons\Android folder.
- *Feature graphic*—The feature graphic is a banner image that's displayed across the top of the Play store listing. This needs to be 1024 × 500 pixels in size and should be something that highlights your app, such as cover art, an app and company logo, or a useful part of a screenshot.
- *Application type and category*—Tell the Play store what type of app you're submitting (an application or a game) and what category to put it under. This way your app will appear in the correct store listing. For Countr, the type would be Applications and the category would be Tools.
- *Contact details*—Provide an email address that your users can use to contact you. This is publicly displayed, so be warned—you may get some spam! You can also provide your website and phone number if you need to provide support to your customers.
- *Privacy policy*—Provide a privacy policy if you're handling any user data, or you need to tick the box to say that you aren't providing a privacy policy at this time. If your app does anything with users' personal data, you have to provide a privacy policy—personal data includes anything that would allow the user to be identified, any financial information, health information, or contact details such as a phonebook.

This is your one chance to hook a user who has discovered your app on the store, so it's worth putting a lot of effort into making this content very high quality, with well-chosen screenshots and well-written text. You can also provide translations of your content into different languages. You can manage translations from the Manage

Translations drop-down, choosing to either manually upload translations or pay someone to do it for you.

Once you've added all the required information, click the Save button.

PRICING AND DISTRIBUTION

The last step before you can publish your app is to set the price for your app and where and how it should be distributed. To do this, head to the Pricing & Distribution tab. We'll be distributing a free app here, but if you want to charge for your app, you need to set up a merchant account first—contact your bank if you want to do this. By default your app will be set to free, so leave it like this for now.

There are a number of options you can set here, including various Google programs for families, education, Android TV, or Android Car, but those are outside the scope of our app. These are the fields you should set:

- *Countries*—From here you can set the countries your app is available in. Which countries you choose is up to you—the more you choose, the more customers you can get, but this could lead to higher support requirements. Also, be aware that the local laws of each country are different, so you'll need to ensure that your app is compliant with the law in all countries. Also, watch out for blocked services, such as Facebook being blocked in China—if your app needs Facebook, you should uncheck China in the Countries list. Countr should be fine everywhere in the world, so you can just select the Available radio button at the top of the country list to select everything.
- *Contains ads*—Declare if your app has any ads in it. This information is shown on the Play store listing so users can decide before they download your app if they want to put up with ads or not. If your app has ads and you don't declare it, you risk being kicked off the store.
- *Content guidelines*—You must tick this box to declare that your app meets Google's content guidelines, which are available at http://mng.bz/Var3. If you don't follow these guidelines, your app will be kicked off the store.
- *U.S. export laws*—Google hosts apps on servers in the United States, so when a user outside the United States downloads your app, it's classed as exporting the software. This means you have to follow the U.S. export laws, especially in regard to encryption (including making web calls over HTTPS). You need to tick this box to say your app complies with all these laws. Google has more information about this at http://mng.bz/yDT3.

PUBLISHING

Once you've provided all the required information, you'll be able to publish your app to the store.

You should see Ready to Publish in the top banner on each page (figure 16.12). If you see a Why Can't I Publish? button at the top right of the page, something hasn't

Figure 16.12 Once your app is ready to publish, the top banner will update to show this.

been set properly. You can click this button to see what to do to finalize your app for publication.

To publish your app, head to the App Releases tab and click the Edit Release button in the Production section. Click the Review button, verify the details, and then click the Start Rollout to Production button (figure 16.13) and confirm the dialog that's displayed. Your app won't be published immediately; instead it will be reviewed and analyzed by Google to ensure that everything is working and that you're not doing anything dodgy inside your app. Most of the time this is automated, but Google may manually verify your app if it's deemed necessary. With an app like Countr, it should pass review pretty swiftly, but if Google finds any problems, you'll be contacted to help resolve them.

Manage your app's APKs, review release history, and rollout your app to production, alpha, or beta. Learn more

Confirm rollout to production: 1.0

Prepare release
Review and rollout

Review summary

This release is ready to be rolled out.

APKs in this release

	Version code	Uploaded	Installs on active devices
1 APK added			
	1	Today, 12:27 PM	No data

What's new in this release?

You should provide release notes for every new release. This helps your users understand the benefits of upgrading to the latest version of your app.
Go back to add release notes

PREVIOUS DISCARD START ROLLOUT TO PRODUCTION

Figure 16.13 After reviewing your release, you can roll it out to the store.

It usually takes anything up to a few hours for the first release of an app to be approved (though it can be much less—I published Countr in about 30 minutes), with updates being approved more quickly. You won't be notified when it's published—only if there are problems—so keep checking back to see if it's been successful. Once it has been published, you should be able to open the Google Play store app on any Android device and install the app (figure 16.14). Be warned, though, there are millions of apps on the store, so it may not be easy to find!

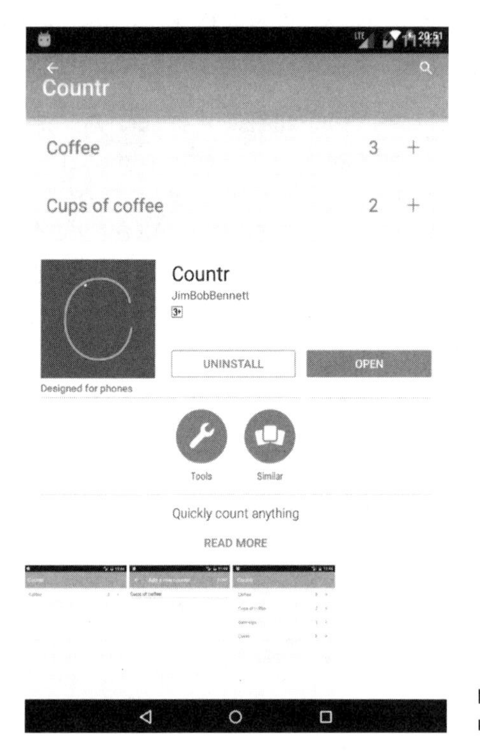

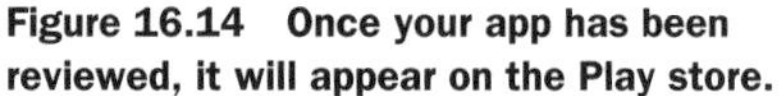
Figure 16.14 Once your app has been reviewed, it will appear on the Play store.

Congratulations! You've published your first Xamarin Android app to the Google Play store. Now is definitely the time to pat yourself on the back and celebrate a job well done. But for an app to be successful, there's still more work to do. You need to monitor the analytics in App Center to see how and where your app is being used, and keep an eye out for crashes or bugs. If a bug is found, you'll have to fix it and get an update out as soon as possible.

> **GOOGLE HAS TOOLS FOR MANAGING APP ROLLOUTS** Google has a huge range of tools and capabilities to help you manage your app, including staged rollouts by country or random percentage of users, A/B testing to evaluate how well features are received, and management for paid apps, in-app purchases, or app subscriptions. You can read more on using the Google Play console to manage and publish your apps in Google's Play Console Help, at http://mng.bz/w99p.

REVIEWS AND RATINGS

Once your app has been released, users can download it, enjoy the fruits of your labor, and give you feedback via the Play store in the form of star ratings and reviews (figure 16.15). The higher the star rating, the more likely people are to download your app and the higher up the search results it will end up. Conversely, if your app has a low rating, people will avoid it. Reviews are also a great way to get detailed feedback—for example, if you get a 1-star rating with a comment about a bug, you can fix it and publish an update.

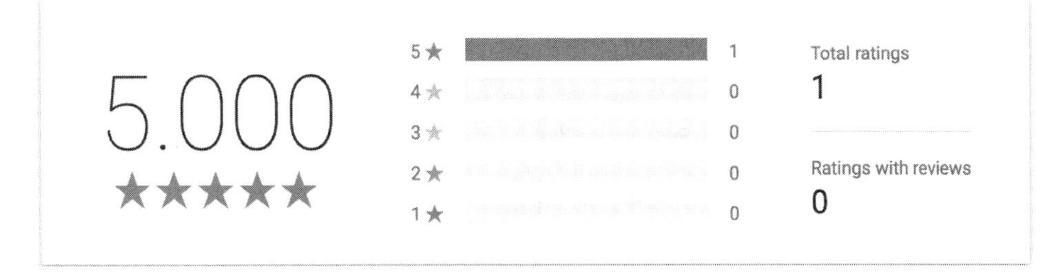

Figure 16.15 Ideally you want to aim for a 5-star rating to get more downloads.

You can monitor reviews from the User Feedback tab in the Play store console. From there you can see ratings broken down by time, app version, country, or other user details. You can also see reviews from users and reply to these, maybe providing support to a user who is having issues with your app, or notifying a user of a bug fix that has been published.

It might be tempting to try to get your rating up by getting people to give you fake ratings (or buying them—there are "click farms" where you can hire people to install and rate your app by the thousand), but if you get caught doing that your app might be kicked off the store, or worse, your developer account might be terminated. This could be a huge problem for an enterprise. If you can't publish mobile apps, it could be the end of your business.

PUBLISHING UPDATES

At some point after your first release, you'll probably want to update your app—to fix bugs or add new features. Once your app has been released to the store, all updates are managed by the store. App Center only provides automatic updates to builds that are distributed via App Center, so anyone who installs your app from the store won't receive any updates unless you push them to the store.

Updates are pushed to the store by creating a new production release in the same way you created the initial release for your app. Once your app is published the Play store, the developer console changes, giving more options to manage your release. To upload a new APK, head to the Release Management section on the left side and select the App Releases tab as you did when uploading the APK the first time around. Work through the same steps as before, clicking Manage Production then Create

Release, and uploading a new APK downloaded from App Center. It's also worth updating the release notes to reflect what has changed. Personally, I feel it's worth providing entertaining and detailed release notes—not the boring "Bug fixes and other improvements" that is usual for apps like Facebook. Once you upload a new APK, you can see which version will be superseded by the new version, and you can enter a new release name to track this new version.

You can only upload APKs that are for apps with the same package name and signed with the same keystore and a higher version code. If the package name of the new APK doesn't match, or the version code is the same or lower, it will be rejected. The same is true if the keystore is different (which is why it's vital to keep the keystore safe).

Once you've uploaded a new APK with an incremented version code, click Save and then Review. Review the release to make sure everything is in order and then click Start Rollout to Production. Once again, Google will analyze your app for compliance, and if everything is successful, the updated APK will be available on the store. Existing users will then be able to download and install your update.

16.2.3 Alternative stores

Although Google Play is the major app store for Android users, it's not the only one—Android is an open OS, which means other stores can be set up to distribute apps. This is important for app developers, as it may make sense to publish your app to multiple stores, especially if you want to target the Chinese market.

At the time of writing, Google Play is not available in China, so if you want to make your app available to a Chinese audience, you'll also need to publish it on at least one of a number of Chinese Android stores. These include Baidu App store (http://shouji.baidu.com/), Tencent App Gem (http://android.app.qq.com/), and Xiaomi App Store (http://app.xiaomi.com/). These stores are all in Chinese, so you'll need access to Chinese translations of both your app and your product details to be successful. If your app accesses a backend, you'll also need to verify that it's available in China—some cloud services are blocked by the "Great Firewall," including some of the big names such as Facebook and Google (but not Microsoft's Azure). If your app relies on a Facebook login, you'll either need to avoid rolling out to China or add a different login method.

Outside of China, the other big app store to be aware of is Amazon's Appstore for Android—found by going to your local Amazon site and looking for "Appstore for Android" under the Departments menu, and this is available worldwide. If you want to publish your apps on this store, you can do so at https://developer.amazon.com.

Publishing to the Chinese and Amazon stores is outside the scope of this book.

16.3 Distributing iOS apps to beta testers

We've looked at Android, and now it's time to look at iOS. Although the principles are the same as for Android, there is, as always, the fly in the ointment that is provisioning profiles.

16.3.1 Enabling app distribution

In the last chapter you set up a Debug build for your iOS app in App Center so that you could run the on-device launch tests, as well as run UI tests in Test Cloud. You also signed it with your development provisioning profile. This served your purposes then, but going forward you'll need different build setups. You need to sign your app with different iOS provisioning profiles depending on where you want to distribute to, and create release builds so that you can enable auto updates.

You can set up distribution groups for your iOS app the same way as previously described for Android. The process for setting up distribution groups in App Center is identical. The only difference is that you need to get a bit more information from your iOS beta test users so that you can create provisioning profiles that include their devices.

Provisioning iOS users

Back in chapter 13 you created a development provisioning profile for your device. This profile was linked to the device UDID (the unique identifier for your device that's set by iOS) and it allowed you to run your app through a debugger on the device. To distribute your app, we need one of two other types of provisioning profile:

- *Ad hoc*—Ad hoc provisioning profiles are used for distributing to beta testers. Just like with development profiles, these are tied to a specific set of device UDIDs and have the same rules about the number of registered devices—a limit of 100 of each type per membership year. When your app is signed with an ad hoc profile, you can install it on any of the registered devices using distribution tools like App Center, Apple's TestFlight, or iTunes. Unlike with Android, there's no need to turn on any permissions to allow users to run your apps. Instead, permissions are enabled via the ad hoc provisioning profile.
- *App Store*—App Store provisioning profiles are used to sign your app for distribution via the store. Apps signed with this profile can run on any compatible device with no limitations, except that you can only distribute these apps via the App Store.

APPLE ALSO HAS ENTERPRISE PROVISIONING PROFILES Apple has an enterprise developer program for large organizations, where you can build apps and provision them for distribution just to a limited number of in-house users, not to the store. This allows you to build internal apps that only work for your users and don't require the full Apple release process or public store distribution. You can read more about this in Apple's Developer library at https://developer.apple.com/programs/enterprise/.

Before you can create these provisioning profiles, you need to create a new certificate—in chapter 13 you created a developer certificate, but for ad hoc and store profiles you require a *distribution certificate*. You can create one in the same way as the developer certificate, using the Apple Developer portal or Fastlane from inside Visual Studio for Mac, but instead of selecting iOS App Development for the certificate type, select App Store and Ad Hoc from the Apple Developer portal, or iOS Distribution from Visual Studio for Mac. Once you have the certificate in your keychain, export it as a .p12 file because you'll need to upload this to App Center later on.

To distribute your app to beta test users, you'll need an ad hoc provisioning profile set up using the UDIDs of all your beta test users' devices. This is where iOS becomes a pain—every time you sign up a new beta test user, you need to get the UDID of their device. You can find it in a number of different ways:

- *From Xcode*—If the device owner has Xcode installed, they can launch it with the device connected, select Window > Devices, and select their device in the left pane. The device UDID will be shown as the identifier on the right, as shown in figure 16.16.

Figure 16.16 You can get device UDIDs from the Devices window in Xcode.

- *From iTunes*—This is the only way to get the UDID on Windows, and it also works on macOS. Plug the device in, select the device in iTunes, and select the Summary tab. You'll see a serial number on the right, and if you click the serial number it will change to show the UDID (figure 16.17).

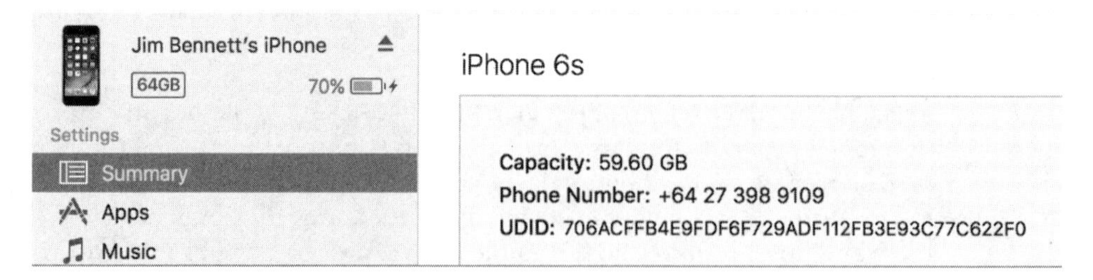

Figure 16.17 You can get device UDIDs from the Device window in iTunes.

- *From the macOS terminal*—If your device is plugged in to your Mac, you can get its details using the Instruments app from the terminal. Launch the terminal and run `instruments -s devices`. This will show a list of all connected devices, both physical and simulators, with their UDIDs (figure 16.18).

```
AT-AT:~ JimBennett$ instruments -s devices
Known Devices:
Jim Bennett's iPhone (10.3.2) [706acffb4e9fdf6f729adf112fb3e93c77c622f0]
```

Figure 16.18 You can get device UDIDs from the macOS terminal using Instruments.

Once you have the UDIDs of your beta testers, enter them into the Devices section of the Apple Developer site, as you did in chapter 13.

Now that you have a certificate and the beta test devices registered, you can create the profiles. Create a new profile as before, but instead of selecting iOS App Development, select Ad Hoc, select your app ID, select the new distribution certificate, check all the devices you want your profile to support, and name it something like *Beta test*. Once it's created, download a copy of it so you can upload it to App Center later.

SETTING UP THE AD HOC BUILD

The next thing to do is to set up an ad hoc build to distribute to beta testers. From your iOS app in App Center, select the Build tab, select the master branch, and open the Configure Build panel by clicking the spanner button at the top right.

> **WE'LL BE REUSING THE SAME BRANCH FOR ALL BUILDS** As discussed earlier for Android, we're going to use the same branch for development, beta test, and store builds. In a production app, you'd ideally set up multiple apps, each with a different provisioning profile, and set the app secrets in different builds using compiler flags.

Configure this branch to build the Countr.sln solution using a release configuration, select Device Build and Build This Branch on Every Push, and then upload the provisioning profile you created for ad hoc distribution and the distribution certificate .p12 file you exported. Make sure the Test on a Real Device setting is unchecked (you can't test release builds on real devices), and check the Distribute Builds option, selecting the distribution group you want your app to be distributed to. Click Save, and this will save the configuration and start a build.

Once the build completes, an email will be sent out to all collaborators in the selected distribution group with a link to install the app, just as for your Android builds.

The steps for installing the app are a bit different than Android. Before you install the app for the first time, install an App Center provisioning profile to allow installs of apps from App Center—this is part of Apple's strict security (figure 16.19). Once you click the See Details button in the email, you'll be guided through the steps. The first page tells you that you need to install the profile and gives instructions about what to do. Tap Install, and you'll be redirected to the Settings app on the device, where you can install the profile (you'll need to enter your passcode to approve the install). You only need to do this the first time you install any app from App Center on a device.

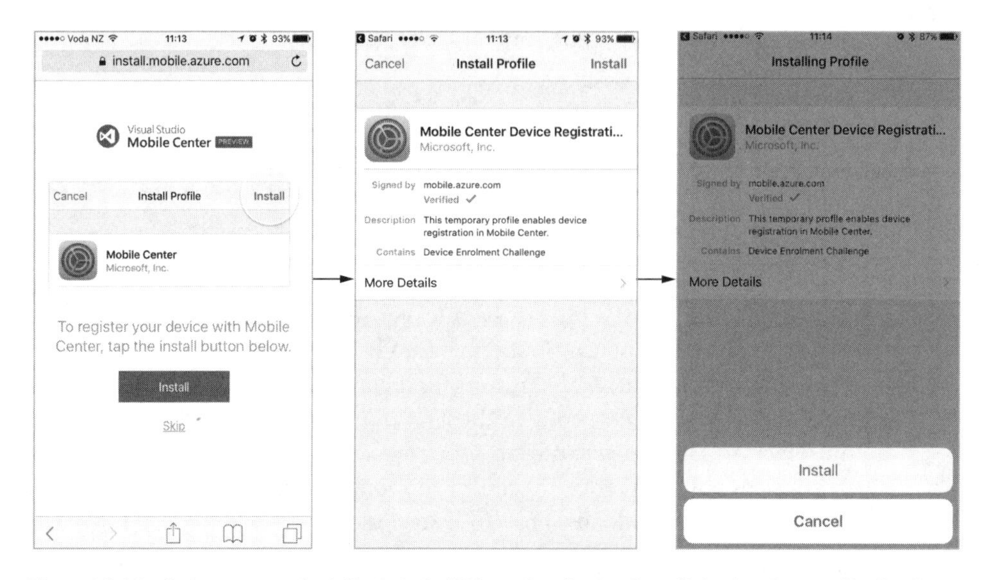

Figure 16.19 Before you can install a beta build from App Center, install the App Center distribution profile.

Once this profile is installed, you'll see the same install page as you did for Android. Tap the Install button, tap Install in the dialog that pops up, and the app will be installed. You'll see it appear on the iOS home screen. This is shown in figure 16.20.

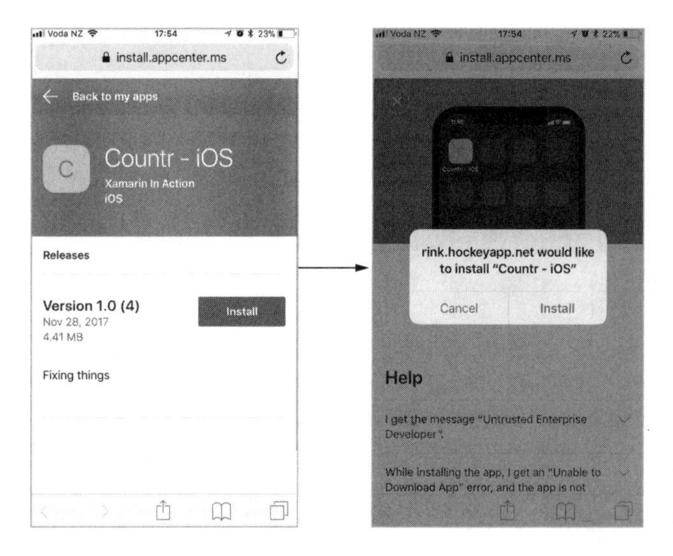

Figure 16.20 Once the App Center profile is installed, you can install the app on your device.

16.3.2 Auto updates

iOS apps support automatic updates in the same way as Android apps, although the setup is a bit more complicated. Start by adding the Microsoft.AppCenter.Distribute NuGet package to the Countr.iOS app. Then enable distribution inside AppDelegate .cs by making the changes shown in the following listing.

Listing 16.2 Adding App Center distribution to Countr.iOS

```
using Microsoft.AppCenter.Distribute;
...
public override bool FinishedLaunching(UIApplication app,
                                       NSDictionary options)
{
    AppCenter.Start("<your app secret>",
                    typeof(Analytics),
                    typeof(Crashes),
                    typeof(Distribute));     // Adds distribution to the App Center startup
   ...
}
```

Once that's done, make a change to the info.plist file to tell your app how to open the App Center updater. Open info.plist and switch to the Advanced tab. Click Add URL Type under the URL Types section, and enter `appcenter-<your app secret>` into the URL Schemes field, where `<your app secret>` is your app secret from App Center (figure 16.21).

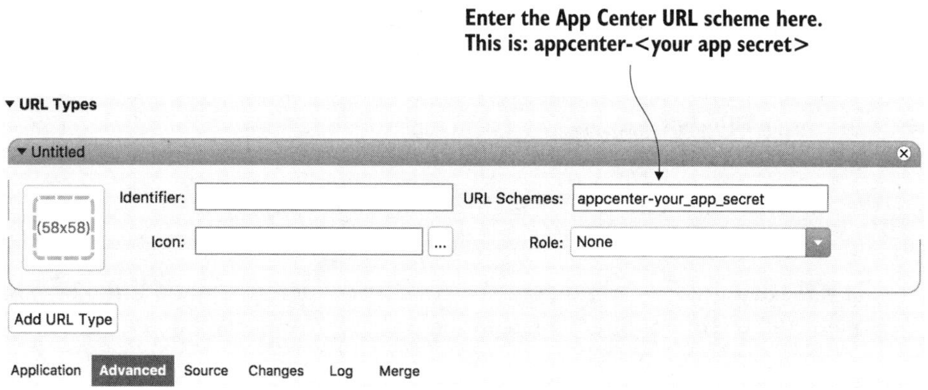

Enter the App Center URL scheme here. This is: appcenter-<your app secret>

Figure 16.21 Adding the App Center URL schema to the info.plist

Once you've made this change, check your code in and push it to your repository to trigger a build. Install this build on your device, and launch it. The first time your app starts, it will open a web page to enable in-app updates, just like the Android version, and then return to your app (figure 16.22).

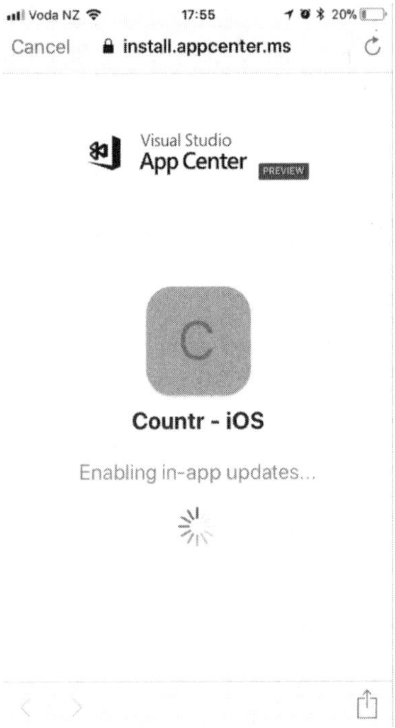

Figure 16.22 The first time your app starts, it will enable in-app updates.

Just like with Android, iOS apps need to have their version numbers incremented so that App Center can detect an update. The version number is defined in the info.plist file and is made up of multiple parts—a version and a build (figure 16.23). The version is a three-part code in the format of *major.minor.revision*, and the build is a single-integer build number for a particular version. An update is defined as one of the following:

- The same version but a higher build number
- A higher version with any build number (higher or lower)

If you keep the version number the same, increment the build number; if you increment the version number, you can increment or reset the build number if you want. This means if you're updating version 1.0 build 1, you can either use 1.1 build 1 or 1.0 build 2.

To test auto updates, increment one of these fields and push your changes to your source code provider. Once the app is built, restart the app on your device and you'll be prompted to install the update (figure 16.24). Tap Update Now and your app will be terminated, the new version downloaded and installed.

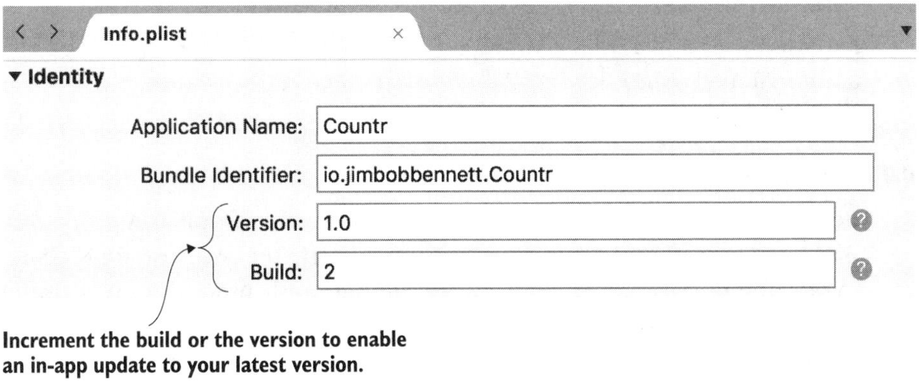

Info.plist

▼ Identity

Application Name: Countr

Bundle Identifier: io.jimbobbennett.Countr

Version: 1.0

Build: 2

Increment the build or the version to enable an in-app update to your latest version.

Figure 16.23 For your app to detect an update, either the build or version needs to be incremented.

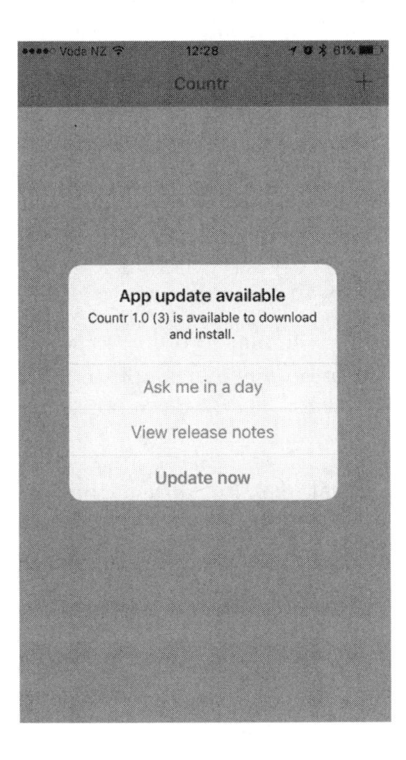

Figure 16.24 When you launch your app after an update is available, you'll be prompted to install the update.

16.4 Publishing iOS apps on the Apple App store

Now that you've beta tested your app, it's time to upload it to the store. All iOS apps are distributed using the iOS App Store. Unlike Android there are no other stores available.

16.4.1 Provisioning your app for publishing

Before you can publish to the App Store, you need an explicit App ID for your app. Back in chapter 13 you created a wildcard App ID that you could use from any app, but for the store you need an explicit one that's only used by a single app. From the Apple Developer site, select the App Ids tab, click the plus button, and create a new explicit app ID using the same prefix that you used for your wildcard ID, but ending in *Countr* instead of *. For example, I would use `io.jimbobbennett.Countr`.

To publish your app to the store, you need an App Store provisioning profile. Create and download one in the Apple Developer site, signed using the distribution certificate you created for an ad hoc profile and using the new explicit App ID. You won't need to specify any device UDIDs for this profile—it will allow any device to run your app, providing it's distributed using the App Store.

The next step is to set up the build in App Center using your App Store provisioning profile and distribution certificate. Ensure the Test on a Real Device and Distribute Builds settings are both turned off. Save this and wait for the build to finish. Once it's finished, click the Download button and select Download Build to download the app's IPA.

16.4.2 Setting up your app

Setting up apps for release to the iOS App Store is similar to doing so for the Google Play store—you need to create an app, set up some metadata, upload a binary, and await approval.

ITUNES CONNECT

iOS apps aren't configured using the Apple Developer site. Instead they're set up in iTunes Connect. This is the Apple portal for configuring apps available on Apple's stores—covering iOS, tvOS, and macOS. You can access it at https://itunesconnect.apple.com, logging in with your Apple ID (figure 16.25).

Click the My Apps button, click the plus button, and select New App to add a new iOS app.

In the dialog that pops up (shown in figure 16.26), select the iOS platform and enter the app name that you want to appear on the App Store (this is limited to 50 characters). This app name has to be unique across all the millions of apps on the store, so you'll need to be creative with the name. For example, *Countr* is already taken, and there are a number of apps with names starting with *Countr*, so I've used the name *Countr - Count anything*.

After entering the name, select the primary language of your app. Then select the bundle ID for your app, using the explicit App ID you set up in the Apple Developer

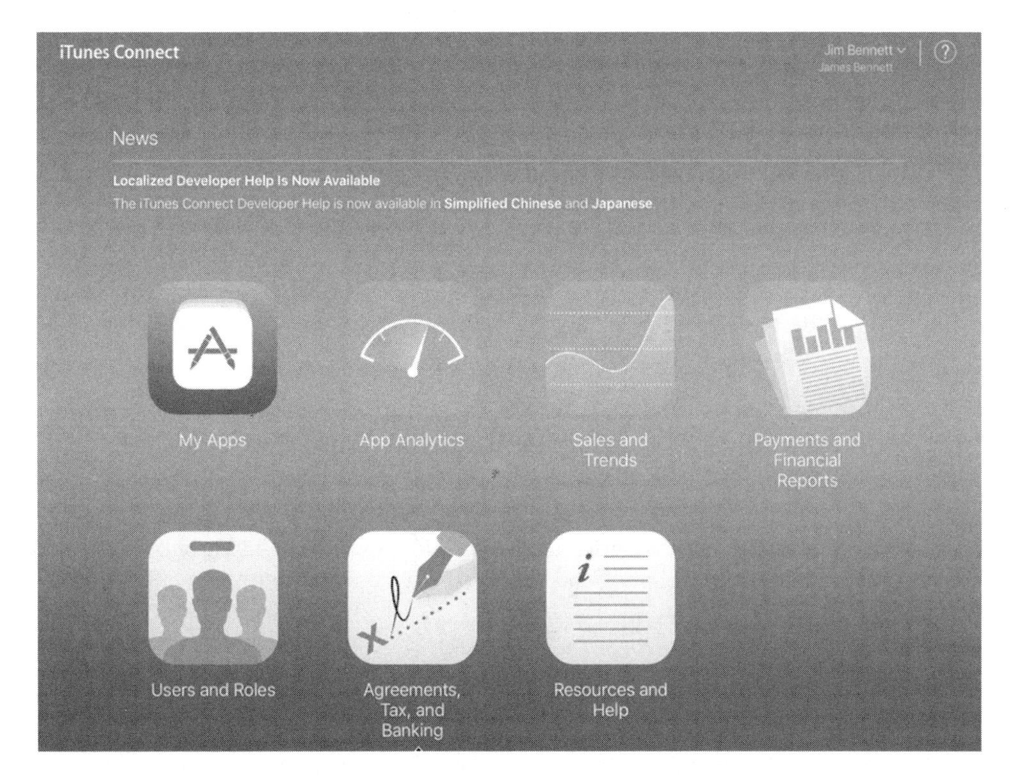

Figure 16.25 iTunes Connect is used to manage all apps released to the Apple App Stores.

New App

Platforms ?
☑ iOS ☐ tvOS

Name ?
Countr - Count anything

Primary Language ?
English (U.S.)

Bundle ID ?
io-jbb-Countr - io.jbb.Countr

SKU ?
Countr 1

Cancel Create

The platform for your app

The name for your app: this has to be unique across the app store.

The primary language for your app: the app information will default to be in this language.

The explicit App ID for your app: this is the App ID used when creating the store provisioning profile.

An internal identifier for your app: this is not shown on the store.

Figure 16.26 To create a new app, enter the name and bundle ID.

site. This *must* match the bundle ID in your info.plist file or you won't be able to upload your IPA. Finally, enter a SKU—a unique identifier for your app, such as a code name for your current release. This is an internal identifier and won't be shown on the App Store.

Once all this information is entered, click Create.

> **WILDCARD APP ID WON'T WORK** You can select a wildcard App ID here, such as *com.mycompany.**, but if you do, it will ask for a suffix and create this as an explicit App ID automatically. This means that if your App Store provisioning profile was signed using a wildcard App ID, it won't match this app, and you won't be able to upload the app.

Once your app is created, you'll see the app management screen where you can configure the store listing and app versions. App management in iTunes Connect is broken down into two parts: general app settings, including app information and pricing, and version settings against different versions of your app. As with the Google Play store, all the metadata and images you add to your app must be suitable for all audiences, or your app will be rejected. Before we set this all up, let's upload the IPA.

UPLOADING THE IPA

Unfortunately, for iOS apps, you can't upload your IPA using iTunes Connect. Instead you need to use a tool on your Mac called Application Loader that comes as part of Xcode. You can launch this either by finding it using Spotlight (it's buried inside the Xcode package, not easily accessible from the Application folder) or by launching Xcode and selecting Xcode > Open Developer Tool > Application Loader. Once it loads up, log in with your Apple ID.

From Application Loader, select Deliver Your App (figure 16.27), click Choose, and then select the IPA you downloaded from App Center. Application Loader will check iTunes Connect for an app that matches the bundle ID and will show a screen with the details of your app. Click Next, and Application Loader will connect to iTunes Connect, validate your IPA, and upload it. This may take a few minutes because it does some static code analysis on your app to make sure you aren't using any private APIs or doing anything you shouldn't.

Once your app has been uploaded, it will be analyzed in more depth by Apple, and if any issues are found you'll be emailed about them. This analysis will take about half an hour. Once your app is ready, you'll receive an email letting you know it's finished processing.

> **YOU MAY GET A WARNING ABOUT PUSH NOTIFICATIONS** Once your app has been submitted in Application Loader, you may get an email warning you that your app registers with the push notification service but doesn't include entitlements for push. Countr doesn't use push notifications, so we haven't set them up, but the App Center SDK includes push-notification code. You can ignore this warning.

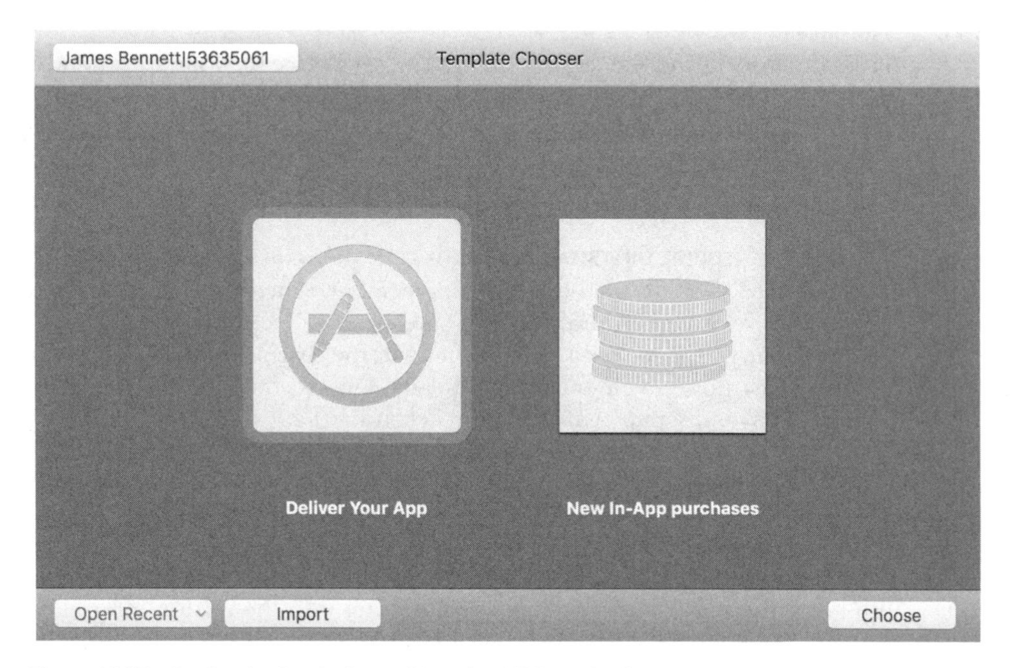

Figure 16.27 Application Loader is used to upload IPAs to Apple.

Once your app has been uploaded, head back to iTunes Connect to finish setting it up.

APP INFORMATION

The first thing to set up is the app information, and you can access this from the App Information tab on the left side of iTunes Connect. In this tab you can set up some basic information about your app. These are the required fields:

- *Subtitle*—This is a short description of your app that's used on the store as a tagline. This should be a short, snappy subtitle to entice users into reading more about your app or installing it. It can be up to 30 characters and is only shown on the App Store on devices running iOS 11.
- *Privacy Policy*—If your app does anything with users' personal data, you have to provide a privacy policy. Personal data includes anything that would allow the user to be identified, such as account registration, any financial information, health information, or contact details such as a phonebook. You can leave this blank for Countr—we don't collect any information.
- *Category*—You can set a primary and (optionally) a secondary category to categorize your app correctly on the App Store. The primary category for Countr would be Utilities, and if you wanted to set a secondary category you could use Productivity.

PRICING AND AVAILABILITY

From the Pricing and Availability tab you can set a price for your app and which countries it's available in. Set the price to be free—it will be labeled as 0 in your local currency (for example, for me it's NZD 0). Once you've set a price, your app will default to being available in all countries. You can leave this as is or click the Edit button to choose a limited set of countries to release your app to.

> **PAID APPS REQUIRE DIFFERENT CONTRACTS** If you want to charge for your app, you'll need to sign a paid developer agreement. When you signed up for the Apple Developer program, you will have signed a free app agreement, so to charge for your app you'll need to head to the first page of iTunes Connect and access the Agreements, Tax, and Banking section to sign the relevant agreement and set up your merchant account.

APP VERSIONS

Once you've set the app information and pricing, the next stage is to set up a new version of your app. Each time you want to release your app, you create a new version, configure any metadata to go out with the version, submit it for review, and then publish it. Versions are numbered and usually tie up with the version information inside your app's info.plist file. Each new version should have a higher version number, and if you have to submit multiple builds for a version (for example, if Apple finds a bug in your app) then you increment the build, leaving the version the same, and push up a new IPA.

When your app was created, an initial 1.0 version was created, and you can see this on the left side of iTunes Connect. If you click on this version, you can set up its metadata, attach a build to it, and submit it for review. This is the required metadata:

- *Screenshots*—You need at least one screenshot from the largest devices of each form factor, so a 5.5" device if your app supports iPhones, and a 12.9" device if your app supports iPads. The easiest way to generate these is either using the simulator or Test Cloud, run on an iPhone 7 Plus and an iPad Pro. You can add other screen sizes if you want to, but if you don't, the larger ones will be scaled down.
- *Description*—This is where you can enter a more detailed description about your app, covering its features, how it can help your users achieve their goals or solve their problems, and anything else required to explain your app to your target audience. You can enter up to 4000 characters here.
- *Keywords*—Keywords are used to help people search for your app. This is a comma-separated list of words or phrases relevant to your app and that will help people find it. For example, you could enter *count, counter, track* as the keywords, and your app would be shown to people searching using any of those three words. How high up the ranking it will be displayed depends on the popularity of your app, how good the reviews are, or if Apple likes you. You can use up to 100 characters here.

- *Support URL*—This is a link to a website providing support for your app. You have to provide this URL, but Apple is pretty flexible about what the URL points to, as long as the URL provides ways to contact you. For example, you could use your Twitter account URL or a Facebook page. I use the URL of my blog, because there are links on there to contact me.
- *Build*—You can upload as many IPAs as you like using Application Loader. From the Build section you can select which build you want to publish with your release. Click Select a Build Before You Submit Your App, select the appropriate build from the popup, and click Done.
- *App Icon*—This is the large app icon that will be shown on the App Store for your app, and it needs to be a PNG or JPEG at a resolution of 1024 × 1024 pixels. If you used MakeAppIcon to generate your app icon, it will have generated an app icon for the store along with the rest of the icons, called iTunesArtwork@ 2x.png, so upload this file. You can also find it in the source code that accompanies this book in the Images\Countr\AppIcons\iOS folder.
- *Version*—This is the public version of your app, and for a first app this will default to 1.0. You should change this to match the version number you set inside your info.plist file to make it easier to track app releases.
- *Rating*—Specify a content rating for your app to ensure it's only made available to the right audience. To set the rating, click the Edit button next to the Rating section and fill in the questionnaire. Countr is suitable for everyone, so you should be able to select None for all categories.
- *Copyright*—Enter a copyright message for your app, such as *2017 - My Company*. You don't need to add the copyright symbol at the start.
- *App Review Information*—Provide additional information to assist Apple with its reviews. This includes contact information, such as your name, phone number, and email. You can also provide a dummy account for Apple to use if your app requires a sign-in, and by default they tick the "Sign-in required" box, so untick this because Countr doesn't need any user sign-in.
- *Version Release*—Once you've set up your app, you submit it for review, and once it's approved it can be published to the store. You can choose how this publishing happens: whether it should happen automatically, as soon as the app is approved; happen automatically after a given date; or require a manual publish. You can set this choice here—the default is to automatically publish as soon as it's approved. You'll normally want to publish immediately unless you have a marketing campaign or release event lined up.

By default, all the content you provide here is in the language you selected as the primary language for your app. You can provide different language versions using the language drop-down at the top right of the Version page.

Once all this metadata is set up, click the Save button, and then click the Submit for Review button at the top right. You'll then need to answer three questions:

- *Export Compliance*—This is to check to see if your app uses any form of encryption. Select No here for this example, as Countr doesn't use any form of encryption, but if you're publishing an app that does use encryption for anything, you'll need to select Yes and answer further questions because the United States has restrictions on the export of encryption. Note that if you make any web calls using HTTPS, you'll need to select Yes, as HTTPS uses encryption. You can read more about this in the iTunes Connect "Resources and Help" at http://mng.bz/brT6.
- *Content Rights*—This is to verify that your app doesn't display any third-party content, and if it does, that you have the relevant permissions to do so. Countr doesn't use any third-party content, so you can select No.
- *Advertising Identifier*—iOS provides a unique identifier for each device, used for advertisement tracking. Countr doesn't show any ads, so select No this time, but if you use this for ad tracking you must answer Yes or your app will be rejected and you'll need to submit a new IPA and start again. Apple will scan your IPA for usage of the API that provides this.

Once you've answered these questions, click Submit. Your version will then move to "Waiting for review" and be reviewed by Apple. You should also get an email confirming this. Most apps are reviewed within 48 hours, so it may take a few days to get approved. If your app is rejected, you'll be told why (and be given a link to the relevant section of their app guidelines), and you can then make any changes that Apple suggests and resubmit your app. The approval process is varied, as real people are involved—you can have one person approve your app, then push up a bug fix before publishing, and have another reject your app for something that was there when the first person approved the app. Apple's decision is final, though, so it's very hard to fight them on anything. You can read the guidelines at http://mng.bz/525T.

You can update your app metadata while it's waiting for review, but not once it is in review. You also can't change the IPA. If you need to upload a new IPA, remove the app from review using the link that will appear at the top of the app version page, upload a new binary, and then resubmit for review.

Apple is really good at keeping you updated—you'll get emails as your app moves through the different states, such as when someone starts the review and when it's approved. You can also install the iTunes Connect app from the iOS App Store, called Connect, that allows you to manage your releases (figure 16.28). Through this app, Apple will send you push notifications when the states change. The different states are shown in table 16.1.

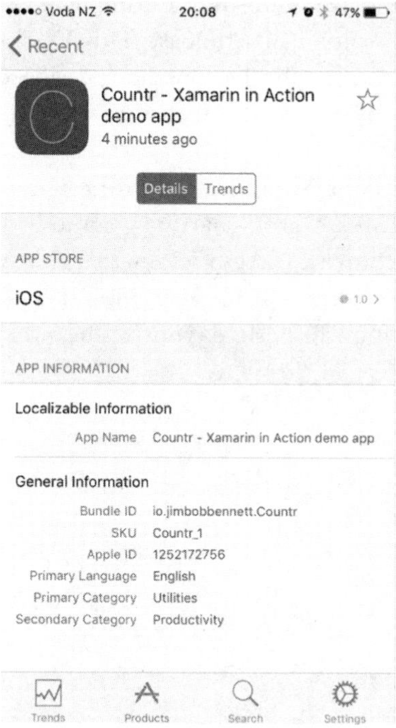

Figure 16.28 Apple is great at updating you about the progress of approving your app. There's even an app to manage it, called Connect.

Table 16.1 The different states for your app in iTunes Connect

State	Description
Prepare for Submission	This is the state all new versions start in.
Waiting for Review	Your app has been submitted for review and is waiting for someone at Apple to start the review. You can change any of the app metadata at this point, but if you want to upload a new IPA, remove your app from review.
In Review	Someone at Apple is currently reviewing your app.
Rejected	Your app has been rejected by Apple. There will be a link on the version page to the resolution center where you can see the issue and reply to the reviewer.
Pending Agreement	Your app can be approved before you've signed the relevant contracts—for example, if your app isn't free and you haven't signed the paid apps agreement. You can find the agreements to sign in the Agreements, Tax, and Banking section available from the iTunes Connect front page.
Ready for Sale	Your app has been released to the store and is available for download.

Once your app has been approved, it should be published automatically, assuming you left the version release option set to Automatically Release This Version. If you need to manually release, select the version from the list on the left side of iTunes Connect and click the Make App Available button at the top right—this button will have replaced the Submit for Review button.

Congratulations—you've now published your Xamarin app to the iOS App Store (figure 16.29) as well as the Google Play store! A cross-platform job well done. You may struggle to find your app on the App Store to begin with—the iOS App Store takes a while to publish your app globally and index it for searching, and even links from inside Apple's Connect app may fail for a while. Be patient, it should show after an hour or so.

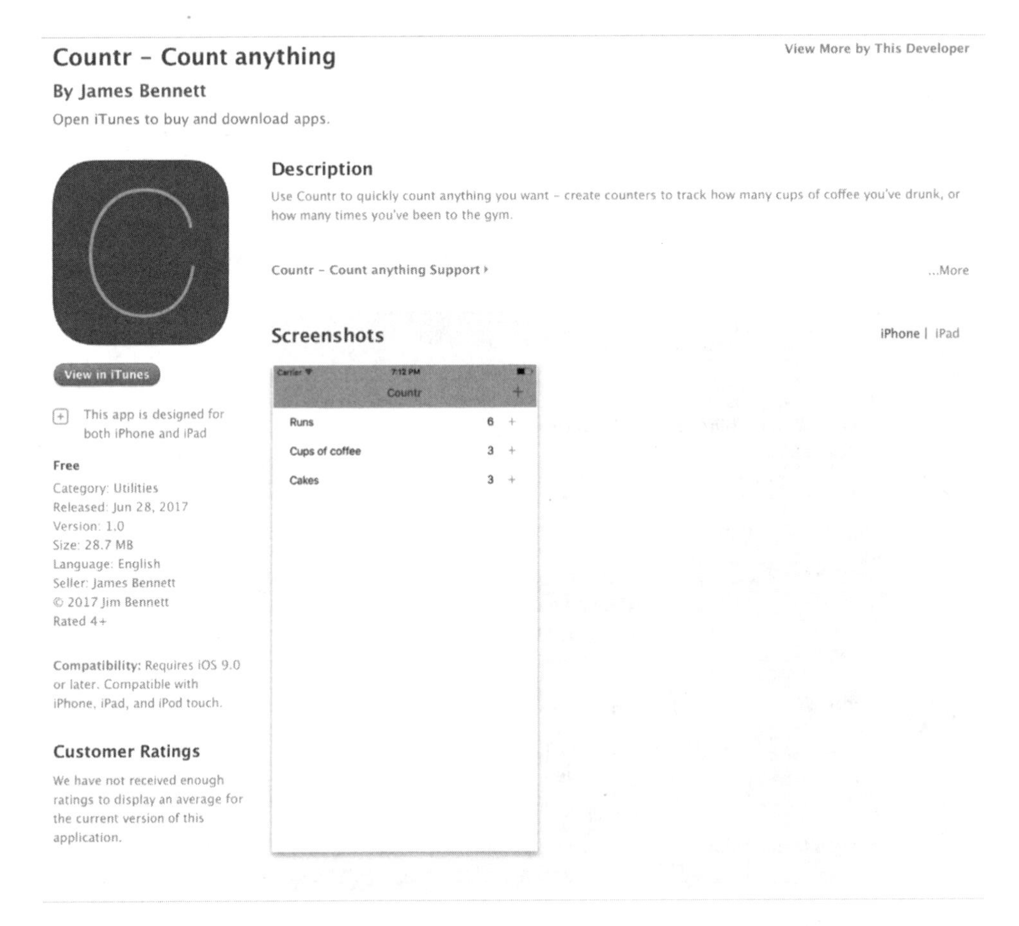

Figure 16.29 The Countr listing on the iOS App Store

> **STORE DISTRIBUTION IS HARD** It's a lot of work with a number of manual steps to distribute to the Apple App Store. To make your life easier, a lot of this process can be automated using Fastlane. You've already used Fastlane to generate provisioning profiles from Visual Studio for Mac, but it can do a whole lot more than just profiles. Head to https://fastlane.tools to learn more, or check out the Xamarin University video about Fastlane at http://mng.bz/e1i0.

Reviews and ratings

You can find reviews and ratings for your app inside iTunes Connect by selecting the Activity tab on the top and choosing Ratings and Reviews on the left side (figure 16.30). You can break down ratings and reviews by app version, user's location, or date. If a user gives a review, you can respond to it, maybe letting them know that their problem is fixed or helping them if they're stuck.

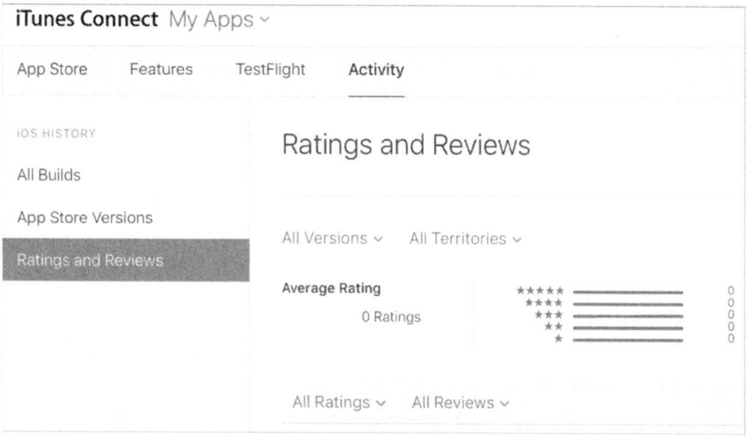

Figure 16.30 Review ratings and reviews from users via the Activity tab.

Apple is very strict on rating manipulation—your developer account will be terminated if you try to fudge the numbers.

Publishing updates

Once your app has been published, it's time to think about updates—bug fixes or more features. All updates are managed by the App Store. Just like with Android, App Center updates are disabled for store builds.

You can create a new version using the + Version or Platform button on the left side of iTunes Connect. You can only have one unreleased version of your app at any time, so you can't create a new version until your previous version has been approved. You also can't delete versions—if a version needs to be fixed up, you have to change that version instead of deleting it and starting again.

YOU CAN ONLY DELETE PUBLISHED APPS If you build an app and then decide to delete it, you'll find you can't unless it has been published. Even if Apple has rejected your app and you can't publish it, you can't delete it.

When you add a new version, all the metadata and screenshots from the previous version are copied over. You'll then need to update this information to reflect your new app version, updating screenshots to match your latest app UI and adding details about what's new to the app description. You'll need to upload a new build as well, with an incremented version number. This increment should be to the version number in the info.plist file, not just the build number. You can increment the build number if you want, leave it, the same or reset it, but you need to always increment the version number to indicate a new app version.

Once your new version is ready, click the Submit for Review button to submit your new version for review, and wait while it goes through the approval process.

MAKE SURE ANYTHING NEEDED FOR REVIEW IS STILL RELEVANT The reviews for updates are usually faster than for the initial version, but Apple still does thorough checks. This means anything you set up to help with the initial review needs to still be valid. For example, if you provided a demo account to use, this account should still be working.

Summary

In this chapter you learned

- App Center can be used to distribute apps to beta testers.
- Apps distributed by App Center can have in-app updates to help push new versions to your testers.
- To publish your app, you can use the Google Play store for Android apps and the iOS App Store for iOS apps.
- There are alternative Android app stores that you may want to target, especially if you want to publish to Chinese users.

You also learned how to

- Set up App Center distribution groups.
- Enable in-app updates in your app using the App Center SDK.
- Create and publish Android apps using the Google Play store.
- Create and publish iOS apps using the iOS App Store.

Where to next?

Over the course of this book you've learned about Xamarin, from developing a simple Hello World app, through learning about the MVVM design pattern, to planning and designing an app, writing a cross-platform model layer and view-model layer, and platform-specific view layers. You've run your apps on devices, tested them with automated UI testing, set them up to track how they're used and detect crashes, and distributed them to beta testers and the store. You've been through the entire mobile-optimized development lifecycle and seen how tools from Xamarin and Microsoft can make this journey easy and fun.

To some, Xamarin is just wrappers around the iOS and Android SDKs and the tooling to compile mobile apps, but really it's a whole lot more. It offers the ability to build a large percentage of your mobile app once, sharing 70–80% of code between iOS and Android. It's a way to write apps for iOS and Android using one language, and a language that in my opinion is the best around—it gives you great power combined with simplicity, allowing you to write clean, easy-to-read code, with a simple syntax for building multithreaded apps. C# is very important to its creators and has an exciting roadmap of features and improvements coming up.

Xamarin is the tooling that allows you to write mobile apps on a Mac or on Windows, easily switching from one to the other if needed. Xamarin gives you the power to automate your mobile app testing, writing your tests in C#, the same language you use to write your apps. It opens up a huge world of NuGet packages providing amazing cross-platform functionality, as well as giving you plugins that allow you to access platform-specific features, like the camera, from cross-platform code.

The marriage of Microsoft and Xamarin has only strengthened these capabilities. Xamarin tools are now built on top of powerful tools from Microsoft, such as the open source Rosyln C# compiler. Microsoft brings more to the mix in the form of App Center, providing a one-stop shop to introduce mobile app devops. It also has Azure, the best cloud service for developers—something you can access using open source, cross-platform NuGet packages from Xamarin apps as easily as Windows developers can from their applications.

Xamarin has an amazing community of passionate developers from all around the globe and all walks of life. As you continue your journey as a Xamarin developer, I urge you to get involved with the community, whether online, through local events like meetups, or thorough big international conferences such as //Build or Microsoft Connect.

If you want some amazing online content, check these out:

- The MvvmCross documentation at http://www.mvvmcross.com.
- The great forums at https://forums.xamarin.com.
- The vibrant Xamarin community Slack team (which you can join) at https://xamarinchat.herokuapp.com/, full of Xamarin developers and support engineers.
- The Xamarin show on Microsoft's Channel 9, with incredible content updated regularly, at https://channel9.msdn.com/Shows/XamarinShow.
- Planet Xamarin, a really useful aggregator of Xamarin blogs from world-class developers, at www.planetxamarin.com.
- The Xamarin podcast at www.xamarinpodcast.com, or MergeConflict by James Montemagno from Xamarin and Frank Krueger (the developer behind,

amongst others, SQLite-Net-PCL, a C# and F# IDE for the iPad called Continuous, and the newly released Xamarin Live Player) at http://www.mergeconflict.fm. MergeConflict covers a wide range of development topics relevant to mobile developers.

The future of Xamarin is exciting. Every year over the past few years has been the best year yet for mobile app developers, a trend I don't see stopping.

Now, go build apps!

appendix A
UI flows and threads for SquareRt and Countr

In chapter 6 we looked at the user flows for SquareRt and Countr, and you saw how to break them down by layer (view, view model, or model), and by thread (UI or background). Let's now look at a full breakdown of these flows with the help of the handy diagram that was introduced in figure 6.19.

A.1 SquareRt

There's only one user flow in SquareRt, shown in figure A.1.

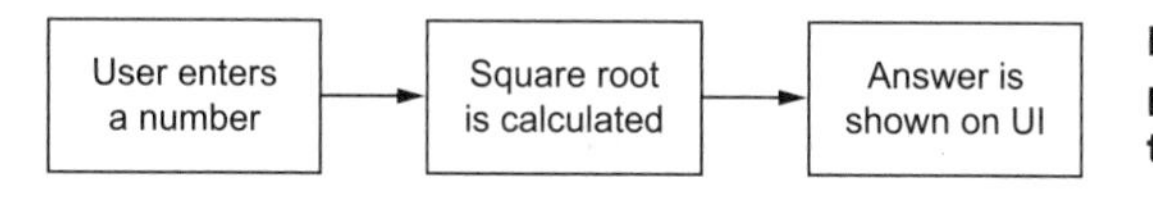

Figure A.1 The SquareRt app is pretty simple, with only one flow that the user can take.

Mapping this to the different layers and threads is relatively simple. The calculation is fast, so it can can run on any thread. Figure A.2 shows this flow broken down.

View	UI thread	User enters a number	Answer is shown on UI
View model	UI thread	View model passes value straight to model	View model passes value straight to view
	Background thread		
Model	UI thread	Square root is calculated	
	Background thread		

Figure A.2 The SquareRt user flow is trivial: the view handles the user interactions, the view model passes values straight through, and the model can calculate on the UI thread.

A.2 Countr

Countr has four user flows, as shown in figure A.3.

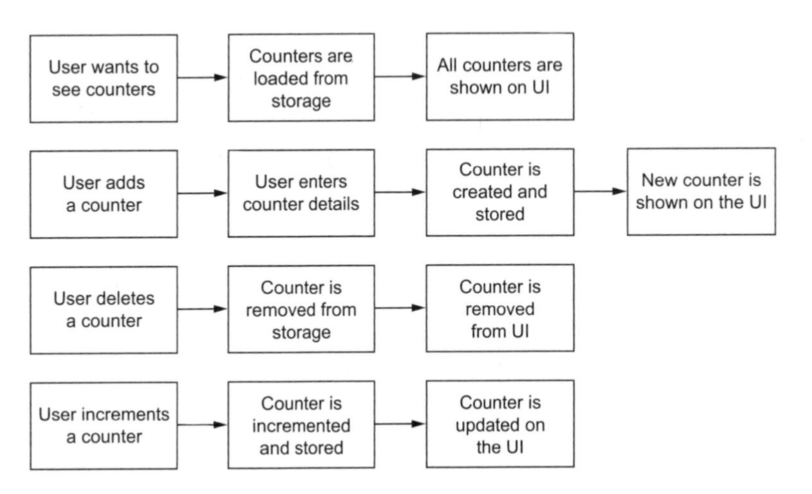

Figure A.3 The user flows for the Countr app: showing, adding, deleting, and incrementing counters

A.2.1 Loading counters

The first user flow is loading counters from storage and showing them on the UI. Loading from storage happens in the model layer and on a background thread. The list of counters is then shown in the UI, back on the UI thread. Figure A.4 shows this flow.

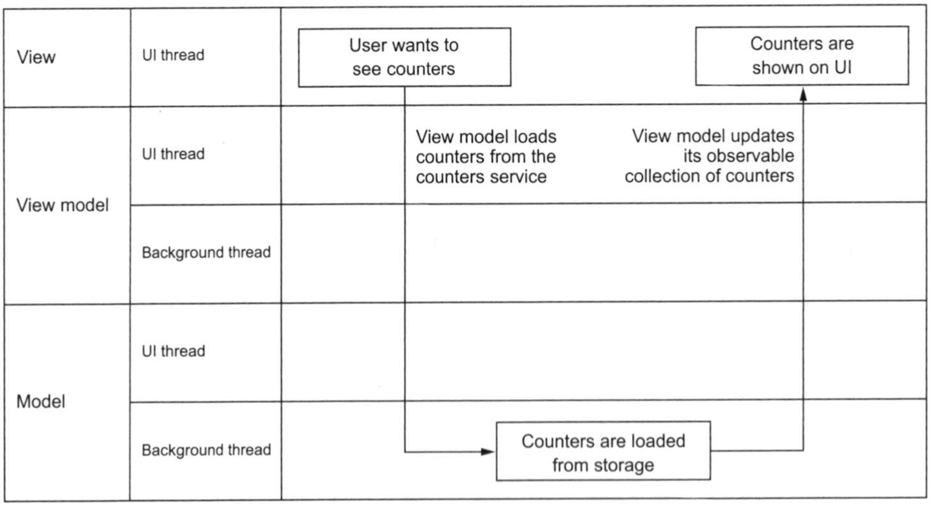

View
UI thread
User wants to see counters
Counters are shown on UI
View model
UI thread
View model loads counters from the counters service
View model updates its observable collection of counters
Background thread
Model
UI thread
Background thread
Counters are loaded from storage

Figure A.4 The first user flow for Countr loads counters on a background thread and then updates the UI from the UI thread.

A.2.2 *Adding a counter*

The second user flow is adding a counter. For this, the counters view model needs to navigate to a new screen where the user can enter the details of a new counter. Then the model layer saves this counter, the counter view model navigates back, and the counters view model updates the UI to show the new counter.

This user flow can be broken down into three parts: navigation to a new screen, creating the counter, and updating the counters list. Figure A.5 shows the flow for navigating to a new screen, figure A.6 shows the flow for entering and saving a new counter, and figure A.7 shows the flow for updating the counters list.

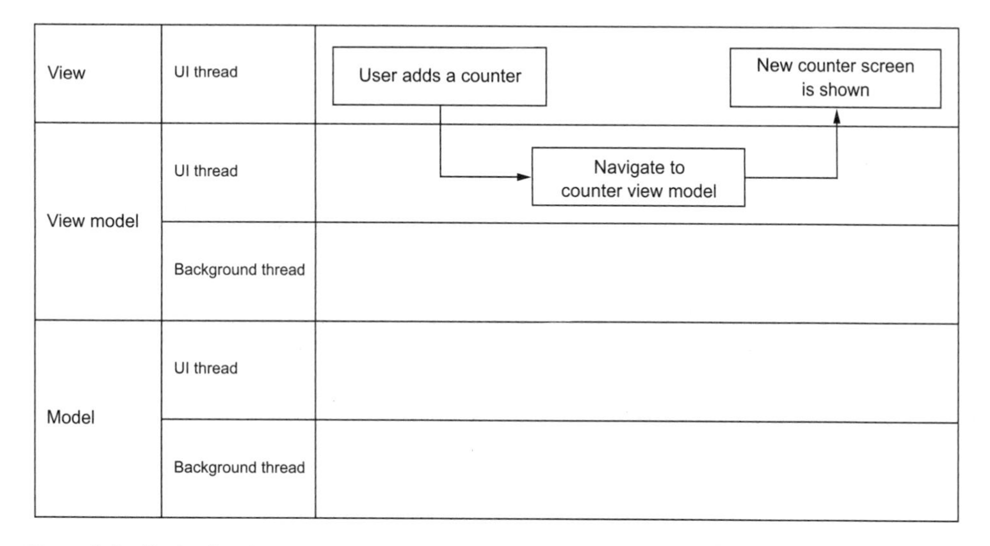

Figure A.5 Navigation to a new screen occurs on the UI thread in the view-model layer.

Figure A.6 Saving the counter happens in the model layer on a background thread.

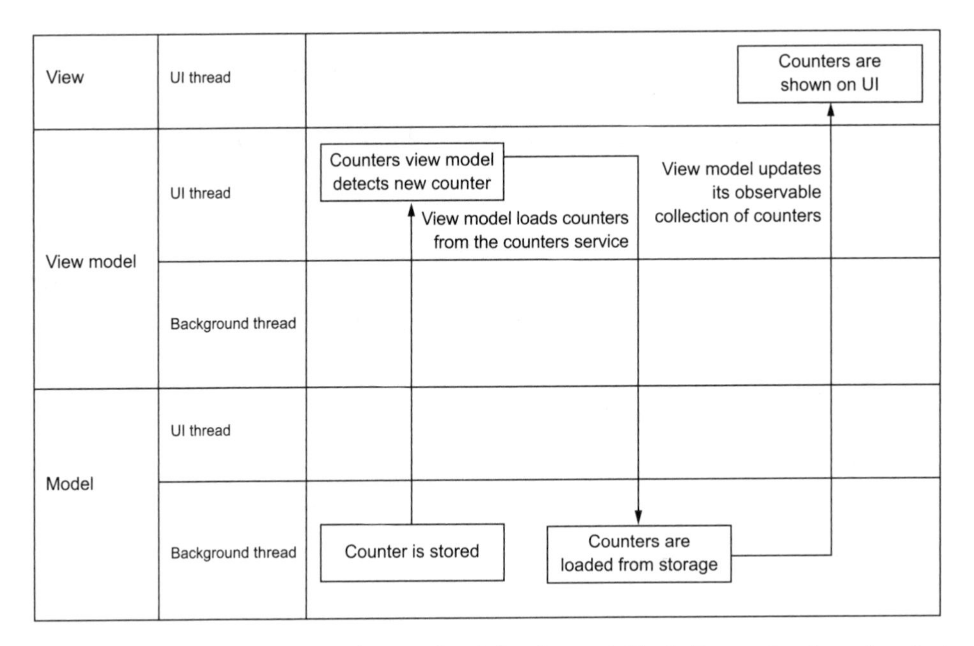

Figure A.7 Once the counters have been updated, the view model loads the counters from storage via the model layer on a background thread, and then it updates the UI from the UI thread.

A.2.3 *Deleting a counter*

The third used flow is deleting a counter. The UI initiates the deletion from the UI thread, which deletes the counter from storage on a background thread, before finally updating the UI back on the UI thread. This is shown in figure A.8.

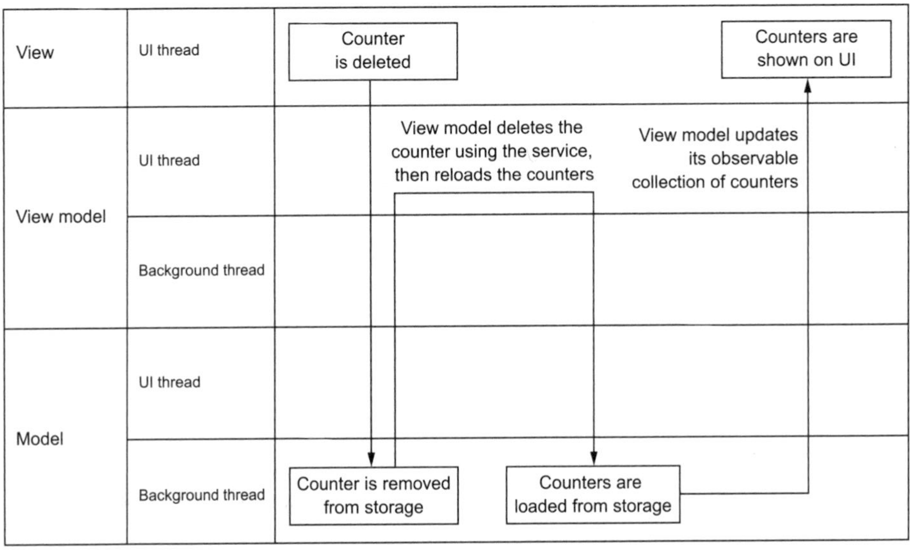

View
UI thread
Counter is deleted
Counters are shown on UI
View model
UI thread
View model deletes the counter using the service, then reloads the counters
View model updates its observable collection of counters
Background thread
Model
UI thread
Background thread
Counter is removed from storage
Counters are loaded from storage

Figure A.8 Counters are deleted from storage on a background thread, the counters are reloaded on a background thread, and the UI is updated back on the UI thread.

A.2.4 Incrementing a counter

The final user flow is incrementing a counter. The counter is incremented on the UI thread, causing the UI to update, and then the updated counter is saved to storage on a background thread. Figure A.9 shows this final user flow.

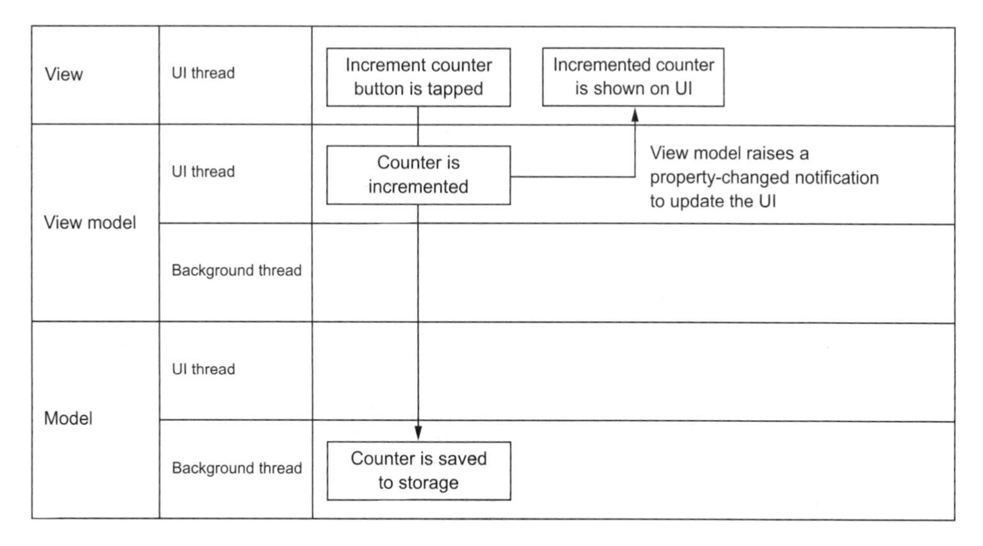

Figure A.9 When a counter is updated, the updated counter is stored on a background thread and the UI is updated on the UI thread.

appendix B *Using MVVM Light instead of MvvmCross*

This book focuses on building cross-platform apps using MVVM, and although the concepts are agnostic to the framework you're using, my examples focused on the MvvmCross framework. There are a range of different MVVM frameworks, each with their own quirks, features, and ways of doing things. You've seen MvvmCross; this appendix looks at a different framework called MVVM Light.

The question of which framework to use has a standard technology answer—it depends! Each framework has its own strengths and weaknesses. MvvmCross is a heavyweight, opinionated framework. It provides a lot for you out of the box, which has the upside of making it easier to get started because you have less code to write, but the downside is that it's harder to do things that are different from the MvvmCross way. MVVM Light, on the other hand, is much more lightweight and provides only what you need to implement the basics of MVVM. You have to do more yourself, but in return you have more control.

Sometimes the best reason for choosing a framework is experience. If in the past you've built Windows apps using MVVM Light, it makes sense to keep using the framework you know. If you don't have experience with any MVVM frameworks that support Xamarin apps, you could try out a simple app in each framework to see which feels more comfortable. You can always switch frameworks if needed, but remember that the lighter the framework, the easier it is to change. It's easier to change from MVVM Light to MvvmCross than the other way around, especially if you've used a lot from the MvvmCross ecosystem.

B.1 MVVM Light

MVVM Light is an open source MVVM framework created by Laurent Bugnion, a Cloud Developer Advocate working at Microsoft. As the name suggests, it's a lightweight framework, in that it doesn't do too much for you. It just provides you with the basics. Although it's lightweight, it does have everything you need to build apps. It's also very mature, having been around for eight years, and it supports all the various Windows technologies as well as Xamarin apps.

Out of the box it provides a base view model to handle property-change notifications, a command implementation, a binding layer, an IoC container, a navigation service to support view-model-first navigation, a dispatcher helper to marshal calls onto the UI thread, and a messenger. For iOS and Android apps it also has helpers for table views and recycler views.

This appendix isn't a full tutorial on MVVM Light. It just looks at the features MVVM Light provides, showing you how to get started porting Countr to MVVM Light. There's an example version of Countr using MVVM Light in the source code that accompanies this book, and the MVVM Light website at http://www.mvvmlight.net has tutorials you can use, and a link to a PluralSight course.

B.2 Installing MVVM Light

The easiest way to create an MVVM Light project is to create a standard Xamarin app and then add the MvvmLight NuGet packages. There are two main packages to choose from: MvvmLight or MvvmLightLibs. The MvvmLight NuGet package installs the required libraries and creates some example view and view model files. The MvvmLightLibs package just installs the required libraries. To port Countr, you would remove the MvvmCross packages and then install MvvmLightLibs.

These libraries provide everything necessary for your core cross-platform project as well as your iOS app. For Android, there are two more NuGet packages to install. MvvmLightAndroidSupport provides support for recycler views, and the third-party JimBobBennett.MvvmLight.AppCompat NuGet package provides support for AppCompat.

B.3 The model layer

The only difference in the model layer is the messenger. Just like MvvmCross, MVVM Light has a messenger—`GalaSoft.MvvmLight.Messaging.Messenger`—and this exposes an interface called `IMessenger`. This is a simple interface, with methods to register and unregister for a message, and to send a message to all registered recipients. Messages can be any class—there's no need to derive from a particular base class, unlike MvvmCross with its base `MvxMessage` class. This means the existing Countr model layer can be reused just by changing the messenger and removing the message base class.

B.4 The view model layer

Just like MvmCross, MVVM Light has a base view-model class, `GalaSoft.MvvmLight.ViewModelBase`. This class has similar capabilities to the base view model in MvvmCross, providing support for property-changed notifications and a `Set` method to update a value inside a property if it has changed, raising the property-changed event.

Commands are provided using `GalaSoft.MvvmLight.Command.RelayCommand`. Just like the MvvmCross `MvxCommand` class, this command wraps an action. One feature that's not provided in MVVM Light is support for async commands—there's no way to create an async `RelayCommand` that you can await the execution on.

This lack of async support also extends to navigation. MVVM Light has a navigation service, exposed via `GalaSoft.MvvmLight.Views.INavigationService`, that provides view-model-first navigation, but the methods on this interface aren't async. Navigation works slightly differently in MVVM Light and MvvmCross. Instead of navigating to a view model, as you do in MvvmCross, you navigate to a page key—a string that defines a view and view-model relationship, and as you'll see later in this appendix, this is defined in the view layer. In our `CountersViewModel`, the `NavigateTo` method would be used when using MVVM Light, with a string-based page key to define where to navigate to, and a parameter can be passed to the target view model. These parameters aren't passed to a particular method on the target view model; instead, the view that's navigated to needs to pull out the parameter. You'll see this later in this appendix.

How you define these page keys is up to you. My preferred way to specify these keys is using the name of the view model, so to navigate to the counter view model, you'd use code such as this:

```
navigationService.NavigateTo(nameof(CounterViewModel), new Counter());
```

Closing a view is done with the `GoBack` method on the navigation service. This will close the current view, showing the previous one.

MVVM Light has an IoC container, accessible using the static `Default` property on the `GalaSoft.MvvmLight.Ioc.SimpleIoc` class. View models, services, and repositories can be registered inside this container and resolved using constructor injection, just like with MvvmCross. The difference is that MVVM Light wraps a lot of this in a view-model locator—a static class used to register services and get view models. MvvmCross has some setup code provided by the framework, and inside this setup code you initialize the content of the IoC container. MVVM Light, on the other hand, relies on you doing this inside your own app code. The traditional way is to create a static view-model locator, and inside the static constructor register everything. You then expose methods or properties on the view-model locator to return view models from the IoC container. The following listing shows an example implementation for Countr.

Listing B.1 Registering services and providing properties to get view-model instances

```
public static class ViewModelLocator        <-- The view model locator is a static class.
{
   static ViewModelLocator()
   {
      SimpleIoc.Default.Register<CountersViewModel>();    The static constructor
      SimpleIoc.Default.Register<CounterViewModel>();     registers view models in
                                                          the IoC container.
```

```
        SimpleIoc.Default.Register<ICountersService, CountersService>();
        SimpleIoc.Default.Register<ICountersRepository, CountersRepository>();
        SimpleIoc.Default.Register<IMessenger, Messenger>();
    }

    public static CountersViewModel CountersViewModel
    {
        get { return SimpleIoc.Default.GetInstance<CountersViewModel>(); }
    }

    public static CounterViewModel CounterViewModel
    {
        get
        {
            return SimpleIoc.Default
                        .GetInstanceWithoutCaching<CounterViewModel>();
        }
    }
}
```

Services and repositories are registered by interface.

Returns a singleton instance of the CountersViewModel

Returns a new instance of the CounterViewModel

In the static constructor, the view models are registered into the IoC container. The static `Default` property on the `SimpleIoc` class returns a singleton instance of the container that you can use anywhere in your code if you want to, although like with the MvvmCross IoC container, constructor injection is preferred as it's easier to test. The constructor also registers your services, repositories, and any other classes you want to resolve, such as the messenger.

The properties that return view models are used by views to get their binding context, and you'll see this in action later in this appendix, when we look at views. The thing to note here, though, is that the IoC container has two methods for retrieving objects from it. The first is `GetInstance`, which returns a singleton, so the same instance every time. The second is `GetInstanceWithoutCaching`, which returns a new instance every time. We only ever want one counters view model, so the property returns the same instance. For the counter view model, we want a new one every time, so we use `GetInstanceWithoutCaching` to return a new instance.

Messages, such as the message sent by the counters service whenever the counters are updated, are handled in the view-model layer by registering an action with the messenger using the `Register` method. This generic method has a generic argument of the type of message you're registering for, and it takes an action to be executed when the message is received. Unlike the MvvmCross messenger, this doesn't return a token that you keep hold of to keep the subscription alive. Instead, you also pass the instance of the owner to it, and as long as the owner hasn't been garbage-collected, the action will be called.

The other difference from MvvmCross is that there's no way to register to receive a message on the UI thread. Instead, all messages are handled on the thread that was used to send them. To handle messages on the UI thread, use the MVVM Light dispatcher helper. This is a class that's only available in your platform-specific app code and can marshal calls onto the UI thread. The trick to making this work inside your cross-platform code project is to register a callback inside your view-model locator that's used to run code on the UI thread, and, as you'll see later in this appendix, set this callback to use the dispatcher helper. The core project's view-model locator code is shown in this listing.

Listing B.2 Registering a callback to run code on the UI thread

```
static Action<Action> dispatcher;
public static void RegisterDispatcher(Action<Action> dispatcherAction)
{
   dispatcher = dispatcherAction;
}

public static void RunOnUIThread(Action action)
{
   dispatcher(action);
}
```

Registers a callback for code to run on the UI thread

Uses the callback to run code

The `RunOnUIThread` method uses the callback to run a given action, so this can be used with messenger to ensure a message is handled on the UI thread:

```
messenger.Register<CountersChangedMessage>(this, m =>
➥ViewModelLocator.RunOnUIThread(async () => await LoadCounters()));
```

B.5 The view layer

As you'd expect, the platform-specific implementation is different on each platform, so let's look at them one by one, starting with Android.

B.5.1 The Android view and application layer

The MVVM Light Android support comes from a separate NuGet package, and there are two packages to use. MvvmLightAndroidSupport provides Android support for non-AppCompat activities and recycler views, and JimBobBennett.MvvmLight.AppCompat provides support for AppCompat activities. I always recommend using AppCompat to provide the largest amount of OS support, so install both NuGet packages. The layout files and activities created in this book can be pretty much reused, with a few tweaks to make them support MVVM Light instead of MvvmCross.

SETTING UP THE NAVIGATION SERVICE

In your initial activity, such as your splash-screen activity, initialize the navigation service and set up the mappings from page keys to views. The code to do this is shown in the following listing.

Listing B.3 Setting up the Android navigation service

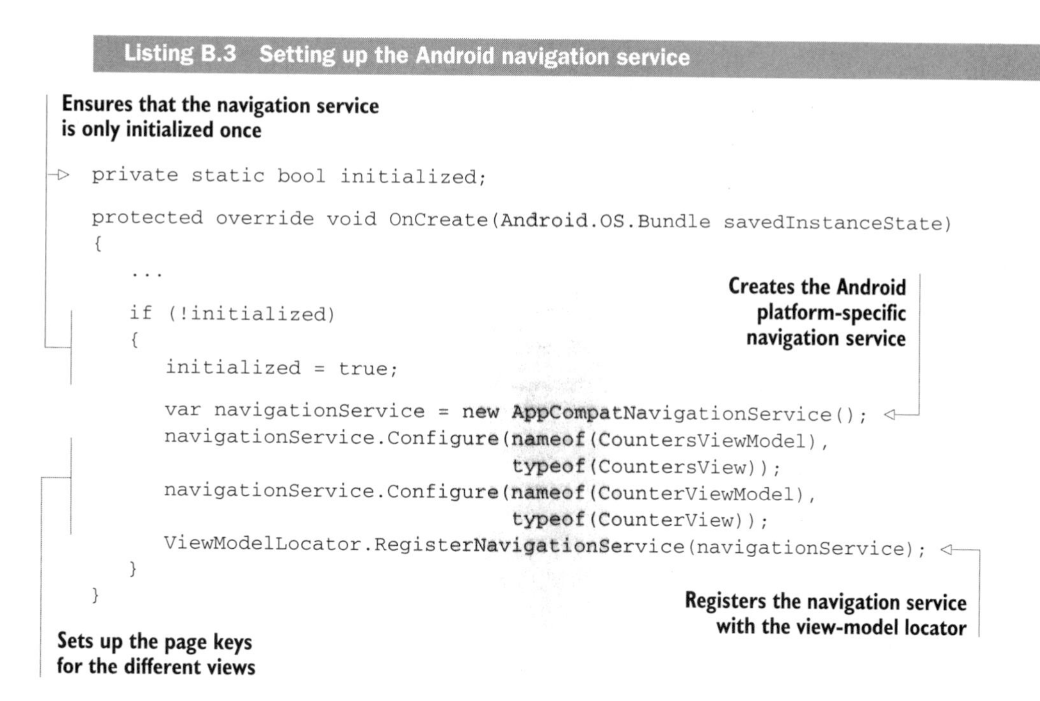
Ensures that the navigation service is only initialized once
Creates the Android platform-specific navigation service
Registers the navigation service with the view-model locator
Sets up the page keys for the different views

```
private static bool initialized;

protected override void OnCreate(Android.OS.Bundle savedInstanceState)
{
   ...
   if (!initialized)
   {
      initialized = true;

      var navigationService = new AppCompatNavigationService();
      navigationService.Configure(nameof(CountersViewModel),
                                  typeof(CountersView));
      navigationService.Configure(nameof(CounterViewModel),
                                  typeof(CounterView));
      ViewModelLocator.RegisterNavigationService(navigationService);
   }
}
```

This code registers all the views with the navigation service using a string-based page key, in this case the name of the relevant view model. When you navigate based on a page key, it will create the relevant activity and show that.

With MvvmCross, you set the app start—the view model to navigate to after the splash screen. MVVM Light doesn't have this. Instead, in the `OnResume` method of the splash screen, you need to manually navigate to the appropriate page key:

```
protected override void OnResume()
{
   base.OnResume();
   ViewModelLocator.NavigationService.NavigateTo(nameof(CountersViewModel));
}
```

RETRIEVING VIEW MODELS AND NAVIGATION PARAMETERS

The view model for the new view will come from the view-model locator. The following listing shows an example of this for the counters view.

Listing B.4 Getting view models inside Android activities

```
CounterViewModel viewModel;

protected override void OnCreate(Bundle savedInstanceState)
{
   ...
   viewModel = ViewModelLocator.CounterViewModel;
}
```

Gets the view model from the view-model locator

When a parameter is passed to the navigation service, it can be retrieved using the platform-specific `GetAndRemoveParameter` method. This method is platform specific—it works slightly differently on iOS and Android to handle the different way data is passed around. When navigating from activity to activity in Android, data is passed using an `Intent`, and the navigation service can use this intent to get the parameter that was passed. The following listing shows how to retrieve the counter parameter in the counter view model.

Listing B.5 Getting the parameter passed to the navigation service

```
var navigationService = (AppCompatNavigationService)ViewModelLocator
➥.NavigationService;
var counter = navigationService.GetAndRemoveParameter<Counter>(Intent);
viewModel.Prepare(counter);
```

Once this parameter has been retrieved, it can be passed to the existing `Prepare` method on the view model. Unlike MvvmCross, there are no lifecycle methods on the view model that are called automatically by the view. You'll need to call methods like `LoadCounters` on the counters view model manually from the `OnCreate` method of your activity, instead of relying on methods such as `Prepare` and `Initialize` being called.

BINDING

When using MVVM Light, binding is configured purely in code in your activity—there's no way to do it in the layout AXML file. Bindings for properties are created using the `SetBinding` extension method from the `GalaSoft.MvvmLight.Helpers` namespace, and this binds a property on the view model to a control. Both the view model and control need to be a field or property on the activity. The bindings that are created aren't stored anywhere by default, so they'll be garbage-collected if you don't explicitly store them somewhere in your code (and once they're garbage-collected, the bindings will no longer work).

The standard pattern is to have a field or property for the view model, a property for the control that retrieves the control from the layout, and a field containing a collection of bindings. The following listing shows how to create the binding for the counter name `EditText` control in the counter view.

Listing B.6 Binding the counter name to an edit text

```
EditText _counterName;
EditText CounterName => _counterName ??
   (_counterName = FindViewById<EditText>(Resource.Id.counter_name));

readonly List<Binding> bindings = new List<Binding>();

protected override void OnCreate(Bundle savedInstanceState)
{
   ...
```

A property that gets the EditText, caching the value

A list of bindings

```
    bindings.Add(this.SetBinding(() => viewModel.Name,
                                 () => CounterName.Text,
                                 BindingMode.TwoWay));
}
```

Creates and stores a binding from the Name property on the view model to the text property on the EditText

The SetBinding extension method must be called on the view.

Commands are bound in a different way than other properties. Instead of using SetBinding, the SetCommand extension method is used. It's called on the widget that you want to configure the command against, such as a button, and the call takes the name of the event to wire up, and the command on the view model to connect to. This mechanism is quite powerful, in that you can wire up any event to a command.

The following listing shows an example of wiring up the click event of the add new counter floating action button to the command on the counters view model.

Listing B.7 Binding the click event of a floating action button to a command

```
AddCounterButton.SetCommand(nameof(FloatingActionButton.Click),
➥viewModel.ShowAddNewCounterCommand);
```

RECYCLER VIEWS

Like MvvmCross, MVVM Light has helpers for recycler views. Instead of providing its own implementation, MVVM Light provides an implementation of a recycler view adapter that will keep the control in sync with an observable collection. The adapter is created using an extension method on ObservableCollection called GetRecycler-Adapter. This method takes a layout for each item and an action that binds an item in the collection to that layout, and it returns an adapter that can be set on the recycler view.

Listing B.8 shows how this adapter is created, and listing B.9 shows an implementation for the action that binds each item.

Listing B.8 Creating an adapter from an observable collection

```
ObservableRecyclerAdapter<CounterViewModel, CachingViewHolder> adapter;

protected override async void OnCreate(Bundle savedInstanceState)
{
   ...
   adapter = viewModel.Counters
                      .GetRecyclerAdapter(BindViewHolder,
                                          Resource.Layout.counter_recycler_view);
   RecyclerView.SetAdapter(adapter);
   ...
}
```

Listing B.9 The BindViewHolder method resets the bindings

```
void BindViewHolder(CachingViewHolder holder,
                    CounterViewModel counterVm,
                    int position)
{
   var name = holder.FindCachedViewById<TextView>
                              (Resource.Id.counter_name);
   var count = holder.FindCachedViewById<TextView>
                              (Resource.Id.counter_count);
   var incrementButton = holder.FindCachedViewById<ImageButton>
                              (Resource.Id.add_image);

   holder.DeleteBinding(name);
   holder.DeleteBinding(count);

   holder.SaveBinding(name,
                      new Binding<string, string>(counterVm,
                                                  () => counterVm.Name,
                                                  name,
                                                  () => name.Text,
                                                  BindingMode.OneWay));
   holder.SaveBinding(count,
                      new Binding<int, string>(counterVm,
                                               () => counterVm.Count,
                                               count,
                                               () => count.Text,
                                               BindingMode.OneWay));
   incrementButton.SetCommand(nameof(ImageButton.Click),
                              counterVm.IncrementCommand);
}
```

When an item in the recycler view is recycled, it needs to have all its bindings reset to stop it showing the old item. The code in `BindViewHolder` is called by the adapter, passing in a view holder, the item view model, and the position in the collection. The view holder is a helper class that stores the underlying controls to avoid a UI lookup each time the item is re-bound, along with a list of bindings. These bindings are deleted, and new bindings are created to the new item.

CONFIGURING THE DISPATCHER HELPER

You have two options for the dispatcher helper, depending on whether you want to support AppCompat or not: `JimBobBennett.MvvmLight.AppCompat.AppCompatDispatcherHelper` is the one to use when using AppCompat, and `GalaSoft.MvvmLight.Threading.DispatcherHelper` is for when you're not using AppCompat. Both variants have a static `CheckBeginInvokeOnUI` method that takes an action and runs it on the UI thread, and you can register this method with the view-model locator to run code on the UI thread:

```
ViewModelLocator.RegisterDispatcher(DispatcherHelper.CheckBeginInvokeOnUI);
```

This code needs to be added to the splash screen when setting up the navigation setting.

B.5.2 The iOS view and application layer

Unlike Android, iOS support is in the standard MvvmLightLibs NuGet package, so there's nothing extra to install. The view controllers can be reused from the MvvmCross version of Countr with a few modifications, and so can the storyboards.

SETTING UP THE NAVIGATION SERVICE

Just like Android, there's a platform-specific navigation service that needs to be configured, with views set up via page keys. The difference is that there's no inherent navigation in iOS like there is in Android. In Android, one activity can navigate to another, but in iOS you need to put your view controllers inside a `UINavigationController` to get the same navigation stack. MvvmCross will create one of these for you, but with MVVM Light you need to create it yourself. MVVM Light also expects the view controllers in your navigation stack to be in the same storyboard, instead of in one storyboard per view, but you can copy and paste from the existing storyboards.

This means that you need only one storyboard for your app, and this storyboard will need to contain a navigation controller marked as the initial view controller, as well as all the view controllers for all your views, as shown in figure B.1. The counters view controller will need to be set as the root view controller in the navigation controller, so that this view is shown on startup (remember, MVVM Light doesn't define an app start view model). This storyboard will also need to be configured as the main interface for your app in the info.plist file (figure B.2).

When you construct the navigation service, pass in the navigation controller, so that it can be used to navigate between views. By the time the `FinishedLaunching` method in the `AppDelegate` is called, the main storyboard will have been loaded, and the root view controller of the app's window will be the navigation controller. The following listing shows how this can be used to configure the navigation controller.

Listing B.10 Navigation service created using the root view controller of the window

```
public override bool FinishedLaunching(UIApplication application,
                                       ➥NSDictionary launchOptions)
{
   var navigationService = new NavigationService();
   navigationService.Initialize((UINavigationController)Window
➥.RootViewController);
   ...
}
```

The views are then registered with the navigation service, and the navigation service is registered with the view-model locator in the same way as on Android.

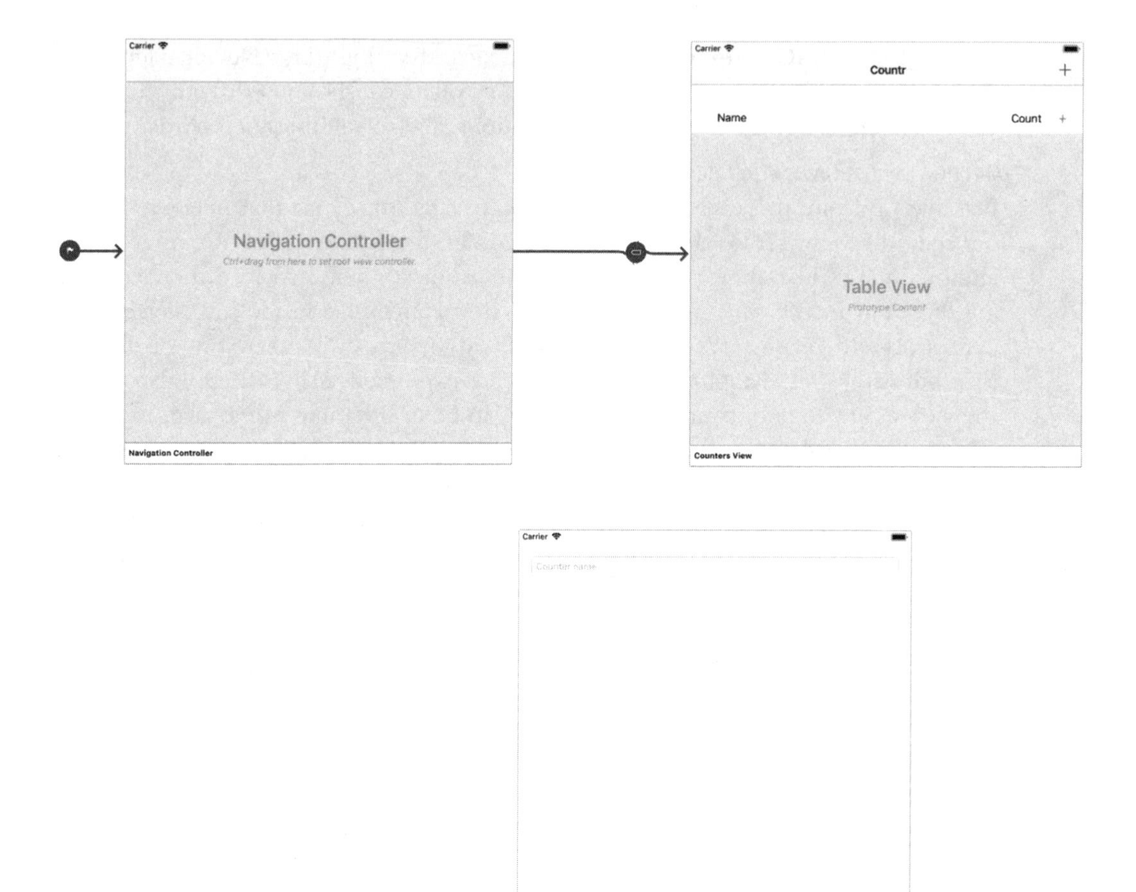

Figure B.1 The main storyboard needs to contain a navigation controller as the initial view controller, have the counters view as the root view controller in the navigation controller, and contain the counter view.

▾ **Deployment Info**

Deployment Target: 9.0

Device family: Universal

Main Interface: Main

Figure B.2 The main interface needs to be set to your storyboard in the info.plist file.

RETRIEVING VIEW MODELS AND NAVIGATION PARAMETERS

Just like on Android, view models are retrieved from the view-model locator. The navigation parameters are also retrieved in a similar way, except the view controller is passed to the `GetAndRemoveParameter` method on the platform-specific navigation service, instead of to an Intent, as shown in the following listing.

Listing B.11 Getting the parameter passed to the navigation service

```
var navigationService = (NavigationService)ViewModelLocator.NavigationService;
var counter = (Counter)navigationService.GetAndRemoveParameter(this);
viewModel.Prepare(counter);
```

BINDING

Binding on iOS uses the same mechanism as Android—extension methods that return bindings that you persist in your view controller. The only real difference is that you don't need to manually create properties for the controls; these are created for you when you name a control in the storyboard designer. Commands are also bound using the same extension method as Android.

TABLE VIEWS

MVVM Light provides helpers to help bind table view controllers to observable collections. Unlike like with Android, there's a base class to use for your table view controller, `ObservableTableViewController<T>`, where the generic parameter `T` is the view model for each item.

The table view source is created using an extension method on an observable collection called `GetTableViewSource`, just like how the recycler view adapter was created on Android. This extension method takes an action to bind a cell and a cell prototype identifier. You can optionally pass a func that returns a new `ObservableTableViewSource<T>`, which is used if you need to override the behavior of the basic table view source (for example, if you need to implement swipe to delete). This method returns a fully configured table view source that you can pass to the table view and that will keep your table in sync with your observable collection. The following listing shows an example of this.

Listing B.12 Creating the table view source from the counters observable collection

```
UITableViewSource tableViewSource;

public override async void ViewDidLoad()
{
   ...
   tableViewSource = viewModel.Counters.GetTableViewSource(BindCounterCell,
                                                           "CounterCell");
   TableView.Source = tableViewSource;
}
```

In this code, BindCounterCell is a method that binds the cell to the item view model, and "CounterCell" is the prototype identifier for the table view cell class that's defined on the storyboard.

Unlike on Android, there's no view holder to store all the bindings against each cell, so it's best to use the cell class to manage the bindings. This way, each cell can store a list of bindings that are then deleted and recreated when the binding context changes. The following listing shows how this can be implemented in the counter cell.

Listing B.13 Binding a counter view model to the counter cell

```
List<Binding> bindings = new List<Binding>();
CounterViewModel viewModel;

public void Bind(CounterViewModel counterVm)
{
   foreach (var binding in bindings)
      binding.Detach();
   bindings.Clear();

   viewModel = counterVm;

   bindings.Add(this.SetBinding(() => viewModel.Name,
                                () => CounterName.Text));
   bindings.Add(this.SetBinding(() => viewModel.Count,
                                () => CounterCount.Text));
   IncrementButton.SetCommand(viewModel.IncrementCommand);
}
```

Clears out any existing bindings

Rebinds the counter name, count, and increment command

This Bind method can then be called from the BindCounterCell action passed to the GetTableViewSource extension method:

```
private void BindCounterCell(UITableViewCell cell,
                             ➥CounterViewModel counterVm,
                             ➥NSIndexPath path)
{
   ((CounterTableViewCell)cell).Bind(counterVm);
}
```

CONFIGURING THE DISPATCHER HELPER

The iOS dispatcher helper is the static class GalaSoft.MvvmLight.Threading .DispatcherHelper, and it's initialized with an object owned by the main thread, so that it knows which thread should be used to dispatch calls to the UI thread. Once initialized, it has a CheckBeginInvokeOnUI method, just as on Android, and you can register this in the view-model locator, as follows.

Listing B.14 Registering the iOS dispatcher helper

```
public override bool FinishedLaunching(UIApplication application,
                                       ➥NSDictionary launchOptions)
{
   ...
   DispatcherHelper.Initialize(application);
   ViewModelLocator.RegisterDispatcher(DispatcherHelper.CheckBeginInvokeOnUI);
   ...
}
```

Summary

MvvmCross and MVVM Light have similarities in that they provide everything you need to build Xamarin apps using MVVM-based view models, a navigation service, a messaging service, commands, and helpers for list controls. They differ in the implementation and the details of what they provide, as outlined in the following tables.

Table B.1 Model layer differences between MvvmCross and MVVM Light

	MvvmCross	MVVM Light
Messaging	`MvxMessenger` Using the MvvmCross messenger, you can subscribe to messages on the UI thread or a background thread. All messages need to derive from `MvxMessage`.	`Messenger` Using the MVVM Light messenger, you can only subscribe to messages on the current thread, and you have to use a platform-specific dispatcher helper to marshal code onto the UI thread. Messages can be any object.

Table B.2 View-model layer differences between MvvmCross and MVVM Light

	MvvmCross	MVVM Light
Base view model class	`MvxViewModel` Provides property-changed notifications and a `SetProperty` method to update a property and raise the notification. Also provides lifecycle methods that are called on navigation and as the view lifecycle happens.	`ViewModelBase` Provides property-changed notifications and a `Set` method to update a property and raise the notification. No lifecycle methods.
Commands	`MvxCommand` and `MvxAsyncCommand` Two command implementations are provided, both taking an action to run when the command is executed and optionally a func to evaluate to see if the command can execute. One implementation is synchronous, and the other is async and supports async and await in the action that's run on execution, meaning that the `Execute` method won't complete until the async implementation has finished.	`RelayCommand` Only one command implementation is provided, taking an action to run when the command is executed and optionally a func to evaluate to see if the command can execute. This doesn't support async, so if the implementation uses async and await, the `Execute` method will complete as soon as the first await is hit.

Table B.2 View-model layer differences between MvvmCross and MVVM Light *(continued)*

	MvvmCross	MVVM Light
Navigation	`IMvxNavigationService` The MvvmCross navigation service is created automatically and provides view model navigation, and has async navigation methods. View models are created on navigation and made available to the views for binding. Parameters passed to the next view model are handled in the view model.	`INavigationService` The MVVM Light navigation service has to be manually created. Navigation is via a string-based page key instead of via view models, and the navigation methods don't have async support. View models aren't created on navigation; a view-model locator is used to get the view model for a view. Parameters passed to the next view model need to be retrieved in the view and passed to the view model.
IoC	`Mvx` An IoC container is provided with a single place to register items in it. View models don't need to be registered, MvvmCross classes (such as the navigation service) are automatically registered, and classes with the same name can be registered in bulk. If the class being registered needs to be a singleton, this is controlled at registration time.	`SimpleIoc` This IoC container is one that you populate manually, usually in the view model locator, but there's no one predefined place to do it. You have to manually register everything, including view models. Access to a singleton instance or multiple instances is handled when retrieving items from the container.

Table B.3 Android view layer differences between MvvmCross and MVVM Light

	MvvmCross	MVVM Light
Views	Views are discovered by name, so the view for `MyViewModel` is called `MyView`. The first view is shown based on the start view model registered in the cross-platform app setup. The view model for a view is automatically set.	Views are registered with the navigation service with a string page key. The first view needs to be manually shown. The view model for a view needs to be manually retrieved from the view-model loader and set.
Binding	Controls can be bound in the layout AXML files or in code.	All binding happens in code.
Recycler views	There's a set of base classes for recycler views and their adapters that provide binding to observable collections.	The standard recycler view is used with a custom adapter that binds to an observable collection.

Table B.4 iOS view layer differences between MvvmCross and MVVM Light

	MvvmCross	MVVM Light
Views	Views are discovered by name, so the view for `MyViewModel` is called `MyView`. The first view is shown based on the start view model registered in the cross-platform app setup. Each view has its own storyboard file. The view model for a view is automatically set.	Views are registered with the navigation service with a string page key. One storyboard is used for everything, and this needs to include a navigation view controller that the navigation service can use. The first view needs to be set as the root of the navigation service or be manually navigated to. The view model for a view needs to be manually retrieved from the view-model loader and set.
Binding	All binding happens in code.	All binding happens in code.
Table views	There's a set of base classes for table view controllers and their data sources that provide binding to observable collections.	There's a set of base classes for table view controllers and their data sources that provide binding to observable collections.

index

Symbols

A

B

C

D

E

F

M

T

U

V

W

X